Koren Talmud Bavli

THE NOÉ EDITION

BAVA KAMMA

Steinsaltz
Center

KOREN

תלמוד בבלי

KOREN TALMUD BAVLI

THE NOÉ EDITION

בבא קמא

BAVA KAMMA

Daf 93b through Daf 111a

COMMENTARY BY

Rabbi Adin Even-Israel Steinsaltz

EDITOR-IN-CHIEF

Rabbi Dr Tzvi Hersh Weinreb

SENIOR CONTENT EDITOR

Rabbi Dr Shalom Z Berger

EXECUTIVE EDITOR

Rabbi Joshua Schreier

STEINSALTZ CENTER

KOREN PUBLISHERS JERUSALEM

Supported by the Matanel Foundation

Koren Talmud Bavli, The Noe Edition
Vol. 21g: Tractate Bava Kamma, Daf 93b through Daf 111a
Paperback, ISBN, 978-965-7766-00-2

First Hebrew/English paperback edition, 2023

Koren Publishers Jerusalem Ltd.
PO Box 4044, Jerusalem 91040, ISRAEL
PO Box 8531, New Milford, CT 06776, USA
www.korenpub.com

Steinsaltz Center

Steinsaltz Center is the parent organization of institutions established by Rabbi Adin Even-Israel Steinsaltz

PO Box 45187, Jerusalem 91450 ISRAEL
Telephone: +972 2 646 0900, Fax +972 2 624 9454
www.steinsaltz-center.org

Printed in Turkey

הִנֵּה יָמִים בָּאִים, נְאֻם אֲדֹנָי יֱהֹוִה, וְהִשְׁלַחְתִּי רָעָב בָּאָרֶץ,
לֹא־רָעָב לַלֶּחֶם וְלֹא־צָמָא לַמַּיִם, כִּי אִם־לִשְׁמֹעַ אֵת דִּבְרֵי יהוה.

Behold, days are coming – says the Lord God – I will send a hunger to the land, not a hunger for bread nor a thirst for water, but to hear the words of the Lord. (AMOS 8:11)

The Noé edition of the Koren Talmud Bavli
with the commentary of Rabbi Adin Even-Israel Steinsaltz
is dedicated to all those who open its covers
to quench their thirst for Jewish Knowledge,
in our generation of Torah renaissance.

This beautiful edition is for the young, the aged,
the novice and the savant alike,
as it unites the depth of Torah knowledge
with the best of academic scholarship.

Within its exquisite and vibrant pages,
words become worlds.

It will claim its place in the library of classics,
in the bookcases of the Beit Midrash,
the classrooms of our schools,
and in the offices of professionals and business people
who carve out precious time to grapple with its timeless wisdom.

For the Student and the Scholar

DEDICATED BY LEO AND SUE NOÉ

Steinsaltz Center

Executive Director, Steinsaltz Center

Rabbi Meni Even-Israel

Managing Editor

Rabbi Jason Rappoport

Senior Content Editor

Rabbi Dr. Shalom Z. Berger

Editors

Rabbi Dr. Joshua Amaru, *Coordinating Editor*
Rabbi Avishai Magence, *Content Curator*
Tal Avrahami
Aryeh Bernstein
Menucha Chwat
Rabbi Yoel Domb
Rabbi Yehoshua Duker
Betzalel Philip Edwards
Rabbi Yonatan Shai Freedman
Raphael Friedman
Rabbi Uri Goldstein
Rabbi Alan Haber
Rabbi Tzvi Chaim Kaye
Stephen Lauber
Sholom Licht
Elisha Loewenstern
Rafi Miller
Rabbi Eli Ozarowski
Rabbi David Sedley
Shira Shmidman
Rabbi Michael Siev
Avi Steinhart

Copy Editors

Aliza Israel, *Coordinator*
Bracha Hermon
Ita Olesker
Debbie Ismailoff
Shira Finson
Ilana Sobel
Deena Nataf
Eliana Kurlantzick Yorav
Erica Hirsch Edvi
Nava Wieder
Sara Henna Dahan

Language Consultants

Dr. Stephanie E. Binder, *Greek & Latin*
Rabbi Yaakov Hoffman, *Arabic*
Dr. Shai Secunda, *Persian*
Shira Shmidman, *Aramaic*

KOREN

Design & Typesetting

Dena Landowne Bailey, *Typesetting*
Tani Bayer, *Jacket Design*
Raphaël Freeman, *Design & Typography*

Images

Eliahu Misgav, *Illustration & Image Acquisition*
Daniel Gdalevich, *Illustration & Image Acquisition*

Introduction by the Publisher

The Talmud has sustained and inspired Jews for thousands of years. Throughout Jewish history, an elite cadre of scholars has absorbed its learning and passed it on to succeeding generations. The Talmud has been the fundamental text of our people.

Beginning in the 1960s, Rabbi Adin Even-Israel Steinsaltz שליט״א created a revolution in the history of Talmud study. His translation of the Talmud, first into modern Hebrew and then into other languages, as well the practical learning aids he added to the text, have enabled millions of people around the world to access and master the complexity and context of the world of Talmud.

It is thus a privilege to present the *Koren Talmud Bavli*, an English translation of the talmudic text with the brilliant elucidation of Rabbi Steinsaltz. The depth and breadth of his knowledge are unique in our time. His rootedness in the tradition and his reach into the world beyond it are inspirational.

Working with Rabbi Steinsaltz on this remarkable project has been not only an honor, but a great pleasure. Never shy to express an opinion, with wisdom and humor, Rabbi Steinsaltz sparkles in conversation, demonstrating his knowledge (both sacred and worldly), sharing his wide-ranging interests, and, above all, radiating his passion. I am grateful for the unique opportunity to work closely with him, and I wish him many more years of writing and teaching

Our intentions in publishing this new edition of the Talmud are threefold. First, we seek to fully clarify the talmudic page to the reader – textually, intellectually, and graphically. Second, we seek to utilize today's most sophisticated technologies, both in print and electronic formats, to provide the reader with a comprehensive set of study tools. And third, we seek to help readers advance in their process of Talmud study.

To achieve these goals, the *Koren Talmud Bavli* is unique in a number of ways:

- The classic *tzurat hadaf* of Vilna, used by scholars since the 1800s, has been reset for great clarity, and opens from the Hebrew "front" of the book. Full *nikkud* has been added to both the talmudic text and Rashi's commentary, allowing for a more fluent reading with the correct pronunciation; the commentaries of *Tosafot* have been punctuated. Upon the advice of many English-speaking teachers of Talmud, we have separated these core pages from the translation, thereby enabling the advanced student to approach the text without the distraction of the translation. This also reduces the number of volumes in the set. At the bottom of each *daf*, there is a reference to the corresponding English pages. In addition, the Vilna edition was read against other manuscripts and older print editions, so that texts which had been removed by non-Jewish censors have been restored to their rightful place.
- The English translation, which starts on the English "front" of the book, reproduces the *menukad* Talmud text alongside the English translation (in bold) and commentary and explanation (in a lighter font). The Hebrew and Aramaic text is presented in logical paragraphs. This allows for a fluent reading of the text for the non-Hebrew or non-Aramaic reader. It also allows for the Hebrew reader to refer easily to the text alongside. Where the original text features dialogue or poetry, the English text is laid out in a manner appropriate to the genre. Each page refers to the relevant *daf*.

- Critical contextual tools surround the text and translation: personality notes, providing short biographies of the Sages; language notes, explaining foreign terms borrowed from Greek, Latin, Persian, or Arabic; and background notes, giving information essential to the understanding of the text, including history, geography, botany, archaeology, zoology, astronomy, and aspects of daily life in the talmudic era.
- Halakhic summaries provide references to the authoritative legal decisions made over the centuries by the rabbis. They explain the reasons behind each halakhic decision as well as the ruling's close connection to the Talmud and its various interpreters.
- Photographs, drawings, and other illustrations have been added throughout the text – in full color in the Standard and Electronic editions, and in black and white in the Daf Yomi edition – to visually elucidate the text.

This is not an exhaustive list of features of this edition, it merely presents an overview for the English-speaking reader who may not be familiar with the "total approach" to Talmud pioneered by Rabbi Steinsaltz.

Several professionals have helped bring this vast collaborative project to fruition. My many colleagues are noted on the Acknowledgments page, and the leadership of this project has been exceptional.

RABBI MENACHEM EVEN-ISRAEL, DIRECTOR OF THE STEINSALTZ CENTER, was the driving force behind this enterprise. With enthusiasm and energy, he formed the happy alliance with Koren and established close relationships among all involved in the work.

RABBI DR. TZVI HERSH WEINREB שליט״א, EDITOR-IN-CHIEF, brought to this project his profound knowledge of Torah, intellectual literacy of Talmud, and erudition of Western literature. It is to him that the text owes its very high standard, both in form and content, and the logical manner in which the beauty of the Talmud is presented.

RABBI JOSHUA SCHREIER, EXECUTIVE EDITOR, assembled an outstanding group of scholars, translators, editors, and proofreaders, whose standards and discipline enabled this project to proceed in a timely and highly professional manner.

RABBI MEIR HANEGBI, EDITOR OF THE HEBREW EDITION OF THE STEINSALTZ TALMUD, lent his invaluable assistance throughout the work process, supervising the reproduction of the Vilna pages.

RAPHAËL FREEMAN, EXECUTIVE EDITOR OF KOREN, created this Talmud's unique typographic design which, true to the Koren approach, is both elegant and user friendly.

It has been an enriching experience for all of us at Koren Publishers Jerusalem to work with the Steinsaltz Center to develop and produce the *Koren Talmud Bavli*. We pray that this publication will be a source of great learning and, ultimately, greater *avodat Hashem* for all Jews.

Matthew Miller, Publisher
Koren Publishers Jerusalem
Jerusalem 5772

Contents

For the vocalized Vilna Shas layout, please open as a Hebrew book.

Introduction to **Perek IX**

And the Lord spoke unto Moses, saying: If anyone sin, and commits a trespass against the Lord, and he defrauds his counterpart with regard to a deposit, or with regard to a pledge, or with regard to a robbery, or if he exploited his counterpart; or he has found that which was lost, and deal falsely with it, and swears to a lie; in any of all these that a man does, sinning therein. Then it shall be, if he has sinned, and is guilty, that he shall restore that which he took by robbery, or the thing that he has gotten by oppression, or the deposit that was deposited with him, or the lost thing that he found. Or anything about which he has sworn falsely, he shall restore it in full, and shall add the fifth part more to it; unto him to whom it appertains shall he give it, in the day of his being guilty. And he shall bring his forfeit unto the Lord, a ram without blemish out of the flock, according to the valuation, for a guilt-offering, unto the priest. And the priest shall make atonement for him before the Lord, and he shall be forgiven, concerning whatsoever he does so as to be guilty thereby.

(Leviticus 5:20–26)

And the Lord spoke unto Moses, saying: Speak unto the children of Israel: When a man or woman shall commit any sin that men commit, to commit a trespass against the Lord, and that soul be guilty. Then they shall confess their sin that they have done; and he shall make restitution for his guilt in full, and add unto it the fifth part thereof, and give it unto him in respect of whom he has been guilty. But if the man have no kinsman to whom restitution may be made for the guilt, the restitution for guilt that is made shall be the Lord's, even the priest's; besides the ram of the atonement, whereby atonement shall be made for him.

(Numbers 5:5–7)

In order to fulfill the obligation detailed in these verses in its most straightforward manner, a robber must return the actual item stolen to the robbery victim. If a stolen item has remained in the possession of the robber for an extended period of time, many practical questions arise: What should the *halakha* be if the stolen item underwent a significant change? Does the robber consequently acquire the stolen item and become liable to pay monetary restitution? What type of change in the item is deemed significant? Additionally, is it sufficient for the robber to return the stolen item, or must the robber also reimburse the robbery victim for his use of the stolen item during the time it was in his possession? What is the *halakha* in a case where the stolen item did not undergo any physical change, but something has happened to reduce or eliminate its value in a manner that is not evident, e.g., a change in the legal or halakhic status of the stolen item?

A related topic is the case of a professional craftsman: What is the *halakha* if he damages or ruins an item that was given to him for the purpose of his work, e.g., an item given to him for repair, or raw material given to him to craft an object? What happens if a craftsman produces a product that is not according to the agreement he entered into with the owner? Is he considered a type of a robber, who acquires the item or materials given to him, in which case he must reimburse the owner with money? Or does the owner retain what he originally owned, while the craftsman must pay compensation calculated in some other manner?

In addition to the monetary obligation that a robber must pay restitution to the robbery victim, there is also a requirement that he atone for committing the sin of robbery. The Gemara discusses a robber who compounded his sin by taking a false oath that he did not in fact commit the robbery, and the means by which he can achieve atonement. He must return the principal value of the stolen item, pay an additional one-fifth penalty, and bring a guilt-offering, known as the guilt-offering for robbery. In this chapter, the Gemara discusses the circumstances in which the robber must pay the additional one-fifth. Is the additional one-fifth payment for the act of robbery or for the act of taking a false oath? What differences in *halakha* are there between the requirement to pay back the principal and the requirement to pay the additional one-fifth payment?

The Torah discusses the case of one who robs a convert, and the convert then dies without heirs. In this case, the robber pays restitution to the priests, then brings his guilt-offering. The Gemara discusses details of this case: When does the obligation to pay the additional one-fifth payment take effect? What is the *halakha* of one who brings his guilt-offering before paying restitution? To which priests does he pay restitution?

This chapter aims to clarify all of these *halakhot* relating to the return of a stolen item.

מתני׳ הַגּוֹזֵל עֵצִים וַעֲשָׂאָן כֵּלִים, צֶמֶר וַעֲשָׂאָן בְּגָדִים – מְשַׁלֵּם כִּשְׁעַת הַגְּזֵלָה.

MISHNA In the case of **one who robs** another **of wood**[H] **and fashions it** into **vessels,** or one who robs another of **wool and fashions it** into **garments,** he **pays** the robbery victim **according to** the value of the goods at the **time of the robbery,** but he need not return the vessels or garments. He has acquired the stolen items because they had undergone a change.

גָּזַל פָּרָה מְעוּבֶּרֶת וְיָלְדָה, רָחֵל טְעוּנָה וּגְזָזָהּ – מְשַׁלֵּם דְּמֵי פָרָה הָעוֹמֶדֶת לֵילֵד, וּדְמֵי רָחֵל הָעוֹמֶדֶת לִיגָּזֵז.

If one **robbed** another **of a pregnant cow and it** then **gave birth** while in his possession, or if one robbed another of **a ewe** that was **laden** with wool **and** the robber then **sheared it,** the robber **pays the value of a cow that is ready to give birth**[N] or **the value of a ewe that is ready to be shorn.** He pays the value of the animal at the time of the robbery, and the calf or the wool remains his.

גָּזַל פָּרָה וְנִתְעַבְּרָה אֶצְלוֹ וְיָלְדָה, רָחֵל וְנִטְעֲנָה אֶצְלוֹ וּגְזָזָהּ – מְשַׁלֵּם כִּשְׁעַת הַגְּזֵלָה. זֶה הַכְּלָל: כָּל הַגַּזְלָנִים מְשַׁלְּמִין כִּשְׁעַת הַגְּזֵלָה.

If one **robbed** another **of a cow, and it became pregnant in his** possession, **and it** then **gave birth;** or if one robbed another **of a ewe, and it became laden** with wool **in his** possession, **and he** then **sheared it,** then the robber **pays according to** the value of the animal at the **time of the robbery. This is the principle: All robbers pay according to** the value of the stolen item at the **time of the robbery.**

גמ׳ אָמְרִי: עֵצִים וַעֲשָׂאָן כֵּלִים – אִין, שִׁיפָּן – לָא. צֶמֶר וַעֲשָׂאָן בְּגָדִים – אִין, לִיבְּנָן – לָא.

GEMARA The Sages **say:** It can be inferred from the mishna that if one robbed another of **wood and fashioned it into vessels, yes,** the robber acquires the wood due to the change. If he merely **sanded it, no,** the robber does not acquire it, as this is not a significant change. Similarly, if one robbed another of **wool and fashioned it** into **garments, yes,** he has acquired the wool due to the change. If **he** merely **washed it, no,** he has not acquired it.

וּרְמִינְהִי: גָּזַל עֵצִים וְשִׁיפָּן, אֲבָנִים וְסִיתְּתָן, צֶמֶר וְלִיבְּנָן, פִּשְׁתָּן וְנִקָּהוּ – מְשַׁלֵּם כִּשְׁעַת הַגְּזֵלָה!

And the Gemara **raises a contradiction** from a *baraita*: If one **robbed** another of **wood and sanded it,** or **stones and smoothed them,** or **wool and washed it,** or **flax and cleaned it, he pays according to** the value of the stolen item at the **time of the robbery.** This *baraita* teaches that even a change such as sanding wood is regarded as a significant change.

אָמַר אַבָּיֵי: תַּנָּא דִּידָן קָתָנֵי שִׁינּוּי דְּרַבָּנַן דְּהָדְרָא, וְכׇל שֶׁכֵּן שִׁינּוּי דְּאוֹרָיְיתָא.

Abaye said: This does not contradict the mishna. **The** *tanna* **of our** mishna **teaches** the *halakha* with regard to **a change** deemed significant **by rabbinic** law, which is not deemed significant by Torah law, **as it is reversible. And all the more so,** if the robber effects **a change** deemed significant **by Torah** law, i.e., an irreversible change, he acquires the stolen item due to the change.

עֵצִים וַעֲשָׂאָן כֵּלִים – בְּעֵצִים מְשׁוּפִּין, וּמַאי נִינְהוּ? נְסָרִים, דְּשִׁינּוּי דַּהֲדַר לִבְרִיָּיתָא הוּא, דְּאִי בָּעֵי מְשַׁלֵּיף לְהוּ. צֶמֶר וַעֲשָׂאָן בְּגָדִים – בְּצֶמֶר טָווּי, דְּשִׁינּוּי דְּהָדַר לִבְרִיָּיתָא הוּא, דְּאִי בָּעֵי סָתַר לֵיהּ, וְכׇל שֶׁכֵּן שִׁינּוּי דְּאוֹרָיְיתָא.

The Gemara explains: Accordingly, it must be that the case in the mishna, where the change is reversible, where one robbed another of **wood and fashioned it into vessels,** is stated **with regard to** one who robbed another of **sanded wood. And what are they? Boards** that the robber used to construct a vessel, **which is a change** in which the item **can revert to its original state, as, if** the robber **desires, he** can **disassemble them.** Similarly, the case of one who robbed another of **wool and fashioned it into garments** refers **to wool** that was already **spun, as** fashioning them into garments **is a change** in which the item **can revert to its original state, as, if** the robber **desires, he** can **unravel them.** The mishna teaches that the robber acquires the stolen item by making these changes, **and all the more so** the robber acquires the stolen item through **a change** deemed significant **by Torah law.**

וְתַנָּא בָּרָא, שִׁינּוּי דְּאוֹרָיְיתָא קָתָנֵי, וְשִׁינּוּי דְּרַבָּנַן לָא קָתָנֵי.

Abaye continues his explanation: **And the** *tanna* **of the** *baraita* **teaches** the *halakha* with regard to **a change** deemed significant **by Torah law,**[H] **but he does not teach** the *halakha* with regard to **a change** deemed significant **by rabbinic law.** It is possible that he maintains that the robber does not acquire the stolen item due to such a change.

HALAKHA

One who robs another of wood, etc. – **הַגּוֹזֵל עֵצִים וכו׳:** If changes occur in a stolen item in a way that the item cannot revert to its previous state, the robber keeps the stolen item and returns the monetary value to its owner (Rambam *Sefer Nezikin, Hilkhot Gezeila VaAveda* 2:1; *Shulḥan Arukh, Ḥoshen Mishpat* 360:1).

A change deemed significant by Torah law – **שִׁינּוּי דְּאוֹרָיְיתָא:** A reversible change is not deemed significant. Consequently, if a robber changes a stolen item in a way that is reversible, e.g., he fashions stolen wood into a box that can be taken apart, he must still return it to its owner. If, however, one robbed another of wood and sanded and cut it, or hollowed it out and fashioned it into a vessel, or if one robbed another of wool and fashioned it into felt, the change is significant, and the robber has acquired the stolen item. The Rema writes that a modification is a significant change only if it results in the item being called by a different name (Rambam *Sefer Nezikin, Hilkhot Gezeila VaAveda* 2:12; *Shulḥan Arukh, Ḥoshen Mishpat* 360:5–6).

NOTES

Pays the value of a cow that is ready to give birth, etc. – **מְשַׁלֵּם דְּמֵי פָרָה הָעוֹמֶדֶת לֵילֵד וכו׳:** The precise meaning of this phrase is unclear. Some explain that the robber is not obligated to return the actual cow or sheep, since it underwent a change by giving birth or being shorn. Instead, the robber must compensate the owner for the value of the animal at the time of the robbery. This is the opinion of the Ba'al HaMaor and the Rosh. Other early commentaries are of the opinion that giving birth or being shorn does not change the body of the animal, so the robber has not acquired the animal itself, but only the newborn animal or the wool that grew. He must therefore return the animal along with additional monetary compensation, which will make his total payment the value of a cow that is ready to give birth or a ewe that is ready to be shorn (see Rashi and *Nimmukei Yosef*).

רַב אַשִׁי אֲמַר: תַּנָּא דִּידַן נַמִּי שִׁינּוּי דְּאוֹרַיְיתָא קָתָנֵי; עֵצִים וַעֲשָׂאָן כֵּלִים – בּוּכָאנֵי, דְּהַיְינוּ שִׁיפָּן. צֶמֶר וַעֲשָׂאָן בְּגָדִים – נַמְטֵי, דְּהַיְינוּ שִׁינּוּי דְּלָא הָדַר.

Rav Ashi stated another answer: **The** ***tanna*** **of our** mishna **is also teaching** the *halakha* with regard to **a change** deemed significant **by Torah law.** The case in the mishna of one who robbed another of **wood and fashioned it** into **vessels** is referring to one who constructed **pestles [*bukhanei*],**[LN] **which is** analogous to the case mentioned in the *baraita* where **one sanded them,** since a pestle is formed by trimming the wood in an irreversible manner. Similarly, the case in the mishna of one who robbed another of **wool and fashioned it into garments** is referring to one who fashioned the wool into pieces of **felt [*namtei*],**[LN] **which is an irreversible change.**

וְלִיבּוּן מִי הָוֵי שִׁינּוּי? וּרְמִינְהִי: לֹא הִסְפִּיק לִיתְּנוֹ לוֹ עַד שֶׁצְּבָעוֹ – פָּטוּר, לִבְּנוֹ וְלֹא צְבָעוֹ – חַיָּיב!

The Gemara asks a question with regard to the *baraita*: **But does washing** effect a significant **change,** so that one who robs another of wool and washes it acquires the wool and pays its value at the time of robbery? **And** the Gemara **raises a contradiction** from a mishna that discusses the *halakhot* of the first of the sheared wool, which one must give to a priest (*Ḥullin* 135a): If the owner of the sheep **did not manage to give**[H] the sheared wool **to** the priest **before he dyed it,**[B] he is **exempt** from giving it to the priest, as the obligation is in effect only with regard to wool remaining in its original state. By contrast, if **he washed it but did not dye it,** he is **obligated** to give it to the priest. This indicates that washing does not effect a significant change.

אֲמַר אַבַּיֵי, לָא קַשְׁיָא: הָא רַבִּי שִׁמְעוֹן, הָא רַבָּנַן. דְּתַנְיָא: גְּזָזוֹ, טְוָואוֹ וַאֲרָגוֹ – אֵין מִצְטָרֵף, לִבְּנוֹ – רַבִּי שִׁמְעוֹן אוֹמֵר: אֵין מִצְטָרֵף, וַחֲכָמִים אוֹמְרִים: מִצְטָרֵף.

Abaye said: It is **not difficult. This** *baraita* is in accordance with the opinion of **Rabbi Shimon,** whereas **that** mishna is in accordance with the opinion of **the Rabbis, as it is taught** in a *baraita* with regard to the first of the sheared wool: If one **sheared it, spun it, and wove it,** the sheared wool **does not combine**[N] with the wool from other sheep to constitute the minimum quantity of wool for which one is obligated to give the first of the sheared wool to the priest. If one **washed it,** then **Rabbi Shimon says** that it **does not combine** with the wool of other sheep, as washing effects a significant change, **and the Rabbis say that** it **combines** with the wool of other sheep, as washing does not effect a significant change. Their opinions correspond to the opinions in the *baraita* and mishna previously quoted.

רָבָא אֲמַר: הָא וְהָא רַבִּי שִׁמְעוֹן, וְלָא קַשְׁיָא: הָא דְּנַפְּצֵיהּ נַפּוּצֵי, הָא דִּסַרְקֵיהּ סְרוּקֵי.

Rava stated another answer: **This and that,** i.e., both the mishna and the *baraita*, are in accordance with the opinion of **Rabbi Shimon, and it is not difficult. This** mishna is referring to a case **where one untangled**[HN] the strands of wool by hand before washing it. In this case, the washing is not fully effective, and does not effect a significant change. **That** *baraita* is referring to a case **where one combed it** before washing it. The washing is more effective and consequently effects a significant change.

רַבִּי חִיָּיא בַּר אָבִין אֲמַר: הָא דְּחַוְּורֵיהּ חַוּוֹרֵי, הָא דְּכַבְרֵיהּ כַּבְרוּיֵי.

Rabbi Ḥiyya bar Avin stated another answer: **This** mishna is referring to a case **where** one merely **whitened it,** which is not a significant change. **That** *baraita* is referring to a case **where one bleached it**[N] with sulfur, which is a significant change.

LANGUAGE

Pestles [*bukhanei*] – בּוּכָאנֵי: The origin of this word is not completely clear. It means a type of utensil, and came to be used to describe any utensil with a long body and round top. The modern Hebrew word *bukhna* has the same meaning.

Felt [*namtei*] – נַמְטֵי: Apparently from the Middle Persian word namat, meaning felt or a bed covering. Felt is generally made from unspun fibers that are combed, layered, and then condensed by applying pressure, heat, and moisture. The fibers combine to make a sheet that cannot subsequently be separated into threads.

HALAKHA

Did not manage to give, etc. – לֹא הִסְפִּיק לִיתְּנוֹ וכו׳: The *halakha* is in accordance with the opinion of the Rabbis. Consequently, if the owner dyed the first of the sheared wool before giving it to a priest, he is exempt from giving it to the priest. If the owner washed the wool but did not dye it, it must be given to the priest (Rambam *Sefer Zera'im*, *Hilkhot Bikkurim* 10:6; *Shulḥan Arukh*, *Yoreh De'a* 333:3).

Where one untangled, etc. – דְּנַפְּצֵיהּ וכו׳: If a thief untangles wool by hand and washes it, he has changed it and has thereby acquired it. The Rema writes in the name of the *Tur* that this applies only if he bleached the wool irreversibly, e.g., with sulfur (Rambam *Sefer Nezikin*, *Hilkhot Gezeila VaAveda* 2:12 and *Leḥem Mishne* there; *Shulḥan Arukh*, *Ḥoshen Mishpat* 360:6–7, and in the comment of Rema, and *Shakh* and *Beur HaGra* there).

BACKGROUND

Did not manage to give the sheared wool to the priest before he dyed it – לֹא הִסְפִּיק לִיתְּנוֹ לוֹ עַד שֶׁצְּבָעוֹ: This refers to the mitzva of first shearing (see Deuteronomy 18:4). The mitzva obligates one who has at least five sheep, each producing twelve *sela* worth of wool, totaling sixty *sela* worth of wool, to give the first part of the sheared wool to a priest. The minimum amount given to the priest is five *sela* worth of wool, a quantity enabling the priest to fashion a small item of clothing from it.

NOTES

Wood and fashioned it into vessels is referring to pestles – עֵצִים וַעֲשָׂאָן כֵּלִים בּוּכָאנֵי: *Tosafot* explain that one acquires an item by making a change to it only if it was altered so significantly that its identity changes and it is now categorized as an item with a different name, as in this case. Similarly, when one steals unfinished wood and fashions it into boards, he has acquired it by changing the material so fundamentally that its identity changes. By contrast, as the Gemara will explain (96a), one who cuts wooden beams into smaller pieces does not acquire them, despite the fact that this change cannot be reversed. This is because they are still referred to as beams, albeit smaller ones (see Rashba).

Garments is referring to one who fashioned them into pieces of felt – בְּגָדִים נַמְטֵי: Making wool into felt is an irreversible change. The mishna did not mention the washing of the wool because generally washing is not performed when producing felt (Rashi; see Ra'avad).

Does not combine – אֵין מִצְטָרֵף: One is required to give the first of the sheared wool to a priest only if he shears wool weighing at least one and a half *maneh* from each of five ewes. If one sheared his sheep and spun or dyed some of the wool before giving it to the priest, the wool that was changed does not combine with the unchanged wool to constitute the minimum quantity of wool for which one is obligated to give the first of the sheared wool to the priest.

Where one untangled, etc. – דְּנַפְּצֵיהּ וכו׳: First he untangled the wool by hand and then washed it. Since the untangling was not thorough, the washing is not thorough either, and therefore it is not a significant change. If one were to comb it with a comb and then wash it, it would be a significant change (*Arukh*).

In its broad sense, this term refers to any manner of separating an item into smaller parts. According to Rashi, it is the process of separating the tangled strands of wool by hand in order to prepare the wool to be combed, after which it can be spun into thread. Since this is done by hand and without great force, it is not a significant change.

Where one bleached it – דְּכַבְרֵיהּ כַּבְרוּיֵי: *Tosafot* and the Rashba write that bleaching the wool with sulfur effects a significant change even according to the opinion of the Rabbis. The Ramah maintains that this distinction is relevant with regard to the opinion of Rabbi Shimon; according to the opinion of the Rabbis, bleaching never effects a significant change. The Meiri distinguishes between the first of the sheared wool, for which bleaching does not effect a significant change, and robbery, for which it does. A possible basis for this distinction is the statement of the Jerusalem Talmud, that several leniencies were applied in the case of robbery in order to encourage the robber to return stolen property as the Gemara will soon note (*Beit Aharon*).

הָשְׁתָּא יֵשׁ לוֹמַר צֶבַע לְרַבִּי שִׁמְעוֹן לָא הָוֵי שִׁינּוּי, לִיבּוּן הָוֵי שִׁינּוּי? דְּתַנְיָא: גָּזַז רִאשׁוֹן רִאשׁוֹן וּצְבָעוֹ, רִאשׁוֹן רִאשׁוֹן וּטְוָואוֹ, רִאשׁוֹן רִאשׁוֹן וַאֲרָגוֹ – אֵין מִצְטָרֵף. רַבִּי שִׁמְעוֹן בֶּן יְהוּדָה אוֹמֵר מִשּׁוּם רַבִּי שִׁמְעוֹן: צְבָעוֹ – מִצְטָרֵף!

Having demonstrated that, according to Rabbi Shimon, washing effects a significant change, the Gemara asks: **Now that it can be said** that, according **to Rabbi Shimon, dye does not** effect a significant **change,** as the Gemara will prove, can it be said that **washing** effects a significant **change? As it is taught** in a *baraita*: If **he sheared** sheep **one by one and dyed** the wool of each sheep before shearing the next sheep, or sheared them **one by one and spun** the wool, or sheared them **one by one and wove** the wool, then the wool sheared from the different sheep **does not combine** to constitute the minimum quantity of wool for which one is obligated to give the first of the sheared wool to the priest. **Rabbi Shimon ben Yehuda says in the name of Rabbi Shimon:** Even if **he dyed it,** it **combines** with the other wool. This indicates that, according to Rabbi Shimon, even dyeing the wool is not a significant change, so how could he maintain that washing it is?

אֲמַר אַבַּיֵי, לָא קַשְׁיָא: הָא רַבָּנַן אַלִּיבָּא דְּרַבִּי שִׁמְעוֹן, הָא רַבִּי שִׁמְעוֹן בֶּן יְהוּדָה אַלִּיבָּא דְּרַבִּי שִׁמְעוֹן.

Abaye said: This is **not difficult. This** statement, that washed wool does not combine with other wool, is the opinion of **the Rabbis in accordance with** the opinion **of Rabbi Shimon,** while **that** statement, that even dyed wool combines with other wool, is the opinion of **Rabbi Shimon ben Yehuda in accordance with** the opinion **of Rabbi Shimon.** There is a dispute as to what Rabbi Shimon rules with regard to this issue.

רָבָא אָמַר: לְעוֹלָם לָא פְּלִיגִי רַבָּנַן עֲלֵיהּ דְּרַבִּי שִׁמְעוֹן בֶּן יְהוּדָה, וְשָׁאנֵי צֶבַע, הוֹאִיל וְיָכוֹל לְהַעֲבִירוֹ עַל יְדֵי צָפוֹן, וְכִי קָתָנֵי הָתָם: לֹא הִסְפִּיק לִיתְּנוֹ לוֹ עַד שֶׁצְּבָעוֹ – פָּטוּר, וְאוֹקִימְנָא כְּדִבְרֵי הַכֹּל – בְּקָלָא אִילָן, דְּלָא עָבַר.

Rava said: Actually, the Rabbis do not disagree with Rabbi Shimon ben Yehuda, and they are also of the opinion that Rabbi Shimon holds that washing effects a significant change. **And** as for the apparent contradiction, **dye is different**[N] and it does not effect a significant change, **since one is able to remove it with soap** [*tzafon*][L] and return the wool to its previous state. **And when it is taught there,** in the mishna cited above, that if **one did not manage to give** the sheared wool **to the** priest **before he dyed it he is exempt, and** this ruling **was established in accordance with all opinions,** it was not stated with regard to ordinary dye but **with regard to indigo,**[H] **which cannot be removed** with soap and therefore effects a permanent and therefore significant change.

אֲמַר אַבַּיֵי: רַבִּי שִׁמְעוֹן בֶּן יְהוּדָה וּבֵית שַׁמַּאי וְרַבִּי אֱלִיעֶזֶר בֶּן יַעֲקֹב וְרַבִּי שִׁמְעוֹן בֶּן אֶלְעָזָר וְרַבִּי יִשְׁמָעֵאל, כּוּלְּהוּ סְבִירָא לְהוּ: שִׁינּוּי בִּמְקוֹמוֹ עוֹמֵד. רַבִּי שִׁמְעוֹן בֶּן יְהוּדָה, הָא דַּאֲמַרַן.

§ **Abaye said: Rabbi Shimon ben Yehuda, and Beit Shammai, and Rabbi Eliezer ben Ya'akov, and Rabbi Shimon ben Elazar, and Rabbi Yishmael all hold** that despite **a change,** the changed item **remains in its place,** i.e., the changed item is still considered to have the status it had before the change. The Gemara proceeds to prove that each of these *tanna'im* holds this way: The opinion of **Rabbi Shimon ben Yehuda is that which we just said.** He says that, according to Rabbi Shimon, even if the wool is dyed it still combines with the wool of other animals to constitute the minimum quantity of wool for which one is obligated to give the first of the sheared wool to the priest.

בֵּית שַׁמַּאי מַאי הִיא? דְּתַנְיָא: נָתַן לָהּ חִטִּין בְּאֶתְנַנָּהּ וַעֲשָׂאָן סוֹלֶת, זֵיתִים – וַעֲשָׂאָן שֶׁמֶן, עֲנָבִים – וַעֲשָׂאָן יַיִן, תָּנֵי חֲדָא: אָסוּר, וְתַנְיָא אִידָּךְ: מוּתָּר. וְאָמַר רַב יוֹסֵף, תָּנֵי גּוּרְיוֹן

What is the source that indicates that **Beit Shammai** maintain that an item that undergoes a change is considered to have the same status that it had before the change? **As it is taught** in a *baraita*: If one **gave** a prostitute **wheat as her payment, and she** ground it and **converted it into flour;** or if he gave her **olives, and she** squeezed them and **converted them into oil;** or if he gave her **grapes, and she** squeezed them and **converted them into wine;** and if, in any of these cases, she subsequently consecrated the final product, **it is taught** in **one** *baraita* that it is **prohibited** to sacrifice them upon the altar as a meal-offering or libation, as the Torah states: "You shall not bring the hire of a harlot or the price of a dog into the House of the Lord your God" (Deuteronomy 23:19). **And it is taught** in **another** *baraita* that it is **permitted,** as the Gemara will explain. **And Rav Yosef says:** It was **taught** by **Guryon**

NOTES

And dye is different – וְשָׁאנֵי צֶבַע: Since dyed wool can revert to its original state, it is not significantly changed. While washed wool may not appear to have been altered significantly, since it cannot be returned to its prior state, it is significantly changed.

LANGUAGE

Soap [*tzafon*] **– צָפוֹן:** Similar to the Greek *σάπων*, *sapon*, which was itself borrowed from a Gallic source. It refers to a substance similar to modern-day soaps, which are based on vegetable or animal oils treated with an alkaline solution. This product was invented by the Gauls and later its use spread to other lands.

HALAKHA

Indigo – קָלָא אִילָן: If one robs another of wool and dyes it, he has significantly changed it and therefore acquired it, even if the dye can be removed (Rabbeinu Yeruḥam; see Rambam), since the Gemara's explanation here is in accordance with the opinion of Rabbi Shimon. The Rema, citing the *Tur*, writes that he acquires it only if the dye cannot be removed, since the *halakha* is in accordance with the statement of Rav Ashi (Rambam *Sefer Nezikin*, *Hilkhot Gezeila VaAveda* 2:12; *Shulḥan Arukh*, *Ḥoshen Mishpat* 360:6–7, and in the comment of Rema, and *Beur HaGra* there).

HALAKHA

These but not in their changed form – הֵם וְלֹא שִׁינּוּיֵיהֶם: If one paid a prostitute for her services with wheat that was then ground into flour, or with olives that were then pressed to produce oil, or with grapes that were then crushed to produce wine, the finished products may be used as offerings, since they were changed. The *halakha* is in accordance with the opinion of Beit Hillel (Rambam *Sefer Avoda, Hilkhot Issurei Mizbe'aḥ* 4:15, 18).

These but not their offspring – הֵם וְלֹא וְלָדוֹתֵיהֶם: Although an animal used to pay a prostitute for her services may not be brought as an offering, its offspring is fit to be brought as an offering (Rambam *Sefer Avoda, Hilkhot Issurei Mizbe'aḥ* 3:12).

This individual is not reciting a blessing, etc. – אֵין זֶה מְבָרֵךְ וכו׳: One who eats a forbidden item, even if it is forbidden only by rabbinic law, does not recite a blessing before or after eating it. The Ra'avad writes that he does recite a blessing, but he cannot be counted as one of the three individuals who together are required to recite the introductory blessing to Grace after Meals. The *Magen Avraham* states that one who has acquired the food by changing it, e.g., he stole wheat and made bread, should recite Grace after Meals, as this blessing is required by Torah law, but not the blessing before eating, which is required by rabbinic law. Similarly, blessings are not recited over mitzvot performed with stolen items, e.g., one would not recite a blessing before donning stolen phylacteries (Rambam *Sefer Ahava, Hilkhot Berakhot* 1:19; *Shulḥan Arukh, Oraḥ Ḥayyim* 25:12, 196:1).

דְּמַאסְפּוּרַק: בֵּית שַׁמַּאי אוֹסְרִין, וּבֵית הִלֵּל מַתִּירִין. מַאי טַעְמֵיהּ דְּבֵית שַׁמַּאי? אָמַר קְרָא: ״גַּם שְׁנֵיהֶם״ – לְרַבּוֹת שִׁינּוּיֵיהֶם. וּבֵית הִלֵּל? אָמַר קְרָא: ״הֵם״ – וְלֹא שִׁינּוּיֵיהֶם.

of Asporak: Beit Shammai prohibit sacrificing these items **and Beit Hillel permit** doing so. The Gemara clarifies: **What is the reason of Beit Shammai?** The Gemara answers: **The verse states:** "You shall not bring the hire of a harlot or the price of a dog into the House of the Lord your God for any vow; for **even both of these** are an abomination unto the Lord your God" (Deuteronomy 23:19). The word "even" is an amplification, which serves **to include** in the prohibition these items in **their changed** form. **And** what is the reason of **Beit Hillel? The verse states "these"** to emphasize that the prohibition applies only to these items in their initial form, **but not** in **their changed** form.[H]

וּבֵית שַׁמַּאי, הָא כְּתִיב ״הֵם״! הַהוּא מִיבְּעֵי לֵיהּ: ״הֵם״ – וְלֹא וְלָדוֹתֵיהֶם. וּבֵית הִלֵּל? תַּרְתֵּי שָׁמְעַתְּ מִינַּהּ: ״הֵם״ – וְלֹא שִׁינּוּיֵיהֶם, ״הֵם״ – וְלֹא וְלָדוֹתֵיהֶם.

The Gemara asks: **And** according to **Beit Shammai, isn't** the word **"these" written** in the verse, indicating an exclusion? The Gemara responds: Beit Shammai **requires that** word to indicate that **"these"** items are forbidden, **but not the offspring** of animals given as payment to the prostitute. The Gemara asks: **And** according to **Beit Hillel,** what is the source of that *halakha*? The Gemara answers: According to Beit Hillel, **you learn two** *halakhot* **from this** word, as follows: **"These"** items are forbidden in their initial form **but not in their changed** form, and **"these"** items are forbidden **but not their offspring.**[H]

וּבֵית הִלֵּל נַמִי, הָכְתִיב ״גַּם״! ״גַּם״ לְבֵית הִלֵּל קַשְׁיָא.

The Gemara asks: **And** according to **Beit Hillel as well, isn't** the word **"even" written** in the verse, indicating an amplification? The Gemara answers: Indeed, the word **"even" is difficult for Beit Hillel.** It is not clear how they would interpret that word.

רַבִּי אֱלִיעֶזֶר בֶּן יַעֲקֹב מַאי הִיא?

The Gemara continues: **What is** the source that indicates that **Rabbi Eliezer ben Ya'akov** holds that an item that undergoes a change is still considered to have the same status that it had before the change?

דְּתַנְיָא, רַבִּי אֱלִיעֶזֶר בֶּן יַעֲקֹב אוֹמֵר: הֲרֵי שֶׁגָּזַל סְאָה שֶׁל חִטִּין, טְחָנָהּ, לְשָׁהּ וַאֲפָאָהּ וְהִפְרִישׁ מִמֶּנָּה חַלָּה, כֵּיצַד מְבָרֵךְ? אֵין זֶה מְבָרֵךְ אֶלָּא מְנָאֵץ, וְעַל זֶה נֶאֱמַר: ״בֹּצֵעַ בֵּרֵךְ נִאֵץ ה׳״.

The Gemara answers: **As it is taught** in a *baraita* that **Rabbi Eliezer ben Ya'akov says:** In the case of one **who robbed** another of **a *se'a* of wheat,** then **ground it, kneaded it, and baked it, and** he then **separated**[N] ***ḥalla* from it,** i.e., he separated the portion of the dough that one is required to separate and then give to a priest, **how can** he **recite the blessing** over the separation of *ḥalla*? **This** individual **is not reciting a blessing,**[H] but **rather** he is **blaspheming.**[N] **And with regard to this it is stated: "The robber who recites a blessing blasphemes the Lord"** (Psalms 10:3), which is referring to a robber who recites a blessing upon performing a mitzva with an item he stole. According to Rabbi Eliezer ben Ya'akov, although this wheat has been significantly changed, it is still considered a stolen item.

NOTES

And baked it and then separated, etc. – וַאֲפָאָהּ וְהִפְרִישׁ וכו׳: *Tosafot* ask why the *baraita* lists separating *ḥalla* after baking, when ordinarily *ḥalla* is separated from the unbaked dough. They give two answers: Either the *baraita* is discussing cakes, whose batter is too thin to be considered dough (see *Tosefot Rabbeinu Peretz*), or the *baraita* is emphasizing the fact that even after all of these changes, this grain maintains its status as having been stolen, and one who recites a blessing over it is in fact blaspheming.

This individual is not reciting a blessing, rather he is blaspheming – אֵין זֶה מְבָרֵךְ אֶלָּא מְנָאֵץ: In this case, it is better to recite no blessing at all. The Rambam rules that no blessing is ever recited over a forbidden item. By contrast, the Rosh on *Berakhot* 7:2 infers from the formulation of the Gemara: He is blaspheming, that one must recite a blessing even if it is blasphemy, since one may not derive any benefit from the world without reciting a blessing. The Meiri writes that although one is required to recite a blessing before eating stolen food, no blessing is recited over the separation of *ḥalla*, as this is a blessing prior to the performance of a mitzva, and it is inappropriate to recite a blessing of this type when the mitzva is performed in this manner. The Jerusalem Talmud indicates that a mitzva performed in this manner is not considered a mitzva at all (*Ḥalla* 1:5).

רַבִּי שִׁמְעוֹן בֶּן אֶלְעָזָר מַאי הִיא? דְּתַנְיָא, כְּלָל זֶה אָמַר רַבִּי שִׁמְעוֹן בֶּן אֶלְעָזָר: כָּל שֶׁבַח שֶׁהִשְׁבִּיחַ גַּזְלָן – יָדוֹ עַל הָעֶלְיוֹנָה, רָצָה – נוֹטֵל שִׁבְחוֹ, רָצָה – אוֹמֵר לוֹ ״הֲרֵי שֶׁלְּךָ לְפָנֶיךָ״.

The Gemara continues: **What is** the source that indicates that **Rabbi Shimon ben Elazar** holds that an item that undergoes a change is still considered to have the same status that it had before the change? **As it is taught** in a *baraita* (*Tosefta* 10:2) that **Rabbi Shimon ben Elazar stated this principle:** With regard to **any enhancement** to the stolen animal in **that it was enhanced** by the actions of the **robber,**[N] **he has the advantage** when repaying the owner. If **he desires, he takes his enhancement,** i.e., when he returns the animal, the robbery victim must pay the difference between its value at the time of the robbery and its current value, and **if he desires** he can return it to the owner and **say to him: That which is yours is before you.**

מַאי קָאָמַר? אֲמַר רַב שֵׁשֶׁת, הָכִי קָאָמַר: הִשְׁבִּיחָהּ – נוֹטֵל שִׁבְחוֹ, כָּחַשׁ – אוֹמֵר לוֹ ״הֲרֵי שֶׁלְּךָ לְפָנֶיךָ״, דְּשִׁינּוּי בִּמְקוֹמוֹ עוֹמֵד.

The Gemara expresses surprise: **What is he saying?** If the robber has a right to demand compensation for the enhancement to the animal, why would he ever return it without stating this demand? **Rav Sheshet said** that **this is** what he **is saying:** If the robber **enhanced it, he takes his enhancement.**[H] If the animal was **weakened,** the robber **says to him: That which is yours is before you,** and no further compensation is required. This is **because** despite **a change,** the changed item **remains in its place.** Since the robber has not acquired it, he simply returns the item to the robbery victim.

אִי הָכִי, אֲפִילּוּ הִשְׁבִּיחַ נַמִי! אָמְרִי: מִפְּנֵי תַּקָּנַת הַשָּׁבִים.

The Gemara asks: **If so,** i.e., if the robber has not acquired it, then **even if he enhanced it** that should be the *halakha* **as well.** The item should still belong to the robbery victim and the robber should not be entitled to compensation. The Sages **say** in response: The fact that the robber has a right to demand compensation for the enhancement is **due to an ordinance** instituted **for the penitent.** In order to ease the burden of one who desires to repent, the Sages instituted that the robber be reimbursed for the increase in the value of the animal. Otherwise, a robber might refrain from returning a stolen item.

רַבִּי יִשְׁמָעֵאל מַאי הִיא? דְּתַנְיָא: מִצְוַת פֵּאָה לְהַפְרִישׁ מִן הַקָּמָה, לֹא הִפְרִישׁ מִן הַקָּמָה – מַפְרִישׁ מִן הָעוֹמָרִים, לֹא הִפְרִישׁ מִן הָעוֹמָרִים – מַפְרִישׁ מִן הַכְּרִי עַד שֶׁלֹּא מֵרְחוֹ,

The Gemara continues: **What is** the source that indicates that **Rabbi Yishmael** holds that an item that undergoes a change is still considered to have the same status that it had before the change? The Gemara answers: **As it is taught** in a *baraita*: The ideal way to fulfill the **mitzva of produce in the corner of the field, which is given to the poor [*pe'a*],** is **to separate**[H] it **from the standing** grain, i.e., grain that has not been harvested. **If** one **did not separate it from the standing** grain, he **separates** it **from the sheaves** of grain that have already been harvested. If he **did not separate** it **from the sheaves,** he **separates** it **from the pile** of grain, **as long as** he **has not** yet **smoothed** the pile.[N]

מֵרְחוֹ – מְעַשֵּׂר וְנוֹתֵן לוֹ. מִשּׁוּם רַבִּי יִשְׁמָעֵאל אָמְרוּ: אַף מַפְרִישׁ מִן הָעִיסָּה וְנוֹתֵן לוֹ.

If he **smoothed** the pile of grain, activating the obligation to tithe the produce, he first **tithes** the grain **and** then **gives** a portion of the tithed produce **to** the poor as *pe'a*, so that the poor will not have to tithe what they receive. Additionally, **they said in the name of Rabbi Yishmael:** If he did not separate *pe'a* during any of the aforementioned stages and he made a dough from the grain, **he separates** *pe'a* **even from the dough**[N] **and gives it to** the poor. This indicates that even if the grain was changed, one is not exempt from the obligation of *pe'a*.

אֲמַר לֵיהּ רַב פַּפָּא לְאַבַּיֵי: אִיכְּפַל כָּל הָנֵי תַּנָּאֵי לְאַשְׁמוֹעִינַן כְּבֵית שַׁמַּאי? אֲמַר לֵיהּ, הָכִי קָאָמְרִי: לֹא נֶחְלְקוּ בֵּית שַׁמַּאי וּבֵית הִלֵּל בְּדָבָר זֶה.

The Gemara has now clarified the sources Abaye alluded to when he listed all the *tanna'im* who hold that despite a change, the changed item remains in its place. **Rav Pappa said to Abaye: Did all these *tanna'im* go to** so much trouble in **an effort [*ikhpal*]**[L] **to teach us** a *halakha* **in accordance with** the opinion of **Beit Shammai,** which is presumably not accepted as normative? Abaye **said to** Rav Pappa: **This is what they are saying: Beit Shammai and Beit Hillel did not engage in a dispute with regard to this matter.** All of the aforementioned *tanna'im* hold that even Beit Hillel agree that a change in the form of an item does not impact its status.

NOTES

Enhancement to the stolen animal in that it was enhanced by the robber – שֶׁבַח שֶׁהִשְׁבִּיחַ גַּזְלָן: The Ra'avad and the Rashba explain that this does not refer to enhancement that resulted from the efforts of the robber, e.g., he fattened the animal, since under those circumstances everyone agrees that the victim is not given the animal without paying the robber for his efforts. The discussion here concerns an animal that was enhanced on its own, i.e., it grew while under the care of the robber. The robber is compensated for this increase in value due to the ordinance instituted for the penitent. The Ra'avad, citing the Rif, infers from Rabbi Shimon ben Elazar's words: That it was enhanced by the robber, that the robber keeps only that which he actively enhanced, though the Rif agrees that the *halakha* does not follow this opinion. Everyone agrees that the robber neither receives nor pays any compensation for a rise or fall in the market price.

Smoothed the pile – מֵרְחוֹ: After it is stacked, the pile of grain is evened out with a special tool, at which point *teruma* and tithes are separated. The owner of the field is obligated to tithe the grain that will be given as *pe'a* because if the poor person had gathered *pe'a* from the field while the grain was still standing, it would be considered as though he acquired it from an ownerless field, which is exempt from tithe. Since it is the owner's actions that cause this grain to be obligated in tithes, he must tithe his portion and then give *pe'a* to the poor person from the tithed grain.

He separates *pe'a* even from the dough – אַף מַפְרִישׁ מִן הָעִיסָּה: One can separate *pe'a* not only from dough, but also from bread that has been baked. The *baraita* presents a case of separating *pe'a* from dough because before wheat is ground and made into dough, no essential change has been made to it. After that point, it is changed completely (Rashi).

HALAKHA

If the robber enhanced it he takes his enhancement, etc. – הִשְׁבִּיחָהּ נוֹטֵל שִׁבְחוֹ וכו׳: If one robbed another of an item, and the victim despaired of recovering it, and the stolen item was not changed, the robber owns any enhancement made to the stolen item after the victim's despair. When he returns the stolen item it is appraised, and the victim must pay the value of the enhancement. If it no longer exists, the robber pays only its value as of the time of the robbery. This is an ordinance instituted by the Sages in order to encourage robbers to repent (Rambam *Sefer Nezikin, Hilkhot Gezeila VaAveda* 2:2; *Shulḥan Arukh, Ḥoshen Mishpat* 362:2).

The mitzva of *pe'a* is to separate, etc. – מצות פאה להפריש וכו׳: One who reaps his field should not reap it completely but should leave one-sixtieth as *pe'a* for the poor. If he did not do so and harvested all the crops, he must give *pe'a* from the crops that he reaped. If he did not give *pe'a* until the completion of the grain harvest, he first tithes his produce and then gives *pe'a* from the tithed produce in the amount required for that field. Even if one ground the wheat into flour, kneaded it, and baked it, he must separate *pe'a* from the bread and give it to the poor. This is in accordance with the opinion of Rabbi Yishmael (Rambam *Sefer Zera'im, Hilkhot Mattenot Aniyyim* 1:1–2, 2:11).

LANGUAGE

Effort [*ikhpal*] – אִיכְּפַל: Some claim that this word is an extension of the root *alef, kaf, peh*, meaning loaded, or packed. Others claim that its root is *kaf, peh, lamed*, meaning to duplicate. The word indicates effort and exertion. The expression therefore means that the *tanna* put effort into phrasing something in a specific way, or to reiterating an idea.

NOTES

One who renounced ownership of his vineyard, etc. – **הַמַּפְקִיר כַּרְמוֹ וכו׳**: Since an ownerless field is exempt from tithes, this owner renounced ownership of his vineyard as an artifice to evade the obligation to tithe.

HALAKHA

One who renounced ownership of his vineyard and arose early, etc. – **הַמַּפְקִיר כַּרְמוֹ וְהִשְׁכִּים וכו׳**: One who renounces ownership of his vineyard, then arises early in the morning, reclaims ownership, and harvests it, is obligated in the mitzvot of *peret*, *olelot*, forgotten clusters, and *pe'a*. In Leviticus 19:9–10, the Torah states that these gifts must be given when harvesting "your field" or "your vineyard." Because this vineyard had belonged to him and belongs to him now, the designation "your vineyard" applies, and the gifts must be given. If one took possession of a field to which others had renounced ownership, he is exempt from giving all of these gifts. In either case, he is exempt from separating tithes (Rambam *Sefer Zera'im*, *Hilkhot Mattenot Aniyyim* 5:27).

BACKGROUND

Peret – **פֶּרֶט**: It is prohibited for the owner of a vineyard to collect individual fallen grapes during the harvest. Those grapes must be left for the poor (see Leviticus 19:10).

Olelot – **עוֹלֵלוֹת**: This term refers to clusters of grapes without a central stalk, or clusters on which the grapes do not hang down one upon the other. The Torah prohibits gathering these incompletely formed clusters of grapes. They must be left for the poor (see Leviticus 19:10 and Deuteronomy 24:21).

Forgotten clusters of grapes left for the poor – **שִׁכְחָה**: One who forgot a sheaf in the field or a cluster in the vineyard while harvesting may not return to collect it. It must be left as one of the agricultural gifts to the poor (see Deuteronomy 24:19).

Pe'a – **פֵּאָה**: The Torah states that it is prohibited for one to harvest the produce in the corner of his field. Rather, he must allow the poor to collect this produce themselves. The Sages decreed that the area of the corner must be at least one-sixtieth of the field. This mitzva is stated in the Torah (see Leviticus 19:9 and 23:22), and tractate *Pe'a* is devoted to exploring its details.

אֲמַר רָבָא: מִמַּאי? דִּלְמָא עַד כָּאן לָא קָאָמַר רַבִּי שִׁמְעוֹן בֶּן יְהוּדָה הָתָם – אֶלָּא בְּצֶבַע, הוֹאִיל וְיָכוֹל לְהַעֲבִירוֹ עַל יְדֵי צָפוֹן;

Rava said: From where can it be proven that all of the aforementioned *tanna'im* hold that an item that undergoes a change is still considered to have the same status that it had before the change? One can say that the reasons for their statements are due to other factors. **Perhaps Rabbi Shimon ben Yehuda states** his opinion, that it is not a significant change, **there,** in the case of the first of the sheared wool, **only with regard to dye,** which is a reversible change, **since one is able to remove it with soap.**

וְעַד כָּאן לָא קָאָמְרִי בֵּית שַׁמַּאי הָתָם – אֶלָּא לַגָּבוֹהַּ, מִשּׁוּם דְּאִימְאִיס;

And perhaps **Beit Shammai state** their opinion **there,** in the case of a harlot, **only** with regard to an offering **to the Most High, because** of the fact **that** the item **has become repugnant,** in being used as payment for the services of a prostitute, and therefore it cannot be used for an offering even if its form has changed.

וְעַד כָּאן לָא קָאָמַר רַבִּי אֱלִיעֶזֶר בֶּן יַעֲקֹב הָתָם – אֶלָּא לְעִנְיַן בְּרָכָה, מִשּׁוּם דַּהֲוָה לֵיהּ מִצְוָה הַבָּאָה בַּעֲבֵירָה;

And perhaps **Rabbi Eliezer ben Ya'akov states** his opinion **there,** where one robbed another of wheat, **only with regard to a blessing, because this is a mitzva** that **is performed through** commission of **a transgression,** but this does not indicate that a change is insignificant with regard to other matters.

וְעַד כָּאן לָא קָאָמַר רַבִּי שִׁמְעוֹן בֶּן אֶלְעָזָר הָתָם – אֶלָּא בְּהַכְחָשָׁה דְּהָדַר;

And perhaps **Rabbi Shimon ben Elazar states** his opinion **there,** where the condition of the animal changed, **only with regard to weakening** of the animal **that is reversible.** Since the animal's value can be restored by fattening it, the weakening is not deemed a significant change.

וְעַד כָּאן לָא קָאָמַר רַבִּי יִשְׁמָעֵאל הָתָם – אֶלָּא לְעִנְיַן פֵּאָה, מִשּׁוּם דִּכְתִיב ״תַּעֲזֹב״ יְתֵירָא! וְכִי תֵּימָא, לִיגְמַר מִינֵּיהּ – מַתְּנוֹת עֲנִיִּים שָׁאנֵי,

And perhaps **Rabbi Yishmael states** his opinion **there,** where one separated *pe'a* at a late stage, **only with regard to** ***pe'a***, **because it is written: "You shall leave** them for the poor" **an additional** time. It is mentioned twice, in Leviticus 19:10 and Leviticus 23:22. One of these terms is superfluous, indicating that *pe'a* must be given to the poor under all circumstances, even if the grain was changed and made into dough. **And if you would say: Let us derive from** ***pe'a*** that in other halakhic domains the status of an item is not affected by its undergoing a change, *pe'a* cannot function as a source because **gifts to the poor are different** from other *halakhot*.

כִּדְבָעֵי רַבִּי יוֹנָתָן. דְּבָעֵי רַבִּי יוֹנָתָן: מַאי טַעֲמָא דְּרַבִּי יִשְׁמָעֵאל? מִשּׁוּם דְּקָסָבַר שִׁינּוּי אֵינוֹ קוֹנֶה, אוֹ דִּלְמָא בְּעָלְמָא קָסָבַר שִׁינּוּי קוֹנֶה, וְהָכָא מִשּׁוּם דִּכְתִיב ״תַּעֲזֹב״ יְתֵירָא?

The Gemara notes: Rava's claim that no definitive conclusion with regard to the opinion of Rabbi Yishmael concerning a changed item is supported by the statement of another *amora* is **like the dilemma raised by Rabbi Yonatan, as Rabbi Yonatan raises a dilemma: What is the reason** for the ruling **of Rabbi Yishmael?** Is it **because he holds** that **change does not** cause one to **acquire** an item? **Or perhaps he generally holds** that **change** does cause one to **acquire** an item, **but here,** in the case of *pe'a*, it is different **because** the term **"You shall leave" is written an additional** time.

וְאִם תִּמְצֵי לוֹמַר, טַעֲמָא דְּרַבִּי יִשְׁמָעֵאל מִשּׁוּם דְּקָסָבַר שִׁינּוּי אֵינוֹ קוֹנֶה, ״תַּעֲזֹב״ יְתֵירָא דִּכְתַב רַחֲמָנָא לָמָּה לִי? וְתוּ, לְרַבָּנַן ״תַּעֲזֹב״ יְתֵירָא דִּכְתַב רַחֲמָנָא לָמָּה לִי?

Having quoted Rabbi Yonatan's dilemma, the Gemara asks: **And if you say** that **the reason** for the ruling **of Rabbi Yishmael is that he holds that change does not** cause one to **acquire** an item, **why do I** need the **additional** term **"You shall leave," which the Merciful One writes** in the Torah? **And furthermore, according to** the opinion of **the Rabbis,** who hold that *pe'a* may not be taken from dough, **why** do I need **the additional** term **"You shall leave" that the Merciful One writes?**

מִבָּעֵי לֵיהּ לְכִדְתַנְיָא: הַמַּפְקִיר כַּרְמוֹ, וְהִשְׁכִּים לַבֹּקֶר וּבְצָרוֹ – חַיָּיב בְּפֶרֶט וּבְעוֹלְלוֹת וּבְשִׁכְחָה וּבְפֵאָה, וּפָטוּר מִן הַמַּעֲשֵׂר.

The Gemara responds: This additional term **is necessary for that which is taught** in a *baraita*: **One who renounced ownership of his vineyard**[N] **and arose early**[H] **in the morning** before anyone else took possession of it **and harvested it is obligated in** the mitzva of **individual fallen** grapes left for the poor [***peret***],[B] **and in** the mitzva of **incompletely formed clusters** of grapes left for the poor [***olelot***],[B] **and in** the mitzva of **forgotten** clusters of grapes left for the poor[B] **and in** the mitzva of ***pe'a***.[B] These are the four gifts to the poor that the Torah requires one to give from a vineyard. **But he is exempt from the** mitzva to **tithe** his produce, because this requirement does not apply to an ownerless field. The obligation to give gifts to the poor in this case is derived from the additional mention of the term "You shall leave."

אָמַר רַב יְהוּדָה אָמַר שְׁמוּאֵל: הֲלָכָה כְּרַבִּי שִׁמְעוֹן בֶּן אֶלְעָזָר.

§ The Gemara returns to the discussion of a stolen item that underwent a change. **Rav Yehuda says that Shmuel says:** The ***halakha*** **is in accordance with** the opinion of **Rabbi Shimon ben Elazar,** who says that even if the stolen animal deteriorated, it is returned to the owner in its current state.

וּמִי אֲמַר שְׁמוּאֵל הָכִי? וְהָאָמַר שְׁמוּאֵל: אֵין שָׁמִין לֹא לְגַנָּב וְלֹא לְגַזְלָן אֶלָּא לִנְזָקִין!

The Gemara expresses surprise: **But did Shmuel** actually **say this? But doesn't Shmuel say: One does not appraise** the change in value, **neither for a thief nor for a robber. Rather,** they keep the stolen animal and pay back the victim with their own money; one appraises the change only for one obligated to pay **for damage?**[N]

בִּשְׁלָמָא לְרָבָא, דְּאָמַר: כִּי קָאָמַר רַבִּי שִׁמְעוֹן בֶּן אֶלְעָזָר הָתָם בְּהַכְחָשָׁה דַּהֲדַר – לָא קַשְׁיָא, כִּי קָאָמַר הֲלָכָה כְּרַבִּי שִׁמְעוֹן בֶּן אֶלְעָזָר דְּשִׁינּוּי בִּמְקוֹמוֹ עוֹמֵד – בְּהַכְחָשָׁה דַּהֲדַר, וְכִי קָאָמַר שְׁמוּאֵל הָתָם: אֵין שָׁמִין לֹא לְגַנָּב וְלֹא לְגַזְלָן אֶלָּא לִנְזָקִין – בְּהַכְחָשָׁה דְּלָא הָדַר.

Granted, according to the opinion of **Rava, who said** earlier in response to Abaye: **When Rabbi Shimon ben Elazar states** his opinion **there,** he stated it only **with regard to weakening** of the animal **that is reversible,** this is **not difficult: When** Shmuel **says** that the ***halakha*** **is in accordance with** the opinion of **Rabbi Shimon ben Elazar,** who holds **that** despite **a change,** the changed item **remains in its place,** he stated this **with regard to weakening** of the animal **which is reversible,** in which case the change is insignificant. **And when Shmuel says there: One does not appraise** the change in value, **neither for a thief nor for a robber,** but rather one appraises the change **only** for one obligated to pay **for damage,** he stated this **with regard to weakening** of the animal **that is irreversible.**

אֶלָּא לְאַבָּיֵי, דְּאָמַר: כִּי קָאָמַר רַבִּי שִׁמְעוֹן בֶּן אֶלְעָזָר – בְּהַכְחָשָׁה דְּלָא הָדַר קָאָמַר, מַאי אִיכָּא לְמֵימַר?

But according to Abaye, who said that **when Rabbi Shimon ben Elazar states** his opinion, **he states it** even **with regard to weakening** of the animal **which is irreversible, what can be said?**

אַבָּיֵי מַתְנֵי הָכִי, אָמַר רַב יְהוּדָה אָמַר שְׁמוּאֵל:

The Gemara responds: **Abaye taught** the statement of Shmuel **like this: Rav Yehuda says** that **Shmuel says:**

NOTES

One does not appraise the damage neither for a thief nor for a robber, rather for damage – אֵין שָׁמִין לֹא לְגַנָּב וְלֹא לְגַזְלָן אֶלָּא לִנְזָקִין: If one person's ox killed another's ox, the owner of the ox that gored returns the carcass to its owner, and the court appraises the difference between the value of this ox when it was alive and the value of its carcass. The owner of the ox that gored then pays the difference. If one stole an animal and it died or its condition deteriorated in his possession, he does not return it. Instead, he pays the value of the animal at the time of the theft. This indicates that he acquires the animal as a result of its deterioration.

אָמְרוּ הֲלָכָה כְּרַבִּי שִׁמְעוֹן בֶּן אֶלְעָזָר. וְלֵיהּ לָא סְבִירָא לֵיהּ.

Some **said** that the ***halakha*** **is in accordance with** the opinion of **Rabbi Shimon ben Elazar, but** Shmuel **himself does not hold accordingly.**

אָמַר רַבִּי חִיָּיא בַּר אַבָּא אָמַר רַבִּי יוֹחָנָן: דְּבַר תּוֹרָה – גְּזֵילָה הַנִּשְׁתַּנֵּית חוֹזֶרֶת בְּעֵינֶיהָ, שֶׁנֶּאֱמַר: ״וְהֵשִׁיב אֶת הַגְּזֵלָה אֲשֶׁר גָּזָל״, מִכָּל מָקוֹם. וְאִם תֹּאמַר: מִשְׁנָתֵנוּ! מִשּׁוּם תַּקָּנַת הַשָּׁבִים.

The Gemara continues the discussion of acquisition of a stolen item due to a change it underwent. **Rabbi Ḥiyya bar Abba says** that **Rabbi Yoḥanan says: By Torah law, a stolen item that has changed is returned as is, as it is stated: "And he shall restore that which he took by robbery"** (Leviticus 5:23). This indicates that he shall return it **in any case,** even if it has been changed. **And if you say:** In **our mishna** it is stated that if the stolen item is changed the robber gives monetary compensation rather than returning the item, that policy was instituted by the Sages **due to the ordinance** instituted **for the penitent.**

וּמִי אֲמַר רַבִּי יוֹחָנָן הָכִי? וְהָאָמַר רַבִּי יוֹחָנָן: הֲלָכָה כִּסְתַם מִשְׁנָה, וּתְנַן: לֹא הִסְפִּיק לִיתְּנוֹ לוֹ עַד שֶׁצְּבָעוֹ – פָּטוּר!

The Gemara asks: **But did Rabbi Yoḥanan** actually **say that? But doesn't Rabbi Yoḥanan say:** The ***halakha*** **is in accordance with an unattributed mishna, and we learned** in a mishna with regard to first of the sheared wool (*Ḥullin* 135a): If the owner of the sheep **did not manage to give** the sheared wool **to** the priest **before he dyed it,** he is **exempt** from giving it to the priest. This indicates that dyeing the wool is a significant change.

אֲמַר לְהוּ הַהוּא מִדְּרַבָּנַן וְרַבִּי יַעֲקֹב שְׁמֵיהּ: לְדִידִי מְפָרְשָׁא לִי מִינֵּיהּ דְּרַבִּי יוֹחָנָן – כְּגוֹן שֶׁגָּזַל עֵצִים מְשׁוּפִּין וַעֲשָׂאָן כֵּלִים, דַּהֲוָה לֵיהּ שִׁינּוּי הַחוֹזֵר לִבְרִיָּיתוֹ.

One of the Rabbis, whose name was Rabbi Ya'akov, said to them: It was explained to me directly **by Rabbi Yoḥanan** that he was referring to a case **where he robbed** another of **sanded wood and fashioned it into vessels, which is a change** in which the item **can revert to its original state.**[H] Consequently, the robber does not acquire the item by Torah law, but rather due to the ordinance instituted for the penitent.

HALAKHA

Which is a change in which the item can revert to its original state – דַּהֲוָה לֵיהּ שִׁינּוּי הַחוֹזֵר לִבְרִיָּיתוֹ: If one robbed another of an item and the victim despaired of retrieving it, even if it was not irreversibly changed, the robber acquires any increase in the value of the item after the victim's despair and pays only the value of the item when the victim despaired of retrieving it. This was instituted by the Sages as part of the ordinance for the penitent. This ruling is in accordance with the opinion of Rabbi Yoḥanan, as explained by Rabbi Ya'akov (Rambam *Sefer Nezikin, Hilkhot Gezeila VaAveda* 2:2; *Shulḥan Arukh, Ḥoshen Mishpat* 362:2).

תָּנוּ רַבָּנַן: הַגַּזְלָנִין וּמַלְוֵי בְּרִבִּית שֶׁהֶחְזִירוּ – אֵין מְקַבְּלִין מֵהֶן, וְהַמְקַבֵּל מֵהֶן – אֵין רוּחַ חֲכָמִים נוֹחָה הֵימֶנּוּ.

§ Having mentioned the ordinance instituted for the penitent, the Gemara discusses other details of this ordinance. **The Sages taught** in a *baraita* (*Tosefta, Shevi'it* 8:11): With regard to **robbers or usurers**[H] **that returned** either the stolen item or the interest to the one from whom they took it, **one should not accept it from them. And** with regard to **one who does accept it from them, the Sages are displeased with him,**[N] since by doing so he discourages those who wish to repent.

אָמַר רַבִּי יוֹחָנָן: בִּימֵי רַבִּי נִשְׁנֵית מִשְׁנָה זוֹ, דְּתַנְיָא: מַעֲשֶׂה בְּאָדָם אֶחָד שֶׁבִּיקֵּשׁ לַעֲשׂוֹת תְּשׁוּבָה, אָמְרָה לוֹ אִשְׁתּוֹ: רֵיקָה, אִם אַתָּה עוֹשֶׂה תְּשׁוּבָה, אֲפִילּוּ אַבְנֵט אֵינוֹ שֶׁלְּךָ! וְנִמְנַע וְלֹא עָשָׂה תְּשׁוּבָה. בְּאוֹתָהּ שָׁעָה אָמְרוּ: הַגַּזְלָנִין וּמַלְוֵי רִבִּיּוֹת שֶׁהֶחְזִירוּ – אֵין מְקַבְּלִין מֵהֶם, וְהַמְקַבֵּל מֵהֶם – אֵין רוּחַ חֲכָמִים נוֹחָה הֵימֶנּוּ.

Rabbi Yoḥanan says: This mishna, i.e., the statement of the *Tosefta*, **was taught in the days of Rabbi** Yehuda HaNasi,[N] **as it is taught in** a *baraita*: There was **an incident with regard to one man who desired to repent** after having been a thief for many years. **His wife said to him: Empty one** [*reika*],[L] **if you repent** you will have to return all the stolen items to their rightful owners, and **even** the **belt** that you are wearing **is not yours, and he refrained and did not repent. At that time,** the Sages **said:** With regard to **robbers or usurers that returned** either the stolen item or the interest to the one from whom they took it, **one should not accept it from them.** And concerning **one who does accept it from them, the Sages are displeased with him.**

מֵיתִיבֵי: הִנִּיחַ לָהֶם אֲבִיהֶם מָעוֹת שֶׁל רִבִּית, אַף עַל פִּי שֶׁהֵן יוֹדְעִין שֶׁהֵן רִבִּית – אֵין חַיָּיבִין לְהַחֲזִיר; אִינְהוּ הוּא דְּלָא, הָא אֲבִיהֶם חַיָּיב לְהַחֲזִיר!

The Gemara **raises an objection**[N] from a *baraita*: With regard to children whose deceased **father left them**[N] **money** paid **as interest, although they know that it is interest, they are not obligated to return** it. The Gemara infers: **They,** the children, **are** the ones **that are not** obligated to return it, **but their father** would have been **obligated to return** it, and his victims may accept his money.

בְּדִין הוּא דַּאֲבִיהֶם נַמִּי אֵינוֹ חַיָּיב לְהַחֲזִיר, וְהָא דְּקָתָנֵי בְּדִידְהוּ – מִשּׁוּם דְּקָא בָּעֵי לְמִתְנֵי סֵיפָא: הִנִּיחַ לָהֶם אֲבִיהֶם פָּרָה וְטַלִּית וְכָל דָּבָר הַמְסוּיָּים – חַיָּיבִין לְהַחֲזִיר מִפְּנֵי כְּבוֹד אֲבִיהֶם – תְּנָא רֵישָׁא נַמִּי בְּדִידְהוּ.

The Gemara responds: **By right,** the *baraita* should have taught **that their father also** would **not** have been **obligated to return** it. **And** the fact **that** the *baraita* **teaches** this *halakha* **with regard to** the children is **because** of the fact **that** the *baraita* **wants to teach** a *halakha* in **the latter clause:** If **their** deceased **father left them a cow, or a garment, or any** other **specific item** he had stolen or taken as interest, **they are obligated to return** it **due to the honor of their father,** so that the item not serve as a reminder to all that their father transgressed. Since this *halakha* needs to be stated specifically with regard to the children, **the first clause** of the *baraita* **is also taught with regard to them.**

וּמִפְּנֵי כְּבוֹד אֲבִיהֶם חַיָּיבִין לְהַחֲזִיר? אִיקְּרֵי כָּאן "וְנָשִׂיא בְעַמְּךָ לֹא תָאֹר", בְּעוֹשֶׂה מַעֲשֵׂה עַמְּךָ!

The Gemara asks: **But** is it true that **due to the honor of their father they are obligated to return** the item or money? **I will read here** the verse: "You shall not revile God, **nor curse a ruler of your people**" (Exodus 22:27), from which the Sages inferred that the prohibition against cursing a ruler is in effect only **with regard to** a ruler that **acts as a member of your people,** i.e., in accordance with Torah law. One who curses a wicked ruler does not violate this prohibition. Similarly, if one's father is wicked, the mitzva to honor him should not apply. Why would his children have to return items that he stole due to his honor?

HALAKHA

Robbers or usurers – **הַגַּזְלָנִין וּמַלְוֵי בְּרִבִּית**: If a robber or usurer whose primary livelihood came from these activities repents, and he attempts to return a stolen item that is no longer in its prior form or a non-distinctive item taken as interest, it should not be accepted. The Sages are displeased with one who does accept it. This ordinance was instituted to assist those who wish to repent, in order to ensure that they do not refrain from repentance due to the difficulty of returning everything they have stolen.

If the robber or usurer wishes to fulfill his obligation to Heaven and return what he has taken, and he states this explicitly to the original owner (*Sma*), the owner may accept it. The Rema writes that if the robber did not volunteer to return the item but was summoned to court after a complaint by the one from whom he stole, he is required to return what he has taken (Rambam *Sefer Nezikin*, *Hilkhot Gezeila VaAveda* 1:13 and *Sefer Mishpatim*, *Hilkhot Malve VeLoveh* 4:5; *Shulḥan Arukh*, *Ḥoshen Mishpat* 366:1 and *Yoreh De'a* 161:7).

LANGUAGE

Empty one [*reika*] – **רֵיקָה**: This expression was apparently quite common, as it appears in external sources as well. It is the Aramaic form of the Hebrew word *reik*, meaning empty, as in: "Then Yiftah fled from his brethren, and dwelt in the land of Tob; and there were gathered empty [*reikim*] fellows to Yiftah, and they went out with him" (Judges 11:3). Using this expression to describe someone implies that he is lacking the basic qualities to be a functional member of society.

NOTES

The Sages are displeased with him [*noḥa heimennu*] – **אֵין רוּחַ חֲכָמִים נוֹחָה הֵימֶנּוּ**: In its literal sense, this means that the Sages are not pleased or do not have peace of mind. Rashi here explains the word *noḥa* somewhat differently, as related to the word resting. The phrase therefore means that the spirit of the Sages does not rest within the heart of one who accepts payment.

In the days of Rabbi Yehuda HaNasi – **בִּימֵי רַבִּי**: *Tosafot* quote the opinion of Rabbeinu Tam, who states that the *halakha* that one should not accept payment from a thief applied only in the generation of Rabbi Yehuda HaNasi, but not during earlier or later generations. *Tosafot* cite numerous instances in the Talmud that indicate that in the days of the *amora'im*, thieves were obligated to return what they had stolen. Alternatively, *Tosafot* suggest that this ordinance was instituted only with regard to a thief who wishes to repent. If a thief was brought to justice and compelled to return what he had taken, one would be allowed to accept it. Rabbi Barukh HaSefaradi, as well as Rabbeinu Yonatan and the Ramah, cite Rav Hai Gaon as having a similar opinion.

The Gemara raises an objection, etc. – **מֵיתִיבֵי וכו׳**: The Ra'avad and the Rid note that throughout this discussion, the Gemara specifically cites *baraitot* as proof rather than the mishna here. Although Rabbi Yehuda HaNasi redacted the Mishna, it was primarily formulated in the generations that preceded him and consequently compiled before the ordinance. It can therefore not be cited as a proof in this discussion. The *baraitot*, by contrast, which were formulated at a later date than the Mishna, can serve as proof of how *halakha* was practiced after the ordinance. Rabbeinu Tam writes a similar idea, in accordance with his opinion that the ordinance was in effect specifically in the time of Rabbi Yehuda HaNasi (see *Tosafot*).

Whose father left them, etc. – **הִנִּיחַ לָהֶם אֲבִיהֶם וכו׳**: The *tanna* of this *baraita* holds that when heirs take possession of an inheritance, it is a transference of ownership from the estate of the father to the child, and not an extension of the father's ownership. Therefore, once the money is in their possession, it is not considered stolen (Rashi).

כְּדַאֲמַר רַב פִּנְחָס: בְּשֶׁעָשָׂה תְּשׁוּבָה, הָכָא נַמִי בְּשֶׁעָשָׂה תְּשׁוּבָה. אִי עָשָׂה תְּשׁוּבָה, מַאי בָּעֵי גַּבֵּיהּ? אִיבָּעֵי לֵיהּ לְאַהְדּוּרֵי! שֶׁלֹּא הִסְפִּיק לְהַחֲזִיר עַד שֶׁמֵּת.

The Gemara responds: It is like that which **Rav Pineḥas said** concerning a different case: This is a case **where he repented. Here too,** it is a case **where** the father **repented,** and since he is no longer wicked, his children are obligated to honor him. The Gemara asks: **If he repented, what was** the stolen item or interest **doing with him?**[N] **He should have returned it** while he was still alive. The Gemara responds: It is a case **where he did not manage to return it before he died.** Consequently, the children must return the items in order to uphold their father's honor.

תָּא שְׁמַע: הַגַּזְלָנִים וּמַלְוֵי בְּרִבִּית, אַף עַל פִּי שֶׁגָּבוּ – מַחֲזִירִין.

The Gemara raises another contradiction: **Come and hear** the statement of another *baraita*: With regard to **robbers and usurers, although they collected** the stolen item or interest, **they return** it.

גַּזְלָנִין מַאי "שֶׁגָּבוּ" אִיכָּא? אִי גְּזוּל – גְּזוּל, וְאִי לָא גְּזוּל – לָא גְּזוּל! אֶלָּא אֵימָא: הַגַּזְלָנִין, וּמַאי נִיהוּ? מַלְוֵי רִבִּיּוֹת, אַף עַל פִּי שֶׁגָּבוּ – מַחֲזִירִין! אָמְרִי: מַחֲזִירִין וְאֵין מְקַבְּלִין מֵהֶם.

The Gemara first clarifies the meaning of the *baraita*: In the case of **robbers, what collection is there,** i.e., why did the *baraita* use the term: Collected, in this context? **If they robbed, they robbed** and did not collect anything; **and if they did not rob, they did not rob** and cannot be called robbers at all. **Rather,** emend the text of the *baraita* to **say:** With regard to **robbers, and who are they,** i.e., what is meant by the term: Robbers? It is referring to **usurers.** The Gemara resumes its citation of the *baraita*: **Although they collected** the interest, **they must return** it. This is contrary to the ruling of the *Tosefta* that if robbers and usurers return what they have taken, it is not accepted. The Gemara explains: **Say** that this *baraita* means that **they return** it, **but one does not accept** it **from them.**

אֶלָּא לָמָּה מַחֲזִירִין? לָצֵאת יְדֵי שָׁמַיִם.

The Gemara asks: **But why do they return** it if it will not be accepted? The Gemara responds: In order **to fulfill** their obligation to **Heaven.**[N] In order to fully repent, they must at least offer to return to the debtors the interest they took unlawfully.

תָּא שְׁמַע: הָרוֹעִים, וְהַגַּבָּאִין, וְהַמּוֹכְסִין – תְּשׁוּבָתָן קָשָׁה, וּמַחֲזִירִין לַמַּכִּירִין!

The Gemara raises a contradiction from another source. **Come and hear** the statement of another *baraita*: With regard to **shepherds** who allow their animals to graze in other people's fields, thereby stealing from the owners; **or** tax **collectors**[H] who are hired to collect taxes on behalf of the government and collect excessive sums; **or tax collectors**[B] who purchase the right to collect taxes themselves and collect unlawfully, **their repentance is difficult,** since they steal from the public. It is difficult for them to find every one of their victims in order to pay them restitution, **and they must return** what they have stolen **to whomever they recognize** as victims of their theft. This *baraita* indicates that thieves do return what they have stolen.

אָמְרִי: מַחֲזִירִין וְאֵין מְקַבְּלִין מֵהֶם. וְאֶלָּא לָמָּה מַחֲזִירִין? לָצֵאת יְדֵי שָׁמַיִם. אִי הָכִי, אַמַּאי תְּשׁוּבָתָן קָשָׁה?

The Gemara answers: **Say** that **they return** it, **but one does not accept it from them.** The Gemara asks: **But why do they return** it if it will not be accepted? The Gemara responds: In order **to fulfill** their obligation to **Heaven.** The Gemara asks: **If so,** if they are not actually obligated to return what they have stolen, **why is their repentance difficult?**

וְעוֹד, אֵימָא סֵיפָא: וְשֶׁאֵין מַכִּירִין – יַעֲשֶׂה בָּהֶן צָרְכֵי צִיבּוּר, וְאָמַר רַב חִסְדָּא: בּוֹרוֹת, שִׁיחִין וּמְעָרוֹת! אֶלָּא, לָא קַשְׁיָא: כָּאן קוֹדֶם תַּקָּנָה, כָּאן לְאַחַר תַּקָּנָה.

And furthermore, say the latter clause of the *baraita*: **And** as for the money belonging to those **that they do not recognize** as their victims, **they should use** that money **for community needs. And Rav Ḥisda says:** This means providing **pits, ditches, and caves,** which benefit the general public. This indicates that a thief actually does pay back what he has stolen. **Rather,** this contradiction must be resolved differently. It is **not difficult: Here,** where the *baraita* states that he must actually return what he has stolen, it is referring to a time **before the ordinance** for the penitent was instituted. **There,** where the *baraita* states that one does not accept the repayment from a robber, it is referring to a time **after the ordinance** was instituted.

וְהַשְׁתָּא דְּאָמַר רַב נַחְמָן: בְּשֶׁאֵין גְּזֵילָה קַיֶּימֶת, אֲפִילּוּ תֵּימָא אִידִי וְאִידִי לְאַחַר תַּקָּנָה, וְלָא קַשְׁיָא.

The Gemara adds: **And now that Rav Naḥman says** that when the Sages say that he does not return what he has stolen, they refer only to a case **where the stolen item does not exist** in its initial form, and **you** can **even say** that **this and that,** both *baraitot*, are referring to a time **after the ordinance** was instituted, **and it is not difficult.**

NOTES

What was it doing with him – מַאי בָּעֵי גַּבֵּיהּ: *Tosafot* explain that if the father kept the stolen item without concern for his own honor, his sons are not required to accord him more honor than he accorded himself.

To fulfill their obligation to Heaven – לָצֵאת יְדֵי שָׁמַיִם: The *Tur* explains that if one goes beyond the letter of the law and returns the interest, it is permitted for the one who paid the interest to receive it from him, and this does not contradict the ordinance for the penitent. The *Yam shel Shlomo* disagrees, arguing that since the Gemara does not reject its previous conclusion that when the interest is returned one may not accept it, one still may not accept it. Nevertheless, he rules that if the usurer entreated the borrower to take back the interest so that he could fulfill his obligation to Heaven, he would be permitted to receive it from him, since the Sages did not enforce their ordinance in such a situation.

HALAKHA

Shepherds or collectors, etc. – הָרוֹעִים וְהַגַּבָּאִין וכו׳: It is impossible for shepherds who allowed their animals to graze in other people's fields, tax collectors who collected taxes illegally in the name of the government, or tax collectors who stole from the masses to compensate all their victims. They should use the money that they must return in the service of communal needs, e.g., providing water cisterns that are open for use by the public (*Shulḥan Arukh*, *Ḥoshen Mishpat* 366:2).

BACKGROUND

Tax collectors – מוֹכְסִין: For centuries, and in some places until relatively recently, it was common for governments to lease the right to collect revenues, e.g., taxes and customs duties, to an individual. He would pay a fixed sum to the government and then collect revenues by its authority. The primary lessee could then delegate the task of collection to other lessees by a similar arrangement, by having them pay him a fixed amount for the right to collect. The collection of revenues was a profitable business for these people, whose earnings were commensurate with the revenues that they collected. This arrangement often resulted in corruption, with the collectors forgoing the debts of friends and family, while placing a heavier burden on others. For this reason, they were generally regarded as thieves.

כָּאן בִּגְזֵילָה קַיֶּימֶת כָּאן בְּשֶׁאֵין גְּזֵילָה קַיֶּימֶת. וְהָא אַבְנֵט, דִּגְזֵילָה קַיֶּימֶת הִיא! מַאי אַבְנֵט? דְּמֵי אַבְנֵט.

Here, the *baraita* that rules that one may accept the stolen item is referring to a case **where the stolen item** still **exists. There,** the *baraita* that rules not to accept it even if the robber seeks only to fulfill his obligation to Heaven is referring to a case where the **stolen item does not** still **exist.** The Gemara asks: **But** the incident in which the robber's wife told him that he would have to return even the **belt,** which was the impetus for instituting the ordinance for the penitents, was a case **where** the **stolen item** still **exists,** in which case the robber would be obligated to return it even after the ordinance was instituted. The Gemara answers: **What** is meant by: Even the **belt? The value of the belt,** but the actual belt was no longer in his possession.

וְכָל הֵיכָא דִּגְזֵילָה קַיֶּימֶת, לָא עֲבוּד רַבָּנַן תַּקַּנְתָּא? וַהֲרֵי מְרִישׁ דִּגְזֵילָה קַיֶּימֶת הִיא, וּתְנַן: עַל הַמְּרִישׁ הַגָּזוּל שֶׁבְּנָאוֹ בַּבִּירָה – שֶׁיִּטּוֹל דָּמָיו, מִפְּנֵי תַּקָּנַת הַשָּׁבִים! שָׁאנֵי הָתָם, דְּכֵיוָן דְּאִיכָּא פְּסֵידָא דְּבִירָה, שַׁוְיוּהּ רַבָּנַן כִּדְלֵיתָא.

The Gemara asks: **And** is it so that **the Sages did not institute an ordinance** for the penitent **anywhere that** the **stolen item** still **exists? But there is** the case of **a beam,**[H] **which is a stolen item that** still **exists, and we learned** in a mishna (*Gittin* 55a): **With regard to a stolen beam that** the robber **built into a building,** the Sages instituted **that** the robbery victim **should take its monetary** value and not the actual beam **because of the ordinance** instituted for **the penitent,** i.e., so that the penitent not be required to destroy his house. This indicates that the ordinance instituted for the penitent is in effect even when the stolen item still exists. The Gemara answers: **There it is different. Since** in that case **there is the loss of the** entire **building,**[N] **the Sages treat** the beam **as though it were not** in existence.

״גָּזַל פָּרָה מְעוּבֶּרֶת וְיָלְדָה״ וכו׳. תָּנוּ רַבָּנַן: הַגּוֹזֵל רָחֵל וּגְזָזָהּ, פָּרָה וְיָלְדָה – מְשַׁלֵּם אוֹתָהּ וְאֶת גִּיזּוֹתֶיהָ וְאֶת וְלָדוֹתֶיהָ, דִּבְרֵי רַבִּי מֵאִיר; רַבִּי יְהוּדָה אוֹמֵר: גְּזֵילָה חוֹזֶרֶת בְּעֵינֶיהָ; רַבִּי שִׁמְעוֹן אוֹמֵר: רוֹאִין אוֹתָהּ כְּאִילּוּ הִיא שׁוּמָא אֶצְלוֹ בְּכֶסֶף.

§ The mishna teaches: If one **robbed** another of **a pregnant cow, and it** then **gave birth** while in the robber's possession, or if one robbed another of a ewe that was laden with wool and the robber then sheared it, he pays the owner the value of a cow that is ready to give birth, or the value of a ewe that is ready to be shorn. In connection with this, **the Sages taught** in a *baraita*: **One who robs** another of **a ewe and sheared it,** and similarly, one who robs another of **a cow and it gave birth,** must **pay it and its sheared wool**[N] **or** it and **its offspring;** this is **the statement of Rabbi Meir. Rabbi Yehuda says: A stolen item is returned as is. Rabbi Shimon says:** A stolen item **is viewed as though it had been monetarily appraised** at the time of the robbery, and the robber pays only that amount.

אִיבַּעְיָא לְהוּ: מַאי טַעְמֵיהּ דְּרַבִּי מֵאִיר? מִשּׁוּם דְּקָסָבַר שִׁינּוּי בִּמְקוֹמוֹ עוֹמֵד, אוֹ דִּילְמָא בְּעָלְמָא שִׁינּוּי קוֹנֶה, וְהָכָא קְנָסָא הוּא דְּקָא קָנֵיס?

The Gemara clarifies the different opinions in this *baraita*. **A dilemma was raised before** the Sages: **What is the reasoning of Rabbi Meir,** who holds that the robber returns the animal and its sheared wool or the animal and its offspring? Is it **due to** the fact **that he holds** that despite **a change,** the changed item **remains in its place?** Despite its changes, the animal always remained in the possession of the robbery victims, and consequently any increase in value belongs to them. **Or, perhaps** Rabbi Meir **generally** holds that one **acquires** an item due to **a change** in it, and therefore the wool or offspring should belong to the robber by right, **but here it is a penalty that he imposes,**[N] which forces the robber to return items that are technically his.

לְמַאי נָפְקָא מִינָּהּ – לְהֵיכָא דְּכָחְשָׁא מִכְחָשׁ.

The Gemara explains: **In what** case does the reasoning of Rabbi Meir make a practical **difference? In** a case **where** the stolen item was **devalued** since the time of the robbery. If Rabbi Meir's reason is that despite a change, the changed item remains in its place, it is returned as is, even if its current value is less than what its value had been at the time of the robbery. But if he requires the robber to return the item itself because of a penalty, and by right the robber acquired the animal due to the change, then in this case where the value decreased, the robber would be required to return what its value had been at the time of the robbery.

HALAKHA

Beam – מְרִישׁ: By Torah law, one who robs another of a beam and builds it into a building must return the beam, even if that necessitates the destruction of the building. Due to the ordinance instituted for the penitent, the Sages ruled that the robber compensates the robbery victim monetarily and need not destroy the building (Rambam *Sefer Nezikin, Hilkhot Gezeila VaAveda* 1:5; *Shulḥan Arukh, Ḥoshen Mishpat* 360:1).

NOTES

Since there is the loss of the building, etc. – דְּכֵיוָן דְּאִיכָּא פְּסֵידָא דְּבִירָה וכו׳: The commentaries note that this Gemara clearly indicates that the robber must nevertheless pay the value of the beam, and the owner may accept the payment. The Ra'avad and Rashba explain that the ordinance instituted for the penitent consists of two elements: One mandates, as in the case of the beam, that if the stolen item still exists but returning it will cause the robber to suffer an excessive loss, the robbery victim should accept monetary restitution and not insist on the return of the actual item. The second element, as mentioned in the Gemara, mandates that if the stolen item no longer exists, payment is not accepted for it even if the robber wishes to repent.

Must pay it and its sheared wool, etc. – מְשַׁלֵּם אוֹתָהּ וְאֶת גִּיזּוֹתֶיהָ וכו׳: The Ra'avad and the Rashba explain that this *baraita* is discussing a case where the stolen animal became pregnant or grew wool while in possession of the robber, in which case Rabbi Yehuda holds that the robber need not make any restitution for the offspring or the wool. All agree, however, that if the animal was pregnant or unshorn at the time of the robbery, then the wool or offspring must be returned to the robbery victim. Other commentaries explain that the *baraita* is discussing a case where the animal was pregnant or unshorn at the time of the robbery. Nevertheless, Rabbi Yehuda holds that any increase in the value of the animal due to an enhancement, e.g., the continued growth of the fetus or additional wool, belongs to the robber, since he acquired this animal through the changes effected by the shearing or birth (Rabbeinu Ḥananel; Rashi; Rosh).

It is a penalty that he imposes – קְנָסָא הוּא דְּקָא קָנֵיס: Although the wool or offspring belongs to the robber, who acquired them through the changes to the animal, Rabbi Meir imposed a penalty and required the robber to return the items to the robbery victim, so that the robber will not benefit from his robbery.

תָּא שְׁמַע: גָּזַל בְּהֵמָה וְהִזְקִינָה, עֲבָדִים וְהִזְקִינוּ – מְשַׁלֵּם כִּשְׁעַת הַגְּזֵילָה. רַבִּי מֵאִיר אוֹמֵר: בַּעֲבָדִים – אוֹמֵר לוֹ ״הֲרֵי שֶׁלְּךָ לְפָנֶיךָ״. וְאִילּוּ בְּהֵמָה – כִּשְׁעַת הַגְּזֵילָה.

The Gemara attempts to find a solution to this question: **Come and hear** what was taught in the mishna (96b): If one **robbed** another of **an animal and it aged** while in his possession, consequently diminishing its value, or if one robbed another of **slaves and they aged, he pays according to** the value of the stolen item at **the time of the robbery. Rabbi Meir says: With regard to slaves,** the robber **says to** the owner: **That which is yours is before you.** The Gemara comments: **But** this indicates that with regard to **an animal** that aged while in the possession of the robber Rabbi Meir concedes to the first *tanna*, and he too holds that **he pays according to** what its value had been at **the time of the robbery.**

וְאִי סָלְקָא דַּעְתָּךְ סָבַר רַבִּי מֵאִיר שִׁינּוּי בִּמְקוֹמוֹ עוֹמֵד, אֲפִילּוּ בְּהֵמָה נַמִי! אֶלָּא לָאו שְׁמַע מִינַּהּ: קָסָבַר רַבִּי מֵאִיר שִׁינּוּי קוֹנֶה, וְהָכָא קְנָסָא הוּא דְּקָא קָנֵיס.

The Gemara continues: **And if it enters your mind** to say that **Rabbi Meir holds** that despite **a change,** the changed item **remains in its place,** then the **animal** should be returned as it is in the case of the animal that aged, **as well. Rather,** must one **not conclude from** the mishna that **Rabbi Meir holds** that one **acquires** an item due to **a change** in the item, **but here,** in the case of a stolen animal that subsequently was shorn or gave birth, the payment of wool or offspring **is a penalty** with **which he penalizes** the robber, so that the robber will not benefit from the increased value of the stolen item?

אָמְרִי, רַבִּי מֵאִיר לְדִבְרֵיהֶם דְּרַבָּנַן קָאָמַר לְהוּ: לְדִידִי שִׁינּוּי אֵין קוֹנֶה, וַאֲפִילּוּ בְּהֵמָה נַמִי, אֶלָּא לְדִידְכוּ דְּאָמְרִיתוּ שִׁינּוּי קוֹנֶה, אוֹדוּ לִי מִיהַת בְּעַבְדָּא דִּכְמַקַּרְקְעֵי דָּמֵי, וְקַרְקַע אֵינָהּ נִגְזֶלֶת! וְאָמְרִי לֵיהּ רַבָּנַן: לָא, עַבְדָּא כְּמִטַּלְטְלֵי דָּמֵי.

The Sages **say** in response: Rabbi Meir's reasoning cannot be proven from the mishna, since it is possible to say that **Rabbi Meir is speaking to** the Rabbis **in accordance with the Rabbis'** own **statement.** His statement should be understood as follows: **According to my own** opinion, one **does not acquire** an item due to **a change** in the item, **and an animal** that was stolen and then aged should be returned as it is now, **as well. But according to you, who say** that one **acquires** an item due to **a change** in it, **agree with me in any event** that **with regard to a slave,** he is returned as is. This is **because his legal status is like** that of **real estate, and real estate cannot be stolen. And the Rabbis say to him** in response: **No,** for the purpose of robbery, **the legal status of a slave is like** that of **movable property.**

תָּא שְׁמַע: לִצְבּוֹעַ לוֹ אָדוֹם וּצְבָעוֹ שָׁחוֹר, שָׁחוֹר וּצְבָעוֹ אָדוֹם – רַבִּי מֵאִיר אוֹמֵר: נוֹתֵן לוֹ דְּמֵי צַמְרוֹ; דְּמֵי צַמְרוֹ אִין, דְּמֵי צַמְרוֹ וְשִׁבְחוֹ לָא. וְאִי סָלְקָא דַּעְתָּךְ סָבַר רַבִּי מֵאִיר שִׁינּוּי אֵין קוֹנֶה, דְּמֵי צַמְרוֹ וְשִׁבְחוֹ בָּעֵי לְמֵיתַב לֵיהּ!

The Gemara again attempts to find a solution to the question: **Come and hear** what was taught in the mishna (100b): If one gave wool to a dyer **to dye it red for him and he dyed it black,** or to dye it **black and he dyed it red, Rabbi Meir says:** The dyer **gives** the owner of the wool the **value of his wool,** since the dyer violated the owner's wishes. It can be inferred from this mishna: The **value of his wool, yes,** he must give it; but the **value of his wool and its enhancement,** i.e., the amount by which the value of the wool increased because it was dyed, **no,** he need not give it. **And if it enters your mind** to say that **Rabbi Meir holds** that one **does not acquire** an item due to a **change** in the item, the dyer should be **required to return** the **value of his wool and its enhancement to** the owner, as it never left the owner's possession.

אֶלָּא לָאו שְׁמַע מִינַּהּ: קָסָבַר רַבִּי מֵאִיר שִׁינּוּי קוֹנֶה, וְהָכָא קְנָסָא הוּא דְּקָא קָנֵיס, שְׁמַע מִינַּהּ.

Rather, isn't it correct to **conclude from** the mishna that **Rabbi Meir holds that** one **acquires** an item due to **a change** in the item, **but here,** in the case of a stolen animal that was subsequently shorn or gave birth, the payment of wool or offspring **is a penalty** with **which he penalizes** the robber, so that the robber will not benefit from the increased value of the stolen item? The Gemara affirms this: **Learn from** the mishna that this is indeed the reasoning of Rabbi Meir.

אִיכָּא דְּאָמְרִי: הָא לָא אִיבָּעֵי לָן, מִדְּאַפֵּיךְ רַב וְתָנֵי: גָּזַל פָּרָה וְהִזְקִינָה, עֲבָדִים וְהִזְקִינוּ – מְשַׁלֵּם כִּשְׁעַת הַגְּזֵילָה, דִּבְרֵי רַבִּי מֵאִיר. וַחֲכָמִים אוֹמְרִים: בַּעֲבָדִים, אוֹמֵר לוֹ ״הֲרֵי שֶׁלְּךָ לְפָנֶיךָ״, וַדַּאי לְרַבִּי מֵאִיר שִׁינּוּי קוֹנֶה, וְהָכָא קְנָסָא הוּא דְּקָא קָנֵיס לֵיהּ.

There are those **who say: This,** i.e., Rabbi Meir's reasoning, **was never in question for us.** Why not? **From** the fact **that Rav reversed** the opinions in the mishna on 96b **and taught** it as follows: If one **robbed** another of **an animal and it aged,** or if one robbed another of **slaves and they aged, he pays according to** what their value had been at **the time of the robbery;** this is **the statement of Rabbi Meir. And the Rabbis say: With regard to slaves,** the robber **says to** the owner: **That which is yours is before you. Certainly,** then, **according to** the opinion of **Rabbi Meir,** one **acquires** an item due to **a change** in the item, which is why the robber pays according to what its value had been at the time of the robbery. **But here,** in the case of the cow that gave birth or the ewe that was shorn, the payment of offspring or wool **is a penalty** with **which he penalizes** the robber.

כִּי קָא אִיבַּעְיָא לָן – הָכִי אִיבַּעְיָא לָן: כִּי קָא קָנֵיס בְּמֵזִיד, אֲבָל בְּשׁוֹגֵג לָא קָנֵיס, אוֹ דִּילְמָא אֲפִילּוּ בְּשׁוֹגֵג נַמִי קָנֵיס?

The Gemara continues the alternative explanation. **When we asked** the question, **this is how we asked** it: **When** Rabbi Meir **penalizes** the robber, is it only for one who robbed **intentionally, but** if one took an item from its owner **unintentionally,** Rabbi Meir **does not penalize** the robber? **Or perhaps he penalizes even** one who took an item from its owner **unintentionally.**

תָּא שְׁמַע: חֲמִשָּׁה גּוֹבִין מִן הַמְּחוֹרָרִין,

The Gemara tries to resolve this question: **Come** and **hear** a proof from a *baraita*: **Five**[N] types of monetary claims **are collected** only **from unsold** [*meḥorarin*][L] property, i.e., property that is still in possession of its owner and has not been sold in the meantime.

וְאֵלּוּ הֵן: פֵּירוֹת, וְשֶׁבַח פֵּירוֹת, וְהַמְקַבֵּל עָלָיו לָזוּן בֶּן אִשְׁתּוֹ וּבַת אִשְׁתּוֹ, וְגֵט חוֹב שֶׁאֵין בּוֹ אַחְרָיוּת, וּכְתוּבַּת אִשָּׁה שֶׁאֵין בָּהּ אַחְרָיוּת.

And these are they: Produce,[H] **and the enhanced** value **of produce.**[H] Even if one has the right to the produce of a particular property, or the gain accrued from that produce, he cannot claim this payment from liened property. The Gemara continues with the list of monetary claims collected from unsold property: **And one who accepts upon himself** at the time of his betrothal the obligation **to provide sustenance for his wife's son**[H] **or his wife's daughter** from a previous marriage; **and a promissory note that has no** property **guarantee,** i.e., a document that does not explicitly state that all of the properties of the debtor will serve to guarantee payment of the debt; **and** similarly, **a woman's marriage contract that has no** property **guarantee.**

מַאן שָׁמְעַתְּ לֵיהּ דְּאָמַר אַחְרָיוּת לָאו טָעוּת סוֹפֵר הוּא? רַבִּי מֵאִיר, וְקָתָנֵי: פֵּירוֹת וְשֶׁבַח פֵּירוֹת.

The Gemara clarifies: **Whom did you hear that says** that omission of the **guarantee** of the sale from the document **is not a scribal error?**[N] It is **Rabbi Meir.** There is a dispute between Rabbi Meir and the Rabbis with regard to a promissory note that does not contain a property guarantee. According to the Rabbis, it was omitted in error and is always considered as having been written in the document. Rabbi Meir holds that a promissory note that does not contain a property guarantee cannot be used to collect property that has been liened or sold; it can be used to collect only unsold property. This *baraita* is therefore in accordance with Rabbi Meir's opinion. **And** the *baraita* **teaches** that **produce and the enhanced** value of **produce** are collected only from unsold property.

שֶׁבַח פֵּירוֹת הֵיכִי דָּמֵי? כְּגוֹן שֶׁגָּזַל שָׂדֶה מֵחֲבֵירוֹ וּמְכָרָהּ לְאַחֵר וְהִשְׁבִּיחָהּ, וַהֲרֵי הִיא יוֹצְאָה מִתַּחַת יָדוֹ, כְּשֶׁהוּא גּוֹבֶה,

The Gemara clarifies: **What are the circumstances** in which he collects the **enhanced** value of **produce?** It is a case **where** one **robbed another** of **a field, and then sold it to another, and the** purchaser **enhanced it, and it is now leaving the possession** of the purchaser because the robbery victim has proved in court that this field is his. **When** the purchaser **collects** from the robber who sold him this field, in order to recoup what he had paid,

NOTES

Five, etc. – **חֲמִשָּׁה וכו׳**: *Tosafot* and other early commentaries note that the list in this *baraita* is not exhaustive, as the Gemara in tractate *Gittin* (48b, 50b) lists other examples of debts collected only from unsold property, including sustenance for one's own wife and daughters.

Omission of the guarantee of the sale from the document is not a scribal error – **אַחְרָיוּת לָאו טָעוּת סוֹפֵר הוּא**: Generally, a contract such as a promissory note, bill of sale, or marriage contract contains a clause in which one of the parties acknowledges that his property will guarantee payment of the debt detailed in the contract. All agree that one can lend money or sell property without this guarantee if that is stated explicitly in the document. There is a disagreement among the Sages, however, with regard to a document that contains no clause concerning this guarantee. Many Sages are of the opinion that the parties intend for there to be a property guarantee, because, as Rashi notes, people generally do not spend money without having the confidence that they will receive something in return, and its omission must be attributed to a scribal error. Rabbi Meir holds that the document must be taken at face value, and the omission of the clause stipulating a guarantee indicates that there was no guarantee.

LANGUAGE

Unsold [*meḥorarin*] – **מְחוֹרָרִין**: Related to the Hebrew *meshuḥrarim*, meaning emancipated. Here it refers to properties that have no lien upon them.

HALAKHA

Produce – **פֵּירוֹת**: The owner of a stolen field can seek recompense for the produce that the robber consumed, but he can collect this only from the robber's unsold property and not from property that has been sold. Similarly, if a field that was stolen and then sold is returned to the robbery victim, the purchaser can collect the value of the field from the robber's liened property that was sold, but he can collect the value of the produce only from unsold property (Rambam *Sefer Nezikin, Hilkhot Gezeila VaAveda* 9:5; *Shulḥan Arukh, Ḥoshen Mishpat* 372:1, 373:2).

Enhanced value of produce – **שֶׁבַח פֵּירוֹת**: If one purchased a field from a robber and enhanced it, and now the field has been returned to the robbery victim and the purchaser seeks recompense, the payment the purchaser receives is as follows: If the value of the improvements made by the purchaser to the field exceed the money outlaid by the purchaser, the owner of the field reimburses the purchaser for his expenses. The robber refunds him the purchase price of the field and the value of the enhancement that was in excess of his expenses. The purchaser can collect the purchase price of the field itself even from the robber's sold properties, but can collect the value of the enhancements only from the robber's unsold properties (Rambam *Sefer Nezikin, Hilkhot Gezeila VaAveda* 9:6; *Shulḥan Arukh, Ḥoshen Mishpat* 373:1).

One who accepts upon himself to provide sustenance for his wife's son, etc. – **הַמְקַבֵּל עָלָיו לָזוּן בֶּן אִשְׁתּוֹ וכו׳**: In the case of one who married a woman and committed to sustain her son or daughter from a previous marriage for a specific period of time and who subsequently died, if the husband and wife had performed an act of acquisition with regard to his commitment, or if he had obligated himself in a document, then the children are considered creditors and can collect sustenance from his property for the duration of the time that he had committed to sustaining them. If they had not performed an act of acquisition but had simply stipulated verbally at the time of the marriage that he would support the children, they can collect sustenance only from unsold property (Rambam *Sefer Nashim, Hilkhot Ishut* 23:18; *Shulḥan Arukh, Even HaEzer* 114:4).

גּוֹבֶה אֶת הַקֶּרֶן מִנְּכָסִים מְשׁוּעְבָּדִים וְאֶת הַשֶּׁבַח מִנְּכָסִים בְּנֵי חוֹרִין, דְּאָתָא בַּעַל אַרְעָא וְשָׁקֵיל אַרְעֵיהּ וְשִׁבְחֵיהּ.

he can **collect the principal,** i.e., what he paid for the field, **from** the robber's **liened property** that has been sold. **But** he can collect **the enhanced** value, i.e., the value of the improvements made to the field, only **from unsold property.** Why are both of these collected from the robber? **Because the owner of the field came and took** both **his land and its enhanced** value.

מַאי לָאו בְּעַם הָאָרֶץ, דְּלָא יָדַע דְּקַרְקַע נִגְזֶלֶת אוֹ אֵינָהּ נִגְזֶלֶת, וַאֲפִילּוּ הָכִי קָאָתֵי בַּעַל קַרְקַע וְשָׁקֵיל לְאַרְעָא וְשִׁבְחָהּ? וּשְׁמַע מִינָּהּ: בְּשׁוֹגֵג נַמִי קָנֵיס. אָמְרִי: לָא, בְּלוֹקֵחַ תַּלְמִיד חָכָם וְיָדַע.

The Gemara clarifies: **What, is it not** speaking **of** a purchaser who is **an ignoramus, who does not know whether property can be stolen or cannot be stolen,** and when he purchased stolen land from the robber, he did so unintentionally, since he was under the mistaken impression that this land belonged to the robber who sold it? **And even so, the owner of the land can come and take the land and its enhanced** value. **And** if so, one may **learn from** the *baraita* that Rabbi Meir **penalizes even** one who acquires stolen items **unintentionally.** The Sages **say** in response: **No,** it is speaking **of a purchaser** who is **a Torah scholar,**[H] **and he knew** that the robber had no right to sell this land. The purchaser is therefore penalized and is required to return the enhanced value of the land as well.

תָּא שְׁמַע: לִצְבּוֹעַ לוֹ אָדוֹם וּצְבָעוֹ שָׁחוֹר, שָׁחוֹר וּצְבָעוֹ אָדוֹם – רַבִּי מֵאִיר אוֹמֵר: נוֹתֵן לוֹ דְּמֵי צַמְרוֹ; דְּמֵי צַמְרוֹ – אִין, דְּמֵי צַמְרוֹ וְשִׁבְחוֹ – לָא.

The Gemara again tries to determine the scope of the penalty: **Come** and **hear** what was taught in a mishna (100b): If one gave wool to a dyer **to dye it red for him and he dyed it black,** or to dye it **black and he dyed it red, Rabbi Meir says:** The dyer **gives** the owner of the wool the **value of his wool,** since the dyer violated the owner's instructions. It can be inferred from the mishna: The **value of his wool, yes,** he must give; **but the value of his wool and its enhanced** value, i.e., the amount by which the value of the wool increased because it was dyed, **no,** he is not required to give.

וְאִי סָלְקָא דַּעְתָּךְ בְּשׁוֹגֵג נַמִי קָנֵיס, דְּמֵי צַמְרוֹ וְשִׁבְחוֹ בָּעֵי לְמֵיתְבָא לֵיהּ! אֶלָּא לָאו שְׁמַע מִינָּהּ: בְּמֵזִיד קָנֵיס, בְּשׁוֹגֵג לָא קָנֵיס, שְׁמַע מִינָּהּ.

And if it enters your mind to say that Rabbi Meir **penalizes** one who acquires a stolen item **unintentionally as well,** the dyer should be **required to return the value of his wool and its enhancement to him. Rather,** must one **not conclude from** the mishna that if it was done **intentionally,** Rabbi Meir **penalizes** the robber, but if it was done **unintentionally he does not penalize** him? The Gemara affirms: **Learn from** the mishna that this indeed is the reasoning of Rabbi Meir.

רַבִּי יְהוּדָה אוֹמֵר: גְּזֵילָה חוֹזֶרֶת בְּעֵינֶיהָ; רַבִּי שִׁמְעוֹן אוֹמֵר: רוֹאִין אוֹתָהּ כְּאִילּוּ הִיא שׁוּמָא אֶצְלוֹ בְּכֶסֶף. מַאי בֵּינַיְיהוּ?

§ The Gemara continues its discussion of the *baraita*. **Rabbi Yehuda says: A stolen item is returned as is. Rabbi Shimon says:** The stolen item **is viewed as though it had been monetarily appraised** at the time of the robbery. The Gemara asks: **What is** the difference **between them,** since ostensibly they agree that the robber does not return the value of the enhancement to the robbery victim?

אָמַר רַב זְבִיד: בְּשֶׁבַח שֶׁעַל גַּבֵּי גְזֵילָה קָמִיפַּלְגִי, רַבִּי יְהוּדָה סָבַר: דְּנִגְזָל הָוֵי, וְרַבִּי שִׁמְעוֹן סָבַר: דְּגַזְלָן הָוֵי.

Rav Zevid says: They disagree with regard to enhancement that is still **upon the stolen item.**[H] The disagreement concerns a case where the enhancement occurred while the stolen item was in the possession of the robber, and when he returned the item it was still enhanced. Therefore, he did not keep any of the enhancement. **Rabbi Yehuda holds** that the enhancement **belongs to the one who was robbed,**[N] **and Rabbi Shimon holds that it belongs to the robber.**

HALAKHA

A purchaser who is a Torah scholar – לוֹקֵחַ תַּלְמִיד חָכָם: In the case of a field that was stolen and then sold, and the purchaser enhanced the value of the field, if he knew that the field was stolen at the time of his purchase he can claim only the principal from the robber. He can claim payment for his expenditures in enhancing the value of the field from the owner of the field. The Rema writes that some say that he cannot claim payment for his expenditures (*Tur*, citing Rabbeinu Yitzḥak and Rosh). The Ramah writes that if the robber explicitly accepted responsibility to reimburse the purchaser for any expenditures and performed an act of acquisition to render that commitment as binding, the robber must then reimburse the purchaser for his expenditures as well (Rambam *Sefer Nezikin, Hilkhot Gezeila VaAveda* 9:7; *Shulḥan Arukh, Ḥoshen Mishpat* 373:1).

Enhancement that is upon the stolen item – שֶׁבַח שֶׁעַל גַּבֵּי גְזֵילָה: If an item was stolen and the owners despaired of recovering it, or if it underwent a change while in the possession of the robber, any enhancement to its value belongs to the robber, be it natural or due to the efforts of the robber. If one robbed another of an animal and it became pregnant while in his possession, he pays only what its value was at the time of the robbery. If the animal gave birth, the offspring belong to the robber. If it did not yet give birth, the court estimates the amount of the increase in value, and the robbery victim pays that sum to the robber and takes the animal. This ruling is in accordance with the opinion of Rabbi Yehuda, as explained by Rav Pappa (Rambam *Sefer Nezikin, Hilkhot Gezeila VaAveda* 2:6; *Shulḥan Arukh, Ḥoshen Mishpat* 362:7).

NOTES

Rabbi Yehuda holds that it belongs to the one who was robbed – רַבִּי יְהוּדָה סָבַר דְּנִגְזָל הָוֵי: Any enhancement in value not present in the animal itself, such as offspring, belongs to the robber, either because he acquired it by virtue of it having been changed, or because of the ordinance instituted for the penitent (see *Tosafot*). According to Rav Zevid, Rabbi Yehuda maintains that even the enhancement in value that is present in the animal itself belongs to the robbery victim, not because he holds that despite a change, the changed item remains in its place but because this change is not significant enough to cause the robber to acquire the animal (Rabbeinu Tam). Others explain that by right the enhancement should belong to the robber, but Rabbi Yehuda penalizes the robber so that he will not profit from the robbery. Unlike the penalty imposed by Rabbi Meir, which would require the robber to return the offspring as well, this is a partial penalty that requires him to return only any enhancement in the animal itself (*Tosafot* 95a; Rashba).

רַב פַּפָּא אָמַר: דְּכוּלֵּי עָלְמָא – שֶׁבַח שֶׁעַל גַּבֵּי גְּזֵילָה דְּגַזְלָן הָוֵי, וְהָכָא – לְמֶחֱצָה, לִשְׁלִישׁ וְלִרְבִיעַ קָמִיפַּלְגִי. רַבִּי יְהוּדָה סָבַר: שֶׁבַח שֶׁעַל גַּבֵּי גְּזֵילָה כּוּלֵּיהּ דְּגַזְלָן הָוֵי, וְרַבִּי שִׁמְעוֹן סָבַר: לְמֶחֱצָה, לִשְׁלִישׁ וְלִרְבִיעַ הוּא דְּשָׁקֵיל גַּזְלָן.

Rav Pappa said that the disagreement between Rabbi Yehuda and Rabbi Shimon can be explained differently: **Everyone** agrees that the **enhancement that is** still **upon the stolen item belongs to the robber, and here they disagree** with regard to whether the robber can keep **one-half,** or **one-third, or one-fourth** of the value of the enhancement, and the remainder is kept by the owner of the animal. **Rabbi Yehuda holds** that the **enhancement that is** still **upon the stolen item belongs entirely to the robber, and Rabbi Shimon holds** that **the robber takes one-half,** or **one-third, or one-fourth** of the value of the enhancement. In other words, he is treated as a shepherd or rancher and receives the share of the enhancement that local custom dictates be paid to that type of laborer.

תְּנַן: גָּזַל פָּרָה וְנִתְעַבְּרָה אֶצְלוֹ וְיָלְדָה, רָחֵל וְנִטְעֲנָה אֶצְלוֹ וּגְזָזָהּ – מְשַׁלֵּם כִּשְׁעַת הַגְּזֵילָה; יָלְדָה – אִין, לָא יָלְדָה – הָדְרָא בְּעֵינָא.

The Gemara cites a proof for Rav Zevid's explanation: **We learned** in the mishna (93b): If one **robbed** another of **a cow, and it became pregnant in his** possession, **and it** then **gave birth**; or if one robbed another of **a ewe, and it became laden** with wool **in his** possession, **and he** then **sheared it,** the robber **pays according to** the value of the animal at **the time of the robbery.** The Gemara infers from the mishna: If the cow **gave birth, yes,** he pays the value of the animal at the time of the theft, but if the cow **did not give birth** and is still pregnant, it is **returned as is.**

בִּשְׁלָמָא לְרַב זְבִיד דְּאָמַר: שֶׁבַח שֶׁעַל גַּבֵּי גְּזֵילָה דְּנִגְזָל הָוֵי לְרַבִּי יְהוּדָה, הָא מַנִּי? רַבִּי יְהוּדָה הִיא. אֶלָּא לְרַב פַּפָּא דְּאָמַר דְּגַזְלָן הָוֵי, הָא מַנִּי? לָא רַבִּי יְהוּדָה וְלָא רַבִּי שִׁמְעוֹן!

Granted, according to the explanation of **Rav Zevid, who says** that **according to** the opinion of **Rabbi Yehuda, enhancement that is** still **upon the stolen item belongs to the one who was robbed,** in accordance with **whose** opinion **is this** mishna? **It is** in accordance with the opinion of **Rabbi Yehuda,** as the pregnant cow is returned as is. **But according to** the explanation of **Rav Pappa, who says** that everyone agrees that the enhancement **belongs to the robber,** in accordance with **whose** opinion **is this** mishna? It is **not** in accordance with the opinion of **Rabbi Yehuda, nor** is it in accordance with the opinion of **Rabbi Shimon,**[N] as the robber does not retain any of the enhanced value.

אָמַר לָךְ רַב פַּפָּא: הוּא הַדִּין אֲפִילּוּ לֹא יָלְדָה נַמִי כִּשְׁעַת הַגְּזֵילָה הוּא דִּמְשַׁלֵּם, וְהָא דְּקָתָנֵי יָלְדָה – אַיְּידֵי דְּנָסֵיב רֵישָׁא יָלְדָה, נְסֵיב סֵיפָא נַמִי יָלְדָה.

The Gemara responds: **Rav Pappa** could have **said to you** that the inference is incorrect: **The same is true** that **even if it did not give birth,** the robber **pays according to** the value of the animal at **the time of the robbery,** and the enhanced value due to the pregnancy is returned to him. **And that which the mishna teaches: It** then **gave birth,** cannot serve as the basis for an inference pertaining to this discussion. **As** the *tanna* needs to **cite** that **it gave birth** in **the first clause** of the mishna, since in that case he acquires the animal due to the change in its condition, therefore **he cites** that **it gave birth** in **the latter clause as well,** but it need not have given birth. It cannot be inferred from this mishna that an animal that has not given birth is returned as is.

תַּנְיָא כְּוָותֵיהּ דְּרַב פַּפָּא, רַבִּי שִׁמְעוֹן אוֹמֵר: רוֹאִין אוֹתָהּ כְּאִילּוּ הִיא שׁוּמָא אֶצְלוֹ בְּכֶסֶף לְמֶחֱצָה, לִשְׁלִישׁ וְלִרְבִיעַ.

The Gemara notes: **It is taught** in a *baraita* **in accordance with** the explanation **of Rav Pappa.** The *baraita* states: **Rabbi Shimon says:** The stolen item **is viewed as though it had been monetarily appraised** at the time of the theft, **for the purpose of** keeping **one-half,** or **one-third, or one-fourth** of the value of the enhancement.

אָמַר רַב אַשִׁי: כִּי הָוֵינַן בֵּי רַב כָּהֲנָא, אִיבַּעְיָא לָן: לְרַבִּי שִׁמְעוֹן דְּאָמַר: לְמֶחֱצָה, לִשְׁלִישׁ וְלִרְבִיעַ הוּא דְּשָׁקֵיל גַּזְלָן, כִּי מְסַלְּקִינַן לֵיהּ – בִּדְמֵי מְסַלְּקִינַן לֵיהּ, אוֹ דִילְמָא מִבִּשְׂרָא שָׁקוֹל?

Rav Ashi said: When we were studying **in the study hall of Rav Kahana, we were asked** a question: **According** to the opinion of **Rabbi Shimon, who says that the robber takes one-half,** or **one-third, or one-fourth** of the value of the enhancement; **when we remove** the robber, taking the stolen animal from him and paying him a portion of the enhanced value, do **we remove him** by paying him his share **with money? Or, perhaps he takes** his portion **from the meat** of the animal.

NOTES

It is not in accordance with Rabbi Yehuda nor is it in accordance with Rabbi Shimon – לָא רַבִּי יְהוּדָה וְלָא רַבִּי שִׁמְעוֹן: It is also not in accordance with the opinion of Rabbi Meir, who holds that in a case like this even the offspring is returned to the robbery victim (Rashi).

וּפְשַׁטְנָא מֵהָא דְּאָמַר רַב נַחְמָן אָמַר שְׁמוּאֵל: שְׁלֹשָׁה שָׁמִין לָהֶן הַשֶּׁבַח וּמַעֲלִין אוֹתָן בְּדָמִים, וְאֵלּוּ הֵן: בְּכוֹר לְפָשׁוּט,

And we resolved the dilemma **from that which Rav Naḥman says that Shmuel says: In three** cases, the court **appraises the** enhanced value for the parties involved in enhancing a field, **and they are paid in money** rather than by being given a portion of the property, **and these are they: A firstborn** son who makes payment **to a regular** son.[NH] This is a case where two sons, one firstborn and the other not, inherit a field from their father. Before it is divided, they both work and enhance the field. When the time comes to divide the field, the firstborn son, who receives a double portion, must pay his brother for the enhancement that the latter contributed to the former's portion. This payment is given in money rather than land.

וּבַעַל חוֹב לַלּוֹקֵחַ, וּבַעַל חוֹב לַיְתוֹמִים.

And the second case is that of **a creditor** who is obligated **to a purchaser,** i.e., a creditor who collects the debt from lands that were sold by the debtor. He pays money to the purchaser for the enhancements generated by the purchaser but does not pay him in land. **And** the third case is that of **a creditor** who is obligated **to orphans,**[NH] i.e., a creditor who collects land from the orphans of his debtor. He must pay them for any enhancements done by the orphans after their father's death. This payment is also given in money rather than land.

אֲמַר לֵיהּ רָבִינָא לְרַב אַשִׁי, מִי אָמַר שְׁמוּאֵל: בַּעַל חוֹב לַלּוֹקֵחַ יָהֵיב לֵיהּ שֶׁבַח? וְהָאָמַר שְׁמוּאֵל: בַּעַל חוֹב גּוֹבֶה אֶת הַשֶּׁבַח! אֲמַר לֵיהּ, לָא קַשְׁיָא: כָּאן בְּשֶׁבַח הַמַּגִּיעַ לִכְתֵפַיִם, וְכָאן בְּשֶׁבַח שֶׁאֵין מַגִּיעַ לִכְתֵפַיִם.

The Gemara discusses Shmuel's statement. **Ravina said to Rav Ashi: Did Shmuel** actually **say** that **a creditor gives the purchaser** any of the **enhanced** value at all? **But doesn't Shmuel say: A creditor collects** all of **the enhanced** value?[H] Rav Ashi **said to him:** This is **not difficult. Here,** where Shmuel stated that a creditor does not collect the enhanced value, it was **with regard to** a case where there was **enhancement that reaches shoulders** [*shevaḥ hammaggia likhtefayim*],[NLH] i.e., the produce that grew due to the improvements made by the purchaser is fully grown and ripened and can now be harvested and carried upon one's shoulders. **But there,** where Shmuel stated that a creditor does collect the enhanced value, it was **with regard to** a case where there was **enhancement that does not reach shoulders,** i.e., its growth is not complete.

אֲמַר לֵיהּ: וְהָא מַעֲשִׂים בְּכׇל יוֹם, וְקָא מַגְבֵּי שְׁמוּאֵל אֲפִילּוּ שֶׁבַח הַמַּגִּיעַ לִכְתֵפַיִם! אֲמַר לֵיהּ, לָא קַשְׁיָא.

Ravina **said to him: But there were daily incidents** of this type, **and Shmuel would collect** from purchasers **even enhancement that reached shoulders.** Rav Ashi **said to him: This is not difficult.**

NOTES

A firstborn son who makes payment to a regular son – בְּכוֹר לְפָשׁוּט: The Torah states that when sons are dividing an inheritance, the firstborn son's portion is double that of the other sons (see Deuteronomy 21:17). The Sages taught that this privilege extends only to property that was in the possession of the father at the time of his death, but not to property that entered the possession of the estate at a later date. Therefore, if the value of the property increased before it was divided among the brothers, the firstborn does not receive a double portion of the property as it stands now. His double portion is calculated from the value of the property as it was at the time of the father's death, and the enhanced value is divided equally among the sons.

And a creditor to orphans – וּבַעַל חוֹב לַיְתוֹמִים: If a creditor seeks to collect payment for a debt from land inherited by the debtor's orphans, he can do so only from the property as it stood at the time of the father's death, not from any subsequent enhancements to the property by the orphans.

Enhancement that reaches shoulders – שֶׁבַח הַמַּגִּיעַ לִכְתֵפַיִם: There are differing explanations of this term. According to Rabbeinu Ḥananel, Rashi, and the Rif, it means that the enhancement has already reached the point where it can be carried upon people's shoulders and removed, i.e., the produce is ripe produce even if it has not yet been harvested. Rabbeinu Tam and the Rashba explain that it means an enhancement that resulted from exertion, as opposed to an enhancement that developed naturally. Rav Tzemaḥ Gaon is quoted as saying that an enhancement that reaches shoulders refers to a tree that has grown as high as one's shoulders.

LANGUAGE

Enhancement that reaches shoulders [*shevaḥ hammaggia likhtefayim*] – שֶׁבַח הַמַּגִּיעַ לִכְתֵפַיִם: The text of most of the commentaries reads *hammaggia likhtefayim*, meaning: Reaches shoulders. Some offer a variant reading: *Hammaggia lakatafim*, which means: That reaches porters, meaning that the enhancement is ready to be given to the porters who carry the harvested produce.

HALAKHA

A firstborn son to a regular son – בְּכוֹר לְפָשׁוּט: A firstborn son does not receive a double portion of the enhancements that were made to the father's estate after his death. Instead, the court appraises the value of the enhancement to his additional portion and he pays his brother his share of that amount in money (Rambam *Sefer Mishpatim, Hilkhot Naḥalot* 3:4; *Shulḥan Arukh, Ḥoshen Mishpat* 278:6).

A creditor to orphans – בַּעַל חוֹב לַיְתוֹמִים: If orphans enhanced the value of property they inherited, their father's creditor cannot collect the value of any of the enhancement. If, however, the properties gained value on their own, the creditor can collect even from the additional value. Some say that a creditor can collect the value of the enhancement only of properties that were set aside as designated repayment. If the orphans claim that they made the enhancements to the field, the burden of proof is upon them. Some say that if the property was not set aside as designated repayment, the burden of proof is upon the creditor (Rema, citing *Tur*). If the orphans prove that they enhanced the property, the value of the enhancement and their expenses are estimated, and they are reimbursed for the lesser of these amounts (Rambam *Sefer Mishpatim, Hilkhot Malve VeLoveh* 21:4, 7; *Shulḥan Arukh, Ḥoshen Mishpat* 115:4–6).

A creditor collects the enhanced value – בַּעַל חוֹב גּוֹבֶה אֶת הַשֶּׁבַח: If a creditor repossessed properties that had been sold by the debtor, and the debtor had written in his promissory note that the lien extends to properties that he will purchase in the future, he can also take the value of the enhancements that were made to the field, whether they came about naturally or were made by the purchaser. There is, however, a difference between these two scenarios: If the field improved naturally, the creditor can take the value of all of the improvements, whereas if the purchaser made the enhancements, the creditor can take only half of the value of the enhancements that are in excess of the purchaser's expenses. Some (Rema, based on Rosh and *Maggid Mishne*) say that in either case the creditor can collect only half of the value of the improvements (Rambam *Sefer Mishpatim, Hilkhot Malve VeLoveh* 21:1; *Shulḥan Arukh, Ḥoshen Mishpat* 115:1).

Enhancement that reaches shoulders – שֶׁבַח הַמַּגִּיעַ לִכְתֵפַיִם: Any produce that was harvested by the purchaser of a field cannot be repossessed by the creditor of the seller. Some say that if the debtor set aside the field as designated repayment, it can be repossessed. Produce that is still attached to the ground, even if it is no longer dependent upon the earth for nutrition, e.g., grapes that are ready to be harvested, can be collected by the creditor. Some (*Shakh*, citing Rosh) say that produce that is no longer dependent upon the earth for nutrition is treated as though it has been harvested (Rambam *Sefer Mishpatim, Hilkhot Malve VeLoveh* 21:2; *Shulḥan Arukh, Ḥoshen Mishpat* 115:1).

LANGUAGE

Se'a [*griva*] – גְּרִיוָא: This word also appears in Syriac. In Arabic it is جريب, *jarīb*. It is the name of a dry measurement called a *se'a* by the Sages.

הָא דְּמַסֵּיק בֵּיהּ כְּשִׁיעוּר אַרְעָא וְשִׁבְחָא, הָא דְּלָא מַסֵּיק בֵּיהּ אֶלָּא כְּשִׁיעוּר אַרְעָא.

This ruling, that Shmuel would collect the enhanced value, is for a case **where** the creditor **is owed**[H] by the debtor **the amount of** the value of **the land and the enhanced value. That** ruling, that Shmuel would not collect the value of the enhancement, is for a case where the creditor **is owed by** the debtor **only the amount of** the value of **the land.**

אֲמַר לֵיהּ, הָנִיחָא לְמַאן דְּאָמַר: אִי אִית לֵיהּ זוּזֵי לְלוֹקֵחַ לָא מָצֵי מְסַלֵּק לֵיהּ לְבַעַל חוֹב – שַׁפִּיר. אֶלָּא לְמַאן דְּאָמַר: אִי אִית לֵיהּ זוּזֵי לְלוֹקֵחַ מָצֵי מְסַלֵּק לֵיהּ לְבַעַל חוֹב, לֵימָא לֵיהּ: אִי הָווּ לִי זוּזֵי הֲוָה מְסַלְּקִינָא לָךְ מִכּוּלֵּיהּ אַרְעָא, הַשְׁתָּא הַב לִי גְּרִיוָא דְּאַרְעָא שִׁיעוּר שִׁבְחַאי!

Ravina **said to him: This works out well according to the one who says: If the purchaser** of the field **has money, he** still **cannot remove the creditor** from the land, i.e., the creditor has the right to collect the land. This is **well. But according to the one who says: If the purchaser** of the field **has money, he can remove the creditor** from the land, i.e., the purchaser can choose to pay him money instead, **let** the purchaser **say: If I had money, I would remove you from all of the land; now** that I do not have sufficient money to pay what you are owed, **give me** at least **a** ***se'a*** [***griva***][L] **of land,** which is **the amount of my enhancement.**

אֲמַר לֵיהּ: הָכָא בְּמַאי עָסְקִינַן – כְּגוֹן דְּשַׁוְיַהּ נִיהֲלֵיהּ אַפּוֹתֵיקִי, דַּאֲמַר לֵיהּ: לֹא יְהֵא לְךָ פֵּרָעוֹן אֶלָּא מִזֶּה.

Rav Ashi **said to him: With what are we dealing here?** We are dealing with a case **where** the debtor **set aside** this field **as designated repayment for him, as he said to him: You shall not be repaid from anything but this,** in which case he clearly has a lien on this field and nothing else.

אָמַר רָבָא: גָּזַל וְהִשְׁבִּיחַ וּמָכַר, וְגָזַל וְהִשְׁבִּיחַ וְהוֹרִישׁ – מַה שֶּׁהִשְׁבִּיחַ מָכַר, מַה שֶּׁהִשְׁבִּיחַ הוֹרִישׁ.

§ The Gemara continues the discussion of a stolen item that has been enhanced. **Rava says:** If one **robbed** another of an item **and enhanced** it **and sold**[H] it to another, and similarly, if one **robbed** another of an item **and enhanced** it and then died **and bequeathed** it, **he sold that which he enhanced and bequeathed that which he enhanced.** And the robbery victim, should he wish to recover the stolen item, must pay the purchaser or heir for the enhanced value.

בָּעֵי רָבָא: הִשְׁבִּיחַ לוֹקֵחַ, מַהוּ? בָּתַר דְּבַעְיָא הֲדַר פַּשְׁטַהּ: מַה מָּכַר רִאשׁוֹן לַשֵּׁנִי? כׇּל זְכוּת שֶׁתָּבֹא לְיָדוֹ.

Rava raises a dilemma related to the aforementioned *halakha*: **What is** the *halakha* **if a purchaser enhanced**[H] the stolen item? Must the robbery victim pay the purchaser for the enhanced value or not? **After** Rava **raised the dilemma, he then resolved it: What has the first** person **sold to the second** in any sale? He has sold **any rights that will come into his possession.** Since the robber had the rights to the value of his enhancements to the stolen item, he sold those rights to the purchaser as well.

HALAKHA

This is where he is owed, etc. – הָא דְּמַסֵּיק בֵּיהּ וכו׳: If a creditor repossessed land from a purchaser, and the valuation of the land when it was sold is commensurate with the debt, the creditor does not keep any of the value of enhancements made to the land. The purchaser can request to be paid for the enhancements or to keep a portion of the land equal in value to the enhancements. This is the case only if the land had not been set aside as designated repayment for the debt. If it was set aside as designated repayment, the creditor takes all of the land, and he compensates the purchaser for either his expenses or the value of the enhancement, whichever amount is the lesser of the two (Rambam *Sefer Mishpatim*, *Hilkhot Malve VeLoveh* 21:6; *Shulḥan Arukh*, *Ḥoshen Mishpat* 115:2, and in the comment of Rema).

One robbed and enhanced and sold, etc. – גָּזַל וְהִשְׁבִּיחַ וּמָכַר וכו׳: If an item was stolen, enhanced, and then sold or bequeathed before the robbery victim had despaired of retrieving it, the purchaser or heir acquires its enhanced value. The purchaser or heir must return the stolen item to the robbery victim and collect the value of the enhancement from him, and he collects the value of the enhancement from the robber (Rambam *Sefer Nezikin*, *Hilkhot Gezeila VaAveda* 2:4 and *Maggid Mishne* there; *Shulḥan Arukh*, *Ḥoshen Mishpat* 362:4 and *Beur HaGra* there).

A purchaser enhanced – הִשְׁבִּיחַ לוֹקֵחַ: If one robbed another of a field and sold it, and the purchaser enhanced the field before it was returned to the robbery victim, then the purchaser collects the value of the enhancement from the robbery victim. This ruling is in accordance with the opinion of Rava, who states that a purchaser assumes all of the rights of the seller. The *Levush* rules that in this scenario, the robbery victim does not collect the value of the enhancements from the robber (Rambam *Sefer Nezikin*, *Hilkhot Gezeila VaAveda* 2:4; *Shulḥan Arukh*, *Ḥoshen Mishpat* 362:4).

בעי רבא: השביח גוי, מהו? אמר ליה רב אחא מדפתי לרבינא: תקנתא לגוי ניקו ונעבוד? אמר ליה: לא צריכא, כגון דזבניה לישראל. סוף סוף הבא מחמת גוי הרי הוא כגוי!

Rava raises a dilemma: What is the *halakha* **if a gentile** robber **enhanced**[HN] the value of a stolen item? **Rav Aḥa of Difti said to Ravina: Shall we arise and institute an ordinance for** the benefit of **a gentile?** Ravina **said to him:** This question **is not necessary** except **where** it was the case **that** a gentile **sold it to a Jew.** Rava was asking if the Jew needs to return the enhanced value. The Gemara comments: **Ultimately, one who comes** to possess an item **due to** purchasing it from **a gentile**[H] **is like a gentile** himself because, as stated previously, in any sale the purchaser's rights are identical to the seller's. Since the Sages did not institute ordinances for the benefit of gentiles, the Jewish purchaser does not have those rights either.

לא צריכא, כגון דגזל ישראל וזבנה ניהליה והשביחה גוי, והדר גוי וזבנה לישראל, מאי? מי אמרינן: כיון דמעיקרא ישראל והדר ישראל – עבדי רבנן תקנתא, או דלמא כיון דאיכא גוי באמצע – לא עבדו ליה רבנן תקנתא? תיקו.

The Gemara explains: This question **is not necessary** except **where** it was the case **that a Jew robbed** another of the item **and sold it to** a gentile, **and the gentile enhanced it, and** then **the gentile went back and sold it to** another **Jew.**[H] **What is** the *halakha* in this case? **Do we say: Since it was initially** stolen by **a Jew and was then** acquired by **a Jew, the Sages did institute an ordinance? Or, perhaps since there is** the ownership of **a gentile intervening, the Sages did not institute an ordinance.** The Gemara comments: The dilemma **shall stand** unresolved.

אמר רב פפא: האי מאן דגזל דיקלא מחבריה וקטליה, אף על גב דשדיא מארעא לארעא דידיה – לא קני, מאי טעמא? מעיקרא דיקלא מיקרי והשתא נמי דיקלא מיקרי, דיקלא ועביד גובי – לא קני, השתא מיהת גובי דדיקלא מיקרי.

§ The mishna teaches that if one robbed another of wood and fashioned it into vessels, he acquired the wood due to the change. The Gemara discusses what qualifies as a change. **Rav Pappa said:** With regard to **this one who robbed another of a palm tree**[H] **and cut it down, although he threw it from the land** of the robbery victim **to his own land, he did not acquire** it. **What is the reason** for this? The tree was **initially called a palm tree, and now,** although it has been cut down, **it is also called a palm tree,** so the change to the item is not sufficiently significant for the robber to acquire it. Moreover, if one robbed another of **a palm tree and made** it into **logs, he did not acquire it,** since **now, in any event, they are called palm tree logs.**

גובי ועבדינהו כשורי – קני; כשורי רברבי ועבדינהו כשורי זוטרי – לא קני; עבדינהו קצוצייתא – קני.

By contrast, if one robbed another of **logs and fashioned them** into **beams, he has acquired** them, since this change is significant. If one robbed another of **large beams and fashioned them** into **small beams, he did not acquire them,** since they are still called beams. If he **fashioned them** into boards, **he did acquire** them.

אמר רבא: האי מאן דגזל לוליבא ועבדינהו הוצי – קני, דמעיקרא לוליבא מיקרי והשתא הוצי; הוצי ועבדינהו חופיא – קני, מעיקרא הוצי והשתא חופיא; חופיא ועבדיה שרשורא – לא קני, מאי טעמא? דהדר סתר ליה והוי חופיא.

Rava said: This one who robbed another **of a palm frond**[H] **and fashioned it** into **leaves [*hutzei*],**[L] i.e., he removed the leaves from the spine, **has acquired** it, **since initially it was called a palm frond and now** it is called **leaves.** One who robbed another **of leaves and fashioned them** into **a broom has acquired them,** since **initially** they were called **leaves, and now** they are called **a broom.** One who robbed another of **a broom** and **fashioned it** into **a rope has not acquired it. What is the reason** for this? The reason is **that** he can **go back** and **unravel it, and it will** once again **be a broom.**

בעי רב פפא: נחלקה התיומת, מהו? תא שמע, דאמר רבי מתון אמר רבי יהושע בן לוי: ניטלה התיומת – פסול.

Rav Pappa raises a dilemma: What is the *halakha* **if the** central **twin-leaf became split,**[N] i.e., is this considered a change through which a stolen *lulav* would be acquired? The Gemara cites a proof: **Come** and **hear** that **which Rabbi Matun says** that **Rabbi Yehoshua ben Levi says: If the** central **twin-leaf was removed,** the *lulav* **is unfit.**

HALAKHA

A gentile enhanced – השביח גוי: If a robber sold a stolen item to a gentile and the gentile enhanced its value, when the stolen item is returned to the robbery victim, the enhancement is returned as well (Rambam *Sefer Nezikin*, *Hilkhot Gezeila VaAveda* 2:5; *Shulḥan Arukh*, *Ḥoshen Mishpat* 362:5).

One who comes to possess an item due to purchasing it from a gentile – הבא מחמת גוי: One who possesses an item due to purchasing it from a gentile has the same legal rights to the item as the gentile had. For example, one who purchases a promissory note from a gentile can collect the debt contained therein, even if this note is invalid according to *halakha*. There are, however, some instances in which the *Shulḥan Arukh* rules that the purchaser does not have the same legal rights to the item as the gentile had. For example, one who purchases a house from a gentile may not obstruct his Jewish neighbor's windows, although the gentile was permitted to do so. The Rema rules that even in this case he has the same legal rights to the item as the gentile had (Rambam *Sefer Mishpatim*, *Hilkhot To'en VeNitan* 14:5 and *Sefer Kinyan*, *Hilkhot Mekhira* 1:17; *Shulḥan Arukh*, *Ḥoshen Mishpat* 45:17, 149:14–15, 154:18, and in the comment of Rema, 194:1).

A Jew robbed and sold it to a gentile, and the gentile enhanced it, and then the gentile went back and sold it to a Jew – גזל ישראל וזבנה ניהליה והשביחה גוי והדר גוי וזבנה לישראל: If a Jewish robber sold a stolen item to a gentile, who enhanced its value and then sold it to a Jew, then the final purchaser acquires the enhanced value. If the robbery victim seizes it, it is not removed from his possession, since the *halakha* in this case remained unresolved in the Gemara. According to the opinion of Rabbeinu Yitzḥak of Dampierre and the Rosh, cited in the *Shakh*, it would be removed from his possession (Rambam *Sefer Kinyan*, *Hilkhot Gezeila VaAveda* 2:5; *Shulḥan Arukh*, *Ḥoshen Mishpat* 362:6).

Robbed another of a palm tree, etc. – גזל דיקלא מחבריה וכו׳: If one robbed another of a palm tree that was attached to the ground by cutting it down, he has not acquired it, even if he cut it into pieces. If he made it into beams, he has acquired it due to the change of its name. If one stole large beams and cut them into smaller beams, he has not acquired them. If he fashioned them into boards, thereby changing their name, he has acquired them (Rambam *Sefer Nezikin*, *Hilkhot Gezeila VaAveda* 2:14; *Shulḥan Arukh*, *Ḥoshen Mishpat* 362:10).

Robbed another of a palm frond, etc. – גזל לוליבא וכו׳: If one robbed another of a palm frond and removed its leaves, he has acquired them due to the change. Similarly, if one robbed another of leaves and fashioned them into a broom, he has acquired them (Rambam *Sefer Nezikin*, *Hilkhot Gezeila VaAveda* 2:13–14; *Shulḥan Arukh*, *Ḥoshen Mishpat* 362:8–9).

LANGUAGE

Leaves [*hutzei*] – הוצי: This word, meaning palm leaf, is the plural form of the Aramaic word *hutza*. It is similar to the Hebrew word *hutz* and the Arabic خوص, *hūṣ*.

NOTES

If a gentile enhanced – השביח גוי: The Ra'avad explains that the Gemara is discussing a case where the gentile stole an item and enhanced it. The Rambam explains the Gemara as referring to a case where a Jew stole the item and sold it to a gentile, who then enhanced its value.

What is the *halakha* if the central twin-leaf became split – נחלקה התיומת מהו: Most of the commentaries note that while the Gemara's question pertains to the *halakhot* of acquisition, i.e., does a robber acquire a palm frond if the central twin-leaf became split, the answer given is based upon the *halakhot* of *lulav*. Since the splitting of the central twin-leaf is significant with regard to the *halakhot* of *lulav*, it is significant with regard to the *halakhot* of acquisition as well.

NOTES

And fashioned it into a brick – וַעֲבְדֵיהּ לִבֵינְתָא: The Rashba explains that in this case the brick was formed but not yet baked in a kiln. Had it been baked, the brick would not be able to revert to its previous state. The early commentaries write that since the robber does not acquire the brick but returns it to its owner as is, the owner must pay for the enhanced value that a brick has relative to earth, either all of the enhanced value or a portion, as discussed by the *tanna'im*. This is because a robber does acquire the enhancement that is still possessed by the stolen item (Ra'avad; Rid).

And fashioned coins – וְעָבֵיד זוּזֵי: *Tosafot* explain that a robber who fashions coins from a bar of silver does not acquire the silver, since it has not been changed significantly. By contrast, if he fashions a vessel, he does acquire the silver, as that is a significant change. The Rashba disagrees with this distinction, since coins are significantly different from a bar of silver, due to their monetary value. In his opinion, the reason the robber does not acquire the silver is that coins can be melted and turned back into a bar of silver without losing value. Consequently, it is not a significant change. Accordingly, the same would apply if he fashioned a vessel from the silver.

LANGUAGE

Bar of silver [*naskha*] – נַסְכָא: The word *nasakh* is the related to the word *natakh*, from which the word *matekhet*, meaning metal, is derived. It refers to lumps of silver of no particular shape. The Sages use this term specifically in reference to hunks of precious metals such as gold and silver.

Black [*sheḥimei*] – שְׁחִימֵי: The literal meaning of this word is dark. Over time, due to small quantities of hydrogen sulfide, H_2S, a gas in the air, the black compound silver sulfide, Ag_2S, is formed. This compound constitutes the tarnish on silver. At times, people would suspect very new-looking coins to be counterfeit, and there were those that would artificially blacken their new coins so that they would be accepted without hesitation.

מַאי לָאו הוּא הַדִּין לְנֶחְלְקָה? לָא, נִיטְּלָה שָׁאנֵי, דְּהָא חָסֵר לָהּ.

What, is it not that the same is true for a case where the central twin-leaf **became split**, i.e., that this *lulav* has been rendered unfit to be used for the mitzva, and the robber has acquired the *lulav* as a result of this change? The Gemara answers: **No,** the case where it **was removed is different, as** the result is that **it is lacking,** and an incomplete *lulav* is certainly unfit. But if the leaf remains in place, albeit split, it does not necessarily render the *lulav* unfit. The *lulav* has not been changed and therefore the robber does not acquire it.

אִיכָּא דְּאָמְרִי: תָּא שְׁמַע, דְּאָמַר רַבִּי מָתוּן אָמַר רַבִּי יְהוֹשֻׁעַ בֶּן לֵוִי: נֶחְלְקָה הַתְּיוֹמֶת – נַעֲשָׂה כְּמִי שֶׁנִּטְּלָה וּפָסוּל, שְׁמַע מִינָּהּ.

There are those **who say** that the question was resolved as follows: **Come and hear** that which **Rabbi Matun says** that **Rabbi Yehoshua ben Levi says: If the central twin-leaf became split,**[H] **it becomes like a** *lulav* whose central **twin-leaf was** completely **removed, and** it is **unfit.** If so, **learn from** his statement that if the central twin-leaf became split, the robber has acquired the *lulav* as a result of the change.

אֲמַר רַב פַּפָּא: הַאי מַאן דִּגְזַל עַפְרָא מֵחַבְרֵיהּ וַעֲבְדֵיהּ לִבֵינְתָא – לָא קָנֵי, מַאי טַעְמָא? דְּהָדַר מְשַׁוֵּי לֵיהּ עַפְרָא; לְבֵינְתָא וַעֲבְדֵיהּ עַפְרָא – קָנֵי. מַאי אָמְרַתְּ? דִּלְמָא הָדַר וְעָבֵיד לֵיהּ לְבֵינְתָא – הַאי לְבֵינְתָא אַחֲרִיתִי הוּא, וּפָנִים חֲדָשׁוֹת בָּאוּ לְכָאן.

§ **Rav Pappa said: This one who robbed another of earth**[H] **and fashioned it into a brick**[N] **has not acquired** it due to the change. **What is the reason** for this? It is **that** he can **return** it **and convert** it back **into earth.** By contrast, if he robbed another of **a brick, and** by crushing it **turned it into earth,**[H] **he has acquired it** due to the change. **If you say: Perhaps** he will **return** it **and fashion it** into a **brick? This is a different brick, and a new entity has arrived,** i.e., entered into existence, **here.**

וַאֲמַר רַב פַּפָּא: הַאי מַאן דִּגְזַל נַסְכָא מֵחַבְרֵיהּ וְעָבֵיד זוּזֵי – לָא קָנֵי, מַאי טַעֲמָא? הָדַר עָבֵיד לְהוּ נַסְכָא; זוּזֵי וַעֲבְדִינְהוּ נַסְכָא – קָנֵי. מַאי אָמְרַתְּ? הָדַר עָבֵיד לְהוּ זוּזֵי – פָּנִים חֲדָשׁוֹת בָּאוּ לְכָאן;

And Rav Pappa also **said: This one who robbed another of a bar of silver** [***naskha***][LH] **and fashioned it into coins**[N] **has not acquired** it due to the change. **What is the reason** for this? He can **return** it and by melting the coins **turn them into a bar of silver.** By contrast, if he robbed another of **coins and fashioned them** into a **bar of silver,**[H] **he has acquired them** due to the change. **What do you say** in response to this, that perhaps he will **return and fashion them** into **coins?** These are new coins, and **a new entity has arrived here.**

שְׁחִימֵי וַעֲבְדִינְהוּ חֲדַתֵּי – לָא קָנֵי, חֲדַתֵּי וַעֲבְדִינְהוּ שְׁחִימֵי – קָנֵי. מַאי אָמְרַתְּ? הֲדַר עָבֵיד לְהוּ חֲדַתֵּי – מֵידַע יְדִיעַ שִׁיחֲמַיְיהוּ.

Rav Pappa continues: If the stolen coins were **black** [***sheḥimei***],[L] i.e., old and used, **and he made them** as **new**[H] by cleaning them thoroughly, **he has not acquired** them. By contrast, if however, they **were new, and he made them black, he has acquired** them. **What do you say** in response to this, that perhaps he will **return** and **make them new** by cleaning them? **Their blackness is already known,** and therefore the coins have been changed irreversibly.

HALAKHA

If the central twin-leaf became split – נֶחְלְקָה הַתְּיוֹמֶת: The leaves of the *lulav* grow as pairs that are connected at their edges. If most of the leaves of the *lulav* are split at the point of their connection, the *lulav* is unfit for use in the performance of the mitzva (*Tur*; *Beit Yosef*). Some explain that even if the central twin-leaf alone is split at the point of its connection all the way down to the spine it is unfit, and the custom is to be stringent (Rema, citing *Terumat HaDeshen*). In practice, the custom is that if the majority of that leaf is split, the *lulav* is considered unfit (Rambam *Sefer Zemanim, Hilkhot Shofar VeSukka VeLulav* 8:4; *Shulḥan Arukh, Oraḥ Ḥayyim* 645:3 and *Mishne Berura* there).

Robbed another of earth, etc. – גָּזַל עַפְרָא וכו׳: One who robbed another of earth and fashioned it into bricks has not acquired it, since it can be returned to its prior form (Rambam *Sefer Nezikin, Hilkhot Gezeila VaAveda* 2:11; *Shulḥan Arukh, Ḥoshen Mishpat* 360:5).

A brick and turned it into earth – לְבֵינְתָא וַעֲבְדֵיהּ עַפְרָא: One who robbed another of a brick and ground it into earth has acquired it by means of the change, as even if he refashions it into a brick it is considered to be a new entity (Rambam *Sefer Nezikin, Hilkhot Gezeila VaAveda* 2:12; *Shulḥan Arukh, Ḥoshen Mishpat* 360:6).

Robbed another of a bar of silver, etc. – גָּזַל נַסְכָא מֵחַבְרֵיהּ וכו׳: One who robbed another of a piece of silver and fashioned it into coins has not acquired the silver, since the coins can be melted down and returned to their prior form (Rambam *Sefer Nezikin, Hilkhot Gezeila VaAveda* 2:11; *Shulḥan Arukh, Ḥoshen Mishpat* 360:5).

Robbed another of coins and fashioned them into a bar of silver – זוּזֵי וַעֲבְדִינְהוּ נַסְכָא: One who robbed another of coins and melted them down into a piece of silver has acquired them due to this change, as even if he refashions them into coins they are considered a new entity (Rambam *Sefer Nezikin, Hilkhot Gezeila VaAveda* 2:12; *Shulḥan Arukh, Ḥoshen Mishpat* 360:6).

Black and he made them new, etc. – שְׁחִימֵי וַעֲבְדִינְהוּ חֲדַתֵּי וכו׳: One who robbed another of old coins and polished them until they appeared new has not acquired them, since they will take on the appearance of old coins again. If he caused new coins to appear old, he has acquired them, as even if he causes them to appear new again, they will be considered a new entity (Rambam *Sefer Nezikin, Hilkhot Gezeila VaAveda* 2:13; *Shulḥan Arukh, Ḥoshen Mishpat* 360:7).

"זה הכלל: כל הגזלנין משלמין כשעת הגזלה". זה הכלל לאתויי מאי? לאתויי הא דאמר רבי אלעא: גנב טלה ונעשה איל, עגל ונעשה שור – נעשה שינוי בידו וקנאו, טבח ומכר – שלו הוא טובח, שלו הוא מוכר.

§ The mishna teaches: **This is the principle: All robbers pay according to** the value of the stolen item at **the time of the robbery.** The Gemara asks: **What is added** by the phrase: **This is the principle?** The Gemara replies: It serves **to add that which Rabbi Ela says:** If one **stole a lamb**[H] **and** during the time that it was in the thief's possession it **became a ram,** or if one stole **a calf** and it **became an ox,** then **a change occurred** while the animal was **in his possession, and he has acquired it** due to the change. If he then **slaughtered or sold** the animal, **he slaughters his own** animal **and he sells his own** animal, and he does not become liable to pay the penalty of four or five times the value of the animal.

ההוא גברא דגזל פדנא דתורי מחבריה, אזל כרב בהו כרבא, זרע בהו זרעא, לסוף אהדרינהו למריה. אתא לקמיה דרב נחמן, אמר להו: זילו שומו שבחא דאשבח.

The Gemara relates: There was **a certain man who robbed another** of **a pair** [*padna*][L] **of oxen.**[H] He then **went** and **plowed** his field **with them,** and **sowed seeds with them, and eventually returned them to their owner.** The robbery victim **came before Rav Naḥman** to claim payment from the robber. Rav Naḥman **said to** the robbery victim and the robber: **Go estimate** the amount by **which** the value of the land **was enhanced** during the time that the pair of oxen was in the possession of the robber, and the robber must pay that amount.

אמר ליה רבא: תורי אשבח, ארעא לא אשבח? אמר: מי קאמינא נשיימו כוליה? פלגא קאמינא. אמר ליה: סוף סוף גזילה הוא, וקא הדרה בעינא, דתנן: כל הגזלנין משלמין כשעת הגזלה!

Rava said to Rav Naḥman: Did **the oxen** alone **enhance** the value of the land? **Did the land not** become **enhanced** in and of itself? Perhaps not all of the enhanced value of the land was due to the labor performed by the oxen. Rav Naḥman **said: Did I say** that **they should estimate** and give him **all of** the enhanced value? **I said** only **half.** Rava **said to him: Ultimately, it is a stolen item and is returned as it was** at the time of the robbery, **as we learned** in a mishna: **All robbers pay according to** the value of the stolen item at **the time of the robbery.** Why should the robber also pay the owner half the value of the enhancement?

אמר ליה, לא אמינא לך: כי יתיבנא בדינא לא תימא לי מידי, דאמר הונא חברין עלאי: אנא ושבור מלכא אחי בדינא? האי איניש גזלנא עתיקא הוא ובעינא דאיקנסיה.

Rav Naḥman **said to** Rava: **Didn't I tell you** that **when I am sitting in judgment, do not say anything to me,** i.e., do not question or comment upon my rulings. An indication that my rulings should not be questioned is **as our friend Huna has said about me,** that **King Shapur**[B] **and I are brothers with regard to** monetary **laws,** i.e., with regard to monetary laws, my opinion is equal to that of Shmuel. **This man is an experienced robber, and I wish to penalize him.** Therefore, I compelled him to pay the enhanced value, although by right he is not obligated to do so.

מתני׳ גזל בהמה והזקינה, עבדים והזקינו – משלם כשעת הגזלה; רבי מאיר אומר: בעבדים – אומר לו "הרי שלך לפניך".

MISHNA If one **robbed** another of **an animal and it aged**[H] while in his possession, consequently diminishing its value, or if one robbed another of Canaanite **slaves and they aged** while in his possession, they have been changed. The robber therefore **pays according to** the value of the stolen item at **the time of the robbery. Rabbi Meir says: With regard to** Canaanite **slaves, he says to**[N] the robbery victim: **That which is yours is before you.**

BACKGROUND

King Shapur – שבור מלכא: Shapur was a name of several of the Persian kings. This King Shapur is King Shapur I (3901–3932; 141–172 CE), the second ruler of the Sassanid dynasty and son of its founder. King Shapur continued the wars against the Romans and conquered extensive territory from them, reaching as far as Syria and beyond. In a battle near Odessa, he defeated the Roman emperor Valerian, took him into captivity, and kept him as a prisoner until the latter's death. He had his captives build several cities and dams. His domestic policy reflected tolerance toward other religions.

Likeness of King Shapur I of Persia, on a coin minted during his reign

HALAKHA

Stole a lamb, etc. – גנב טלה וכו׳: If one stole a lamb that grew into a ram while in his possession, or if one stole a calf that grew into an ox while in his possession, he has acquired the animal through this change (Rambam *Sefer Nezikin, Hilkhot Gezeila VaAveda* 2:14; *Shulḥan Arukh, Ḥoshen Mishpat* 360:10, in the comment of Rema).

Who robbed another of a pair of oxen, etc. – דגזל פדנא דתורי מחבריה וכו׳: If one robs another of an animal, utilizes it for work, and then returns it to its owner, although he has transgressed a prohibition, he is not obligated to pay anything to the owner, provided the animal was not weakened and its value was not diminished (see *Sma* and *Netivot HaMishpat*). If this is a known robber, the court penalizes him. It estimates his profits from his use of the animal and compels him to give that amount to the robbery victim. This penalty can be imposed even outside of Eretz Yisrael if imposed by the leading judge of the generation or by a court that has been elected by the community (Rosh). The *Baḥ* and Gra explain that if the robber used the animal to plow, he must pay half of the enhanced value of the field (Rambam *Sefer Nezikin, Hilkhot Gezeila VaAveda* 3:6; *Shulḥan Arukh, Ḥoshen Mishpat* 363:3).

Robbed another of an animal and it aged, etc. – גזל בהמה והזקינה וכו׳: If one robbed another of an animal that subsequently was weakened irreversibly or aged, or of a coin that broke or was invalidated by the government, or of produce that all rotted, or of wine that fermented, in all of these cases he pays the value of the item at the time of the robbery. Some hold that this does not apply in the case of a coin that was invalidated by the government (Rema, citing Rosh). If one robbed another of Canaanite slaves who aged, or animals that were weakened but can regain their strength, or of coins that were invalidated only in some locations, or of produce that part of it rotted, or of leavened bread over which Passover then elapsed, or of *teruma* that became impure, or of an ox that was disqualified to be sacrificed as an offering, or of an ox that was sentenced to be stoned, in all of these cases the robber can return the stolen item and say: That which is yours is before you. This ruling is in accordance with the mishna and the opinion of Rabbi Meir, since Rav ruled in accordance with his opinion (Rambam *Sefer Nezikin, Hilkhot Gezeila VaAveda* 3:4; *Shulḥan Arukh, Ḥoshen Mishpat* 363:1).

LANGUAGE

Pair [*padna*] – פדנא: In Aramaic this means a pair of cattle as well as the yoke that is upon them. This is similar to the Arabic word فدان, *faddān*.

NOTES

With regard to slaves he says to, etc. – בעבדים אומר לו וכו׳: Because, as will be explained, Canaanite slaves have the legal status of real estate, then, just as real estate cannot be stolen but remains in the possession of its robbery victim even if it was changed, so too, Canaanite slaves remain in the possession of the robbery victim, and if they age they do so in his possession. See 97a for a discussion of payment for a slave's labor.

גזל מטבע ונסדק, פירות והרקיבו, יין והחמיץ – משלם כשעת הגזלה.

If one **robbed** another of **a coin and it cracked,** thereby reducing its value; or if one robbed another of **produce and it rotted;** or if one robbed another of **wine and it fermented,** then **he pays according to** the value of the stolen item at **the time of the robbery.**

מטבע ונפסל, תרומה ונטמאת, חמץ ועבר עליו הפסח, בהמה ונתעבדה בה עבירה, או שנפסלה מעל גבי המזבח, או שהיתה יוצאה ליסקל – אומר לו "הרי שלך לפניך".

If he robbed another of **a coin and it was invalidated** by the government; or if he robbed another of ***teruma* and it became ritually impure;** or if he robbed another of **leavened bread and Passover elapsed over it,** and therefore it is prohibited to derive benefit from it; or if he robbed another of **an animal and a sin was performed with it,**[N] thereby disqualifying it for use as an offering; **or if** the animal **was disqualified**[N] **from** being sacrificed **upon the altar** for some other reason; **or if** the animal **was going out to be stoned** because it gored and killed a person at some point after the robbery, the robber **says to** the robbery victim: **That which is yours is before you.** In all of these cases, although the value of the stolen item has been diminished or altogether lost, since the change is not externally discernible, the robber returns the item in its current state.

גמ׳ אמר רב פפא: לא הזקינה – הזקינה ממש, אלא אפילו כחשה. והא אנן הזקינה תנן! כחשה כגון הזקינה, דלא הדר בריא.

GEMARA With regard to the mishna's statement that one who robbed another of an animal that aged pays what its value was at the time of the robbery, **Rav Pappa says:** It is **not** so that **aged** means that it **actually aged. But even** if the animal was **weakened,** which is a less significant change, it is still considered changed, and the robber has acquired the animal. The Gemara asks: **But didn't we learn** in the mishna that it **aged,** indicating that a lesser change, e.g., weakening, is not significant? The Gemara responds: Rav Pappa was speaking of **weakening** that is **like aging,** i.e., the animal became so weak **that it will not return** to its former **health.**

אמר ליה מר קשישא בריה דרב חסדא לרב אשי, הכי קאמרי משמיה דרבי יוחנן: אפילו גנב טלה ונעשה איל, עגל ונעשה שור – נעשה שינוי בידו וקנאו, טבח ומכר – שלו הוא טובח, שלו הוא מוכר. אמר ליה, לאו אמינא לך: לא תחליף גברי? ההוא משמיה דרבי אלעא איתמר.

Mar Kashisha,[P] son **of Rav Ḥisda, said to Rav Ashi: This is what they say in the name of Rabbi Yoḥanan: Even if one stole a lamb and it became a ram, or a calf and it became an ox,** it is considered that **a change occurred** while the animal was **in** the robber's **possession, and he has acquired it** due to this change. If he then **slaughtered or sold** the animal, **he slaughters his own** animal **and he sells his own** animal, and he does not become liable to pay the penalty of four or five times the value of the animal. Rav Ashi **said to him: Didn't I say to you: Do not exchange** the names of the **men** in whose name you are transmitting words of Torah? **That** statement **was stated in the name of Rabbi Ela,** not in the name of Rabbi Yoḥanan.

"רבי מאיר אומר: בעבדים – אומר לו "הרי שלך לפניך"". אמר רב חנינא בר אבדימי אמר רב: הלכה כרבי מאיר. ורב שביק רבנן ועביד כרבי מאיר? אמרי: משום דברייתא איפכא תניא. ורב שביק מתניתין ועביד כברייתא? רב, מתניתין נמי איפכא תני.

§ The mishna teaches that **Rabbi Meir says: With regard to** Canaanite **slaves, he says to** the robbery victim: **That which is yours is before you.** The Gemara comments: **Rav Ḥanina bar Avdimi says** that **Rav says:** The ***halakha* is in accordance with** the opinion of **Rabbi Meir.** The Gemara asks: **And would Rav set aside** the opinion of **the Rabbis,** who are the majority, **and practice** the *halakha* **in accordance with** the opinion of **Rabbi Meir?** The **Sages say:** It is **because it is taught** in a *baraita* in the **opposite** manner, i.e., with the opinions reversed, so that the Rabbis, rather than Rabbi Meir, hold that with regard to slaves the robber says: That which is yours is before you. The Gemara asks: **And would Rav set aside the mishna and practice** the *halakha* **in accordance with** the statement of **the *baraita*?** The Gemara responds: **Rav also teaches the mishna** in the **opposite** manner.[N]

ומאי טעמיה דרב דאפיך מתניתין מקמי דברייתא? אדרבה, ניפוך לברייתא מקמי מתניתין! אמרי: רב נמי מתניתין איפכא אתניה.

And what is the reasoning of Rav, who reversed the opinions in **the mishna in light of the *baraita*? On the contrary, let him reverse** the opinions in **the *baraita* in light of the mishna.** The Sages **say** in response: **Rav also learned the mishna** in the **opposite** manner. Rav did not decide to reverse the opinions in the mishna. In the text of the mishna that he utilized, the opinions were the same as in the *baraita*.

NOTES

And a sin was performed with it – **ונתעבדה בה עבירה**: If, for example, a person engaged in sexual intercourse with this animal, or if the animal was worshipped as idolatry, even if there are not two witnesses who can testify to this, the animal is disqualified for use as an offering. The value of the animal has been diminished as a result.

Or if the animal was disqualified – **או שנפסלה**: *Tosafot* (98a) note that this is a case where the animal had already been consecrated. They therefore rule that only if the blemish developed naturally can the robber say: That which is yours is before you. If, however, the robber blemished the animal, he must pay the damages.

Also teaches the mishna in the opposite manner – **מתניתין נמי איפכא תני**: According to this interpretation, Rav himself reversed the attributions in the mishna, so that the statement with regard to Canaanite slaves is made by the Rabbis, not Rabbi Meir, and, consequently, Rav rules in accordance with the majority.

PERSONALITIES

Mar Kashisha – **מר קשישא**: It appears that Rav Ḥisda had two sons, both of whom were called Mar. In order to distinguish between them, one was known as Mar Kashisha, i.e., Mar the Elder, and the other as Mar Yenuka, i.e., Mar the Younger. According to Rashi, Mar Kashisha was the older brother and Mar Yenuka the younger. According to *Tosafot*, Mar Yenuka was the older brother but was known as Mar the Younger because he was born when his father, Rav Ḥisda, was young, while his brother was known as Mar the Elder because he was born in Rav Ḥisda's later years.

ואי בעית אימא: כי לא אפיך – חדא מקמי חדא, חדא מקמי תרתי אפיך.

And if you wish, say instead that Rav did in fact decide to reverse the opinions in the mishna, based upon the principle: **When he does not reverse** a mishna due to a *baraita*, it is when there is **one** mishna that he will not reverse **in light of one** *baraita*. But **he would reverse one** mishna **in light of two** *baraitot*, and in this case there is a second *baraita* in which the opinions are the reverse of those found in the mishna.

דתניא: המחליף פרה בחמור וילדה, וכן המוכר שפחתו וילדה, זה אומר "ברשותי ילדה" והלה שותק – זכה בה. זה אומר "איני יודע" וזה אומר "איני יודע" – יחלוקו.

The second *baraita* is **as it is taught** in the *Tosefta* (*Bava Metzia* 8:23–24): In the case of **one who exchanges a cow for a donkey,**[H] **and** in the meantime the cow **gave birth; and similarly,** in the case of **one who sells his** Canaanite **maidservant, and** in the meantime **she gave birth,** if in either of these cases the purchaser and seller have a dispute as to when the birth took place, where **this one says: She gave birth** at the time that she was **in my possession** and therefore the offspring is mine, **and the other is silent,**[N] then the one who stated definitively that she gave birth while in his possession **has acquired** the offspring. If **this** one **says: I do not know, and that** one **says: I do not know,**[N] then **they shall divide** the value of the offspring.

זה אומר "ברשותי" וזה אומר "ברשותי" – ישבע המוכר שברשותו ילדה, לפי שכל הנשבעין שבתורה נשבעין ולא משלמין, דברי רבי מאיר.

The *baraita* continues: If **this** one **says:** She gave birth while **in my possession, and that** one **says:** She gave birth while **in my possession,** then **the seller must take an oath that she gave birth** while **in his possession, as anyone who** is obligated to **take an oath that** is enumerated **in the Torah**[H] **takes an oath and does not pay;** this is **the statement of Rabbi Meir.** In this case, since the seller initially had possession of the animal or the maidservant, he is considered the defendant, and therefore it is sufficient for him to take an oath to exempt himself from payment and maintain possession of the offspring.

וחכמים אומרים: אין נשבעין לא על העבדים ולא על הקרקעות.

The *baraita* continues: **And the Rabbis say** that **one does not take an oath**[H] **concerning either** Canaanite **slaves or concerning land.** This indicates that according to the opinion of the Rabbis, Canaanite slaves have the legal status of land, whereas according to the opinion of Rabbi Meir, they do not. It follows, then, that in the mishna here as well, it is the Rabbis, and not Rabbi Meir, who maintain that, with regard to slaves, one says: That which is yours is before you, as one does with regard to land.

האי הלכה כרבי מאיר, הלכה כרבנן מיבעי ליה! הכי קאמר: למאי דאפכיתו ותניתו, הלכה כרבי מאיר.

The Gemara asks: If it is true that the opinion that the mishna attributed to Rabbi Meir was attributed by Rav to the Rabbis, then **this** phrase: The ***halakha*** **is in accordance with** the opinion of **Rabbi Meir,** is imprecise. Rav **should have** said that the ***halakha*** **is in accordance with** the opinion of **the Rabbis.** The Gemara responds: **This is** what Rav **is saying: According to** the way **that you have reversed** the opinions in the mishna, **and you taught** that Rabbi Meir says that the robber says to the robbery victim: That which is yours is before you, then the ***halakha*** is **in accordance with** the opinion of **Rabbi Meir,** despite the fact that according to Rav, this is the opinion of the Rabbis.

NOTES

And the other is silent – והלה שותק: Rashi explains that silence is tantamount to an uncertain claim, and this ruling follows the principle that when there is a definite claim and an uncertain claim, the definite claim is superior. *Tosafot* disagree with this interpretation, and explain instead that since he was silent and did not even say: I do not know, his silence is tantamount to an admission that the offspring is not his.

I do not know – איני יודע: This is a case where the cow or the maidservant was not in the possession of either party, and since there is no other way to resolve the dispute they must divide the value of the offspring.

HALAKHA

One who exchanges a cow for a donkey, etc. – המחליף פרה בחמור וכו׳: If a cow was exchanged for a donkey or a Canaanite maidservant was sold, and the cow or the maidservant gave birth but it is unknown in whose possession the mother was when the birth took place, then if one party claims that she gave birth while in his possession and the other party is silent, the one who stated the claim keeps the offspring.

If both parties claim that they do not know in whose possession the mother was when the offspring was born, and the offspring is not in the possession of either one, some say that the burden of proof is upon the purchaser. Others, based upon the Rambam, say that they should divide the value of the offspring.

If each party claims that the offspring was born when the mother was in his possession, the offspring remains in the possession of the seller unless the purchaser proves his claim, even if the seller does not make his claim with certainty. If the purchaser cannot bring proof, the seller must take an oath. In the case of an animal, it is a Torah-mandated oath, which he takes while holding a sacred object. If his claim is to the offspring of a Canaanite maidservant, he takes an oath of inducement, mandated by rabbinic law (Rambam *Sefer Kinyan, Hilkhot Mekhira* 20:10–11; *Shulḥan Arukh, Ḥoshen Mishpat* 223:1–2).

As anyone who is obligated to take an oath that is enumerated in the Torah, etc. – שכל הנשבעין שבתורה וכו׳: Anyone obligated by Torah law to take an oath does so in order to exempt himself from paying a claim that was registered against him. There are instances where one would take an oath by rabbinic law in order to remove property from one in whose possession it currently stands (Rambam *Sefer Mishpatim, Hilkhot To'en VeNitan* 1:4; *Shulḥan Arukh, Ḥoshen Mishpat* 89:1).

One does not take an oath, etc. – אין נשבעין וכו׳: There are some matters with regard to which, by Torah law, one does not take an oath while holding a sacred object. They are matters concerning land, slaves, documents, and consecrated property. The Sages mandated that an oath of inducement be taken in these cases (Rambam *Sefer Mishpatim, Hilkhot To'en VeNitan* 5:1; *Shulḥan Arukh, Ḥoshen Mishpat* 95:1).

וּמִי אֲמַר רַב עַבְדָּא כִּמְקַרְקְעֵי דָּמֵי? וְהָאָמַר רַב דָּנִיאֵל בַּר רַב קְטִינָא אָמַר רַב: הַתּוֹקֵף בְּעַבְדּוֹ שֶׁל חֲבֵירוֹ וְעָשָׂה בּוֹ מְלָאכָה – פָּטוּר. וְאִי סָלְקָא דַּעְתָּךְ עַבְדָּא כִּמְקַרְקְעֵי דָּמֵי, אַמַּאי פָּטוּר? בִּרְשׁוּתָא דְּמָרֵיהּ קָאֵי!

And did Rav actually **say** that the legal status of a Canaanite **slave is like** that of **real estate? But doesn't Rav Daniel bar Rav Ketina say** that **Rav says: One who seizes another's** Canaanite **slave**[H] **and performs labor with him is exempt** from paying the master for the labor of the slave? **And if it enters your mind** to say that, in Rav's opinion, the legal status of **a slave is like** that of **real estate, why** is he **exempt** from paying? A slave, like real estate, **is** always **in the possession of his owner,** wherever he might be. Therefore, the one who seized him did not steal the slave, in which case he could simply return him. Rather, he made use of a slave belonging to another and should be liable to pay for the master's loss of the slave's labor.

הָכָא בְּמַאי עָסְקִינַן – שֶׁלֹּא בִּשְׁעַת מְלָאכָה. כִּי הָא דִּשְׁלַח לֵיהּ רַבִּי אַבָּא לְמָרִי בַּר מָר, בְּעִי מִינֵּיהּ מֵרַב הוּנָא: הַדָּר בַּחֲצַר חֲבֵירוֹ שֶׁלֹּא מִדַּעְתּוֹ, צָרִיךְ לְהַעֲלוֹת לוֹ שָׂכָר אוֹ אֵין צָרִיךְ לְהַעֲלוֹת לוֹ שָׂכָר? וְשָׁלְחוּ לֵיהּ: אֵינוֹ צָרִיךְ לְהַעֲלוֹת לוֹ שָׂכָר.

The Gemara answers: **With what are we dealing here?** We are dealing with a case where the one who seized the slave forced him to perform labor when it was **not during** regular **working hours.** Consequently, he did not prevent the slave from performing labor for his master. Since the owner did not incur any loss, the one who seized the slave is not obligated to pay for the benefit that he derived from the slave. This is **like that** message **that Rabbi Abba sent to Mari bar Mar:**[P] **Ask Rav Huna** concerning **one who resides in another's courtyard**[N] **without** the owner's **knowledge: Does he need to pay him rent, or does he not need to pay him rent? And they sent to him** in response: **He does not need to pay him rent,** since the owner of the property did not incur any monetary loss.

הָכִי הָשְׁתָא!? בִּשְׁלָמָא הָתָם, בֵּין לְמַאן דְּאָמַר בֵּיתָא מִיתְּבָא יָתֵיב – נִיחָא לֵיהּ, בֵּין לְמַאן דְּאָמַר "וּשְׁאִיָּה יֻכַּת שָׁעַר" – נִיחָא לֵיהּ,

The Gemara rejects this comparison: **How can these cases be compared? Granted, there,** in the case of a courtyard, **whether** the reasoning for that *halakha* is **according to the one who says: An inhabited house**[N] remains **habitable,** and it is therefore **satisfactory for** the owner of the property to have someone residing in his courtyard, or **whether** the reasoning is **according to the one who says** that since the verse states: "In the city is left desolation, **and the gate is smitten unto ruin**" (Isaiah 24:12), which indicates that a desolate house will fall into ruin but an inhabited house will be maintained, either way it is satisfactory **for** the owner that one stay in his courtyard. Consequently, the one who resides there need not pay rent.

אֶלָּא הָכָא מִי נִיחָא לֵיהּ דְּנִכְחוּשׁ עַבְדֵיהּ? אָמְרִי: הָכִי נַמִי נִיחָא לֵיהּ, דְּלָא לִיסְתְּרִי עַבְדֵיהּ.

But here, in the case of a slave, **is it satisfactory for him that his slave be weakened** by performing labor for another? The Sages **say: Indeed, it is satisfactory for him that** the work habits of **his slave not be undone.**[N]

בֵּי רַב יוֹסֵף בַּר חָמָא הָווּ תָּקֵיף עַבְדֵי דְּאִינָשֵׁי דְּמַסֵּיק בְּהוּ זוּזֵי וְעָבְדִי בְּהוּ מְלָאכָה, אֲמַר לֵיהּ רַבָּה בְּרֵיהּ: מַאי טַעְמָא עָבֵיד מָר הָכִי? אֲמַר לֵיהּ, דְּאָמַר רַב נַחְמָן: עַבְדָּא – נְהוּם כְּרֵיסֵיהּ לָא שָׁוֵי. אֲמַר לֵיהּ: אֵימָא דַּאֲמַר רַב נַחְמָן, כְּגוֹן דָּארוּ עַבְדֵיהּ דִּמְרַקֵּיד בֵּי כּוּבֵי, כּוּלְּהוּ עַבְדֵי מִעֲבַד עָבְדִי?

The Gemara records a related incident. Members of the **house of Rav Yosef bar Hama**[P] **would,** with his approval, **seize the slaves of people who owed him money, and they would work them** against the will of the owners. **Rabba,**[N] **son of** Rav Yosef bar Hama, **said to him: What is the reason that** the **Master does this,** i.e., seizes and uses these slaves? Rav Yosef bar Hama **said to him:** As **Rav Nahman says: A slave is not worth** even **the bread in his stomach.** When the slaves work for me and eat in my home, I am not causing the owners any monetary loss. Rav Yosef bar Hama's son **said to him: I will say that Rav Nahman said** this with regard to specific slaves, **such as his slave Daru,**[L] **who** only **dances among** the wine **barrels** [*kuvei*][NL] and does not perform any labor. **All** other **slaves perform labor,** and their labor is worth more than their board.

HALAKHA

One who seizes another's slave, etc. – הַתּוֹקֵף בְּעַבְדּוֹ שֶׁל חֲבֵירוֹ וכו׳: If one seizes another's slave and performs labor with him but does not prevent the slave from performing the labor he normally performs for his master, he is exempt from payment, since people prefer that their slaves not be idle. If the slave was prevented from performing the labor he normally performs for his master, then the one who seized him must pay the slave's owner the amount that a worker would be paid to perform the labor that the one who seized him had the slave perform (Rambam *Sefer Nezikin, Hilkhot Gezeila VaAveda* 3:7; *Shulhan Arukh, Hoshen Mishpat* 363:4).

PERSONALITIES

Mari bar Mar – מָרִי בַּר מָר: A contemporary of Rav Hisda and a disciple of Rav Huna and Rav, Mari bar Mar is quoted both for his own statements and for those of his teachers. Some commentaries suggest that his father is called Mar, or Master, because his name was Huna, and Mari's colleagues, the other disciples of Rav Huna, did not want to mention their teacher's name.

Rav Yosef bar Hama – רַב יוֹסֵף בַּר חָמָא: A third-generation Babylonian *amora*, Rav Yosef bar Hama lived in Mehoza and may have served as leader of that community. He was a student of Rav Sheshet but also had discussions on Torah topics and *halakha* with other Sages, including Rav Zeira. Rav Yosef bar Hama's son was the great *amora* Rava, who was already regarded as one of the leading Sages during his father's lifetime. At times, Rava would comment upon his father's halakhic rulings or discuss them with him, always utilizing the respectful language appropriate for a child speaking to a parent, and the father would, on occasion, agree with his son.

NOTES

One who resides in another's courtyard – הַדָּר בַּחֲצַר חֲבֵירוֹ: The Gemara explains that this refers to a case where the courtyard is not commonly available for rental (21a). Since in any event the owners would not have earned any money from its use, they do not suffer a loss when someone lives there.

An inhabited house, etc. – בֵּיתָא מִיתְּבָא וכו׳: There is a difference between the two explanations: According to the first explanation, if a house is inhabited, its residents will take care of its upkeep and maintenance. According to the second, an abandoned property will be neglected and will ultimately fall into disrepair on its own. Essentially, both express the same concept: It is beneficial to the owner of a property that someone reside there.

Be undone – לִיסְתְּרִי: Rashi explains that a slave who does not perform labor becomes accustomed to idleness, and therefore the owner prefers that his slave perform labor for another rather than be idle. Rabbeinu Hananel explains that an idle slave acts as though he were an authority figure, and consequently it becomes difficult to induce him to perform labor in the future. The Rashba, quoting another interpretation of Rabbeinu Hananel, writes that this slave is one who becomes physically weakened if he does not perform labor.

Rabba – רַבָּה: Based on other versions of the text, this should read Rava, who was in fact the son of Rav Yosef bar Hama.

Dances among the barrels – מְרַקֵּיד בֵּי כּוּבֵי: The literal translation of this phrase is: Dances among the barrels of wine. It refers to a jester who entertains guests at a tavern in exchange for food and wine.

LANGUAGE

Daru – דָּארוּ: Some say that this name derives from the Greek Δῶρος, *Doros*. Since this individual lived in Babylonia, it is likely an abbreviation of the Persian name Darius.

Barrels [*kuvei*] – כּוּבֵי: The origin of this word appears to be Semitic, similar to the Arabic كوب, *kūb*, meaning a large goblet without handles. It also bears some semblance to the Hebrew word *kubba'at*, meaning a beaker or cup.

אֲמַר לֵיהּ: אֲנָא כְּרַב דָּנִיֵּאל סְבִירָא לִי, דְּאָמַר רַב דָּנִיֵּאל בַּר רַב קְטִינָא אָמַר רַב: הַתּוֹקֵף בְּעַבְדּוֹ שֶׁל חֲבֵירוֹ וְעָשָׂה בּוֹ מְלָאכָה – פָּטוּר, אַלְמָא נִיחָא לֵיהּ דְּלָא לִיסַּתְּרֵי עַבְדֵּיהּ.

Rav Yosef bar Ḥama **said to him: I hold in accordance with** the opinion **of Rav Daniel, as Rav Daniel bar Rav Ketina says** that **Rav says: One who seizes another's slave and performs labor with him is exempt** from paying the master for the labor of the slave. **Apparently,** it is **satisfactory for** the master **that** the work habits of **his slave not be undone.**

אֲמַר לֵיהּ: הָנֵי מִילֵּי הֵיכָא דְּלָא מַסֵּיק בְּהוּ זוּזֵי, מָר כֵּיוָן דְּמַסֵּיק בְּהוּ זוּזֵי מִחְזֵי כְּרִבִּית, דְּאָמַר רַב יוֹסֵף בַּר מְנִיוּמִי אָמַר רַב נַחְמָן: אַף עַל פִּי שֶׁאָמְרוּ הַדָּר בַּחֲצַר חֲבֵירוֹ שֶׁלֹּא מִדַּעְתּוֹ אֵין צָרִיךְ לְהַעֲלוֹת לוֹ שָׂכָר, הִלְוָהוּ וְדָר בַּחֲצַר חֲבֵירוֹ – צָרִיךְ לְהַעֲלוֹת לוֹ שָׂכָר! אֲמַר לֵיהּ: הֲדַרִי בִּי.

Rabba **said to him: This statement** of Rav Daniel applies **when** the one who seizes the slave **is not owed money** by the owner of the slave. But **since the Master is owed money by**[H] the owner of the slave, this **has the appearance of interest,**[N] **as Rav Yosef bar Minyumi says that Rav Naḥman says: Although** the Sages **said that one who resides in another's courtyard without his knowledge does not need to pay him rent,** if one **lent** money to another, **and** then **resided in the courtyard of another,** i.e., that of his creditor, **he needs to pay him rent,** to avoid the appearance of interest. Rav Yosef **bar Ḥama said to him: I retract** my opinion, and will no longer seize the slaves of my debtors.

אִיתְּמַר: הַתּוֹקֵף סְפִינָתוֹ שֶׁל חֲבֵירוֹ וְעָשָׂה בָּהּ מְלָאכָה, אָמַר רַב: רָצָה – שְׂכָרָהּ נוֹטֵל, רָצָה – פְּחָתָהּ נוֹטֵל; וּשְׁמוּאֵל אָמַר: אֵינוֹ נוֹטֵל אֶלָּא פְּחָתָהּ.

It **was stated:** In the case of **one who seizes another's ship**[H] and **performs labor with it,** what payment can the ship's owner claim? **Rav says** that he may choose: If he **wishes,** he can **take** the cost of the ship's **rent,** and if he **wishes,** he can **take** the amount by which the value of the ship was **diminished** by being used for this labor, whichever amount is larger. **And Shmuel says: He** can **take only** the amount by which the value of the ship was **diminished.**

אֲמַר רַב פַּפָּא: לָא פְּלִיגִי, הָא דַּעֲבִידָא לְאַגְרָא, הָא דְּלָא עֲבִידָא לְאַגְרָא. וְאִיבָּעֵית אֵימָא: הָא וְהָא דַּעֲבִידָא לְאַגְרָא, הָא דְּנָחֵית לֵיהּ אַדַּעְתָּא דְּאַגְרָא, וְהָא דְּנָחֵית לֵיהּ אַדַּעְתָּא דִּגְזָלָנוּתָא.

Rav Pappa said: They **do not disagree.** They were addressing different cases: **This,** i.e., Rav's statement, is referring to a ship **that is commonly** available **for rental. That,** i.e., Shmuel's statement, is referring to a ship that **is not commonly** available **for rental. And if you wish, say** instead: **This and that** statement are both referring to a ship **that is commonly** available **for rental. This,** Rav's statement, is referring to a case **where** the one who seized the ship **descended,** i.e., took possession, **with the intention of renting** the ship. He pays for the rental. **That,** Shmuel's statement, is referring to a case **where** the one who seized the ship **descended with the intention of robbery,** to use it without paying. He is regarded as a robber and pays only the amount by which its value was diminished.

"גָּזַל מַטְבֵּעַ וְנִסְדַּק" [וכו׳]. אָמַר רַב הוּנָא: נִסְדַּק – נִסְדַּק מַמָּשׁ, נִפְסַל – פְּסָלַתּוּ מַלְכוּת.

§ The mishna teaches: If one **robbed** another of **a coin and it cracked,**[H] he pays the value of the coin at the time of the robbery, as he has acquired it due to its change. But if the coin was invalidated, he says: That which is yours is before you. Since this is not a significant change, he has not acquired it. The Sages disagree with regard to the explanation of this *halakha*. **Rav Huna says:** When the mishna states that the coin **cracked,** it means that it **actually cracked;** when it says that the coin was **invalidated,** it means that it was **invalidated by the government**[B] and is therefore unfit for use.

NOTES

The appearance of interest – מִחְזֵי כְּרִבִּית: It appears that the debtor is giving the creditor an additional benefit in exchange for the loan: The right to live in his property. This has the appearance of interest but is not actual interest, since there was no stipulation that the creditor be permitted to live in this property in exchange for granting the loan (Ramah). *Tosafot* note that one should not infer from this *halakha* that it is not permitted for one who borrows money to perform any favors for the creditor. The prohibition in this case is due to the fact that allowing the creditor to live in the debtor's property in a public manner creates the impression on others that interest has been paid. By contrast, a private favor is permitted. *Tosafot* also note that if the two parties are familiar with one another and would habitually perform favors for one another, they may continue to do so even if one lent money to the other.

BACKGROUND

Invalidated by the government, etc. – פְּסָלַתּוּ מַלְכוּת וכו׳: In talmudic times the government on occasion prohibited the use of certain coins. Sometimes the motive was economic, as when a government would outlaw the use of foreign currencies to preserve the value of its own currency. Generally, though, the motive was political. Coins issued by rebel forces or by a city or province that did so illegally would be banned by the central government. At other times, such as when large quantities of copper or lead were mixed with the precious metals or the government issued coins of less than standard weight, the government's official currency was invalidated, so to speak, by the people, who would essentially invalidate the coins by refusing to accept them as payment.

HALAKHA

Is owed money by, etc. – מַסֵּיק בְּהוּ זוּזֵי וכו׳: One who lends money to another may not seize the debtor's slave and have him perform labor, even if the slave would not have been performing any other labor at that time. Similarly, he may not dwell in the debtor's courtyard free of charge, nor may he rent the courtyard from the debtor at a reduced rate, even if this courtyard was not commonly rented. If the creditor did dwell in a courtyard that was not commonly rented, he is not obligated pay for it, even to fulfill his obligation toward Heaven. The Rambam holds that in this case the creditor must pay rent to the owner of the field, in order to avoid any trace of interest. In any event, all agree that if the courtyard was commonly rented, the creditor must pay rent (Rambam *Sefer Mishpatim*, *Hilkhot Malve VeLoveh* 6:2; *Shulḥan Arukh*, *Yoreh De'a* 166:1).

One who seizes another's ship – הַתּוֹקֵף סְפִינָתוֹ שֶׁל חֲבֵירוֹ: If one seized another's ship, and it was not commonly rented, and he performed labor with it, then the court estimates the amount by which the value of the ship diminished due to this action, and the one who seized the ship must pay that amount to its owner. If the ship was commonly rented and the one who seized it had intended to pay rent, the owner may choose to be paid either the rental price or the amount by which the value of the ship diminished, since it was seized without permission. If one seized the ship with the intention of stealing it or of borrowing it without the owner's knowledge, he pays the amount by which the value of the ship diminished (Rambam *Sefer Nezikin*, *Hilkhot Gezeila VaAveda* 3:8; *Shulḥan Arukh*, *Ḥoshen Mishpat* 363:5).

Robbed another of a coin and it cracked – גָּזַל מַטְבֵּעַ וְנִסְדַּק: One who stole a coin that later cracked or was invalidated by the government pays its value at the time of the robbery, in accordance with the opinion of Rav Yehuda. This is the ruling of the Rambam, based on the *ge'onim*, who held that the *halakha* follows Rav Yehuda in his disputes with Rav Huna. The Rema cites the *Tur*, quoting the Rosh, who says that if the coin was invalidated by the government, the robber can say: That which is yours is before you. The ruling is in accordance with the opinion of Rav Huna, since Rav and Shmuel both ruled in accordance with his opinion, and it is also the opinion of Rabba (Rambam *Sefer Nezikin*, *Hilkhot Gezeila VaAveda* 3:4; *Shulḥan Arukh*, *Ḥoshen Mishpat* 363:1 and *Beur HaGra* there).

HALAKHA

Invalidated in this province, etc. – **פְּסָלַתּוּ מְדִינָה זוֹ וכו׳**: If one robbed another of a coin that was then invalidated in one province but remains valid in another province, the robber can return the coin and say: That which is yours is before you. For those who rule in accordance with the opinion of Rav Huna, the same applies if the coin is not valid in any province (Rambam *Sefer Nezikin, Hilkhot Gezeila VaAveda* 3:4; *Shulḥan Arukh, Ḥoshen Mishpat* 363:1 and *Shakh* there).

וְרַב יְהוּדָה אָמַר: פְּסָלַתּוּ מַלְכוּת נַמִי הַיְינוּ נִסְדַּק. אֶלָּא הֵיכִי דָּמֵי נִפְסַל? שֶׁפְּסָלַתּוּ מְדִינָה זוֹ וְיוֹצְאָה בִּמְדִינָה אַחֶרֶת.

And Rav Yehuda says: A coin **invalidated by the government is the same as** a coin that is **cracked,** because its complete loss of value is a significant change. **But what are the circumstances** of the mishna, in which a coin that was **invalidated** is not considered changed? It is a case **where** a coin **was invalidated** by the government in **this province,**[H] and the residents there can no longer use it, **but** the coin still **circulates** and is in use **in another province.**

אֲמַר לֵיהּ רַב חִסְדָּא לְרַב הוּנָא: לְדִידָךְ דְּאָמְרַתְּ נִפְסַל – פְּסָלַתּוּ מַלְכוּת, הֲרֵי פֵּירוֹת וְהִרְקִיבוּ, יַיִן וְהֶחְמִיץ, דִּכְי פְּסָלַתּוּ מַלְכוּת דָּמֵי, וְקָתָנֵי: מְשַׁלֵּם כִּשְׁעַת הַגְּזֵילָה!

The Gemara clarifies Rav Huna's opinion. **Rav Ḥisda said to Rav Huna: According to your** opinion, **that you said** that the term **invalidated** means that the coin was **invalidated** by the **government,** and the mishna rules that in that case the robber can return it as is, there is a difficulty. **But** what of the cases in the mishna of one who robbed another of **produce and it rotted** or one who robbed another of **wine and it fermented, which are similar to** a coin that was **invalidated by the government,** since none of these items are fit for use, **and** the mishna **teaches** that the robber **pays according to** their value at **the time of the robbery** because they underwent a change? Why would the *halakha* be different in the case of a coin that was invalidated by the government?

אֲמַר לֵיהּ: הָתָם נִשְׁתַּנָּה טַעְמוֹ וְרֵיחוֹ, הָכָא לֹא נִשְׁתַּנָּה.

Rav Huna **said to him: There,** in the cases of produce and wine, **its taste and its smell changed. Here,** in the case of the coin that was invalidated, the coin itself **did not change.**

אֲמַר לֵיהּ רָבָא לְרַב יְהוּדָה: לְדִידָךְ דְּאָמְרַתְּ פְּסָלַתּוּ מַלְכוּת נַמִי הַיְינוּ נִסְדַּק, הֲרֵי תְּרוּמָה וְנִטְמֵאת דִּכְי פְּסָלַתּוּ מַלְכוּת דָּמֵי, וְקָתָנֵי: אוֹמֵר לוֹ ״הֲרֵי שֶׁלְּךָ לְפָנֶיךָ״!

The Gemara clarifies Rav Yehuda's opinion. **Rava said to Rav Yehuda: According to your** opinion, **that you said** that a coin that was **invalidated by the government is** the same as one that **cracked,** and the mishna rules that in that case the robber pays according to its value at the time of the robbery, there is a difficulty. **But** what of the case in the mishna of one who robbed another of ***teruma*** **and it became impure, which is similar to** a coin that was **invalidated by the government, and** the mishna **teaches** that the robber **says** to the robbery victim: **That which is yours is before you.**

אֲמַר לֵיהּ: הָתָם לָא מִינְכַּר הֶיזֵּיקָהּ, הָכָא מִינְכַּר הֶיזֵּיקָהּ.

Rav Yehuda **said to him: There,** in the case of *teruma*, **the damage is not evident,** since it is impossible to tell the difference between pure and impure items. **Here,** in the case of the coin, **the damage is evident,** since one can tell by looking at it that it is the type of coin that was invalidated.

אִיתְּמַר: הַמַּלְוֶה אֶת חֲבֵירוֹ עַל הַמַּטְבֵּעַ וְנִפְסְלָה הַמַּטְבֵּעַ, רַב אָמַר:

§ With regard to a coin that was invalidated, it **was stated** that there was a dispute concerning the question: In the case of **one who lends** money to **another on** the condition that he repay the loan using a particular kind of **coin,**[N] **and that coin becomes invalidated, Rav says:**

NOTES

One who lends money to another on the condition that he repay the loan using a coin – **הַמַּלְוֶה אֶת חֲבֵירוֹ עַל הַמַּטְבֵּעַ**: Rabbeinu Barukh explains this statement as follows: One lent money to another, with the assumption that the loan be repaid in the same coin, i.e., the same form of currency. According to Rashi, the Gemara is discussing a case where one lent merchandise to another with the stipulation that it be repaid with a specific coin, and that coin was subsequently invalidated. If money was lent, per the explanation of Rabbeinu Barukh, the debtor would be able to claim that had he never borrowed the money, as the coins would in any event have been invalidated while in the possession of the creditor. Therefore, he should not have to repay the loan (Meiri). *Tosafot* discuss this at length and claim that there is no difference between loans of merchandise and money, since in either case the creditor expects to be paid in currency that is valid at the time of payment. They explain that the Gemara is discussing a case where the debtor commits to repay the loan specifically with coins and not with merchandise. Similarly, the Ra'avad explains that in this case, a contract stated that the loan would be repaid with coins that are in circulation (see *Penei Yehoshua*).

נוֹתֵן לוֹ מַטְבֵּעַ הַיּוֹצֵא בְּאוֹתָהּ שָׁעָה. וּשְׁמוּאֵל אָמַר: יָכוֹל לוֹמַר לוֹ ״לֵךְ הוֹצִיאוֹ בְּמֵישָׁן״. אָמַר רַב נַחְמָן: מִסְתַּבְּרָא מִילְּתֵיהּ דִּשְׁמוּאֵל – דְּאִית לֵיהּ אוֹרְחָא לְמֵיזַל לְמֵישָׁן, אֲבָל לֵית לֵיהּ אוֹרְחָא – לָא.

The debtor **gives him a coin that is in circulation at that time** with which he repays the loan. **And Shmuel says** that the debtor **can say to the creditor:**[H] I am giving you a coin like the one you gave me, although you cannot utilize it here. **Go spend it in Meishan,**[NB] i.e., a distant place where this coin is still in circulation. **Rav Naḥman said: Shmuel's statement is reasonable when** the creditor **has a way to go to Meishan,** i.e., he intends to travel there, and therefore the debtor can tell him to spend the coin when he arrives at his destination. **But if he has no way** to go to Meishan, i.e., he does not intend to go there, the debtor may **not** give him these coins. Rather, he must give him coins that are in circulation in their current location.

אֵיתִיבֵיהּ רָבָא לְרַב נַחְמָן: אֵין מְחַלְּלִין עַל הַמָּעוֹת שֶׁאֵינָם יוֹצְאוֹת, כֵּיצַד? הָיוּ לוֹ מָעוֹת כּוֹזְבִיּוֹת, יְרוּשַׁלְמִיּוֹת, אוֹ שֶׁל מְלָכִים הָרִאשׁוֹנִים – אֵין מְחַלְּלִין; הָא שֶׁל אַחֲרוֹנִים דּוּמְיָא דְּרִאשׁוֹנִים – מְחַלְּלִין!

Rava raised an objection to Rav Naḥman from a *baraita* (*Tosefta, Ma'aser Sheni* 1:6): **One cannot desacralize**[N] second-tithe produce by transferring its sanctity **onto coins that are not in circulation.**[H] **How so? If one had coins of bar Kokheva** [*Kozeviyyot*],[NB] **coins of Jerusalem,**[B] **or** coins **of earlier kings,** all of which are no longer in use, one **cannot desacralize** second-tithe produce by transferring its sanctity onto them. Rava infers: **But** if one had coins **of later,** i.e., current, kings, that are **similar to** the coins of the **earlier** kings in that they have been invalidated in his location, since they are still valid elsewhere, one **can desacralize** the second-tithe produce by transferring its sanctity onto them. The *baraita* does not make a distinction as to whether the owner of the produce intends to travel to the location where those coins are in use or not.

HALAKHA

The debtor can say to the creditor, etc. – יָכוֹל לוֹמַר לוֹ וכו׳: If one lends to another on the condition that he be repaid with a specific currency, and that currency becomes invalidated in one province but can still be used in another province, then if the creditor intends to travel to that province, the debtor can repay him with the currency that was stipulated. If the creditor does not intend to travel there, or if the government is restricting use of this currency (Rema, citing *Tur*), the debtor must give the creditor currency that is valid in their current location. This ruling is in accordance with the opinion of Shmuel, as interpreted by Rav Naḥman. The *halakha* follows Shmuel's opinion in cases of monetary law, and this is also the conclusion of the Gemara's discussion. The *halakha* is the same with regard to the payment of a marriage contract.

The Rema writes that this *halakha* applies if the loan was given on condition that the debtor pay it with a specific currency. If there was no stipulation, the debtor pays with the currency that he borrowed (*Tur*). The Mordekhai rules that if there was a stipulation that the repayment be with a coin that is in circulation, the debtor must repay the debt in this manner (Rambam *Sefer Mishpatim, Hilkhot Malve VeLoveh* 4:12; *Shulḥan Arukh, Ḥoshen Mishpat* 74:7).

One cannot desacralize second-tithe produce onto coins that are not in circulation – אֵין מְחַלְּלִין עַל הַמָּעוֹת שֶׁאֵינָם יוֹצְאוֹת: Second-tithe produce can be redeemed only with a coin that is in circulation at that time and in that place, including the coins of previous kings that are still in circulation. The *Shulḥan Arukh* notes that perhaps in the present day, one need not be particular about this, since in any event the coins will not actually be used, but the practical *halakha* is that one should be careful to redeem second tithe with a coin that is in circulation (Rambam *Sefer Zera'im, Hilkhot Ma'aser Sheni* 4:10; *Shulḥan Arukh, Yoreh De'a* 331:138).

NOTES

In Meishan – בְּמֵישָׁן: The Ra'avad explains that in Meishan all coins were accepted, even those that were considered invalid by the government.

One cannot desacralize – אֵין מְחַלְּלִין: One who is unable to bring his second-tithe produce to Jerusalem to consume it there can redeem it, i.e., desacralize it, by exchanging the produce for money, which is then brought to Jerusalem and used to purchase food. This is as the verse states: "Then you shall turn it into money, and bind up the money in your hand, and shall go to the place that the Lord your God shall choose" (Deuteronomy 14:25). One of the requirements of redemption is that the produce be exchanged for money that is legal tender in Jerusalem, and the money must be metal that has been minted as a coin, not just a piece of silver (Rashi).

Coins of bar Kokheva [*Kozeviyyot*] – מָעוֹת כּוֹזְבִיּוֹת: Some explain that these are coins from a different province, such as the city Keziv (Rav Tzemaḥ Gaon). Rashi explains that these are coins minted by bar Kokheva, also referred to as ben Koziva. Similarly, it is stated in the Jerusalem Talmud that these are coins minted during the time of a rebellion.

BACKGROUND

Meishan – מֵישָׁן: The Meishan region was south of the major Jewish population centers in Babylonia. It was viewed as a place with little Torah, and was populated by people with unfit lineage.

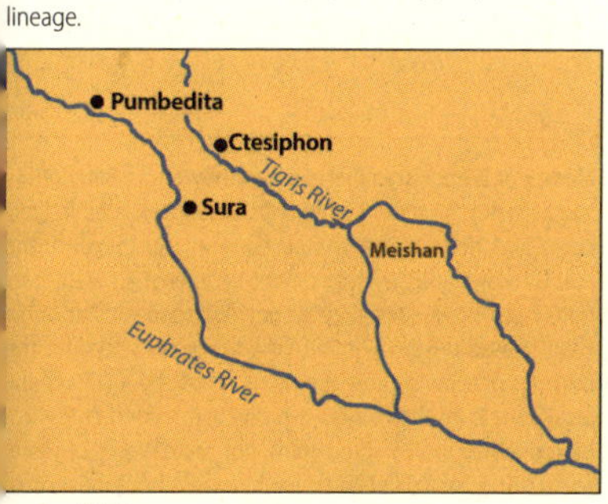

Location of Meishan

Coins of bar Kokheva [*Kozeviyyot*] – מָעוֹת כּוֹזְבִיּוֹת: This refers to coins that were minted by bar Kokheva, also referred to as ben Koziva, during the time that he ruled in Eretz Yisrael. Since these coins were issued by one who was viewed as the leader of a rebellion, they were completely banned by the Roman government. Consequently, they had the status of coins that are not in circulation.

Two sides of a *sela* coin minted during the bar Kokheva revolt

Coins of Jerusalem – יְרוּשַׁלְמִיּוֹת: This refers either to coins that were minted in Jerusalem during the period of Jewish autonomy during the Second Temple period. They were not considered valid currency, either because they had the status of the coins of previous kings, or because they were deemed invalid for political reasons, as coins that were minted during the Great Revolt.

BACKGROUND

Kingdoms are particular – מַלְכְיוֹת מַקְפִּידוֹת: There are several reasons that governments are particular with regard to foreign currency. Politically, they may not wish to support foreign governments or people who are as seen as enemies. For economic reasons, they may want to encourage people to use domestic currency so that it retains its value relative to foreign currencies.

אֲמַר לֵיהּ: הָכָא בְּמַאי עָסְקִינַן – כְּשֶׁאֵין מַלְכְיוֹת מַקְפִּידוֹת זוֹ עַל זוֹ.

Rav Naḥman **said to him: With what are we dealing here** in the *baraita*? We are dealing with a case **where the kingdoms are not particular with one another.**[N] They allow a coin that has been invalidated in their province to be taken out of their borders and spent in a province where it is valid. Since these coins can be given to those planning to travel to the location where it is valid, it is considered to be a valid coin even in the location of the one desacralizing the second-tithe produce.

אֶלָּא כִּי אֲמַר שְׁמוּאֵל – כְּשֶׁמַּלְכְיוֹת מַקְפִּידוֹת זוֹ עַל זוֹ? הֵיכִי מָצֵי מַמְטֵי לְהוּ? דְּמַמְטֵי לָהּ עַל יְדֵי הַדְּחָק, דְּלָא בָּחְשִׁי, וְאִי מַשְׁכְּחִי קָפְדִי.

The Gemara asks: **But,** according to this explanation, **when Shmuel said** that the debtor can repay his debt with invalidated coins only if the creditor intends to travel to a location where they are valid, he is speaking of a case **where the kingdoms are particular**[B] **with each other.** If so, **how can he bring** these coins to Meishan without the authorities confiscating them? The Gemara responds: Shmuel is discussing a case **where** the creditor can **bring them with difficulty,** as in a case **where** the authorities **do not search, but if they find** any invalid coins **they are particular** to confiscate them. It is therefore possible to bring these coins into the other kingdom. Nevertheless, since the authorities are particular, one who does not plan to travel there will not be able to exchange these coins with anyone in his location.

תָּא שְׁמַע: אֵין מְחַלְּלִין עַל מָעוֹת שֶׁל כָּאן וְהֵן בְּבָבֶל, וְשֶׁל בָּבֶל וְהֵן כָּאן. שֶׁל בָּבֶל וְהֵן בְּבָבֶל – מְחַלְּלִין. קָתָנֵי מִיהַת: אֵין מְחַלְּלִין עַל מָעוֹת שֶׁל כָּאן וְהֵן בְּבָבֶל, אַף עַל גַּב דְּסוֹפוֹ לְמֵיסַק לְהָתָם!

The Gemara questions Shmuel's opinion: **Come and hear** what was taught in a *baraita* (*Tosefta, Ma'aser Sheni* 1:6): **One cannot desacralize** second-tithe produce by transferring its sanctity **onto money of** Eretz Yisrael, i.e., **here,** when **they,** the coins and their owner, **are in Babylonia.**[N] **And** one cannot do so onto money **of Babylonia when they,** the coins and their owner, **are here** in Eretz Yisrael. If one uses money **of Babylonia and they are in Babylonia,** one **can desacralize** the second-tithe produce. **In any event,** the *baraita* **teaches:** One **cannot desacralize** second-tithe produce by transferring its sanctity **onto money of** Eretz Yisrael, **here,** when **they are in Babylonia.** And this is stated **even though they will ultimately ascend to there,** Eretz Yisrael, as the very purpose of transferring the sanctity to the coins is to spend them in Jerusalem.

הָכָא בְּמַאי עָסְקִינַן – כְּשֶׁמַּלְכְיוֹת מַקְפִּידוֹת זוֹ עַל זוֹ. אִי הָכִי, שֶׁל בָּבֶל וְהֵן בְּבָבֶל לְמַאי חֲזוּ? חֲזוּ דְּזָבֵין בְּהוּ בְּהֵמָה וּמַסֵּיק לִירוּשָׁלַיִם.

The Gemara answers: **With what are we dealing here?** We are dealing with a case **where** the **kingdoms are** especially **particular with one another,** and it is impossible to transport coins from one location to the other. The Gemara asks: **If so,** if the kingdoms are especially particular with one another, then with regard to the case in the *baraita,* in which sanctity is transferred onto money **of Babylonia and they are in Babylonia, for what are these** coins **fit?** In any case they cannot be brought to Jerusalem. The Gemara responds: **They are fit for purchasing an animal with them** in Babylonia **that will be brought up to Jerusalem.**

NOTES

Where kingdoms are not particular with one another – כְּשֶׁאֵין מַלְכְיוֹת מַקְפִּידוֹת זוֹ עַל זוֹ: The Ra'avad explains that the kingdom allows currency to be removed from its borders. Therefore, it can be used to purchase an animal elsewhere. A government might restrict the removal of coins from its boundaries to prevent an increase in the price of silver that may result from a scarcity of silver for minting new coins. They therefore keep and melt down old coins. *Tosafot,* by contrast, explain that the government is not particular about the use of old, invalid coins, in which case these coins can be used to purchase an animal in Jerusalem.

Money of Eretz Yisrael here, when they are in Babylonia – מָעוֹת שֶׁל כָּאן וְהֵן בְּבָבֶל: The *baraitot* were formulated in Eretz Yisrael and therefore refer to Eretz Yisrael as: Here. Second tithe that is located in Babylonia cannot be redeemed with coins from Eretz Yisrael, since they are not legal tender in Babylonia. Rashi, based on the Gemara on 98a, explains that for the purpose of second tithe, the money must be a coin of the locale one is in. The Ra'avad explains that second tithe must be redeemed with minted coins, not mere pieces of metal and a coin from a different region is regarded as a mere piece of metal.

והתניא: התקינו שיהו המעות יוצאות בירושלים מפני כך! אמר רבי זירא, לא קשיא: כאן בזמן שיד ישראל תקיפה על אומות העולם, כאן בזמן שיד אומות העולם תקיפה על עצמן.

With regard to the statement of the *baraita*, that one cannot desacralize second-tithe produce by transferring its sanctity onto Babylonian money when in Eretz Yisrael, the Gemara asks: **But isn't it taught** in a *baraita*: The Sages **instituted that** all **money shall circulate in Jerusalem because of this reason,** i.e., so that Jews from all locations will be able to use their local currencies? **Rabbi Zeira said:** This is **not difficult. Here,** the *baraita* that states that all money is valid in Jerusalem is referring to **a time when the authority of the Jewish people is dominant**[N] **over the nations of the world** and could enforce the rabbinic enactments. **There,** the *baraita* that states that sanctity may not be transferred onto Babylonian money when in Eretz Yisrael, is referring to **a time when the authority of the nations of the world is dominant over them,** i.e., the Jews, at which time foreign currency was not usable in Jerusalem.

תנו רבנן: איזהו מטבע של ירושלים? דוד ושלמה מצד אחד, וירושלים עיר הקודש מצד אחר. ואיזהו מטבע של אברהם אבינו? זקן וזקינה מצד אחד, ובחור ובתולה מצד אחר.

Having mentioned the coins of Jerusalem, the Gemara notes: **The Sages taught: What is the coin of** ancient **Jerusalem?**[B] The names **David and Solomon**[N] were inscribed **on one side, and Jerusalem the Holy City** was on the **other side. And what is the coin of Abraham our forefather? An old man and an old woman,**[N] representing Abraham and Sarah, were inscribed **on one side, and a young man and a young woman,** representing Isaac and Rebecca, were **on the other side.**

בעא מיניה רבא מרב חסדא: המלוה את חבירו על המטבע, והוסיפו עליו, מהו? אמר לו: נותן לו מטבע היוצא באותה שעה. אמר ליה: ואפילו כי נפיא? אמר ליה: אין. אמר ליה: אפילו כי תרטיא? אמר ליה: אין.

§ **Rava inquired of Rav Ḥisda: What is** the *halakha* in the case of **one who lends** money **to another**[N] **on** the condition that he repay the loan in **coin,** i.e., with the specific denomination of a currency, **and** the government **added to**[N] the size of the coin,[H] so that a coin of the same denomination now weighs more? Is the debtor obligated to return the newly adjusted coin, or can he repay the debt according to the prior weight of the coin that he borrowed? Rav Ḥisda **said to him: He gives him the coin that is in circulation at the time** of the payment. Rava **said to him: And** is this the *halakha* **even** if the new coin is as large **as a sieve?**[N] Rav Ḥisda **said to him: Yes.** Rava **said to him:** And is this the *halakha* **even** if it is as large **as a quarter-*kav* [*tartiya*]?**[L] Rav Ḥisda **said to him: Yes.**

והא קא זיילין פירי! אמר רב אשי: חזינן, אי מחמת טיבעא זיל – מנכינן ליה,

Rava challenged: **But** by increasing the weight of this coin, the **produce has decreased in price,** and since more produce can be purchased with this coin, giving it to the creditor as repayment is a form of interest. **Rav Ashi said: We examine** the situation: **If** the produce **decreased in price due to** the change in the weight of **the coin,** the debt **is reduced for** the debtor and the creditor is repaid with coins that equal the prior value of the loan.

BACKGROUND

Coin of ancient Jerusalem, etc. – מטבע של ירושלים וכו׳: It is generally accepted that coins in their current form, i.e., small pieces of metal stamped with an image, were first minted in Lydia of Asia Minor, at the end of the First Temple period. This has not been fully proven, and pieces of metal bearing inscriptions that attest to their weight and purity exist from long before that time. The only real difference between those and later coins is the presence of an image. Nevertheless, the Gemara's descriptions of ancient coins should not be taken literally. They are suggestions as to what could have appeared on a coin minted during the reign of King David or in the days of Abraham. This approach solves some of the halakhic difficulties related to these coins.

HALAKHA

One who lends money to another on condition that he repay in coin and the government added to the coin – המלוה את חבירו על המטבע והוסיפו עליו: If one lends money to another on the condition that he repay with a particular type of coin, or if a marriage contract stipulates that it will be paid with a particular type of coin, and the weight of that coin was increased, leading to a reduction, however significant, in the price of produce, then the appropriate amount is subtracted from the payment. If there was no reduction in the value of produce, the debtor pays in the currently circulating coin without any subtraction. This applies if the value of the coin increased by up to one-fifth. If the value increased by more than one-fifth, the full difference in value between the former weight of the coin and its current weight is subtracted. The same principles apply if the value of the coin decreased. If the weight of the coin remained the same but its value increased or decreased, the debtor pays in the same coin that he was lent (Rambam *Sefer Mishpatim, Hilkhot Malve VeLoveh* 4:11; *Shulḥan Arukh, Yoreh De'a* 165:1, *Ḥoshen Mishpat* 74:7, and in the comment of Rema, and *Sma* there).

LANGUAGE

Quarter-*kav* – תרטיא: Apparently from the Greek τρίτη, *tritē*, meaning one-third. It refers to a large coin that was one-third of some larger measurement, or to a coin that was larger than most other coins by one-third.

NOTES

When the authority of the Jewish people is dominant, etc. – שיד ישראל תקיפה וכו׳: The straightforward explanation of the Gemara is that when the authority of the Jewish people was dominant, they could compel the governments of the areas surrounding Eretz Yisrael to allow Jews to bring local currency to Eretz Yisrael. The Ra'avad offers an alternative explanation: When the authority of the Jewish people was dominant, many pilgrims came to Jerusalem from outside of Eretz Yisrael, which necessitated an ordinance allowing the use of foreign currency in Jerusalem. Later, when the authority of the Jewish people was not dominant, most of the pilgrims came to Jerusalem from within Eretz Yisrael, and this ordinance was no longer necessary.

The Ramah understands the Gemara in the opposite manner: When the authority of the Jewish people was dominant, they would maintain the roads leading to Jerusalem so that pilgrims could bring their actual produce to Jerusalem in such a manner that it would not spoil along the way. When the authority of the Jewish people was not dominant, the roads fell into disrepair, and Jews would have to desacralize their produce and bring money instead. It then was permitted for all currency to circulate in Jerusalem.

David and Solomon, etc. – דוד ושלמה וכו׳: Rashi explains that it was their names and not their faces that appeared on the coin, since it is prohibited to fashion a human image.

An old man and an old woman – זקן וזקינה: *Tosafot* comment that here too it was the names rather than the images that appeared on the coin. It is not necessary to make this assumption, though, as Abraham and Sarah lived before the Torah was given, and there may not have been a restriction on fashioning human images. *Tosefot Rabbeinu Peretz* explains that the young man and woman on the other side of the coin are also representative of Abraham and Sarah after they returned to their youth (see Genesis 18:12–14).

One who lends money to another, etc. – המלוה את חבירו וכו׳: The Ra'avad and Rashi explain that this question is in accordance with the opinion of Rav: Would Rav maintain that the debtor must pay with coins that are currently circulating even if it will result in interest being paid? The Rashba notes that this question can be asked even according to the opinion of Shmuel, in a case where the old coins can no longer be used.

And the government added to – והוסיפו עליו: In talmudic times, the value of a coin was based upon its weight. Occasionally the government would decide that new coins of a certain denomination, e.g., a dinar, would now contain a greater quantity of precious metal. While the name of the coin remained the same, the new coins were more valuable than the old ones.

As a sieve – כי נפיא: This is hyperbole. Rabbeinu Barukh writes that in some versions this question appears last, since a sieve is larger than a quarter-*kav*. That is the version of the Gemara recorded by the *Halakhot Gedolot*.

LANGUAGE

Agardamis – אַגַּרְדָּמִיס: From the Greek ἀγορανόμος, *agoranomos*, meaning: One appointed over the marketplace. It may be that the Gemara is using the term to describe this individual's role, and it may also be that it was the name or nickname of the individual.

Arab merchant [*tayya'a*] – טַיָּיעָא: The origin of this word appears to be the name of a specific Arab tribe called الطائي, *al-tā'ī*. The Arab tribes that resided in the desert area between Arabia and Babylonia would come to trade even as far as Babylonia.

Fortress [*kastera*] – קַסְטְרָא: From the Latin castra, meaning a fortress, a place where soldiers encamp.

NOTES

Up to ten to be the equivalent of eight – עַד עֲשָׂרָה בִּתְמָנְיָא: Rashi explains that they discovered that the weight of ten old coins was equal to that of eight new coins, and they paid eight new coins in place of the ten old coins that had been stipulated. A similar explanation is given by the *ge'onim*.

One who throws another's coin – הַזּוֹרֵק מַטְבֵּעַ שֶׁל חֲבֵירוֹ: The Gemara cites four *halakhot* taught by Rabba that appear to have a common denominator, that one who causes another to lose money in a way that is not an absolute loss is not liable to pay damages. Most of the commentaries note that these statements are stated specifically according to the opinion of Rabba, who rules that there is no liability for damage caused by indirect action. However, since the *halakha* is that there is liability for damage caused by indirect action, the *halakha* does not follow Rabba's opinion in these cases. By contrast, Rashi and the Ra'avad hold that two of the cases, that of one who throws a coin into the sea, and that of one who slits the ear of another's cow, are not cases of indirect action, but mere causation, and the *halakha* is that one is exempt from paying damages brought about by causation.

HALAKHA

One who throws another's coin, etc. – הַזּוֹרֵק מַטְבֵּעַ שֶׁל חֲבֵירוֹ וכו׳: One who pushes another's coin and rolls it into the sea, or who throws it into the sea, is liable to pay damages, since the *halakha* is that one incurs liability for damage caused by indirect action. This ruling is counter to the statement of Rabba. Some hold that if he did not pick up the coin, and it fell into translucent water, this is merely a case of causation, and he is exempt from liability (Rambam *Sefer Nezikin, Hilkhot Hovel UMazik* 7:11; *Shulhan Arukh, Hoshen Mishpat* 386:1, 386:3, and in the comment of Rema, and *Shakh* there).

One cannot desacralize onto money that is not in his possession – אֵין מְחַלְּלִין עַל מָעוֹת שֶׁאֵינָן בִּרְשׁוּתוֹ: Second tithe may be redeemed only with coins that are in the possession of the one who seeks to redeem it. Coins that fell into a pit from which they can be retrieved can be used to redeem second tithe (Rambam *Sefer Zera'im, Hilkhot Ma'aser Sheni* 4:11; *Shulhan Arukh, Yoreh De'a* 331:113).

וְאִי מְחַמַּת תַּרְעָא זִיל לָא מְנַכֵּינַן לֵיהּ.

And if the produce **decreased in price due to the market** value, the debt **is not reduced for him.**

וְהָא קָא שָׁבַח לְעִנְיַן נִסְכָּא! אֶלָּא, כִּי הָא דְּרַב פַּפָּא וְרַב הוּנָא בְּרֵיהּ דְּרַב יְהוֹשֻׁעַ עָבְדִי עוּבְדָא בְּזוּזֵי דַּאֲגַרְדָּמִיס טַיָּיעָא עַד עֲשָׂרָה בִּתְמָנְיָא.

The Gemara challenges: **But** the value of the coin **has been enhanced for the purpose of** melting it down into **a bar of metal.** Since this coin now contains a larger quantity of metal, if it were to be melted it would be worth more than an earlier coin of the same type, so it should be considered interest. **Rather,** in this case one must act **in accordance with how Rav Pappa and Rav Huna, son of Rav Yehoshua,** acted when they **performed an action with the dinars of Agardamis**[L] **the Arab merchant** [*tayya'a*]:[L] They considered **up to ten** old coins to be the equivalent **of eight**[N] new coins. Since ten old coins were equivalent in value to eight new coins, they paid eight new coins in exchange for ten old ones.

אָמַר רַבָּה: הַזּוֹרֵק מַטְבֵּעַ שֶׁל חֲבֵירוֹ לַיָּם הַגָּדוֹל – פָּטוּר; מַאי טַעְמָא? אָמַר: הָא מַנַּח קַמָּךְ, אִי בָּעֵית שְׁקַלֵיהּ. וְהָנֵי מִילֵּי בִּצְלוּלִין, דְּקָא חָזֵי לֵיהּ, אֲבָל עֲכוּרִין דְּלָא קָחָזֵי לֵיהּ – לָא; וְהָנֵי מִילֵּי דְּאַדְיֵיהּ אַדּוֹיֵי, אֲבָל שְׁקַלֵיהּ בִּידֵיהּ – מִיגְזַל גְּזַלֵיהּ, הֲשָׁבָה בָּעֵי מִיעֲבַד.

§ **Rabba says: One who throws another's coin**[NH] **into the Great Sea is exempt** from liability. **What is the reason** for this? He can **say:** The coin **is resting before you; if you wish, take it.** The Gemara comments: **And this statement** applies only if the coin is **in translucent** water, **where** the owner of the coin **can see** the coin, **but** in **turbid** water, **where he cannot see** the coin, it does **not** apply, and the one that threw it will be liable to compensate the owner. **And this statement** applies only **when he rolled** the coin into the sea without picking it up, **but** if he **took** the coin **with his hands** and threw it into the sea, **he has robbed** the owner of **it, and** the robber **is required to perform** the mitzva of **returning** the coin to its owner.

מְתִיב רָבָא: אֵין מְחַלְּלִין עַל מָעוֹת שֶׁאֵינָן בִּרְשׁוּתוֹ, כֵּיצַד? הָיוּ לוֹ מָעוֹת בְּקַסְטְרָא אוֹ בְּהַר הַמֶּלֶךְ, אוֹ שֶׁנָּפַל כִּיסוֹ לַיָּם הַגָּדוֹל – אֵין מְחַלְּלִין! אֲמַר רַבָּה: שָׁאנֵי לְעִנְיַן מַעֲשֵׂר, דְּבָעֵינַן מָצוּי בְּיָדְךָ, דְּרַחֲמָנָא אָמַר: ״וְצַרְתָּ הַכֶּסֶף בְּיָדְךָ״, וְלֵיכָּא.

Rava raises an objection to the statement of Rabba from a *baraita* (*Tosefta, Ma'aser Sheni* 1:6): One **cannot desacralize** second tithe by transferring its sanctity **onto money that is not in his possession.**[H] **How so? If he had money in a fortress** [*kastera*],[L] **or in the King's Mountain** [*Har HaMelekh*],[B] **or if his purse fell into the Great Sea,** one **may not desacralize** second tithe by transferring its sanctity onto that money. This indicates that money that fell into the Great Sea is considered lost. **Rabba said:** This is not difficult; it **is different with regard to** second **tithe, since it is necessary** that the money be **found in the hand** of the one who wishes to desacralize the tithe, **as the Merciful One states** in the Torah: "Then you shall turn it into money, **and bind up the money in your hand,** and shall go to the place that the Lord your God shall choose" (Deuteronomy 14:25), **and if** it is in the Great Sea, **it is not** in his hand, but nevertheless it is not considered lost.

BACKGROUND

The King's Mountain – הַר הַמֶּלֶךְ: The term the King's Mountain is occasionally used to refer to the entire mountainous region of Judea, while it sometimes refers to only the southern portion of that region. It is possible that the Hasmonean kings built private estates in the southern hills, and as a result the entire region was named the King's Mountain. Elsewhere in rabbinic literature, this region is described as a dangerous one, perhaps in the aftermath of the bar Kokheva revolt.

Location of the King's Mountain

וְאָמַר רַבָּה: הַשָּׁף מַטְבֵּעַ שֶׁל חֲבֵירוֹ – פָּטוּר; מַאי טַעְמָא? דְּהָא לָא עֲבַד וְלָא מִידֵּי. וְהָנֵי מִילֵּי דְּמַחְיֵיהּ בְּקוּרְנָסָא וְטַרְשֵׁיהּ, אֲבָל שַׁיְיפָא בְּשׁוֹפִינָא – חַסּוּרֵי חַסְרֵיהּ.

And Rabba also says: One who effaces the image **of another's coin**[H] **is exempt** from paying damages, even though he caused the coin to lose value. **What is the reason** for this? **As he did not do anything,** the coin remains the same size as before. The Gemara comments: **And this statement** applies only in a case where **he struck it with a hammer** [*kurnesa*][L] **and flattened it; but if he filed it with a file** [*shofina*][L] he must pay the amount of the reduction in value, since **he caused it to diminish**[N] in size.

מְתִיב רָבָא: הִכָּהוּ עַל עֵינוֹ וְסִמְּאָהּ, עַל אׇזְנוֹ וְחֵירְשׁוֹ – עֶבֶד יוֹצֵא בָּהֶן לְחֵירוּת; כְּנֶגֶד עֵינוֹ וְאֵינוֹ רוֹאֶה, כְּנֶגֶד אׇזְנוֹ וְאֵינוֹ שׁוֹמֵעַ – אֵין עֶבֶד יוֹצֵא בָּהֶן לְחֵירוּת!

Rava raises an objection to the statement of Rabba from a *baraita* (*Tosefta* 9:26): If a master **struck** his slave **on his eye and blinded it,** or **on his ear and deafened it, the slave is emancipated by means of these** injuries. If he struck the slave **near his eye and** as a result **he does not see, or near his ear and he does not hear, the slave is not emancipated by means of these** injuries. The first clause indicates that one is liable for damage caused even if it is not visible damage.

רַבָּה לְטַעְמֵיהּ, דְּאָמַר רַבָּה: חֵירְשׁוֹ לְאָבִיו – נֶהֱרָג, שֶׁאִי אֶפְשָׁר לַחֲרִישָׁה בְּלֹא חַבּוּרָה, דְּטִפְּתָא דְּדָמָא נָפְלַת לֵיהּ בְּאוּנֵּיהּ.

The Gemara responds: **Rabba** conforms **to his** standard line of **reasoning, as Rabba says: One who deafens his father is put to death,** even though no bruise is visible, **because it is impossible for deafening** to occur **without a bruise,** as it is certain **that a drop of blood fell into his ear** from the blow, even if it is not visible from the outside. Striking someone in the ear in a manner that causes deafness results in a significant physical change, while striking a coin with a hammer does not detract from the actual size of the coin.

וְאָמַר רַבָּה: הַצּוֹרֵם אוֹזֶן פָּרָתוֹ שֶׁל חֲבֵירוֹ – פָּטוּר; מַאי טַעְמָא? פָּרָה כִּדְקַיְימָא קַיְימָא, דְּלָא עֲבַד וְלָא מִידֵּי, וְכוּלְּהוּ שְׁוָורִים לָאו לְגַבֵּי מִזְבֵּחַ קַיְימִי.

And Rabba also **says: One who slits**[N] **the ear of another's cow**[H] **is exempt** from paying damages, even though this cow is no longer fit to be sacrificed as an offering due to the injury. **What is the reason** for this? As **the cow was available** for many uses until now, so **it is** still **available** for those uses now, **since** the one who slit its ear **did not do anything** to damage the cow in a substantial way. **And** concerning the fact that it is rendered disqualified from being sacrificed as an offering, **not all oxen stand near the altar,** i.e., most animals are not sacrificed as offerings anyway, so it is not considered a loss.

מְתִיב רָבָא: הָעוֹשֶׂה מְלָאכָה בְּמֵי חַטָּאת וּבְפָרַת חַטָּאת – פָּטוּר מִדִּינֵי אָדָם וְחַיָּיב בְּדִינֵי שָׁמַיִם. מְלָאכָה הוּא דְּלָא מִינְּכַר הֶיזֵּיקָהּ, אֲבָל צוֹרֵם דְּמִינְּכַר הֶיזֵּיקָהּ, הָכִי נַמִי דְּמִחַיַּיב בְּדִינֵי אָדָם!

Rava raises an objection from a *baraita*: **One who performs a task with the water of purification,**[H] i.e., the water that is mixed with the ashes of the red heifer and sprinkled upon one who has become impure as part of the purification ritual, **or with** the red **heifer of purification,** whose ashes are mixed with springwater and sprinkled on those who have contracted impurity imparted by a corpse on the third and seventh days of their impurity, is **exempt according to human laws,** since he has not caused any discernible damage, **but** is **liable according to the laws of Heaven.** It may be inferred from here that one is exempt from liability according to human laws only if he performed **a task** with those items, **since the damage** that he caused **is not evident, but** in the case of one who **slits** the ear, **where the damage is evident,** he is **indeed liable according to human laws.**

אָמְרִי: הוּא הַדִּין דַּאֲפִילּוּ צוֹרֵם פָּטוּר, וְהָא קָא מַשְׁמַע לַן, דַּאֲפִילּוּ מְלָאכָה דְּלָא מִינְּכַר הֶיזֵּיקָהּ – חַיָּיב בְּדִינֵי שָׁמַיִם.

The Sages **say** in response: **The same is true that even one who slits** the ear **is exempt** according to human laws, **and** the *baraita* that specified cases where the damage is not evident **teaches us this: That even** one who performs **a task** with the water of purification or the red heifer, **where the damage is not evident, is liable according to the laws of Heaven.**

וְאָמַר רַבָּה: הַשּׂוֹרֵף שְׁטָרוֹ שֶׁל חֲבֵירוֹ – פָּטוּר; דְּאָמַר לֵיהּ: נְיָירָא קְלַאי מִינָּךְ. מַתְקִיף לַהּ רָמִי בַּר חָמָא: הֵיכִי דָּמֵי?

And Rabba also **says: One who burns another's** promissory **note**[H] **is exempt,** as the one who burned it can **say to him: I have burned** only **your paper,** and he is not held liable for the fact that the creditor will no longer be able to prove that he had provided the loan. **Rami bar Ḥama objects to this: What are the circumstances?**

HALAKHA

One who effaces another's coin – הַשָּׁף מַטְבֵּעַ שֶׁל חֲבֵירוֹ: One who effaces the image of another's coin, even if he did not diminish the volume of the coin, is liable to pay damages, because there is liability for damage caused by indirect action, contrary to the opinion of Rabba. Some say that this is a case of damage caused by indirect action, and he is exempt from liability, unless he diminished the volume of the coin (Rambam *Sefer Nezikin, Hilkhot Ḥovel UMazik* 7:11; *Shulḥan Arukh, Ḥoshen Mishpat* 386:1, 386:3, and in the comment of Rema, and *Ketzot HaḤoshen* there).

One who slits the ear of another's cow – הַצּוֹרֵם אוֹזֶן פָּרָתוֹ שֶׁל חֲבֵירוֹ: One who slits the ear of another's cow is liable to pay damages, since by rendering it unfit for use as an offering, he has diminished its value. This ruling is in accordance with the opinion that there is liability for damage caused by indirect action (Rambam *Sefer Nezikin, Hilkhot Ḥovel UMazik* 7:11).

One who performs a task with water of purification, etc. – הָעוֹשֶׂה מְלָאכָה בְּמֵי חַטָּאת וכו׳: One who places a red heifer into a stall so that it will suckle from its mother and thresh at the same time, and similarly, one who diverts his attention from the waters of purification, thereby disqualifying them, is exempt according to human laws, but is liable according to the laws of Heaven (Rambam *Sefer Nezikin, Hilkhot Ḥovel UMazik* 7:5 and *Sefer Tahara, Hilkhot Para Aduma* 1:7 and *Maggid Mishne* and *Mishne LaMelekh* there).

One who burns another's promissory note – הַשּׂוֹרֵף שְׁטָרוֹ שֶׁל חֲבֵירוֹ: One who burns another's promissory note is liable to pay him the sum of the debt recorded therein, since the *halakha* is that there is liability for damage caused by indirect action (Rambam *Sefer Nezikin, Hilkhot Ḥovel UMazik* 7:9; *Shulḥan Arukh, Ḥoshen Mishpat* 386:2).

NOTES

He caused it to diminish – חַסּוּרֵי חַסְרֵיהּ: One who files another's coin must pay not only for the particles of silver that he filed away, but for the entire loss incurred, as the owner previously had a coin and now he has only a piece of silver. This is considered a full-fledged act of damage and not mere causation (see Rashi).

One who slits, etc. – הַצּוֹרֵם וכו׳: The mishna (96b) rules that if one robbed another of an animal and it naturally became disqualified from being sacrificed as an offering, it can it be returned as is, indicating that if the robber caused its disqualification, he would be liable to pay compensation. This seems to contradict the ruling of Rabba concerning one who slits the ear of another's cow. *Tosafot* and the Rashba explain that Rabba is referring to one who slits the ear of a non-sacred cow, while the mishna discusses a consecrated cow that became unfit. Since it was already consecrated, the robber would be liable if he actively caused it to be disqualified from being sacrificed as an offering. Rashi, commenting on the mishna on 96b, explains that the mishna is also discussing a non-sacred cow. He does not accept the inference drawn by the other early commentaries that there is a distinction between an animal that became unfit on its own and one that is rendered unfit as a result of an action.

LANGUAGE

Hammer [*kurnesa*] **– קוּרְנָסָא:** Apparently from the Greek **κέαρνον**, *kearnon*, meaning a hammer, specifically of the variety used by carpenters and other craftspeople.

File [*shofina*] **– שׁוֹפִינָא:** This is similar to the Hebrew word *shofin*, which was apparently borrowed from Aramaic. It refers to a type of file used primarily with metal.

אִי דְּאִיכָּא סָהֲדֵי דְּיָדְעִי מַאי הֲוָה בִּשְׁטָרָא – לִיכְתְּבוּ לֵיהּ שְׁטָרָא מְעַלְּיָא, וְאִי דְּלֵיכָּא סָהֲדֵי – אֲנַן מְנָא יָדְעִינַן? אָמַר רָבָא: תֶּיהְוֵי בְּמַאֲמִינוֹ.

If there are witnesses who know what was written in the promissory **note, they should write a** new, **proper,** promissory **note for him,** and there will not be any loss. **And if there are no witnesses, how do we know** what was written in the promissory note in order to assess liability? **Rava says: Let it** refer to a case **where** the one who burned the promissory note **trusts**[H] the creditor with regard to the details of the promissory note. Despite the concession of the one who burned the promissory note with regard to the amount of the debt, Rabba holds that he is exempt, since the value of the debt is not inherent in the actual paper.

אָמַר רַב דִּימִי בַּר חֲנִינָא: הָא דְּרַבָּה – מַחֲלוֹקֶת רַבִּי שִׁמְעוֹן וְרַבָּנַן הִיא; לְרַבִּי שִׁמְעוֹן דְּאָמַר: דָּבָר הַגּוֹרֵם לְמָמוֹן כְּמָמוֹן דָּמֵי – מִחַיַּיב, לְרַבָּנַן דְּאָמְרִי: דָּבָר הַגּוֹרֵם לְמָמוֹן לָאו כְּמָמוֹן דָּמֵי – לָא מִחַיַּיב.

Rav Dimi bar Ḥanina said: This statement **of Rabba is the** subject of **a dispute** between **Rabbi Shimon and the Rabbis. According** to the opinion **of Rabbi Shimon, who says** that **an item that causes financial loss**[N] **is considered** to have **monetary** value, the one who burned the promissory note **is liable. According** to the opinion **of the Rabbis, who say** that **an item that causes financial loss is not considered** to have **monetary** value, he **is not liable.** Rabba holds in accordance with the Rabbis, and therefore rules that one who burns a promissory note is exempt from liability.

מַתְקִיף לַהּ רַב הוּנָא בְּרֵיהּ דְּרַב יְהוֹשֻׁעַ: אֵימַר דְּשָׁמְעַתְּ לֵיהּ לְרַבִּי שִׁמְעוֹן דָּבָר הַגּוֹרֵם לְמָמוֹן כְּמָמוֹן דָּמֵי – בְּדָבָר שֶׁעִיקָּרוֹ מָמוֹן, כִּדְרַבָּה, דְּאָמַר רַבָּה: גָּזַל חָמֵץ לִפְנֵי הַפֶּסַח, וּבָא אַחֵר וּשְׂרָפוֹ בַּמּוֹעֵד – פָּטוּר, שֶׁהַכֹּל מְצוּוִּים עָלָיו לְבַעֲרוֹ. לְאַחַר הַפֶּסַח – מַחֲלוֹקֶת רַבִּי שִׁמְעוֹן וְרַבָּנַן,

Rav Huna, son of Rav Yehoshua, objects to this: Say that you heard the opinion **of Rabbi Shimon,** that **an item that causes financial loss is considered** to have **monetary** value, **with regard to** a case where he damaged **an item that** has **intrinsic monetary** value, **in accordance with** the statement **of Rabba. As Rabba says:** If one **robbed** another of **leavened bread before Passover,**[H] **and another came and burned it during the festival** of Passover, when the leavened bread had already become forbidden, the one who burned it is **exempt** from paying the robber, **as all are commanded to destroy** the leavened bread, and he therefore performed a mitzva. If he burned it **after Passover,** that is the matter of **dispute** between **Rabbi Shimon and the Rabbis.**

לְרַבִּי שִׁמְעוֹן דְּאָמַר: דָּבָר הַגּוֹרֵם לְמָמוֹן כְּמָמוֹן דָּמֵי – חַיָּיב, לְרַבָּנַן דְּאָמְרִי: דָּבָר הַגּוֹרֵם לְמָמוֹן לָאו כְּמָמוֹן דָּמֵי – פָּטוּר. בְּדָבָר שֶׁאֵין עִיקָּרוֹ מָמוֹן מִי אָמְרִינַן?

Rav Huna, son of Rav Yehoshua, explains: **According to** the opinion of **Rabbi Shimon, who says** that **an item that causes financial loss is considered** to have **monetary** value, the one who burned it is **liable,** and he must pay the robber. Although it is prohibited to derive benefit from leavened bread, the robber could have returned it to the victim and been exempt from liability. Now that it has been burned, the robber will have to pay the monetary value of the leavened bread at the time of the theft. **According to** the opinion of **the Rabbis, who say** that **an item that causes financial** loss **is not considered** to have **monetary** value, he is **exempt. But with regard to an item** such as a promissory note, **which has no intrinsic monetary** value, **do we say** that in Rabbi Shimon's opinion it too is considered to have monetary value?

אָמַר אַמֵּימָר: מַאן דְּדָאֵין דִּינָא דְּגַרְמֵי – מַגְבֵּי בֵּיהּ דְּמֵי שְׁטָרָא מְעַלְּיָא, וּמַאן דְּלָא דָּאֵין דִּינָא דְּגַרְמֵי – מַגְבֵּי בֵּיהּ דְּמֵי נְיָירָא בְּעָלְמָא. הֲוָה עוּבְדָא, וְכַפְיֵיהּ רַפְרָם לְרַב אַשִׁי, וְאַגְבֵּי בֵּיהּ כִּי כְּשׁוּרָא לְצַלְמָא.

The Gemara cites a ruling for the case where one burns the promissory note of another. **Ameimar said: The one who rules** that there is **liability** for damage caused by **indirect action**[N] **collects in this** case, the **value of a proper** promissory **note,** i.e., the amount of the debt, from the one who burned the promissory note. **The one who rules** that there is **no liability** for damage caused by **indirect** action **collects, in this** case, **merely the value of the paper.** The Gemara relates that **there was an incident** like this one, **and Rafram forced Rav Ashi,** who had burned a document in his youth, to pay damages, **and he collected** payment, **in this** case, **as if** he had damaged **a beam** used **for crafting a sculpture,**[B] i.e., he paid him the value of the debt listed in the promissory note.

HALAKHA

Let it refer to a case where he trusts – **תֶּיהְוֵי בְּמַאֲמִינוֹ:** One who burns another's promissory note is liable to pay him the full value of the debt that was recorded therein. This is in accordance with the opinion of Rafram, and contrary to the opinion of Rabba, as the *halakha* is that there is liability for damage caused by indirect action. This applies in a case where the one who caused the damage admits that the promissory note had been ratified and does not dispute the details of the debt recorded therein. If, however, he does not trust the owner of the promissory note, he pays only the value of the paper, as stated by Rava. The *Tur* rules that if there are witnesses who can testify concerning the contents of the promissory note, they should testify to this effect before a court, and the judges can then write a new promissory note based on their testimony (Rambam *Sefer Nezikin, Hilkhot Ḥovel UMazik* 7:9; *Shulḥan Arukh, Ḥoshen Mishpat* 386:2).

If one robbed another of leavened bread before Passover, etc. – **גָּזַל חָמֵץ לִפְנֵי הַפֶּסַח וכו׳:** The Ramban writes that if one robbed another of leavened bread and Passover elapsed over it, one who burns it is liable to pay the robber, since by eliminating the possibility of returning the bread he caused the robber to suffer a monetary loss, as the robber must now pay the owner the value of the bread at the time of the robbery. The Maharshal holds that this matter is the subject of a dispute between Rabbi Shimon and the Rabbis, and the *halakha* is generally determined in accordance with the opinion of the Rabbis, who ruled in this case that he is exempt. The *Shakh* writes that although according to the Ramban this is a case of damage caused by indirect action, for which the one who caused the damage should be liable, since this is an uncommon case, he is exempt from liability (*Shulḥan Arukh, Ḥoshen Mishpat* 386:2 and *Shakh* there).

NOTES

An item that causes financial loss – **דָּבָר הַגּוֹרֵם לְמָמוֹן:** This is discussed primarily earlier in this tractate (76a), with regard to the question of one who steals a consecrated animal from the one who consecrated it. While the latter does not own the animal, he bears financial responsibility for its loss, as he must replace it if it is subsequently lost. Therefore, according to the opinion of Rabbi Shimon, the thief is considered to have stolen that person's animal, as he holds that an item whose loss causes a person to lose money is considered that person's property for the purpose of collecting damages. The Sages disagree with the opinion of Rabbi Shimon (Meiri; Rashba).

The one who rules that there is liability for damage caused by indirect action – **מַאן דְּדָאֵין דִּינָא דְּגַרְמֵי:** There are at least three closely related concepts with regard to the *halakhot* of damages: Causation [*gerama*], for which one is exempt; indirect action [*garmi*], for which, according to most commentaries, one is liable; and damaging an item that causes financial loss [*davar hagorem lemamon*]. The Ra'avad explains the distinction between them: Causation, for which one is exempt, refers to when the damage is caused by something else; indirect action refers to when one indirectly causes damage himself, including by means of his thought or speech; and damaging an item that causes financial loss refers to when the damage is caused directly to an item whose loss may, although not necessarily, cause its owner to incur a financial loss.

BACKGROUND

A beam used for crafting a sculpture – **כְּשׁוּרָא לְצַלְמָא:** The tradition quoted by the commentaries explains that this refers to a beam used for crafting sculptures, which, due to the demands of the artistry involved, would be of the highest-quality wood, without any flaws. A similar description of idol-making appears in Isaiah 40:20. Consequently, a debt collected in its entirety, without discount or compromise, is likened to a beam used for crafting idols.

"חָמֵץ וְעָבַר עָלָיו הַפֶּסַח – אוֹמֵר לוֹ הֲרֵי שֶׁלְּךָ לְפָנֶיךָ". מַאן תַּנָּא: אוֹמְרִין בְּאִיסּוּרֵי הֲנָאָה "הֲרֵי שֶׁלְּךָ לְפָנֶיךָ"? אֲמַר רַב חִסְדָּא: רַבִּי יַעֲקֹב הִיא, דְּתַנְיָא: שׁוֹר שֶׁהֵמִית, עַד שֶׁלֹּא נִגְמַר דִּינוֹ, מְכָרוֹ – מָכוּר, הִקְדִּישׁוֹ – מוּקְדָּשׁ, שְׁחָטוֹ – בְּשָׂרוֹ מוּתָּר, הֶחֱזִירוֹ שׁוֹמֵר לִבְעָלָיו – מוּחְזָר;

§ The mishna teaches that if one robbed another of **leavened bread, and Passover elapsed over it,** and it is therefore prohibited to derive benefit from it, the robber **says to** his victim: **That which is yours is before you.** The Gemara asks: **Who** is the *tanna* who **taught** that **with regard to items from which benefit is forbidden** one **says: That which is yours is before you? Rav Ḥisda said: It is** the opinion of **Rabbi Ya'akov, as it is taught** in a *baraita* (*Tosefta* 5:4): If there was **an ox that killed** a person and is consequently liable to be stoned, and **before** the court **sentenced it** the owner **sold** the ox, the **sale** is valid; if **he consecrated it,** the **consecration** is valid; if **he slaughtered it, its flesh is permitted; if a bailee returned it to its owner, it is returned.**

מִשֶּׁנִּגְמַר דִּינוֹ, מְכָרוֹ – אֵינוֹ מָכוּר, הִקְדִּישׁוֹ – אֵינוֹ מוּקְדָּשׁ, שְׁחָטוֹ – בְּשָׂרוֹ אָסוּר, הֶחֱזִירוֹ שׁוֹמֵר לִבְעָלָיו – אֵינוֹ מוּחְזָר. רַבִּי יַעֲקֹב אוֹמֵר: אַף מִשֶּׁנִּגְמַר דִּינוֹ, הֶחֱזִירוֹ שׁוֹמֵר לִבְעָלָיו – מוּחְזָר;

The *baraita* continues: By contrast, **from when it was sentenced** to be stoned it is prohibited to derive benefit from it, and if the owner **sold it,** the **sale** is **not** valid; if **he consecrated it,** the **consecration** is **not** valid; if **he slaughtered it, its flesh is forbidden; if a bailee returned it to its owner, it is not returned,** as once it is prohibited to derive benefit from it, the ox is worthless. **Rabbi Ya'akov says: Even after it was sentenced,** if **a bailee returned it to its owner, it is returned.**

מַאי לָאו בְּהָא קָמִיפַּלְגִי, דְּרַבִּי יַעֲקֹב סָבַר: אוֹמְרִין בְּאִיסּוּרֵי הֲנָאָה "הֲרֵי שֶׁלְּךָ לְפָנֶיךָ", וְרַבָּנַן סָבְרִי: אֵין אוֹמְרִין בְּאִיסּוּרֵי הֲנָאָה "הֲרֵי שֶׁלְּךָ לְפָנֶיךָ"?

Rav Ḥisda completes his analysis: **What, is it not that they disagree about this** issue, **that Rabbi Ya'akov holds** that **with regard to items from which benefit is forbidden** one can **say: That which is yours is before you, and the Rabbis hold** that **with regard to items from which benefit is forbidden** one **cannot say: That which is yours is before you?**

אֲמַר לֵיהּ רַבָּה: לָא, דְּכוּלֵּי עָלְמָא – אָמְרִינַן בְּאִיסּוּרֵי הֲנָאָה "הֲרֵי שֶׁלְּךָ לְפָנֶיךָ", דְּאִם כֵּן, נִפְלְגוּ בְּחָמֵץ בְּפֶסַח. אֶלָּא אֲמַר רַבָּה: הָכָא בְּגוֹמְרִין דִּינוֹ שֶׁל שׁוֹר שֶׁלֹּא בְּפָנָיו קָא מִיפַּלְגִי,

Rabba said to him in response: **No.** It may be **that everyone** agrees that **with regard to items from which benefit is forbidden** one can **say: That which is yours is before you,** and the ruling of the mishna is also in accordance with the opinion of the Rabbis. **As if so,** i.e., if it were true that the dispute in the *baraita* between the Rabbis and Rabbi Ya'akov concerns the general question of returning an item from which benefit is forbidden, **they should disagree with regard to** the case of **leavened bread on Passover** and whether it can be returned as is, since this is a clear case of an item from which benefit is forbidden. **Rather, Rabba said: Here,** in the *baraita*, **they disagree with regard to** a different issue: Can **an ox be sentenced in its absence?**

רַבָּנַן סָבְרִי: אֵין גּוֹמְרִין דִּינוֹ שֶׁל שׁוֹר שֶׁלֹּא בְּפָנָיו, דְּאָמַר לֵיהּ: אִי אַיְיתִיתֵיהּ נִיהֲלִיהּ הֲוָה מַעֲרִיקְנָא לֵיהּ לְאַגְמָא, הַשְׁתָּא מְסַרְתֵּיהּ בְּיַד מַאן דְּלָא מָצֵינָא לְאִישְׁתַּעוּיֵי דִּינָא בַּהֲדֵיהּ; וְרַבִּי יַעֲקֹב סָבַר: גּוֹמְרִין דִּינוֹ שֶׁל שׁוֹר שֶׁלֹּא בְּפָנָיו, דְּאָמַר לֵיהּ: מַאי עֲבַדִי לֵיהּ? סוֹף סוֹף הֲוָה גָּמְרִי לֵיהּ דִּינָא שֶׁלֹּא בְּפָנָיו.

Rabba explains the dispute: **The Rabbis hold** that **an ox may not be sentenced in its absence,**[N] and therefore the bailee is liable to pay. The reason is **that** when the ox is returned after its sentencing, the owner may **say to** the bailee: **Had you brought** the ox **to me** before sentencing, **I would have chased it away into the marsh,** preventing the sentencing from taking place. **Now,** since you did not return it to me before it was given to the court, **you have given it to one with whom I cannot litigate,** as the court was sure to sentence it. Therefore you must pay me and not return the ox. **And Rabbi Ya'akov holds** that **an ox may be sentenced** even **in its absence,** and the claim of the owner of the ox is not accepted. The reason is **that** the bailee may **say to** the owner in response: **What did I do** to the ox? **Ultimately it would have been sentenced in its absence** and rendered forbidden.

NOTES

An ox may not be sentenced in its absence – אֵין גּוֹמְרִין דִּינוֹ שֶׁל שׁוֹר שֶׁלֹּא בְּפָנָיו: According to the Rabbis, since the Torah juxtaposes the ox's punishment with that of its master, it must be judged like its master, and people can be judged only in their presence. Rabbi Ya'akov maintains that the reason that people can be judged only in their presence is to enable them to assert a claim for themselves that might affect the court's decision. Since this does not apply to an ox, there is no requirement that it be present for its verdict to be issued (*Tosafot*).

אַשְׁכַּחֵיהּ רַב חִסְדָּא לְרַבָּה בַּר שְׁמוּאֵל, אֲמַר לֵיהּ: תָּנֵית מִידֵּי בְּאִיסּוּרֵי הֲנָאָה? אֲמַר לֵיהּ: אִין, תָּנֵינָא: ״וְהֵשִׁיב אֶת הַגְּזֵלָה״ – מַה תַּלְמוּד לוֹמַר ״אֲשֶׁר גָּזָל״? יַחֲזִיר כְּעֵין שֶׁגָּזַל.

The Gemara relates an incident: **Rav Ḥisda,** who stated that the mishna is in accordance with the opinion of Rabbi Ya'akov and not the Rabbis, **found Rabba bar Shmuel** and **said to him: Did you learn anything** with regard to the *halakhot* of returning stolen **items from which benefit is forbidden?** Rabba bar Shmuel **said to him: Yes, we learned a** *baraita*: The verse states: "Then it shall be, if he has sinned, and is guilty, **that he shall restore the item** that he robbed" (Leviticus 5:23). **What is the meaning** when **the verse states: "That he robbed"?** It means that the robber must **return the same item that he robbed.**

מִכָּאן אָמְרוּ: גָּזַל מַטְבֵּעַ וְנִפְסַל, פֵּירוֹת וְהִרְקִיבוּ, יַיִן וְהֶחְמִיץ, תְּרוּמָה וְנִטְמֵאת, חָמֵץ וְעָבַר עָלָיו הַפֶּסַח, בְּהֵמָה וְנֶעֶבְדָה בָּהּ עֲבֵירָה, וְשׁוֹר עַד שֶׁלֹּא נִגְמַר דִּינוֹ – אוֹמֵר לוֹ ״הֲרֵי שֶׁלְּךָ לְפָנֶיךָ״.

The *baraita* continues: **From here** the Sages **stated** that if one **robbed** another of **a coin and it was invalidated,** or of **produce and it rotted,** or of **wine and it fermented,** or of *teruma* **and it became ritually impure,** or of **leavened bread and Passover elapsed over it,** or of **an animal and a sin was performed with it, or of an ox that had not been sentenced, he** can **say to** the robbery victim: **That which is yours is before you.**

מַאן שָׁמְעַתְּ לֵיהּ דְּאָמַר: עַד שֶׁלֹּא נִגְמַר דִּינוֹ אִין, מִשֶּׁנִּגְמַר דִּינוֹ לָא – רַבָּנַן, וְקָתָנֵי: חָמֵץ וְעָבַר עָלָיו הַפֶּסַח – אוֹמֵר לוֹ ״הֲרֵי שֶׁלְּךָ לְפָנֶיךָ״. אֲמַר לֵיהּ: אִי מַשְׁכַּחַתְּ לְהוּ, לָא תֵּימָא לְהוּ וְלָא מִידֵּי.

The Gemara notes: **Who did you hear say** that **before the ox was sentenced** it can be returned, but **after it was sentenced it cannot?** It is **the Rabbis,** who disagree with Rabbi Ya'akov in the *baraita*; **and** this *baraita* **teaches** that if one robbed another of **leavened bread and Passover elapsed over it, he** can **say to** the robbery victim: **That which is yours is before you.** This disproves the analysis of Rav Ḥisda, as even the Rabbis agree that an item from which benefit is forbidden is returned as is. Rav Ḥisda **said to** Rabba bar Shmuel: **If you find** the Sages, **do not say anything to them,** i.e., do not publicize that I erred.

פֵּירוֹת וְהִרְקִיבוּ – אוֹמֵר לוֹ ״הֲרֵי שֶׁלְּךָ לְפָנֶיךָ״. וְהָתְנַן: פֵּירוֹת וְהִרְקִיבוּ – מְשַׁלֵּם כִּשְׁעַת הַגְּזֵילָה! אֲמַר רַב פַּפָּא: כָּאן שֶׁהִרְקִיבוּ כּוּלָּן, כָּאן שֶׁהִרְקִיבוּ מִקְצָתָן.

§ The Gemara discusses the *baraita*, which states that if one robbed another of **produce and it rotted,**[H] **he** can **say to** the robbery victim: **That which is yours is before you.** The Gemara asks: **But didn't we learn** in the mishna (96b): If one robbed another of **produce and it rotted, he pays** compensation **according to** the value of the stolen item at **the time of the robbery? Rav Pappa said: Here,** the mishna is referring to a case where the stolen produce **all rotted,**[N] which constitutes a significant change. The robber acquires the produce and must pay what its value was at the time of the robbery. **There,** the *baraita* is referring to a case where **part of** the stolen produce **rotted.** In such a case the robber may return it and say: That which is yours is before you.

מתני׳ נָתַן לָאוּמָּנִין לְתַקֵּן וְקִלְקְלוּ – חַיָּיבִין לְשַׁלֵּם. נָתַן לְחָרָשׁ שִׁידָּה תֵּיבָה וּמִגְדָּל לְתַקֵּן וְקִלְקֵל – חַיָּיב לְשַׁלֵּם. וְהַבַּנַּאי שֶׁקִּיבֵּל עָלָיו לִסְתּוֹר אֶת הַכּוֹתֶל, וְשִׁיבֵּר הָאֲבָנִים אוֹ שֶׁהִזִּיקָן – חַיָּיב לְשַׁלֵּם; הָיָה סוֹתֵר מִצַּד זֶה וְנָפַל מִצַּד אַחֵר – פָּטוּר, וְאִם מֵחֲמַת הַמַּכָּה – חַיָּיב.

MISHNA If one **gave** items **to craftsmen to fix**[H] **and they damaged** them, the craftsmen are **liable to pay** for the damage. For example, if one **gave a chest, a box, or a cabinet**[B] **to a carpenter to fix, and he damaged** it, he is **liable to pay. And a builder who committed to demolish a wall**[H] and while demolishing it he **broke the stones, or who damaged them,**[N] **is liable to pay. If he was demolishing on this side** of the wall, **and** the wall **fell from another side** and caused damage, he is **exempt**[N] from liability. **But if** a stone fell and caused damage **due to** the force **of the blow, he is liable.**

NOTES

Here the produce all rotted, etc. – כָּאן שֶׁהִרְקִיבוּ כּוּלָּן וכו׳: The *Nimmukei Yosef* explains that if all the produce has rotted, the damage is evident, like wine that fermented, but if only part of the produce has rotted it is considered normal, and this is considered a case where the damage is not evident.

Or who damaged them – אוֹ שֶׁהִזִּיקָן: Since the builder accepted upon himself to demolish the wall, the homeowner is completely exempt from responsibility. The builder is not even considered a hired laborer, as, if he were, he and the homeowner would share responsibility equally (Rabbeinu Yehonatan of Lunel; Meiri).

And the wall fell from another side, he is exempt – וְנָפַל מִצַּד אַחֵר פָּטוּר: The Rambam writes that if he struck the wall and the damage resulted from the impact, he is liable, since this is like damage caused by shooting an arrow.

BACKGROUND

A chest [*shidda*], a box [*teiva*], or a cabinet [*migdal*] – שִׁידָּה תֵּיבָה וּמִגְדָּל: The difference between these terms is not clarified by the early commentaries. Based on the few sources that do explain their meaning, it seems that a *teiva* was a simple box with a covering or a door on top. A *shidda* contained several drawers. A *migdal* was apparently what is now called a cabinet, i.e., a box whose height is usually greater than its width, with doors on its front.

HALAKHA

Produce and it rotted – פֵּירוֹת וְהִרְקִיבוּ: If one robbed another of produce and the produce rotted entirely, he pays the owner its value at the time of the robbery. If part of the produce rotted, he returns it as is, and he says to the robbery victim: That which is yours is before you. This is in accordance with the opinion of Rav Pappa. The *Haggahot Asheri*, cited by the *Shakh*, writes that this applies if the produce rotted as the result of aphids, i.e., a common garden pest. If it rotted as the result of worms, it is treated as regular produce, and the robber may say: That which is yours is before you (Rambam *Sefer Nezikin*, *Hilkhot Gezeila VaAveda* 3:4; *Shulḥan Arukh*, *Ḥoshen Mishpat* 363:1).

If one gave items to craftsmen to fix, etc. – נָתַן לָאוּמָּנִין לְתַקֵּן וכו׳: If a craftsman damaged a vessel he was given to fix, or if a craftsman damaged a vessel that he had constructed from raw materials belonging to the one that hired him, he is liable to pay the full value of a vessel, since a craftsman does not acquire ownership rights through the enhancement of the vessel. The *Halakhot Gedolot*, and the *Tur*, citing the Ri, maintain that a craftsman does acquire ownership rights through the enhancement of the vessel. The *Shakh* concludes that this is treated as an uncertainty (Rambam *Sefer Mishpatim*, *Hilkhot Sekhirut* 10:4; *Shulḥan Arukh*, *Ḥoshen Mishpat* 306:2 and *Even HaEzer* 28:15, and in the comment of Rema).

A builder who committed to demolish a wall – הַבַּנַּאי שֶׁקִּיבֵּל עָלָיו לִסְתּוֹר אֶת הַכּוֹתֶל: If a builder hired to demolish a wall broke the stones or caused damage, he is liable to pay for the damage. If he was demolishing the wall on one side and a stone came out of the wall and fell onto the other side, he is exempt from liability. If it fell directly as a result of his striking the wall, he is liable (Rambam *Sefer Nezikin*, *Hilkhot Ḥovel UMazik* 6:11; *Shulḥan Arukh*, *Ḥoshen Mishpat* 306:2, and in the comment of Rema; and 384:3).

גמ׳ אָמַר רַב אַסִי: לֹא שָׁנוּ אֶלָּא שֶׁנָּתַן לְחָרָשׁ שִׁידָּה תֵּיבָה וּמִגְדָּל לִנְעוֹץ בָּהֶן מַסְמֵר, וְנָעַץ בָּהֶן מַסְמֵר וְשִׁיבְּרָן. אֲבָל נָתַן לְחָרָשׁ עֵצִים לַעֲשׂוֹת שִׁידָּה תֵּיבָה וּמִגְדָּל, וְעָשָׂה מֵהֶן שִׁידָּה תֵּיבָה וּמִגְדָּל וְשִׁיבְּרָן – פָּטוּר;

GEMARA The mishna teaches that if one gave a carpenter a chest, a box, or a cabinet to fix, and he damaged it, the carpenter is liable to pay for the damage. **Rav Asi says:** The Sages **taught** that a carpenter is liable to pay damages **only** in a case where one **gave the carpenter a chest, a box, or a cabinet to drive a nail into them,** i.e., he gave the carpenter complete vessels to repair, **and he drove the nail into them and broke them. But if** one **gave wood to a carpenter to build a chest, a box, or a cabinet, and he built a chest, a box, or a cabinet from** the wood, **and** before giving it to the owner the carpenter **broke them,** he is **exempt** from paying for the damage caused to these vessels, and must pay only for the damage caused to the wood.

מַאי טַעֲמָא? אוּמָּן קוֹנֶה בְּשֶׁבַח כְּלִי.

What is the reason for this? It is because **a craftsman acquires** ownership rights **through** the **enhancement of the vessel.**[N] The craftsman is considered to have acquired the vessel through his work, which enhances its value, and it remains in his possession until he returns it to the owners. Consequently, if he damages the vessel in any way, he is damaging his own item, and must return only the value of the raw materials to the owners.

תְּנַן: נָתַן לָאוּמָּנִין וְקִלְקְלוּ – חַיָּיבִין לְשַׁלֵּם; מַאי לָאו דְּיָהֵיב לְהוּ עֵצִים? לָא, שִׁידָּה תֵּיבָה וּמִגְדָּל.

The Gemara attempts to contradict Rav Asi's statement: **We learned** in the mishna that if one **gave** items **to craftsmen** to fix **and they damaged** them, they are **liable to pay** for the damage. **What, is it not** referring to a case **where he gave them wood,** and they nevertheless pay the owner the value of a vessel? The Gemara responds: **No,** it is referring to a case where he gave them **a chest, a box, or a cabinet** to repair.

הָא מִדְּקָתָנֵי סֵיפָא שִׁידָּה תֵּיבָה וּמִגְדָּל, מִכְּלָל דְּרֵישָׁא עֵצִים! אָמְרִי: פֵּרוּשֵׁי קָא מְפָרֵשׁ לָהּ: כֵּיצַד נָתַן לָאוּמָּנִין לְתַקֵּן וְקִלְקְלוּ חַיָּיבִין לְשַׁלֵּם? כְּגוֹן שֶׁנָּתַן לְחָרָשׁ שִׁידָּה תֵּיבָה וּמִגְדָּל.

The Gemara asks: **But from** the fact **that the latter clause** of the mishna **teaches** about **a chest, a box, or a cabinet, it may be inferred that the first clause** of the mishna is referring to **wood.** The Sages **say** in response: The latter clause **is explaining** the first clause. After stating that the craftsmen are liable to pay damages, the mishna explains: **In what** case is it so that if one **gave** items **to craftsmen to fix, and they damaged** them, they are **liable to pay?** It is with regard to a case **where** one **gave a carpenter a chest, a box, or a cabinet.**

וְהָכִי נָמֵי מִסְתַּבְּרָא דְּ״כֵּיצַד״ קָתָנֵי, דְּאִי סָלְקָא דַּעְתָּךְ רֵישָׁא עֵצִים, הַשְׁתָּא אַשְׁמַעִינַן עֵצִים חַיָּיבִין לְשַׁלֵּם, וְלָא אָמְרִינַן אוּמָּן קוֹנֶה בְּשֶׁבַח כֵּלִים, שִׁידָּה תֵּיבָה וּמִגְדָּל מִבַּעְיָא?

The Gemara notes: **And so too, it is reasonable** to say **that** the latter clause of the mishna **teaches in what** case the first clause deems them liable, **as, if it enters your mind** to think that **the first clause** is referring to a case where he gave **wood,** one could ask: **Now that** the mishna **told us** that if one gave **wood,** the craftsman **is liable to pay** the value of a vessel, **and we do not say** that **a craftsman acquires** ownership rights **through** the **enhancement of vessels, is** it **necessary** to tell us that if one gave **a chest, a box, or a cabinet,** the craftsman is liable to pay damages?

אִי מִשּׁוּם הָא לָא אִירְיָא, תְּנָא סֵיפָא לְגַלּוּיֵי רֵישָׁא; שֶׁלֹּא תֹּאמַר רֵישָׁא שִׁידָּה תֵּיבָה וּמִגְדָּל, אֲבָל עֵצִים לָא – תְּנָא סֵיפָא שִׁידָּה תֵּיבָה וּמִגְדָּל, מִכְּלָל דְּרֵישָׁא עֵצִים, וַאֲפִילּוּ הָכִי חַיָּיב לְשַׁלֵּם.

The Gemara dismisses this proof: **If it is due to that** reason, i.e., if that is the manner in which the explanation of the mishna is refuted, **there is no** conclusive **argument,** because that claim can be refuted by saying that the *tanna* **taught the latter clause to shed light on the first clause, so that you would not say** that **the first clause** is referring to a case where one gave the carpenter **a chest, a box, or a cabinet, but** had he given **wood,** the carpenter would **not** be liable. Therefore, the mishna **teaches** the case of one who gave a carpenter **a chest, a box, or a cabinet** in **the latter clause,** and it follows **by inference that the first clause** discusses one who gave the carpenter **wood, and even so** the carpenter **is liable to pay** damages. It is therefore impossible to prove Rav Asi's statement from the mishna.

לֵימָא מְסַיַּיע לֵיהּ: הַנּוֹתֵן צֶמֶר לַצַּבָּע

The Gemara suggests: **Let us say** that a mishna (100b) **supports** the opinion of Rav Asi: With regard to **one who gives wool to a dyer**

NOTES

A craftsman acquires ownership rights through enhancement of the vessel – אוּמָּן קוֹנֶה בְּשֶׁבַח כְּלִי: Some explain this to mean that a craftsman acquires a share of the enhanced value of the vessel (see Rashba). Others (Rabbeinu Barukh) explain it to mean that a craftsman acquires ownership of the vessel by enhancing it. The Rid writes that this principle means only that the craftsman does not bear responsibility for the enhanced value if the vessel is damaged. It does not mean that he owns any share of the actual product. Later commentaries (see *Ketzot HaḤoshen* and *Netivot HaMishpat*) explain that the ownership rights of a craftsman are similar to the rights that a creditor has to collateral, i.e., he has certain rights but does not fully own the item.

BACKGROUND

It was burned in the cauldron – הִקְדִּיחוֹ יוֹרָה: In its broader sense, this means that the wool was ruined because of conditions in the cauldron, e.g., the presence of other substances. In its narrower sense, it means that the water of the cauldron was so hot that it burned the dye and adversely affected its color.

HALAKHA

One who gives his garment to a craftsman, etc. – הַנּוֹתֵן טַלִּיתוֹ לָאוּמָּן וכו׳: One who gives his garment to a craftsman for repairs on a contractual basis does not violate the prohibition against delaying the payment of wages as long as the garment remains in the possession of the craftsman, even if the latter had informed the owner that the task was complete. If the owner was given his garment, even in the middle of the day, he violates the prohibition against delaying the payment of wages once the sun sets, since with regard to that prohibition contractors have the same status as hired laborers (Rambam *Sefer Mishpatim, Hilkhot Sekhirut* 11:3; *Shulḥan Arukh, Ḥoshen Mishpat* 339:6).

וְהִקְדִּיחוֹ יוֹרָה – נוֹתֵן לוֹ דְּמֵי צַמְרוֹ; דְּמֵי צַמְרוֹ – אִין, דְּמֵי צַמְרוֹ וְשִׁבְחוֹ – לָא. לָאו שֶׁהִקְדִּיחוֹ לְאַחַר נְפִילָה, דְּאִיכָּא שְׁבָחָא, וּשְׁמַע מִינָּהּ: אוּמָּן קוֹנֶה בְּשֶׁבַח כֵּלִי?

and it was burned in the cauldron[B] in which it was dyed, the dyer **gives** the owner the **value of his wool.** The Gemara infers: The **value of his wool, yes,** the dyer must pay that amount, but the **value of the wool and its enhanced** value, **no,** he need not pay. The Gemara suggests: Is this **not** referring to a case where the wool **was burned after falling** into the cauldron and the dye had taken hold, so **that there is enhanced** value, **and** one can **learn from** the mishna that **a craftsman acquires** ownership rights **through** the **enhancement of the vessel,** and therefore the dyer need not pay the enhanced value?

אָמַר שְׁמוּאֵל: הָכָא בְּמַאי עָסְקִינַן – כְּגוֹן שֶׁהִקְדִּיחוֹ בִּשְׁעַת נְפִילָה, דְּלֵיכָּא שְׁבָחָא. אֲבָל הִקְדִּיחוֹ לְאַחַר נְפִילָה מַאי, נוֹתֵן לוֹ דְּמֵי צַמְרוֹ וְשִׁבְחוֹ? לֵימָא, שְׁמוּאֵל לֵית לֵיהּ דְּרַב אַסִי?

Shmuel said: This is not a proof. **With what are we dealing here?** We are dealing with a case **where** the wool **was burned at the moment of falling** into the cauldron, before the dye had taken hold, so **that there is no enhancement.** The Gemara asks: **But** according to this opinion, **what** would the *halakha* be **if** it **was burned after falling** into the cauldron, when the dye had taken hold? Would the dyer **give** the owner the **value of his wool and its enhancement? Shall we say** that **Shmuel does not accept** the statement **of Rav Asi,** and holds that a craftsman does not acquire ownership rights through the enhancement of the vessel?

אָמַר לָךְ שְׁמוּאֵל: הָכָא בְּמַאי עָסְקִינַן – כְּגוֹן דְּצֶמֶר וְסַמָּנִין דְּבַעַל הַבַּיִת, וְצַבָּע אֲגַר יָדֵיהּ הוּא דְּשָׁקֵיל.

The Gemara rejects this statement. **Shmuel** could have **said to you: With what are we dealing here** in the mishna? We are dealing with a case **where the wool and herbs** used in the dye both **belong to the homeowner, and the dyer is taking** only the **payment of his hand,** i.e., the wages for his labor, and nothing else. In this case, the craftsman does not acquire ownership rights through the enhancement of the vessel, but in a case where the craftsman provides the materials, he does acquire such rights.

אִי הָכִי, נוֹתֵן לוֹ דְּמֵי צַמְרוֹ וְסַמָּנִין מִיבְּעֵי לֵיהּ! אֶלָּא, שְׁמוּאֵל דַּחוּיֵי קָא מַדְחֵי לֵיהּ.

The Gemara asks: **If so,** i.e., if the homeowner's herbs were also ruined by the dyer, the mishna **should have** said that the dyer **gives** the owner the **value of his wool and herbs,** not just the value of his wool. **Rather, Shmuel is** merely **dismissing** the Gemara's proof with regard to the statement of Rav Asi that a craftsman acquires a vessel through its enhancement, by saying that the mishna could be understood otherwise. He does not, however, state his own opinion on this matter.

תָּא שְׁמַע: הַנּוֹתֵן טַלִּיתוֹ לָאוּמָּן, גְּמָרוֹ וְהוֹדִיעוֹ – אֲפִילּוּ מִכָּאן וְעַד עֲשָׂרָה יָמִים אֵינוֹ עוֹבֵר עָלָיו מִשּׁוּם ״לֹא תָלִין״, נְתָנָהּ לוֹ בַּחֲצִי הַיּוֹם – כֵּיוָן שֶׁשָּׁקְעָה עָלָיו הַחַמָּה עוֹבֵר עָלָיו מִשּׁוּם ״בַּל תָּלִין״.

The Gemara offers another suggestion: **Come** and **hear** a proof from a *baraita*: With regard to **one who gave his garment to a craftsman,**[H] and the craftsman **concluded** the work **and notified** the owner that the work was complete, **even** if the owner delays paying the craftsman **from now until ten days** henceforth, **he does not violate, for this** delay, the prohibition **of:** "You shall not oppress your neighbor, nor rob him; the wages of a hired worker **shall not abide with you all night** until the morning" (Leviticus 19:13). If the craftsman **gave** the garment **to him at midday,** then **once the sun has set** and the owner has not paid him, the owner **does violate, for this** delay, the prohibition **against delaying** the payment of wages.

וְאִי סָלְקָא דַּעְתָּךְ אוּמָּן קוֹנֶה בְּשֶׁבַח כֵּלִי, אַמַּאי עוֹבֵר מִשּׁוּם ״בַּל תָּלִין״?

The Gemara concludes: **And if it enters your mind** to say that a **craftsman acquires** ownership rights **through** the **enhancement of the vessel, why does** the owner **violate** the prohibition **against delaying** the payment of wages? It is as if the craftsman acquired the garment, and the payment is considered to be a purchase of the garment by the owner, rather than a wage.

אָמַר רַב מָרִי בְּרֵיהּ דְּרַב כָּהֲנָא: בְּגַרְדָּא דְּסַרְבָּלָא, דְּלֵיכָּא שְׁבָחָא.

The Gemara responds: **Rav Mari, son of Rav Kahana, said:** The *baraita* is stating the *halakha* **with regard to the laundering of a thick garment, where there is no enhancement** of the garment. Therefore, the craftsman does not acquire it.

סוֹף סוֹף לְמַאי יָהֲבָהּ נִהֲלֵיהּ? לְרַכּוּכֵי, כֵּיוָן דְּרַכְּכֵיהּ הַיְינוּ שְׁבָחָא! לָא צְרִיכָא, דְּאַגְרֵיהּ לְבִיטְשֵׁי, בִּיטְשָׁא בִּיטְשָׁא בְּמָעֲתָא, דְּהַיְינוּ שְׂכִירוּת.

The Gemara asks: **Ultimately, to what** end **did** the owner of the garment **give it to** the craftsman? He gave it to him in order **to soften** it. **Once he has softened it, that is its enhancement,** and the craftsman has therefore acquired it. The Gemara responds: **No;** it is **necessary** to teach this *halakha* in a case **where** the owner **hired** the craftsman **for treading,**[B] i.e., to forcefully tread on the garment in water until it softens, with the owner paying the craftsman **a** ***ma'a***[B] **coin for each tread.** The difference is **that this is** considered **hired** labor, where the craftsman is paid based on the amount of times he performed an action, and not contractual labor, where he is paid based on the outcome, in this case, a softened garment.

וּלְמַאי דְּסָלֵיק אַדַּעְתִּין מֵעִיקָּרָא דְּלָא אַגְרֵיהּ לְבִיטְשֵׁי, מְסַיַּיע לֵיהּ לְרַב שֵׁשֶׁת. דְּבָעוּ מִינֵּיהּ מֵרַב שֵׁשֶׁת: קַבְּלָנוּת, עוֹבֵר עָלָיו מִשּׁוּם ״בַּל תָּלִין״ אוֹ אֵינוֹ עוֹבֵר? וַאֲמַר לְהוּ רַב שֵׁשֶׁת: עוֹבֵר.

The Gemara comments: **And with regard to what entered our minds initially, that** the owner **did not hire** the worker **for treading** but rather he hired him like a craftsman based on the assumption that the garment would be returned laundered, this **supports** the opinion **of Rav Sheshet. As they asked Rav Sheshet:** If one hires **a contractor,** who is not paid an hourly wage but is paid upon the completion of his task, and the one who hired him does not pay him on the day that he completes the work, does he **violate, for this** delay, the **prohibition against delaying** the payment of wages, **or** does he **not violate** the prohibition? **And Rav Sheshet said to them:** He does **violate** the prohibition.

לֵימָא, דְּרַב שֵׁשֶׁת פְּלִיגָא אַדְּרַב אַסִּי? אֲמַר שְׁמוּאֵל בַּר אַחָא: בִּשְׁלִיחָא דְּאִיגַּרְתָּא.

The Gemara asks: **Shall we say** based on this statement **that Rav Sheshet disagrees with** the statement **of Rav Asi,** who holds that a craftsman acquires ownership rights through the enhancement of the vessel, and his payment is not considered to be a wage? **Shmuel bar Aḥa said:** Rav Sheshet is discussing a specific type of contractor, and he stated his ruling **with regard to an agent** tasked with the delivery **of a letter,** in which case, since the contractor's only task is to deliver the letter, there is no enhancement through which he might acquire ownership rights. Consequently the prohibition against delaying the payment of wages applies.

לֵימָא כְּתַנָּאֵי: ״עֲשֵׂה לִי שֵׁירִים, נְזָמִין וְטַבָּעוֹת וְאֶקַּדֵּשׁ לָךְ״, כֵּיוָן שֶׁעֲשָׂאָן – מְקוּדֶּשֶׁת, דִּבְרֵי רַבִּי מֵאִיר. וַחֲכָמִים אוֹמְרִים: אֵינָהּ מְקוּדֶּשֶׁת עַד שֶׁיַּגִּיעַ מָמוֹן לְיָדָהּ;

The Gemara suggests: **Let us say** that the statement of Rav Asi, that a craftsman acquires ownership rights through the enhancement of the vessel, is the **subject of** a dispute between ***tanna'im***. As it is taught in a *baraita*: If a woman gave gold to a goldsmith, instructing him: **Fashion bracelets, earrings, or rings for me,**[H] **and I will be betrothed to you** as payment for your work, then **once he has fashioned them she is betrothed;** this is **the statement of Rabbi Meir. And the Rabbis say: She is not betrothed until money enters her possession.**

מַאי מָמוֹן? אִילֵימָא אוֹתוֹ מָמוֹן, מִכְּלָל דְּרַבִּי מֵאִיר סָבַר אוֹתוֹ מָמוֹן לָא? אֶלָּא בְּמַאי מִקַּדְּשָׁא? אֶלָּא פְּשִׁיטָא. מַאי מָמוֹן? מָמוֹן אַחֵר.

The Gemara asks: **What** is this **money** mentioned by the Rabbis? **If we say** it means **that** very **money,** i.e., the rings she ordered, then **by inference Rabbi Meir holds** that even **that** very **money is not** required in order for the betrothal to take effect. **But with what** does **he betroth her?** He has given her nothing but the jewelry. **Rather, it is obvious.** To **what money** are the Rabbis referring? They must be referring to when he betroths her via **other money,** i.e., the payment she owes him for his service. According to the opinion of the Rabbis, in order for the betrothal to take effect he must give her additional money, while according to Rabbi Meir the betrothal takes effect when he gives her the jewelry.

BACKGROUND

Treading – בִּיטְשֵׁי: After launderers would soak a garment in water, they would step on it repeatedly to soften the fabric and to remove any dirt that adhered to it or was stuck between its fibers. The Gemara here discusses a case where the launderer was a contractor who was hired not for cleaning a garment, but for the task of stepping on the garment a specific number of times.

Roman fresco depicting adults and children treading on laundry in tubs

***Ma'a* – מָעָה:** The *ma'a* is a small silver coin generally identified, both in weight and significance, with the *gera*, the smallest denomination of currency mentioned in the Torah. Originally, the biblical sacred shekel, equal in worth to the mishnaic *sela*, was worth twenty *ma'a*, but the *sela* was later increased by 20 percent to twenty-four *ma'a*. The mishnaic shekel, half of a biblical shekel, was worth twelve *ma'a*.

HALAKHA

Fashion bracelets…for me, etc. – עֲשֵׂה לִי שֵׁירִים וכו׳: If a man betroths a woman with the payment of labor that he will perform for her, and he performed the labor, the betrothal does not take effect unless he gives her an item worth one *peruta*, since a craftsman does not acquire ownership rights through the enhancement of the vessel (Gra). Based on the opinion that a craftsman does acquire ownership rights through the enhancement of the vessel, some say that if he is a contractor, the betrothal is valid (Rema, citing *Tur* and Rabbeinu Yitzḥak of Dampierre). Others say that if the vessel is still in his possession, and he betroths her with his wages, it is as though he has betrothed her with a collateral-based loan, and the betrothal is valid (Rema, citing Rabbeinu Yeruḥam). The later commentaries indicate that this applies only in a case where the collateral is specifically taken for the purpose of the loan (Rambam *Sefer Nashim, Hilkhot Ishut* 5:20; *Shulḥan Arukh, Even HaEzer* 28:15).

HALAKHA

The obligation to pay a wage, etc. – **יֶשְׁנָהּ לִשְׂכִירוּת וכו׳**: A laborer is entitled to wages from the time that he commences his work, and he becomes entitled progressively to additional payment as he completes the work (Rambam *Sefer Nashim*, *Hilkhot Ishut* 5:20).

One who betroths a woman with a loan – **הַמְקַדֵּשׁ בְּמִלְוֶה**: If a man lent money to a woman, even with a promissory note, and betroths her with this loan, the betrothal is not valid, even if the money is still in her possession and has not yet been spent. The same is true if she owes him wages for labor that he performed for her, even if he betrothed her at the moment that she was to pay him. This is in accordance with the ruling of the Gemara (Rambam *Sefer Nashim*, *Hilkhot Ishut* 5:13; *Shulḥan Arukh*, *Even HaEzer* 28:7).

וְסָבְרוּהָ, דְּכוּלֵּי עָלְמָא – יֶשְׁנָהּ לִשְׂכִירוּת מִתְּחִילָּה וְעַד סוֹף, וּדְכוּלֵּי עָלְמָא – הַמְקַדֵּשׁ בְּמִלְוֶה אֵינָהּ מְקוּדֶּשֶׁת.

The Gemara prefaces its explanation of the connection to the issue at hand by delineating two assumptions: **And** those who say that Rabbi Meir and the Rabbis are engaging in a dispute with regard to the issue of a craftsman acquiring ownership rights through the enhancement of a vessel **assumed** that **everyone** agrees that the obligation to pay **a wage**[H] is incurred continuously **from the beginning** of the period he was hired **to its end**, i.e., the obligation to pay for a service begins when the hired party commences work, and the sum owed increases as he proceeds. The fact that he is not paid from the time he commences work establishes the wages as a debt. Consequently, the wages now have the status of a loan. **And** they also assumed that **everyone** agrees that with regard to **one who betroths** a woman **with a loan**[H] that **she is not betrothed.** She therefore cannot be betrothed to him by not having to pay the wages for his work.

מַאי לָאו בְּאוּמָּן קוֹנֶה בְּשֶׁבַח כְּלִי קָמִיפַּלְגִי, דְּרַבִּי מֵאִיר סָבַר: אוּמָּן קוֹנֶה בְּשֶׁבַח כְּלִי, וְרַבָּנַן סָבְרִי: אֵין אוּמָּן קוֹנֶה בְּשֶׁבַח כְּלִי?

Based on these assumptions, the Gemara asks: **What, is it not that they disagree with regard to** whether **a craftsman acquires** ownership rights **through** the **enhancement of the vessel? As Rabbi Meir holds** that **a craftsman acquires** ownership rights **through** the **enhancement of the vessel,** and since he owns the enhanced value of the vessel, when he gives the jewelry to her he is giving her something valuable of his own, and she is betrothed. **And the Rabbis hold** that **a craftsman does not acquire** ownership rights **through** the **enhancement of the vessel,** and since a craftsman, in this case, the goldsmith, does not own the jewelry, he cannot betroth a woman with it.

לָא, דְּכוּלֵּי עָלְמָא – אֵין אוּמָּן קוֹנֶה בְּשֶׁבַח כְּלִי, אֶלָּא הָכָא בְּיֶשְׁנָהּ לִשְׂכִירוּת מִתְּחִילָּה וְעַד סוֹף קָא מִיפַּלְגִי,

The Gemara rejects this explanation of the dispute: **No,** it is possible that **everyone** agrees that **a craftsman does not acquire** ownership rights **through** the **enhancement of the vessel, but here they disagree with regard to** the issue of whether the obligation to pay **a wage** is incurred continuously **from the beginning** of the period he was hired **to** its **end.**

רַבִּי מֵאִיר סָבַר: אֵין לִשְׂכִירוּת אֶלָּא לְבַסּוֹף, וְרַבָּנַן סָבְרִי: יֵשׁ לִשְׂכִירוּת מִתְּחִילָּה וְעַד סוֹף.

Rabbi Meir holds that the obligation to pay **a wage** is incurred **only at the end** of the period for which he was hired, i.e., the owner is obligated to pay only when the work is complete, and therefore the goldsmith's wages do not have the status of a loan, but of a sum of money that she becomes obligated to give him at that time. If he gives her the jewelry without asking for that money, it is as though he gave the money from his wages to her, and she may be betrothed with it. **And the Rabbis hold** that the obligation to pay **a wage** is incurred continuously **from the beginning** of the period he was hired **to** its **end,** and therefore his wages have the status of a loan, and she cannot be betrothed with them and must be given additional money.

וְאִי בָּעֵית אֵימָא: דְּכוּלֵּי עָלְמָא – יֶשְׁנָהּ לִשְׂכִירוּת מִתְּחִילָּה וְעַד סוֹף, וְהָכָא בִּמְקַדֵּשׁ בְּמִלְוֶה קָמִיפַּלְגִי, דְּרַבִּי מֵאִיר סָבַר: הַמְקַדֵּשׁ בְּמִלְוֶה – מְקוּדֶּשֶׁת, וְרַבָּנַן סָבְרִי: הַמְקַדֵּשׁ בְּמִלְוֶה – אֵינָהּ מְקוּדֶּשֶׁת.

And if you wish, say instead that **everyone** agrees that the obligation to pay **a wage is** incurred continuously **from the beginning** of the period he was hired **to** its **end, and here they disagree with regard to one who betroths** a woman **with a loan. As Rabbi Meir holds** that with regard to **one who betroths** a woman **with a loan, she is betrothed. And the Rabbis hold** that with regard to **one who betroths** a woman **with a loan, she is not betrothed.**

Perek **IX**
Daf **99** Amud **b**

רָבָא אָמַר: דְּכוּלֵּי עָלְמָא יֶשְׁנָהּ לִשְׂכִירוּת מִתְּחִילָּה וְעַד סוֹף, וּדְכוּלֵּי עָלְמָא – הַמְקַדֵּשׁ בְּמִלְוֶה אֵינָהּ מְקוּדֶּשֶׁת, וּדְכוּלֵּי עָלְמָא – אֵין אוּמָּן קוֹנֶה בְּשֶׁבַח כְּלִי.

Rava said another interpretation: **Everyone** agrees that the obligation to pay **a wage** is incurred continuously **from the beginning** of the period a craftsman is hired **to** its **end; and everyone** agrees that with regard to **one who betroths** a woman **with a loan, she is not betrothed; and everyone** agrees that **a craftsman does not acquire** ownership rights **through** the **enhancement of the vessel.**

אֶלָּא הָכָא בְּמַאי עָסְקִינַן – כְּגוֹן שֶׁהוֹסִיף לָהּ נוֹפֶךְ מִשֶּׁלּוֹ, רַבִּי מֵאִיר סָבַר: מִלְוֶה וּפְרוּטָה – דַּעְתָּהּ אַפְּרוּטָה, וְרַבָּנַן סָבְרִי: מִלְוֶה וּפְרוּטָה – דַּעְתָּהּ אַמִּלְוֶה.

But with what are we dealing here? We are dealing with a case **where he added a jewel [*nofekh*]**[B] **of his own for her. Rabbi Meir holds** that if a man betroths a woman with **a loan and one *peruta*,**[H] **her mind is** focused **on the *peruta*.** Therefore, in this case the jewel serves as the betrothal money. **And the Rabbis hold** that if a man betroths a woman with **a loan and one *peruta* her mind is** focused **on the loan,** so the loan serves as the betrothal money, and if one betroths a woman with a loan, she is not betrothed.

וּבִפְלוּגְתָּא דְּהָנֵי תַּנָּאֵי; דְּתַנְיָא: ״בִּשְׂכַר שֶׁעָשִׂיתִי עִמָּךְ״ – אֵינָהּ מְקוּדֶּשֶׁת, ״בִּשְׂכַר שֶׁאֶעֱשֶׂה עִמָּךְ״ – מְקוּדֶּשֶׁת; רַבִּי נָתָן אוֹמֵר: ״בִּשְׂכַר שֶׁאֶעֱשֶׂה עִמָּךְ״ – אֵינָהּ מְקוּדֶּשֶׁת, וְכׇל שֶׁכֵּן ״בִּשְׂכַר שֶׁעָשִׂיתִי עִמָּךְ״;

And Rabbi Meir and the Rabbis disagree **in the dispute** between **these *tanna'im*. As it is taught** in the *Tosefta* (*Kiddushin* 3:4): If one says to a woman: Be betrothed to me **with the payment for which I have worked for you, she is not betrothed,** as the payment is a loan, since she already owes him this money. But if he says: Be betrothed to me **with the payment for which I will work for you, she is betrothed,** as from the moment he is entitled to the money, he gives it to her for her betrothal. **Rabbi Natan says:** If he says: Be betrothed to me **with the payment for which I will work for you, she is not betrothed,** as Rabbi Natan holds that the obligation to pay a wage is incurred continuously from the beginning of the period he was hired to its end, which means that upon the completion of the labor it is a loan, **and all the more so** if he says: Be betrothed to me **with the payment for which I have worked for you.**

וְרַבִּי יְהוּדָה הַנָּשִׂיא אוֹמֵר, בֶּאֱמֶת אָמְרוּ: בֵּין ״בִּשְׂכַר שֶׁעָשִׂיתִי עִמָּךְ״ וּבֵין ״בִּשְׂכַר שֶׁאֶעֱשֶׂה עִמָּךְ״ – אֵינָהּ מְקוּדֶּשֶׁת, וְאִם הוֹסִיף לָהּ נוֹפֶךְ מִשֶּׁלּוֹ – מְקוּדֶּשֶׁת.

The *baraita* cites a third opinion: **And Rabbi Yehuda HaNasi says: Actually they said** that the *halakha* is that regardless of **whether** he said: **With the payment for which I have worked**[H] **for you, or whether** he said: **With the payment for which I will work for you, she is not betrothed. But if he added a jewel of his own for her, she is betrothed.**

מַאי אִיכָּא בֵּין תַּנָּא קַמָּא לְרַבִּי נָתָן – אִיכָּא בֵּינַיְיהוּ שְׂכִירוּת, בֵּין רַבִּי נָתָן לְרַבִּי יְהוּדָה הַנָּשִׂיא – אִיכָּא בֵּינַיְיהוּ מִלְוֶה וּפְרוּטָה.

The Gemara clarifies the dispute: **What difference is there between the first *tanna* and Rabbi Natan?** The difference **between them** is with regard to **a wage:** Is the obligation incurred continuously or only upon the completion of the work? The difference **between Rabbi Natan and Rabbi Yehuda HaNasi** is the issue of **a loan and one *peruta*.** Rabbi Natan holds that if a man betroths a woman with a loan and one *peruta* her mind is focused on the loan, and in this case his jewel is disregarded; and Rabbi Yehuda HaNasi holds that her mind is focused on the *peruta*, in this case the jewel, and she is betrothed with the jewel.

אָמַר שְׁמוּאֵל: טַבָּח אוּמָּן שֶׁקִּלְקֵל – חַיָּיב לְשַׁלֵּם, מַזִּיק הוּא, פּוֹשֵׁעַ הוּא, נַעֲשָׂה כְּאוֹמֵר לוֹ ״שְׁחוֹט לִי מִכָּאן״ וְשָׁחַט לוֹ מִכָּאן.

§ The Gemara now returns to the topic of a craftsman who damages the item with which he is working. **Shmuel says: An expert butcher who damaged** an animal by slaughtering it incorrectly, thereby rendering it non-kosher, **is liable to pay** the owner of the animal for the damage. Why? **He is one who causes damage; he is negligent; he is like one who is told** by the animal's owner to **slaughter it from here,** i.e., the area of the throat where ritual slaughter is performed, **and he slaughtered it from there,** i.e., a different area of the throat, in violation of the owner's wishes.

לָמָּה לֵיהּ לְמֵימַר ״מַזִּיק הוּא, פּוֹשֵׁעַ הוּא״? אִי אָמַר ״מַזִּיק הוּא״, הֲוָה אָמִינָא: הָנֵי מִילֵּי הֵיכָא דְּקָא עָבֵיד בְּשָׂכָר, אֲבָל הֵיכָא דְּקָא עָבֵיד בְּחִנָּם – לָא, קָא מַשְׁמַע לַן: פּוֹשֵׁעַ הוּא.

The Gemara asks: **Why must he say** both that the butcher **is one who causes damage** and that **he is negligent?** The Gemara explains: If Shmuel had **said** only that **he is one who causes damage, I would say** that **this statement** applies only in a case where the butcher slaughtered the animal **for pay,** in which case, due to the extra responsibility that he bears, he is considered to be one who caused damage and is liable to pay even in a case where the damage was unintentional; **but** in a case **where he does** the work **for free,** I would say **no,** he is exempt from liability in a case where the damage was unintentional. Shmuel therefore **teaches us** that the butcher **is negligent,** and one who works without pay is analogous to an unpaid bailee, who is liable to pay for damage caused by negligence.

BACKGROUND

Jewel [*nofekh*] – נוֹפֶךְ: This refers to one of the stones in the breastplate of the High Priest (see Exodus 28:18), and like most of those stones, its precise identity is unknown. Rav Se'adya Gaon writes that it is a black precious stone. Others maintain that it refers to turquoise, a semiprecious, blue-green stone. Contextually, it can be understood that the *nofekh* is a semiprecious stone. A small one is not very valuable, and serves primarily as an addition to jewelry.

HALAKHA

A loan and one *peruta* – מִלְוֶה וּפְרוּטָה: If a man who lent money to a woman gave her one *peruta* and said: You are hereby betrothed with the loan and this *peruta*, she is betrothed (Rambam *Sefer Nashim*, *Hilkhot Ishut* 5:16; *Shulḥan Arukh*, *Even HaEzer* 28:14).

Whether he said, with the payment for which I have worked – בֵּין בִּשְׂכַר שֶׁעָשִׂיתִי: If a man betroths a woman in exchange for labor that he performs for her, she is not betrothed unless he adds one *peruta* of his own, whether he already completed the labor or will complete it in the future (Rambam *Sefer Nashim*, *Hilkhot Ishut* 5:20; *Shulḥan Arukh*, *Even HaEzer* 28:15).

HALAKHA

One who gives an animal to a butcher – הַנּוֹתֵן בְּהֵמָה לְטַבָּח: If an animal is given to a butcher who slaughters it improperly so that it becomes non-kosher; and similarly, if wheat is brought to a miller who does not soak it and consequently it becomes bran; and similarly, if flour is brought to a baker who underbakes it, in all these cases, if the craftsman is performing paid labor, he is liable to pay for the item in its entirety. If the labor is performed for free, then an expert butcher is exempt, while a non-expert one is liable. This is in accordance with the opinion of Rabbi Yoḥanan, as explained by the Gemara (Rambam *Sefer Mishpatim, Hilkhot Sekhirut* 10:5; *Shulḥan Arukh, Ḥoshen Mishpat* 306:4).

אֵיתִיבֵיהּ רַב חָמָא בַּר גּוּרְיָא לִשְׁמוּאֵל: הַנּוֹתֵן בְּהֵמָה לְטַבָּח וְנִבְלָהּ, אוּמָּן – פָּטוּר, הֶדְיוֹט – חַיָּיב, וְאִם נוֹתֵן שָׂכָר, בֵּין הֶדְיוֹט בֵּין אוּמָּן – חַיָּיב! אֲמַר לֵיהּ: לֶיעְכַּר מוֹחָךְ!

Rav Ḥama bar Gurya raised an objection to Shmuel from the *Tosefta* (10:10): With regard to **one who gives an animal to a butcher,**[H] **and** the butcher killed it in a way that **rendered it an animal carcass,** if the butcher is **an expert,** then he is **exempt** from liability; if he is **an ordinary** person, without particular expertise in the act of ritual slaughter, he is **liable. And if** the owner of the animal **paid** the butcher, then regardless of **whether** he is **an ordinary** person or **whether** he is **an expert,** the butcher is **liable** to pay for the damage. This indicates that an expert butcher who slaughtered the animal improperly is exempt if he slaughtered it without pay. Shmuel **said to him: May your mind be muddled**[N] for raising a ridiculous objection.

אֲתָא הַהוּא מֵרַבָּנַן קָא מוֹתִיב לֵיהּ, אֲמַר לֵיהּ: הַשְׁתָּא שְׁקָלְתְּ מַאי דִּשְׁקַל חַבְרָךְ, קָאָמֵינָא לְכוּ אֲנָא רַבִּי מֵאִיר, וְקָאָמְרִיתוּ לִי רַבָּנַן. אַמַּאי לָא דָּיְיקַת מִילַּי? שֶׁאֲנִי אוֹמֵר: מַזִּיק הוּא, פּוֹשֵׁעַ הוּא, נַעֲשָׂה כְּאוֹמֵר לוֹ שְׁחוֹט לִי מִכָּאן וְשָׁחַט לוֹ מִכָּאן. מַאן אִית לֵיהּ הַאי סְבָרָא – רַבִּי מֵאִיר, דְּאָמַר: מִבָּעֵי לֵיהּ לְמִירְמֵי אַנַּפְשֵׁיהּ.

One of the Sages came and raised the same **objection to** Shmuel. Shmuel **said to him: Now you shall receive what your friend received** from me, since **I say to you** my statement in accordance with the opinion of **Rabbi Meir, and you say to me,** i.e., you raise an objection, based upon the opinion of **the Rabbis. Why were you not precise** in your consideration of **my** choice of **words?** As **I say: He is one who causes damage; he is negligent; he is like one who is told** by the animal's owner to **slaughter it from here, and he slaughtered it from there. Who accepts this reasoning?** It is **Rabbi Meir, who says: He should have taken upon himself** the responsibility to perform his task properly, and if he did not, he is liable to pay for the damage that he caused. The other *baraita* is in accordance with the opinion of the Rabbis, who exempt him from liability.

הֵי רַבִּי מֵאִיר? אִילֵּימָא [הָא] רַבִּי מֵאִיר (קל"ן סִימָן),

The Gemara asks: **Which** statement of **Rabbi Meir** is Shmuel referring to? **If we say** it is **this** statement of **Rabbi Meir,** that is difficult. Parenthetically, the Gemara states that the letters *kuf, lamed, nun* serve as a **mnemonic** device for the three statements of Rabbi Meir that will be cited. It stands for: He tied it [*kesharo*], to dye [*litzboa*], and broke [*nishbera*].

דִּתְנַן: קְשָׁרוֹ בְּעָלָיו בְּמוֹסֵירָה וְנָעַל בְּפָנָיו כָּרָאוּי, וְיָצָא וְהִזִּיק, בֵּין תָּם בֵּין מוּעָד – חַיָּיב, דִּבְרֵי רַבִּי מֵאִיר;

The Gemara returns to the matter at hand: **As we learned** in a mishna (45b): If **the** ox's **owner tied it with reins** to a fence **or locked** the gate **before it in an appropriate manner, but** nevertheless the ox **emerged and caused damage, whether** the ox is **innocuous or forewarned** the owner is **liable,** since this is not considered sufficient precaution to prevent damage; this is **the statement of Rabbi Meir.** As the Gemara explains on 45b, Rabbi Meir holds that a forewarned ox requires a heightened level of safeguarding, and since the owner did not safeguard it, he is liable. The same would apply here, that one who agrees to perform a task must exercise care in executing it. Otherwise, he will be held liable to pay for damage.

הָתָם בִּקְרָאֵי פְּלִיגִי!

The Gemara explains why this cannot be the statement of Rabbi Meir that Shmuel was referring to: **There,** in that mishna, the Sages **disagree with regard to** the interpretation of biblical **verses,**[N] not logical reasoning, as the Gemara explains there, and conclusions cannot be drawn from that *halakha* to this one.

NOTES

May your mind become muddled – לֶיעְכַּר מוֹחָךְ: The reason for this sharp response was that Rav Ḥama bar Gurya demonstrated disrespect for his teacher. Instead of asking his teacher why he had added more words, Rav Ḥama bar Gurya inferred from them a certain point and then quoted the *baraita* to the contrary, as if Shmuel had forgotten it. Shmuel noticed this and saw it as an obligation to chastise him for dishonoring a Torah scholar (*Ḥazon Ish*).

Disagree with regard to the interpretation of biblical verses – בִּקְרָאֵי פְּלִיגִי: According to the opinion of Rabbi Yehuda an innocuous ox requires a greater degree of safeguarding than a forewarned ox, since with regard to the latter the Torah states: "And the owner has not secured it" (Exodus 21:36), which indicates that as long as the animal's owner provides sufficient safeguarding, he is exempt from liability for damage caused by the ox. According to the opinion of Rabbi Meir, this verse emphasizes the requirement that the owner of a forewarned ox provide a greater degree of safeguarding for his animal.

אֶלָּא הָא רַבִּי מֵאִיר, דִּתְנַן: לִצְבּוֹעַ לוֹ אָדוֹם וּצְבָעוֹ שָׁחוֹר, שָׁחוֹר וּצְבָעוֹ אָדוֹם – רַבִּי מֵאִיר אוֹמֵר: נוֹתֵן לוֹ דְּמֵי צַמְרוֹ; הָתָם בְּיָדַיִם קַלְיָאו מִינֵּיהּ!

Rather, it is this statement of **Rabbi Meir** that Shmuel is referring to, **as we learned** in a mishna (100b): If one gave wool to a dyer **to dye it red for him, and he dyed it black,** or to dye it **black, and he dyed it red, Rabbi Meir says:** The dyer **gives** the owner **the value of his wool,** indicating that he is liable to pay for the damage. The Gemara rejects this opinion: This statement also does not prove that according to Rabbi Meir a worker is liable to pay for a job performed improperly, since **there,** the dyer **burned** the wool, thereby removing it **from** the owner **by direct action.**[N]

אֶלָּא הָא רַבִּי מֵאִיר, דִּתְנַן: נִשְׁבְּרָה כַּדּוֹ וְלֹא סִילְּקָהּ, נָפְלָה גְּמַלּוֹ וְלֹא הֶעֱמִידָהּ – רַבִּי מֵאִיר אוֹמֵר: חַיָּיב בְּנִזְקָן, וַחֲכָמִים אוֹמְרִים: פָּטוּר מִדִּינֵי אָדָם וְחַיָּיב בְּדִינֵי שָׁמַיִם, וְקַיְּימָא לָן, דִּבְנִתְקַל פּוֹשֵׁעַ הוּא פְּלִיגִי.

Rather, it is **this** statement of **Rabbi Meir** that Shmuel is referring to, **as we learned** in a *baraita*: If one's **jug broke** on the road **and he did not remove it,** or if **his camel fell** on the road **and he did not stand it up, Rabbi Meir says: He is liable for the damage** that they cause, **and the Rabbis say: He is exempt according to human laws but liable according to the laws of Heaven.** The Gemara notes: **And we maintain** that they **disagree with regard to** the question of whether **one who stumbles** is considered **negligent.** According to the opinion of Rabbi Meir, one who stumbles is considered negligent, since he should have paid attention while walking. He is therefore liable for whatever damage he causes. In the case of an expert butcher as well, Rabbi Meir holds that he is considered negligent when damaging the animal he slaughtered, and the Rabbis hold that he is not negligent and therefore exempt from liability.

אָמַר רַבָּה בַּר בַּר חָנָה אָמַר רַבִּי יוֹחָנָן: טַבָּח אוּמָּן שֶׁקִּלְקֵל – חַיָּיב, וַאֲפִילּוּ הוּא אוּמָּן כְּטַבָּחֵי צִיפּוֹרִי. וּמִי אֲמַר רַבִּי יוֹחָנָן הָכִי? וְהָאֲמַר רַבָּה בַּר בַּר חָנָה: עוּבְדָּא הֲוָה קַמֵּיהּ דְּרַבִּי יוֹחָנָן בִּכְנִישְׁתָּא דְּמָעוֹן, וַאֲמַר לֵיהּ: זִיל אַיְיתֵי רְאָיָה דִּמְמַחֵית לְתַרְנְגוֹלִים וְאֶפְטְרָךְ!

The Gemara discusses Rabbi Yoḥanan's opinion concerning the case of an expert butcher. **Rabba bar bar Ḥana says** that **Rabbi Yoḥanan says: An expert butcher who damaged** an animal by slaughtering it incorrectly, thereby rendering it non-kosher, is **liable** to pay the owner of the animal, **and even if he is as expert as the butchers of Tzippori,**[B] it is not considered an accident, and he is considered to be at fault. The Gemara asks: **And did Rabbi Yoḥanan** actually **say this? But didn't Rabba bar bar Ḥana say** that **there was an incident** in which a butcher who damaged an animal was brought to court **before Rabbi Yoḥanan in the synagogue of** the town **Maon,**[B] **and** Rabbi Yoḥanan **said to** the butcher: **Go bring proof that you are an expert**[H] **at** slaughtering **chickens, and I will exempt you** from payment.

לָא קַשְׁיָא: כָּאן בְּחִנָּם, כָּאן בְּשָׂכָר; כִּי הָא דְּאָמַר רַבִּי זֵירָא: הָרוֹצֶה שֶׁיִּתְחַיֵּיב לוֹ טַבָּח, יַקְדִּים לוֹ דִּינָר.

The Gemara responds: This is **not difficult. Here,** in the aforementioned incident, the butcher slaughtered the animal **for free,** and he is therefore exempt, while **there,** in Rabba bar bar Ḥana's previous statement, he slaughtered the animal **for pay,** and is therefore liable to pay for the damage. This is **in accordance with that which Rabbi Zeira says: One who wants a butcher to be liable to** pay **him** in the event that he damages the animal during slaughter should **advance him a dinar,** so that he is paid for his services, and he is consequently liable to pay damages.

מֵיתִיבֵי: הַמּוֹלִיךְ חִטִּים לִטְחוֹן, וְלֹא לְתָתָן, וַעֲשָׂאָן סוּבִּין אוֹ מוּרְסָן, קֶמַח לְנַחְתּוֹם וַעֲשָׂאוֹ פַּת נִיפּוּלִין, בְּהֵמָה לְטַבָּח וְנִיבְּלָהּ, חַיָּיב, מִפְּנֵי שֶׁהוּא כְּנוֹשֵׂא שָׂכָר! אֵימָא: מִפְּנֵי שֶׁהוּא נוֹשֵׂא שָׂכָר.

The Gemara **raises an objection** from the *Tosefta* (10:9): **One who brought wheat** to another **to grind** for him, and the miller **did not wet** the grains sufficiently for the grinding to be performed effectively, **and** as a result **he converted** the grain **into bran**[B] **or coarse bran;** or if one gave **flour to the baker and he made bread** that is **underbaked**[B] and tends to crumble; or if one gave **an animal to a butcher** and the butcher killed it in a way that **rendered it** an unslaughtered **animal carcass,** the worker is **liable, because he is like a paid bailee.** This indicates that even if the work was done for free, the worker has the legal status of one who is paid, and he is liable to pay for the damage. The Gemara answers by emending the *baraita*: **Say** instead: **Because he is a paid bailee** and actually receives payment.

הַהוּא מַגְרוּמְתָּא דַּאֲתַאי לְקַמֵּיהּ דְּרַב, טַרְפַהּ, וּפַטְרֵיהּ לְטַבָּח מִלְּשַׁלּוּמֵי דָּמֵי; פַּגְעוּ בֵּיהּ רַב כָּהֲנָא וְרַב אַסִּי בְּהַהוּא גַּבְרָא, אֲמַרוּ לֵיהּ: עֲבֵיד בָּךְ רַב תַּרְתֵּי.

The Gemara relates: There was a **certain** animal that was **slaughtered** with an incision **not in the neck**[NH] **that was brought before Rav.** He **declared it non-kosher, and exempted the butcher from paying its value. Rav Kahana and Rav Asi encountered that man,** i.e., the owner of the animal, and **they said to him: Rav did two for you.**

NOTES

Burned it…by direct action – בְּיָדַיִם קַלְיָאו: Rashi explains that the dyer intended to effect a change in the item. By contrast, in the case of the butcher, it can be assumed that he intended to slaughter the animal properly. The Ra'avad explains that the difference between the case of a butcher and that of a dyer is that dying wool the wrong color is a major change. The dyer is therefore regarded as a robber, and he acquires the wool due to the change. The butcher damaged the animal by deviating slightly from the correct area of ritual slaughter, while the actual change to the animal is minor and insignificant.

Slaughtered not in the neck – מַגְרוּמְתָּא: One of the ways that an act of ritual slaughter is rendered invalid is when the incision is not made in the proper area of the animal's throat and is made too close to its head. This is known as *hagrama*.

BACKGROUND

Tzippori – צִיפּוֹרִי: Tzippori was a large town in the Upper Galilee, and the perennial rival of Tiberias for recognition as the spiritual capital of the Galilee. During the Second Temple period it enjoyed special status among the towns of the Galilee because of its large and learned Jewish community.

Synagogue of the town Maon – כְּנִישְׁתָּא דְּמָעוֹן: This refers to the large synagogue in the town of Maon, also called Beit Maon, which was a suburb of Tiberias, situated to the east of Tiberias. Beit Maon was the hometown of the priestly watch of Ḥuppa.

Did not wet them and he converted the grain into bran – לֹא לְתָתָן וַעֲשָׂאָן סוּבִּין: For grinding to be effective, the millstones are first separated from each other, and occasionally the wheat is wetted so that when the grinding begins, the chaff is separated from the wheat kernel, and the kernel is then ground without the chaff. If the miller is not skilled, he might grind the kernel along with the chaff, which results in bran flour.

Bread that is underbaked – פַּת נִיפּוּלִין: This refers to bread that has not risen. Dough that is properly kneaded and baked will rise due to the yeast or leavening agent. Bread that did not rise sufficiently or collapsed during the baking process is therefore harder and has less flavor.

HALAKHA

Bring proof that you are an expert – אַיְיתֵי רְאָיָה דִּמְמַחֵית: A butcher who slaughters for free, and similarly, any craftsman who does work without receiving pay, must bring proof of his expertise in order to be exempt from liability for payment of damages. If they cannot bring proof, they are liable to pay (Rambam *Sefer Mishpatim*, *Hilkhot Sekhirut* 10:5; *Shulḥan Arukh*, *Ḥoshen Mishpat* 306:7).

A certain animal slaughtered not in the neck, etc. – הַהוּא מַגְרוּמְתָּא וכו׳: When is a butcher held liable? He is held liable if he slaughtered an animal in a way that is definitely not halakhically valid. By contrast, if he committed an error that leaves the animal unfit due to an uncertainty over its status, e.g., by pausing while slaughtering a minor portion of the trachea or esophagus, he is exempt from liability. Even in cases where it is customary to deem the slaughtered animal forbidden, the butcher is exempt due to the uncertainty. Some (*Terumat HaDeshen*) disagree with this ruling, and the *halakha* is in accordance with the dissenting opinion (*Shakh*). If this occurs, the slaughterer forfeits his wages (*Shulḥan Arukh*, *Ḥoshen Mishpat* 306:5, and in the comment of Rema).

מאי תרתי? אילימא תרתי לגריעותא, דאיבעי ליה לאכשורי כרבי יוסי ברבי יהודה וטרפה כרבנן, ואי נמי כרבנן, דאיבעי ליה חיובא לטבחא, ומי שרי למימר כי האי גונא?

The Gemara asks: **What are the two? If we say** there were **two unfavorable** rulings, what are they? One is that **he should have declared** the animal **kosher, in accordance with** the opinion of **Rabbi Yosei, son of Rabbi Yehuda,** who says that an animal that has been slaughtered in this manner is kosher, **and** instead he **declared it non-kosher, in accordance with** the opinion of **the Rabbis,** who hold that it is not kosher. **And** the second is that **even** if he holds **in accordance with** the opinion of **the Rabbis, he should have** ruled that **the butcher** is **liable** to pay for the damage. The Gemara challenges this explanation: **But** if these are the two that Rav Kahana and Rav Asi are referring to, **is it permitted** for them **to say this type** of statement to the owner of the animal?

והתניא: לכשיצא, לא יאמר: "אני מזכה וחבירי מחייבין, אבל מה אעשה שחבירי רבו עלי", ועל זה נאמר: "הולך רכיל מגלה סוד"!

But isn't it taught in a *baraita* that **when** a judge **leaves** the courthouse, **he should not say** to the litigant: **I found you innocent**[H] **and my colleagues found you liable, but what can I do, since my colleagues outnumber me? And** it is **concerning** a circumstance such as **this** that it **is stated: "He that goes about as a talebearer reveals secrets;** but he that is of a faithful spirit conceals a matter" (Proverbs 11:13).

אלא תרתי למעליותא, דלא אוכלך ספק איסורא, ומנעך מספק גזילה.

Rather, the intention is that they told him that there were **two favorable** rulings: First, **that** by declaring the animal to be non-kosher, **he did not allow you to eat** an item about which there is **uncertainty** as to whether it is **forbidden, and** second, by exempting the butcher from paying you, **he prevented you** from being in a situation where there is **uncertainty** as to whether receiving payment from the butcher constitutes **robbery,** since you would have been given the butcher's money when he may be exempt, as the animal may in fact be kosher.

איתמר: המראה דינר לשולחני ונמצא רע, תני חדא: אומן – פטור, הדיוט – חייב, ותניא אידך: בין אומן בין הדיוט – חייב!

§ The Gemara continues the discussion of an expert who erred, thereby causing a loss. **It was stated:** With regard to **one who presents a dinar to a money changer**[H] to assess its value or authenticity and the money changer declares it valid, **and it is found to be bad,** i.e., invalid, causing its owner a monetary loss, it **is taught** in **one** *baraita* that if the money changer is **an expert,** he is **exempt,**[N] while if he is **an ordinary** person he is **liable. And it is taught** in **another** *baraita* that irrespective of **whether** he is **an expert** or **whether** he is **an ordinary** person, he is **liable** to pay for the owner's loss.

אמר רב פפא: כי תניא אומן פטור – כגון דנכו ואיסור, דלא צריכי למיגמר כלל. אלא במאי טעו? טעו בסיכתא חדתא, דההיא שעתא דנפק מתותי סיכתא.

To reconcile the *baraitot*, **Rav Pappa said: When** the *baraita* **teaches** that **an expert is exempt** from liability, it is referring to renowned experts **such as** the money changers **Dankhu and Issur,** whose expertise is so great **that they do not need to learn** about assessing currency **at all.** The Gemara asks: **But** if they are so proficient, **in what did they err?** The Gemara answers: **They erred with regard to** a coin from **a new press,**[BN] **which at that time was leaving the press,** and they did not know its value.

ההיא איתתא דאחזיא דינרא לרבי חייא, אמר לה: מעליא הוא. למחר אתאי לקמיה ואמרה ליה: אחזיתיה ואמרו לי בישא הוא, ולא קא נפיק לי. אמר ליה לרב: זיל חלפיה ניהלה, וכתוב אפנקסי: "דין עסק ביש".

The Gemara relates: There was **a certain woman who presented a dinar to Rabbi Ḥiyya** to assess its authenticity. **He said to her: It is a proper coin. The next day she came before him and said to him: I presented it** to others, **and they told me** that **it is a bad** dinar, **and I am not able to spend it.** Rabbi **Ḥiyya said to Rav: Go exchange it for her, and write on my tablet** [*apinkasi*]:[L] This was **a bad transaction,** as I should not have assessed the coin.

HALAKHA

He should not say, I found you innocent, etc. – לא יאמר אני מזכה וכו׳: Upon leaving the court, one of the judges may not say to a litigant: I ruled that you are innocent, or guilty, but was outnumbered by my colleagues. One who does so is considered a talebearer who reveals secrets, in accordance with the statement in the Gemara. The *Shakh* writes that one also violates this prohibition if he says: The judge was wrong for finding you liable (Rambam *Sefer Shofetim, Hilkhot Sanhedrin* 22:7; *Shulḥan Arukh, Ḥoshen Mishpat* 19:1).

One who presents a dinar to a money changer – המראה דינר לשולחני: If a money changer who was paid to evaluate a coin says that it is valid and it is found to be invalid, he is liable to pay even if he is an expert who does not need to learn more. If he was not paid, he is exempt, provided that he is an expert who does not need to learn more. If he is not an expert, he is liable to pay even if he evaluated the coin without being paid (Rambam *Sefer Mishpatim, Hilkhot Sekhirut* 10:5; *Shulḥan Arukh, Ḥoshen Mishpat* 306:6).

BACKGROUND

A new press – סיכתא חדתא: The primary meaning of this word is a spike or nail. Rashi explains that it refers to a die, which is a piece of hard metal upon which is engraved an inversion of the image that will appear on the coin, and when struck will imprint the image upon the coin. A new press refers to a new die used to mint a new type of coin.

LANGUAGE

Tablet [*pinkas*] – פנקס: From the Greek πίναξ, *pinax*. Its primary meaning is a tablet used for writing. Over time, the *pinax* developed into a group of several tablets that were connected to form a small book. Although writing tablets in talmudic times took on different forms and were made from various materials, it seems that the most popular kind was a wooden board coated with wax, so that the writing could be easily etched into the wax and then erased after each use.

Wax-coated tablet with stylus

NOTES

An expert is exempt, etc. – אומן פטור וכו׳: *Tosafot* note that the difference between the case of a money changer, where the Gemara does not make a distinction between paid and unpaid work, and a butcher, where it does make that distinction, is that assessing coins requires a greater level of expertise. Therefore, a money changer who lacks the requisite level of knowledge should not offer an opinion, even without pay. The Rashba draws a different distinction: Even the most expert butcher may occasionally slaughter an animal incorrectly, as a physical act cannot be performed with precision every time, but a money changer relies exclusively upon his knowledge, and therefore, when he commits an error, he reveals that he is not an expert. If, however, one as expert as Issur and Dankhu errs, it must be completely due to circumstances beyond his control.

A new press – סיכתא חדתא: Rashi explains that a completely new coin had been issued, and the old one was invalidated. In other words, Issur and Dankhu examined a coin that had previously been valid, and had not yet been made aware of the fact that the coin had been invalidated (*Arukh*).

וּמַאי שְׁנָא דַּנְכוּ וְאִיסּוּר דִּפְטִירִי, מִשּׁוּם דְּלָא צְרִיכִי לְמִיגְמַר? רַבִּי חִיָּיא נַמִּי לָאו לְמִיגְמַר קָא בָּעֵי! רַבִּי חִיָּיא לִפְנִים מִשּׁוּרַת הַדִּין הוּא דַּעֲבַד; כִּדְתָנֵי רַב יוֹסֵף: ״וְהוֹדַעְתָּ לָהֶם״ – זֶה

The Gemara asks: **But what is different** about **Dankhu and Issur, who are exempt due to** the fact **that they do not need to learn** about assessing currency? **Rabbi Ḥiyya too did not need to learn,**[N] as he was also an expert. The Gemara responds: **Rabbi Ḥiyya** was not actually required to return a dinar to this woman, but when he did so **he acted beyond the letter of the law.**[H] This is **as that** which **Rav Yosef taught** concerning the verse: "And you shall show them the way wherein they must walk, and the work that they must do" (Exodus 18:20): **"And you shall show them"; this** is referring to

NOTES

Did not need to learn – לָאו לְמִיגְמַר קָא בָּעֵי: The Rashba writes that the Gemara had a tradition that Rabbi Ḥiyya was an expert on coinage on the level of Issur and Dankhu. He also quotes the Ra'avad, who says that Rabbi Ḥiyya would not have involved himself in this matter had he not had the necessary expertise.

HALAKHA

Beyond the letter of the law – לִפְנִים מִשּׁוּרַת הַדִּין: Because of his stature, a wise person must conduct himself beyond the letter of the law (Rambam *Sefer HaMadda*, *Hilkhot Yesodei HaTorah* 5:11 and see *Hilkhot Deot* 1:5).

Perek **IX**
Daf **100** Amud **a**

בֵּית חַיֵּיהֶם, ״אֶת הַדֶּרֶךְ״ – זוֹ גְּמִילוּת חֲסָדִים, ״יֵלְכוּ״ – זוֹ בִּיקּוּר חוֹלִים, ״בָּהּ״ – זוֹ קְבוּרָה, ״אֶת הַמַּעֲשֶׂה״ – זֶה הַדִּין, ״אֲשֶׁר יַעֲשׂוּן״ – זוֹ לִפְנִים מִשּׁוּרַת הַדִּין.

the core of their existence,[N] i.e., Torah study, which is the source of life. **"The way"; this** is referring to **acts of kindness.**[N] **"They must walk"; this** is referring to **visiting the sick. "Wherein"; this** is referring to the **burial** of the dead. **"The work"; this** is referring to conducting oneself in accordance with **the law. "That they must do"; this** is referring to conducting oneself **beyond the letter of the law.** This indicates that the Torah mandates that people conduct themselves beyond the letter of the law.

רֵישׁ לָקִישׁ אַחֲוִי לֵיהּ דִּינָרָא לְרַבִּי אֶלְעָזָר. אֲמַר: מְעַלְּיָא הוּא. אֲמַר לֵיהּ: חֲזִי, דַּעֲלָךְ קָא סָמֵיכְנָא. אֲמַר לֵיהּ: כִּי סָמְכַתְּ עֲלַי מַאי לְמֵימְרָא, דְּאִי מִשְׁתַּכַּח בִּישָׁא בָּעֵינָא לְאִיחְלוּפֵי לָךְ? וְהָא אַתְּ הוּא דְּאָמְרַתְּ: רַבִּי מֵאִיר הוּא דְּדָאֵין דִּינָא דְּגַרְמֵי, מַאי לָאו רַבִּי מֵאִיר וְלָא סְבִירָא לַן כְּוָותֵיהּ?

The Gemara relates: **Reish Lakish presented a dinar to Rabbi Elazar** so that the latter would assess it. Rabbi Elazar **said: It is a proper** coin. Reish Lakish **said to him: Realize that I am relying on you.**[NH] Rabbi Elazar **said to him: What** is the purpose **of stating that you are relying on me?** Is it so **that if** this dinar **is** later **found** to be **bad, I will be required to exchange it for you** with a good dinar? **But it is you who said** that **it is Rabbi Meir** who is of the opinion **that** there is **liability** for damage caused by **indirect** action, even if he did not directly cause damage to the property. **What, is it not** that you intended to say: This is the opinion of **Rabbi Meir, but we do not hold in accordance with his** opinion?

אֲמַר לֵיהּ: לָא, רַבִּי מֵאִיר וּסְבִירָא לַן כְּוָותֵיהּ.

Reish Lakish **said to him: No,** I intended to say that this is the opinion of **Rabbi Meir, and we do hold in accordance with his** opinion.[H]

הֵי רַבִּי מֵאִיר? אִילֵימָא רַבִּי מֵאִיר (ד׳ ל׳ מ׳ פ׳ סִימָן),

The Gemara asks: **Which** statement **of Rabbi Meir** is Rabbi Elazar referring to? **If we say** it is **this** statement **of Rabbi Meir,** that is difficult. Parenthetically, the Gemara states that the letters ***dalet, lamed, mem, peh*** serve as **a mnemonic** device for the four statements of Rabbi Meir that will be cited. It stands for: Judged [*dan*], to dye [*litzboa*], covers [*mesakekh*], and broke open [*pirtza*].

NOTES

The core of their existence – בֵּית חַיֵּיהֶם: Rashi explains that the use of this phrase here is referring to Torah study, while in his commentary to the parallel passage in tractate *Bava Metzia* (30b), he explains that it is referring to a trade, which enables people to provide for themselves.

The way, this is referring to acts of kindness – אֶת הַדֶּרֶךְ זוֹ גְּמִילוּת חֲסָדִים: The Riaf explains that this means to conduct oneself as the verse states: "That they may keep the way of the Lord, to do righteousness and justice" (Genesis 18:19). Alternatively, the Maharsha explains that this is in accordance with the verse: "After the Lord your God shall you walk" (Deuteronomy 13:5), which the Sages interpret to mean that one should strive to emulate God's attributes, e.g., just as God clothes the naked, so should you.

Realize that I am relying on you – חֲזִי דַּעֲלָךְ קָא סָמֵיכְנָא: There is a dispute among the commentaries with regard to the meaning of this statement. Some say that like Rabbi Ḥiyya, Rabbi Elazar was an expert in assessing coins, and he became liable to pay for any potential damage through Reish Lakish stating that he relies upon his assessment. According to this, even an expert is liable to pay a person who, in asking his opinion, states that he is relying upon his answer (*Haggahot Asheri*, citing Maharih). Others explain the Rabbi Elazar was not an expert, and they understand from this Gemara that even a non-expert is exempt from liability unless he is told that his opinion is being relied upon (Rif). According to the opinion of *Tosafot*, who also say that Rabbi Elazar was not an expert, a non-expert is always liable, and Reish Lakish was simply warning Rabbi Elazar of his liability, despite there being no need to do so. *Tosafot* further explain that if he had been an expert, even if he had been told explicitly that he is being relied upon, he would still be exempt from liability.

HALAKHA

Realize that I am relying on you – חֲזִי דַּעֲלָךְ קָא סָמֵיכְנָא: If a non-expert is shown a dinar even without being paid for his assessment, he is liable to pay for his error only if he was told: Realize that I am relying on you, as demonstrated by the incident with Rabbi Elazar (Gra). This is because one who informs an expert of this fact demonstrates that only the expert's judgment, and not that of anyone else, is being relied upon (Rif; Rambam). Some say that even if he is not told that he is being relied upon he is still liable (*Tur*, citing Rosh), but the *halakha* is in accordance with the first opinion (Rambam *Sefer Mishpatim*, *Hilkhot Sekhirut* 10:5; *Shulḥan Arukh*, *Ḥoshen Mishpat* 306:6).

And we do hold in accordance with his opinion – וּסְבִירָא לַן כְּוָותֵיהּ: The *halakha* is in accordance with the opinion of Rabbi Meir, who rules that there is liability for damage caused by indirect action, which, according to the Rambam, means that anyone who causes damage to another's property, even if not by any direct action, is liable to pay for the damage. Some distinguish between the cases attributed to Rabbi Meir that are cited in the Gemara, where there is liability for indirect action, and other similar cases in which the damage is merely attributed to causation (*gerama*), and the one who caused the damage is exempt (Rabbeinu Yitzḥak; Rosh). Some hold that one who regularly causes damage by causation is penalized and held liable (Rema, citing Rabbi Yitzḥak ben Avraham), but the *Shakh* writes that liability should not extend beyond the cases specified in the Gemara (Rambam *Sefer Nezikin*, *Hilkhot Ḥovel UMazik* 7:11; *Shulḥan Arukh*, *Ḥoshen Mishpat* 386:1–3).

דִּתְנַן: דָּן אֶת הַדִּין, זִיכָּה אֶת הַחַיָּיב, חִיֵּיב אֶת הַזַּכַּאי, טִימֵּא אֶת הַטָּהוֹר, טִיהֵר אֶת הַטָּמֵא – מַה שֶּׁעָשָׂה עָשׂוּי וִישַׁלֵּם מִבֵּיתוֹ;

The Gemara returns to the matter at hand. **As we learned** in a mishna (*Bekhorot* 28b): If a judge **issued a judgment**[H] and erred, and he **acquitted** one who was in fact **liable,** or **deemed liable** one who should have in fact been **acquitted,** or if he **ruled** that **a pure** item **is impure,** or **ruled** that **an impure** item is **pure,** and by doing so he caused a litigant a monetary loss, **what he did is done,** i.e., the judgment stands, **and** the judge **must pay** damages **from his home,** i.e., from his personal funds. He is therefore liable to pay the damages even though he caused the loss indirectly.

הָא אִיתְּמַר עֲלַהּ, אָמַר רַבִּי אִילְעָא אָמַר רַב: וְהוּא שֶׁנָּטַל וְנָתַן בַּיָּד!

The Gemara explains why this cannot be the statement of Rabbi Meir that Shmuel was referring to: **But wasn't it stated with regard to that** mishna that **Rabbi Ile'a says** that **Rav says: And this** mishna is discussing a case **where** the judge not only issued a ruling, but actively **took** the money from the one whom he found liable, **and gave** it to the other party **by** his own **hand.**[N] This is not a case of causation but of direct action.

אֶלָּא הָא רַבִּי מֵאִיר, דִּתְנַן: לִצְבּוֹעַ לוֹ אָדוֹם וּצְבָעוֹ שָׁחוֹר, שָׁחוֹר וּצְבָעוֹ אָדוֹם – רַבִּי מֵאִיר אוֹמֵר: נוֹתֵן לוֹ דְּמֵי צַמְרוֹ; הָתָם קָא עָבֵיד בְּיָדַיִם!

Rather, Rabbi Elazar must be referring to **this** statement **of Rabbi Meir, as we learned** in a mishna (100b): If one gave wool to a dyer **to dye it red for him, and he dyed it black,** or to dye it **black, and he dyed it red, Rabbi Meir says:** The dyer **gives** the owner the **value of his wool.** The Gemara responds: This too does not prove that according to the opinion of Rabbi Meir one is liable even if the loss was brought about by causation, since **there he does** cause damage **through** direct **action.**

אֶלָּא הָא רַבִּי מֵאִיר, דִּתְנַן: הַמְסַכֵּךְ גַּפְנוֹ עַל גַּבֵּי תְּבוּאָתוֹ שֶׁל חֲבֵירוֹ – הֲרֵי זֶה קִידֵּשׁ וְחַיָּיב; הָתָם נַמִי קָא עָבֵיד בְּיָדַיִם!

Rather, Rabbi Elazar must be referring to **this** statement **of Rabbi Meir, as we learned** in a mishna (*Kilayim* 7:4): **One who drapes his grapevine**[H] **atop another's grain has rendered** them **forbidden**[N] due to the prohibition against growing diverse kinds in a vineyard, **and he is liable** to pay the owner of the grain for the damage. The Gemara responds: This too does not prove that according to the opinion of Rabbi Meir one is liable even if the loss was brought about by causation, since **there too he does** cause damage **by** direct **action.**

אֶלָּא הָא רַבִּי מֵאִיר, דְּתַנְיָא: מְחִיצַת הַכֶּרֶם שֶׁנִּפְרְצָה;

Rather, it must be referring to **this** statement **of Rabbi Meir, as it is taught** in the *Tosefta* (*Kilayim* 3:4): If there was **a partition of a vineyard** that is adjacent to a wheat field, and **that** partition **broke open,**

HALAKHA

Issued a judgment – דָּן אֶת הַדִּין: If a non-expert judge who was not accepted as an arbitrator by the litigants, even though he has been granted permission to rule on halakhic matters, errs in a matter that is not an explicit *halakha*, but with regard to which there is a consensus among his fellow judges, and he personally transfers the payment, he is liable to pay for the damage from his own funds. He may then collect that amount from the litigant in whose favor he ruled erroneously, but if the latter cannot pay, the judge suffers the loss. This is because he caused damage by indirect action. The Rema writes that some say that even if he did not personally transfer the payment, the verdict cannot be retracted, and he must pay from his personal funds (Rambam *Sefer Shofetim, Hilkhot Sanhedrin* 5:4; *Shulḥan Arukh, Ḥoshen Mishpat* 25:4).

One who drapes his grapevine, etc. – הַמְסַכֵּךְ גַּפְנוֹ וכו׳: If one drapes his grapevine atop another's grain, the grain is not forbidden, since one cannot render forbidden that which he does not own. This is in accordance with the opinion of Rabbi Yosei and Rabbi Shimon in the mishna in tractate *Kilayim*, and not in accordance with the opinion of Rabbi Meir. The grapevine is forbidden, as Rabbi Yoḥanan rules in the Jerusalem Talmud (Rambam *Sefer Zera'im, Hilkhot Kilayim* 5:8; *Shulḥan Arukh, Yoreh De'a* 296:4).

NOTES

Where he took and gave it by his own hand – שֶׁנָּטַל וְנָתַן בַּיָּד: Rashi gives a detailed explanation of how exactly the judge executed his ruling by his own hand: When he found the innocent party liable, he took the money from one party and gave it to the other. When he found the liable party innocent, he took collateral away from a creditor. When he ruled that a pure item is impure, he personally put it in contact with an impure item in order to strengthen his ruling; and when he ruled that an impure item is pure, he mixed it in with pure produce in a way that it could not be identified in the mixture. In the latter case, not only is the forbidden item not nullified, it actually causes the entire mixture to be forbidden.

Has rendered them forbidden – הֲרֵי זֶה קִידֵּשׁ: Draping vines in this manner is tantamount to planting them. The commentaries explain that both the grain and the grapevine become forbidden. While the mishna does not state explicitly that this is the opinion of Rabbi Meir, it is a principle that an unattributed mishna is attributed to Rabbi Meir (*Tosafot*, citing Rabbeinu Tam). In that mishna, Rabbi Yosei and Rabbi Shimon disagree with the opinion of Rabbi Meir, and state that one cannot render forbidden an item that is not his.

אוֹמֵר לוֹ ״גְּדוֹר״, נִפְרְצָה – אוֹמֵר לוֹ ״גְּדוֹר״. נִתְיָיאֵשׁ מִמֶּנָּה וְלֹא גְּדָרָהּ – הֲרֵי זֶה קִידֵּשׁ וְחַיָּיב בְּאַחֲרָיוּתוֹ.

the owner of the wheat field may **tell** the owner of the vineyard[N] to **repair** the breach[N] before the vines intermingle with the grain and cause it to become forbidden. If the partition **broke open** again, he may again **tell him** to **repair** it. If the owner of the vineyard **abandoned** the partition **and did not repair it, he has rendered** the grain **forbidden,**[H] **and is obligated** to pay **restitution for it.**[N] This demonstrates that one is liable to pay damages even if he did not perform any action at all, and consequently proves that Rabbi Meir rules there is liability for damage caused by indirect action.

מתני׳ הַנּוֹתֵן צֶמֶר לַצַּבָּע וְהִקְדִּיחוֹ יוֹרָה – נוֹתֵן לוֹ דְּמֵי צַמְרוֹ. צְבָעוֹ כָּאוּר, אִם הַשֶּׁבַח יָתֵר עַל הַיְּצִיאָה – נוֹתֵן לוֹ אֶת הַיְּצִיאָה, וְאִם הַיְּצִיאָה יְתֵירָה עַל הַשֶּׁבַח – נוֹתֵן לוֹ אֶת הַשֶּׁבַח.

MISHNA In the case of **one who gives wool**[H] **to a dyer and it was burned in the cauldron** during the dyeing process, thereby completely ruining the wool so that there is no enhancement, only loss, the dyer **gives the** owner **the value of his wool. If he dyed it unattractively** [***ka'ur***][LN] so that the dye is not absorbed well by the wool, **if the enhancement,** i.e., the amount that the value of the wool has increased by being dyed, **exceeds the** dyer's **expenses,**[N] the owner of the wool **gives** the dyer **the expenses. And if the expenses exceed the enhancement, he gives him** the value of **the enhancement.**

לִצְבּוֹעַ לוֹ אָדוֹם וּצְבָעוֹ שָׁחוֹר, שָׁחוֹר וּצְבָעוֹ אָדוֹם – רַבִּי מֵאִיר אוֹמֵר: נוֹתֵן לוֹ דְּמֵי צַמְרוֹ; רַבִּי יְהוּדָה אוֹמֵר: אִם הַשֶּׁבַח יָתֵר עַל הַיְּצִיאָה – נוֹתֵן לוֹ אֶת הַיְּצִיאָה, וְאִם הַיְּצִיאָה יְתֵירָה עַל הַשֶּׁבַח – נוֹתֵן לוֹ אֶת הַשֶּׁבַח.

If the owner gave wool to a dyer **to dye it red for him**[N] **and** instead **he dyed it black,**[B] or to dye it **black and he dyed it red, Rabbi Meir says:** The dyer **gives** the owner of the wool **the value of his wool. Rabbi Yehuda says:** Here too, **if the** value of the **enhancement exceeds the** dyer's **expenses,** the owner of the wool **gives** the dyer **the expenses. And if the expenses exceed the enhancement, he gives him** the value of **the enhancement.**

גמ׳ מַאי כָּאוּר? אָמַר רַב נַחְמָן אָמַר רַבָּה בַּר בַּר חָנָה: כְּלַבּוּס. מַאי כְּלַבּוּס? אָמַר רַבָּה בַּר שְׁמוּאֵל:

GEMARA The Gemara clarifies: **What** does the mishna **mean by unattractively? Rav Naḥman said** that **Rabba bar bar Ḥana said:** ***Kelabus***.[L] The Gemara asks: **What** does ***kelabus*** mean? **Rabba bar Shmuel said:**

LANGUAGE

Unattractively [*ka'ur*] – **כָּאוּר**: According to most commentaries this word means ugly, related to a similar word, spelled with the letter *ayin*. Some explain that the word derives from the word for fire, *ur*, and means charred or burned.

Kelabus – **כְּלַבּוּס**: From the Latin clavus, which among other definitions is the term for a metal nail or stripes on cloth. The word is ordinarily used in rabbinic literature for a pair of tongs. The *ge'onim* explain that it means the color was not absorbed into the wool in a consistent fashion, but has stripes running in different directions, making the wool look similar to a pair of tongs. Some suggest that the word is related to the Greek χίλιοι, *khilioi*, meaning a thousand colors, indicating an inferior dye job that resulted in one garment being of many different shades.

BACKGROUND

To dye it red for him and instead he dyed it black – **לִצְבּוֹעַ לוֹ אָדוֹם וּצְבָעוֹ שָׁחוֹר**: In mishnaic times, wool was ordinarily dyed rather than bleached or used in its natural color. Most often, professional dyers would receive laundered fleece and would dye the wool according to the customer's specifications. Occasionally accidents would occur and even an expert dyer could produce wool that had a darker hue than was ordered, which the mishna refers to as black. For example, if the pot had been used previously there may be some remnants of the previous dye absorbed in a clay pot, or a metal pot itself might alter the hue of the dye. If the shade of the wool turned out to be unacceptable, the final product may turn out to be worthless or, at any rate, worth less than the cost of the dye that was used.

HALAKHA

He has rendered it forbidden, etc. – **הֲרֵי זֶה קִידֵּשׁ וכו׳**: If the partition of a vineyard is breached near a field of grain the owner of the vineyard is told to repair it. If it is breached a second time he is told to repair it again. If he was not warned to fix it he is not liable for any damage caused (*Tosafot*). If he abandoned the partition and did not repair it he has rendered the grain forbidden (Rambam *Sefer Zera'im*, *Hilkhot Kilayim* 7:17 and *Kesef Mishne* and Mahari Kurkus there; *Shulḥan Arukh*, *Yoreh De'a* 296:47).

One who gives wool, etc. – **הַנּוֹתֵן צֶמֶר וכו׳**: If one gave wool to a dyer and it was burned in the cauldron, the dyer must give the value of the wool to its owner. If the dyer dyed it in an unattractive way, or if he was asked to dye it red but he dyed it black, if the value of the enhancement exceeds the expenses, the owner pays the dyer for the expenses and keeps the wool. If the expenses exceeded the value of the enhancement, the owner pays for the enhancement and keeps the wool.

Some say that the amount the value of the item would have appreciated had the dyer not deviated from the instructions is considered part of the principal and not part of the enhancement (*Tur*, citing Rosh), but the *halakha* does not follow this opinion. Neither the owner of the wool nor the dyer may insist that the dyer pay the value of the wool to its owner, since a craftsman does not acquire ownership rights through the enhancement of a vessel (Rambam *Sefer Mishpatim*, *Hilkhot Sekhirut* 10:4; *Shulḥan Arukh*, *Ḥoshen Mishpat* 306:3 and *Shakh* and *Beur HaGra* there).

NOTES

May tell him – **אוֹמֵר לוֹ**: *Tosafot* note that the Gemara does not simply state that the owner of the vineyard is obligated to repair the breach; he is also told to repair it, since in order to be liable to pay for the damage he must be warned. The Gemara presents a scenario in which he was warned twice to repair it in order to clarify that if he repaired it once he is will become obligated to repair it again should it break. Rabbeinu Tam writes that the repeated scenario serves to teach the *halakha* that the growth of the grain during the first time the partition was breached is not combined with the growth of the grain during the second breach with regard to the assessment of whether the grain grew a sufficient amount to render it forbidden.

Repair the breach – **גְּדוֹר**: The prohibition against diverse kinds applies to grain that grows in the proximity of a vineyard. If one two-hundredth of the extant quantity of grain grew under those circumstances, it is not nullified and both the vineyard and the grain are forbidden. *Tosafot* explain that the instruction to repair the partition is given specifically to the owner of the vineyard since he is the one who causes damage in this case, as according to *halakha* a space of four cubits is designated surrounding a vineyard to enable the owner to properly tend to the vines, and the owner of the vineyard is obligated to keep his vineyard four cubits away from the field unless there is a fence. Rabbeinu Yehonatan of Lunel writes that the directive is given to the owner of the vineyard alone only if there are no grapes on the vine, as in that case only the grain becomes forbidden, and the owner of the vineyard is viewed as the one causing the damage. If there are grapes on the vine that will become forbidden as well, both owners are obligated to repair the partition.

And is obligated to pay restitution for it – **וְחַיָּיב בְּאַחֲרָיוּתוֹ**: *Tosafot* write that this is not considered damage that is not evident, because even though no damage can be seen in the grain, the breach in the partition is considered damage that is evident. *Tosafot* reject the suggestion that the liability here is a penalty and not restitution for actual damage, because if that were the case liability would apply only if the partition was breached intentionally, and not if it happened unwittingly. By contrast, the *Gilyon HaShas* notes that according to the opinion of Rabbi Meir, a penalty can be imposed even in a case of unwitting damage.

If he dyed it unattractively – **צְבָעוֹ כָּאוּר**: Rashi explains that he dyed the wool using the residue of dye remaining in the cauldron. The dyer is therefore considered to have caused damage by direct action, and is at a disadvantage according to all opinions, even according to the opinion of Rabbi Meir cited in the continuation of the discussion. Rambam's Commentary on the Mishna explains that the dyer dyed the wool a different shade of color than that requested by the owner.

If the enhancement exceeds the expenses – **אִם הַשֶּׁבַח יָתֵר עַל הַיְּצִיאָה**: *Tosafot*, citing the Jerusalem Talmud, imply that the expenses are the dyer's wages. If the enhancement of the wool is less than his wage, he receives only the value of the enhancement. Rashi on *Bava Metzia* 78b explains the word expenses as referring to the amount spent by the dyer to purchase the materials needed to dye the wool.

To dye it red for him – **לִצְבּוֹעַ לוֹ אָדוֹם**: Rabbi Meir holds that since the dyer deviated from the request of the owner, he has the status of a robber and acquires the wool due to the change. He therefore returns only the value of the wool to the owner. According to Rabbi Yehuda, he is considered a hired laborer (Ra'avad).

HALAKHA

One who gives wood to a carpenter – הַנּוֹתֵן עֵצִים לֶחָרָשׁ: With regard to one who gives wood to a carpenter to fashion a chair for him and instead he fashions a bench, or if he gives him wood to fashion a beautiful chair and he fashions an ugly one, if the value of the enhancement exceeds the carpenter's expenses, the owner of the wood pays the carpenter for his expenses. If the expenses exceeded the value of the enhancement, he pays only the value of the enhancement, in accordance with the opinion of Rabbi Yehuda (Rambam *Sefer Mishpatim, Hilkhot Sekhirut* 10:4; *Shulḥan Arukh, Ḥoshen Mishpat* 306:3).

Enhancement dye provides to the wool – שֶׁבַח סַמָּנִין עַל הַצֶּמֶר: One who robs another of wool and dye and then proceeds to dye the wool with the stolen dye is obligated to pay only the value of the wool, assuming that its value did not increase due to the dye. If the robbery victim seizes the dyed wool, the court will not interfere, as no conclusion was reached in the Gemara with regard to the *halakha* in such a case. If one robbed another of pigments and wool, then converted the pigments into dye and then dyed the wool, he is liable to compensate the owner for the pigments, according to their value at the time of the robbery (*Sma*). Similarly, if one robbed another of dye and used it to dye his own wool, he is obligated to reimburse him for the dye, in accordance with the Gemara (Rambam *Sefer Nezikin, Hilkhot Gezeila VaAveda* 3:10; *Shulḥan Arukh, Ḥoshen Mishpat* 363:11 and *Shakh* there).

כַּפְּרָא דוּדֵי.

The sediments of dye in **the cauldrons,** that is, the dyer took the dye remaining in the cauldron from previous use, and used that dye for this garment, leading to an inferior result.

תָּנוּ רַבָּנַן: הַנּוֹתֵן עֵצִים לֶחָרָשׁ לַעֲשׂוֹת מֵהֶן כִּסֵּא וְעָשָׂה מֵהֶן סַפְסָל, סַפְסָל וְעָשָׂה מֵהֶן כִּסֵּא – רַבִּי מֵאִיר אוֹמֵר: נוֹתֵן לוֹ דְּמֵי עֵצָיו; רַבִּי יְהוּדָה אוֹמֵר: אִם הַשֶּׁבַח יָתֵר עַל הַיְּצִיאָה – נוֹתֵן לוֹ אֶת הַיְּצִיאָה, וְאִם הַיְּצִיאָה יְתֵירָה עַל הַשֶּׁבַח – נוֹתֵן לוֹ אֶת הַשֶּׁבַח;

§ **The Sages taught** (*Tosefta* 10:8): With regard to **one who gives wood to a carpenter**[H] **to fashion a chair from it and he fashioned a bench from it** instead, or one who gives him wood to fashion **a bench and he fashioned a chair from it** instead, **Rabbi Meir says:** The carpenter **gives him the value of his wood** and keeps the chair or bench, as he has acquired it due to the change. **Rabbi Yehuda says:** He does not acquire the item. Rather, **if the** value of the wood's **enhancement exceeds the** carpenter's **expenses** the owner **gives** the carpenter **the expenses, and if the expenses exceed the enhancement** of the wood **he gives him** the value of **the enhancement.** Since the carpenter deviated from the customer's order, he is entitled to either his expenses or the enhancement, the smaller amount of the two.

וּמוֹדֶה רַבִּי מֵאִיר: אִם נָתַן עֵצִים לֶחָרָשׁ לַעֲשׂוֹת מֵהֶן כִּסֵּא נָאֶה וְעָשָׂה מֵהֶן כִּסֵּא כָּעוּר, סַפְסָל נָאֶה וְעָשָׂה סַפְסָל כָּעוּר, אִם הַשֶּׁבַח יָתֵר עַל הַיְּצִיאָה – נוֹתֵן לוֹ דְּמֵי הַיְּצִיאָה, וְאִם הַיְּצִיאָה יְתֵירָה עַל הַשֶּׁבַח – נוֹתֵן לוֹ דְּמֵי הַשֶּׁבַח.

The *baraita* continues: **And Rabbi Meir concedes** that **if he gave wood to a carpenter to fashion a beautiful chair from it and he fashioned an ugly chair from it,** or to fashion **a beautiful bench** from it **and he fashioned an ugly bench** from it, then **if the** value of the wood's **enhancement exceeds the** carpenter's **expenses** the owner **gives** the carpenter **the value of the expenses, and if the expenses exceed the enhancement he gives him the value of the enhancement.** Since the carpenter did not deviate significantly from the customer's instructions, Rabbi Meir concedes that the carpenter does not acquire the item due to the change.

אִיבַּעְיָא לְהוּ: יֵשׁ שֶׁבַח סַמָּנִין עַל הַצֶּמֶר, אוֹ אֵין שֶׁבַח סַמָּנִין עַל הַצֶּמֶר?

§ In connection with the discussion of the halakhic implications of the enhancement of a garment quoted above, the Gemara records that **a dilemma was raised before** the Sages: What is the *halakha*? That **the enhancement** which **dye** provides **to the wool**[H] **is** substantive, i.e., the dye is considered a separate entity from the wool it dyed? **Or is** the *halakha* that **the enhancement** which **dye** provides **to the wool is not substantive,** i.e., the dye does not remain an independent entity, and it is viewed as if there is only colored wool?

הֵיכִי דָּמֵי? אִילֵימָא דִּגְזַל סַמָּנִין וְדַקִּינְהוּ וּתְרַנְהוּ וְצָבַע בָּהֶן, תֵּיפוֹק לֵיהּ מִשּׁוּם דְּקַנִינְהוּ בְּשִׁינּוּי!

The Gemara asks: **What are the circumstances** in which this dilemma is relevant? **If we say that** the dilemma arises **where one robbed** another of **pigments, and ground them** up **and soaked them** in water, converting them into dye, **and** then **dyed** wool **with them,** then the dilemma would be concerning how the robber returns the pigments. In this case, **derive** the *halakha* **due to** the fact that the robber **acquired** the pigments **due to a change** of form, which occurred when he ground the pigments, and in any event will be obligated to return the value of the pigments at the time of the robbery.

לָא צְרִיכָא, דִּגְזַל סַמָּנִין שְׁרוּיִין וּצְבַע בְּהוּ, מַאי? יֵשׁ שֶׁבַח סַמָּנִין עַל גַּבֵּי צֶמֶר, דְּאָמַר לֵיהּ: הַב לִי סַמָּנַאי דִּשְׁקַלְתִּינְהוּ, אוֹ דִּלְמָא אֵין שֶׁבַח סַמָּנִין עַל גַּבֵּי הַצֶּמֶר, דְּאָמַר לֵיהּ: לֵית לָךְ גַּבַּאי וְלָא מִידֵּי?

The Gemara answers: **No,** it is **necessary** to resolve the dilemma in a case **where** one **robbed** another of **pigments** that had already been **soaked** in water, **and** then **dyed** wool **with them. What** is the *halakha* here? Is **the enhancement** which **dye** provides **to the wool** substantive, i.e., a separate entity, so **that** the owner can **say to** the robber: **Give me my dyes that you took? Or perhaps the enhancement** which **dye** provides **to the wool is not substantive,** but becomes one with the wool, so **that** the robber can **say to** the owner: **I have nothing at all of yours,** since the dyes are no longer considered extant.

אָמְרִי: וְאִי אֵין שֶׁבַח סַמָּנִין עַל גַּבֵּי צֶמֶר, מִי מָצֵי אָמַר לֵיהּ לֵית לָךְ גַּבַּאי וְלָא מִידֵּי? נֵימָא לֵיהּ: הַב לִי סַמָּנַאי דְּאַפְסֵדְתִּינְהוּ!

The Gemara rejects this understanding of the application of the dilemma. The Sages **say: And** even **if the enhancement** which **dye** provides **to the wool is not substantive, can** the robber really **say to him: I have nothing at all of yours? Let** the owner **say to him: Give me my dyes that you have** caused to be **lost.** Even if the dyes are no longer considered extant, the owner is still entitled to monetary compensation for the robbery.

אֶלָּא לְהַךְ גִּיסָא: אֵין שֶׁבַח סַמָּנִין עַל גַּבֵּי הַצֶּמֶר וּבָעֵי שַׁלּוּמֵי לֵיהּ, אוֹ דִּלְמָא יֵשׁ שֶׁבַח סַמָּנִין עַל גַּבֵּי צֶמֶר, וְאָמַר לֵיהּ: הָא מַנְחֵי קַמָּךְ, שְׁקַלִינְהוּ? שְׁקַלִינְהוּ?! בְּמַאי שָׁקְלֵיהּ, בְּצָפוֹן? צָפוֹן עֲבוֹרֵי מִיעֲבַר, הֲשָׁבָה לָא עָבֵיד!

Rather, the dilemma is relevant **to that** other **side** of the question: Is the *halakha* that the **enhancement** which **dye** provides **to the wool is not substantive, and** therefore the robber **needs** to **pay him? Or perhaps** the **enhancement** which **dye** provides **to the wool is substantive, and** the robber **can say to him:** The dyes absorbed into the wool **lie before you; take them.** The Gemara rejects this as well: **Take them? With what** should he **take** the dyes, **with soap?** While **soap does remove** dye from the wool, **it does not return** the dye to the robbery victim, as the dye cannot be recovered.

אֶלָּא הָכָא בְּמַאי עָסְקִינַן – כְּגוֹן דִּגְזַל צֶמֶר וְסַמָּנִין דְּחַד, וּצְבַעֵיהּ לְהַהוּא צֶמֶר בְּהָנַךְ סַמָּנִין, וְקָא מַהֲדַר לֵיהּ נִיהֲלֵיהּ לַצֶּמֶר; יֵשׁ שֶׁבַח סַמָּנִין עַל גַּבֵּי הַצֶּמֶר, וְקָא מַהֲדַר לֵיהּ סַמָּנִין וְצֶמֶר, אוֹ דִּלְמָא אֵין שֶׁבַח סַמָּנִין עַל גַּבֵּי צֶמֶר, וְצֶמֶר מַהֲדַר לֵיהּ, סַמָּנִין לָא מַהֲדַר לֵיהּ?

The Gemara suggests another scenario: **Rather, with what are we dealing here?** We are dealing with a case **where he robbed one** person **of wool and dyes, and dyed that wool with those dyes, and he is returning the** dyed **wool to him.** The dilemma is: Is the *halakha* that **enhancement** which **dye** provides **to the wool is substantive, and** he is therefore **returning** both the **dye and** the **wool to him? Or perhaps enhancement** which **dye** provides **to the wool is not substantive, and** it is only **the wool** that **he is returning to him,** but **he is not returning the dye to him,** since it is no longer extant.

אָמְרִי: תֵּיפּוֹק לֵיהּ דְּאִייַּקַר לֵיהּ נִיהֲלֵיהּ בְּדָמֵי! לָא צְרִיכָא, דְּזַל צִיבְעָא. וְאִיבָּעֵית אֵימָא: כְּגוֹן שֶׁצָּבַע בְּהוּ קוֹפָא.

The Gemara rejects this understanding of the application of the dilemma as well. The Sages **say: Derive** the *halakha* in this case based on the fact **that he increased the value** of the wool **for him,** as dyed wool is more expensive than undyed wool. Consequently, even if the robber has not returned the dye, he reimburses the owner for it when he returns the appreciated wool. The Gemara suggests: **No,** it is **necessary** to resolve the dilemma in a case **where** the cost of **the dye has depreciated.** If the dye is viewed as an independent entity the robber is returning both the wool and the dye. If it is not, he must reimburse the robbery victim for the value of the dye at the time of the robbery. **And if you wish, say** instead: The dilemma is relevant in a case **where** he robbed another of dye and a basket, and **dyed** the **basket with** the dye,[N] in which case the dye does not increase the value of the dyed item.

רָבִינָא אָמַר: הָכָא בְּמַאי עָסְקִינַן – כְּגוֹן דְּצֶמֶר דְּחַד וְסַמָּנִין דְּחַד, וְקָאָתֵי קוֹף וּצְבַעֵיהּ לְהַהוּא צֶמֶר בְּהָנַךְ סַמָּנִין; יֵשׁ שֶׁבַח סַמָּנִין עַל גַּבֵּי צֶמֶר, דְּאָמַר לֵיהּ: הַב לִי סַמָּנַאי דְּגַבָּךְ נִינְהוּ. אוֹ דִּלְמָא אֵין שֶׁבַח סַמָּנִין עַל גַּבֵּי צֶמֶר, וְאָמַר לֵיהּ: לֵית לָךְ גַּבַּאי כְּלוּם?

The Gemara presents an alternative understanding of the case where the dilemma applies. **Ravina said: With what are we dealing here?** We are dealing with a case **where** there was **wool** that belonged to **one** person **and dyes that** belonged to **one** other person, **and a monkey came and dyed that wool with those dyes.** The dilemma is as follows: Is the *halakha* that **enhancement** which **dye** provides **to the wool is substantive,** so **that** the owner of the dye can **say to** the owner of the wool: **Give me my dyes that are with you? Or perhaps enhancement** which **dye** provides **to the wool is not substantive and** the owner of the wool can **say to** the owner of the dye: **There is nothing** of yours **with me,** and he is exempt from liability because the dyes are no longer extant.

תָּא שְׁמַע: בֶּגֶד שֶׁצְּבָעוֹ בִּקְלִיפֵּי עָרְלָה – יִדָּלֵק; אַלְמָא חֲזוּתָא מִילְּתָא הִיא.

Having determined the scenario in which the dilemma is relevant, the Gemara proceeds to resolve the dilemma. **Come** and **hear** a solution from a mishna (*Orla* 3:1): **A garment that one dyed with** dye extracted from **peels of *orla*,**[BH] i.e., fruit that grows on a tree during its first three years, **must be burned,** as it is prohibited to derive benefit from *orla*. **Apparently,** the enhancement of an item's **appearance is** considered a significant **matter,** and the dye therefore remains an independent substance even after having been absorbed by the wool.

אָמַר רָבָא: הֲנָאָה הַנִּרְאָה לָעֵינַיִם אָסְרָה תּוֹרָה, דְּתַנְיָא: "עֲרֵלִים לֹא יֵאָכֵל" – אֵין לִי אֶלָּא אִיסּוּר אֲכִילָה, מִנַּיִן שֶׁלֹּא יֵהָנֶה מִמֶּנּוּ, וְלֹא יִצְבַּע [בּוֹ], וְלֹא יַדְלִיק בּוֹ אֶת הַנֵּר?

The Gemara rejects this resolution. **Rava said:** The reason the garment must be burned is not because the dye remains an independent substance. Rather, it is because **the Torah prohibited benefit that is visible to the eye, as it is taught** in a *baraita*: The verse states: "And shall have planted all manner of trees for food, then you shall count the fruit thereof as forbidden; three years shall it be as **forbidden** [*areilim*] to you; **it shall not be eaten**" (Leviticus 19:23). From this verse **I have** derived **only a prohibition** against **eating** it; **from where** is it derived that one **may not** even derive **benefit**[H] **from it, and** that **one may not dye with** dyes extracted from the fruit, **and** that **one may not light a lamp with** oil extracted from the fruit?

NOTES

He dyed the basket [*kofa*] with the dye – שֶׁצָּבַע בְּהוּ קוֹפָא: Rashi offers two translations for the word *kofa*: Basket and monkey, and explains that in either case the value of the dyed item does not increase. Others understand that a monkey, owned by the robber, dyed the wool, and such a haphazard process certainly would not have increased the wool's value (*Arukh*). *Tosafot* suggest that the Gemara means the wool was dyed in an ugly fashion, similar to the ugliness of a monkey. The Ba'al HaMaor notes that this entire discussion is relevant only according to the opinion that one is exempt from paying for indirect damage. According to the opinion that one is liable to pay for indirect damage, the robber would be obligated to pay for the damage to the dye.

BACKGROUND

Peels of *orla* – קְלִיפֵּי עָרְלָה: It is prohibited to eat or derive benefit from the fruit that grows during the first three years after a tree has been planted (see Leviticus 19:23). This prohibition applies only to the fruit, including its peel, but not to the other parts of the tree. In addition, the prohibition does not apply to trees planted as a fence for property or as a wind buffer rather than for their fruit.

The Gemara is referring primarily to pomegranate peels, from which a very durable, reddish-brown dye can be extracted, and also to peels of walnuts, from which a green dye can be extracted. While any pomegranate or walnut peel could have been used for this purpose, dyers often preferred to use fruits that would in any case not be eaten.

HALAKHA

A garment that one dyed with peels of *orla* – בֶּגֶד שֶׁצְּבָעוֹ בִּקְלִיפֵּי עָרְלָה: A garment that was dyed with dye made from peels of *orla* must be burned (Rambam *Sefer Kedusha*, *Hilkhot Ma'akhalot Assurot* 16:20).

From where is it derived that one may not even derive benefit, etc. – מִנַּיִן שֶׁלֹּא יֵהָנֶה וכו׳: All fruit that a tree produces during the first three years after its planting is *orla*, and it is prohibited to derive benefit from any part of such fruit, including the peel (Rambam *Sefer Kedusha*, *Hilkhot Ma'akhalot Assurot* 10:9; *Shulhan Arukh*, *Yoreh De'a* 294:1).

תַּלְמוּד לוֹמַר: ״וַעֲרַלְתֶּם עָרְלָתוֹ אֶת פִּרְיוֹ...עֲרֵלִים לֹא יֵאָכֵל״, לְרַבּוֹת אֶת כּוּלָּם.

The *baraita* answers: **The verse states: "Then you shall count the fruit thereof [*orlato*] as forbidden [*araltem*].** Three years shall it be as **forbidden [*areilim*]** to you; **it shall not be eaten"** (Leviticus 19:23), **to include all these** types of benefit in the prohibition. Consequently, there is an explicit derivation that an item dyed with *orla* dye is forbidden.

HALAKHA

A garment that one dyed with the peels of produce from the Sabbatical Year – בֶּגֶד שֶׁצְּבָעוֹ בִּקְלִיפֵּי שְׁבִיעִית: It is prohibited to dye wool using the peels of produce from the Sabbatical Year and then receive payment for the dyeing process (Rambam *Sefer Zera'im, Hilkhot Shemitta VeYovel* 6:2).

תָּא שְׁמַע: בֶּגֶד שֶׁצְּבָעוֹ בִּקְלִיפֵּי שְׁבִיעִית – יִדָּלֵק. שָׁאנֵי הָתָם, דְּאָמַר קְרָא: ״תִּהְיֶה״, בַּהֲוָיָתָהּ תְּהֵא.

The Gemara attempts another resolution of the dilemma. **Come** and **hear** a resolution from that which was taught in a *baraita*: **A garment that one dyed with** dye extracted from **the peels of** produce from the **Sabbatical** Year[H] must be **burned** when the time for the elimination of Sabbatical Year produce arrives. This indicates that the dye evidently remains an independent substance. The Gemara rejects this proof: It **is different there, as the verse states: "Shall** all the increase thereof **be"** (Leviticus 25:7), and the phrase: "Shall be," teaches that it **will** always **remain as it is,** i.e., it retains its status as Sabbatical Year produce despite any change to its form.

Perek **IX**
Daf **101** Amud **b**

רָבָא רָמֵי, תְּנַן: בֶּגֶד שֶׁצְּבָעוֹ בִּקְלִיפֵּי עָרְלָה – יִדָּלֵק; אַלְמָא חֲזוּתָא מִילְּתָא הִיא. וּרְמִינְהִי: רְבִיעִית דָּם שֶׁנִּבְלְעָה בְּבַיִת – הַבַּיִת טָמֵא, וְאָמְרִי לַהּ: הַבַּיִת טָהוֹר. וְלָא פְּלִיגִי, הָא בְּכֵלִים דַּהֲווֹ מֵעִיקָּרָא, הָא בְּכֵלִים דְּאָתוּ לְבַסּוֹף;

The Gemara states that **Rava raises a contradiction: We learned** in a mishna (*Orla* 3:1): **A garment that one dyed with** dye extracted from **peels of *orla* must be burned. Apparently,** the change in **appearance** precipitated by the *orla* peels **is** considered a significant **matter,** and the dye retains its status as *orla*. **And raise a contradiction** from another mishna (*Oholot* 3:2): With regard to **a quarter-*log* of blood**[N] from a corpse **that was absorbed in** the floor of **a house,**[NH] every vessel in **the house is ritually impure** by virtue of being under the same roof as the blood. **And some say** that any vessel in **the house is ritually pure. And** these two statements **do not disagree,** as **this** first statement was **in reference to vessels that were** in the house **at the outset,** before the blood was absorbed; and **this** second statement was **in reference to vessels that came** into the house **at the end,** after the blood had already been absorbed.

נִבְלְעָה בִּכְסוּת, רוֹאִין, אִם מִתְכַּבֶּסֶת הַכְּסוּת וְיוֹצֵא מִמֶּנָּה רְבִיעִית דָּם – טְמֵאָה, וְאִם לָאו – טְהוֹרָה!

The mishna continues: If the blood **was absorbed in a garment,**[H] it is **examined,** and **if the garment is washed and a quarter-*log* of blood emerges from it, it is ritually impure,** and the garment imparts ritual impurity to the vessels in the house as well. **But if not,** i.e., if less than a quarter-*log* of blood emerges, then it **is pure,** and it does not impart impurity. Apparently, only the blood that can be removed from the garment is considered blood, while the blood absorbed in the garment is insignificant. If this is the case, the change in appearance precipitated by the blood is not considered a significant matter, and the blood absorbed in the garment does not remain an independent substance.

NOTES

A quarter-*log* of blood – רְבִיעִית דָּם: A quarter-*log* of blood from a corpse renders items impure just as a corpse itself would, imparting impurity by contact or carrying, and, as in this case, by virtue of being under the same roof. The mishna is referring to a case where there was precisely one quarter-*log* of blood.

That was absorbed in a house, etc. – שֶׁנִּבְלְעָה בְּבַיִת וכו׳: Vessels that were in a house which contained a quarter-*log* of blood that had not yet been absorbed by the floor are rendered impure. Vessels that were brought into the house after the blood was absorbed are not rendered impure. The Ra'avad explains that while blood in the floor of the house continues to render items impure, the assumption is that some of the blood evaporates during the absorption process, and since there was precisely a quarter-*log* of blood to begin with, there is insufficient blood remaining to render the vessels impure. The Meiri, by contrast, simply understands that blood that was absorbed in the ground ceases to render items impure.

HALAKHA

A quarter-*log* of blood that was absorbed in a house – רְבִיעִית דָּם שֶׁנִּבְלְעָה בְּבַיִת: A quarter-*log* of blood in a house renders all of the vessels in the house impure until the blood is absorbed in the floor of the house. Items that were in the house prior to the blood becoming absorbed remain impure even after the blood has been absorbed (Rambam *Sefer Tahara, Hilkhot Tumat Met* 4:11).

Was absorbed in a garment – נִבְלְעָה בִּכְסוּת: If blood was absorbed in a garment such that a quarter-*log* would flow out of it when it was washed, the garment imparts ritual impurity to items that come in contact with it, to one who carries it, and to any items that are found under the same roof with it. If less than a quarter-*log* of blood would flow out of it when washed, it would not impart ritual impurity to items that are found under the same roof but would be subject to the *halakhot* of an item that came in contact with a corpse. This is because an absorbed substance that cannot be removed is ritually pure (Rambam *Sefer Tahara, Hilkhot Tumat Met* 4:13).

אֲמַר רַב כָּהֲנָא: מִקּוּלֵּי רְבִיעִיּוֹת שָׁנוּ כָּאן, בְּדַם תְּבוּסָה דְּרַבָּנַן.

The Gemara presents an answer. **Rav Kahana said:** A *halakha* **from** among **the leniencies** applied to the measurements **of a quarter-*log*** was **taught here,** as the mishna is written **in reference to the blood of submission**[NH] that is discharged from a body at the time of death, and such blood is ritually impure **by rabbinic law,** but in general, a change in appearance precipitated by blood is significant.

רָבָא רָמֵי, תְּנַן: מִמִּין הַצּוֹבְעִין – סְפִיחֵי סָטִים וְקוֹצָה, יֵשׁ לָהֶן שְׁבִיעִית וְלִדְמֵיהֶן שְׁבִיעִית, יֵשׁ לָהֶן בִּיעוּר וְלִדְמֵיהֶן בִּיעוּר; אַלְמָא, עֵצִים יֵשׁ בָּהֶן מִשּׁוּם קְדוּשַּׁת שְׁבִיעִית.

§ Having cited a contradiction raised by Rava, the Gemara proceeds to cite another. **Rava raises** another **contradiction. We learned** in a mishna (*Shevi'it* 7:1): Concerning plants **from** among **the species that** are used as **dyes,**[NH] for example the ***sefiḥin***, i.e., produce that grew without being intentionally planted, **of woad**[B] **and safflower;**[B] **they have** sanctity of the **Sabbatical** Year **and money** exchanged for **them has** sanctity of the **Sabbatical** Year. Additionally, **they are** subject to the *halakha* of **eradication,**[B] **and money** exchanged for **them is** subject to the *halakha* of **eradication. Apparently, wood,** a type of inedible growth, **is subject to the sanctity of the Sabbatical** Year despite the fact that it is not edible.

NOTES

The blood of submission – **דַּם תְּבוּסָה**: The *tanna'im* in the mishna (*Oholot* 3:5) disagree with regard to the precise definition of this blood. According to Rabbi Akiva, it is the last one-eighth of a *log* emitted before death, from the body of a person who was killed, and the first one-eighth of a *log* emitted after the death. Rabbi Yishmael defines the blood of submission in the same manner but extends it to a quarter-*log* of blood emitted before and after death. Other *tanna'im* offer different definitions. The blood of submission imparts impurity by rabbinic decree (see *Tosefta*, *Oholot* 4:12; Rabbi Shimshon of Saens, *Oholot* 3:5).

From among the species that are used as dyes – **מִמִּין הַצּוֹבְעִין**: The sanctity of the Sabbatical Year applies to all produce that is fit for consumption by people or animals, as well as plants that are used as dyes. The halakhic ramifications of this sanctity include the following *halakhot*: One may not use such produce for any unconventional purpose, and if the produce is exchanged with some other item, that item is endowed with the sanctity of the Sabbatical Year.

HALAKHA

The blood of submission – **דַּם תְּבוּסָה**: Blood from a living body that was mixed with blood from a corpse so that there is in total a quarter-*log* of blood is considered blood of submission, unless it is known that the majority of the blood came from the living body. The Sages instituted that such blood imparts ritual impurity to one who touches it, to one who carries it, and to items that are found under the same roof with it (Rambam *Sefer Tahara*, *Hilkhot Tumat Met* 2:13).

From among the species that are used as dyes – **מִמִּין הַצּוֹבְעִין**: A plant that is used as a dye is subject to the sanctity of the Sabbatical Year and must be eradicated once it is no longer found in the fields. The same applies to any money exchanged for this plant (Rambam *Sefer Zera'im*, *Hilkhot Shemitta VeYovel* 7:13).

BACKGROUND

Safflower – **קוֹצָה**: Safflower, also known as *Carthamus tinctorius* L., is referred to in the Talmud as either *ḥariya*, *morika*, or as it appears here, *kotza*. It is a thorny plant from the Asteraceae family, whose flowers were used to make yellow dye. Today its leaves are used as a high-quality fodder for animals and its seeds are used to produce oil.

Safflower

Eradication – **בִּיעוּר**: There are two primary opinions with regard to the requirement to eradicate produce of the Sabbatical Year. Moreover, among those who hold each opinion there is disagreement with regard to the details. Rashi, the Rambam, and the Ra'avad hold that eradication must be performed after a given type of produce is no longer found in the field. It is performed by destroying any of that same species of produce that remains in one's house, by burning it, throwing it into the sea, or the like.

Tosafot, the *Smag*, and the Ramban maintain that the process of eradication entails removing the produce from one's house and then declaring it ownerless: When a given type of produce is no longer in the field one removes it from his home, and then declares it ownerless and renders it available to both the poor and the wealthy to eat in the field. At that point anyone may consume it, including the owner if he reacquires it from its ownerless state. According to some authorities, it may be consumed only by the poor.

BACKGROUND

Woad – **סָטִים**: Known as *Isatis tinctoria* L., and colloquially as woad, this is a biannual or multiannual plant from the Brassicaceae family which reaches up to a meter in height, with simple leaves and yellow flowers. By means of various compressing and fermenting processes, a very durable indigo blue dye can be extracted from its leaves. Nowadays, the use of woad for dye production has all but ceased, as dye producers now make a less expensive, synthetic indigo dye. Although woad is not cultivated, it can be found growing naturally in many places in Eretz Yisrael, and it is occasionally referred to as the Asp of Jerusalem.

Woad flowers

Old woad mill in Thörey, Germany

Indigo from woad

HALAKHA

Reed leaves, etc. – עלי קנים וכו׳: The halakhic status of growths from the Sabbatical Year that are not generally eaten is dependent on the owner's intention. If he plans to use them as firewood they are considered firewood, and if he wishes to eat them they are considered produce of the Sabbatical Year (Rambam *Sefer Zera'im, Hilkhot Shemitta VeYovel* 5:11).

BACKGROUND

Storage – חבא: It seems that the reference here is to a method of crop storage where the produce is piled up and then covered with stubble and straw. This method is still practiced in many places in the world, and is also mentioned in the Jerusalem Talmud.

NOTES

Wood used to provide heat – עצים דמשחן: Rashi explains that this is a particular type of oily wood used specifically as kindling. The Rid adds that it could also include any wood used for cooking. Rabbeinu Ḥananel writes that the Gemara is not referring to a specific type of wood. Rather, it is making a general observation that wood is often used to provide warmth, in which case the benefit and consumption coincide.

ורמינהי: עלי קנים ועלי גפנים שגיבבן בחבא על פני השדה, לקטן לאכילה – יש בהן משום קדושת שביעית, לעצים – אין בהן משום קדושת שביעית!

And raise a contradiction from a *baraita*: With regard to **reed leaves**[H] **and vine leaves that one piled for storage**[B] **upon the field,** if he **gathered them for eating, they are subject to the sanctity of the Sabbatical** Year; if he gathered them **for** use as **wood,** e.g., for kindling a fire, **they are not subject to the sanctity of the Sabbatical** Year. Apparently, wood or any other non-food product is not subject to the sanctity of the Sabbatical Year.

ומשני, אמר קרא: ״לאכלה״, במי שהנאתו וביעורו שוין, יצאו עצים שהנאתן אחר ביעורן.

And Rava **answers** the contradiction, as **the verse states:** "And the Sabbath produce of the land shall be **for food** for you" (Leviticus 25:6), indicating that the sanctity of the Sabbatical Year takes effect only **with regard to those** items **whose benefit and whose consumption coincide,** as is the case with regard to food. **Wood is excluded, as its benefit follows its consumption.** The primary purpose of kindling wood is not accomplished with the burning of the wood; rather, it is with the charcoal that heats the oven. Therefore, wood is not subject to the sanctity of the Sabbatical Year.

והא איכא עצים דמשחן, דהנאתן וביעורן שוין!

The Gemara objects: **But isn't there wood** that is used to provide **heat,**[N] **whose benefit coincides with its consumption,** as one enjoys the warmth provided by the fire while the wood is burned?

אמר רבא:

Rava said:

Perek **IX**
Daf **102** Amud **a**

HALAKHA

One may not transfer Sabbatical Year produce, etc. – אין מוסרין פירות שביעית וכו׳: It is prohibited to use produce of the Sabbatical Year for laundering, sprinkling, as a poultice, or as an emetic. The *halakha* is in accordance with the opinion of the Rabbis (Rambam *Sefer Zera'im, Hilkhot Shemitta VeYovel* 5:10).

BACKGROUND

Laundering – כבוסה: In talmudic times, clothes were laundered with a variety of substances. Soda and potash, found in various plants and rocks, and the ash of burnt plants were all used for this purpose.

Ore containing potash

סתם עצים להסקה הן עומדין.

Unspecified wood exists for fuel, i.e., charcoal, so its benefit follows its consumption.

אמר רב כהנא: ועצים להסקה תנאי היא; דתניא: אין מוסרין פירות שביעית לא למשרה ולא לכבוסה, ורבי יוסי אומר: נותנין פירות שביעית לתוך המשרה ולתוך הכבוסה.

Rav Kahana says: And the matter of whether **kindling wood,** whose benefit follows its consumption, is subject to the sanctity of the Sabbatical Year **is** a dispute among the ***tanna'im*****, as it is taught** in the *Tosefta* (*Shevi'it* 6:25): **One may not transfer Sabbatical Year produce,**[H] e.g., wine, to another person; **neither for soaking** flax to prepare it for spinning, as the benefit derived from the flax follows its soaking, when the soaked and spun thread is woven into a garment; **nor or for laundering**[B] with it, as the benefit derived follows the laundering when one wears the clean clothes. Soaking the flax or laundering the garment in wine is considered the consumption of the wine, as it is no longer potable. **And Rabbi Yosei says: One may transfer** to another **Sabbatical** Year **produce for soaking and for laundering.**

מאי טעמא דרבנן? אמר קרא: ״לאכלה״ – ולא למשרה, ״לאכלה״ – ולא לכבוסה; ורבי יוסי אומר, אמר קרא: ״לכם״, לכל צרכיכם.

The Gemara asks: **What is the reasoning** for the statement **of the Rabbis? The verse states** with regard to Sabbatical Year produce: **"For food"** (Leviticus 25:6), from which it is inferred: **But not for soaking; "for food," but not for laundering. And Rabbi Yosei says** that it is permitted, as **the verse** also **states: "For you,"** from which it is inferred: For you, **for all your needs,** even for soaking and for laundering.

ורבנן נמי, הכתיב ״לכם״! ״לכם״ דומיא ד״לאכלה״ – במי שהנאתו וביעורו שוין, יצאו משרה וכבוסה שהנאתן אחר ביעורן.

The Gemara asks: **And** according to **the Rabbis as well, isn't it written: "For you"?** How do they explain that term? The Gemara answers: From that term "for you" it is derived: **"For you," similar to "for food,"** i.e., the sanctity of the Sabbatical Year takes effect **with regard to those** items **whose benefit and whose consumption coincide,** which **excludes soaking and laundering, where** the items' **benefit follows their consumption.**

וְרַבִּי יוֹסֵי נַמִי, הָכְתִיב "לְאׇכְלָה"! אָמַר לָךְ: הַהוּא מִיבְּעֵי לֵיהּ לְכִדְתַנְיָא, דְּתַנְיָא: "לְאׇכְלָה" – וְלֹא לְמְלוֹגְמָא; אַתָּה אוֹמֵר: "לְאׇכְלָה" וְלֹא לְמְלוֹגְמָא, אוֹ אֵינוֹ אֶלָּא "לְאׇכְלָה" וְלֹא לִכְבוּסָה? כְּשֶׁהוּא אוֹמֵר: "לָכֶם" – הֲרֵי כְּבוּסָה אָמוּר, הָא מָה אֲנִי מְקַיֵּים "לְאׇכְלָה"? "לְאׇכְלָה" – וְלֹא לְמְלוֹגְמָא.

The Gemara asks: **And according to Rabbi Yosei as well, isn't it written: "For food"?** Rabbi Yosei could have **said to you: That** term **is necessary for that which is taught** in a *baraita*, **as it is taught:** The verse states: **"For food," but not for a poultice** [*melogema*].[NL] The *baraita* continues: Do **you say "for food" but not for a poultice, or** perhaps **it is only "for food" but not for laundering? When** the verse **says: "For you," laundering is** already **stated** as permitted since it includes all of one's bodily needs. **How do I realize** the meaning of that which the verse states: **"For food"?** It is **"for food" but not for a poultice.**

וּמָה רָאִיתָ לְרַבּוֹת הַכְּבוּסָה וּלְהוֹצִיא אֶת הַמְּלוֹגְמָא? מְרַבֶּה אֲנִי אֶת הַכְּבוּסָה שֶׁשָּׁוָה בְּכׇל אָדָם, וּמוֹצִיא אֲנִי אֶת הַמְּלוֹגְמָא שֶׁאֵינוֹ שָׁוֶה בְּכׇל אָדָם.

The *baraita* continues. Should one ask: **And what did you see** that led you **to include the** use of Sabbatical Year produce for **laundering and to exclude the** use of Sabbatical Year produce as **a poultice?** Perhaps the opposite should be said. The *baraita* answers: **I include the** use for **laundering, which** applies **equally to every person,** as everyone needs clean clothes, **and I exclude the** use as **a poultice, which** does **not** apply **equally to every person;** it is only for the ill wounded.

כְּמַאן אָזְלָא הָא דְּתַנְיָא: "לְאׇכְלָה" – וְלֹא לְמְלוֹגְמָא, "לְאׇכְלָה" – וְלֹא לְזִילּוּף, "לְאׇכְלָה" – וְלֹא לַעֲשׂוֹת מִמֶּנָּה אַפִּיקְטְוִיזִין, כְּמַאן? כְּרַבִּי יוֹסֵי, דְּאִי כְּרַבָּנַן – אִיכָּא נַמִי מִשְׁרָה וּכְבוּסָה.

In accordance with whose opinion is **that which is taught** in a *baraita* with regard to Sabbatical Year produce: **"For food," but not for a poultice;** "**for food," but not for sprinkling**[NB] wine in one's house to provide a pleasant fragrance; **"for food," but not to make an emetic** [*apiktevizin*][L] **from it** to induce vomiting? **In accordance with whose** opinion is this *baraita*? It is **in accordance with** the opinion of **Rabbi Yosei, as, if** it were **in accordance with** the opinion of **the Rabbis, is there** not **also soaking and laundering** that should have been excluded from the *baraita*, as in the Rabbis' opinion the use of Sabbatical Year produce for those purposes is forbidden?

"רַבִּי יְהוּדָה אוֹמֵר: אִם הַשֶּׁבַח" כו'. (סִימָן סבן.)

§ The mishna (100b) teaches that if the owner gave wool to a dyer to dye it red and instead he dyed it black, Rabbi Meir says: The dyer gives the owner of the wool the value of his wool. **Rabbi Yehuda says: If** the value of **the enhancement** exceeds the dyer's expenses, the owner of the wool gives the dyer the expenses. If the expenses exceed the enhancement, he gives him the value of the enhancement. The Gemara provides **a mnemonic** device, the acrostic ***saban***, for the names of the Sages involved in the following incident; each letter in the acrostic represents the middle letter of one of the names: *Samekh*, Rav Yosef; *beit*, Rabbi Abba; *nun*, Rav Huna.

יָתֵיב רַב יוֹסֵף אֲחוֹרֵי דְּרַבִּי אַבָּא קַמֵּיהּ דְּרַב הוּנָא, וְיָתֵיב רַב הוּנָא וְקָאָמַר: הֲלָכָה כְּרַבִּי יְהוֹשֻׁעַ בֶּן קׇרְחָה וַהֲלָכָה כְּרַבִּי יְהוּדָה.

The Gemara relates: **Rav Yosef was sitting behind Rabbi Abba,** and they were both sitting **before Rav Huna. And Rav Huna was sitting and saying:** The ***halakha*** **is in accordance with the** opinion of **Rabbi Yehoshua ben Korḥa and the *halakha* is in accordance with** the opinion of **Rabbi Yehuda.**

אַהַדְרִינְהוּ רַב יוֹסֵף לְאַפֵּיהּ, אֲמַר: בִּשְׁלָמָא רַבִּי יְהוֹשֻׁעַ בֶּן קׇרְחָה אִצְטְרִיךְ, סָלְקָא דַּעְתָּךְ אָמֵינָא יָחִיד וְרַבִּים הֲלָכָה כְּרַבִּים, קָא מַשְׁמַע לַן הֲלָכָה כְּיָחִיד.

Rav Yosef **turned his face** in disdain of Rav Huna's statement. **He said: Granted,** stating that the *halakha* is in accordance with the opinion of **Rabbi Yehoshua ben Korḥa is necessary,** as it would **enter your mind to say** that there is a principle that when there is a dispute between **an individual and the many,** the ***halakha*** is **in accordance with** the opinion of **the many.** Rav Huna therefore **teaches us** that in this case the ***halakha*** **is in accordance with** the opinion of Rabbi Yehoshua ben Korḥa, despite the fact that he is **an individual.**

רַבִּי יְהוֹשֻׁעַ בֶּן קׇרְחָה מַאי הִיא? דְּתַנְיָא, רַבִּי יְהוֹשֻׁעַ בֶּן קׇרְחָה אוֹמֵר: מִלְוָה בִּשְׁטָר אֵין נִפְרָעִין מֵהֶן, מִלְוָה עַל פֶּה נִפְרָעִין מֵהֶן, מִפְּנֵי שֶׁהוּא כְּמַצִּיל מִיָּדָם.

The Gemara interrupts Rav Yosef's remark and asks: **What is** the ruling of **Rabbi Yehoshua ben Korḥa** to which Rav Huna is referring? It is **as it is taught** in a *baraita*: **Rabbi Yehoshua ben Korḥa says** that with regard to **a loan with** a promissory **note, one may not collect**[NH] the loan **from** gentiles near the time of their holidays, but with regard to **a loan by oral** agreement, **one may collect from** gentiles even near the time of their holidays, **because** the creditor is considered **as one who salvages** money **from their possession.**

NOTES

Poultice [*melogema*] – מְלוֹגְמָא: Rashi interprets *melogema* as a poultice, i.e., a soft, moist mass of cloth and herbs applied hot as a medicament to the body, while Rav Naḥshon Gaon explains that it is a kind of rinse used to clean one's mouth.

But not for sprinkling – וְלֹא לְזִילּוּף: In talmudic times, fragrant liquids such as wine would be sprinkled around a residence to infuse the air with a pleasant aroma. Since this was done primarily by the affluent, it was not considered a practice which applies equally to every person, and it was therefore prohibited to use produce of the Sabbatical Year for this purpose (Rashi).

One may not collect – אֵין נִפְרָעִין: One may not collect a loan from gentiles or provide them with loans near the time of their holidays, because it is likely that they will thank their deities for granting them either the loan or the wherewithal to repay their debts. Rabbi Yehoshua ben Korḥa limits this prohibition to the collection of loans granted with a promissory note, because they can be collected at a later time. He allows one to collect a loan granted by oral agreement because there is no guarantee that one will be able to collect it after the holiday.

LANGUAGE

Poultice [*melogema*] – מְלוֹגְמָא: From the Greek μάλαγμα, *malagma*, meaning a bandage for a wound.

Emetic [*apiktevizin*] – אַפִּיקְטְוִיזִין: Possibly from the Greek ἔκπτυσις, *ekptusis*, meaning expectoration.

BACKGROUND

Sprinkling – זִילּוּף: In talmudic times, people employed various methods to infuse the air of their homes with a pleasant smell and to neutralize unwanted odors. At times they would burn incense, and other times they would sprinkle wine. A special wine with a strong smell was used for this purpose. Sprinkling was a luxurious practice, held in such high regard by wealthy individuals that they would often spend more on wine for sprinkling than on wine for drinking.

HALAKHA

With regard to a loan with a promissory note one may not collect, etc. – מִלְוָה בִּשְׁטָר אֵין נִפְרָעִין וכו׳: One may not collect a loan with a promissory note from a gentile during the three days preceding a gentile holiday. The same applies to a loan granted in exchange for collateral. By contrast, it is permitted to collect a loan given by oral agreement, because the creditor is considered as one who salvages his money, since he may not be able to collect it after the holiday. In a time and place where the gentiles rule over the Jews, one may collect even a loan with a promissory note, as the gentile courts may not enforce the agreement (*Shakh*, citing *Tosafot*). Nowadays, the accepted practice is to allow the collection of loans at any time (Rambam *Sefer HaMadda*, *Hilkhot Avoda Zara* 9:1; *Shulḥan Arukh*, *Yoreh De'a* 148:1 and *Shakh* there).

HALAKHA

Whoever reneges – כָּל הַחוֹזֵר: Whoever reneges on an agreement before its terms have been fulfilled is at a disadvantage, so that if the purchaser reneges after paying a portion of the money, the seller may decide to cancel the transaction entirely and return what has been paid. Alternatively, he may provide the purchaser with inferior-quality land equal in value to the amount that the purchaser already paid. If the seller reneges, the purchaser may cancel the transaction and claim a refund, which the seller must provide with either money or his superior-quality land (Rambam *Sefer Kinyan, Hilkhot Mekhira* 8:2; *Shulḥan Arukh, Ḥoshen Mishpat* 190:10).

אֶלָּא הֲלָכָה כְּרַבִּי יְהוּדָה לָמָּה לִי? מַחֲלוֹקֶת וְאַחַר כָּךְ סְתָם הִיא, וּמַחֲלוֹקֶת וְאַחַר כָּךְ סְתָם הֲלָכָה כִּסְתָם!

But with regard to the statement that the ***halakha*** **is in accordance with** the opinion of **Rabbi Yehuda, why do I** need it? This **is** an example of the Mishna recording **a dispute, and afterward** recording only one side of that dispute as **an unattributed opinion. And** the principle is that when the Mishna records **a dispute, and afterward** records only one side of that dispute as **an unattributed opinion,** then **the *halakha*** **is in accordance with the unattributed opinion.**

מַחֲלוֹקֶת בְּבָבָא קַמָּא: לִצְבּוֹעַ לוֹ אָדוֹם וּצְבָעוֹ שָׁחוֹר, שָׁחוֹר וּצְבָעוֹ אָדוֹם – רַבִּי מֵאִיר אוֹמֵר: נוֹתֵן לוֹ דְּמֵי צַמְרוֹ, רַבִּי יְהוּדָה אוֹמֵר: אִם הַשֶּׁבַח יָתֵר עַל הַיְצִיאָה – נוֹתֵן לוֹ אֶת הַיְצִיאָה, וְאִם הַיְצִיאָה יְתֵירָה עַל הַשֶּׁבַח – נוֹתֵן לוֹ אֶת הַשֶּׁבַח; וּסְתָם בְּבָבָא מְצִיעָא, דִּתְנַן: כׇּל הַמְשַׁנֶּה – יָדוֹ עַל הַתַּחְתּוֹנָה, וְכׇל הַחוֹזֵר בּוֹ – יָדוֹ עַל הַתַּחְתּוֹנָה.

The Gemara identifies the dispute and the unattributed mishna. The **dispute** is found **in** tractate ***Bava Kamma***: If one gave wool to a dyer **to dye it red for him and** instead **he dyed it black,** or to dye it **black and he dyed it red, Rabbi Meir says:** The dyer **gives** the owner of the wool **the value of his wool. Rabbi Yehuda says: If** the value of **the enhancement exceeds the expenses,** the owner of the wool **gives the expenses to** the dyer. **And if the expenses exceed the enhancement, he gives him** the value of **the enhancement. And the unattributed** mishna appears **in** tractate ***Bava Metzia*****, as we learned** in a mishna there (76a): **Whoever changes** from the terms of an agreement **is at a disadvantage, and whoever reneges**[H] **from** an agreement **is at a disadvantage.** This unattributed mishna accords with the opinion of Rabbi Yehuda, who holds that a craftsman who deviates from his assignment receives either the expenses or the enhancement, whichever is of lesser value.

וְרַב הוּנָא? אִצְטְרִיךְ, סָלְקָא דַּעְתָּךְ אָמֵינָא אֵין סֵדֶר לַמִּשְׁנָה, וּסְתָם וְאַחַר כָּךְ מַחֲלוֹקֶת הִיא. וְרַב יוֹסֵף? אִי הָכִי, כׇּל מַחֲלוֹקֶת וְאַחַר כָּךְ סְתָמָא, נֵימָא: אֵין סֵדֶר לַמִּשְׁנָה, וּסְתָם וְאַחַר כָּךְ מַחֲלוֹקֶת הִיא.

The Gemara asks: **And** being that this is a dispute and afterward an unattributed opinion, why did **Rav Huna** find it necessary to state that the *halakha* follows the opinion of Rabbi Yehuda? **It is necessary,** as it would **enter your mind to say** that **the Mishna is not sequential and,** in fact, this **is** a case of **an unattributed** ruling **followed by a dispute. And** why does **Rav Yosef** disagree? He disagrees because **if that is so,** then with regard to **every** case where **a dispute** is recorded **and afterward an unattributed** opinion is recorded, **let us say: The Mishna is not sequential, and** this **is** a case of **an unattributed** ruling **followed by a dispute.**

וְרַב הוּנָא? כִּי לָא אָמְרִינַן אֵין סֵדֶר לַמִּשְׁנָה – בַּחֲדָא מַסֶּכְתָּא, אֲבָל בִּתְרֵי מַסֶּכְתּוֹת אָמְרִינַן. וְרַב יוֹסֵף? כּוּלָּהּ נְזִיקִין חֲדָא מַסֶּכְתָּא הִיא.

And Rav Huna would respond: The situation **where we do not say** that **the Mishna is not sequential,** i.e., where we say that the Mishna is sequential, is only when both *mishnayot* appear **in one tractate, but** when they appear **in two** different **tractates we say** that the Mishna is not sequential. Since these *mishnayot* are found in two different tractates, *Bava Kamma* and *Bava Metzia*, the assumption is that the Mishna is not sequential. **And Rav Yosef** would respond: **All of *Nezikin*****,** i.e., *Bava Kamma, Bava Metzia,* and *Bava Batra*, **is one tractate.**[B]

וְאִיבָּעֵית אֵימָא, מִשּׁוּם דְּקָתָנֵי לַהּ גַּבֵּי הִלְכְתָא פְּסִיקָתָא: כׇּל הַמְשַׁנֶּה – יָדוֹ עַל הַתַּחְתּוֹנָה, וְכׇל הַחוֹזֵר בּוֹ – יָדוֹ עַל הַתַּחְתּוֹנָה.

And if you wish, say that even if *Bava Kamma* and *Bava Metzia* are to be considered two separate tractates, Rav Yosef would still hold that Rav Huna's statement was unnecessary **because it is taught** as one of a pair **of established *halakhot*: Whoever changes** from the terms of an agreement **is at a disadvantage, and whoever reneges** on an agreement **is at a disadvantage.** Since this ruling was taught with another, established *halakha*, it is apparent that this is also an established *halakha*.

תָּנוּ רַבָּנַן: הַנּוֹתֵן מָעוֹת לִשְׁלוּחוֹ

§ The Gemara notes another dispute concerning one who deviates from the terms of an agreement. **The Sages taught** in the *Tosefta* (*Bava Metzia* 4:20): **One who gives money to his agent**

BACKGROUND

***Nezikin* is one tractate – נְזִיקִין חֲדָא מַסֶּכְתָּא הִיא:** Rav Sherira Gaon writes that this statement applies to the first three tractates in the order of *Nezikin*: *Bava Kamma, Bava Metzia,* and *Bava Batra*. The rest of *Nezikin* has no specific order. Most early authorities accept this assertion. By contrast, the Ri Migash maintains that indeed the entire order of *Nezikin* is one long tractate.

לִיקַּח לוֹ חִטִּין – וְלָקַח מֵהֶם שְׂעוֹרִין, שְׂעוֹרִין – וְלָקַח מֵהֶם חִטִּין, תַּנְיָא חֲדָא: אִם פָּחֲתוּ – פָּחֲתוּ לוֹ, וְאִם הוֹתִירוּ – הוֹתִירוּ לוֹ, וְתַנְיָא חֲדָא: אִם פָּחֲתוּ – פָּחֲתוּ לוֹ, וְאִם הוֹתִירוּ – הוֹתִירוּ לָאֶמְצַע.

to purchase wheat for him, which he plans to sell at a profit, **and** instead the agent **purchased barley with** the money, or if he gave his agent money to purchase **barley and** instead **he purchased wheat with** the money, two *baraitot* issue discordant rulings with regard to the *halakha*. **It is taught** in **one** *baraita* that **if there was a loss,**[H] **the loss is for** the agent, **and if there was a profit,** the **profit is for** the agent as well, as he is considered to have abrogated his status as an agent by deviating from the instructions. **And it is taught** in **one** *baraita* (*Tosefta, Bava Metzia* 4:20) that if there was an agreement that both parties would split the profits from the transaction, **if there was a loss, the loss is for** the agent, **and if there was a profit,** the **profit** goes **to the middle,** i.e., the agent and the investor split the profit.

אָמַר רַבִּי יוֹחָנָן: לָא קַשְׁיָא; הָא – רַבִּי מֵאִיר, וְהָא – רַבִּי יְהוּדָה.

To reconcile the *baraitot*, **Rabbi Yoḥanan said:** This is **not difficult. This** first *baraita* is in accordance with the opinion of **Rabbi Meir, and this** second *baraita* is in accordance with the opinion of **Rabbi Yehuda.**

הָא רַבִּי מֵאִיר דְּאָמַר שִׁינּוּי קוֹנֶה, וְהָא רַבִּי יְהוּדָה דְּאָמַר שִׁינּוּי אֵינוֹ קוֹנֶה.

Rabbi Yoḥanan explains his rationale: **This** first *baraita* is in accordance with the opinion of **Rabbi Meir, who says** that **a change** by an agent that deviates from the terms of his assignment means that the agent **acquires** the item in question for himself, as in the case of one who was paid to dye wool red but dyed it black. In this case as well, when the agent purchases wheat instead of barley, or vice versa, he acquires the grain for himself. **And this** second *baraita* is in accordance with the opinion of **Rabbi Yehuda, who says** that **a change** by an agent which deviates from the terms of his assignment does **not** mean that the agent **acquires** the item in question for himself. It is acquired by the one who appointed the agent, and they split the profits as agreed. But the agent is held responsible for any loss incurred, due to his deviation from the instructions.

מַתְקִיף לַהּ רַבִּי אֶלְעָזָר: מִמַּאי? דִּלְמָא עַד כָּאן לָא קָאָמַר רַבִּי מֵאִיר – אֶלָּא בְּמִידֵּי דַּחֲזֵי לֵיהּ לְגוּפֵיהּ, אֲבָל לִסְחוֹרָה – לָא אָמַר!

Rabbi Elazar objects to this explanation: From where do you say that the dispute between Rabbi Meir and Rabbi Yehuda extends to the case of these *baraitot*? **Perhaps Rabbi Meir says** that a change by an agent from the terms of his assignment results in the acquisition of the item by the agent **only with regard to an item that is fit for** use by the one who appointed the agent **himself,** such as wool dyed the wrong color, which is now not usable for its intended purpose. **But** Rabbi Meir **does not say** his ruling with regard to an item purchased **for** subsequent sale as **merchandise,** since it is intended to be sold for a profit in any event, and the transaction would take effect as agreed upon initially, with the agent held responsible for any loss incurred.

אֶלָּא אָמַר רַבִּי אֶלְעָזָר: הָא וְהָא רַבִּי מֵאִיר, וְלָא קַשְׁיָא: כָּאן – לַאֲכִילָה, כָּאן – לִסְחוֹרָה.

Rather, Rabbi Elazar said: Both **this** *baraita* **and that** *baraita* are written in accordance with the opinion of **Rabbi Meir, and** it is **not difficult. Here,** in the first *baraita*, it is discussing grain purchased **for eating,** and since the one who appointed the agent desired wheat, he does not acquire the barley. **There,** in the second *baraita*, it is discussing grain purchased **for** subsequent sale as **merchandise,** and the transaction takes effect as agreed upon initially, with the agent held responsible for any loss incurred.

HALAKHA

If there was a loss, etc. – **אִם פָּחֲתוּ וכו׳**: If one gives money to an agent to purchase wheat, whether to resell it or to consume it, and the agent purchased barley, any loss caused by this action is suffered by the agent. If the transaction resulted in a financial gain, then the profit is distributed according to their prior arrangement, whether as a partnership or as a standard agency, as the *halakha* is in accordance with the opinion of Rabbi Yehuda, as explained by Rabbi Yoḥanan (Rif; Rambam; Rosh). The *Shakh*, citing *Sefer HaIttur*, holds that in any case where the agent deviated from his instructions the profits are to be divided between him and the one who appointed him (Rambam *Sefer Kinyan, Hilkhot Sheluḥin VeShutafin* 1:5, 5:2; *Shulḥan Arukh, Ḥoshen Mishpat* 176:11, 183:5).

מְחַכוּ עֲלָהּ בְּמַעַרְבָא, לְרַבִּי יוֹחָנָן אַלִּיבָּא דְּרַבִּי יְהוּדָה: וְכִי מִי הוֹדִיעוֹ לְבַעַל חִטִּין שֶׁיַּקְנֶה חִטִּין לְבַעַל מָעוֹת? מַתְקִיף לָהּ רַב שְׁמוּאֵל בַּר סַסְרָטִי: אִי הָכִי, אֲפִילּוּ חִטִּין וְחִטִּין נַמִי לָא!

The Gemara notes that **they laughed at it in the West**, Eretz Yisrael, at the explanation **of Rabbi Yoḥanan**, who said that **according to** the opinion **of Rabbi Yehuda**, a deviation by an agent from the terms of his assignment does not result in the acquisition of the item for the agent himself: **And who informed the owner of the wheat**, i.e., the seller, **that he should transfer the wheat to the owner of the money?** If the seller was unaware that the agent was acting on someone else's behalf, how would the one who appointed the agent acquire the wheat? **Rav Shmuel bar Sasrati objects to this** rationale: **If so,** then **even** in a case where the agent was sent to purchase **wheat and** he purchased **wheat,**[N] the one who appointed the agent should **not** acquire the wheat, since the seller was unaware that the agent was acting on someone else's behalf.

אֲמַר רַבִּי אַבָּהוּ: שָׁאנֵי חִטִּין וְחִטִּין, דִּשְׁלִיחוּתֵיהּ קָא עָבֵיד, וְכִי בַּעַל הַבַּיִת דָּמֵי.

Rabbi Abbahu said: The case of an agent who was assigned to purchase **wheat and** purchased **wheat is different, as** the agent **is performing his assignment** and, as such, **he is like the customer,**[N] i.e., the one who appointed him, and it is as though the latter has purchased the grain himself.

תֵּדַע, דִּתְנַן: אֶחָד הַמַּקְדִּישׁ נְכָסָיו וְאֶחָד הַמַּעֲרִיךְ אֶת עַצְמוֹ, אֵין לוֹ בִּכְסוּת אִשְׁתּוֹ, וְלֹא בִּכְסוּת בָּנָיו, וְלֹא בְּצֶבַע שֶׁצָּבַע לִשְׁמָן, וְלֹא בְּסַנְדָּלִים חֲדָשִׁים שֶׁלְּקָחָן לִשְׁמָן;

Rabbi Abbahu further explains: **Know** that the agent is viewed as an extension of the one who appointed him, **as we learned** in a mishna (*Arakhin* 24a): Concerning both **one who consecrates his property**[H] **and one who valuates himself** by donating his fixed value to the Temple, the Temple treasury **does not have**[N] any rights **with regard to** the donor's **wife's clothing; and not with regard to his children's clothing; and not with regard to** new clothes colored with **dye that the** donor **dyed for** his wife or children; **and not with regard to new sandals**[N] **that** the donor **purchased for** his wife or children. Presumably, the treasurer has no right to these items because they are for the personal use of the donor's wife and children, and are considered as if owned by them.

וְאַמַּאי? לֵימָא הָכָא נַמִי: מִי הוֹדִיעוֹ לַצַּבָּע שֶׁיַּקְנֶה צִבְעוֹ לָאִשָּׁה? אֶלָּא לָאו מִשּׁוּם דְּאָמְרִינַן [דִּשְׁלִיחוּתֵיהּ קָא עָבֵיד, וּכְיַד אִשְׁתּוֹ דָּמֵי? הָכָא נַמִי] – שְׁלִיחוּתֵיהּ קָא עָבֵיד, וּכְיַד בַּעַל הַבַּיִת דָּמֵי.

Rabbi Abbahu continues: **And why** is it so, i.e., why is it that the wife is considered the owner of the dyed clothing for which the husband paid? **Here also, let us say: Who informed the dyer that he should transfer his dye to the wife? Rather, is it not because we say that** the husband **is performing his assignment and,** as such, he **is like** an extension of **his wife's hand? Here also,** in the case of one who purchases grain for another, the agent **is performing his assignment, and is like** an extension of the **customer's hand.**

אֲמַר רַבִּי אַבָּא: לֹא, כָּל הַמַּקְדִּישׁ נְכָסָיו אֵין דַּעְתּוֹ עַל כְּסוּת אִשְׁתּוֹ וּבָנָיו.

The Gemara rejects this explanation. **Rabbi Abba said: No,** the reason for the ruling of the mishna is that **the intention of anyone who consecrates his property is not upon the clothing of his wife and his children,** i.e., he does not intend to consecrate those items.

מַתְקִיף לָהּ רַבִּי זֵירָא: וְכִי דַּעְתּוֹ שֶׁל אָדָם עַל תְּפִילָּיו? וּתְנַן: הַמַּקְדִּישׁ נְכָסָיו – מַעֲלִין לוֹ תְּפִילִּין! אֲמַר לֵיהּ אַבַּיֵי: אִין, דַּעְתּוֹ שֶׁל אָדָם עַל תְּפִילִּין – הַמַּקְדִּישׁ נְכָסָיו סָבַר: מִצְוָה קָא עָבֵידְנָא. וְאֵין דַּעְתּוֹ שֶׁל אָדָם עַל כְּסוּת אִשְׁתּוֹ וּבָנָיו – מִשּׁוּם אֵיבָה.

Rabbi Zeira objects to Rabbi Abba's explanation: **And is it the intention of a person** who consecrates his property to do so **upon his phylacteries?** Presumably not. **And we learned** in a mishna (*Arakhin* 23b) that with regard to **one who consecrates** all of **his property,** his **phylacteries are evaluated for him**[H] and consecrated. Apparently, lack of intent to consecrate a particular item does not prevent its consecration. **Abaye said to** Rabbi Zeira: **Yes, the intention of a person** who consecrates his property **is upon** his **phylacteries,**[N] because **one who consecrates his property thinks** to himself: **I am performing a mitzva,** and he therefore intends to include his phylacteries; **but the intention of a person is not upon the clothing of his wife and his children, due to the enmity** that would be engendered if he consecrated their clothing.

מַתְקִיף לָהּ רַב אוֹשַׁעְיָא: וַהֲלֹא חַיָּיבֵי עֲרָכִין שָׁנוּ כָּאן, וּתְנַן: חַיָּיבֵי עֲרָכִין מְמַשְׁכְּנִין אוֹתָן;

Rav Oshaya also **objects to** Rabbi Abba's explanation: **But is it not** so that the matter of **those who are obligated in valuations was taught here** in the mishna, **and we learned** in a mishna (*Arakhin* 21a): Concerning **those who are obligated in valuations,** the Temple treasury **seizes collateral from them** to force them to fulfill their vow.

NOTES

Even where he was sent to purchase wheat and purchased wheat – אֲפִילּוּ חִטִּין וְחִטִּין נַמִי: *Tosefot Rabbeinu Peretz* explains that the Sages of Eretz Yisrael understood that the default assumption of any seller is that he is completing the sale with the one who is giving him payment. In this case, since the payment is given by the agent, and not the actual purchaser, the seller will not have the intention of completing the sale with the purchaser. Rav Shmuel bar Sasrati counters that if this were so, even if the agent is purchasing wheat as instructed, the seller is still under the impression that he is selling it to the agent, and if the Sages of Eretz Yisrael are correct the sale would not take effect in this case as well. Therefore, it must be that although the seller assumes that he is selling the grain to the one actually providing the money, in this case, the agent, the sale does take effect.

It follows, then, that it should take effect even when the agent purchases barley instead of wheat, as the agreement between the seller and the agent is paramount, and according to the opinion of Rabbi Yoḥanan this deviation from the instructions is not enough to nullify the agency.

As the agent is performing his assignment and he is like the customer – דִּשְׁלִיחוּתֵיהּ קָא עָבֵיד וְכִי בַּעַל הַבַּיִת דָּמֵי: *Tosefot Rabbeinu Peretz* explains that Rabbi Abbahu counters Rav Shmuel bar Sasrati, maintaining that in fact the seller must intend to sell the item to the actual purchaser for the sale to take effect. Nevertheless, in the case where the agent was instructed to purchase wheat and purchased wheat, his status as an agent renders him an extension of the one who appointed him, and it is as if the seller has the customer in mind.

When the agent deviates from his instructions he is not considered an extension of the one who appointed him, and the opinion of the Sages of Eretz Yisrael, i.e., that the lack of intention on the part of the seller to complete the sale with the correct purchaser should prevent the sale from taking effect, would stand.

He does not have – אֵין לוֹ: Rashi understands that the pronoun here refers to the Temple treasury, and consequently they have no claim to these items. Others explain that it refers to the donor of the items. Accordingly, the mishna teaches that the donor does not own his family's clothing, and it therefore remains in their possession.

New sandals – סַנְדָּלִים חֲדָשִׁים: Rashi understands that the added novelty in describing the sandals as new is to teach that even if the sandals had not been worn by any member of the donor's family, the fact that the donor purchased the sandals for them is sufficient for the sandals to be considered their property.

The intention of a person is upon his phylacteries – דַּעְתּוֹ שֶׁל אָדָם עַל תְּפִילִּין: Rashi explains that since the one consecrating his property is performing a mitzva by giving it to the Temple, it is presumed that he wishes to donate all of his property, even those items used to perform mitzvot. He will then find other means of acquiring or borrowing phylacteries.

HALAKHA

One who consecrates his property, etc. – אֶחָד הַמַּקְדִּישׁ נְכָסָיו וכו׳: One who consecrates his property or otherwise is indebted to the Temple treasury is compelled to pay his debt, and collateral is seized until he does so. If one does not have money with which to pay, he must sell all of his property in order to do so, with the exception of his family's shoes and clothing (Rambam *Sefer Hafla'a*, *Hilkhot Arakhin VaḤaramim* 3:14).

His phylacteries are evaluated for him – מַעֲלִין לוֹ תְּפִילִּין: The Temple treasurer collects all of the belongings of one who consecrates all of his property, including the phylacteries on his head (Rambam *Sefer Hafla'a*, *Hilkhot Arakhin VaḤaramim* 6:3).

וְכִי דַּעְתּוֹ שֶׁל אָדָם עַל עַצְמוֹ לְמַשְׁכְּנוֹ?!

And is the intention of a person upon himself to allow the treasurer **to seize collateral from him?** Presumably not. Nevertheless, collateral is seized from him, proving that one's intention does not prevent consecration. Accordingly, even if it is assumed that he does not intend to consecrate the clothing of his wife or children, the clothing should nevertheless be consecrated. Why, then, is the clothing of his wife or children not consecrated?

אֶלָּא אָמַר רַבִּי אַבָּא: כָּל הַמַּקְדִּישׁ נְכָסָיו – נַעֲשֶׂה כְּמִי שֶׁהִקְנָה לָהֶן כְּסוּת אִשְׁתּוֹ וּבָנָיו מֵעִיקָּרָא.

Rather, Rabbi Abba also holds that the reason the clothing is not consecrated is not due to his intent, and he **said** a different explanation: **Anyone who consecrates his property becomes as one who transferred his wife's and his children's clothing to them at the outset.** Therefore, the clothing did not belong to him at the time that he consecrated his property.

תָּנוּ רַבָּנַן: הַלּוֹקֵחַ שָׂדֶה בְּשֵׁם חֲבֵירוֹ – אֵין כּוֹפִין אוֹתוֹ לִמְכּוֹר, וְאִם אָמַר לוֹ "עַל מְנָת" – כּוֹפִין אוֹתוֹ לִמְכּוֹר.

§ The Gemara presents another situation in which one makes a purchase involving a third party. **The Sages taught:** In the case of **one who purchases a field in the name of another, he is not compelled to sell** it. **But if he said to him** at the time of the sale: I will purchase the field **on the condition** that he will sell it to me, **he is compelled to sell** it.

מַאי קָאָמַר? אָמַר רַב שֵׁשֶׁת, הָכִי קָאָמַר: הַלּוֹקֵחַ שָׂדֶה מֵחֲבֵירוֹ בְּשֵׁם רֵישׁ גָּלוּתָא – אֵין כּוֹפִין אוֹתוֹ רֵישׁ גָּלוּתָא לִמְכּוֹר, וְאִם אָמַר "עַל מְנָת" – כּוֹפִין אֶת רֵישׁ גָּלוּתָא לִמְכּוֹר.

Noting the ambiguity of this statement, the Gemara asks: **What is it saying? Rav Sheshet said** that **this** is what it **is saying:** With regard to **one who purchases a field from another,** claiming that he is acting **in the name of the Exilarch**[B] or another dominant figure, so that others will be discouraged from contesting the sale, **the Exilarch is not compelled to sell** it to him, i.e., the Exilarch is not required to provide the purchaser with documentation that the field belongs to the purchaser. **But if** the purchaser **said** to the seller: I will purchase the field **on the condition** that the Exilarch will provide me with that documentation, **the Exilarch is compelled to sell** it to him, i.e., to provide him with the documentation.

אָמַר מָר: הַלּוֹקֵחַ שָׂדֶה בְּשֵׁם רֵישׁ גָּלוּתָא – אֵין כּוֹפִין אוֹתוֹ רֵישׁ גָּלוּתָא לְחַזּוֹר; מִכְּלָל דִּמִקְנָא קַנְיָא לֵיהּ. לֵימָא פְּלִיגָא דִּבְנֵי מַעַרְבָא, דְּאָמְרִי: וְכִי מִי הוֹדִיעוֹ לְבַעַל חִטִּין שֶׁיַּקְנֶה חִטִּין לְבַעַל הַבַּיִת?

The Gemara questions Rav Sheshet's interpretation. **The Master said:** With regard to **one who purchases a field in the name of the Exilarch, the Exilarch is not compelled to sell** it to him. Since the *baraita* teaches only that the Exilarch is not required to provide the purchaser with documentation that the field is his, it can be understood **by inference that** the purchaser **has** nevertheless **acquired** the field **for himself.**[H] **Let us say that** this interpretation of the *baraita* **disagrees with** the statement of **the residents of the West,** Eretz Yisrael, **who say: And who informed the owner of the wheat that he should transfer the wheat to the customer?** Since the seller assumed he was selling the field to the Exilarch, the Sages of Eretz Yisrael would hold that the sale does not take effect.

אִי מִשּׁוּם הָא לָא קַשְׁיָא, כְּגוֹן דְּאוֹדְעֵיהּ לְבַעַל שָׂדֶה, וְאוֹדְעִינְהוּ לְסָהֲדֵי.

The Gemara rejects this: **If** it is **due to this** inference that it is surmised that the *baraita* is in conflict with the opinion of the Sages of Eretz Yisrael, it is **not difficult,** as it can be said that the *baraita* is discussing a case **where** the purchaser **informed the owner of the field and informed the witnesses** that he intends to purchase the field for himself.

אֶלָּא אֵימָא סֵיפָא: "עַל מְנָת" – כּוֹפִין אוֹתוֹ רֵישׁ גָּלוּתָא לִמְכּוֹר, אַמַּאי? וְלֵימָא רֵישׁ גָּלוּתָא: לָא יְקָרַיְיכוּ בָּעֵינָא, וְלָא זִילוּתַיְיכוּ בָּעֵינָא!

The Gemara rejects Rav Sheshet's interpretation for a different reason. **Rather, say** that **the latter clause** is difficult, as it states that if the purchaser said to the seller: I will purchase the field **on the condition** that the Exilarch will sell it to me, **the Exilarch is compelled to sell** it to him. **Why** should the Exilarch be compelled to provide the purchaser with documentation? **But let the Exilarch say: I do not desire your esteem nor do I desire your disgrace,** i.e., I am not involved in your affairs. Since the Exilarch had not been party to the negotiations, how can a stipulation stated by the purchaser render him obligated?

אֶלָּא אָמַר אַבָּיֵי, הָכִי קָאָמַר: הַלּוֹקֵחַ שָׂדֶה בְּשֵׁם חֲבֵירוֹ רֵישׁ גָּלוּתָא

Rather, Abaye said: This is what the *baraita* **is saying:** With regard **to one who purchases a field in the name of his friend, the Exilarch,**[N]

BACKGROUND

In the name of the Exilarch – בְּשֵׁם רֵישׁ גָּלוּתָא: Not only was the Exilarch the civil authority over the Jewish community in Persia, he served in an official capacity and was considered a government minister. Being that the Exilarch had great power, at times people would claim to be purchasing property on his behalf, so as to prevent others from contesting the sale.

HALAKHA

By inference that he has acquired the field for himself – מִכְּלָל דְּמִקְנָא קַנְיָא לֵיהּ: A seller cannot renege on a sale even if the purchaser deceitfully claimed that he was purchasing the item on behalf of another, as long as the purchaser paid for the purchase himself. This ruling stands in opposition to the opinion of the Sages of Eretz Yisrael (*Shulḥan Arukh*, *Ḥoshen Mishpat* 184:2 and *Beur HaGra* there).

NOTES

In the name of his friend the Exilarch – בְּשֵׁם חֲבֵירוֹ רֵישׁ גָּלוּתָא: There are versions of the text that do not mention the Exilarch here, as he is not relevant to this explanation.

NOTES

The seller is not compelled – אֵין כּוֹפִין אֶת הַמּוֹכֵר: The seller is not compelled to write a second deed in the purchaser's name. The Rosh explains that the seller may not wish to provide the purchaser with an additional deed, as people are hesitant to have legal documents circulating in their name.

On the condition – עַל מְנָת: Rashi explains that the purchaser states to the seller: I will purchase the field on the condition that you will provide a deed in my name. Accordingly, it is clear why the Exilarch is not compelled to provide the purchaser with a document stating his ownership, as the Exilarch was not involved in the transaction.

Others explain that the statement was made by the purchaser to the Exilarch, meaning: I will purchase the field in your name on the condition that you will later provide documentation that it belongs to me. Nevertheless, Abaye holds that the Exilarch is still not compelled to write the document, as he has the right to say: I do not desire your esteem and I do not wish to participate in such a transaction.

HALAKHA

The seller is not compelled, etc. – אֵין כּוֹפִין אֶת הַמּוֹכֵר וכו׳: If one purchased a field from another, stating that he is purchasing it on behalf of a third party, and received a bill of sale to that effect, and then stated that he in fact purchased it for himself, the seller is not compelled to provide an additional bill of sale. If the purchaser had informed the seller, or even just witnesses, that he is purchasing the field for himself, but requires a bill of sale in the name of another for whatever reason, the seller must provide him with an additional bill of sale in his own name. This is in accordance with Abaye's explanation of the *baraita* (Rambam *Sefer Kinyan*, *Hilkhot Sheluḥin VeShutafin* 2:5; *Shulḥan Arukh*, *Ḥoshen Mishpat* 184:2).

LANGUAGE

Protection [*panaḥya*] – פַּנַחְיָא: Apparently from the Middle Persian panāhīh, also meaning protection.

אֵין כּוֹפִין אֶת הַמּוֹכֵר לִמְכּוֹר זִימְנָא אַחֲרִיתִי, וְאִם אָמַר לוֹ ״עַל מְנָת״ – כּוֹפִין אֶת הַמּוֹכֵר לִמְכּוֹר.

the seller is not compelled[N][H] **to sell** the field **another time,** i.e., to provide the purchaser with a document denoting him as the owner of the field. **But if he said to him:** I will purchase the field **on the condition**[N] that you will provide a deed in my name, **the seller is compelled to sell** the field again, i.e., to provide the purchaser with a document denoting him as the owner.

אָמַר מָר: הַלּוֹקֵחַ שָׂדֶה בְּשֵׁם חֲבֵירוֹ – אֵין כּוֹפִין אֶת הַמּוֹכֵר לִמְכּוֹר זִימְנָא אַחֲרִיתִי. פְּשִׁיטָא! מַהוּ דְּתֵימָא מָצֵי אָמַר לֵיהּ: מֵידַע יָדַעַתְּ דַּאֲנָא לְנַפְשַׁאי שָׁקֵילְנָא, וּפַנַחְיָא בְּעָלְמָא הוּא דְּקָבָעֵינָא, וְזוּזֵי בִּכְדִי לָא שָׁדֵינָא, אֶלָּא אַדַּעְתָּא דְּכָתַב לֵיהּ שְׁטָרָא אַחֲרִינָא – קָא מַשְׁמַע לָן דְּאָמַר לֵיהּ: עִנְיָינָא עָבְדִי לָךְ בַּהֲדֵי הַהוּא דְּזַבְנַתְּ לֵיהּ בִּשְׁמֵיהּ, וְיִכְתּוֹב לָךְ שְׁטָרָא אַחֲרִינָא.

The Gemara clarifies the *baraita*: **The Master said:** In the case of **one who purchases a field in the name of another, the seller is not compelled to sell** the field **another time.** The Gemara asks: **Isn't this obvious?** The Gemara answers: **Lest you say** that the purchaser **can say to** the seller: **You knew that I took,** i.e., purchased, the field **for myself, and it was merely** for **protection** [*ufanaḥya*][L] **that I desired** to obtain ownership by claiming to purchase it in the name of the other person, **and I do not throw out money for naught. Rather,** it was **with the intention that you will write another document for him,** i.e., the seller, stating that I purchased the field. The *baraita* therefore **teaches us that** the seller can **say to him: I have performed a matter for you together with the one in whose name you purchased** the field, **and let him write you another document.**

וְאִם אָמַר לוֹ ״עַל מְנָת״ – כּוֹפִין אֶת הַמּוֹכֵר לִמְכּוֹר. פְּשִׁיטָא! לָא צְרִיכָא, דַּאֲמַר לְהוּ לְסָהֲדֵי קַמֵּיהּ דִּידֵיהּ: חֲזוּ דִּשְׁטָרָא אַחֲרִינָא קָא בָּעֵינָא; מַהוּ דְּתֵימָא, מָצֵי אָמַר לֵיהּ: אָמִינָא שְׁטָרָא מֵהֵיאַךְ דְּקָא שָׁקַלְתְּ בִּשְׁמֵיהּ קָאָמְרַתְּ, קָא מַשְׁמַע לָן דְּאָמַר לֵיהּ: לְהָכִי טָרְחִי וְאָמְרִי לְהוּ לְעֵדִים קַמָּךְ, דְּמִינָּךְ הוּא דְּקָא בָּעֵינָא.

The Gemara discusses Abaye's interpretation of the latter clause of the *baraita*, which states: **But if he said to him:** I will purchase the field **on the condition** that you will provide a deed in my name, **the seller is compelled to sell** the field again. Isn't that **obvious? No,** it is **necessary** to state this *halakha* in a case **where** the purchaser **said to the witnesses in front of** the seller: You can **see that I require another document. Lest you say** that the seller **can say to him: I thought** that it was **a document from the one in whose name you purchased** the field that **you were saying** you required, and not from me. Therefore, the *baraita* **teaches us that** the purchaser can **say to him:** It was **for this that I took the trouble and said to the witnesses, in front of you,** that I require another document, **as it is from you that I require** the document.

רַב כָּהֲנָא יְהַב זוּזָא אַכִּיתָּנָא, לְסוֹף אִייַּקַּר כִּיתָּנָא, זַבְנֵיהּ מָרְוָותֵיהּ דְּכִיתָּנָא. אֲתָא לְקַמֵּיהּ דְּרַב, אֲמַר לֵיהּ: מָה אַעֲבֵיד, אִיזִיל אִישְׁקִיל זוּזָאי? אֲמַר לֵיהּ: אִי כִּי קָא זָבְנִי אָמְרִי ״הַאי כִּיתָּנָא דְּכָהֲנָא הוּא״ – זִיל שְׁקוֹל, וְאִי לָא – לָא תִּשְׁקוֹל.

§ The Gemara mentions a related incident: **Rav Kahana gave money** to a salesman in exchange **for flax,** and temporarily left the flax in the possession of the seller. **Ultimately,** the **flax appreciated** in value and the **owner of the flax sold it** for a greater profit on behalf of Rav Kahana, intending to give him all of the money. Rav Kahana then **came before Rav,** and **said to him: What should I do? Should I go and take my money,** or would doing so have the appearance of collecting interest for a loan? Rav **said to** Rav Kahana: **If, when they sold** the flax, **they said: This flax is Kahana's, go take** the money, as in such a case it is as though the flax was purchased directly from you. **But if** they did **not** say this, **do not take** the money, since you would be receiving a greater sum of money than you provided, and this would appear to be a loan repaid with interest.

כְּמַאן? כִּבְנֵי מַעְרְבָא, דְּאָמְרִי: מִי הוֹדִיעוֹ לְבַעַל חִטִּין שֶׁיַּקְנֶה חִטִּין לְבַעַל מָעוֹת?

The Gemara asks: **In accordance with whose** opinion was Rav's ruling? Was it only **in accordance with** the opinion of **the people of the West,** Eretz Yisrael, **who say: Who informed the owner of the wheat that he should transfer the wheat to the owner of the money?** As the Gemara taught earlier, the Sages of Eretz Yisrael hold that the sale can be performed on another's behalf only if such an arrangement is explicitly stated at the time of the transaction. In this case as well, if the seller did not explicitly state that the money would belong to Rav Kahana, all the money from the sale would be acquired by the seller, who would then be prohibited to give it to Rav Kahana due to the appearance of paying interest.

אטו מי יהיב רב כהנא ארבע ושקיל תמני? כיתנא ממילא הוא דאייקר, מיגזל גזלוה, ותנן: כל הגזלנין משלמין כשעת הגזלה!

The Gemara rejects this: **Is that to say that Rav Kahana gave four** dinars **and took eight** in return? He did not lend money to the seller. Rather, **the flax appreciated** in value **by itself,** and when the seller sold it **he robbed** Rav Kahana of his flax, **and we learned** in a mishna (93b) that **all robbers pay** compensation **according to** the value of the stolen item at **the time of the robbery.** Therefore, according to all opinions the seller owes Rav Kahana the value of the flax at the time the seller sold it for its appreciated value, and Rav Kahana's accepting the money would not constitute collecting interest for a loan.

אמרי: התם אמנה הואי, ולא משכיה רב כהנא לכיתנא. ורב לטעמיה, דאמר רב: עושין אמנה בפירות, ואין עושין אמנה בדמים.

Having rejected the previous explanation of Rav's ruling, the Gemara presents an alternative understanding of the case. The Sages **say: There, it was** a matter of **trust,** as the seller was paid in advance **and Rav Kahana did not pull the flax** as an act of acquisition, or perform any other formal act of acquisition. Consequently, at the time of the second sale the flax belonged to the seller. **And Rav** conforms **to his** standard line of **reasoning, as Rav says: One may make** an arrangement of **trust with regard to** the delivery of items such as **produce,**[H] i.e., one may pay the money in advance with the agreement that he will receive the produce at a later date, **but one may not make** an arrangement of **trust with regard to money,**[N] i.e., one may not pay the money in advance with the agreement that he will receive the value of the produce at a later date, as this has the appearance of collecting interest.

מתני׳ הגוזל את חבירו שוה פרוטה ונשבע לו – יוליכנו אחריו למדי. לא יתן לא לבנו ולא לשלוחו, אבל נותן לשליח בית דין. ואם מת – יחזיר ליורשיו.

MISHNA **One who robs another**[H] of an item having **the value of** at least **one *peruta* and takes** a false **oath to** the robbery victim claiming his innocence, and then later wishes to repent, must **bring** the money, which includes the principal together with an additional one-fifth payment, to the robbery victim, even if this necessitates following **after him to** a distant place like **Medea.**[NB] The robber **may not give** the payment **to** the robbery victim's **son**[H] to return it to the robbery victim, **and neither** may he give it **to his agent, but he may give** the payment **to an agent of the court.**[HN] **And if** the robbery victim **dies, he returns it to his heirs.**[HN]

HALAKHA

One may make an arrangement of trust with regard to produce, etc. – עושין אמנה בפירות וכו׳: One who received advance payment for an item that then appreciated in value may deliver the item to the purchaser. Rabbeinu Tam permits him to deliver the monetary value of the appreciated item, in accordance with the opinion of Rabbi Yannai in *Bava Metzia* 63a, while the Rashbam and the Rosh rule that he may not, in accordance with the opinion of Rav (*Shulḥan Arukh*, *Yoreh De'a* 175:6).

One who robs another, etc. – הגוזל את חבירו וכו׳: One who robs another of an item worth one *peruta* or more and then takes a false oath claiming his innocence must pursue the robbery victim as far as necessary in order to return the stolen item (Rambam *Sefer Nezikin*, *Hilkhot Gezeila VaAveda* 7:9; *Shulḥan Arukh*, *Ḥoshen Mishpat* 367:1).

He may not give the payment to the son, etc. – לא יתן לא לבנו וכו׳: One who robbed another and then took a false oath claiming his innocence cannot fulfill his obligation to return the stolen item by giving it to the son or agent of the robbery victim. If the robbery victim appointed an agent in the presence of witnesses, the robber may give the payment to that agent (Rambam *Sefer Nezikin*, *Hilkhot Gezeila VaAveda* 7:10; *Shulḥan Arukh*, *Ḥoshen Mishpat* 367:2).

He may give it to an agent of the court – נותן לשליח בית דין: One who robbed another and then took a false oath claiming his innocence may give the principal and the additional one-fifth payment to the court, or to a court-appointed agent. If he does so, he has fulfilled his obligation to return the stolen item and may bring his guilt-offering immediately. There is a dispute among the later commentaries with regard to whether a robber has fulfilled his obligation if the court ultimately fails to deliver the payment to the robbery victim (Rambam *Sefer Nezikin*, *Hilkhot Gezeila VaAveda* 7:10; *Shulḥan Arukh*, *Ḥoshen Mishpat* 367:2).

And if the robbery victim dies he returns it to his heirs – ואם מת יחזיר ליורשיו: If the robbery victim dies, the robber must return the principal and the additional one-fifth payment to the heirs of the robbery victim (Rambam *Sefer Nezikin*, *Hilkhot Gezeila VaAveda* 8:1; *Shulḥan Arukh*, *Ḥoshen Mishpat* 367:4).

BACKGROUND

Medea – מדי: In talmudic times, Medea was one of the provinces of the Iranian kingdom. During the First Temple period, Medea was still a strong, independent country, situated largely east of the Tigris River. Medea was considered a faraway land even in the days of the Mishna, and traveling there required considerable time and effort.

NOTES

One may not make an arrangement of trust with regard to money – אין עושין אמנה בדמים: According to Rav, it is permitted to pay in advance for a particular item only if an arrangement is made with the seller that he will eventually deliver the item. It is forbidden for the seller to later give the purchaser the cash value of the item in lieu of the item itself, as this has the appearance of paying interest, since, ostensibly, one gives another a sum of money and receives a greater sum in return (see Rabbeinu Ḥananel). *Tosafot* note that in the discussion of this issue in tractate *Bava Metzia* (63a), Rabbi Yannai permits such a transaction, as he holds that since there was technically a sale rather than a loan, the prohibition against paying interest does not apply, even by rabbinic law.

To Medea – למדי: Some explain that the Gemara's use of Medea to exemplify a distant place is not incidental, but is actually an allusion to the verse: "Behold, I will stir up the Medes against them, who shall not regard silver" (Isaiah 13:17). Accordingly, the Talmud intimates that even if the item one is returning is considered worthless to its owner, the robber must nevertheless ensure that it is returned (*Tiferet Yisrael*).

But he may give it to an agent of the court – אבל נותן לשליח בית דין: The mishna teaches that once the robber has transferred the stolen item to a court agent, he is considered to have returned it and may bring his guilt-offering immediately. Rashi explains that this leniency is due to the ordinance instituted for the penitent, so that one wishing to return a stolen item need not expend more money in returning it than the stolen item is worth. Consequently, the robber may present the payment to an agent of the court, who will hold it until the robbery victim comes to claim it. *Tosafot*, however, contend that this refers to an agent appointed by the court to convey the payment to the robbery victim. *Tosefot HaRash* add that the robber must pay for this agent's efforts.

And if the robbery victim dies he returns it to his heirs – ואם מת יחזיר ליורשיו: Some explain that the novelty here is that the robber must seek out his victim's heirs, just as he must seek out the victim himself (first explanation in *Tosafot*; Rashba). Others explain that the novelty is that the robber is not exempt from paying the additional one-fifth payment if his victim dies. This is in contrast to the *halakha* that if the robber dies, his own heirs are exempt from paying the additional one-fifth payment (second explanation in *Tosafot*). According to the Meiri, the mishna teaches that if the robbery victim has many heirs scattered in various places, the robber needs to convey the payment to only one of them, rather than tracking down each heir separately.

נָתַן לוֹ אֶת הַקֶּרֶן וְלֹא נָתַן לוֹ אֶת הַחוֹמֶשׁ, מָחַל לוֹ עַל הַקֶּרֶן וְלֹא מָחַל לוֹ עַל הַחוֹמֶשׁ, מָחַל לוֹ עַל זֶה וְעַל זֶה חוּץ מִפָּחוֹת שָׁוֶה פְּרוּטָה בְּקֶרֶן – אֵינוֹ צָרִיךְ לֵילֵךְ אַחֲרָיו. נָתַן לוֹ אֶת הַחוֹמֶשׁ וְלֹא נָתַן לוֹ אֶת הַקֶּרֶן, מָחַל לוֹ עַל הַחוֹמֶשׁ וְלֹא מָחַל לוֹ עַל הַקֶּרֶן, מָחַל לוֹ עַל זֶה וְעַל זֶה חוּץ מִשָּׁוֶה פְּרוּטָה בְּקֶרֶן – צָרִיךְ לֵילֵךְ אַחֲרָיו.

If **he gave** the robbery victim **the principal**[H] value of the stolen item **but did not give him** the additional **one-fifth** payment, or if the owner **forgave him concerning the principal but did not forgive him concerning** the additional **one-fifth** payment, or if **he forgave him concerning this and concerning that, with the exception of the value of less than one *peruta* of the principal, he need not pursue him** to repay the remaining debt. By contrast, if **he gave** the robbery victim the additional **one-fifth** payment[H] **but did not give him the principal,** or if the robbery victim **forgave him concerning** the additional **one-fifth** payment **but did not forgive him concerning the principal,** or if **he forgave him concerning this and concerning that, with the exception of the value of one *peruta* of the principal, he must pursue him** to repay the remaining debt.

נָתַן לוֹ אֶת הַקֶּרֶן וְנִשְׁבַּע לוֹ עַל הַחוֹמֶשׁ,

If the robber **gave** the robbery victim **the principal and took** a false **oath to him concerning** the additional **one-fifth** payment, asserting that he had already paid it,

HALAKHA

If he gave him the principal – נָתַן לוֹ אֶת הַקֶּרֶן: In any situation where the robber is no longer obligated to pay at least the value of one *peruta* of the principal, he need not pursue the robbery victim in order to return the additional one-fifth payment. Accordingly, if the robber had already paid or was forgiven the principal, he need not pursue the victim (Rambam *Sefer Nezikin, Hilkhot Gezeila VaAveda* 7:11; *Shulḥan Arukh, Ḥoshen Mishpat* 367:3).

He gave him the additional one-fifth payment, etc. – נָתַן לוֹ אֶת הַחוֹמֶשׁ וכו׳: If the robber paid or was forgiven the additional one-fifth payment he must nevertheless pursue the robbery victim to repay the principal, provided that the remaining debt is at least the value of one *peruta* (Rambam *Sefer Nezikin, Hilkhot Gezeila VaAveda* 7:11; *Shulḥan Arukh, Ḥoshen Mishpat* 367:2).

Perek **IX**
Daf **103** Amud **b**

הֲרֵי זֶה מְשַׁלֵּם חוֹמֶשׁ עַל חוֹמֶשׁ עַד שֶׁיִּתְמַעֵט הַקֶּרֶן מִשָּׁוֶה פְּרוּטָה.

then the additional one-fifth is considered a new principal obligation. The robber **pays** an additional **one-fifth** payment **apart from** the additional **one-fifth**[H] payment about which he had taken a false oath. If he then takes a false oath concerning the second one-fifth payment, he is assessed an additional one-fifth payment for that oath, **until the principal,** i.e., the additional one-fifth payment about which he has most recently taken the false oath, **is reduced to less than the value of one *peruta*.**

וְכֵן בְּפִקָּדוֹן, שֶׁנֶּאֱמַר: ״אוֹ בְפִקָּדוֹן אוֹ בִתְשׂוּמֶת יָד אוֹ בְגָזֵל אוֹ עָשַׁק אֶת עֲמִיתוֹ, אוֹ מָצָא אֲבֵדָה וְכִחֶשׁ בָּהּ וְנִשְׁבַּע עַל שָׁקֶר״ – הֲרֵי זֶה מְשַׁלֵּם קֶרֶן וְחוֹמֶשׁ וְאָשָׁם.

And such is the *halakha* **with regard to a deposit,**[N] **as it is stated:** "If anyone sins, and commits a trespass against the Lord, and he defrauds his counterpart **with regard to a deposit, or with regard to a pledge, or with regard to a robbery, or if he exploited his counterpart; or he has found that which was lost, and deals falsely with it, and swears to a lie**...he shall restore it in full, and shall add the fifth part more to it" (Leviticus 5:21–24). **This** one must pay the **principal and** an additional **one-fifth** payment, **and bring a guilt-offering.**[H]

גמ׳ נִשְׁבַּע לוֹ – אִין, לֹא נִשְׁבַּע לוֹ – לָא, מַנִּי? לָא רַבִּי טַרְפוֹן וְלָא רַבִּי עֲקִיבָא. דְּתַנְיָא: גָּזַל אֶחָד מֵחֲמִשָּׁה וְאֵינוֹ יוֹדֵעַ אֵיזֶה מֵהֶן, וְכָל אֶחָד אוֹמֵר ״אוֹתִי גָּזַל״ – מַנִּיחַ גְּזֵילָה בֵּינֵיהֶם וּמִסְתַּלֵּק, דִּבְרֵי רַבִּי טַרְפוֹן; רַבִּי עֲקִיבָא אוֹמֵר: לֹא זוֹ דֶּרֶךְ מוֹצִיאָתוֹ מִידֵי עֲבֵירָה, עַד שֶׁיְּשַׁלֵּם גְּזֵילָה לְכָל אֶחָד [וְאֶחָד];

GEMARA The mishna teaches that if a robber took a false oath that he did not rob, he must travel even as far as Medea in order to repay the robbery victim. This indicates that if **he takes an oath to** the robbery victim, **yes,** he is required to go to any length to repay his obligation, but if **he did not take an oath to him, no,**[H] he does not have to do so. **Whose** opinion is this? It is **not** the opinion of **Rabbi Tarfon and not** the opinion **of Rabbi Akiva, as it is taught** in a mishna (*Yevamot* 118b): If one **robbed one of five**[H] people **and he does not know which of them** he robbed, **and each one** of the five **says: He robbed me,** the robber **places** the **stolen item between them**[N] **and withdraws** from them; this is **the statement of Rabbi Tarfon. Rabbi Akiva says: This is not the way to spare him from transgression.** He is not considered to have returned the stolen item **until he pays** the value of the **stolen item to each and every one** of the five.

HALAKHA

Pays an additional one-fifth payment apart from the additional one-fifth – מְשַׁלֵּם חוֹמֶשׁ עַל חוֹמֶשׁ: If a robber returned the principal amount of the robbery, then took a false oath stating that he had returned the additional one-fifth payment, the additional one-fifth is considered a new principal obligation. The robber therefore owes an additional fifth apart from the additional one-fifth payment. If he pays the new principal, then took a false oath stating that he had returned the new additional one-fifth payment, this process can continue until the principal is reduced to less than the value of one *peruta* (Rambam *Sefer Nezikin, Hilkhot Gezeila VaAveda* 7:12).

The principal and an additional one-fifth payment and a guilt-offering – קֶרֶן וְחוֹמֶשׁ וְאָשָׁם: One who owes another money for whatever reason and takes a false oath that he does not owe the money is obligated to pay his creditor the principal amount owed and an additional one-fifth payment, and is also obligated to bring a guilt-offering (Rambam *Sefer Nezikin, Hilkhot Gezeila VaAveda* 7:1–2).

If he did not take an oath to him, no – לֹא נִשְׁבַּע לוֹ לָא: A robber who orally denies his debt but has not taken a false oath that he does not owe the victim is not obligated to pursue the latter in order to return the stolen item to him, but may wait for the robbery victim to come and claim it from him. The Rema, citing the Rosh and the *Tur*, writes that the robber must notify the robbery victim that his payment is ready for him to collect (Rambam *Sefer Nezikin, Hilkhot Gezeila VaAveda* 7:9; *Shulḥan Arukh, Ḥoshen Mishpat* 367:1).

Robbed one of five – גָּזַל אֶחָד מֵחֲמִשָּׁה: One who robbed one of five people but does not know which, must pay all of them who take an oath that they were the victim of the robbery. This is the *halakha* even if the robber did not take a false oath concerning his obligation, as the *halakha* is in accordance with the opinion of Rabbi Akiva. Some halakhic authorities rule in accordance with the opinion of Rabbi Tarfon that the robber may place the stolen item between the claimants and withdraw (Rambam *Sefer Nezikin, Hilkhot Gezeila VaAveda* 4:9; *Shulḥan Arukh, Ḥoshen Mishpat* 365:1 and *Shakh* there).

NOTES

And such is the *halakha* with regard to a deposit – וְכֵן בְּפִקָּדוֹן: The verse discusses not only one who actively robs money from another, but also one who withholds payment in any form. Consequently, one who was appointed as a bailee for a deposit and takes a false oath that he was not the bailee is also included in the *halakha* obligating one to pay an additional one-fifth and bring a guilt-offering. The *halakha* is the same for one who withholds payment of a loan by taking an oath that he does not owe it.

Between them – בֵּינֵיהֶם: The early commentaries note that this does not mean that the robber physically places the stolen item between them, as one of the five could then seize it unlawfully. Rather, it means that the robber leaves the money with the court until they clarify to whom it belongs or holds on to it as a deposit for its rightful owner.

מַנִּי? אִי רַבִּי טַרְפוֹן – אַף עַל גַּב דְּאִישְׁתְּבַע, אָמַר: מַנִּיחַ גְּזֵילָה בֵּינֵיהֶם וּמִסְתַּלֵּק, אִי רַבִּי עֲקִיבָא – אַף עַל גַּב דְּלָא אִישְׁתְּבַע, אָמַר: עַד שֶׁיְּשַׁלֵּם גְּזֵילָה לְכׇל אֶחָד וְאֶחָד!

The Gemara clarifies: In accordance with **whose** opinion is the mishna written? **If** one suggests that it is in accordance with the opinion of **Rabbi Tarfon,** it is not so, because **even though** the robber **took** a false **oath** that he did not rob, Rabbi Tarfon **says: He places** the **stolen item between them and withdraws;** it is not his responsibility to ensure that it reaches the robbery victim. **If** one suggests that it is in accordance with the opinion of **Rabbi Akiva,** it is also not so, because **even though** the robber **did not** necessarily **take** a false **oath,** Rabbi Akiva **says:** He is not considered to have returned the stolen item **until he pays** the value of the **stolen item to each and every one** of the five, while the mishna rules that his obligation is contingent upon his having taken the false oath.

לְעוֹלָם רַבִּי עֲקִיבָא הִיא, וְכִי קָאָמַר רַבִּי עֲקִיבָא עַד שֶׁיְּשַׁלֵּם גְּזֵילָה לְכׇל אֶחָד וְאֶחָד, הֵיכָא דְּאִישְׁתְּבַע הוּא דְּקָאָמַר; מַאי טַעְמָא? דְּאָמַר קְרָא: "לַאֲשֶׁר הוּא לוֹ יִתְּנֶנּוּ בְּיוֹם אַשְׁמָתוֹ".

The Gemara answers: **Actually, it is** in accordance with the opinion of **Rabbi Akiva, and when Rabbi Akiva says** that the robber is not considered to have returned the stolen item **until he pays** the value of the **stolen item to each and every one** of the five, it is only in a case **where** the robber **took** a false **oath that** Rabbi Akiva **says** this. **What is the reason? As the verse states** with regard to one who takes a false oath concerning a financial obligation: **"Unto him to whom it appertains shall he give it, on the day of his being guilty"** (Leviticus 5:24). The *halakha* that the guilty party must make a rigorous effort to return what he owes is stated in the case of one who took a false oath, and Rabbi Akiva would state his ruling only in that case.

וְרַבִּי טַרְפוֹן? אַף עַל גַּב דְּאִישְׁתְּבַע עֲבוּד רַבָּנַן תַּקַּנְתָּא; דְּתַנְיָא, רַבִּי אֶלְעָזָר בְּרַבִּי צָדוֹק אוֹמֵר: תַּקָּנָה גְּדוֹלָה הִתְקִינוּ, שֶׁאִם הָיְתָה הוֹצָאָה יְתֵירָה עַל הַקֶּרֶן – מְשַׁלֵּם קֶרֶן וְחוֹמֶשׁ לְבֵית דִּין, וּמֵבִיא אֲשָׁמוֹ וּמִתְכַּפֵּר לוֹ.

The Gemara asks: **And** how does **Rabbi Tarfon** rule that a robber who took a false oath is not required to pay all claimants, being that the verse indicates otherwise? The Gemara answers: **Even though he took** a false **oath** and by Torah law is obligated to return the stolen item to the robbery victim, **the Sages instituted an ordinance** allowing him to place it between the five possible victims, **as it is taught** in a *baraita* that **Rabbi Elazar, son of Rabbi Tzadok, says:** The Sages **instituted a great ordinance**[N] stating **that if the expense** required to return a stolen item to the victim **is greater than the principal,** the robber may **pay the principal and** the additional **one-fifth** payment **to the court, and** he then **brings his guilt-offering and achieves atonement for himself.** This ordinance would apply here as well, as the expense required to pay all five claimants is greater than the principal.

וְרַבִּי עֲקִיבָא? כִּי עֲבוּד רַבָּנַן תַּקַּנְתָּא – הֵיכָא דְּיָדַע לְמַאן גַּזְלֵיהּ, דְּקָא מַהְדַּר לֵיהּ מָמוֹנָא לְמָרֵיהּ. גָּזַל אֶחָד מֵחֲמִשָּׁה, דְּלָא יָדַע לְמַאן גַּזְלֵיהּ, דְּלָא הָדַר מָמוֹנָא לְמָרֵיהּ – לָא עֲבוּד רַבָּנַן תַּקַּנְתָּא.

The Gemara asks: **And** doesn't **Rabbi Akiva** agree that the Sages instituted this ordinance? The Gemara answers: Rabbi Akiva holds that **when the Sages instituted the ordinance,** they did so only for cases **where** the robber **knows whom he robbed, as** in such cases **he is** definitely **returning the money to its owner** by depositing it with the court, who will convey it to the robbery victim. But in the case of one who **robbed one of five** people, **where he does not know whom he robbed,** and **where,** by merely placing the stolen item between the five of them **the money is not returned to its owner, the Sages did not institute an ordinance.**

מֵתִיב רַב הוּנָא בַּר יְהוּדָה: אָמַר רַבִּי שִׁמְעוֹן בֶּן אֶלְעָזָר: לֹא נֶחְלְקוּ רַבִּי טַרְפוֹן וְרַבִּי עֲקִיבָא עַל שֶׁלָּקַח אֶחָד מֵחֲמִשָּׁה וְאֵינוֹ יוֹדֵעַ מֵאֵיזֶה מֵהֶן לָקַח, שֶׁמַּנִּיחַ דְּמֵי מִקָּח בֵּינֵיהֶם וּמִסְתַּלֵּק. עַל מָה נֶחְלְקוּ? שֶׁגָּזַל אֶחָד מֵחֲמִשָּׁה בְּנֵי אָדָם וְאֵינוֹ יוֹדֵעַ מֵאֵיזֶה מֵהֶן גָּזַל, שֶׁרַבִּי טַרְפוֹן אוֹמֵר: מַנִּיחַ דְּמֵי גְזֵילָה בֵּינֵיהֶם וּמִסְתַּלֵּק, וְרַבִּי עֲקִיבָא אוֹמֵר: אֵין לוֹ תַּקָּנָה עַד שֶׁיְּשַׁלֵּם גְּזֵילָה לְכׇל אֶחָד וְאֶחָד;

Rav Huna bar Yehuda raises an objection to the explanation that Rabbi Akiva stated his opinion specifically in a case where the robber took an oath. The *baraita* in the *Tosefta* (*Yevamot* 14:2) states that **Rabbi Shimon ben Elazar says: Rabbi Tarfon and Rabbi Akiva did not disagree with regard to one who purchased** an item **from** one of **five**[H] people **and does not know from which of them he purchased** it, as both agree **that** in this case **he places the money of the purchase between them and withdraws.** Since the purchaser has not transgressed, he is not penalized by being required to suffer the loss of paying each of them. **With regard to what did they disagree?** They disagree with regard to one **who robbed one of five people, and he does not know from which of them he robbed** the item, **as Rabbi Tarfon says: He places the stolen item between them and withdraws, and Rabbi Akiva says: He has no remedy,** i.e., he has not fulfilled his obligation to return the stolen item, **until he pays** the value of **the stolen item to each and every one** of them.

NOTES

They instituted a great ordinance – **תַּקָּנָה גְּדוֹלָה הִתְקִינוּ**: The Meiri explains that this ordinance was instituted for circumstances in which the return of the stolen item would entail a significantly greater expense on the part of the robber than the value of the stolen item itself. Nevertheless, once the Sages instituted the ordinance, it applies to all cases in which the expense would exceed the value of the stolen item, even if by only a little. Maharatz Ḥayyut, based on Rashi in tractate *Shevuot* 47a, writes that this ordinance is referred to as great because the Sages were audacious enough to override the Torah law that a robber must return the stolen item at any cost. This ordinance was instituted for the sake of the robbers, in order to encourage repentant robbers to return others' items, and to this end the Sages also allowed a robber to deliver his payment to the court.

HALAKHA

Purchased from one of five – **לָקַח אֶחָד מֵחֲמִשָּׁה**: One who purchased an item from one of five people, but does not remember from whom, is not obligated to pay every one of them that claims he was the seller. Rather, he may place the purchase money between them in a manner that the money will remain secure and he may then withdraw. When the true seller is identified, he will take the money. There is disagreement among the halakhic authorities concerning whether the money should remain in the possession of the purchaser or if it is transferred to the court (see *Shakh*). It is considered an act of piety for the purchaser to pay all of the five, provided that they claim to be the seller (Rambam *Sefer Kinyan*, *Hilkhot Mekhira* 20:2; *Shulḥan Arukh*, *Ḥoshen Mishpat* 222:2).

וְאִי סָלְקָא דַּעְתָּךְ דְּאִישְׁתַּבַּע, מָה לִי לָקַח מָה לִי גָּזַל?

Rav Huna bar Yehuda states his objection: **And if it enters your mind that** Rabbi Akiva stated his ruling specifically **with regard to** one who **took** a false **oath, what** is the difference **to me** if he **purchased** an item from another, and **what** is the difference **to me** if he **robbed**[H] him? In either case he has transgressed the prohibition against taking a false oath denying his obligation, and he should be penalized by being required to ensure that the one to whom he owes the money receives it.

וְעוֹד מְתִיב רָבָא: מַעֲשֶׂה בְּחָסִיד אֶחָד שֶׁלָּקַח מִשְּׁנֵי בְּנֵי אָדָם וְלֹא הָיָה יוֹדֵעַ מֵאֵיזֶה מֵהֶן לָקַח, וּבָא לִפְנֵי רַבִּי טַרְפוֹן, אָמַר לוֹ: הַנַּח דְּמֵי מִקָּחֲךָ בֵּינֵיהֶם וְהִסְתַּלֵּק. בָּא לִפְנֵי רַבִּי עֲקִיבָא, אָמַר לוֹ: אֵין לְךָ תַּקָּנָה עַד שֶׁתְּשַׁלֵּם לְכׇל אֶחָד וְאֶחָד; וְאִי סָלְקָא דַּעְתָּךְ דְּמִישְׁתַּבַּע, חָסִיד מִי מִישְׁתַּבַּע בְּשִׁיקְרָא?

And Rava raises another objection to the explanation that Rabbi Akiva stated his opinion specifically in a case where the robber took an oath. There was **an incident involving a certain pious** man **who purchased** an item **from** one of **two people, and he did not know from which of them he purchased** the item, **and he came before Rabbi Tarfon** for a ruling. Rabbi Tarfon **said to him: Place the money of your purchase between them and withdraw. He** then **came before Rabbi Akiva,** who **said to him: You have no remedy until you pay each and every one,** i.e., both of them. **And if it enters your mind** that Rabbi Akiva stated his ruling specifically **where** the purchaser **took** a false **oath, does a pious** man **take a false oath?** It seems from this incident that Rabbi Akiva rules he must pay all potential owners regardless of whether or not he took a false oath.

וְכִי תֵּימָא, דְּמִישְׁתַּבַּע וַהֲדַר הֲוֵי חָסִיד, וְהָא כׇּל הֵיכָא דְּאָמְרִינַן ״מַעֲשֶׂה בְּחָסִיד אֶחָד״ – אוֹ רַבִּי יְהוּדָה בֶּן בָּבָא אוֹ רַבִּי יְהוּדָה בְּרַבִּי אִילְעַאי, וְרַבִּי יְהוּדָה בֶּן בָּבָא וְרַבִּי יְהוּדָה בְּרַבִּי אִילְעַאי חֲסִידִים דְּמֵעִיקָּרָא הָווּ!

And if you would say that perhaps **he took** a false **oath and** later **became a pious man, but** isn't there a tradition that **anywhere that we say: There was an incident involving a certain pious** man, the pious man is **either Rabbi Yehuda ben Bava**[P] **or Rabbi Yehuda, son of Rabbi Elai,**[P] **and Rabbi Yehuda ben Bava and Rabbi Yehuda, son of Rabbi Elai, were** both **pious** men **from the beginning.**

אֶלָּא לְעוֹלָם רַבִּי טַרְפוֹן הִיא, וּמוֹדֶה רַבִּי טַרְפוֹן הֵיכָא דְּאִישְׁתַּבַּע, מַאי טַעְמָא? דְּאָמַר קְרָא: ״לַאֲשֶׁר הוּא לוֹ יִתְּנֶנּוּ בְּיוֹם אַשְׁמָתוֹ״. וְרַבִּי עֲקִיבָא, דְּאָמַר אַף עַל גַּב דְּלָא מִישְׁתַּבַּע – קְנָיס.

Due to these objections, the Gemara offers an alternative explanation. **Rather,** the mishna here **is actually** in accordance with the opinion of **Rabbi Tarfon, and Rabbi Tarfon concedes** that a robber must pay every potential owner in a case **where he took** a false **oath,** as is the case in the mishna here. **What is the reason? As the verse states: "Unto him to whom it appertains shall he give it, in the day of his being guilty"** (Leviticus 5:24). This verse, which requires one to go to any length to return money owed, is referring specifically to one who takes a false oath concerning his financial obligation. **And Rabbi Akiva, who said** in the mishna in tractate *Yevamot* that a robber must pay all potential owners **even though he did not take** a false **oath,** agrees that the verse is referring specifically to one who takes a false oath, but holds that the Sages **penalize** the robber by obligating him to pay them all in any event.

וְרַבִּי טַרְפוֹן, מִכְּדֵי הֵיכָא דְּמִישְׁתַּבַּע לָא סַגִּיא דְּלָא הוֹדָה, מַאי אִירְיָא וְנִשְׁבַּע? אֲפִילּוּ בְּלָא שְׁבוּעָה נָמֵי! דְּתַנְיָא: מוֹדֶה רַבִּי טַרְפוֹן, בְּאוֹמֵר לִשְׁנַיִם ״גָּזַלְתִּי אֶחָד מִכֶּם מָנֶה וְאֵינִי יוֹדֵעַ אֵיזֶה מִכֶּם״ – נוֹתֵן לָזֶה מָנֶה וְלָזֶה מָנֶה,

The Gemara questions this explanation of the mishna: **But** if the mishna is in accordance with the opinion of **Rabbi Tarfon, after all,** the mere fact that it is a case **where he took** a false **oath is not sufficient** to obligate him to pay the additional one-fifth and to bring a guilt-offering if it is a case **where he did not** also **admit**[N] that he took a false oath and owes the money. Therefore, **why** would the mishna here **specifically** state: **And he took** a false **oath? Even without** taking the false **oath,** the robber should **also** be obligated to pursue the owner as a result of his having admitted his obligation. **As it is taught** in a *baraita*: **Rabbi Tarfon concedes** that in a case where a robber **says to two** people: **I robbed one of you of one hundred dinars and I do not know which of you** it was, **he gives one hundred dinars to this** person **and one hundred dinars to that** person,

HALAKHA

What is the difference to me if he purchased, and what is the difference to me if he robbed – מָה לִי לָקַח מָה לִי גָּזַל: One who purchased an item from one of five people and took a false oath that he did not do so must pay each one of them that claims to be the seller. The court enforces this obligation (Rambam *Sefer Kinyan*, *Hilkhot Mekhira* 20:3; *Shulḥan Arukh*, *Ḥoshen Mishpat* 222:3 and *Taz* there).

PERSONALITIES

Rabbi Yehuda ben Bava – רַבִּי יְהוּדָה בֶּן בָּבָא: Rabbi Yehuda ben Bava was one of the *tanna'im* active during the period between the destruction of the Second Temple and the destruction of the city of Beitar. He began his studies while the Temple was still standing, but was most active during the years when the Sanhedrin was located in Yavne. His testimonies and other statements are mentioned in many sources. He was famous for his piety.

According to the Gemara in tractate *Sanhedrin*, he was cruelly executed by the Romans after ordaining five Rabbis to serve as judges. It was said about him: If not for him, the *halakhot* of fines would have disappeared from among the Jewish people. According to the calculations, he must have been over the age of ninety when he died.

Rabbi Yehuda son of Rabbi Elai – רַבִּי יְהוּדָה בְּרַבִּי אִילְעַאי: When the Mishna refers to Rabbi Yehuda without any addition, it means Rabbi Yehuda, son of Rabbi Elai, one of the greatest of the fourth-generation *tanna'im*. He was one of the last five disciples of Rabbi Akiva, while his father, Rabbi Elai, was a student of Rabbi Eliezer. Rabbi Yehuda learned Rabbi Eliezer's Torah statements from his father. Rabbi Yehuda's foremost teacher was Rabbi Akiva, and it was in accordance with his opinion that he laid the foundations for the halakhic exegesis of Leviticus known as the *Sifra*, or *Torat Kohanim*. According to tradition, any unattributed statement in the *Sifra* was authored by Rabbi Yehuda.

Rabbi Yehuda was ordained by Rabbi Yehuda ben Bava and is frequently quoted in aggadic sources alongside Rabbi Neḥemya. His disciples included Rabbi Elazar, son of Rabbi Shimon; Rabbi Yishmael, son of Rabbi Yosei; and Rabbi Yehuda HaNasi. His son, Rabbi Yosei, son of Rabbi Yehuda, was also a renowned Sage.

NOTES

It is not sufficient where he did not admit – לָא סַגִּיא דְּלָא הוֹדָה: *Tosafot* and the Ra'avad explain that since the court had already exempted the robber from payment based on his oath, it is clear that he is admitting his obligation in order to repent, without any ulterior motives. If this is the case, even Rabbi Tarfon would agree that the robber must return the stolen item to its owner in order to atone for his act, just as he concedes that a robber who does not know whom he robbed must pay all claimants if he wishes to atone for his robbery, as the Gemara will now note. Rashi explains that the Torah describes a robber's obligation to return a stolen item in order to achieve atonement only after it mentions his admission of guilt. Therefore, anyone who admits that he must return a stolen item is included in the Torah's obligation to pay the principal and additional one-fifth payment, and to bring a guilt-offering.

שֶׁכְּבָר הוֹדָה מִפִּי עַצְמוֹ!

as he has already admitted his obligation on his own.[H] Rabbi Tarfon concedes that a robber who wishes to repent must go to any length to return the stolen item to its owner. If the mishna here is in accordance with his opinion, it should not have stated its ruling specifically in a case where the robber took a false oath.

אֶלָּא אָמַר רָבָא: שָׁאנֵי מַתְנִיתִין, דְּכֵיוָן דְּיָדַע לְמַאן גַּזְלֵיהּ וְאוֹדֵי לֵיהּ, כֵּיוָן דְּאֶפְשָׁר לְאַהֲדוּרֵי מָמוֹנָא לְמָרֵיהּ הָוֵה לֵיהּ כְּמַאן דְּאָמַר לֵיהּ ״יְהֵיו לִי בְּיָדְךָ״. הִלְכָּךְ: נִשְׁבַּע, אַף עַל גַּב דְּקָאָמַר לֵיהּ ״יְהֵיו לִי בְּיָדְךָ״, כֵּיוָן דְּבָעֵי כַּפָּרָה – לָא סַגֵּי עַד דְּמָטֵי לִידֵיהּ; הָא לָא אִישְׁתַּבַּע – הָוֵי גַּבֵּיהּ פִּקָּדוֹן עַד דְּאָתֵי וְשָׁקֵיל לֵיהּ.

Rather, Rava said: The case of **the mishna is different,**[N] and the *halakha* stated here could be in accordance with the opinions of both Rabbi Tarfon and Rabbi Akiva. **For as** the robber **knows whom he robbed and admitted to him** that he robbed him, **since it is possible to return the money to its owner,** the robbery victim **is as the one who says to** the robber: The money you owe me **will be** kept **in your possession** as a deposit **for me. Therefore,** in a case where the robber **took** a false **oath, even though** the owner is considered to have **said to him:** The money you owe me **will be** kept **in your possession** as a deposit **for me, since** the robber **requires atonement** for his false oath, **it is not possible** for him to achieve atonement **until** the money **reaches the possession of** the robbery victim. **But** in a case where the robber **did not take** a false **oath,**[H] the money **is** considered as a **deposit** given **to** the robber **until** the owner **comes and takes it.**

״לֹא יִתֵּן לֹא לִבְנוֹ וְלֹא לִשְׁלוּחוֹ״. אִיתְּמַר: שָׁלִיחַ שֶׁעֲשָׂאוֹ בְּעֵדִים, רַב חִסְדָּא אָמַר: הָוֵי שָׁלִיחַ, רַבָּה אָמַר: לָא הָוֵי שָׁלִיחַ.

§ The mishna teaches that if the robber wishes to return the stolen item, he **may not give** the payment **to** the robbery victim's **son** to return it to the robbery victim, **nor to his agent.** The Gemara comments: It **was stated** with regard to **an agent who was appointed in** the presence of **witnesses**[H] to collect a debt from another: **Rav Ḥisda said:** Such an agent **is** a legally recognized **agent,** so that the debtor is considered to have repaid his debt as soon as he transfers the money to the agent, and the debtor will not be held responsible if an accident occurs causing the loss of the money before the agent gives it to the creditor. **Rabba said:** Such an agent **is not** a legally recognized **agent,** and the debtor remains responsible until the money reaches the creditor's possession.

רַב חִסְדָּא אָמַר הָוֵי שָׁלִיחַ; לְהָכִי טַרְחֵי וְאוֹקְמֵיהּ בְּעֵדִים – דְּלֵיקוּ בִּרְשׁוּתֵיהּ. רַבָּה אָמַר לָא הָוֵי שָׁלִיחַ; הָכִי קָאָמַר: אִינִישׁ מְהֵימְנָא הוּא, אִי סָמְכַתְּ – סְמוֹךְ, אִי בָּעֵית לְשַׁדּוּרֵיהּ בִּידֵיהּ – שַׁדַּר בִּידֵיהּ.

The Gemara explains their respective opinions: **Rav Ḥisda said** that he **is an agent** because it was **for this** reason that the creditor **took the trouble and appointed** the agent **in** the presence of **witnesses, in order to place** the matter **under** the agent's **domain. Rabba said** that he **is not an agent** because **this is** what the creditor is assumed to be **saying** to the debtor: This individual **is a trustworthy person. If you** are willing to **rely** on him, then **rely** on him to convey the payment to me. Similarly: **If you wish to send** the debt **in his possession,** then **send** it **in his possession.**

NOTES

Rather, Rava said, the case of the mishna is different, etc. – אֶלָּא אָמַר רָבָא שָׁאנֵי מַתְנִיתִין וכו׳: Rashi, Rabbeinu Ḥananel, and many early commentaries accept this version of the text in the Gemara, and understand that Rava is offering a new explanation of the mishna. According to this interpretation, the mishna can be in accordance with both the opinion of Rabbi Tarfon and Rabbi Akiva, as they both agree that a robber who takes a false oath must return payment directly to the owner and that one who does not take a false oath is considered as a bailee of the stolen item.

The Ra'avad, Ba'al HaMaor, and *Tosafot* had an alternate version of the text that omits the word: Rather. According to this version, Rava is adding to the previous explanation, and posits that the mishna is in accordance with the opinion of Rabbi Tarfon, who requires a robber to return payment directly to the owner only if he has admitted his guilt after taking a false oath. Rabbeinu Peretz suggests the opposite explanation: Rava is suggesting that the mishna is in accordance with the opinion of Rabbi Akiva exclusively. According to him, Rabbi Akiva holds that the Sages imposed a fine only upon a robber who took a false oath; otherwise, the robber is considered a bailee of the stolen item.

HALAKHA

As he has already admitted on his own – שֶׁכְּבָר הוֹדָה מִפִּי עַצְמוֹ: If a robber says to two people: I robbed one of you but do not know which, if he desires to fulfill his obligation to Heaven, he should pay the full amount to each of them. According to *halakha*, he may pay the full amount to the two of them, and they will divide it (Rambam *Sefer Nezikin, Hilkhot Gezeila VaAveda* 4:10; *Shulḥan Arukh, Ḥoshen Mishpat* 365:2).

But in a case where the robber did not take a false oath – הָא לָא אִישְׁתַּבַּע: One who robs another and denies having done so without taking a false oath is not obligated to pursue the robbery victim in order to return the stolen item. Rather, he holds on to it as a deposit until the robbery victim arrives to claim it. Some hold that the robber is not even obligated to send messengers to inform the robbery victim of his willingness to return the stolen item, but may wait until the robbery victim returns to the robber's location (Maharshal), though others disagree (*Shakh*). The Rema, citing the Rosh and the *Tur*, writes that the robber must send messengers to inform the robbery victim that he may collect the stolen item. This ruling is based on Rava's emphasis that the robber admitted his guilt to the robbery victim (Rambam *Sefer Nezikin, Hilkhot Gezeila VaAveda* 7:9; *Shulḥan Arukh, Ḥoshen Mishpat* 367:1 and *Beur HaGra* there).

An agent who was appointed in the presence of witnesses – שָׁלִיחַ שֶׁעֲשָׂאוֹ בְּעֵדִים: If one who is owed money by another appoints an agent in the presence of witnesses and authorizes him to collect the debt, the debtor has fulfilled his obligation to return the debt once he transfers the money to the agent. This is in accordance with the opinions of Rav Ḥisda, Rabbi Yoḥanan, and Rabbi Elazar (Rambam *Sefer Nezikin, Hilkhot Gezeila VaAveda* 7:10 and *Sefer Kinyan, Hilkhot Sheluḥin VeShutafin* 3:5; *Shulḥan Arukh, Ḥoshen Mishpat* 121:1, 367:2; see also 123).

תְּנַן: הַשּׁוֹאֵל אֶת הַפָּרָה, וְשִׁילְּחָהּ בְּיַד בְּנוֹ בְּיַד עַבְדּוֹ בְּיַד שְׁלוּחוֹ, אוֹ בְּיַד בְּנוֹ בְּיַד עַבְדּוֹ בְּיַד שְׁלוּחוֹ שֶׁל שׁוֹאֵל, וּמֵתָה – פָּטוּר;

The Gemara cites a mishna that poses a difficulty to the opinion of Rav Ḥisda. **We learned** in a mishna (*Bava Metzia* 98b): With regard to **one who** enters into an agreement to **borrow a cow**[H] from another, **and** the owner **sent it** to the borrower **in the possession of his** own **son,** or **in the possession of his** own **slave,** or **in the possession of his** own **agent, or** if he sent it **in the possession of the borrower's son,** or **in the possession of** the borrower's **slave,** or **in the possession of** the borrower's **agent, and** the cow **died,** the borrower is **exempt** from paying for the cow, as it never entered his possession.

הַאי שְׁלוּחוֹ הֵיכִי דָּמֵי? אִי דְּלָא עָשָׂה בְּעֵדִים, מְנָא יָדְעִינַן? אֶלָּא דְּעָשָׂה בְּעֵדִים, וְקָתָנֵי דְּפָטוּר, קַשְׁיָא לְרַב חִסְדָּא!

The Gemara explains the case of the mishna: With regard to **this agent of** the borrower, **what are the circumstances** surrounding his appointment? **If** the mishna is discussing a case **where he did not appoint** him as his agent **in** the presence of **witnesses, how do we know** that he was appointed as an agent? **Rather,** it must be that it is a case **where he appointed** him as his agent **in** the presence of **witnesses, and** yet the mishna **teaches that** the borrower is **exempt.** This poses **a difficulty to** the opinion of **Rav Ḥisda,** who holds that one acquires property through his agent. According to his reasoning, the borrower should be held responsible for the cow once it reaches the possession of the agent.

כִּדְאָמַר רַב חִסְדָּא: בִּשְׂכִירוֹ וּלְקִיטוֹ, הָכָא נַמִי בִּשְׂכִירוֹ וּלְקִיטוֹ.

The Gemara answers: It is **as that** which **Rav Ḥisda said** concerning a different mishna: This is stated **with regard to his hired** hand **or his** regular **harvester;**[N] **here also** the mishna in *Bava Metzia* is **with regard to his hired** hand **or his** regular **harvester.** The mishna discusses a case where there were no witnesses to the appointment of the agent, and therefore it does not pose a difficulty to the opinion of Rav Ḥisda. Yet, since it is well known that this person is constantly in the owner's service, he is assumed to be acting as his agent.

תְּנַן: לֹא יִתֵּן לֹא לִבְנוֹ וְלֹא לִשְׁלוּחוֹ; הַאי שְׁלוּחוֹ הֵיכִי דָּמֵי? אִי דְּלָא עֲשָׂאוֹ בְּעֵדִים, מְנָא יָדְעִינַן? אֶלָּא לָאו דַּעֲשָׂאוֹ בְּעֵדִים! תִּרְגְּמָא רַב חִסְדָּא: בִּשְׂכִירוֹ וּלְקִיטוֹ.

The Gemara poses a difficulty to the opinion of Rav Ḥisda from the mishna here. **We learned** in the mishna: If the robber wishes to return the stolen item, he **may not give** the payment **to** the robbery victim's **son** to return it to the robbery victim, **nor to his agent.** With regard to **this agent of** the robbery victim, **what are the circumstances** surrounding his appointment? **If** the mishna is discussing a case **where** the robbery victim **did not appoint him** as his agent **in** the presence of **witnesses, how do we know** that he was appointed as an agent? **Rather, is it not** discussing a case **where** the robbery victim **appointed him** as his agent **in** the presence of **witnesses,** and the robber nevertheless does not fulfill his obligation to return the stolen item by giving it to this agent? The Gemara answers: **Rav Ḥisda interpreted** the ruling of the mishna **with regard to his hired** hand **or his** regular **harvester,** who do not require witnesses to validate their appointment as his agent.

אֲבָל שָׁלִיחַ שֶׁעֲשָׂאוֹ בְּעֵדִים, מַאי? הָכִי נַמִי דְּהָוֵי שָׁלִיחַ? אַדְּתָנֵי סֵיפָא: אֲבָל נוֹתֵן הוּא לִשְׁלִיחַ בֵּית דִּין, לִפְלוֹג וְלִיתְנֵי בְּדִידֵיהּ: שָׁלִיחַ שֶׁעֲשָׂאוֹ בְּעֵדִים הָכִי נַמִי דְּהָוֵי שָׁלִיחַ!

The Gemara asks: **But** with regard to **an agent who** the robbery victim **appointed in** the presence of **witnesses, what** is the *halakha*? Would one say that **indeed,** one appointed before witnesses **is** a legally recognized **agent?** If that is the case, **instead of teaching in the latter clause: But he may give** the payment **to an agent of the court,** which indicates that this is the only agent to whom he may give it, **let** the mishna **make a distinction within** the case of an agent appointed by the robbery victim **itself and teach: An agent who** the robbery victim **appointed in** the presence of **witnesses is indeed** a legally recognized **agent.** If an agent appointed in the presence of witnesses is a legally recognized agent, why does the mishna shift to discuss an agent of the court?

HALAKHA

One who enters into an agreement to borrow a cow, etc. – **הַשּׁוֹאֵל אֶת הַפָּרָה וכו׳**: One who arranges to borrow a cow, which is then delivered by an agent, is not responsible for the animal until it reaches his possession, regardless of whether the agent is the owner's or his own. Nevertheless, if the borrower appointed the agent in the presence of witnesses (*Leḥem Mishne*), or had agreed with the owner to have the animal delivered, the borrower is responsible for the cow as soon as it enters the agent's possession (Rambam *Sefer Mishpatim, Hilkhot She'ela UFikadon* 3:1; *Shulḥan Arukh, Ḥoshen Mishpat* 340:5).

NOTES

His hired hand or his regular harvester – **שְׂכִירוֹ וּלְקִיטוֹ**: All are aware that these people are affiliated with the owner and would be considered as his agents even without an appointment in the presence of witnesses. Nevertheless, one who transferred an item to them could still be responsible for any mishaps or accidents.

אָמְרִי: לָא פְּסִיקָא לֵיהּ; שְׁלִיחַ בֵּית דִּין, לָא שְׁנָא עֲשָׂאוֹ נִגְזָל וְלָא שְׁנָא עֲשָׂאוֹ גַּזְלָן הָוֵי שָׁלִיחַ – פְּסִיקָא לֵיהּ. שָׁלִיחַ שֶׁעֲשָׂאוֹ בְּעֵדִים, דְּכִי עֲשָׂאוֹ נִגְזָל הוּא דְּהָוֵי שָׁלִיחַ, עֲשָׂאוֹ גַּזְלָן לָא הָוֵי שָׁלִיחַ – לָא פְּסִיקָא לֵיהּ;

The Sages **say** in response: Although the *tanna* of the mishna could have stated the case of an agent appointed by the robbery victim in the presence of witnesses, **he** could **not** have stated this *halakha* **definitively,** as with regard to **an agent of the court,** there **is no difference** whether the **robbery victim appointed him** as an agent, i.e., the court appointed him at the behest of the robbery victim, **and** there **is no difference** whether the **robber appointed him** as an agent, i.e., the court appointed him at the behest of the robber. In both cases **he is** a legally recognized **agent.** Therefore, **he** could state the *halakha* concerning an agent of the court **definitively.** By contrast, with regard to **an agent who was appointed in** the presence of **witnesses, that** only **when** the **robbery victim appointed him** as an agent **he is an agent,** but when the **robber appointed him** as an agent, **he is not an agent,** as the robber cannot appoint an agent to receive payment on behalf of the robbery victim, **he** could **not** have stated this *halakha* **definitively.**

וּלְאַפּוּקֵי מֵהַאי תַּנָּא, דְּתַנְיָא, רַבִּי שִׁמְעוֹן בֶּן אֶלְעָזָר אוֹמֵר: שְׁלִיחַ בֵּית דִּין שֶׁעֲשָׂאוֹ נִגְזָל וְלֹא עֲשָׂאוֹ גַּזְלָן, אוֹ עֲשָׂאוֹ גַּזְלָן וְשָׁלַח הַלָּה וְנָטַל אֶת שֶׁלּוֹ מִיָּדוֹ – פָּטוּר.

The Gemara comments: **And** this mishna, which rules that an agent of the court is an agent even if appointed only by the robber, serves **to exclude** the opinion of **this** following ***tanna*****, as it is taught** in the *Tosefta* (10:11) that **Rabbi Shimon ben Elazar says:** If there was **an agent of the court who was appointed by** the **robbery victim but not appointed by** the **robber, or** an agent who **was appointed by** the **robber, and** subsequently **the other,** i.e., the robbery victim, **sent** for **and took his** payment **from** the agent's **possession,** the robber is **exempt** from paying for any accidental damage to the payment during the delivery. Rabbi Shimon ben Elazar states that the robber is exempt from paying for any accidental damage when he gave the payment to a court agent he appointed only if the robbery victim sent for and took possession of the payment. This is in opposition to the ruling of the mishna that the robber is exempt whenever he gives the payment to an agent of the court.

רַבִּי יוֹחָנָן וְרַבִּי אֶלְעָזָר דְּאָמְרִי תַּרְוַיְיהוּ: שָׁלִיחַ שֶׁעֲשָׂאוֹ בְּעֵדִים הָוֵי שָׁלִיחַ, וְאִם תֹּאמַר: מִשְׁנָתֵנוּ!

The Gemara cites the opinion of two other *amora'im* with regard to the status of an agent appointed in the presence of witnesses. **Rabbi Yoḥanan and Rabbi Elazar both say: An agent who was appointed in** the presence of **witnesses is** a legally recognized **agent. And if you say: Our mishna** contradicts this assertion, as it rules that the stolen item is not considered returned if given to an agent of the robbery victim, this is of no concern.

בְּמַמְצִיא לוֹ שָׁלִיחַ, דְּאָמַר לֵיהּ: אִית לִי זוּזֵי גַּבֵּי פְּלָנְיָא וְלָא קָא מְשַׁדַּר לְהוּ, אִיתְחֲזֵי לֵיהּ, דִּלְמָא אִינִישׁ הוּא דְּלָא מַשְׁכַּח לְשַׁדּוּרֵי לֵיהּ;

The Gemara explains: The mishna does not mean to disqualify an agent appointed by the robbery victim in the presence of witnesses, but rather is referring to a case **where** the robbery victim **provides** the robber **with an agent**[H] without appointing him in the presence of witnesses, in **that he says to** someone: **I have money** owed to me that is currently **with so-and-so, and he is not sending it. Present yourself to him,** as **perhaps** he wishes to return it but **cannot find a person with whom to send it.**

אִי נַמִי, כִּדְרַב חִסְדָּא: בִּשְׂכִירוֹ וּלְקִיטוֹ.

The Gemara offers a second explanation: **Alternatively,** it is **in accordance with** the statement **of Rav Ḥisda,** that the mishna is not discussing a case where he appointed the agent in the presence of witnesses, but it is still known that the agent acts on behalf of the robbery victim, as the ruling of the mishna is stated **with regard to the victim's hired** hand **or his** regular **harvester.** That is why the robber is still liable after having given the payment to the agent.

אָמַר רַב יְהוּדָה אָמַר שְׁמוּאֵל:

§ The Gemara discusses another matter relating to the appointment of an agent. **Rav Yehuda says** that **Shmuel says:**

HALAKHA

Where the robbery victim provides him with an agent – בְּמַמְצִיא לוֹ שָׁלִיחַ: An agent that was not formally appointed and was simply instructed to present himself to a particular debtor so that the latter will have an opportunity to repay his debt is not a legally recognized agent. This is the *halakha* even if he was given instructions about how to proceed in the presence of witnesses (*Sma*). Therefore, the borrower is held responsible for the payment even after it has entered such an agent's possession (*Shulḥan Arukh*, *Ḥoshen Mishpat* 121:2).

אֵין מְשַׁלְּחִין מָעוֹת בִּדְיוֹקָנִי, וַאֲפִילּוּ עֵדִים חֲתוּמִים עָלֶיהָ; וְרַבִּי יוֹחָנָן אָמַר: אִם עֵדִים חֲתוּמִים עָלֶיהָ – מְשַׁלְּחִין.

One who owes a debt **may not send money** with another to the creditor **on the basis of a figure** [*deyokani*][LHN] or sign used in place of a signature that is associated with the creditor. The possession of this sign on the part of the other is not sufficient proof that he has been appointed as an agent. **And** this is the *halakha* **even if witnesses** verifying that this is the creditor's sign **are signed on it. And Rabbi Yoḥanan says: If** there are **witnesses signed on it, one may send** the money with the other.

אָמְרִי: לִשְׁמוּאֵל מַאי תַּקַּנְתָּא? כִּי הָא דְּרַבִּי אַבָּא הֲוֵי מַסֵּיק זוּזֵי בְּדְרַב יוֹסֵף בַּר חָמָא, אֲמַר לֵיהּ לְרַב סָפְרָא: בַּהֲדֵי דְּאָתֵית אַיְיתִינְהוּ נִיהֲלִי. כִּי אֲזַל לְהָתָם, אֲמַר לֵיהּ רָבָא בְּרֵיהּ: מִי כְּתַב לָךְ "הִתְקַבַּלְתִּי"? אֲמַר לֵיהּ: לָא. אִי הָכִי, זִיל בְּרֵישָׁא וְלִכְתּוֹב לָךְ "הִתְקַבַּלְתִּי".

The Sages say: **According to Shmuel, what is the rectification,** i.e., what recourse is available to one who wishes to collect a debt without traveling to the debtor's location? The Gemara answers: One may act **like that** course of action **of Rabbi Abba, who was owed money**[N] **by Rav Yosef bar Ḥama.** Rabbi Abba **said to Rav Safra: When you come** back from Rabbi Yosef bar Ḥama's locale, **bring** my money **to me. When** Rav Safra **went there, Rava,** Rav Yosef bar Ḥama's **son, said to him: Did** Rabbi Abba **write you** a document stating: **I have received** payment, so that my father will have proof that he has absolved himself of the debt? Rav Safra **said to him: No.** Rava responded: **If so, first go** to him **and let him write you** a document stating: **I have received** payment, and then my father will pay you.

לַסּוֹף אֲמַר לֵיהּ: אִי כְּתַב לָךְ נַמִּי "הִתְקַבַּלְתִּי" לָאו כְּלוּם הוּא, דִּלְמָא אַדְּאָתֵית שָׁכֵיב רַבִּי אַבָּא וְנָפְלוּ זוּזֵי קַמֵּי יַתְמֵי, וְ"הִתְקַבַּלְתִּי" דְּרַבִּי אַבָּא לָאו כְּלוּם הוּא. אֲמַר לֵיהּ: וְאֶלָּא מַאי תַּקַּנְתָּא? זִיל נַקְנִינְהוּ לָךְ אַגַּב אַרְעָא, וְתָא אַתְּ כְּתוֹב לָן "הִתְקַבַּלְתִּי".

Ultimately, Rava **said to him: Even if he writes you** a document stating: **I have received** payment, **it is nothing,** since **perhaps by** the time **you arrive** back here, **Rabbi Abba will have died and the money will fall before** his **orphans** as an inheritance, **and the** document stating: **I have received** payment, that was written **by Rabbi Abba, will be nothing,** as the debt is no longer owed to him, but rather, to his heirs. Rav Safra **said to him: Rather, what is the rectification?** Rava replied: **Go,** and Rabbi Abba **will transfer to you**[H] the rights to the money owed to him **by means of** acquisition **of land**[N] from him, **and** then **you** should **come and write for us** a document stating: **I have received** payment.[N] Then, we will pay you.

LANGUAGE

Figure [*deyokani*] – דְּיוֹקָנִי: Apparently from the Greek δείκανον, *deikanon*, meaning a drawn or woven figure.

HALAKHA

One may not send money on the basis of a figure – אֵין מְשַׁלְּחִין מָעוֹת בִּדְיוֹקָנִי: One who was not appointed as an agent in the presence of witnesses to collect another's debt or deposit is not a legally recognized agent, even if he possesses signs authenticated by witnesses indicating that the creditor sent him. Accordingly, a debtor who transfers payment to such an agent is still responsible for the payment until it reaches the creditor's possession, as the *halakha* is in accordance with the opinion of Shmuel (Rambam *Sefer Kinyan, Hilkhot Sheluḥin VeShutafin* 1:8; *Shulḥan Arukh, Ḥoshen Mishpat* 121:3; see 121:4).

Go, and Rabbi Abba will transfer to you, etc. – זִיל נַקְנִינְהוּ לָךְ וכו׳: Although a creditor's legally recognized agent is able to accept payment transferred to him by the debtor, his agency is immediately terminated in the event of the creditor's death. If this happens before the agent is paid, the debtor remains responsible to pay the heirs of the creditor. Therefore, the debtor has the right to refuse to transfer payment to the agent. As Rava suggests, if the creditor transferred the debt to his agent by means of the acquisition of land, then the debtor has fulfilled his obligation to pay his debt by giving the payment to the agent, and he will have no further obligation even in the event of the original creditor's death (*Shulḥan Arukh, Ḥoshen Mishpat* 122:1).

NOTES

Money on the basis of a figure, etc. – מָעוֹת בִּדְיוֹקָנִי וכו׳: Most commentaries explain that the Gemara is referring to a case where a creditor sends another to collect a debt and provides him with a figure or sign, e.g., the creditor's signature or seal, to verify his status as the creditor's agent. This method of authentication is not accepted even if there are witnesses who testify that the signature or seal belongs to the creditor. Others understand that the reference here is not to an image per se, but to a set of signs or a code, known only to the debtor and creditor, which the latter shares with his agent (Rabbeinu Ḥananel; Rabbeinu Yehonatan of Lunel).

Tosafot explain that although it is proven that the creditor relies upon the one whom he entrusted with the sign, that person does not have the status of an agent. Consequently, the debtor would still be liable were an accident to occur causing the money to be lost before being delivered to the creditor. Accordingly, if one possesses a document signed by witnesses appointing him as the creditor's agent and authorizing him to collect payment, the debtor would be able to fulfill his obligation by paying this agent. There is uncertainty, however, whether the agent must be appointed in the debtor's presence. The *ge'onim* write that the *halakha* is dependent upon societal conventions, so that if documents of authorization are generally relied upon, or even if they had been relied upon by these specific people, they are accepted in this case.

Others write that the Gemara is referring to a case where witnesses signed a document authorizing its bearer to act as the creditor's agent. Accordingly, Shmuel does not assert that such an agent is not legally recognized. Rather, he advises debtors against transmitting payment via such an agent due to the concern Rava raises later, that in the event of the creditor's death, his heirs may be able to claim the debt a second time (Ra'avad; Ba'al HaMaor).

Was owed money – הֲוֵי מַסֵּיק זוּזֵי: The Rashba finds this version of the text troubling because there is a principle that while money can be transferred from one person to another, an abstract debt cannot, even by means of the acquisition of land. Accordingly, it should have been impossible for Rabbi Abba to transfer the debt to Rav Safra. The Rashba therefore prefers a different version of the text that reads: He had money, meaning that Rabbi Abba had left an actual deposit in Rav Yosef bar Ḥama's possession, as deposited money can be transferred from one person to another by means of the acquisition of land.

Will transfer to you by means of acquisition of land – נַקְנִינְהוּ לָךְ אַגַּב אַרְעָא: Movable property cannot be acquired by the payment of money or through the giving of a document. It must be transferred through pulling, which is a formal act of acquisition. In order to enable the acquisition of money without the need to perform a physical action, money may be transferred from one person to another along with one's land, as Rava suggested to Rav Safra.

Write for us, I have received payment – כְּתוֹב לָן הִתְקַבַּלְתִּי: This document stating: I received payment, is not identical to the one mentioned earlier. The former refers to a document certifying that responsibility for the payment has been transferred to the agent, while the latter verifies that the money itself has been returned directly to its legal owner (*Shita Mekubbetzet*).

כִּי הָא דְּרַב פַּפָּא הֲוָה מַסֵּיק תְּרֵיסַר אַלְפֵי זוּזֵי בֵּי חוֹזַאי, אַקְנִינְהוּ נִיהֲלֵיהּ לְרַב שְׁמוּאֵל בַּר אַבָּא אַגַּב אַסֵּיפָא דְּבֵיתֵיהּ. כִּי אֲתָא, נְפַק לְאַפֵּיהּ עַד תָּוָאךְ.

The Gemara notes: And this is **like that** course of action **of Rav Pappa, who was owed twelve thousand dinars** by a resident of **Bei Ḥozai,**[B] and **he transferred** his claim to the money **to Rav Shmuel bar Abba by means of** the acquisition of **the threshold of his house.**[N] **When** Rav Shmuel bar Abba **came** from Bei Ḥozai with the money in hand, Rav Pappa **went out as far as Tavakh**[B] **toward him** in his excitement to receive the money.

״נָתַן לוֹ אֶת הַקֶּרֶן״ וכו׳. אַלְמָא חוֹמֶשׁ מָמוֹנָא הוּא, וְאִם מָיֵית – מְשַׁלְּמִי לֵיהּ יוֹרְשִׁין.

§ The mishna teaches that if the robber **gave** the robbery victim **the principal** value of the stolen item, but did not give him the additional one-fifth payment required of a robber, he is not required to pursue the robbery victim in order to return the additional one-fifth payment. The Gemara comments: **Apparently,** the additional **one-fifth** payment **is** considered **monetary restitution**[N] rather than a fine. **And** accordingly, **if** the robber **died,** the **heirs** of the robber must **pay it** to the robbery victim.

וּתְנַן נַמִי: נָתַן אֶת הַקֶּרֶן וְנִשְׁבַּע עַל הַחוֹמֶשׁ – הֲרֵי מוֹסִיף חוֹמֶשׁ עַל חוֹמֶשׁ; אַלְמָא חוּמְשָׁא מָמוֹנָא הוּא.

And we also learned in the mishna that if the robber **gave** the robbery victim **the principal and takes** a false **oath** to him **concerning** the additional **one-fifth** payment, asserting that he had already paid it, the robber **adds** an additional **one-fifth** payment **apart from** the additional **one-fifth** payment about which he had taken a false oath. **Apparently,** the additional **one-fifth** payment **is monetary restitution,** as one is obligated to pay an additional one-fifth for taking a false oath only with regard to monetary restitution, not with regard to fines.

וְתַנְיָא נַמִי הָכִי: הַגּוֹזֵל אֶת חֲבֵירוֹ, וְנִשְׁבַּע לוֹ וּמֵת – יוֹרְשִׁין מְשַׁלְּמִים קֶרֶן וְחוֹמֶשׁ וּפְטוּרִין מִן הָאָשָׁם.

And this is also taught in a *baraita*: With regard to **one who robs another and takes** a false **oath to him** that he did not rob him, **and** then **dies,** his **heirs pay the principal and** additional **one-fifth** payments to the robbery victim, **but are exempt from** the obligation to bring **the guilt-offering.**[NH]

וְיוֹרְשִׁין בְּנֵי שַׁלּוּמֵי חוּמְשָׁא דַּאֲבוּהוֹן הָווּ, אַלְמָא חוֹמֶשׁ מָמוֹנָא הוּא וּבָעֵי שַׁלּוּמֵי יוֹרְשִׁין? וּרְמִינְהוּ: עֲדַיִין אֲנִי אוֹמֵר: אֵימָתַי אֵינוֹ מְשַׁלֵּם חוֹמֶשׁ עַל גֶּזֶל אָבִיו – בִּזְמַן שֶׁלֹּא נִשְׁבַּע לֹא הוּא וְלֹא אָבִיו;

The Gemara asks: **But are heirs obligated to pay the** additional **one-fifth** payment **of their father,** indicating that **apparently** the additional **one-fifth** payment **is monetary restitution, and** therefore the **heirs must pay** it? **But** one could **raise a contradiction** from a *baraita*. After having stated that one is required to add the additional one-fifth payment only for a robbery he commits himself, and not for a robbery committed by his father, the *baraita* states: **I** would **still say** that **when does** an heir **not pay** the additional **one-fifth** payment **for his father's robbery?**[H] It is only **when neither he nor his father took** a false **oath.**

הוּא וְלֹא אָבִיו, אָבִיו וְלֹא הוּא, הוּא וְאָבִיו מִנַּיִן? תַּלְמוּד לוֹמַר: ״אֲשֶׁר גָּזָל״ וַ״אֲשֶׁר עָשָׁק״, וְהוּא לֹא גָּזַל וְלֹא עָשַׁק!

But if **he** took a false oath, **but not his father;** or if **his father** took a false oath, **but not he;** or if **he and his father** both took false oaths; **from where** is the heir's exemption derived? **The verse states:** "He shall restore the item **that he robbed,"** and "the item **that he has acquired through exploitation"** (Leviticus 5:23), **and** in this case the heir **did not rob and did not exploit.** Since the verse states the obligation to pay the additional one-fifth payment when discussing one who robbed or exploited another, and the heir has done neither, he is exempt from payment. This *baraita* states that heirs are not obligated to pay the additional one-fifth payment.

BACKGROUND

Bei Ḥozai – בֵּי חוֹזַאי: This is a province in Persia, known today by the similar name of Khuzestan, which is located near where the Tigris and Euphrates rivers flow into the Persian Gulf. Although the province was home to a Jewish community, it never developed as a center of Torah scholarship due to its distance from the Babylonian academies. The residents of Bei Ḥozai were primarily occupied with international trade and, as evidenced in several sources, were rather violent people with little connection to Torah.

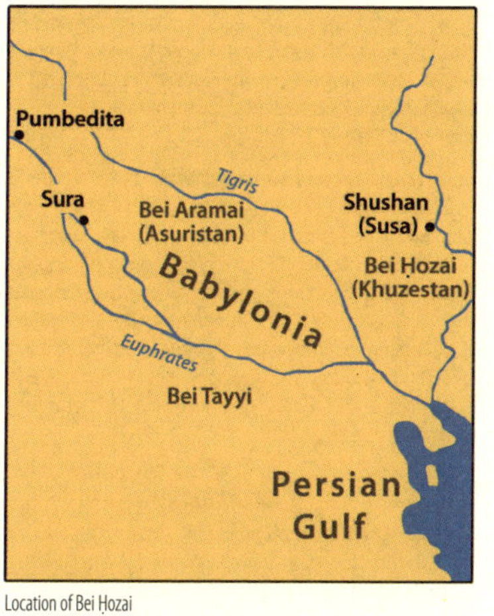

Location of Bei Ḥozai

Tavakh – תָּוָאךְ: Apparently this is the name of a town near Neresh (Nares) located on the caravan routes to Bei Ḥozai. A similar place name found in Babylonia is Tauk.

NOTES

By means of the acquisition of the threshold of his house – אַגַּב אַסֵּיפָא דְּבֵיתֵיהּ: According to most commentaries, the case in this Gemara is one where an individual was merely appointed as another's agent. If the creditor provided another with a document of authorization giving the latter full power of attorney, the ruling might be different (see Ra'avad and *Shita Mekubbetzet*).

Apparently the additional one-fifth payment is considered monetary restitution – אַלְמָא חוֹמֶשׁ מָמוֹנָא הוּא: Since the additional one-fifth payment is monetary restitution, one's obligation to pay it is transferred to the heirs in the event of the debtor's death (Rashi; *Shita Mekubbetzet*).

But are exempt from the obligation to bring the guilt-offering – וּפְטוּרִין מִן הָאָשָׁם: Even if the debtor had designated a particular animal to be brought as a guilt-offering, his heirs cannot sacrifice it in the Temple due to the *halakha* that an offering whose owner has died is no longer a valid offering. If their father had not designated an offering, the heirs have no responsibility to bring an offering, because atonement cannot be achieved for the dead (Rashi).

HALAKHA

Heirs are exempt from the guilt-offering – יוֹרְשִׁין פְּטוּרִין מִן הָאָשָׁם: One who inherits a stolen item cannot incur an obligation to bring a guilt-offering due to the robbery (Rambam *Sefer Nezikin, Hilkhot Gezeila VaAveda* 7:6).

When does an heir not pay the additional one-fifth for his father's robbery – אֵימָתַי אֵינוֹ מְשַׁלֵּם חוֹמֶשׁ עַל גֶּזֶל אָבִיו: If one took a false oath that he did not commit a robbery and later admitted his guilt before dying, his heir is responsible to pay the principal and one-fifth payments to the robbery victim. If the robber did not admit to the robbery, but the heir did, he is exempt from paying the additional one-fifth. If the heir himself took a false oath and later admitted his guilt, he is obligated to pay both the principal and one-fifth payments, provided that the stolen item is still extant. If the stolen item is no longer extant, he pays only the principal (Rambam *Sefer Nezikin, Hilkhot Gezeila VaAveda* 7:3–6).

אֲמַר רַב נַחְמָן, לָא קַשְׁיָא: כָּאן שֶׁהוֹדָה, כָּאן שֶׁלֹּא הוֹדָה.

The Gemara answers: **Rav Naḥman said** that it is **not difficult. Here,** in the mishna and the first *baraita*, they discuss a case **where** the robber **admitted** his obligation and therefore was required to pay the additional one-fifth payment, and this obligation is transferred to his heir; **there,** in the latter *baraita*, it discusses a case **where he did not admit** his obligation and was never required to pay the additional one-fifth payment.

אִי לֹא הוֹדָה, קֶרֶן נַמִּי לָא מְשַׁלֵּם! וְכִי תֵּימָא הָכִי נַמִּי דְּלָא מְשַׁלֵּם, וְהָא מִדְּקָא מַהֲדַר אַחוֹמֶשׁ, לְמֵימְרָא דְּקֶרֶן מְשַׁלֵּם!

The Gemara rejects this answer: **If** the latter *baraita* discusses a case where **he did not admit** his obligation, then the *halakha* would be that the heir **would not pay even the principal,** as the obligation is not known by anyone. **And if you would say** that **indeed it is so that he does not pay** the principal, **but** isn't it understood **from** the fact that the *tanna* **searches for** a source to teach the heir's exemption from only the additional **one-fifth** payment, **that** it means **to say that he does pay the principal.**

וְעוֹד תַּנְיָא: וַעֲדַיִין אֲנִי אוֹמֵר: אֵימָתַי הוּא מְשַׁלֵּם קֶרֶן עַל גֶּזֶל אָבִיו – בִּזְמַן שֶׁנִּשְׁבַּע הוּא וְאָבִיו; אָבִיו וְלֹא הוּא, הוּא וְלֹא אָבִיו, לֹא הוּא וְלֹא אָבִיו מִנַּיִן? תַּלְמוּד לוֹמַר: גְּזֵילָה וְעוֹשֶׁק אֲבֵידָה וּפִקָּדוֹן יֵשׁ תַּלְמוּד;

The Gemara also proves that the heir must pay the principal from the continuation of the same *baraita*. **And further, it is taught** in that *baraita*: **And I** would **still say: When does** the heir **pay the principal for his father's robbery?** It is only **when he and his father** both **took** false **oaths.** But if **his father** took a false oath, **and not he;** or if **he** took a false oath, **but not his father;** or if **neither he nor his father** took false oaths; **from where** is the heir's obligation to pay the principal derived? **The verse states** the following terms: **"Robbery," and "exploitation," "lost item," and "deposit"** (Leviticus 5:23); and **there is a derivation** [*yesh talmud*] here to derive that the heir is obligated to pay the principal in all of these cases.

וִיתֵיב רַב הוּנָא וְקָאָמַר לְהָא שְׁמַעְתָּא, אֲמַר לֵיהּ רַבָּה בְּרֵיהּ: ״יֵשׁ תַּלְמוּד״ קָאָמַר מָר, אוֹ ״יִשְׁתַּלְּמוּ״ קָאָמַר מָר? אֲמַר לֵיהּ: ״יֵשׁ תַּלְמוּד״ קָאָמִינָא, וּמֵרִיבּוּיָא דִּקְרָאֵי אֲמַרִי!

The Gemara clarifies: **And Rav Huna sat and stated this *halakha*,** and **Rabba, his son, said to him:** Was **the Master saying** that **there is a derivation** [*yesh talmud*], or was **the Master saying** that **they will be paid** [*yishtalmu*]? Rav Huna **said to him: I am saying: There is a derivation, and it is from the additional** expressions in the **verses**[N] that **I say** it can be derived. It is apparent that an heir is obligated to pay the principal, and this refutes Rav Naḥman's attempted resolution.

אֶלָּא מַאי ״לֹא הוֹדָה״ – לֹא הוֹדָה אָבִיו וְהוֹדָה בְּנוֹ.

Rather, what did Rav Naḥman mean when he suggested that the second *baraita* is referring to a case where **he did not admit** his obligation and exempts his heir from paying the additional one-fifth but obligates him to pay the principal? The *baraita* is referring to a case where the **father did not admit, but his son did admit,** and therefore he is obligated to pay the principal.

וְנִחַיַּיב בְּנוֹ חוֹמֶשׁ אַשְּׁבוּעָה דִּידֵיהּ! אָמְרִי: בְּשֶׁאֵין גְּזֵילָה קַיֶּימֶת. אִי בְּשֶׁאֵין גְּזֵילָה קַיֶּימֶת, אֲפִילּוּ קֶרֶן נַמִּי לֹא מְשַׁלֵּם! לָא צְרִיכָא, דְּאִיכָּא אַחֲרָיוּת.

The Gemara asks: **And let his son be liable** to pay the additional **one-fifth** payment **for his own** false **oath.** The Sages **say: In the** case of the *baraita*, it is **where the stolen item is no longer extant.** Although the false oath was taken, it is not the type of obligation for which one must pay an additional one-fifth payment. The Gemara asks: **If** in the case of the *baraita* it is **where the stolen item is no longer extant,**[H] the *halakha* should be that the heir **does not pay even the principal,**[N] as the *halakha* is that while heirs must return an item stolen by their father, they are not obligated to compensate the owner if the item is no longer extant. The Gemara answers: **No,** the ruling **is necessary** in a case **where there is guaranteed** property, i.e., land, which the heirs inherited from the robber. Heirs are obligated to compensate the owner of a stolen item with inherited land, even if the stolen item itself is no longer extant.

וְכִי אִיכָּא אַחֲרָיוּת נְכָסִים מַאי הָוֵי? מִלְוֶה עַל פֶּה הִיא, וּמִלְוֶה עַל פֶּה אֵינוֹ גּוֹבֶה לֹא מִן הַיּוֹרְשִׁין וְלֹא מִן הַלָּקוֹחוֹת!

The Gemara asks: **And even when there is**[N] **guaranteed property,** i.e., land, **what of it?** After all, such a debt **is** legally considered a **loan by oral** agreement, and the creditor of a **loan by oral** agreement **cannot collect from the heirs** of the debtor, **nor** can he collect **from those who purchased** land from the debtor.

אָמְרִי:

The Sages **say** in response:

NOTES

And it is from the additional expressions in the verses – וּמֵרִיבּוּיָא דִּקְרָאֵי: The additional terms referred to here are the words "robbery," "exploitation," and "lost item." Since these expressions are all included in the phrase: "Anything about which he has sworn falsely" (Leviticus 5:24), they are superfluous, and additional *halakhot* may be derived from them (Rashi; *Shita Mekubbetzet*).

Does not pay even the principal – אֲפִילּוּ קֶרֶן נַמִּי לֹא מְשַׁלֵּם: Since heirs are generally exempt from repaying loans by oral agreement that their father received, they are exempt from paying for a stolen item that is no longer extant. Although the heir took a false oath, such an oath is considered a regular false oath, and one does not pay the additional one-fifth payment for taking this oath (Rashi).

And even when there is, etc. – וְכִי אִיכָּא וכו׳: Rashi preferred a different version of the text, in which this exchange does not appear. He prefers it because the Gemara (111b) states that heirs who inherit land must compensate one whom their father had robbed. Other commentaries, however, accept this version of the text and suggest that the Gemara here is discussing the implication that the heirs are obligated by Torah law to compensate the robbery victim, while the Gemara later on refers to an ordinance instituted by the Sages obligating heirs to do so.

HALAKHA

The stolen item is no longer extant – אֵין גְּזֵילָה קַיֶּימֶת: Heirs who inherit a stolen item from their father must return it to its owner unless it has been altered significantly, in which case they must provide monetary restitution. If the stolen item had been consumed before the robbery victim despaired of recovering it, the heirs are obligated to pay restitution. If it was consumed after the robbery victim had despaired of recovering it, they are obligated to pay restitution only if they had inherited land from their father. The *ge'onim* instituted an ordinance that they must pay restitution even with moveable property they had inherited, as they instituted in cases where the father died without having paid a loan contracted by oral agreement (Rambam *Sefer Nezikin*, *Hilkhot Gezeila VaAveda* 5:5–7; *Shulḥan Arukh*, *Ḥoshen Mishpat* 361:7 and *Sma* there).

בְּשֶׁעָמַד בַּדִּין. אִי בְּשֶׁעָמַד בַּדִּין אֲפִילּוּ חוֹמֶשׁ נַמִּי מְשַׁלֵּם! אָמַר רַב הוּנָא בְּרֵיהּ דְּרַב יְהוֹשֻׁעַ: לְפִי שֶׁאֵין מְשַׁלְּמִין חוֹמֶשׁ עַל כְּפִירַת שִׁעְבּוּד קַרְקָעוֹת.

The reference here is to a case **in which** the father had already **stood trial** and was obligated to pay. In such a case, the debt is considered like a loan with a promissory note, which a creditor may collect from the debtor's heirs. The Gemara rejects this: **If** it is a case **in which** the father had already **stood trial** and was obligated to pay, then the heir, who took a false oath and later confessed, would have to **pay even** the additional **one-fifth** payment **as well,** as this would be akin to any monetary obligation; but the *baraita* rules that he is obligated to pay only the principal. **Rav Huna, son of Rav Yehoshua, said:** The heir is exempt **because one does not pay** the additional **one-fifth** payment **for the denial of** a debt that is secured by **a lien on land.**[NH]

רָבָא אָמַר: הָכָא בְּמַאי עָסְקִינַן – כְּגוֹן שֶׁהָיְתָה דִּיסַקַּיָּיא שֶׁל אָבִיו מוּפְקֶדֶת בְּיַד אֲחֵרִים, קֶרֶן מְשַׁלֵּם – דְּהָא אִיתֵיהּ, חוֹמֶשׁ לָא מְשַׁלֵּם – דְּכִי אִישְׁתְּבַע בְּקוּשְׁטָא אִישְׁתְּבַע, דְּהָא לָא הֲוָה יָדַע.

Rava said a different explanation: **With what are we dealing here?** We are dealing with a case **where** the stolen item is still extant, yet the heir is exempt because **his father's sack** [*disakaya*][L] containing the stolen item **was deposited in the possession of others.** Accordingly, the heir **pays the principal, since** the stolen item **is extant,** but **he does not pay** the additional **one-fifth** payment **because when he took an oath** that it was not in his possession, **he took an oath truthfully, as he did not know** that his father had stolen the item.

״חוּץ מִפָּחוֹת שָׁוֶה פְּרוּטָה בְּקֶרֶן״ כּו׳. אָמַר רַב פָּפָּא: לֹא שָׁנוּ אֶלָּא שֶׁאֵין גְּזֵילָה קַיֶּימֶת, אֲבָל גְּזֵילָה קַיֶּימֶת – צָרִיךְ לֵילֵךְ אַחֲרָיו, חָיְישִׁינַן שֶׁמָּא תְּיַיקֵּר.

§ The mishna teaches that if the robbery victim forgave the robber concerning both payments, **excepting less than** the value **of one** *peruta* **of the principal,** he need not pursue him in order to return the remaining debt. **Rav Pappa says: They taught** that the robber is not obligated to pursue the robbery victim **only when** the **stolen item is not extant, but** if the **stolen item** is still **extant, he must pursue him** to return it, as **we are concerned** that **perhaps** the stolen item **will appreciate** in value, and the debt he owes will exceed the value of one *peruta*.

אִיכָּא דְּאָמְרִי, אָמַר רַב פָּפָּא: לָא שְׁנָא גְּזֵילָה קַיֶּימֶת, וְלָא שְׁנָא שֶׁאֵין גְּזֵילָה קַיֶּימֶת – אֵינוֹ צָרִיךְ לֵילֵךְ אַחֲרָיו, לְשֶׁמָּא תְּיַיקֵּר לָא חָיְישִׁינַן.

There are those who say that **Rav Pappa said:** The *halakha* **is not different** when the **stolen item is extant,**[H] and it **is not different when** the **stolen item is not extant.** In either case **he does not need to pursue him** because **we are not concerned that perhaps it will appreciate** in value.

אָמַר רָבָא. גָּזַל שָׁלֹשׁ אֲגוּדּוֹת בְּשָׁלֹשׁ פְּרוּטוֹת וְהוּזְלוּ וְעָמְדוּ עַל שְׁתַּיִם, אִם הֶחֱזִיר לוֹ שְׁתַּיִם – חַיָּיב לְהַחֲזִיר לוֹ אַחֶרֶת. וְתָנָא תּוּנָא: גָּזַל חָמֵץ וְעָבַר עָלָיו הַפֶּסַח – אוֹמֵר לוֹ ״הֲרֵי שֶׁלְּךָ לְפָנֶיךָ״;

The Gemara cites another ruling with regard to a stolen item worth less than one *peruta*. **Rava says:** If one **robbed** another of **three bundles**[H] of goods that were worth **three** *perutot* in total, **and they depreciated** in value **and** their value **stood at two** *perutot*, even **if he returned two** bundles **to** the robbery victim he **is obligated to return the other** bundle. **And the** *tanna* of the mishna also **taught** (96b): If one **robbed** another of **leavened bread, and Passover elapsed over it,** and it is therefore prohibited to derive benefit from it, the robber **says to** the victim: **That which is yours is before you,** and he is not required to pay compensation, despite the fact that the robbery victim has suffered a monetary loss.

NOTES

The denial of a debt that is secured by a lien on land – כְּפִירַת שִׁעְבּוּד קַרְקָעוֹת: The *halakha* is that in a case where the stolen item is no longer extant, an heir is obligated to pay only from land inherited from the robber; therefore, his denial is essentially of a debt of liened land, and the Sages taught that the *halakhot* of the oath on a deposit apply only when the deposit is moveable property. Accordingly, he is not obligated to pay the additional one-fifth payment for the denial of this debt. The Rambam notes that while he is exempt from the additional one-fifth payment, he is nevertheless liable for taking a false oath.

LANGUAGE

Sack [*disakaya*] – **דִּיסַקַּיָּיא:** From the Greek δισάκκιον, *disakkion*, meaning double sack, a saddlebag placed on an animal.

Donkey with a traditional two-sided pack

HALAKHA

One does not pay the additional one-fifth payment for the denial of a debt that is secured by a lien on land – אֵין מְשַׁלְּמִין חוֹמֶשׁ עַל כְּפִירַת שִׁעְבּוּד קַרְקָעוֹת: Land, slaves, and documents are not included in the *halakhot* of the additional one-fifth payment. Consequently, one who denies owing money that is secured by one of these entities is not obligated to pay an additional one-fifth (Rambam *Sefer Nezikin, Hilkhot Gezeila VaAveda* 8:14).

It is not different when the stolen item is extant – לָא שְׁנָא גְּזֵילָה קַיֶּימֶת: There is no concern that a stolen item currently worth less than one *peruta* will appreciate in value. Accordingly, a robber who retains a stolen item worth less than one *peruta* is not obligated to return it to the robbery victim. The robbery victim may locate the robber and collect his item. The *halakha* is therefore in accordance with the second version of Rav Pappa's statement (Rambam *Sefer Nezikin, Hilkhot Gezeila VaAveda* 7:11; *Shulḥan Arukh, Ḥoshen Mishpat* 367:3).

If one robbed another of three bundles, etc. – גָּזַל שָׁלֹשׁ אֲגוּדּוֹת וכו׳: One who robbed another of three bundles worth three *perutot* in total and then returned two of them after the value had depreciated to two *perutot* in total is obligated to return the third bundle to the robbery victim, since it was worth one *peruta* at the time of robbery (Rambam *Sefer Nezikin, Hilkhot Gezeila VaAveda* 1:6; *Shulḥan Arukh, Ḥoshen Mishpat* 360:3).

טַעֲמָא דְּאִיתֵיהּ בְּעֵינֵיהּ, הָא לֵיתֵיהּ בְּעֵינֵיהּ, אַף עַל גַּב דְּהָשְׁתָּא לָאו מָמוֹנָא, כֵּיוָן דְּמֵעִיקָּרָא מָמוֹנָא הוּא – בָּעֵי שַׁלּוֹמֵי. הָכָא נַמִי, אַף עַל גַּב דְּהָשְׁתָּא לָא שָׁוֶה פְּרוּטָה, [כֵּיוָן דְּמֵעִיקָּרָא הָוֵי שָׁוֶה פְּרוּטָה] – בָּעֵי שַׁלּוֹמֵי.

The Gemara explains the proof from the mishna: It may be inferred that **the reason** that he is not required to pay compensation is **that** the bread is still **there in its unadulterated** form; **but if it is not there in its unadulterated** form, **even though now it is not** worth **money, since it was** worth **money initially,** at the time of the robbery, **he is required to pay. Here too, even though** the third bundle is **not worth one *peruta* now, since initially it was worth one *peruta*, he is required to pay.**

בָּעֵי רָבָא: גָּזַל שְׁתֵּי אֲגוּדוֹת בִּפְרוּטָה וְהֶחֱזִיר לוֹ אַחַת מֵהֶן, מַהוּ? מִי אָמְרִינַן הָשְׁתָּא לֵיכָּא גְּזֵילָה, אוֹ דִּלְמָא הָא לָא הֲדַר גְּזֵילָה דַּהֲוַאי גַּבֵּיהּ?

Rava raises a dilemma: If one **robbed** another of **two bundles** of goods that **were worth one *peruta***[H] in total, **and he returned one of them to** the robbery victim, **what is** the *halakha*? **Do we say** that **now there is no** longer **a stolen item** in the possession of the robber, as the remaining bundle is worth less than one *peruta*, and he has therefore fulfilled his obligation to return the stolen item; **or perhaps** we say that since the robber **did not return the stolen item that was in his possession** in its entirety, he is obligated to return the second bundle?

הֲדַר פְּשַׁטַהּ: גְּזֵילָה אֵין כָּאן, הֲשָׁבָה אֵין כָּאן. אִי גְּזֵילָה אֵין כָּאן, הֲשָׁבָה יֵשׁ כָּאן! הָכִי קָאָמַר: אַף עַל פִּי שֶׁגְּזֵילָה אֵין כָּאן, מִצְוַת הֲשָׁבָה אֵין כָּאן.

Rava himself **then resolves** the dilemma: **There is no stolen item here,** as the remaining bundle is worth less than one *peruta*; **there is no returning** of a stolen item **here.** The Gemara expresses surprise at this expression: **If there is no stolen item here,** as what remains is insignificant, it follows that **there is** fulfillment of the mitzva of **returning** the stolen item **here,** and the robber ought to be exempt, as he is no longer considered to be in possession of a stolen item. The Gemara explains that **this is** what Rava **is saying: Even though** the robber is exempt from returning the second bundle, as **there is no stolen item here, there is** nevertheless **no** fulfillment of the **mitzva of returning** a stolen item **here,**[N] since the returned bundle was worth less than one *peruta* as well.

וְאָמַר רָבָא, הֲרֵי אָמְרוּ: נָזִיר שֶׁגִּילֵּחַ וְשִׁיֵּיר שְׁתֵּי שְׂעָרוֹת – לֹא עָשָׂה וְלֹא כְּלוּם. בָּעֵי רָבָא: גִּילֵּחַ אַחַת וְנָשְׁרָה אַחַת, מַהוּ? אֲמַר לֵיהּ רַב אַחָא מִדִּיפְתִּי לְרָבִינָא: נָזִיר שֶׁגִּילֵּחַ אַחַת אַחַת קָא מִבַּעְיָא לֵיהּ לְרָבָא?!

§ Following Rava's previous dilemma, the Gemara cites a similar dilemma raised by Rava. **And Rava says:** The Sages **said** that **a nazirite who shaved**[B] his head as required **but left two hairs**[H] uncut **has done nothing,** and his obligation to shave his head has not been fulfilled. **Rava raises a dilemma:** If a nazirite shaved and left two hairs, and afterward he **shaved one** of them, **and** the other **one fell out**[H] of its own accord, **what is** the *halakha*? Is this considered shaving one's entire head or not? **Rav Aḥa of Difti said to Ravina: Is Rava raising a dilemma** as to whether one can **shave** his head **one** hair **by one** hair? How does this case differ from that of one who shaves his entire head one hair at a time, which is a fulfillment of his obligation?

אֲמַר לֵיהּ: לָא צְרִיכָא, כְּגוֹן שֶׁנָּשַׁר אַחַת מֵהֶן וְגִילֵּחַ אַחַת; מִי אָמְרִינַן: הָשְׁתָּא מִיהַת הָא לֵיכָּא שִׁיעוּר, אוֹ דִּלְמָא הָא לָאו גִּילּוּחַ הוּא, דְּמֵעִיקָּרָא הָא שִׁיֵּיר שְׁתֵּי שְׂעָרוֹת, וְהָשְׁתָּא כִּי גִּילֵּחַ לָא הָוֵי שְׁתֵּי שְׂעָרוֹת?

Ravina **said to him: No,** a resolution to Rava's dilemma **is necessary** in a case **where one of** the hairs **fell out** first, **and** then **he shaved** the other **one. Do we say** that **now, in any event, there is no measure**[N] of hair left on his head that requires shaving, as one remaining hair is not significant, and he has therefore fulfilled his obligation; **or perhaps** we say that **this is not** considered **shaving, as initially he left** the significant amount of **two hairs** uncut, **and now when he shaves** a second time, **there are not two hairs** left for him to shave, and this does not qualify as shaving?

HALAKHA

If one robbed another of two bundles that were worth one *peruta* – גָּזַל שְׁתֵּי אֲגוּדוֹת בִּפְרוּטָה: One who robbed another of two bundles worth one *peruta* in total and then returned one of them is not obligated to return the second, although he is not considered to have fulfilled the mitzva of returning a stolen item (Rambam *Sefer Nezikin, Hilkhot Gezeila VaAveda* 1:6; *Shulḥan Arukh, Ḥoshen Mishpat* 360:4).

A nazirite who shaved his head but left two hairs – נָזִיר שֶׁגִּילֵּחַ וְשִׁיֵּיר שְׁתֵּי שְׂעָרוֹת: A nazirite who shaved his head but left two hairs uncut has not fulfilled the mitzva of shaving and must shave again (Rambam *Sefer Hafla'a, Hilkhot Nezirut* 8:6).

If he shaved one of them and the other one fell out, etc. – גִּילֵּחַ אַחַת וְנָשְׁרָה אַחַת וכו׳: If a nazirite shaved his head but left two hairs uncut, and he later shaved one of the remaining hairs, after which the second fell out, he has fulfilled the mitzva of shaving. If one of the remaining hairs fell out before he shaved the other, he has not fulfilled the mitzva of shaving, though he is not required to shave again (Rambam *Sefer Hafla'a, Hilkhot Nezirut* 8:7 and *Leḥem Mishne* there).

NOTES

There is no fulfillment of the mitzva of returning a stolen item here – מִצְוַת הֲשָׁבָה אֵין כָּאן: The Ba'al HaMaor understands this to mean that since there is no stolen item in the robber's possession, the mitzva to return a stolen item does not apply. Rabbeinu Ḥananel explains that Rava meant that if the robber does not return the second bundle, he does not fulfill the mitzva of returning a stolen item. The early commentaries note that this indicates that if one stole an item worth less than one *peruta* to begin with, he is not obligated to return the stolen item. The Meiri writes that even if the stolen item is worth less than one *peruta*, there is nevertheless a mitzva to return it. The Rashba notes that regardless of the mitzva to return a stolen item, it is prohibited to steal any item, even one worth less than one *peruta*.

There is no measure – לֵיכָּא שִׁיעוּר: Since only one hair remains and one is not required to shave a single hair, it is possible that the nazirite has fulfilled his obligation. Yet, since he initially left two hairs that required shaving and did not actually shave them, it is also possible that he has not fulfilled his obligation (Ramah).

BACKGROUND

A nazirite who shaved – נָזִיר שֶׁגִּילֵּחַ: There are several circumstances in which the Torah requires an individual to shave his head or entire body as part of a process of purification or the assumption of a different status. One of these cases is that of a nazirite who completes his term of naziriteship (see Numbers 6:18–19). Upon the conclusion of the period of his vow, a nazirite shaves his head. This was performed in a special chamber within the Women's Courtyard in the Temple. Afterward, his hair was placed in the fire over which his peace-offering was cooked. No benefit may be derived from his hair. A nazirite who, during his term, became ritually impure with impurity imparted by a corpse must shave his head on the day he purifies himself. On the following day, he brings the required offerings and begins his term of naziriteship anew (see Numbers 6:9).

הָדַר פְּשְׁטָהּ: שֵׂעָר אֵין כָּאן, גִּילּוּחַ אֵין כָּאן. אִי שֵׂעָר אֵין כָּאן, גִּילּוּחַ יֵשׁ כָּאן! הָכִי קָאָמַר: אַף עַל פִּי שֶׁשֵּׂעָר אֵין כָּאן, מִצְוַת גִּילּוּחַ אֵין כָּאן.

Rava himself **then resolves** the dilemma: **There is no hair here; there is no shaving here.** The Gemara expresses surprise at this expression: **If there is no hair here,** then **there is shaving here,** as no hair remains. The Gemara explains that **this is what** Rava **is saying: Even though there is no hair here,** as only one hair remains, nevertheless **there is no mitzva of shaving here,**[N] as he failed to shave it all on the first attempt, and the second time he shaved less than the required amount.

וְאָמַר רָבָא, הֲרֵי אָמְרוּ: חָבִית שֶׁנִּיקְּבָה וּסְתָמוּהָ שְׁמָרִים – הִצִּילוּהָ. בָּעֵי רָבָא: אָגַף חֶצְיָהּ, מַהוּ?

§ The Gemara cites another dilemma raised by Rava. **And Rava says:** The Sages **said** (*Kelim* 10:6) that with regard to a sealed earthenware **barrel that was punctured**[NH] **and** was then **sealed by sediments**[B] from its contents, the sediments have effectively **saved** the contents of the barrel from contracting ritual impurity if the barrel were to come into contact with an impure item, as it is once again considered a sealed barrel. **Rava raises a dilemma:** If one **sealed half of** the hole,[NH] **what is** the *halakha*? Do we say that since the hole is not currently large enough to allow ritual impurity to penetrate, the barrel is considered sealed; or perhaps we say that since the hole was initially large enough to allow impurity to penetrate, and it has not yet been sealed completely, the barrel retains its status and is not considered sealed?

אֲמַר לֵיהּ רַב יֵימַר לְרַב אַשִׁי: לָאו מַתְנִיתִין הִיא זוֹ? דִּתְנַן: חָבִית שֶׁנִּיקְּבָה וּסְתָמוּהָ שְׁמָרִים – הִצִּילוּהָ, פְּקָקָהּ בִּזְמוֹרָה – עַד שֶׁיְּמָרֵחַ, הָיוּ בָּהּ שְׁתַּיִם – עַד שֶׁיְּמָרֵחַ מִן הַצְּדָדִים וּבֵין זְמוֹרָה לַחֲבֶירְתָּהּ;

The Gemara notes that **Rav Yeimar said to Rav Ashi: Isn't this** *halakha* stated explicitly in **our mishna,** quoted by Rava above? **As we learned** in the continuation of that mishna: With regard to an earthenware **barrel that was punctured and** was then **sealed by sediments,** the sediments have effectively **saved** the contents of the barrel from contracting ritual impurity. If it was not sealed by sediments and instead one **plugged** the hole **with a vine,** its contents remain susceptible to contracting ritual impurity **until he smears** clay around the uncovered parts of the hole. If **there were two** vines placed in the hole in order to plug it, its contents remain susceptible to contracting ritual impurity **until he smears** clay **from the sides** of the hole inward, **and between one vine and the other.**

טַעְמָא דְּמָרַח, הָא לָא מָרַח לָא, אַמַּאי? וְתֶיהֱוֵי כִּי אָגַף חֶצְיָהּ!

Rav Yeimar explains: **The reason** its contents become impervious to contracting ritual impurity is **that he smeared** clay over the uncovered sections of the hole, **but if he did not smear** clay over the uncovered sections, the contents would **not** be impervious to contracting ritual impurity. **Why** should this not be like the case in Rava's dilemma? **But let it be** considered, when one plugs the hole with the vine, **as though** one had **sealed half of** the hole, since there is no apparent difference between a hole that is half-sealed and a hole that is partially plugged with a vine. Accordingly, Rava should not have stated his dilemma, as it is clear from the mishna that if the hole is only partially covered, the contents of the barrel are susceptible to contracting ritual impurity.

אָמְרִי: הָכִי הַשְׁתָּא?! הָתָם אִי לָא מָרַח לָא קָאֵי, אָגַף חֶצְיָהּ – בְּמִידֵּי דְּקָאֵי קָאֵי.

The Sages **say** in response: **How can these** cases **be compared? There, if he does not smear** clay around the vines, the vine **will not remain** in place. By contrast, in a case where **he sealed half of it with a substance that remains** in place, as in Rava's dilemma, the seal **remains** in place and could be considered a seal. Rava's dilemma remains unresolved.

וְאָמַר רָבָא, הֲרֵי אָמְרוּ: גָּזַל חָמֵץ וְעָבַר עָלָיו הַפֶּסַח – אוֹמֵר לוֹ ״הֲרֵי שֶׁלְּךָ לְפָנֶיךָ״. בָּעֵי רָבָא:

§ The Gemara cites another dilemma raised by Rava. **And Rava says:** The Sages **said** that if one **robbed** another of **leavened bread, and Passover elapsed over it,**[H] and it is therefore prohibited to derive benefit from it, the robber **may say to** the victim: **That which is yours is before you. Rava raises a dilemma:**

NOTES

There is no mitzva of shaving here – מִצְוַת גִּילּוּחַ אֵין כָּאן: *Tosafot* note that there is a dispute in tractate *Nazir* concerning whether failure to perform the mitzva of shaving precludes the completion of one's term of naziriteship, or if it is only a mitzva to be performed *ab initio*.

An earthenware barrel that was punctured – חָבִית שֶׁנִּיקְּבָה: Rashi explains that the reference here is to a barrel that was placed beneath an opening in the ceiling, in order to prevent the ritual impurity of a corpse located beneath the upper story from imparting impurity to the upper story. By contrast, the majority of the early commentaries understand that the Gemara is referring to a barrel placed together with a corpse under a roof. The contents of the barrel remain protected from contracting ritual impurity provided that it is sealed with a tightly bound cover, and Rava wishes to ascertain whether this barrel is sealed.

If one sealed half of the hole – אָגַף חֶצְיָהּ: A vessel that has been punctured with a hole of a certain size cannot serve as a barrier to prevent its contents from contracting ritual impurity. Rashi explains that when the hole is partially sealed, that is sufficient to protect its contents from contracting impurity. *Tosafot* ask: If the hole is now of an insignificant size, why would the barrel not be able to serve as a barrier? *Tosefot HaRash* cites Rabbeinu Tam, who offers a different interpretation, namely that Rava is referring to a case where one sealed half of the hole, and the other half was sealed by sediments. The dilemma is whether one would be required to smear clay or not in order to combine the two sealants. According to this interpretation, this dilemma is not similar to the others raised by Rava.

HALAKHA

An earthenware barrel that was punctured, etc. – חָבִית שֶׁנִּיקְּבָה וכו׳: An earthenware vessel that has been punctured and then sealed by the sediment of its contents is considered a sealed barrel and protects its contents from contracting ritual impurity, provided that it has a tightly sealed cover. If the hole was plugged with a vine, the contents remain susceptible to contracting ritual impurity until the sides of the hole are smeared with clay. If the hole was plugged with two vines, the sides of the hole and the space between the two vines must be smeared with clay (Rambam *Sefer Tahara*, *Hilkhot Tumat Met* 22:8).

If one sealed half of the hole – אָגַף חֶצְיָהּ: The *halakha* with regard to a tightly covered barrel that was punctured and partially sealed remains uncertain, as Rava's dilemma stands unresolved (Rambam *Sefer Tahara*, *Hilkhot Tumat Met* 22:8).

If one robbed another of leavened bread and Passover elapsed over it – גָּזַל חָמֵץ וְעָבַר עָלָיו הַפֶּסַח: If one robbed another of leavened bread and Passover then elapsed over it, the robber may return it to the victim as is, despite the fact that the victim now has no use for it (Rambam *Sefer Nezikin*, *Hilkhot Gezeila VaAveda* 3:4; *Shulḥan Arukh*, *Ḥoshen Mishpat* 363:1).

BACKGROUND

Sealed by sediments – סְתָמוּהָ שְׁמָרִים: Yeast consists of single-celled fungi that cause grape juice to ferment and become wine. These fungi proliferate and then stick together in clumps, some of which are heavier than the wine and therefore sink to the bottom of the barrel in a layer impermeable to the wine. Since yeast develops faster with exposure to air, it is reasonable that the sediment would proliferate in a punctured barrel, and could very well seal the hole.

נִשְׁבַּע עָלָיו מַהוּ? מִי אָמְרִינַן: כֵּיוָן דְּאִי מִיגְּנַב בָּעֵי שַׁלּוּמֵי לֵיהּ – מָמוֹנָא קָא כָּפַר לֵיהּ. אוֹ דִּלְמָא הָשְׁתָּא מִיהַת הָא מַנַּח, וְעַפְרָא בְּעָלְמָא הוּא, וְלָא כָּפַר לֵיהּ מָמוֹנָא?

If the robber **took** a false **oath concerning** the robbery of the leavened bread, **what is the** *halakha*? **Do we say** that **since, if it** were to be **stolen** from the robber, the robber **would need to pay** the initial value of the bread **to** the robbery victim, as he can no longer say: That which is yours is before you, and therefore **he has denied** a claim **of a monetary matter to** the robbery victim[H] and must consequently pay the additional one-fifth payment and bring a guilt-offering? **Or perhaps** we say that **now, in any event, it is resting** in the robber's possession **and it is** considered as **mere dust,** since it is prohibited to derive benefit from it, and as such **he has not denied** a claim **of a monetary matter,** and the *halakhot* concerning a false oath do not apply.

מִילְּתָא דְּאִיבַּעְיָא לֵיהּ לְרָבָא, פְּשִׁיטָא לֵיהּ לְרַבָּה; דְּאָמַר רַבָּה: "שׁוֹרִי גָּנַבְתָּ", וְהוּא אוֹמֵר "לֹא גָּנַבְתִּי".

The Gemara comments: **The matter that was a dilemma for Rava is obvious to Rabba, as Rabba says** that in a scenario where one says to another: **You stole my ox,**[H] **and the other says: I did not steal** it.

"מַה טִּיבוֹ אֶצְלְךָ"? "שׁוֹמֵר חִנָּם אֲנִי עָלָיו" – חַיָּיב, שֶׁהֲרֵי פָּטַר עַצְמוֹ מִגְּנֵיבָה וַאֲבֵידָה;

The first asks: **What is the nature of its** presence **in your** possession? The second responds: **I am an unpaid bailee**[B] **over it.**[N] If the defendant then takes a false oath to that effect, after which he confesses that he stole the ox, he is **liable** to bring a guilt-offering for denying a claim of a monetary matter, **as he exempted himself from** liability in cases of **theft and loss.**

"שׁוֹמֵר שָׂכָר אֲנִי עָלָיו" – חַיָּיב, שֶׁהֲרֵי פָּטַר עַצְמוֹ מִשְּׁבוּרָה וּמֵתָה;

If he responds instead: **I am a paid bailee over it,** and takes a false oath to that effect, after which he confesses that he stole the ox, he is **liable** to bring a guilt-offering for denying a claim of a monetary matter, **as he exempted himself from** liability in cases of **breakage and death.**

"שׁוֹאֵל אֲנִי עָלָיו" – חַיָּיב, שֶׁהֲרֵי פָּטַר עַצְמוֹ מִמֵּתָה מֵחֲמַת מְלָאכָה;

If he responds instead: **I am a borrower of it,** and takes a false oath to that effect, after which he confesses that he stole the ox, he is **liable** to bring a guilt-offering for denying a claim of a monetary matter, as **he exempted himself from** liability in cases where the ox **died due to** ordinary **labor.**

אַלְמָא, אַף עַל גַּב דְּהָא קָאֵים, כֵּיוָן דְּאִי מִיגְּנִיב מָמוֹנָא קָא כָּפַר, הָשְׁתָּא נַמִי מָמוֹנָא קָא כָּפַר – הָכָא נַמִי, אַף עַל גַּב דְּעַפְרָא בְּעָלְמָא הוּא, כֵּיוָן דְּאִי מִיגְּנִיב בָּעֵי שַׁלּוּמֵי לֵיהּ מָמוֹנָא מְעַלְּיָא, הָשְׁתָּא נַמִי מָמוֹנָא קָא כָּפַר לֵיהּ.

In all of these cases, the ox is in the possession of the one who took the false oath, and he admits that it belongs to the other. The Gemara analyzes Rabba's statement: **Apparently,** Rabba holds that **even though** the ox is now **extant** and can be returned to its owner, **since, if it were to be stolen,** the robber **would** be found to **be denying** a claim of **a monetary matter,** as according to his claim he would then be exempt from paying, he is **now** considered to **be denying** a claim of **a monetary matter as well. Here,** in the case of the bread **also, even though it is** considered **mere dust, since, if it were to be stolen, he would be required to pay** the robbery victim **full-fledged monetary restitution,** he is **now** considered to **be denying** a claim of a **monetary matter as well.**

יָתֵיב רָבָא וְקָאָמַר לְהָא שְׁמַעְתָּא, אֵיתִיבֵיהּ רַב עַמְרָם לְרָבָא: "וְכִחֶשׁ בָּהּ" – פְּרָט לְמוֹדֶה בְּעִיקָּר,

Rava sat and said this *halakha*, that one who protected himself from potential liability for payment by taking a false oath that he is a bailee is liable to pay the additional one-fifth payment and bring a guilt-offering. **Rav Amram raised an objection to Rava** from a *baraita*: The verse states concerning one who is liable for taking a false oath concerning a monetary matter: **"And deals falsely with it"** (Leviticus 5:22); this serves to **exclude one who admits to the primary** feature of a claim.

HALAKHA

He has denied a claim of a monetary matter to the robbery victim – מָמוֹנָא קָא כָּפַר לֵיהּ: If one robbed another of bread that was later burned or lost, he is obligated to pay the owner the amount that the bread was worth at the time of robbery. Accordingly, if the robber takes a false oath that he did not rob another of the bread, he is obligated to pay the additional one-fifth payment and bring a guilt-offering even if his oath was taken after the bread had become forbidden. This is in accordance with the resolution of Rava's dilemma (Rambam *Sefer Nezikin, Hilkhot Gezeila VaAveda* 3:5).

You stole my ox, etc. – שׁוֹרִי גָּנַבְתָּ וכו׳: If one steals another's ox and then takes a false oath that he is an unpaid bailee of it, he is liable to bring a guilt-offering for taking a false oath on a deposit, as, by doing so, he has exempted himself from liability for theft and loss. Similarly, if he took a false oath that he is a paid bailee he is also liable, since he has exempted himself from liability in cases of breakage and death. Even if he takes a false oath that he is a borrower he is liable, since he exempts himself from liability should the animal die or deteriorate due to ordinary labor (Rambam *Sefer Hafla'a, Hilkhot Shevuot* 8:8–9).

BACKGROUND

Bailee – שׁוֹמֵר: A bailee is one who received an item from its owner and accepted responsibility for it. The extent of this responsibility depends on the status of the bailee. An unpaid bailee is held responsible for a deposit only if he is negligent or misappropriates the item (see Exodus 22:6–8); a paid bailee is held responsible for theft and loss, but is exempt from paying for the item if was taken by force or was damaged due to circumstances beyond his control (see Exodus 22:9–12); and a borrower is obligated for all of these, but is exempt from liability where the item is destroyed or damaged due to the borrower's use of it in a conventional manner (see Exodus 22:13). A bailee who misappropriates an item is obligated to pay in all cases. Accordingly, when the robber claims to be one of these bailees, he is exempting himself from a certain degree of responsibility, and the Gemara cites these exemptions one by one.

NOTES

I am an unpaid bailee over it – שׁוֹמֵר חִנָּם אֲנִי עָלָיו: In general, a robber would be liable to bring an offering for taking a false oath concerning a deposit if he attempted to keep the animal in his possession by taking the oath. Here he admits that the ox belongs to its owner. Nevertheless, due to the fact that his claim carries with it the potential to save him money, he is considered as one who took a false oath on a deposit, and he is liable to bring an offering. Accordingly, the same would apply to one who takes a false oath concerning leavened bread over which Passover has elapsed, as in both cases the robber gains potential financial benefit.

כֵּיצַד? ״שׁוֹרִי גָּנַבְתָּ״, וְהוּא אוֹמֵר ״לֹא גָּנַבְתִּי״.

The *baraita* continues: **How is this so?** In a scenario where one says to another: **You stole my ox, and** the latter **says: I did not steal** it.

״מַה טִּיבוֹ אֶצְלְךָ״? ״אַתָּה מְכַרְתּוֹ לִי, אַתָּה נְתַתּוֹ לִי בְּמַתָּנָה, אָבִיךָ מְכָרוֹ לִי, אָבִיךָ נְתָנוֹ לִי בְּמַתָּנָה, אַחַר פָּרָתִי רָץ, מֵאֵלָיו בָּא אֶצְלִי, תּוֹעֶה בַּדֶּרֶךְ מְצָאתִיו, שׁוֹמֵר חִנָּם אֲנִי עָלָיו, שׁוֹמֵר שָׂכָר אֲנִי עָלָיו, שׁוֹאֵל אֲנִי עָלָיו״, וְנִשְׁבַּע וְהוֹדָה, יָכוֹל יְהֵא חַיָּיב? תַּלְמוּד לוֹמַר: ״וְכִחֵשׁ בָּהּ״ – פְּרָט לְמוֹדֶה בָּעִיקָּר!

The first asks: **What is the nature of its** presence **in your** possession? The second responds with any of the following replies: **You sold it to me; you gave it to me as a gift; your father sold it to me; your father gave it to me as a gift; it chased after my cow** and entered my domain; **it came to me on its own; I found it straying on the road** and I brought it home; **I am an unpaid bailee over it; I am a paid bailee over it;** or **I am a borrower of it; and** the second **takes** a false **oath** to that effect, **and** then **admits** that he had done so; one **might** have thought that he **should be liable. The verse states: "And deals falsely with it,"** which serves to **exclude one who admits to the primary** feature of a claim. The *baraita* states explicitly that one who takes a false oath that he is a bailee is not liable; how can Rava state otherwise?

אֲמַר לֵיהּ: תְּדוּרָא! כִּי תַּנְיָא הַהִיא – דְּקָאָמַר לֵיהּ ״הֵילָךְ״, כִּי קָאָמִינָא – דְּקַיְימָא בַּאֲגַם.

Rava **said to him: Fool, when that** *baraita* **is taught,** it is referring to a case **where** the robber **said to** the owner: **Here you are,**[H] and presented the ox to him immediately, so that he did not profit by claiming that he was a bailee. **When I spoke,** I was referring to a case **where** the ox **was standing in** a different place, such as **a swamp,** and was not returned to the owner.

״אַתָּה מְכַרְתּוֹ לִי״, מַאי מוֹדֶה בָּעִיקָּר אִיכָּא? לָא צְרִיכָא, דַּאֲמַר לֵיהּ: לֹא נָתַתִּי לָךְ דָּמֵי, שְׁקֵיל תּוֹרָךְ וְזִיל.

Several examples of an oath in which the robber admits to the primary feature of a claim were cited in the *baraita* above. The Gemara analyzes some of these examples. When the robber says: **You sold** the ox **to me,** he has asserted that it belongs to him, so **what admission to the primary** feature of the claim **is there?** The Gemara explains: **No,** it is **necessary** to teach this in a case **where he said to him:** You sold the animal to me, but **I did not give you the money,**[N] **take your ox and go.**

״אַתָּה נְתַתּוֹ לִי, אָבִיךָ נְתָנוֹ לִי״, מַאי מוֹדֶה בָּעִיקָּר אִיכָּא? דַּאֲמַר לֵיהּ: עַל מְנָת דְּעָבֵידְנָא לָךְ נַיְיח דְּנַפְשָׁא, וְלָא עֲבַדִי לָךְ, שְׁקֵיל תּוֹרָךְ וְזִיל.

When the robber says: **You gave it to me,** or: **Your father gave it to me,** he has asserted that it belongs to him, so **what admission to the primary feature of the claim is there?** The Gemara explains: It is a case **where he said to him:** It was given to me **on the condition that I will afford you satisfaction, and I did not do** anything **for you; take your ox and go.**

״תּוֹעֶה בַּדֶּרֶךְ מְצָאתִיו״, לֵימָא: אִיבָּעֵי לָךְ לְאַהֲדוּרֵיהּ לִי! אָמַר אֲבוּהּ דִּשְׁמוּאֵל: בְּאוֹמֵר: ״שְׁבוּעָה, אֲבֵידָה מָצָאתִי, וְלֹא הָיִיתִי יוֹדֵעַ שֶׁהִיא שֶׁלְּךָ שֶׁאַחֲזִירֶנָּה לָךְ״.

When the robber says: **I found it straying on the road** and I brought it home, **let** the owner **say** to him: **You should have returned it**[N] **to me. Shmuel's father said:** The *baraita* is referring to a case **in which he says:** I take **an oath** that **I found** the ox **as a lost item, and I did not know that it was yours so that I could return it to you.**

תַּנְיָא: אָמַר בֶּן עַזַּאי, שָׁלֹשׁ שְׁבוּעוֹת הֵן: הִכִּיר בָּהּ וְלֹא בְּמוֹצְאָהּ, בְּמוֹצְאָהּ וְלֹא בָּהּ, לֹא בָּהּ וְלֹא בְּמוֹצְאָהּ.

§ After discussing a false oath taken by a robber in which he admits to the primary feature of a claim, the Gemara discusses a false oath taken by witnesses. **It is taught** in a *baraita*: When a witness takes an oath that he has no knowledge of the status of a lost item, **ben Azzai says** that **there are three** possible false **oaths,** i.e., the oath may be false for one of three reasons: The witness may have **recognized** the lost item **but** did **not** recognize **its finder,** or he may have recognized **its finder but** did **not** recognize the item, or he may have recognized **neither** the item **nor its finder.** In each of these cases, the witness took a false oath that he had no knowledge of the lost item, when in fact he had limited knowledge of it.

לֹא בָּהּ וְלֹא בְּמוֹצְאָהּ, קוּשְׁטָא אִשְׁתַּבַּע! אֵימָא: בָּהּ וּבְמוֹצְאָהּ.

The Gemara asks: In the third case cited above, where the witnesses recognized **neither** the item **nor its finder, he took his oath in truth** when he claimed that he did not have knowledge of the lost item. Why is this cited as an example of a false oath? The Gemara emends the *baraita*: **Say** that the reference here is to a case where he recognized both the item **and its finder.**

HALAKHA

Where the robber said to the owner, here you are – דְּקָאָמַר לֵיהּ הֵילָךְ: If one steals an ox from another and takes a false oath that he found it and did not know to whom it belongs, or that he purchased it from the owner but did not yet pay, or that he received it as a gift in return for some future favor that he did not yet perform, or that he is a borrower or a bailee, and then offers the animal to its owner, he is exempt from liability to bring a guilt-offering for taking a false oath on a deposit. He is liable to bring an offering for taking a false oath on an utterance (Rambam *Sefer Hafla'a, Hilkhot Shevuot* 8:10–11).

NOTES

I did not give you the money – לֹא נָתַתִּי לָךְ דָּמֵי: In general, a sale cannot be nullified if one of the parties decides to renege on the sale. The Rashba discusses the legal mechanics by which this particular sale would be nullified based on the robber's statement. One explanation is that the Gemara is referring to a case where he claims that the sale agreement included a stipulation that the transaction would be nullified if the money was not paid by a certain time. Therefore, since he did not pay, the sale is void. Alternatively, even if no stipulation was included, the sale may be canceled due to the fact that the owner denies having sold it. The Ramah learns from here that any sale that includes the assumption that payment will be provided is not fulfilled without payment. The same applies to a gift that is based on the stipulation that the recipient will perform a favor for the giver.

You should have returned it – אִיבָּעֵי לָךְ לְאַהֲדוּרֵיהּ: This question is unlike the Gemara's earlier inquiries, as it does not relate to Rava's interpretation of the *baraita* but to the actual ruling of the *baraita*. Therefore, the question is answered by Shmuel's father, who preceded Rava by several generations. Some early commentaries note that it would be inaccurate to infer from the *baraita* that the finder of a lost item must pursue its owner to return it to him. Rather, the reference here is to a case where the owner was actively searching for his ox and inquired as to its location, and the finder did not respond (Ra'avad; Rashba).

לְמַאי הִלְכְתָא? רַב אַמִי אָמַר רַבִּי חֲנִינָא: לִפְטוּר, וּשְׁמוּאֵל אָמַר: לְחִיּוּב.

The Gemara asks: **For which *halakha*** did ben Azzai cite these examples? **Rav Ami says** that **Rabbi Ḥanina says:** They were cited **to** teach that there is **exemption**[N] in these cases from bringing an offering for taking a false oath of testimony. **And Shmuel says** that these examples were cited **to** teach that the witness incurs **liability** to bring an offering in these cases.

וּבִפְלוּגְתָּא דְּהָנֵי תַּנָּאֵי, דְּתַנְיָא: הַמַּשְׁבִּיעַ עֵד אֶחָד – פָּטוּר, וְרַבִּי אֶלְעָזָר בְּרַבִּי שִׁמְעוֹן מְחַיֵּיב;

The Gemara comments: **And** Rav Ami and Shmuel disagree **with** regard **to** the issue that is the subject of **the dispute** between **these *tanna'im*, as it is taught** in a *baraita*: With regard to **one who administers an oath** to **a single witness**[H] and the witness takes a false oath that he has no awareness of the monetary matter at hand, the witness is **exempt** from bringing a sin-offering; **and Rabbi Elazar, son of Rabbi Shimon, deems** the witness **liable** to bring a sin-offering.

בְּמַאי קָא מִיפַּלְגִי, מָר סָבַר: דָּבָר הַגּוֹרֵם לְמָמוֹן כְּמָמוֹן דָּמֵי, וּמָר סָבַר: לָאו כְּמָמוֹן דָּמֵי.

The Gemara asks: **With regard to what do they disagree?** One **Sage,** Rabbi Elazar, son of Rabbi Shimon, **holds** that **an item that causes financial** loss **is considered** to have **monetary** value.[N] Similarly, the potential monetary benefit that the witness can generate by causing the defendant to admit to the debt and pay the owner is considered to have monetary value. Therefore, the witness is considered to have taken a false oath with regard to a monetary matter. **And one Sage,** the first *tanna*, **holds** that an item that causes financial loss **is not considered** to have **monetary** value. Similarly, the potential monetary benefit that the witness can generate by causing the defendant to admit to the debt and pay the owner is not considered to have monetary value. Therefore, the witness is not considered to have taken a false oath with regard to a monetary matter.

אָמַר רַב שֵׁשֶׁת: הַכּוֹפֵר בְּפִקָּדוֹן – נַעֲשָׂה עָלָיו גַּזְלָן וְחַיָּיב בְּאוֹנָסִין. וְתָנָא תּוּנָא: "וְכִחֶשׁ בָּהּ" – לָמַדְנוּ עוֹנֶשׁ, אַזְהָרָה מִנַּיִן? תַּלְמוּד לוֹמַר: "לֹא תְכַחֲשׁוּ"; מַאי לָאו לְעוֹנֶשׁ מָמוֹן?

§ The Gemara discusses the *halakha* concerning a bailee who denies having a deposit in his possession. **Rav Sheshet says:** A bailee who falsely **denies** a claim **concerning a deposit**[H] **becomes as a robber with regard to it, and** he is therefore **liable** to pay even **for** damage that is the result of **accidents.** The Gemara notes that **the *tanna*** also **taught** this *halakha* in a *baraita*. The verse states: **"And deals falsely with it"** (Leviticus 5:22–24), and **we learned** from this verse the **punishment** for one who denies having a deposit. **From where** is the **prohibition** itself derived? **The verse states: "Neither shall you deal falsely"** (Leviticus 19:11). The Gemara explains: **What, is** the *baraita* **not** referring **to** the **punishment of** having to pay **money** due to his denial even for accidental damage, in accordance with the statement of Rav Sheshet?

לָא, לְעוֹנֶשׁ שְׁבוּעָה. הָא מִדְּקָתָנֵי סֵיפָא וְאִישְׁתַּבַּע, מִכְּלָל דְּרֵישָׁא דְּלָא אִישְׁתַּבַּע! דְּקָתָנֵי סֵיפָא: "וְנִשְׁבַּע עַל שָׁקֶר" – לָמַדְנוּ עוֹנֶשׁ, אַזְהָרָה מִנַּיִן? תַּלְמוּד לוֹמַר: "לֹא תְשַׁקְּרוּ"; וּמִדְּסֵיפָא דְּאִישְׁתַּבַּע, רֵישָׁא דְּלָא אִישְׁתַּבַּע!

The Gemara rejects this: **No,** the *baraita* is referring **to the punishment** for taking a false **oath,**[N] i.e., the additional one-fifth payment and the bringing of the offering. The Gemara challenges: **From the** fact **that the latter clause** of the *baraita* **teaches** a case **where he took an oath, it may be inferred that the first clause** teaches a case **where he did not take an oath,** and the punishment referred to by the *baraita* is the imposition of liability for accidental damage. **As the latter clause teaches** that the verse states: **"And swear to a lie"** (Leviticus 5:22), and **we learned** from this that there is **a punishment** for taking a false oath. **From where** is the **prohibition** itself derived? **The verse states: "Nor lie"** (Leviticus 19:11). **And from the** fact **that the latter clause** teaches the *halakha* **where he took an oath, the first clause** must be teaching the *halakha* in a case **where he did not take an oath.**

אָמְרִי: אִידִי וְאִידִי דְּאִישְׁתַּבַּע, כָּאן שֶׁהוֹדָה, כָּאן שֶׁבָּאוּ עֵדִים; אָתוּ עֵדִים – חַיָּיב בְּאוֹנָסִין, אוֹדוּיֵי אוֹדֵי – חַיָּיב בְּקֶרֶן וְחוֹמֶשׁ וְאָשָׁם.

The Gemara answers: The Sages **say** in response that both **this** clause **and that** clause are referring to a case **where he took an oath,** but **here,** in the latter clause, it is **where** the bailee **admitted** his false oath, while **there,** in the first clause, it is **where witnesses came** and testified that the deposit is in his possession. Where **witnesses came,** he is **liable** only **for** damage that is a result of **accidents,** and **where he admitted** his false oath, he is **obligated** to pay for the **principal and** an additional **one-fifth** payment, **and** to bring **a guilt-offering.** Since the *baraita* is referring in both clauses to a case where the bailee took an oath, it offers no support for Rav Sheshet's statement.

NOTES

To teach that there is an exemption – לִפְטוּר: Though the witness is exempt from bringing an offering for taking a false oath of testimony, he is nevertheless liable to bring an offering for taking a false oath on an utterance.

An item that causes financial loss is considered to have monetary value – דָּבָר הַגּוֹרֵם לְמָמוֹן כְּמָמוֹן דָּמֵי: The commentaries offer different explanations of this discussion. According to one understanding, the dispute between Rav Ami and Shmuel would apply only to a single witness, as the testimony of a single witness is considered only a matter that causes potential monetary benefit, since it cannot impose a direct financial obligation. There is potential monetary benefit, as the testimony of even one witness could encourage the finder to return the lost item to avoid opprobrium. If there were two witnesses, who are generally able to force a monetary payment, both Rav Ami and Shmuel agree that they would be liable for their false oath, since their testimony could have obligated the finder to return the animal.

By contrast, the Rosh understands that the dispute may apply even to two witnesses in the first two cases mentioned by ben Azzai, i.e., where the animal was recognized but not the finder, or vice versa, because their testimony in these cases is not sufficient to force the return of the animal, but merely to encourage its return. Accordingly, the dispute between Rav Ami and Shmuel is limited to a single witness only in the case where both the finder and the lost animal were recognized, as in such a case two witnesses would be liable according to all opinions, since their testimony would have secured payment for the claimant. The Maharam of Rothenburg offers a third explanation, that both Rav Ami and Shmuel agree that a single witness is exempt in the first two cases cited by ben Azzai, as a single witness who offers partial testimony is considered to be an indirect cause of a mere loss of potential monetary benefit and is therefore certainly exempt. Accordingly, the question: For which *halakha*, refers exclusively to the third case mentioned by ben Azzai.

To the punishment for taking a false oath – לְעוֹנֶשׁ שְׁבוּעָה: Rashi understands that the punishment referred to here is the bailee's responsibility to pay for accidental damage, as Rashi holds that this obligation is imposed only if he took a false oath. Others explain that the Gemara is referring to the punishment of having to bring an offering for taking a false oath (*Tosafot*; Ra'avad).

HALAKHA

One who administers an oath to a single witness – הַמַּשְׁבִּיעַ עֵד אֶחָד: A single witness who took a false oath that he does not know of any testimony is exempt from bringing an offering for taking a false oath of testimony. This is because the testimony of a single witness cannot impose financial liability. The *halakha* is therefore in accordance with the opinion of the Rabbis (Rambam *Sefer Hafla'a*, *Hilkhot Shevuot* 10:5).

One who falsely denies a claim concerning a deposit – הַכּוֹפֵר בְּפִקָּדוֹן: A bailee who falsely denies in court having received a deposit is considered a robber even if he did not take an oath (*Sma*), provided that there are witnesses who testify that they saw the deposit in his possession at the time of his denial. Accordingly, the bailee is held responsible even for accidental damage, and he is disqualified from bearing witness (Rambam *Sefer Nezikin*, *Hilkhot Gezeila VaAveda* 3:14; *Shulḥan Arukh*, *Ḥoshen Mishpat* 294:1).

מְתִיב רָמִי בַּר חָמָא: וְשֶׁכְּנֶגְדּוֹ חָשׁוּד עַל הַשְּׁבוּעָה, כֵּיצַד? אֶחָד שְׁבוּעַת הָעֵדוּת וְאֶחָד שְׁבוּעַת הַפִּקָּדוֹן, וַאֲפִילּוּ שְׁבוּעַת שָׁוְא;

After dismissing the attempted proof for Rav Sheshet's statement that a bailee who denies possession of a deposit is considered a robber even without having taken a false oath, the Gemara now attempts to disprove the statement itself. **Rami bar Ḥama raises an objection** to Rav Sheshet's statement: Though it is usually the defendant who is required to take an oath in order to avoid having to pay a claim, there are cases in which the plaintiff takes an oath to receive payment. The mishna in *Shevuot* (44b) lists these cases: **And** one such case is **where** the plaintiff's **opponent,** i.e., the defendant, **is suspect with regard to an oath,** i.e., there is reason for the court to believe that he would take a false oath. **How** would the defendant have become suspect? It would be by having taken a false oath with regard to **either an oath of testimony**[HB] **or an oath on a deposit, or even for an oath** taken **in vain.**

וְאִם אִיתָא, בִּכְפִירָה הוּא דְּאִיפְּסֵיל לֵיהּ!

The Gemara comments: Since the mishna states that he becomes suspect only as a result of having taken a false oath, it can be inferred that he does not become suspect by virtue of denial of a claim alone. **And if it is so** that a bailee who denies having taken the deposit is considered a robber even without having taken an oath, then **it is with** his **denial that he** ought to be **disqualified,** as a robber does not have the credibility to take an oath.

אָמְרִי: הָכָא בְּמַאי עָסְקִינַן – דְּקָאֵי בַּאֲגַם, דְּלָאו כְּפִירָה הוּא, דְּסָבַר: אֶשְׁתַּמֵּיטְנָא לֵיהּ אַדְּאָזֵילְנָא וּמַיְיתִינָא לֵיהּ;

The Sages **say** in defense of Rav Sheshet's opinion: **With what are we dealing here,** in the case of the mishna in *Shevuot*? We are dealing with a case **where** the deposit **stands in** a place not in the bailee's possession, e.g., **a swamp, as** in this case his statement **is not** considered a complete **denial, because he thinks** to himself: **I will evade** the owner by claiming that I never took the deposit **until I go and bring it to him.** Therefore, he is not considered to be a robber. By contrast, Rav Sheshet is referring to a case where the bailee denied responsibility for the item while it was in his possession, as he intended to keep it for himself.

תֵּדַע, דְּאָמַר רַב אִידִי בַּר אָבִין: הַכּוֹפֵר בְּמִלְוָה כָּשֵׁר לְעֵדוּת,

The Gemara adds: **Know** that one who denies possession of an item only so that he may later return it is not considered a robber, **as Rav Idi bar Avin says: One who denies** a claim **concerning** having taken **a loan**[H] **is fit to bear witness,**

HALAKHA

Either an oath of testimony, etc. – אֶחָד שְׁבוּעַת הָעֵדוּת וכו׳: One who takes a false oath, whether an oath of testimony, an oath on an utterance, or an oath on a deposit, assumes the status of one who is suspect with regard to the concern that he may take a false oath (Rambam *Sefer Mishpatim, Hilkhot To'en VeNitan* 2:2; *Shulḥan Arukh, Ḥoshen Mishpat* 92:2).

One who denies a claim concerning having taken a loan – הַכּוֹפֵר בְּמִלְוָה: One does not become suspect with regard to the concern that he may take a false oath unless he has taken a false oath in the past. Accordingly, one who denies having taken a loan and is contradicted by witnesses does not assume the status of one who is suspect with regard to the concern that he may take a false oath (Rambam *Sefer Mishpatim, Hilkhot To'en VeNitan* 2:12; *Shulḥan Arukh, Ḥoshen Mishpat* 92:4).

BACKGROUND

Oath of testimony – שְׁבוּעַת הָעֵדוּת: The *halakhot* concerning an oath of testimony are mentioned in the Torah (Leviticus 5:1) and are explored in depth in the fourth chapter of tractate *Shevuot*. If a plaintiff claims that witnesses have information supporting his case and he requests that they testify on his behalf, and they refuse to testify and deny that they have this information, they are required to take an oath to that effect. If the oath of testimony was taken falsely, they are required to bring a sin-offering as atonement.

Perek **IX**
Daf **106** Amud **a**

בְּפִקָּדוֹן פָּסוּל לְעֵדוּת.

but one who denies a claim **concerning** having taken **a deposit**[H] **is disqualified from bearing witness,** because if it is clear that the deposit is in his possession, yet he denies it, he must be lying.

וְהָאָמַר אִילְפָא: שְׁבוּעָה קוֹנָה; שְׁבוּעָה הִיא דְּקָנְיָא, אֲבָל כְּפִירָה לָא קָנְיָא! הָכָא נַמִי דְּקַיְימָא בַּאֲגַם.

The Gemara raises a further difficulty with regard to Rav Sheshet's opinion: **But didn't Ilfa say** that **an oath effects acquisition,** meaning that once he testified falsely that he did not become a bailee, the item in question becomes his property, rendering him liable as a robber even for damage or loss resulting from accidents? The Gemara infers: **It is** the taking of **an oath that effects acquisition, but** mere **denial** of having become a bailee **does not effect acquisition.** The Gemara rejects this distinction: **Here too,** Ilfa must be referring to a case **where** the deposit **stands in** a place not in the bailee's possession, e.g., **a swamp,** and as long as he does not take an oath, it can be assumed that his intention is simply to be evasive. But if the animal was standing in his house, then he acquires it as soon as he denies the claim.

HALAKHA

One who denies a claim concerning a deposit – הַכּוֹפֵר בְּפִקָּדוֹן: If one denies a claim concerning a deposit, even without taking a false oath, he is considered suspect with regard to the concern that he may take a false oath. This applies provided that there are witnesses who saw the deposit in his possession at the time he denied having it, or in any other case in which there is no plausible basis to claim that he was merely being evasive to buy time but intended to return the deposit (*Shulḥan Arukh, Ḥoshen Mishpat* 92:4 and *Sma* there).

ואיבעית אימא: מאי שבועה קונה – כדרב הונא, דאמר רב הונא אמר רב: "מנה לי בידך", והלה אומר: "אין לך בידי", ונשבע, ואחר כך באו עדים – פטור, שנאמר: "ולקח בעליו ולא ישלם" – כיון שקבלו הבעלים שבועה, שוב אין משלם ממון.

And if you wish, say instead: **What is the meaning of** Ilfa's statement that **an oath effects acquisition?** It is **in accordance with** the statement **of Rav Huna, as Rav Huna says** that **Rav said** that if one party says: I have **one hundred dinars in your possession, and the other** party **says: You do not** have any money **in my possession,** and the latter **took an oath** to that effect, **and later, witnesses came**[H] and testified that his oath was false, he is **exempt, as it is stated:** "The oath of the Lord shall be between them both, to see whether he has not put his hand unto his neighbor's goods; **and the owner thereof shall accept it, and he shall not make restitution**" (Exodus 22:10); teaching that **once the owner received an oath,**[N] the one who took the oath **no longer pays monetary restitution.** Ilfa's statement that an oath effects acquisition means that the bailee will no longer have to pay monetary restitution, and it does not relate to Rav Sheshet's statement that the bailee becomes responsible for damage resulting from accidents as soon as he denies the claim.

גופא, אמר רב הונא אמר רב: "מנה לי בידך", והלה אומר "אין לך בידי כלום", ונשבע ובאו עדים – פטור, שנאמר: "ולקח בעליו ולא ישלם", כיון שקבלו בעלים שבועה, שוב אין משלמין ממון.

§ Having mentioned Rav's ruling, the Gemara addresses **the** matter **itself: Rav Huna says** that **Rav says** that if one party says: I have **one hundred dinars in your possession, and the other** party **says: You do not** have any money **in my possession,** and the latter **takes an oath** to that effect, **and later, witnesses came** and testified that his oath was false, he is **exempt, as it is stated: "And the owner thereof shall accept it, and he shall not make restitution"** (Exodus 22:10); teaching that **once the owner received an oath,** the one who took the oath **no longer pays monetary restitution.**

אמר רבא: מסתברא מילתיה דרב במלוה, דלהוצאה ניתנה, אבל פקדון – ברשותיה דמריה קאי; והאלהים! אמר רב אפילו בפקדון, דכי כתיב קרא – בפקדון כתיב.

Rava said: Rav's statement is reasonable in the case of one who denies having taken **a loan, which is intended for expenditure.**[N] Since the money is no longer in his possession, the Torah exempts him from monetary restitution once he takes an oath. **But** in the case of one who denies having accepted **a deposit, it remains in the owner's possession** and must be returned intact, and it is not considered to be monetary restitution. Rava continues: **But, by God, Rav said** his statement **even in** the case of one who denies having accepted **a deposit, as when** this verse exempting him from payment **is written, it is written** in the case of one who denies having accepted **a deposit.**

יתיב רב נחמן וקאמר להא שמעתא. איתיביה רב אחא בר מניומי לרב נחמן: "היכן פקדוני"? אמר לו: "אבד", "משביעך אני", ואמר: "אמן", והעדים מעידים אותו שאכלו – משלם את הקרן. הודה מעצמו – משלם קרן וחומש ואשם!

§ The Gemara relates that **Rav Naḥman was sitting and saying this *halakha*. Rav Aḥa bar Minyumi raised an objection to Rav Naḥman** from that which was taught in a mishna (108b): If the owner asked the bailee: **Where is my deposit, and** the bailee **said to him:** It **is lost,** and the owner said: **I administer an oath to you,** and the bailee **said: Amen,** thereby accepting the oath, **and the witnesses testify about** the bailee **that he consumed** the deposit, then he must **pay the principal.** If he **admitted of his own** accord that he had taken a false oath, then he must **pay the principal and** the additional **one-fifth** payment, **and** bring **a guilt-offering.** This indicates that one is required to pay monetary restitution for a deposit even after taking an oath.

אמר ליה רב נחמן: הכא במאי עסקינן – כגון דנשבע חוץ לבית דין. אמר ליה: אי הכי, אימא סיפא: "היכן פקדוני"? אמר לו: "נגנב", "משביעך אני", ואמר: "אמן", והעדים מעידים אותו שגנבו – משלם תשלומי כפל, הודה מעצמו – משלם קרן וחומש ואשם; ואי סלקא דעתך חוץ לבית דין, מי איכא כפל?

Rav Naḥman said to him: With what are we dealing here? We are dealing with a case **where one takes an oath outside of court,**[N] which does not exempt him from paying restitution. Rav Aḥa bar Minyumi **said to him: If so, say the latter clause** of the mishna: If the owner asked the bailee: **Where is my deposit,** and the bailee **said to him:** It was **stolen,** and the owner said: **I administer an oath to you, and** the bailee **said: Amen,** thereby accepting the oath; **and the witnesses testify about** the bailee **that he stole it,** he must **pay the payment of double** the principal. If he **admitted of his own** accord that he had taken a false oath, then he must **pay the principal and** the additional **one-fifth** payment, **and** bring **a guilt-offering. And if it enters your mind** that this oath was taken **outside of court, is there** an obligation of **double payment** in such a circumstance?

HALAKHA

He took an oath, and later witnesses came – נשבע ואחר כך באו עדים: If one denies a claim lodged against him and takes an oath to that effect, and witnesses then testify that his oath had been false, he must pay the principal and an additional one-fifth of the principal, and he is henceforth considered suspect with regard to the concern that he may take a false oath. This is not in accordance with the opinion of Rav, but rather that of Rav Naḥman, whose rulings are followed in matters of monetary law (Rambam *Sefer Mishpatim, Hilkhot To'en VeNitan* 2:11; *Shulḥan Arukh, Ḥoshen Mishpat* 87:30).

NOTES

Once the owner received an oath – כיון שקבלו הבעלים שבועה: One explanation of this ruling is that once he takes an oath denying possession, the owner no longer has any legal claim against him. Since his oath was false, he receives the relevant punishments, by both human laws and the laws of Heaven. These punishments are more severe than monetary redress, and there is a halakhic principle that when subject to two punishments, one lesser and one greater, one receives only the greater punishment; therefore, he is given only the punishments for taking a false oath.

Which is intended for expenditure – דלהוצאה ניתנה: Since people borrow money in order to spend it, there is a presumption that loan money might be spent immediately following the loan. Even if the actual money lent is still in the debtor's possession, the loan money is not considered to be extant, as other money will be used to repay the loan, and the debtor pays restitution. By contrast, the actual deposit is given back to the owner as is, so the verse: "And he shall not make restitution" (Exodus 22:10) does not apply to it.

Where one takes an oath outside of court – דנשבע חוץ לבית דין: Rashi explains that such an oath is not significant enough to exempt one from paying restitution.

אֲמַר לֵיהּ: יָכֵילְנָא לְשַׁנּוּיֵי לָךְ: רֵישָׁא חוּץ לְבֵית דִּין, וְסֵיפָא בְּבֵית דִּין, מִיהוּ שִׁינּוּיָא דְּחִיקָא לָא מְשַׁנֵּינַן לָךְ; אִידִי וְאִידִי בְּבֵית דִּין, וְלָא קַשְׁיָא: כָּאן בְּקָפַץ, כָּאן בְּשֶׁלֹּא קָפַץ.

Rav Naḥman **said to him: I am able to answer you** by saying that **the first clause** of the mishna is referring to one who took an oath **outside of court, and the latter clause** of the mishna is referring to one who took an oath **in court, but we will not answer you with a forced answer.**[N] Instead, I will explain it in this manner: Both **this** clause **and that** clause are referring to an oath taken **in court, and** it is **not difficult. Here,** the ruling of the first clause is **with regard to** one who **leaped**[N] to take an oath as soon as the other litigant stated his claim, even though the court had not yet required him to do so, which is not considered a full-fledged oath. **There,** the ruling of the latter clause is **with regard to** one **who did not leap** but took an oath only when required by the court.

אֲמַר לֵיהּ רָמִי בַּר חָמָא לְרַב נַחְמָן: מִכְּדִי דְּרַב לָא סְבִירָא לָךְ, מַשְׁכּוּנֵי נַפְשָׁךְ אַדְּרַב לָמָּה לָךְ? אֲמַר לֵיהּ: לְפָרוּשָׁה לִדְרַב, דְּרַב הָכִי מְתָרֵץ לָהּ לְמַתְנִיתִין.

Rami bar Ḥama said to Rav Naḥman: After all, you do not hold in accordance with the statement **of Rav; why are you pledging yourself to** explain the statement **of Rav** so that it not be contradicted by the mishna? Rav Naḥman **said to him:** I said this not to justify Rav's ruling but **to clarify** the statement **of Rav, as Rav** would **explain the mishna in this** manner, as I did.

וְהָא רַב קְרָא קָאָמַר! אָמְרִי: קְרָא, לְכָל הַנִּשְׁבָּעִין שֶׁבַּתּוֹרָה נִשְׁבָּעִין וְלֹא מְשַׁלְּמִין הוּא דַּאֲתָא, "וְלָקַח בְּעָלָיו וְלֹא יְשַׁלֵּם" – מִי שֶׁעָלָיו לְשַׁלֵּם הוּא נִשְׁבָּע.

The Gemara asks: **But Rav quoted a verse,** so how could Rav Naḥman not agree with his statement? The Sages **said** in response: This **verse** was not written to teach the ruling of Rav; rather, **it comes to** teach the *halakha* that **all those** discussed **in the Torah** who are required to **take oaths,**[H] **take oaths and do not pay;** as the verse should be interpreted as follows: **"And the owner thereof shall accept it, and he shall not make restitution"** (Exodus 22:10), teaching that **one who has** the obligation **to pay**[N] **is** the one who **takes an oath,** and not the one demanding payment.

מְתִיב רַב הַמְנוּנָא: הִשְׁבִּיעַ עָלָיו חֲמִשָּׁה פְּעָמִים, בֵּין בִּפְנֵי בֵּית דִּין וּבֵין שֶׁלֹּא בִּפְנֵי בֵּית דִּין, וְכָפַר עָלָיו – חַיָּיב עַל כָּל אַחַת וְאַחַת, וְאָמַר רַבִּי שִׁמְעוֹן: מַה טַּעַם? הוֹאִיל וְיָכוֹל לַחֲזוֹר וּלְהוֹדוֹת;

Rav Hamnuna raises an objection to Rav's statement from a different mishna (*Shevuot* 36b), which states: If an owner requested the return of his deposit and the purported bailee denied having received it, and the owner **administered an oath** to the bailee **about** the deposit **five times,**[H] **whether before the court or not before the court, and** the bailee **denied** the claim each time, **he is liable for each and every one** of the oaths and must pay the additional one-fifth payment and bring a guilt-offering for each one. **And Rabbi Shimon says: What is the reason? Since he is able to retract and admit** after each oath, at which point he would be liable to pay, therefore each subsequent false oath is a denial of that liability. It can be seen from this mishna that one who admits liability after having taken a false oath is liable to pay, counter to the statement of Rav.

וְהָכָא קָפַץ לָא מָצֵית אָמְרַתְּ – "הִשְׁבִּיעַ עָלָיו" קָתָנֵי, חוּץ לְבֵית דִּין לָא מָצֵית אָמְרַתְּ – "בִּפְנֵי בֵּית דִּין" קָתָנֵי!

And here, you cannot say that the mishna in *Shevuot* is referring to a case where the bailee **leaped** to volunteer his oath, because it **teaches** explicitly that the owner **administered an oath** to the bailee **about** the deposit. And **you cannot say** that the mishna in *Shevuot* is referring to a case where the bailee took his oath **outside of court,** because it **teaches** explicitly that the *halakha* applies whether the oath was taken **before the court** or not before the court.

NOTES

A forced answer – שִׁינּוּיָא דְּחִיקָא: Rashi explains that Rav Naḥman finds it more forced to read the two clauses of the mishna as referring to two different locations than to read them as referring to one location, the court, but with two different types of legal proceedings: One in which the bailee taking the oath did so of his own accord without it being administered, and the other in which the oath was administered to him.

Here, with regard to one who leaped – כָּאן בְּקָפַץ: Just as the oath must take place in court in order to exempt him, it must also be administered by the court, as opposed to a case where the bailee takes an oath of his own volition or in response to the owner's request. Some early commentaries explain that an oath taken of one's own accord and not administered by the court is entirely irrelevant in terms of monetary law, and is viewed as nothing more than a personal vow that one takes in order to lend credence to his statement (Rabbeinu Ḥananel; see Ramah). By contrast, the Rashba explains that such an oath does have legal significance with regard to other cases of monetary liability, but it is not sufficient to exempt the defendant from the obligation to pay restitution or double payment for theft.

One who has the obligation to pay, etc. – מִי שֶׁעָלָיו לְשַׁלֵּם וכו׳: The oath is not considered proof of one's claim, since if that were to be the case, either party could take the oath. Rather, it serves either to add gravity to the proceedings so that the defendant, fearful of taking a false oath, will not defend himself with a false claim, or to convince the other party of his sincerity, so as to appease him. By rabbinic law, there are certain situations in which a plaintiff takes an oath to collect what he claims is owed to him, e.g., if the defendant is not trusted by the court, or in a case where the court assesses that the defendant is not sufficiently clear in his claim. The Sages also instituted a plaintiff's oath in certain cases where the defendant was a suspected criminal and they wished to penalize him by enabling the plaintiff to collect from him.

HALAKHA

All those in the Torah who are required to take oaths, etc. – כָּל הַנִּשְׁבָּעִין שֶׁבַּתּוֹרָה וכו׳: All oaths mandated by Torah law are taken by the one against whom a claim has been lodged, in order to exempt himself from payment. The Sages instituted additional oaths, some of which are taken by the plaintiff to enable him to collect the debt he claims he is owed. The circumstances in which these oaths are taken include cases of employees who claim that they are owed wages; one who claims to have been robbed but the thief does not know what he stole; a victim of physical assault; storekeepers with record books; and cases where the one against whom a claim has been lodged is considered suspect with regard to the concern that he may take a false oath (Rambam *Sefer Mishpatim, Hilkhot To'en VeNitan* 1:4; *Shulḥan Arukh, Ḥoshen Mishpat* 89:1).

Administered an oath to the bailee about the deposit five times – הִשְׁבִּיעַ עָלָיו חֲמִשָּׁה פְּעָמִים: One who falsely denies another's monetary claim and takes multiple oaths to that effect is liable to bring a separate guilt-offering for each false oath, whether he took the oaths of his own accord or because the claimant had him do so, and whether or not the oath was taken in court. The reason he is liable for a separate offering for each false oath is that had he admitted his liability after any individual denial, he would thereby have been required to pay; therefore, each denial with a false oath has the potential result of exempting him from payment, and it is monetarily significant in its own right (Rambam *Sefer Hafla'a, Hilkhot Shevuot* 7:9).

הוּא מוֹתִיב לַהּ, וְהוּא מְפָרֵק לַהּ: לְצַדְדִין קָתָנֵי; הִשְׁבִּיעַ עָלָיו חוּץ לְבֵית דִּין, וּבְבֵית דִּין קָפַץ.

The Gemara explains: **He,** Rav Hamnuna, **raised the objection and he resolved it:** The *tanna* **teaches it disjunctively,** i.e., the rulings of the mishna are stated with regard to different circumstances. Where it teaches that the owner **administered an oath** to the bailee **about** the deposit, that is referring to **outside of court, and** when it discusses an oath taken **before the court,** it is referring to a case where the bailee **leaped** and volunteered his oath. Therefore, the mishna does not discuss the case with regard to which Rav issued his ruling, where the bailee was forced to take an oath before the court.

מְתִיב רָבָא: בַּעַל הַבַּיִת שֶׁטָּעַן טַעֲנַת גַּנָּב בְּפִקָּדוֹן, וְנִשְׁבַּע וְהוֹדָה וּבָאוּ עֵדִים, אִם עַד שֶׁלֹּא בָּאוּ עֵדִים הוֹדָה – מְשַׁלֵּם קֶרֶן וְחוֹמֶשׁ וְאָשָׁם, וְאִם מִשֶּׁבָּאוּ עֵדִים הוֹדָה – מְשַׁלֵּם תַּשְׁלוּמֵי כֶפֶל וְאָשָׁם;

Rava raises an objection to Rav's statement from a *baraita*: In the case of **a homeowner** acting as a bailee **who** falsely **claimed, with regard to a deposit,** that **a thief** stole it, **and he took an oath** to that effect **and** subsequently **admitted** that he was lying and that in fact he took the item himself, **and witnesses came** and testified that the bailee himself indeed took the item, then **if he admitted** his guilt **before** the **witnesses came** and testified, **he pays** the **principal** value of the item **and** the additional **one-fifth** payment, **and** he must also bring **a guilt-offering. But if he admitted** his guilt **after** the **witnesses came** and testified, **he pays** the **double payment and** brings **a guilt-offering.** This *baraita* rules that one who takes an oath is not exempt from payment, counter to the statement of Rav.

וְהָכָא חוּץ לְבֵית דִּין וְקָפַץ לָא מָצֵית אָמְרַתְּ – ״כֶּפֶל״ קָתָנֵי!

And here, in this *baraita*, **you cannot say that** it is referring to an oath taken **outside of court or** that he **leaped** and volunteered his oath, because **double payment is taught** in the *baraita*, and one is obligated to pay double payment only when the accused has an oath administered to him before the court.

אֶלָּא אָמַר רָבָא: כׇּל הוֹדָה, לָא שְׁנָא טוֹעֵן טַעֲנַת אָבַד וְלָא שְׁנָא טוֹעֵן טַעֲנַת גַּנָּב נָמֵי – לָא אָמַר רַב, דְּהָא כְּתִיב ״וְהִתְוַדָּה״, דִּבְעֵי שַׁלּוֹמֵי קֶרֶן וְחוֹמֶשׁ;

The Gemara cites a new version of Rava's statement. **Rather, Rava said:** In **any** case where one **admits** to having taken a false oath, there **is no difference** whether one falsely **states the claim** that the deposit **was lost, and** there **is no difference** whether one falsely **states the claim** that **a thief** stole the deposit **as well;** in these cases, **Rav did not say** that taking an oath exempts the bailee from restitution, **because it is written** in the Torah portion discussing a false oath taken with regard to a deposit: "**And they shall confess** the sin that they performed, and he shall return the principal for his guilt, and he shall add to it one-fifth, and he gives it to the one with regard to whom is guilty" (Numbers 5:7), teaching **that** anyone who admits to a false oath concerning a deposit **is required to pay the principal and** the additional **one-fifth** payment.

טוֹעֵן טַעֲנַת גַּנָּב וּבָאוּ עֵדִים נָמֵי – לָא אָמַר רַב, דְּהָא כְּתִיב תַּשְׁלוּמֵי כֶפֶל; כִּי קָאָמַר – כְּגוֹן שֶׁטּוֹעֵן טַעֲנַת אָבַד, וְנִשְׁבַּע וְלֹא הוֹדָה וּבָאוּ עֵדִים.

The Gemara continues the new version of Rava's statement: Additionally, in a case where one falsely **states the claim** that **a thief** stole the deposit and takes an oath to that effect **and witnesses come** and say that he had stolen it, **as well, Rav did not say** that taking an oath exempts the bailee from restitution, **because double payment is written** in the Torah (see Exodus 22:8). **When he says** that taking an oath exempts the bailee from restitution, it is in a case **where one** falsely **states the claim that** the deposit **was lost and takes an oath** to that effect, **and did not admit it, and witnesses come** and testify that he had stolen it.

אֲזַל רַב גַּמְדָּא וַאֲמָרָהּ לִשְׁמַעְתָּא קַמֵּיהּ דְּרַב אָשֵׁי. אֲמַר לֵיהּ: הַשְׁתָּא וּמָה רַב הַמְנוּנָא תַּלְמִידֵיהּ דְּרַב, וְיָדַע דְּאָמַר רַב הוֹדָה וְקָמוֹתֵיב הוֹדָה, וְאַתְּ אָמְרַתְּ: הוֹדָה לָא אָמַר רַב?!

The Gemara relates that **Rav Gamda went and said that** *halakha* **before Rav Ashi.** Rav Ashi **said to him: Now** consider: **And even Rav Hamnuna,** who was **Rav's student and knew that Rav says** that one who takes a false oath is exempt from paying restitution even in a case where he **admitted** it; **and** Rav Hamnuna therefore **challenged** him from a mishna that teaches that one is not exempt in a case where he **admitted** it. **And you say** that **Rav did not say** his *halakha* in a case where one **admitted** that he took a false oath? Presumably, Rav Hamnuna, as Rav's student, was aware of the scope of his teacher's ruling. How, then, can you limit it as being narrower than Rav Hamnuna's interpretation?

אֲמַר לֵיהּ רַב אַחָא סָבָא לְרַב אָשֵׁי, רַב הַמְנוּנָא הָכִי קָא קַשְׁיָא לֵיהּ:

Rav Aḥa the Elder said to Rav Ashi: Rav Hamnuna did not raise a difficulty against Rav with regard to the case of one admitting to having taken a false oath, rather, with regard to the case where witnesses came after he took the oath, and **this is** what **is difficult for him:**

אִי אָמְרַתְּ בִּשְׁלָמָא: נִשְׁבַּע כִּי אָתוּ עֵדִים מִיחַיַּיב, אַמְּטוּ לְהָכִי מְחַיְּיבִינַן לֵיהּ קׇרְבָּן אַשְּׁבוּעָה בַּתְרַיְיתָא, הוֹאִיל וְיָכוֹל לַחֲזוֹר וּלְהוֹדוֹת.

Granted, if you say that when **one takes** a false **oath** and then **witnesses come, he is liable** to pay, **that is why we hold him liable** for **a guilt-offering for the final oath, since he can** still **retract and admit**[N] his liability and incur an obligation to pay. Consequently, the fact that he took another false oath constitutes an additional false denial of his monetary liability.

אֶלָּא אִי אָמְרַתְּ: כִּי אָתוּ עֵדִים פָּטוּר, מִי אִיכָּא מִידֵּי דְּאִילּוּ אָתֵי סָהֲדֵי וּמַסְהֲדֵי בֵּיהּ פָּטוּר, וַאֲנַן נֵיקוּ נִיחַיְּיבֵיהּ קׇרְבָּן אַשְּׁבוּעָה, הוֹאִיל וְיָכוֹל לַחֲזוֹר וּלְהוֹדוֹת? הָשְׁתָּא מִיהַת לָא אוֹדֵי!

But if you say, as Rav did, that even **when witnesses come he is exempt** from paying, then the mishna's ruling is difficult, as **is there any** similar case **where if witnesses come and testify with regard to it, he would be exempt, and yet we would stand and obligate him** to bring **a guilt-offering for a** later **oath,** for no reason other than **since he can** still **retract and admit** his liability? As of **now, in any event, he has not admitted**[N] to any liability and has no extant debt, and any further oaths that he takes are not denials of monetary liability. It follows, then, that Rava's explanation of Rav's opinion cannot be undermined by Rav Hamnuna's challenge.

אָמַר רַבִּי חִיָּיא בַּר אַבָּא אָמַר רַבִּי יוֹחָנָן: הַטּוֹעֵן טַעֲנַת גַּנָּב בְּפִקָּדוֹן – מְשַׁלֵּם תַּשְׁלוּמֵי כֶפֶל, טָבַח וּמָכַר – מְשַׁלֵּם תַּשְׁלוּמֵי אַרְבָּעָה וַחֲמִשָּׁה;

§ The Gemara cites another ruling concerning the topic of a bailee who claims that a deposit in his possession was stolen. **Rabbi Ḥiyya bar Abba says** that **Rabbi Yoḥanan says: One who** falsely **states the claim, with regard to a deposit,** that a **thief**[H] stole it, and it becomes clear that he stole it himself, **pays double payment. If he slaughtered or sold** it, **he must pay fourfold or fivefold payment.**

הוֹאִיל וְגַנָּב מְשַׁלֵּם תַּשְׁלוּמֵי כֶפֶל, וְטוֹעֵן טַעֲנַת גַּנָּב מְשַׁלֵּם תַּשְׁלוּמֵי כֶפֶל, מַה גַּנָּב שֶׁהוּא מְשַׁלֵּם כֶּפֶל – טָבַח וּמָכַר מְשַׁלֵּם תַּשְׁלוּמֵי אַרְבָּעָה וַחֲמִשָּׁה, אַף טוֹעֵן טַעֲנַת גַּנָּב בְּפִקָּדוֹן כְּשֶׁהוּא מְשַׁלֵּם תַּשְׁלוּמֵי כֶפֶל – טָבַח וּמָכַר מְשַׁלֵּם תַּשְׁלוּמֵי אַרְבָּעָה וַחֲמִשָּׁה.

He explains his ruling by means of a comparison: **Since a thief pays double payment, and** one who falsely **states the claim** that **a thief** stole the deposit also **pays double payment,** it follows that **just as a thief, who** ordinarily **pays double payment,** and if he **slaughtered or sold** an animal he stole **pays fourfold or fivefold payment, so too,** one who falsely **states the claim** that **a thief stole a deposit, who** ordinarily **pays double payment,** if he **slaughtered or sold** the animal he received as a deposit **pays fourfold or fivefold payment.**

מָה לְגַנָּב – שֶׁכֵּן מְשַׁלֵּם תַּשְׁלוּמֵי כֶפֶל שֶׁלֹּא בִּשְׁבוּעָה, תֹּאמַר בְּטוֹעֵן טַעֲנַת גַּנָּב – שֶׁאֵין מְשַׁלֵּם תַּשְׁלוּמֵי כֶפֶל אֶלָּא בִּשְׁבוּעָה!

The Gemara asks: **What** is notable **about** the *halakha* **of a thief?** It is notable **in that** he **pays double payment** even **without** having taken a false **oath; will you say** that this stringency should apply **with regard to** one who falsely **states the claim** that **a thief** stole the deposit, **who pays double payment only upon** taking a false **oath?** Therefore, one cannot derive from the obligation of a thief to pay fourfold or fivefold payment to the case of one who falsely states the claim that the deposit was stolen.

אָמְרִי: הֶיקֵּישָׁא הִיא, וְאֵין מְשִׁיבִין עַל הֶיקֵּישָׁא.

The Sages **say** in response: Rabbi Yoḥanan did not base his ruling on a logical inference; rather, **it is** a derivation based upon **a juxtaposition,**[N] as the verses discussing a thief and one who falsely states the claim that a deposit was stolen are juxtaposed, **and one cannot refute** through analysis a derivation based upon **juxtaposition.**[B]

הָנִיחָא לְמַאן דְּאָמַר: חַד בְּגַנָּב וְחַד בְּטוֹעֵן טַעֲנַת גַּנָּב – שַׁפִּיר. אֶלָּא לְמַאן דְּאָמַר: הַאי "אִם יִמָּצֵא הַגַּנָּב" וְ"אִם לֹא יִמָּצֵא" תַּרְוַיְיהוּ בְּטוֹעֵן טַעֲנַת גַּנָּב, מַאי אִיכָּא לְמֵימַר?

The Gemara asks: **This works out well according to the one who says** that **one** verse is stated **with regard to a thief and one** verse is stated **with regard to** one who falsely **states the claim** that **a thief** stole the deposit. According to him, there is a juxtaposition, and one can **well** derive one from the other. **But according to the one who says** that **both this** verse: **"If the thief shall be found,** he shall pay double" (Exodus 22:6), **and: "If the thief shall not be found"** (Exodus 22:7), are referring to one who falsely **states the claim** that **a thief** stole the deposit, and neither verse is referring to a thief, **what is there to say?**

NOTES

Since he can still retract and admit – הוֹאִיל וְיָכוֹל לַחֲזוֹר וּלְהוֹדוֹת: The mere fact that he repeated his false oath is not sufficient to render him liable to bring another offering, as one oath does not take effect when another is already in effect. The obligation resulting from the second oath must be due to the fact that it also served the legal function of denying a monetary claim. Since an admission would have been sufficient for the court to require him to pay, each successive oath is considered, according to this opinion, a new denial of a monetary claim (Rashi). The Ra'avad notes that the reason that the Gemara specifies his retraction, and not witness testimony, as the potential cause for his obligation is because only through a retraction would he be liable to bring an offering and pay the additional one-fifth payment as well.

Now, in any event, he has not admitted – הָשְׁתָּא מִיהַת לָא אוֹדֵי: If there has been no actual admission, there is no actual monetary obligation. Therefore, each subsequent oath is merely a repetition of the first oath (Rashi).

It is a juxtaposition – הֶיקֵּישָׁא הִיא: The Gemara notes earlier (63b) that some explain that the verse: "If the thief shall be found, he shall pay double" (Exodus 22:6), is referring to an actual thief, and the following verse: "If the thief shall not be found" (Exodus 22:7), is referring to a bailee who claims that the deposit was stolen and was found to have stolen it himself. The juxtaposition of these two clauses teaches that all the *halakhot* stated in the case of a thief apply equally to one who makes a false claim that a deposit was stolen, including the obligation to pay the fourfold or fivefold payment for selling or slaughtering a stolen animal (see Exodus 21:37).

HALAKHA

One who states the claim with regard to a deposit that a thief, etc. – הַטּוֹעֵן טַעֲנַת גַּנָּב בְּפִקָּדוֹן וכו׳: If one claims that a deposit in his possession was stolen and took an oath to that effect, and witnesses testify that the deposit had been in his possession the entire time, he is considered a thief and is liable to pay double payment. If the deposit was an animal and he had slaughtered or sold it after taking the false oath, he is liable to pay fourfold or fivefold payment (Rambam *Sefer Nezikin*, *Hilkhot Geneiva* 4:1; *Tur*, *Ḥoshen Mishpat* 352).

BACKGROUND

One cannot refute a juxtaposition – אֵין מְשִׁיבִין עַל הֶיקֵּישָׁא: The reason for this is that the *halakhot* derived from a juxtaposition are considered to be explicitly stated in the Torah and therefore no analysis can refute them. A derivation by analogy or by verbal analogy can be refuted unless the verbal analogy is based on a word that is superfluous in both verses.

אָמְרִי: ״גַּנָּב״ ״הַגַּנָּב״.

The Sages say in response: Rabbi Yoḥanan's ruling is derived from an amplification indicated by the verse not employing the term **"thief** [*gannav*]," and instead employing the expanded term **"the thief** [*hagannav*]." This teaches that the *halakha* of the fourfold and fivefold payment applies to one who falsely states the claim that the deposit was stolen, as well.

אֵיתִיבֵיהּ רַבִּי חִיָּיא בַּר אַבָּא לְרַבִּי יוֹחָנָן: ״הֵיכָן שׁוֹרִי״? ״נִגְנַב״, ״מַשְׁבִּיעֲךָ אֲנִי״, וְאָמַר: ״אָמֵן״, וְהָעֵדִים מְעִידִים אוֹתוֹ שֶׁאֲכָלוֹ – מְשַׁלֵּם תַּשְׁלוּמֵי כֶפֶל. וְהָא הָכָא דְּאִי אֶפְשָׁר לְכַזַּיִת בָּשָׂר בְּלֹא שְׁחִיטָה, וְקָתָנֵי: מְשַׁלֵּם תַּשְׁלוּמֵי כֶפֶל; תַּשְׁלוּמֵי כֶפֶל – אִין, תַּשְׁלוּמֵי אַרְבָּעָה וַחֲמִשָּׁה – לָא!

Rabbi Ḥiyya bar Abba raised an objection to the statement of **Rabbi Yoḥanan** from a *baraita*: In a scenario where one said to an unpaid bailee: **Where is my ox?** Then the bailee responded: It **was stolen.** And the owner said: **I administer an oath to you, and** the bailee **said: Amen. And the witnesses testify about** the bailee **that he ate it,** he **pays double payment. But here,** the *halakha* is **that it is impossible to** eat even **an olive-bulk of meat without slaughtering** the animal first, indicating that it must have been slaughtered, **and** nevertheless **it teaches** that he **pays double payment.** It can be inferred that **double payment, yes,** he pays; but **fourfold or fivefold payment, no,** he does not pay.

הָכָא בְּמַאי עָסְקִינַן – כְּגוֹן שֶׁאֲכָלוֹ נְבֵילָה.

Rabbi Yoḥanan answers: **With what are we dealing here?** We are dealing with a case **where he ate it** as an unslaughtered **animal carcass.** Since it was not killed according to the *halakhot* of ritual slaughter, the thief does not pay the fourfold or fivefold payment.

וְלִישְׁנֵי לֵיהּ: כְּגוֹן שֶׁאֲכָלוֹ טְרֵיפָה! כְּרַבִּי מֵאִיר, דְּאָמַר: שְׁחִיטָה שֶׁאֵינָהּ רְאוּיָה שְׁמָהּ שְׁחִיטָה.

The Gemara asks: **And let** Rabbi Yoḥanan **answer** Rabbi Ḥiyya bar Abba by saying that it is a case **such as where he ate it** as an **animal with a wound that will cause it to die within twelve months** [*tereifa*], in accordance with Rabbi Shimon's opinion that the legal status of an act of slaughter that is not fit for accomplishing its full ritual purpose is not considered an act of slaughter for which the thief must pay the fourfold or fivefold payment. The Gemara responds that Rabbi Yoḥanan holds **in accordance with** the opinion of **Rabbi Meir, who says** that the legal status of an act of **slaughter that is not fit** for accomplishing its full ritual purpose **is considered** an act of **slaughter,** and the thief would pay the fourfold or fivefold payment.

וְלִישְׁנֵי לֵיהּ: בְּבֶן פְּקוּעָה! כְּרַבִּי מֵאִיר, דְּאָמַר: בֶּן פְּקוּעָה טָעוּן שְׁחִיטָה.

The Gemara further asks: **And let** Rabbi Yoḥanan **answer** Rabbi Ḥiyya bar Abba by saying that the ruling of the *baraita* is stated **with regard to an animal removed from its mother's womb after the mother was ritually slaughtered** [***ben pekua***],[NBL] which is permitted for consumption without slaughter, so that there is a possibility that the thief ate it without first slaughtering it. The Gemara responds that Rabbi Yoḥanan holds **in accordance with** the opinion of **Rabbi Meir, who says** that **a *ben pekua* requires slaughter.**

וְלִישְׁנֵי לֵיהּ: כְּגוֹן שֶׁעָמַד בַּדִּין, וְאָמְרוּ לוֹ: ״צֵא תֵּן לוֹ״. דְּהָא אָמַר רָבָא: ״צֵא תֵּן לוֹ״, טָבַח וּמָכַר – פָּטוּר, מַאי טַעְמָא? כֵּיוָן דִּפְסַקֵיהּ לְמִילְּתֵיהּ וְטָבַח וּמָכַר הָוֵי גַּזְלָן, וְגַזְלָן לָא מְשַׁלֵּם תַּשְׁלוּמֵי אַרְבָּעָה וַחֲמִשָּׁה;

The Gemara further asks: **And let** Rabbi Yoḥanan **answer** Rabbi Ḥiyya bar Abba by saying that it is a case **where** the bailee **stood in judgment** in court, **and** the judges **said to him: Go out** and **give him** the stolen animal, and he did not do so, and subsequently slaughtered or sold it? In this case he would not pay the fourfold or fivefold payment, **as doesn't Rava say** that if the judges instruct a thief: **Go out** and **give him** the stolen animal, **and he** instead **slaughtered or sold** it, he is **exempt** from paying the fourfold or fivefold payment. **What is the reason** for this? **Once** the court **ruled on his matter,** requiring him to give the animal to the owner, and he did not heed the court's ruling **but slaughtered or sold** the animal, **he is** considered **a robber,** and not a thief; **and a robber does not pay fourfold or fivefold payment.**

״חַיָּיב אַתָּה לִיתֵּן לוֹ״, וְטָבַח וּמָכַר – חַיָּיב, מַאי טַעְמָא? כָּל כַּמָּה דְּלָא פְּסִיקָא לֵיהּ מִילְּתָא, אַכַּתִּי גַּנָּב הוּא!

Rava continues: But if the judges say only: **You are obligated to give** the animal **to him,** and he did not heed the court's statement **but slaughtered or sold** the animal, then he is **obligated** to pay the fourfold or fivefold payment. **What is the reason** for this? **Since** the court **has not issued a definitive ruling in this matter, he is still** considered **a thief** rather than a robber.

NOTES

Ben pekua – בֶּן פְּקוּעָה: A *ben pekua* is an animal fetus removed alive from its mother's womb after the mother underwent ritual slaughter. If this occurred in the case of a large mammal, such as a cow, during the first eight months of pregnancy, the offspring is considered as though it was a limb of its mother's body when the act of slaughter was performed, and is therefore permitted for consumption without being slaughtered itself. There is a dispute among the Sages with regard to a fetus removed in the ninth month of pregnancy. Rabbi Meir holds that in that case, it is considered an independent entity, and one may not eat it without first slaughtering it, like any other animal. Rabbi Shimon Shezuri holds that a ninth-month fetus is no different than an earlier-term one. The *halakhot* of this topic are discussed at length in the fourth chapter of tractate *Ḥullin*.

BACKGROUND

Ben pekua – בֶּן פְּקוּעָה: Like humans, animals can be born either by vaginal birth or by Caesarean section. When the surgical incision for a Caesarean section is made while the mother is alive, the offspring is termed: An animal delivered through the abdominal wall [*yotzei dofen*]. Even if the mother is slaughtered, the fetus does not die immediately when its mother dies; therefore, if the mother's womb is cut open within a short time after she is slaughtered, it is possible to extract the offspring, who can live like any other animal.

LANGUAGE

Ben pekua – בֶּן פְּקוּעָה: As the letters *peh* and *beit* are both bilabial plosives, i.e., letters pronounced by bringing the lips together and expelling air in a burst, with the difference being that the *beit* is voiced while the *peh* is not voiced, the word *paka* is related to *baka*, which means to cut open. Here, it refers to an animal born via the cutting open of the mother animal's womb in order to remove it.

אָמְרִי: וְלִיטַעְמֵיךְ, לִישַׁנֵּי לֵיהּ: בְּשׁוּתָּף שֶׁטָּבַח שֶׁלֹּא מִדַּעַת חֲבֵירוֹ! אֶלָּא, חֲדָא מִתְּרֵי וּתְלָתָא נָקַט.

The Sages **say** in response: **And according to your reasoning, let** Rabbi Yoḥanan **answer** Rabbi Ḥiyya bar Abba by saying that the ruling of the *baraita* is stated **with regard to a partner who slaughtered** an animal stolen by him and his partner **without the other** partner's **knowledge,**[N] as the *halakha* is that in such a case, the thief, i.e., the partner who slaughtered the animal, does not pay fourfold or fivefold payment. **Rather,** Rabbi Yoḥanan **selected one of two or three** possible answers but did not mean to say that it was the only possible answer.

וְאָמַר רַבִּי חִיָּיא בַּר אַבָּא אָמַר רַבִּי יוֹחָנָן: הַטּוֹעֵן טַעֲנַת גַּנָּב בַּאֲבֵידָה – מְשַׁלֵּם תַּשְׁלוּמֵי כֶפֶל; מַאי טַעְמָא? דִּכְתִיב: "עַל כׇּל אֲבֵדָה אֲשֶׁר יֹאמַר".

§ The Gemara cites a related ruling: **And Rabbi Ḥiyya bar Abba says** that **Rabbi Yoḥanan says:** With regard to **one who** falsely **states the claim, with regard to a lost item,** that **a thief**[H] stole it, i.e., he found a lost item, and when the owner requested its return, he claimed that it had been stolen from him, and it became known that he lied and had taken the item himself, **he pays double payment. What is the reason** for this? **As it is written** in the verse concerning double payment for a thief: "For any matter of trespass, from an ox, for a donkey, for a sheep, for a garment, or **for any lost item about which one shall say:** This is it, the claims of both of them shall come before the judges; the one whom the judges convict shall pay double to his neighbor" (Exodus 22:8). It can be seen from here that double payment applies to a false claim of theft even with regard to a lost item.

אֵיתִיבֵיהּ רַבִּי אַבָּא בַּר מֶמֶל לְרַבִּי חִיָּיא בַּר אַבָּא: "כִּי יִתֵּן אִישׁ" – אֵין נְתִינַת קָטָן כְּלוּם; וְאֵין לִי אֶלָּא שֶׁנְּתָנוֹ כְּשֶׁהוּא קָטָן וּתְבָעוֹ כְּשֶׁהוּא קָטָן, נְתָנוֹ כְּשֶׁהוּא קָטָן וּתְבָעוֹ כְּשֶׁהוּא גָּדוֹל מִנַּיִן? תַּלְמוּד לוֹמַר: "עַד הָאֱלֹהִים יָבֹא דְּבַר שְׁנֵיהֶם" – עַד שֶׁתְּהֵא נְתִינָה וּתְבִיעָה שָׁוִין כְּאֶחָד;

Rabbi Abba bar Memel raised an objection to Rabbi Ḥiyya bar Abba from a *baraita*: The verse states: **"If a man gives** his neighbor money or vessels to safeguard, and it was stolen from the house of the man, if the thief shall be found, he shall pay double" (Exodus 22:6). The use of the word "man" indicates that the **giving** of a deposit **by a minor is nothing.**[H] **And I have** derived **only** a case **where he gives** the deposit **when he is a minor and lodges the claim** concerning it **against** the bailee **when he is** still **a minor. From where** is it derived that the *halakha* would be the same in a case where **he gives** the deposit **when he is a minor and lodges the claim** concerning it **against** the bailee **when he is an adult? The verse states: "The claims of both of them shall come before the judges"** (Exodus 22:8), i.e., the claim is valid **only when** the **giving** of the deposit **and the claim are equal,** both done when he is an adult.

וְאִם אִיתָא, תֶּיהֱוֵי נָמֵי כַּאֲבֵידָה! אֲמַר לֵיהּ: הָכָא בְּמַאי עָסְקִינַן – כְּגוֹן שֶׁאֲכָלוֹ כְּשֶׁהוּא קָטָן.

Based on the ruling of this *baraita*, Rabbi Abba bar Memel raises his objection: **And if it is so** that even one who finds a lost item pays double payment for claiming falsely that it was stolen, indicating that the giving of the item as a deposit by the owner is not an essential condition to render the thief liable for double payment, then the claim of a minor **should be like a lost item as well,** and one who received a deposit from a minor should be liable for double payment. Rabbi Ḥiyya bar Abba **said to him: With what are we dealing here?** We are dealing with a case **where** the bailee **consumed** the deposit **when** the owner **was** still **a minor,** so that at the time it was consumed, the owner had no legal standing. Therefore, the bailee is not obligated to pay.

NOTES

Who slaughtered without the other partner's knowledge – שֶׁטָּבַח שֶׁלֹּא מִדַּעַת חֲבֵירוֹ: The penalty of paying four or five times the principal is imposed only when this amount is paid in full. In this case, he would be liable to pay only four or five times the value of half the principal, as his partner is liable for the other half of the principal. Therefore, there is no fourfold or fivefold payment.

HALAKHA

One who falsely states the claim with regard to a lost item that a thief, etc. – הַטּוֹעֵן טַעֲנַת גַּנָּב בַּאֲבֵידָה וכו׳: If one finds a lost item and then claims that it was stolen from him and took an oath to that effect, and witnesses testify that it had been in his possession the entire time, he is considered a thief and is liable to pay double payment. If the lost item was an animal and he had slaughtered or sold it after taking the false oath, he is liable to pay fourfold or fivefold payment. According to the Rambam, this is the *halakha* only if he had claimed that it had been stolen from him by armed bandits, which is a case of duress. By contrast, the *Tur* holds that this is the *halakha* even if he had claimed that it was a standard theft (Rambam *Sefer Nezikin*, *Hilkhot Geneiva* 4:4; *Tur*, *Ḥoshen Mishpat* 352).

Giving of a deposit by a minor is nothing – אֵין נְתִינַת קָטָן כְּלוּם: If one claims that a deposit he was safeguarding for a minor was stolen and took an oath to that effect, and witnesses testify that the deposit had been in his possession the entire time, he is not liable to pay double payment, even if the owner was already an adult by the time he lodged the claim for his deposit to be returned, as the giving of a deposit by a minor is nothing in terms of rendering one liable to pay double payment (Rambam *Sefer Nezikin*, *Hilkhot Geneiva* 4:9).

PERSONALITIES

Rabbi Ḥiyya bar Yosef – רַבִּי חִיָּיא בַּר יוֹסֵף: Rabbi Ḥiyya bar Yosef was a second-generation Babylonian *amora* who ascended to Eretz Yisrael. During his residence in Babylonia he assumed the title of Rav, which was customarily used in Babylonia, and after he immigrated to Eretz Yisrael he assumed the title of Rabbi, which was customarily used in Eretz Yisrael.

אֲבָל כְּשֶׁהוּא גָּדוֹל, מַאי? הָכִי נַמִי דִּמְשַׁלֵּם? אִי הָכִי, אַדְּתָנָא: עַד שֶׁתְּהֵא נְתִינָה וּתְבִיעָה שָׁוִין כְּאֶחָד, לִיתְנֵי: עַד שֶׁתְּהֵא אֲכִילָה וּתְבִיעָה שָׁוִין כְּאֶחָד! אֲמַר לֵיהּ, תְּנֵי: עַד שֶׁתְּהֵא אֲכִילָה וּתְבִיעָה שָׁוִין כְּאֶחָד.

Rabbi Abba bar Memel questions this answer: **But** had the bailee consumed it **when** the owner was already **an adult, what** is the *halakha*; **indeed,** would the *halakha* be **that** the bailee **pays? If so, rather than teaching:** The claim is valid **only when** the **giving** of the deposit **and** the **claim are equal, let** the *baraita* **teach:** The claim is valid **only when** the **consumption** of the deposit **and** the **claim are equal,** which would be a more precise ruling. Rabbi Ḥiyya bar Abba **said to him:** Emend the *baraita* and **teach:** The claim is valid **only when** the **consumption** of the deposit **and** the **claim are equal.**

רַב אַשִׁי אֲמַר: לָא דָּמֵי, אֲבֵידָה קָא אָתְיָא מִכֹּחַ בֶּן דַּעַת, וְהָא לָא אָתְיָא מִכֹּחַ בֶּן דַּעַת.

Rav Ashi said a different answer to Rabbi Abba bar Memel's objection: The two cases **are not comparable,** so an objection to Rabbi Ḥiyya bar Abba's statement concerning a lost item cannot be derived from the case of a minor giving a deposit, because the **lost item came** into the possession of the finder **by** the **power of one** who is **mentally competent,** as the one who lost it is presumed to be an adult, though he did not personally give it to the finder; **but this** deposit given by a minor **did not come** into his possession **by** the **power of one** who is **mentally competent,** as from a halakhic perspective, a minor is not considered mentally competent. Therefore, he has no grounds for a claim.

וְאָמַר רַבִּי חִיָּיא בַּר אַבָּא אָמַר רַבִּי יוֹחָנָן: הַטּוֹעֵן טַעֲנַת גַּנָּב בְּפִקָּדוֹן – אֵינוֹ חַיָּיב עַד שֶׁיִּכְפּוֹר בְּמִקְצָת וְיוֹדֶה בְּמִקְצָת; מַאי טַעֲמָא? דְּאָמַר קְרָא: ״כִּי הוּא זֶה״. וּפְלִיגָא דְּרַבִּי חִיָּיא בַּר יוֹסֵף, דְּאָמַר רַבִּי חִיָּיא בַּר יוֹסֵף:

§ The Gemara quotes a related ruling: **And Rabbi Ḥiyya bar Abba says** that **Rabbi Yoḥanan says:** With regard to **one who** falsely **states the claim, with regard to a deposit,** that a **thief** stole it, **he is not obligated** to take an oath, nor to pay double payment, **until he denies part of** the claim **and admits to part of** the claim. **What is the reason** for this? **As the verse states:** "About which one shall say: **This is it**" (Exodus 22:8), indicating an admittance of only this part, but no more. The Gemara notes: **And** this **disagrees** with the ruling **of Rabbi Ḥiyya bar Yosef,**[P] **as Rabbi Ḥiyya bar Yosef says:**

Perek **IX**
Daf **107** Amud **a**

HALAKHA

It is written concerning a loan – אַמִּלְוֶה הוּא דִּכְתִיב: If Reuven claims that Shimon owes him money or movable property, and Shimon has the legal ability to absolve himself of any monetary obligation to Reuven by claiming to have purchased or returned the money or property, or by completely denying having taken it in the first place, but in fact Shimon admits to part of the claim, he is obligated to pay the amount he admits to owing, and by Torah law he takes an oath with regard to the rest of the claim and is exempt from paying the remainder. If a bailee or one who rented or borrowed an item denies a claim, he takes an oath by Torah law to exempt himself from payment whether he admitted to a part of the claim or denied it entirely. This is in accordance with the ruling of Rabbi Ḥiyya bar Yosef that the verse is written with a merging of Torah portions (Rambam *Sefer Mishpatim*, *Hilkhot Sekhirut* 2:8 and *Hilkhot To'en VeNitan* 1:1; *Shulḥan Arukh*, *Ḥoshen Mishpat* 87:1, 295:3).

עֵירוּב פָּרָשִׁיּוֹת כָּתוּב כָּאן, וְכִי כְּתִיב ״כִּי הוּא זֶה״ – אַמִּלְוֶה הוּא דִּכְתִיב. וּמַאי שְׁנָא מִלְוֶה?

A merging of Torah **portions is written here,**[N] and the *halakha* written in this passage is in fact meant to be applied to a different passage. **And when it is written: "This is it,"** from which the *halakha* of a partial admission is derived, **it is written concerning a loan,**[H] not a deposit. The Gemara asks: **And what is different** about **a loan**[N] that this *halakha* would apply only there?

NOTES

A merging of Torah portions is written here – עֵירוּב פָּרָשִׁיּוֹת כָּתוּב כָּאן: There is a dispute among the early commentaries as to the correct understanding of this idea, which then informs their understanding of the discussion on this *amud*. The most straightforward understanding, held by Rashi and some of the *ge'onim*, is that a detail stated in one passage in fact applies to a different passage. In this case, the clause: "This is it" (Exodus 22:8), which is the source for the principle that one is obligated to take an oath only when admitting to a part of a claim, is referring not to a deposit, which is the subject of this passage, but to a loan.

By contrast, *Tosafot*, citing Rabbeinu Tam, understand the merging of Torah portions to mean that the *halakha* written in the context of deposits also extends to loans. They therefore hold that one is obligated to take an oath with regard to a deposit only when one's claim that the deposit was lost or stolen, or that he never received it, is associated with an admission that one still owes some other part of the deposit.

Other early commentaries explain that the Gemara is not differentiating between a loan and a deposit; rather, within the domain of deposits it is differentiating between a claim that is also applicable to a loan and a claim that is not. The *halakha* derived from the merging of Torah portions, that the obligation to take an oath applies only when one admitted to a part of the claim, would apply to deposits when the exculpatory claim is one that could also be stated with regard to a loan, e.g., that the exchange never occurred, but not those claims specific to the domain of deposits, e.g., that the item was lost in circumstances beyond the bailee's control. Consequently, if a bailee states a claim with regard to a deposit that could be stated only with regard to a deposit, he is obligated to take an oath even when denying his liability entirely, but if the claim is one that could be stated with regard to a loan, then the bailee is obligated to take an oath only when he admits to part of his liability (*Tosafot* citing Riva; Rashba; Meiri; see *Sefer HaYashar*).

And what is different about a loan – וּמַאי שְׁנָא מִלְוֶה: Rashi explains that the question is why this principle applies to loans and not deposits. *Tosafot*, citing Rabbeinu Tam, explain that the question is why one who admits to part of a claim is liable. The Riva, in accordance with his understanding of the previous stage of the discussion, explains that the question is why this *halakha*, when applied to deposits, is stated only with regard to claims when it could be stated in the case of a loan as well.

כְּדְרַבָּה, דְּאָמַר רַבָּה: מִפְּנֵי מָה אָמְרָה תּוֹרָה מוֹדֶה בְּמִקְצָת הַטַּעֲנָה יִשָּׁבַע? חֲזָקָה אֵין אָדָם מֵעִיז פָּנָיו בִּפְנֵי בַּעַל חוֹבוֹ; וְהַאי בְּכוּלֵּיהּ בָּעֵי דְּנִכְפְּרֵיהּ, וְהַאי דְּלָא כָּפְרֵיהּ – מִשּׁוּם דְּאֵין אָדָם מֵעִיז פָּנָיו;

The Gemara answers: It is **in accordance with** the statement **of Rabba, as Rabba says: For what** reason **did the Torah say** that one who **admits to a part of the claim must take an oath?** It is because there is **a presumption** that **a person does not exhibit insolence**[N] by lying **in the presence of his creditor,** who had done him a favor by lending money to him. **And this** person who denies part of the claim actually **wants to deny all of** the debt, so as to be exempt, **and this** fact **that he does not deny** all **of it** is **because a person does not exhibit insolence.**

וּבְכוּלֵּי בָּעֵי דְּלוֹדֵי לֵיהּ, וְהַאי דְּכָפַר לֵיהּ בְּמִקְצָת – סָבַר: אִי מוֹדֵינָא לֵיהּ בְּכוּלֵּיהּ תָּבַע לִי בְּכוּלֵּיהּ, אִישְׁתַּמֵּיט לִי מִיהָא הָשְׁתָּא אַדְּהָווּ לִי זוּזֵי וּפָרַעְנָא; הִלְכָּךְ רְמָא רַחֲמָנָא שְׁבוּעָה עִילָּוֵיהּ כִּי הֵיכִי דְּלוֹדֵי לֵיהּ בְּכוּלֵּיהּ.

Rabba continues: **And** in order not to exhibit insolence, he **wants to admit to** the creditor **with** regard to **all of** the debt, **and this** fact **that he denies** owing **him in part** is because he **reasons: If I admit to him with regard to all of** the debt, **he will lodge a claim against me with regard to all of it,** and right now I do not have the money to pay. **I will evade him at least** for **now until I have money, and** then **I will pay** him all of it. This rationalization enables one to falsely deny part of a claim. **Therefore, the Merciful One imposes an oath on him,** in order to ensure **that he will admit to him with regard to all of** the debt.

וְגַבֵּי מִלְוֶה הוּא דְּאִיכָּא לְמֵימַר הָכִי, אֲבָל גַּבֵּי פִּקָּדוֹן מֵעִיז וּמֵעִיז.

The Gemara completes its answer: **And it is with regard to a loan that this can be said,** as the basis for this explanation is that one will not exhibit insolence before his creditor, who did him a favor by lending him money; **but with regard to a deposit, one will certainly exhibit insolence,**[N] as the claimant did him no favor. Therefore, there is no reason to say that one who completely denies a claim concerning a deposit is deemed credible any more than one who admitted to part of it, and he is obligated to take an oath in either case.

תָּנֵי רָמִי בַּר חָמָא: אַרְבָּעָה שׁוֹמְרִין

§ **Rami bar Ḥama teaches** this *baraita*: **All four** types of **bailees**

NOTES

A person does not exhibit insolence, etc. – אֵין אָדָם מֵעִיז וכו׳: Here too, the commentaries provide different explanations. Some understand this to mean that one would not exhibit insolence before his creditor, who did him a favor by lending him money without charging interest or deriving any other financial advantage. This interpretation applies specifically to loans, but not to deposits, where no favor has been done for the bailee (Rashi; Rabbeinu Ḥananel; Rabbeinu Barukh).

Other early commentaries cited above explain it to mean that one would not be so insolent as to deny a matter outright, having the knowledge that the other party knows for a fact that he is lying, which applies to all of the claims that could be stated both with regard to loans and deposits. For example, if one denies having borrowed money or having received a deposit, or claims to have returned it, the other party knows for a fact that his statement is not true. That is not the case for those claims that are unique to deposits: If one claims that it was stolen or lost from one's possession, or broken, the owner does not know whether that is true or false (Riva; Ramah; Rashba; Rosh; Meiri).

But with regard to a deposit one will certainly exhibit insolence – אֲבָל גַּבֵּי פִּקָּדוֹן מֵעִיז וּמֵעִיז: According to the explanation of Rashi, one is obligated to take an oath even after denying all liability with regard to a deposit. According to the explanation of the Riva, one is obligated to take an oath after stating any claim with regard to a deposit, as the owner cannot know for certain whether it is a lie. Rabbeinu Tam holds that this line should be deleted from the Gemara text, in accordance with his explanation that this *halakha* applies both to a loan and to a deposit (see *Tosafot*).

Perek **IX**
Daf **107** Amud **b**

צְרִיכִין כְּפִירָה בְּמִקְצָת וְהוֹדָאָה בְּמִקְצָת, וְאֵלּוּ הֵן: שׁוֹמֵר חִנָּם וְהַשּׁוֹאֵל, נוֹשֵׂא שָׂכָר וְהַשּׁוֹכֵר.

require denial of a part[N] of the claim **and admittance of a part of** the claim in order to be obligated to take an oath when someone claims to have given them an item as a deposit, **and these are they: An unpaid bailee, and a borrower,**[N] **a paid bailee, and a renter.**

אֲמַר רָבָא: מַאי טַעֲמָא דְּרָמִי בַּר חָמָא? שׁוֹמֵר חִנָּם, בְּהֶדְיָא כְּתִיב בֵּיהּ ״כִּי הוּא זֶה״; שׁוֹמֵר שָׂכָר, יָלֵיף נְתִינָה נְתִינָה מִשּׁוֹמֵר חִנָּם;

The Gemara quotes the source for this statement. **Rava said: What is the reasoning** for the statement **of Rami bar Ḥama?** Concerning **an unpaid bailee, it is explicitly written with regard to him: "This is it,"** as explained earlier. Concerning **a paid bailee,** Rami bar Ḥama **learns** by means of a verbal analogy to the term **giving** used with regard to a paid bailee **from** the term **giving** used with regard to **an unpaid bailee,** since the verses about both a paid and an unpaid bailee begin: "If a man gives his neighbor" (Exodus 22:6, 9).

שׁוֹאֵל, ״וְכִי יִשְׁאַל״ – וי״ו מוֹסִיף עַל עִנְיָן רִאשׁוֹן; שׁוֹכֵר, אִי לְמַאן דְּאָמַר כְּשׁוֹמֵר שָׂכָר – הַיְינוּ שׁוֹמֵר שָׂכָר, אִי לְמַאן דְּאָמַר כְּשׁוֹמֵר חִנָּם – הַיְינוּ שׁוֹמֵר חִנָּם.

Rava continues: Rami bar Ḥama learns the *halakha* concerning a **borrower** from the verse: **"And if [*vekhi*] a man borrow"** (Exodus 22:13). There is a principle that the conjunction "and," represented by the letter ***vav*, adds to the previous topic.** Based on this principle, the *halakhot* of a borrower are connected to those of the subject of the previous verse, the bailee. Concerning **a renter, if** Rami bar Ḥama is stating his ruling **according to the one who says** that a renter is **like a paid bailee,** this **is** the same as **a paid bailee; if** he is stating his ruling **according to the one who says** that a renter is **like an unpaid bailee,** this **is** the same as **an unpaid bailee.**

NOTES

Denial of a part, etc. – כְּפִירָה בְּמִקְצָת וכו׳: According to this *baraita*, bailees are not obligated to take an oath if they state a full denial, nor if they state a partial admission without a denial, but only when they state claims that include both a partial denial and a partial admission. The Gemara in *Bava Metzia* (98a) explains that this can transpire when a bailee receives multiple items or animals to safeguard and denies having received one of them, admits his obligation with regard to another, and states a claim justifying why he is not returning the third, e.g., an unpaid bailee claiming it had been stolen, or a paid bailee claiming that it was damaged by accident. This *baraita* apparently contradicts Rabbi Ḥiyya bar Yosef's statement that there is no need for a partial admission to render a bailee obligated to take an oath.

And a borrower – וְהַשּׁוֹאֵל: Though most claims are not exculpatory with regard to borrowers, as they are liable even for accidental damage or loss, they are nevertheless included here, because they can claim that the animal died due to ordinary labor (*Penei Yehoshua*).

וְאָמַר רַבִּי חִיָּיא בַּר יוֹסֵף: הַטּוֹעֵן טַעֲנַת גַּנָּב בְּפִקָּדוֹן, אֵינוֹ חַיָּיב עַד שֶׁיִּשְׁלַח בּוֹ יָד; מַאי טַעְמָא? ״וְנִקְרַב בַּעַל הַבַּיִת אֶל הָאֱלֹהִים אִם לֹא שָׁלַח יָדוֹ בִּמְלֶאכֶת רֵעֵהוּ״, מִכְּלָל דְּאִי שָׁלַח בָּהּ יָד – מִיחַיַּיב; לְמֵימְרָא דְּבְשָׁלַח בָּהּ יָד עָסְקִינַן.

§ **And Rabbi Ḥiyya bar Yosef says:** With regard to an unpaid bailee **who** falsely **states the claim, with regard to a deposit,** that **a thief** stole it, and is discovered to have lied, **he is not liable** to pay double payment **unless he misappropriates it,** i.e., uses it for his own needs, before taking his oath. **What is the reason** for this? The verse states: "If the thief shall not be found, **the owner of the house shall approach the judges to determine if he misappropriated his neighbor's goods**" (Exodus 22:7), and the following verse concludes: "The one whom the judges convict shall pay double to his neighbor." **By inference,** one can learn **that if he misappropriated it, he is liable** for double payment; **that is to say that we are dealing** only **with** a case **where he misappropriates it.**

אֲמַר לְהוּ רַבִּי חִיָּיא בַּר אַבָּא, הָכִי אָמַר רַבִּי יוֹחָנָן: בְּעוֹמֶדֶת עַל אֵבוּסָהּ שָׁנוּ. אֲמַר לֵיהּ רַבִּי זֵירָא לְרַבִּי חִיָּיא בַּר אַבָּא: דַּוְקָא בְּעוֹמֶדֶת עַל אֵבוּסָהּ קָאָמַר, אֲבָל שָׁלַח בָּהּ יָד – קָנָה, וּשְׁבוּעָה לָא מְהַנְיָא בֵּיהּ כְּלוּם. אוֹ דִּלְמָא אֲפִילּוּ עוֹמֶדֶת עַל אֵבוּסָהּ קָאָמַר?

Rabbi Ḥiyya bar Abba said to his students: **This is** what **Rabbi Yoḥanan says: They taught** this *halakha* that one who falsely claims that the deposit was stolen is liable for double payment **with regard to** an animal still **standing over its** feeding **trough,** i.e., the bailee is still safeguarding it for its owner. **Rabbi Zeira said to Rabbi Ḥiyya bar Abba: Is he stating** his ruling **specifically with regard to** an animal **standing over its** feeding **trough, but if the** bailee **misappropriated it** before taking an oath, he has **acquired it, and an oath is not effective for him**[N] **at all,** not even to cause him to be liable to pay double payment? **Or perhaps he is stating** his ruling **even with regard to** an animal **standing over its** feeding **trough,** in addition to an animal that the bailee misappropriated?

אֲמַר לֵיהּ: זוֹ לֹא שָׁמַעְתִּי, כַּיּוֹצֵא בָּהּ שָׁמַעְתִּי, דְּאָמַר רַבִּי אַסִּי אָמַר רַבִּי יוֹחָנָן: הַטּוֹעֵן טַעֲנַת אָבַד וְנִשְׁבַּע, וְחָזַר וְטָעַן טַעֲנַת גַּנָּב וְנִשְׁבַּע, וּבָאוּ עֵדִים – פָּטוּר; מַאי טַעְמָא, לָאו מִשּׁוּם דְּקָנָה בִּשְׁבוּעָה רִאשׁוֹנָה?

Rabbi Ḥiyya bar Abba **said to him: I did not hear this** ruling, so I cannot transmit Rabbi Yoḥanan's opinion, but **I did hear** something **similar to it, as Rabbi Asi says** that **Rabbi Yoḥanan says:** With regard to an unpaid bailee **who** falsely **states the claim** that the deposit **was lost and takes an oath** to that effect, **and retracted and** falsely **states the claim** that **a thief** stole the deposit **and takes an oath** to that effect, **and witnesses came** and testified that he lied, he is **exempt** from double payment for the second claim. **What is the reason; is it not due to** the fact **that** he already **acquired** the item **with the first oath,**[N] and therefore the second oath is disregarded, which is why he is not liable for double payment for a false claim of theft? So too, one who misappropriates the deposit thereby acquires it and is no longer obligated to take an oath.

אֲמַר לֵיהּ: לָא, הוֹאִיל וְיָצָא יְדֵי בְעָלִים בִּשְׁבוּעָה רִאשׁוֹנָה.

Rabbi Zeira **said to him: No,** there is no proof from there, because one could argue that the reason is not because he acquired the item with the first oath; rather, **since it left the owner's possession**[N] **with** the bailee taking the **first oath,** he is exempt from taking an additional oath with regard to the same claim, but his oath will be significant even after having misappropriated the item.

אִיתְּמַר נַמִּי, אָמַר רַבִּי אָבִין אָמַר רַבִּי אֶילְעָא אָמַר רַבִּי יוֹחָנָן: הַטּוֹעֵן טַעֲנַת אֲבֵידָה בְּפִקָּדוֹן וְנִשְׁבַּע, וְחָזַר וְטָעַן טַעֲנַת גְּנֵיבָה וְנִשְׁבַּע, וּבָאוּ עֵדִים – פָּטוּר, הוֹאִיל וְיָצָא יְדֵי בְעָלִים בִּשְׁבוּעָה רִאשׁוֹנָה.

It was also stated: Rabbi Avin says that **Rabbi Ile'a says** that **Rabbi Yoḥanan says:** With regard to **one who** falsely **states the claim, with regard to a deposit, that** it is now **lost,**[H] **and takes an oath** to that effect, **and retracts and** falsely **states the claim that** the deposit was taken through **theft and takes an oath** to that effect, **and witnesses come** and testify that he lied with regard to the claim of theft, he is **exempt** from double payment for the second claim, **since it left the owner's possession with** the bailee taking the **first oath.**

NOTES

And an oath is not effective for him – **וּשְׁבוּעָה לָא מְהַנְיָא בֵּיהּ:** Rashi explains that by misappropriating the animal the bailee is considered like a robber, and from that point onward he is liable for any damage that may befall it, even by accident. Therefore, there is no longer any efficacy to the bailee's claim that it was stolen, because it now belongs to him and any claim or denial is a statement about his own property. Rabbi Akiva Eiger explains (responsum 192) that the point of the Gemara is that one who falsely claims that the item was stolen and takes an oath to that effect is liable only when that oath would exempt him from payment, but in a case where he had misappropriated the animal, he is liable in any event, and therefore this claim is not included in the category of one who claims an item was stolen.

Due to the fact that he already acquired the item with the first oath – **מִשּׁוּם דְּקָנָה בִּשְׁבוּעָה רִאשׁוֹנָה:** As Rav Sheshet stated earlier (105b), once a bailee falsely denies responsibility for a deposit, he is considered to be a robber. Similarly, in denying responsibility for the deposit by claiming that it was lost, and all the more so in taking a false oath to that effect, the bailee is seen as a robber vis-à-vis the deposit, and he cannot be subsequently held liable for its theft or a false claim about its theft. The *halakha* would be the same in the case of a bailee who misappropriates the deposit, thereby acquiring it just as the robber does.

Since it left the owner's possession – **הוֹאִיל וְיָצָא יְדֵי בְעָלִים:** Rashi understands that by taking the first oath, the bailee has released himself from any obligation to the owner, and the court cannot require him to take another oath. Therefore, his subsequent claim that the deposit was stolen has no effect, neither strengthening nor weakening his case, and the second oath is not considered a court-mandated oath but a personal guarantee to the owner. *Tosafot* add that even if the bailee were to admit to having lied and were to be summoned to a different court, he still would not be required to take another oath, and if the second court were to administer an oath to him, that oath would not render him liable.

HALAKHA

One who falsely states the claim with regard to a deposit that it is now lost, etc. – **הַטּוֹעֵן טַעֲנַת אֲבֵידָה בְּפִקָּדוֹן וכו׳:** If a bailee claims that a deposit was lost and takes an oath to that effect, and subsequently he claims that it was stolen and takes an oath to that effect, and then witnesses contradict his claim, he is exempt from paying double payment usually incumbent on thieves, as the deposit is considered to have departed the owner's possession upon the bailee taking the first oath (Rambam *Sefer Nezikin*, *Hilkhot Geneiva* 4:3; *Tur*, *Ḥoshen Mishpat* 352).

אָמַר רַב שֵׁשֶׁת: הַטּוֹעֵן טַעֲנַת גַּנָּב בְּפִקָּדוֹן, כֵּיוָן שֶׁשָּׁלַח בּוֹ יָד – פָּטוּר; מַאי טַעְמָא? הָכִי קָאָמַר רַחֲמָנָא: ״וְנִקְרַב בַּעַל הַבַּיִת אֶל הָאֱלֹהִים אִם לֹא שָׁלַח יָדוֹ״ וגו׳, הָא שָׁלַח יָדוֹ – פָּטוּר.

The Gemara cites an *amora* who disputes the ruling of Rabbi Ḥiyya bar Yosef. **Rav Sheshet says:** With regard to an unpaid bailee **who** falsely **states the claim, with regard to a deposit,** that **a thief** stole it, and is discovered to have lied, **once he misappropriated it**[H] before he took an oath he is **exempt. What is the reason** for this? **This is what the Merciful One is saying,** i.e., this is how the verse is to be understood: "If the thief shall not be found, **the owner of the house shall approach the judges if he has not misappropriated** his neighbor's goods" (Exodus 22:7), indicating that this verse speaks specifically with regard to a case where he did not misappropriate the deposit; **consequently,** if **he misappropriated it,** he is **exempt** from double payment.

אֲמַר לֵיהּ רַב נַחְמָן: וַהֲלֹא שָׁלֹשׁ שְׁבוּעוֹת מַשְׁבִּיעִין אוֹתוֹ: ״שְׁבוּעָה שֶׁלֹּא פָּשַׁעְתִּי בָּהּ״, ״שְׁבוּעָה שֶׁלֹּא שָׁלַחְתִּי בָּהּ יָד״, ״שְׁבוּעָה שֶׁאֵינָהּ בִּרְשׁוּתִי״; מַאי לָאו ״שְׁבוּעָה שֶׁלֹּא שָׁלַחְתִּי בָּהּ יָד״ דּוּמְיָא דִ״שְׁבוּעָה שֶׁאֵינָהּ בִּרְשׁוּתִי״, מָה ״שְׁבוּעָה שֶׁאֵינָהּ בִּרְשׁוּתִי״, כִּי מִיגַּלְיָא מִילְּתָא דְּאִיתֵיהּ בִּרְשׁוּתֵיהּ – חַיָּיב, אַף ״שְׁבוּעָה שֶׁלֹּא שָׁלַחְתִּי בָּהּ יָד״, כִּי מִיגַּלְיָא מִילְּתָא דְּשָׁלַח בָּהּ יָד – חַיָּיב?

Rav Naḥman said to Rav Sheshet: **But aren't three oaths administered**[H] by the court **to** any unpaid bailee who claims that the deposit was stolen from him? The first is: **An oath that I was not negligent in** safeguarding **it,**[N] thereby enabling it to be stolen; the second is: **An oath that I did not misappropriate it;** the third is: **An oath that it is not in my possession.**[N] **What, is it not** so that: **An oath that I did not misappropriate it,** is **similar to: An oath that it is not in my possession,** in the following manner: **Just as** with regard to: **An oath that it is not in my possession, when the matter becomes revealed that it is in his possession,** he is **liable, so too,** with regard to: **An oath that I did not misappropriate it, when the matter becomes revealed that he did misappropriate it,** he should be **liable?**

אֲמַר לֵיהּ: לָא, ״שְׁבוּעָה שֶׁלֹּא שָׁלַחְתִּי בָּהּ יָד״ דּוּמְיָא דְ״שֶׁלֹּא פָּשַׁעְתִּי בָּהּ״; מָה ״שְׁבוּעָה שֶׁלֹּא פָּשַׁעְתִּי בָּהּ״, כִּי מִיגַּלְיָא מִילְּתָא דְּפָשַׁע בָּהּ – פָּטוּר מִכֶּפֶל, אַף ״שְׁבוּעָה שֶׁלֹּא שָׁלַחְתִּי בָּהּ יָד״, כִּי מִיגַּלְיָא מִילְּתָא דְּשָׁלַח בָּהּ יָד – פָּטוּר מִכֶּפֶל.

Rav Sheshet **said to him: No,** there is no proof from there, because one could say that the *halakha* of: **An oath that I did not misappropriate it,** is **similar to** the *halakha* of: An oath **that I was not negligent in** safeguarding **it,** in the following manner: **Just as** with regard to: **An oath that I was not negligent in** safeguarding **it, when the matter becomes revealed that he was negligent in** safeguarding **it,** he is **exempt from double payment, so too,** with regard to: **An oath that I did not misappropriate it, when the matter becomes revealed that he did misappropriate it,** he is **exempt from double payment.** Since the comparison can be made between different pairings of the oaths to suggest opposite conclusions, none of these comparisons are definitive.

בָּעֵי רָמִי בַּר חָמָא: מָמוֹן הַמְחַיְּיבוֹ כֶּפֶל פּוֹטְרוֹ מִן הַחוֹמֶשׁ, אוֹ דִּלְמָא שְׁבוּעָה הַמְחַיַּיבְתּוֹ כֶּפֶל פּוֹטַרְתּוֹ מִן הַחוֹמֶשׁ?

§ **The** *baraita* quoted earlier (65b) teaches that a bailee who would be liable for double payment if witnesses were to testify that he had in fact stolen a deposit about which he had taken an oath attesting to its theft does not pay the additional one-fifth payment normally imposed upon one who takes a false oath with regard to a monetary claim. The Gemara explores the reason for this *halakha*. **Rami bar Ḥama raises a dilemma:** Is it the **monetary** obligation **that renders him liable** for **double payment** which **exempts him from the** additional **one-fifth** payment, **or perhaps** is it the taking of the **oath that renders him liable for double payment** which **exempts him from the** additional **one-fifth** payment?

הֵיכִי דָּמֵי – כְּגוֹן שֶׁטָּעַן טַעֲנַת גַּנָּב וְנִשְׁבַּע, וְחָזַר וְטָעַן טַעֲנַת אָבַד וְנִשְׁבַּע,

The Gemara explains: **What are the circumstances** in which there is a practical difference between these possibilities? It is in a case **where he** falsely **states the claim** that **a thief** stole the deposit **and takes an oath** to that effect, **and retracts and** falsely **states the claim** that it was lost **and takes an oath** to that effect,

HALAKHA

One who falsely states the claim with regard to a deposit that a thief stole it, once he misappropriated it – הַטּוֹעֵן טַעֲנַת גַּנָּב בְּפִקָּדוֹן כֵּיוָן שֶׁשָּׁלַח בּוֹ יָד: If a bailee claims that the deposit was stolen, but takes an oath to that effect only after misappropriating it, and after he takes the oath it is contradicted by witness testimony, he is not required to pay double payment, in accordance with Rav Sheshet's ruling (*Maggid Mishne*). The Ra'avad and the Rosh rule that he is required to pay double payment, following Rabbi Zeira's inference from Rabbi Yoḥanan's opinion, and noting that this is also Rav Naḥman's opinion, as he challenges Rav Sheshet (Rambam *Sefer Nezikin, Hilkhot Geneiva* 4:2; *Tur, Ḥoshen Mishpat* 352).

Three oaths administered – שָׁלֹשׁ שְׁבוּעוֹת מַשְׁבִּיעִין: The oath of a bailee includes three elements: That the bailee safeguarded the item in the standard manner; that the circumstance that he claimed to have occurred did actually transpire, whether theft, loss, or death, such that the item is not presently in the bailee's possession; and that the bailee did not misappropriate the item prior to its loss (Rambam *Sefer Mishpatim, Hilkhot She'ela UFikadon* 6:1; *Shulḥan Arukh, Ḥoshen Mishpat* 295:2 and *Sma* and *Taz* there).

NOTES

That I was not negligent in safeguarding it – שֶׁלֹּא פָּשַׁעְתִּי בָּהּ: This oath is required since even unpaid bailees are liable for theft or loss if they were so negligent in safeguarding the deposit that the loss or theft could have reasonably resulted from their negligence.

That it is not in my possession – שֶׁאֵינָהּ בִּרְשׁוּתִי: This vow is required because it is plausible that a deposit could be truly lost or stolen and then found by the bailee, and he might have the opportunity to say, deceptively, but technically truthfully, that it was lost or stolen, and keep it for himself. Therefore, the oath must not only state that it was lost or stolen, but that it is still not in the bailee's possession.

וּבָאוּ עֵדִים אַקַּמַּיְיתָא וְהוֹדָה אַבַּתְרַיְיתָא, מַאי?

and witnesses come and testify **with regard to** his **first** claim that at the time he took an oath that the deposit had been stolen, it was actually in his possession; **and he admits with regard to** his **second** claim that it had been a lie and that it had not actually been lost, **what is the** ***halakha***: Is he obligated to pay the additional one-fifth payment?

מָמוֹן הַמְחַיַּיבְתּוֹ כֶּפֶל פּוֹטְרוֹ מִן הַחוֹמֶשׁ, וְהָא אִיחַיַּיב לֵיהּ עִילָּוֵיהּ כְּפֵילָא, אוֹ דִּלְמָא: שְׁבוּעָה הַמְחַיַּיבְתּוֹ כֶּפֶל פּוֹטַרְתּוֹ מִן הַחוֹמֶשׁ, וְהָא שְׁבוּעָה בַּתְרַיְיתָא הוֹאִיל דְּלָא קָא מְחַיְּיבָא לֵיהּ כְּפֵילָא – תְּחַיְּיבֵיהּ חוּמְשָׁא?

The Gemara explains the two possibilities: Is it being obligated in a **monetary** obligation **that renders him liable for double payment**[H] which **exempts him from the** additional **one-fifth** payment, **and** in this case **he is liable for the double payment for** the deposit due to the witness testimony and would therefore be exempt from the additional one-fifth payment? **Or perhaps** is it admitting to a false **oath**[N] **that renders him liable** for **double payment** which **exempts him from the** additional **one-fifth** payment, **and** with regard to **this latter oath** that the item was lost, **since it does not render him liable** for **the double payment,** as he took an oath that it had been lost, not stolen, **will it render him liable** for **the** additional **one-fifth** payment?

אָמַר רָבָא, תָּא שְׁמַע: אָמַר לְאֶחָד מִן הַשּׁוּק: "הֵיכָן שׁוֹרִי שֶׁגְּנַבְתָּ"? וְהוּא אוֹמֵר: "לֹא גְּנַבְתִּי", "מַשְׁבִּיעֲךָ אֲנִי" וְאָמַר: "אָמֵן", וְהָעֵדִים מְעִידִים אוֹתוֹ שֶׁגְּנָבוֹ – מְשַׁלֵּם תַּשְׁלוּמֵי כֶּפֶל, וְאִם הוֹדָה מֵעַצְמוֹ – מְשַׁלֵּם קֶרֶן וְחוֹמֶשׁ וְאָשָׁם;

Rava said: Come and **hear** a solution to this dilemma from a mishna (*Shevuot* 49b): In a scenario where one **said to someone from the marketplace:**[N] **Where is my ox that you stole? And the** accused **says** in response: **I did not steal** it; whereupon the owner of the ox said: **I administer an oath to you, and the** accused **said: Amen,** accepting the oath; **and the witnesses testify about** the accused **that he stole it,** he must **pay double payment. And if he admitted of his own** accord that he stole it, then he must **pay the principal and** the additional **one-fifth** payment, **and** bring **a guilt-offering.**

וְהָא הָכָא עֵדִים הוּא דִּמְחַיְּיבִי לֵיהּ כְּפֵילָא, הוֹדָה מֵעַצְמוֹ – אִין, אֲבָל הוֹדָה אַחַר עֵדִים – לָא;

Rava explains the proof: **But here,** it is **witnesses who render him liable** for **the double payment,** as since the accused was not a bailee, the oath does not render him liable, and yet the mishna teaches that if **he admitted of his own** accord that he stole it, then **yes,** he must pay the additional one-fifth payment, **but** if **he admitted after witnesses** testified, then **no,** he is not required to pay the additional one-fifth.

וְאִי סָלְקָא דַּעְתָּךְ שְׁבוּעָה הַמְחַיַּיבְתּוֹ כֶּפֶל פּוֹטַרְתּוֹ מִן הַחוֹמֶשׁ, אַמַּאי הוֹדָה אַחַר עֵדִים לָא? מִכְּדִי הָא שְׁבוּעָה לָא קָא מִיחַיְּיבָא לֵיהּ כְּפֵילָא, תְּחַיְּיבֵיהּ חוּמְשָׁא!

Rava continues: **And if it enters your mind** to say that it is **an oath that renders him liable** for **double payment** which **exempts him from the** additional **one-fifth** payment, **why** does he **not** pay the additional one-fifth payment if **he admitted** that it was a false oath **after witnesses** testified? **After all, this oath does not render him liable** to pay **the double payment,** as the *halakha* that one who falsely takes an oath that the item was stolen pays double payment applies only in the case of a bailee; therefore, the oath **should render him liable** to pay **the** additional **one-fifth** payment, as does any false oath taken with regard to a monetary claim.

אֶלָּא לָאו שְׁמַע מִינָּהּ: מָמוֹן הַמְחַיַּיבְתּוֹ כֶּפֶל פּוֹטַרְתּוֹ מִן הַחוֹמֶשׁ, שְׁמַע מִינָּהּ.

Rava completes the proof: **Rather,** must one **not conclude from** this mishna that it is the **monetary** obligation **that renders him liable** to pay the **double payment** which **exempts him from the** additional **one-fifth** payment? The Gemara affirms: **Conclude from** the mishna that the additional one-fifth payment is dependent upon the type of monetary obligation, and not an oath, resolving Rami bar Ḥama's dilemma.

בָּעֵי רָבִינָא: חוֹמֶשׁ וּכְפֵילָא בִּתְרֵי גַּבְרֵי, מַאי? הֵיכִי דָּמֵי – כְּגוֹן שֶׁמָּסַר שׁוֹרוֹ לִשְׁנֵי בְּנֵי אָדָם וְטָעֲנוּ בּוֹ טַעֲנַת גַּנָּב, חַד נִשְׁבַּע וְהוֹדָה, וְחַד נִשְׁבַּע וּבָאוּ עֵדִים, מַאי?

§ Concerning the additional one-fifth payment, **Ravina raises a dilemma:** If the additional **one-fifth** payment **and the double payment** are split **among two men, what is the** ***halakha***? The Gemara explains the dilemma: **What are the circumstances?** This is referring to a case **where** one **transferred his ox to two people**[H] to safeguard, **and they stated the claim** that **a thief** stole **it** from them; **one of them took an oath** that it had been stolen **and** subsequently **admitted** of his own accord that he had lied, **and one of them took an oath** that it had been stolen **and** subsequently **witnesses came** and testified that he had lied. **What is the** ***halakha*** in this case?

HALAKHA

A monetary obligation that renders him liable for double payment, etc. – **מָמוֹן הַמְחַיַּיבְתּוֹ כֶּפֶל וכו׳**: If a bailee claims that a deposit was stolen and takes an oath to that effect, and then retracts and claims that it was lost and takes an oath to that effect, and then witnesses testify that it was not stolen and the bailee admits that it was not lost, he is not required to pay the additional one-fifth payment for the latter false oath, since he is required to pay double payment as a result of the witness testimony. This ruling is in accordance with the conclusion of the Gemara (Rambam *Sefer Nezikin, Hilkhot Geneiva* 4:6; *Tur*, *Ḥoshen Mishpat* 352).

Transferred his ox to two people, etc. – **מָסַר שׁוֹרוֹ לִשְׁנֵי בְּנֵי אָדָם וכו׳**: If one transferred his ox to two people to act as bailees together, and they subsequently claimed that the ox had been stolen and took oaths to that effect, and then one of them admitted that their claim was false, and witnesses testified that their claim was false as well, invalidating the second bailee's claim, the two of them are required to pay only the principal, but not double payment. If the owner seizes double payment from the second bailee, the court does not intervene to return it to the bailee, as there is an uncertainty with regard to the *halakha* in this case.

The Ra'avad holds that in cases of uncertainty with regard to the imposition of a fine, such as double payment, the court does intervene to return the money to the one from whom it had been seized (*Maggid Mishne*). The *Tur* holds that the second bailee is obligated in double payment, as he had a different understanding of the unresolved dilemma of the Gemara (see *Beit Yosef*, *Baḥ*, and Gra). The bailee who admitted that his oath was false pays the additional one-fifth payment, as in any case of one who takes a false oath about deposits and admits to it of his own accord (Rambam *Sefer Nezikin, Hilkhot Geneiva* 4:7; *Shulḥan Arukh*, *Ḥoshen Mishpat* 352:1).

NOTES

Or perhaps an oath, etc. – **אוֹ דִּלְמָא שְׁבוּעָה וכו׳**: Rashi explains that had the bailee admitted that his first oath, that the deposit was stolen, had been false, after witnesses already testified to that effect, he certainly would have been exempt from the additional one-fifth payment, since the testimony had already negated his oath and rendered him liable to pay double payment. In this case, he admitted that his oath was false only concerning his second oath, that the deposit was lost. There is no double payment for this claim. Therefore, perhaps he should be required to pay the additional one-fifth payment, in addition to bringing a guilt-offering. Rashi further notes that the logic of: It left the owner's possession with the bailee taking the first oath, affects neither his obligation to pay the additional one-fifth payment nor his obligation to sacrifice a guilt-offering, as is explained in the mishna in tractate *Shevuot* (36b), cited earlier in this chapter (106a).

Someone from the marketplace – **אֶחָד מִן הַשּׁוּק**: Rashi emphasizes that this person from the marketplace was not a bailee, and his obligation to pay double payment is as a thief, not as a bailee who took a false oath stating that a thief stole the deposit. His oath was therefore not one of a bailee but one of a person who has had a monetary claim lodged against him, which, if taken falsely, renders him liable to bring a guilt-offering and pay the additional one-fifth payment.

מי אמרינן: בחד גברא קפיד רחמנא דלא משלם חומשא וכפילא, האי נשלם כפילא והאי נשלם חומשא. או דלמא: עלויה חד ממונא קפיד רחמנא דלא נשלם עלה חומשא וכפילא, והכא נמי חד ממונא הוא? תיקו.

Ravina clarifies the possibilities: **Do we say that the Merciful One is particular with regard to one man that he does not pay** both **the** additional **one-fifth** payment **and the double payment,** whereas in this case, **this one** about whom the witnesses testified **will pay the double payment and that one** who admitted of his own accord **will pay the** additional **one-fifth** payment? **Or perhaps the Merciful One is particular that the** additional **one-fifth** payment **and the double payment will not be paid for one monetary** obligation, **and here too, it is one monetary** obligation? The Gemara comments: The dilemma **shall stand** unresolved.

בעי רב פפא: תרי חומשי או תרי כפילי בחד גברא, מאי? היכי דמי – שטען טענת אבד ונשבע והודה, וחזר וטען טענת אבד ונשבע והודה; אי נמי, כגון שטען טענת גנב ונשבע ובאו עדים, וחזר וטען טענת גנב ונשבע ובאו עדים, מאי?

§ Concerning the additional one-fifth payment, **Rav Pappa raises a dilemma:** In a case of **two** additional **one-fifth** payments **or two double payments with regard to one man, what** is the *halakha*; must he pay twice for the same monetary obligation? The Gemara explains: **What are the circumstances?** This is referring to a case **where** one **stated the claim** that the deposit **was lost and took an oath and** then **admitted**[N] that it was not lost, **and returned and** again **stated the claim** that the same deposit **was lost, and took** another **oath** supporting this claim **and** again **admitted** that it was not lost. **Alternatively,** this is referring to a case **where** one **stated the claim** that a **thief** stole the deposit **and took an oath and** then **witnesses came** and testified that he had taken it, **and he returned** and again **stated the claim** that a **thief** stole the same deposit **and** again **took an oath and** then **witnesses came** and again testified that he had taken it; **what** is the *halakha*?

מי אמרינן: תרי גווני ממונא קאמר רחמנא דלא נשתלמו עילוי חד ממונא, והכא חד גוונא הוא. או דלמא: תרי ממונא אמר רחמנא דלא לשתלמו עילוי חד ממונא, והכא נמי תרי ממונא נינהו?

Rav Pappa clarifies the possibilities: **Do we say that the Merciful One states** concerning **two types of monetary restitution,** e.g., double payment and the additional one-fifth payment, **that they will not be paid for one monetary** obligation, **but here, it is** only **one type,** merely doubled; **or perhaps the Merciful One states** concerning **two** payments **of monetary restitution that they will not be paid for one monetary** obligation, **and here too, they are two** payments **of monetary restitution,**[H] whether in the case of two additional one-fifth payments or two double payments?

תא שמע, דאמר רבא: "וחמשתיו יסף עליו" – התורה ריבתה חמישיות הרבה לקרן אחת, שמע מינה.

The Gemara suggests resolution to Rav Pappa's dilemma. **Come and hear, as Rava says.** The verse states: "Or anything about which he has sworn falsely, he shall restore it in full, **and shall add the fifth part [*ḥamishitav*] more thereto"** (Leviticus 5:24). By employing a plural term, *ḥamishitav*, and not the singular *ḥamishito*, **the Torah added many** additional **one-fifths for one principal,**[N] meaning that one can become obligated in multiple one-fifth payments for the same principal. The Gemara affirms: **Conclude from** Rava's statement that this is the *halakha*.

תבעוהו בעלים לשומר ונשבע ושילם, והוכר הגנב, כפל למי? אביי אמר: לבעל הפקדון, רבא אמר: למי שהפקדון אצלו.

§ The Gemara discusses an amoraic dispute concerning a similar case: If **an owner demanded of** an unpaid **bailee** that he return a deposit, and he claimed that it had been stolen from him **and took an oath** to that effect, **and** despite being exempt from payment, **he paid** of his own volition, **and** subsequently **the thief was identified,**[H] **to whom** is **double payment** paid, the owner or the bailee? **Abaye says: To the owner of the deposit. Rava says: To the one in whose** possession **the deposit** was when it was stolen, i.e., the bailee.

NOTES

And admitted – והודה: *Tosafot* posit that he did not in fact admit that he had lied until he had already taken the second oath, and the text of the Gemara should be emended to reflect this. The reasoning of *Tosafot* is that as soon as he admits that it had not been lost, he is obligated, due to his false oath, to pay the owner regardless of what would occur to the deposit, and his second claim that it had been lost would not exempt him. The *Torat Ḥayyim* suggests that the text of the Gemara can be maintained, and it can be referring to claims lodged in two different courts. Since each court hearing stands on its own, his second claim that it was lost would have exempted him in the second court.

Tosafot question what the dilemma of Rav Pappa is, as the mishna in *Shevuot* (36b) explicitly teaches that one who takes a false oath multiple times in response to one claim is liable for each one. *Tosefot HaRosh* answers that the mishna is referring to a case where the bailee admitted to his deceit only at the end, after having taken five false oaths. Since at the point when his liability was established, his obligation had been to pay the principal, this meets the qualification (see 65b) that when monetary restitution is paid exactly according to the principal, the additional one-fifth payment can be added. By contrast, Rav Pappa is asking with regard to a case where he became liable to pay the principal and an additional one-fifth payment after the first oath, by admitting the oath was false. Therefore, when he takes his second oath, his obligation is to pay more than the principal. *Torat Ḥayyim* suggests that the mishna could be understood as referring to liability to bring multiple guilt-offerings, not multiple one-fifth payments.

The Torah added many one-fifths for one principal, etc. – התורה ריבתה חמישיות הרבה לקרן אחת וכו׳: Rashi, the Ramah, and the Rambam understand this to answer both parts of Rav Pappa's dilemma, affirming that one may be required to pay the additional one-fifth payment twice and one may also be required to pay the double payment twice. Rabbeinu Ḥananel and the Ra'avad disagree, holding that Rava answers the dilemma concerning the additional one-fifth payment, but leaves the dilemma concerning double payment unresolved.

HALAKHA

Two payments of monetary restitution, etc. – תרי ממונא וכו׳: If one took a false oath stating the claim that a deposit was lost, then admits that it is still in his possession, and then takes another false oath stating the claim that it was lost, and once again admits that it is still in his possession, he must pay an additional one-fifth payment for each false oath. Similarly, if a bailee took a false oath stating the claim that a thief stole a deposit, and then witnesses testified that it was still in his possession, and the bailee then claimed in a different court (*Maggid Mishne*) that a thief stole it, and witnesses again testified that the deposit is in his possession, the bailee is liable to pay a separate double payment for each false claim, no matter how many times this occurs, in accordance with the ruling of Rava (Rambam *Sefer Nezikin*, *Hilkhot Gezeila VaAveda* 7:13; *Tur*, *Ḥoshen Mishpat* 352).

He paid and the thief was identified, etc. – שילם והוכר הגנב וכו׳: If an owner requests that his unpaid bailee return a deposit and the bailee takes an oath that it had been stolen but pays despite not being obligated to do so, and then the thief is apprehended, the thief pays double payment to the bailee, since the latter paid the owner of his own volition, in accordance with the ruling of Rava (Rambam *Sefer Mishpatim*, *Hilkhot She'ela UFikadon* 8:4).

אַבַּיֵי אָמַר לְבַעַל הַפִּקָּדוֹן, כֵּיוָן דְּאַטְרְחֵיהּ בִּשְׁבוּעָה לָא מַקְנֵי לֵיהּ כְּפֵילָא; רָבָא אָמַר לְמִי שֶׁהַפִּקָּדוֹן אֶצְלוֹ, כֵּיוָן דְּשִׁילֵּם מַקְנֵי לֵיהּ כְּפֵילָא.

The Gemara explains their opinions: **Abaye says** that the double payment is paid **to the owner of the deposit; since** the bailee **troubled him by** taking **an oath** instead of paying immediately, the owner is **not** willing to **grant acquisition of the double payment to** the bailee,[N] so it is paid to the owner. **Rava says** that the double payment is paid **to the one in whose** possession **the deposit** was when it was stolen; **once he paid,** the owner **grants acquisition of the double payment to** the bailee.

וְקָא מִיפַּלְגִי בְּדִיּוּקָא דְּמַתְנִיתִין, דִּתְנַן: הַמַּפְקִיד אֵצֶל חֲבֵירוֹ בְּהֵמָה אוֹ כֵּלִים וְנִגְנְבוּ אוֹ שֶׁאָבְדוּ, שִׁילֵּם וְלֹא רָצָה לִישָּׁבַע, שֶׁהֲרֵי אָמְרוּ שׁוֹמֵר חִנָּם נִשְׁבָּע וְיוֹצֵא, נִמְצָא הַגַּנָּב – מְשַׁלֵּם תַּשְׁלוּמֵי כֶּפֶל, טָבַח וּמָכַר – מְשַׁלֵּם תַּשְׁלוּמֵי אַרְבָּעָה וַחֲמִשָּׁה, לְמִי הוּא מְשַׁלֵּם? לְמִי שֶׁהַפִּקָּדוֹן אֶצְלוֹ;

The Gemara explains: **And they disagree with regard to the** deductive **inference** to be drawn from the wording **of the mishna, as we learned** in a mishna (*Bava Metzia* 33b): In the case of **one who deposits with another,** i.e., an unpaid bailee, **an animal**[H] **or vessels, and they were stolen or lost,** and the bailee **paid** the owner **and did not wish to take an oath,** which he may decide to do, as the Sages **said** that **an unpaid bailee takes an oath** that he is exempt **and is released** from the obligation to pay the owner, but may also opt to pay; in such a case the *halakha* is that if **the thief was found he pays double payment,** or if the deposited item was a sheep or an ox and the thief **slaughtered or sold** it **he pays** the **fourfold or fivefold payment. To whom does** the thief **pay** those payments? He pays them **to the one in whose** possession **the deposit** was when it was stolen or lost. When the bailee paid the owner for the stolen item, he acquired it and therefore is entitled to any payment of principal or fine paid by the thief.

נִשְׁבַּע וְלֹא רָצָה לְשַׁלֵּם, וְנִמְצָא הַגַּנָּב – מְשַׁלֵּם תַּשְׁלוּמֵי כֶּפֶל, טָבַח וּמָכַר – מְשַׁלֵּם תַּשְׁלוּמֵי אַרְבָּעָה וַחֲמִשָּׁה, לְמִי הוּא מְשַׁלֵּם? לְבַעַל הַפִּקָּדוֹן.

The mishna continues: If the bailee **took an oath and did not wish to pay,** and **the thief was** later **found** and was required to **pay double payment,** or he **slaughtered or sold** the sheep or ox and was required to **pay** the **fourfold or fivefold payment, to whom does** the thief **pay** the money? He pays it **to the owner of the deposit,** not to the bailee.

אַבַּיֵי דָּיֵיק מֵרֵישָׁא, רָבָא דָּיֵיק מִסֵּיפָא. אַבַּיֵי דָּיֵיק מֵרֵישָׁא, דְּקָתָנֵי: שִׁילֵּם וְלֹא רָצָה לִישָּׁבַע; טַעְמָא דְּלֹא רָצָה לִישָּׁבַע,

The Gemara explains the dispute: **Abaye inferred** the *halakha* **from** the wording **of the first clause,** and **Rava inferred** the *halakha* **from** the wording **of the latter clause. Abaye inferred** it **from** the wording **of the first clause, as it teaches:** If the bailee **paid** the owner **and did not wish to take an oath,** the thief pays the double, fourfold, or fivefold payment to the bailee. Abaye infers from here that **the reason** the thief pays the bailee is specifically **that** he **did not wish to take an oath,**

Perek **IX**
Daf **108** Amud **b**

הָא נִשְׁבַּע – אַף עַל פִּי שֶׁשִּׁילֵּם, לְמִי מְשַׁלֵּם? לְבַעַל הַפִּקָּדוֹן.

but if he **took an oath, even though** he subsequently **paid,** to **whom does** the thief **pay** double payment? **To the owner of the deposit.**

רָבָא דָּיֵיק מִסֵּיפָא: נִשְׁבַּע וְלֹא רָצָה לְשַׁלֵּם; טַעְמָא דְּלֹא רָצָה לְשַׁלֵּם, הָא שִׁילֵּם – אַף עַל פִּי שֶׁנִּשְׁבַּע, לְמִי מְשַׁלֵּם? לְמִי שֶׁהַפִּקָּדוֹן אֶצְלוֹ.

Rava inferred the *halakha* **from** the wording **of the latter clause.** It teaches: If the bailee **took an oath and did not want to pay,** the thief must pay the penalty to the owner of the deposit. Rava infers from here that **the reason** the thief pays the owner is specifically **that** he **did not want to pay, but** if he **did pay, even though** he **took an oath** previously, **to whom does** the thief **pay** double payment? **To the one in whose** possession **the deposit** was when it was lost.

NOTES

Not willing to grant acquisition of the double payment to the bailee – לָא מַקְנֵי לֵיהּ כְּפֵילָא: The Rid explains that the bailee's payment to the owner does not in and of itself transfer ownership of the stolen item to the bailee, since if the item is found in the thief's possession, it is returned to the owner and the owner returns the bailee's payment. What the Gemara is saying here is that in appreciation for the bailee's decision not to inconvenience the owner and instead to pay for the loss despite not being obligated to do so, the owner is willing to grant acquisition of the potential double payment to the bailee. Therefore, in a case where the bailee inconvenienced the owner to come to court for the imposition of the oath, the owner might not be willing to grant acquisition of the potential double payment.

HALAKHA

One who deposits with another an animal, etc. – הַמַּפְקִיד אֵצֶל חֲבֵירוֹ בְּהֵמָה וכו׳: If one deposits an animal or vessels with an unpaid bailee and they were stolen or lost, and the bailee opted to pay rather than take an oath that they were stolen or lost, and then the thief is apprehended, the thief pays the double, fourfold, or fivefold payment to the bailee. If the bailee took an oath to exempt himself from payment rather than pay, and then the thief is apprehended, the thief pays the double, fourfold, or fivefold payment to the owner of the deposit. In any event, the bailee must take an oath that the deposit is not in his possession (Rambam *Sefer Mishpatim*, *Hilkhot She'ela UFikadon* 8:1; *Tur*, *Ḥoshen Mishpat* 295).

לְאַבַּיֵי קַשְׁיָא סֵיפָא! אָמַר לָךְ אַבַּיֵי, הָכִי קָתָנֵי: נִשְׁבַּע, וְלֹא רָצָה לְשַׁלֵּם קוֹדֶם הַשְּׁבוּעָה אֶלָּא לְאַחַר הַשְּׁבוּעָה, לְמִי מְשַׁלֵּם? לְבַעַל הַפִּקָּדוֹן. לְרָבָא קַשְׁיָא רֵישָׁא! אָמַר לָךְ רָבָא, הָכִי קָתָנֵי: שִׁילֵּם, וְלֹא רָצָה לַעֲמוֹד בִּשְׁבוּעָתוֹ אֶלָּא שִׁילֵּם, לְמִי מְשַׁלֵּם? לְמִי שֶׁהַפִּקָּדוֹן אֶצְלוֹ.

The Gemara notes: The inference from **the latter clause is difficult** for the opinion of **Abaye.** The Gemara explains. **Abaye** could have **said to you: This is what** the latter clause of the mishna **is teaching:** If the bailee **took an oath and did not want to pay** initially **before** taking **the oath,** but **rather** wanted to pay only **after** having taken **the oath,** in this case **to whom does** the thief **pay** double payment? **To the owner of the deposit.** Similarly, the Gemara notes: The inference from **the first clause is difficult** for the opinion of **Rava.** The Gemara explains. **Rava** could have **said to you: This is what** the first clause of the mishna **is teaching:** If he **paid,** meaning he had taken an oath **and did not want to stand by his oath, but** instead **paid** in order to nullify the oath he had taken, **to whom does** the thief **pay** double payment? **To the one in whose** possession **the deposit** was when it was lost.

תְּבָעוּהוּ בְּעָלִים לְשׁוֹמֵר וְנִשְׁבַּע, וְהוּכַּר הַגַּנָּב, תְּבָעוֹ שׁוֹמֵר וְהוֹדָה, תְּבָעוּהוּ בְּעָלִים וְכָפַר, וְהֵבִיאוּ עֵדִים, מִי נִפְטָר הַגַּנָּב בְּהוֹדָאַת שׁוֹמֵר אוֹ לֹא נִפְטָר הַגַּנָּב בְּהוֹדָאַת שׁוֹמֵר?

§ The Gemara relates another dilemma concerning the status of a bailee and stolen deposits. If the **owner** of a deposit **demanded from a bailee** that he return their deposit, and he claimed that it had been stolen from him **and took an oath**[H] to that effect; **and** then **the thief was recognized,** and **the bailee demanded of** the thief to pay **and he admitted** to having stolen it; and then the **owner demanded of** the thief to pay **and he denied** the claim, **and** the owner **brought witnesses** that he had stolen it, **did the thief become exempt**[N] from double payment **through** his **admission** to the **bailee,** as is the *halakha* when one admits liability to a penalty? Does the bailee have standing vis-à-vis the thief despite having exempted himself by taking an oath to the owner, **or did the thief not become exempt through** his **admission** to the **bailee?**

אָמַר רָבָא: אִם בֶּאֱמֶת נִשְׁבַּע – נִפְטָר הַגַּנָּב בְּהוֹדָאַת שׁוֹמֵר, אִם בְּשֶׁקֶר נִשְׁבַּע – לֹא נִפְטָר הַגַּנָּב בְּהוֹדָאַת שׁוֹמֵר.

Rava says: If he **took an oath truthfully,**[N] i.e., if it now becomes clear through the testimony of witnesses that the bailee's oath was true, he is assumed to be someone the owner would rely on to collect the stolen item for him, and he remains a bailee. Therefore, **the thief became exempt through** his **admission** to the **bailee.** If his **oath** was **taken falsely,** e.g., he took an oath that the animal given as a deposit died naturally and it is now clear that his oath was false, he is assumed to be someone whom the owner would not rely on to collect the stolen item for them, and he is no longer a bailee. In this case, **the thief did not become exempt through** his **admission** to the **bailee.**

בָּעֵי רָבָא: עָמַד לִישָּׁבַע בְּשֶׁקֶר וְלֹא הִנִּיחוּהוּ, מַהוּ? תֵּיקוּ. רַב כָּהֲנָא מַתְנֵי הָכִי. רַב טַבְיוּמֵי מַתְנֵי, בָּעֵי רָבָא: נִשְׁבַּע לַשֶּׁקֶר, מַהוּ? תֵּיקוּ.

Rava raises a dilemma concerning the previous ruling: If a bailee **rose to take a false oath but** the owner **did not let him,**[N] **what is** the *halakha*? Should he be considered as one who had taken a false oath, as that was his intention, and he is no longer a bailee, or, since he never actually took the false oath, he is still a bailee? The Gemara comments: The question **shall stand** unresolved. The Gemara notes that **Rav Kahana** would **teach** Rava's question **like this,** as quoted above. **Rav Tavyumei** would **teach** Rava's question differently: **Rava raises a dilemma:** If he actually **took a false oath, what is** the *halakha*?[N] Is he still a bailee or not? The Gemara comments: The question **shall stand** unresolved.

HALAKHA

If the owner demanded from a bailee and he took an oath, etc. – תְּבָעוּהוּ בְּעָלִים לְשׁוֹמֵר וְנִשְׁבַּע: A deposit was stolen from a bailee and the owner demanded its return. The bailee took an oath that it had been stolen, and then the thief was recognized. The bailee demanded that the thief return the stolen item, and the thief admitted having stolen it. The owner then demanded that the thief return the stolen item, and the thief denied having stolen it; but then witnesses testified that he had stolen it. If the bailee's oath had been truthful, the thief is exempted from double payment due to his admission to the bailee. If the bailee had taken a false oath, the court does not force payment of the double, fourfold, or fivefold payment. If instead the owner seizes the item, the court does not intervene to restore it to the thief. This is the *halakha* concerning unresolved dilemmas concerning monetary matters, and in accordance with Rav Tavyumei's version of Rava's statement (Rambam *Sefer Nezikin, Hilkhot Geneiva* 4:8).

NOTES

Did the thief become exempt, etc. – מִי נִפְטָר הַגַּנָּב וכו׳: This dilemma is based on the principle that admission of liability to pay a fine exempts one from paying only if it is stated in the presence of the other litigant. An admission stated in the presence of a third party, even in court, does not exempt him (Rid). The dilemma here is whether the bailee still has standing as the litigant, such that an admission in his presence will exempt the thief. Similarly, in the following case, the dilemma is whether the owner has such standing.

If he took an oath truthfully – אִם בֶּאֱמֶת נִשְׁבַּע: If the oath that the bailee took that he did not misappropriate the deposit was taken truthfully, then the thief is exempt from the fine due to his admission to the bailee. The reason is that it is assumed that the owner would continue to allow the bailee to safeguard the property, and he still has standing. If the bailee lied it is assumed that the owner would not continue to allow him to safeguard the property, and he had no standing as litigant when the thief admitted his liability to him (Rashi).

But they did not let him – וְלֹא הִנִּיחוּהוּ: Rashi, consistent with his position throughout the passage, explains the dilemma as follows: Is it assumed that as long as the bailee has not yet taken a false oath, the owner desires that he continue to act as bailee and therefore the bailee has standing when the thief admits liability? Alternatively, does the bailee's intention to take a false oath undercut his reliability and, in turn, his standing as a bailee?

The Ra'avad, following the text and explanation of Rabbeinu Ḥananel (see also *Tosafot*), explains Rava's dilemma as follows: Do we say that by the owner's not allowing the bailee to take an oath he has effectively absolved him of all liability, and his guardianship has been terminated, or not? *Tosafot* quote the opinion of the *Halakhot Gedolot* that even if the owner were to absolve the bailee from liability for the oath, this does not mean that he forgives liability for payment as well, all the more so when he did not expressly absolve the bailee from liability for the oath but merely prevented him from taking one.

The Ramah explains the dilemma as follows: Does the bailee's willingness to take a false oath render him liable for even accidental damage, as a false oath would, which in turn means that he has standing with regard to the deposit; or is this liability engendered only by actually taking a false oath?

If he took a false oath what is the *halakha* – נִשְׁבַּע לַשֶּׁקֶר מַהוּ: Rashi explains the dilemma to be whether it should be assumed that a bailee who takes a false oath will later regret it and pay for the item, in which case the false oath did not terminate his status as a bailee. The Ra'avad explains it differently: If a bailee testifies that he was not negligent, and plausibly believed, at the time of the oath, that he had not been negligent, is he still considered trustworthy by the owner?

תְּבָעוּהוּ בְּעָלִים לַשּׁוֹמֵר וְשִׁילֵּם, וְהוּכַּר הַגַּנָּב, תְּבָעוּהוּ בְּעָלִים וְהוֹדָה, תְּבָעוֹ שׁוֹמֵר וְכָפַר, וְהֵבִיא עֵדִים, נִפְטָר גַּנָּב בְּהוֹדָאַת בְּעָלִים אוֹ לֹא?

The Gemara relates another dilemma concerning the status of a bailee and stolen deposits: If the **owners** of a deposit **demanded from a bailee** that he return their deposit **and he paid**[H] them instead of taking an oath, **and then the thief was recognized,** and **the owners demanded of** the thief to pay **and he admitted** to having stolen it; and then the **bailee demanded of** the thief to pay **and he denied** the claim, **and** the bailee **brought witnesses** that he had stolen it, did **the thief become exempt** from double payment **through** his **admission** to the **owners,** as is the *halakha* when one admits liability to a penalty, **or not?**

מִי אָמְרִינַן, מָצֵי אָמַר לֵיהּ שׁוֹמֵר לַבְּעָלִים: אַתּוּן כֵּיוָן דְּשָׁקְלִיתוּ לְכוּ דְּמֵי אִסְתַּלֵּיקְתוּ לְכוּ מֵהָכָא, אוֹ דִּלְמָא מָצֵי אָמְרִי לֵיהּ: כִּי הֵיכִי דְּאַתְּ עֲבַדְתְּ לָן מִילְּתָא אֲנַן נַמִי עֲבַדִינַן לָךְ, טְרַחִינַן בָּתַר גַּנָּבָא, שָׁקְלְנָא אֲנַן דִּידָן, וּשְׁקוֹל אַתְּ דִּידָךְ? תֵּיקוּ.

The Gemara explains: **Do we say** that the **bailee can say to the owners: Once you took your money** from me **you removed yourselves from here** and have no further connection to this deposit. Therefore, I am now considered the owner of the stolen item and the right to the double payment is mine, and the thief's admission to you is meaningless. **Or perhaps** the owners **can say to him: Just as you performed a service for us** by paying us when you were not obligated, **we performed** a service **for you as well.** Instead of granting acquisition of the double payment to you, to enable you to be repaid **we took the trouble** to search **after the thief. We will take** what is **ours,**[N] i.e., the stolen item, **and you take** what is **yours,** the money you paid us. The Gemara comments: The question **shall stand** unresolved.

אִתְּמַר: נִגְנְבָה בְּאוֹנֶס וְהוּכַּר הַגַּנָּב, אָמַר אַבַּיֵי: אִם שׁוֹמֵר חִנָּם הוּא – רָצָה עוֹשֶׂה עִמּוֹ דִּין, רָצָה נִשְׁבָּע. אִם שׁוֹמֵר שָׂכָר הוּא – עוֹשֶׂה עִמּוֹ דִּין וְאֵינוֹ נִשְׁבָּע; רָבָא אָמַר: אֶחָד זֶה וְאֶחָד זֶה – עוֹשֶׂה עִמּוֹ דִּין וְאֵינוֹ נִשְׁבָּע.

§ **It was stated:** If an animal given as a deposit **was stolen in circumstances beyond the control** of the bailee, who is therefore exempt from liability regardless of whether he was paid, **and the thief was recognized,**[H] **Abaye says: If he is an unpaid bailee,** then if **he** so **desires** he can choose to **enter** into **judgment with** the thief,[N] i.e., the bailee will pay the owner and then get reimbursed by the thief; and if **he** so **desires** he can **take an oath** that he was not responsible and the owner can demand his money from the thief. **If he is a paid bailee he enters** into **judgment with** the thief[N] **and does not** have the option to **take an oath** to become exempt, as the responsibility to collect payment from the thief is part of his duty as a paid bailee. **Rava says: Whether this** unpaid bailee **or that** paid bailee **enters** into **judgment with** the thief, **he does not** have the option to **take an oath.**

לֵימָא, פְּלִיגָא אַדְּרַב הוּנָא בַּר אָבִין, דְּשָׁלַח רַב הוּנָא בַּר אָבִין: נִגְנְבָה בְּאוֹנֶס וְהוּכַּר הַגַּנָּב, אִם שׁוֹמֵר חִנָּם הוּא – רָצָה עוֹשֶׂה עִמּוֹ דִּין, רָצָה נִשְׁבָּע, וְאִם שׁוֹמֵר שָׂכָר הוּא – עוֹשֶׂה עִמּוֹ דִּין וְאֵינוֹ נִשְׁבָּע?

The Gemara suggests: **Shall we say** that Rava **disagrees with** the ruling **of Rav Huna bar Avin? As Rav Huna bar Avin sent** this ruling: If an animal given as a deposit **was stolen in circumstances beyond the control** of the bailee **and the thief was recognized, if he is an unpaid bailee,** then if **he** so **desires** he can choose to **enter** into **judgment with** the thief; and if **he** so **desires** he can **take an oath** that he was not responsible, and the owner can demand his money from the thief. **And if he is a paid bailee,** then **he enters** into **judgment with** the thief **and does not** have the option to **take an oath.**

HALAKHA

If the owners demanded from a bailee that he return their deposit and he paid – תְּבָעוּהוּ בְּעָלִים לַשּׁוֹמֵר וְשִׁילֵּם: A deposit was stolen from a bailee and the owner demanded its return. The bailee paid the owner but then the thief was recognized. The owner demanded that the thief return it and he admitted having stolen it. Then the bailee demanded of the thief that he reimburse him and the thief denied having stolen it. Then witnesses testified that the thief did steal it. In this case, the court does not force payment of the double, fourfold, or fivefold payment. If the bailee seizes the double, fourfold, or fivefold payment, the court does not intervene to restore it to the thief. This is the *halakha* concerning unresolved dilemmas with regard to monetary matters (Rambam *Sefer Nezikin, Hilkhot Geneiva* 4:8).

Was stolen in circumstances beyond the control of the bailee and the thief was recognized – נִגְנְבָה בְּאוֹנֶס וְהוּכַּר הַגַּנָּב: If a deposit was stolen in circumstances beyond the bailee's control, e.g., by armed bandits (*Tur*), and then the thief was recognized, the bailee, whether he was paid or not, does not take an oath, but enters into judgment with the thief; this is in accordance with the opinion of Rava. If the bailee first took an oath before the thief was recognized, if he was an unpaid bailee he may choose whether to remain with his oath or to enter into judgment with the thief. If he was a paid bailee, then he must enter into judgment with the thief (Rambam *Sefer Mishpatim, Hilkhot She'ela UFikadon* 8:6; *Shulḥan Arukh, Ḥoshen Mishpat* 294:6).

NOTES

We will take what is ours – שָׁקְלְנָא אֲנַן דִּידָן: That is, in this case we did not grant you the right to the double payment. Therefore, the owner has standing, and when the thief admits liability in his presence he is exempt (Ramah).

Enter into judgment with him – עוֹשֶׂה עִמּוֹ דִּין: Rashi explains that the bailee is sued by the owner and pays him. The Ra'avad writes similarly: The bailee and owner are instructed to reach a compromise; this enables the bailee to collect double payment from the thief. The Ra'avad quotes an additional explanation, found in other early commentaries, that the bailee sues the thief directly, which is an extra inconvenience.

If he is a paid bailee he enters into judgment with the thief – אִם שׁוֹמֵר שָׂכָר הוּא עוֹשֶׂה עִמּוֹ דִּין: Some commentaries explain that this refers to a regular case of theft, which is referred to as a circumstance beyond the control of the bailee in that the bailee was not negligent in safeguarding the deposit. A paid bailee is liable for this type of theft, so an oath that he was not negligent would not exempt him, and he therefore does not take an oath (*Shita Mekubbetzet*, citing *Ge'onim*; Rabbeinu Barukh). According to this explanation, the bailee enters into judgment with the owner.

Rashi understands that the theft described here is the type for which even paid bailees are exempt, e.g., by an armed bandit, and, as the Ra'avad explains, the bailee enters into judgment with the thief. The latter is obviously a difficult party to summon to court since he is presumed to be violent. Accordingly, Abaye holds that one of the responsibilities of a paid bailee is to repay the principal to the owner and to attempt to recover the item or obtain payment for its value from the bandit.

אמר לך רבא: הכא במאי עסקינן – כגון שקדם ונשבע. והא רצה עושה עמו דין, רצה נשבע קאמר! הכי קאמר: רצה שומר חנם עומד בשבועתו, רצה עושה עמו דין.

The Gemara responds: **Rava** could have **said to you: With what are we dealing here?** We are dealing with a case **where** it happened **that first** the bailee **took an oath,** before the thief was recognized. The Gemara questions this explanation: **But** Rav Huna bar Avin **says:** If **he** so **desires** he can choose to **enter** into **judgment with** the thief; and if **he** so **desires** he can **take an oath** that he was not responsible, indicating that the bailee had not yet taken an oath. The Gemara answers: Rather, **this is** what Rav Huna bar Avin **is saying:** Having first taken an oath before the thief was recognized, if **an unpaid bailee** so **desires** he can **remain with his oath** and not pay the owner, and if he so **desires** he can choose to **enter** into **judgment with** the thief.

רבה זוטי בעי לה הכי: נגנבה באונס, והחזיר גנב בבית שומר ומתה בפשיעה, מהו? מי אמרינן: כיון דנגנבה באונס כליא ליה שמירתו, או דלמא כיון דהדרה הדרה לשמירתו? תיקו.

Rabba Zuti[P] **raises the dilemma like this:** If an animal given as a deposit **was stolen in circumstances beyond the control** of the bailee, **and the thief returned**[H] the animal to the place from where he had stolen it, and it is now **in the house of the bailee, and it** then **died through** the bailee's **negligence, what is** the *halakha*? **Do we say** that **once it was stolen in circumstances beyond** the bailee's **control his guardianship is completed** and he has no more responsibility for the animal, even for subsequent negligence? **Or perhaps once it** was **returned, it returned to his guardianship,** and an unpaid bailee is liable for loss resulting from negligence? The Gemara comments: The question **shall stand** unresolved.

מתני׳ ״היכן פקדוני?״ אמר לו: ״אבד״, ״משביעך אני״ ואמר: ״אמן״, והעדים מעידים אותו שאכלו – משלם קרן, [הודה מעצמו – משלם קרן וחומש ואשם].

MISHNA If the owner asked the bailee: **Where is my deposit?** And the bailee **said to him:** It was **lost.**[H] And the owner said: **I administer an oath to you, and the** bailee **said: Amen,** therefore accepting the oath; **and the witnesses testify about** the bailee **that he consumed it,** then he must **pay** the **principal.** If the bailee **admitted on his own**[H] that he had taken a false oath, then he must **pay** the **principal and** the additional **one-fifth** payment, **and** bring **a guilt-offering.**[B]

״היכן פקדוני?״ אמר לו: ״נגנב״, ״משביעך אני״, ואמר: ״אמן״, והעדים מעידים אותו שגנבו – משלם תשלומי כפל, הודה מעצמו – משלם קרן וחומש ואשם.

If the owner asked the bailee: **Where is my deposit,** and the bailee **said to him: It was stolen;**[H] and the owner said: **I administer an oath to you, and** the bailee **said: Amen,** therefore accepting the oath; **and the witnesses testify about** the bailee **that he stole it,** he must **pay** the **payment of double** the **principal.** If the bailee **admitted on his own** that he had taken a false oath, then he must **pay the principal,** the additional **one-fifth** payment, **and** bring **a guilt-offering.**

PERSONALITIES

Rabba Zuti – רבה זוטי: A colleague of Rav Ashi, Rabba Zuti was involved in editing the Talmud as well, citing proofs for various *halakhot*. He was known by this name, meaning Rabba the Small, to distinguish him from other *amora'im* with the same first name.

HALAKHA

Was stolen in circumstances beyond the control of the bailee and the thief returned, etc. – נגנבה באונס והחזיר גנב וכו׳: If an animal given as a deposit was stolen in circumstances beyond the bailee's control, and the thief returned it to the bailee's house, where it subsequently died through the bailee's negligence, it is uncertain whether the bailee's guardianship had been terminated. Therefore, the court does not force payment by the bailee, but if the owner seizes payment from the bailee the court does not intervene to restore it to the bailee. This is the *halakha* concerning unresolved dilemmas with regard to monetary matters (Rambam *Sefer Mishpatim, Hilkhot She'ela UFikadon* 8:6).

Where is my deposit and the bailee said to him it was lost – היכן פקדוני, אמר לו אבד: If a bailee claims that a deposit was lost and takes an oath to that effect, and then witnesses testify that he stole it, he is required to pay only the principal (Rambam *Sefer Nezikin, Hilkhot Geneiva* 4:3; *Tur, Ḥoshen Mishpat* 352).

Admitted on his own – הודה מעצמו: A bailee who claims that a deposit was lost or stolen, takes an oath to that effect, and then admits on his own that he had in fact stolen it must pay the principal and the additional one-fifth payment, along with bringing a guilt-offering (Rambam *Sefer Hafla'a, Hilkhot Shevuot* 1:8–9).

Where is my deposit and the bailee said to him it was stolen – היכן פקדוני, אמר לו נגנב: If a bailee claims that a deposit was stolen, takes an oath to that effect, and then witnesses testify that it is, in fact, in his possession, he must pay double payment (Rambam *Sefer Nezikin, Hilkhot Geneiva* 4:1; *Tur, Ḥoshen Mishpat* 352).

BACKGROUND

Pay the principal and the additional one-fifth and bring a guilt-offering – משלם קרן וחומש ואשם: The reason one does not give the additional one-fifth payment and bring a guilt-offering when he did not admit his guilt is because it is written: "And they will admit their transgression" (Numbers 5:7) in the context of one who stole from a convert. It is derived from there that one gives the additional one-fifth payment and brings a guilt-offering only through his own admission, not when witnesses testified against him. This is because the additional one-fifth payment and the guilt-offering serve as atonement, and one cannot fully atone for his transgression unless he himself admits to it.

הַגּוֹזֵל אֶת אָבִיו וְנִשְׁבַּע לוֹ וּמֵת – הֲרֵי זֶה מְשַׁלֵּם קֶרֶן וְחוֹמֶשׁ וְאָשָׁם לְבָנָיו אוֹ לְאֶחָיו, וְאִם אֵינוֹ רוֹצֶה אוֹ שֶׁאֵין לוֹ – לֹוֶה וּבַעֲלֵי חוֹב בָּאִין וְנִפְרָעִים.

The mishna continues: In the case of **one who robs his father**[H] and the father demands that he return the stolen item, **and he takes an oath to** his father that he did not rob him; **and** then the father **dies;**[N] and then the son admits that he robbed him and took a false oath, necessitating the return of the principal and the giving of the additional one-fifth payment to his father's heirs, of which he is either one of several or the only one; what should he do? **This** son **pays** the **principal and** the additional **one-fifth** payment **to his** father's **sons or brothers,**[N] **and** brings **a guilt-offering** and does not keep his own share. **And if he does not want** to forfeit his share **or where he does not have** sufficient funds to pay the other heirs while forfeiting his share, he **borrows** money in the amount of the value of the stolen item **and the creditors come**[N] **and are repaid** in part from his share in the stolen item.

הָאוֹמֵר לִבְנוֹ ״קוֹנָם אִי אַתָּה נֶהֱנֶה מִשֶּׁלִּי״, אִם מֵת – יִרָשֶׁנּוּ;

In the case of **one who says to his son** in a vow: It is forbidden **like an offering** [***konam***],[HN] and for that reason **you may not derive benefit from my property, if** the father then **dies** the son **inherits** from **him,** because it is no longer the father's property once he dies.

HALAKHA

One who robs his father, etc. – הַגּוֹזֵל אֶת אָבִיו וכו׳: In the case of one who robs his father, then takes an oath that he did not do so, and then the father dies and the stolen item is no longer extant, the robber must pay his brothers, or his father's brothers (Rema, citing *Tur*), for the value of the principal and the additional one-fifth payment. If the stolen item is extant, then the robber must give it to his brothers, along with the additional one-fifth payment, and then reach a financial settlement with them so as to receive his portion of the stolen item by other means (see *Sma*). Some commentaries say that the robber is not entitled to any inheritance from the value of the stolen item.

If the robber is poor and cannot afford to give the value of even part of the stolen item, he should borrow from others, and they can collect repayment from what would have been his portion of the stolen item that he now returns to his brothers (Rema, citing *Tur*). If the robber has no sons or brothers, he should borrow from others and they can collect repayment from the stolen item, or he can donate the stolen item to charity (Rambam *Sefer Nezikin, Hilkhot Gezeila VaAveda* 8:2; *Shulḥan Arukh, Ḥoshen Mishpat* 367:5).

If one says to his son *konam*, etc. – הָאוֹמֵר לִבְנוֹ קוֹנָם וכו׳: If one says to his son as a vow: It is hereby prohibited for you to derive benefit from me, or if one takes an oath that his son shall not derive benefit from him, and then dies, the son still inherits his estate (Rambam *Sefer Hafla'a, Hilkhot Nedarim* 5:6; *Shulḥan Arukh, Yoreh De'a* 216:7, 223:2).

NOTES

And dies – וּמֵת: Rashi is of the opinion that the son admits to the theft after his father's death. The Rid states that this is not necessarily the case, and that the same *halakha* would apply even if the son admitted to the theft while his father was still alive, but did not manage to pay before his father died.

To his sons or brothers – לְבָנָיו אוֹ לְאֶחָיו: Rashi and the Meiri explain that this refers to the father's sons or, if he has no sons, to the father's brothers. In other words, the robber-son must return the stolen item to the heirs, according to who has priority in terms of inheritance. By contrast, the Rambam explains that the robber-son gives the stolen item to his own sons or brothers, as the essential point is that he must not keep possession of the stolen item. The Ra'avad adds that this is not a basic requirement of the *halakha* but is done in order to fulfill one's obligation with regard to the laws of Heaven.

Tosafot combine these two opinions, explaining, like the Rambam, that the robber gives the stolen item to his own sons or brothers, but base this on the *halakhot* of inheritance, as they would stand in place of the robber-son in inheriting from his father, who was the victim of the robbery, were the robber to die.

He borrows money and the creditors come, etc. – לֹוֶה וּבַעֲלֵי חוֹב בָּאִין וכו׳: Rashi explains that he borrows money from others for his own needs and pays the stolen item or its monetary equivalent to his brothers or uncles; the creditors can collect their debt from the stolen item. *Tosafot* explain that if the stolen item is not extant the robber borrows money using unspecified land in his inheritance as collateral. If the stolen item is extant he sets it aside as designated repayment, from which the creditors are paid.

The Meiri writes that this *halakha* demonstrates that in principle the son could have taken his portion in the inheritance by keeping the stolen item, as he inherits from his father, but in order to encourage repentance he is required to fulfill the mitzva to return the stolen item by transferring it to others, even though in practice he will ultimately share in its benefit.

One who says to his son *konam*, etc. – הָאוֹמֵר לִבְנוֹ קוֹנָם וכו׳: This *halakha* is taught here despite the fact that it is not connected to the topics of this tractate because a son who has been prohibited by a vow relates to his inheritance from his father in the same way that a son relates to an item that he stole from his father (Meiri).

בְּחַיָּיו וּבְמוֹתוֹ – אִם מֵת לֹא יִירָשֶׁנּוּ, וְיַחֲזִיר לְבָנָיו אוֹ לְאֶחָיו, וְאִם אֵין לוֹ – לֹוֶה וּבַעֲלֵי חוֹב בָּאִים וְנִפְרָעִים.

The mishna continues: If the father stated in his vow that his son may not derive benefit from his property **in his life and in his death,**[HN] then even **if** the father then **dies** the son **does not inherit from him,**[N] as the prohibition is still in effect. **And** instead of taking his inheritance, **he returns** his portion in the estate **to his sons**[H] **or to his brothers. And if he does not have**[N] sufficient funds to subsist without his inheritance, he **borrows** money in the amount of the value of his share in the inheritance **and the creditors come and are repaid**[N] from his share.

גמ׳ אָמַר רַב יוֹסֵף: אֲפִילּוּ לְאַרְנְקִי שֶׁל צְדָקָה. אָמַר רַב פַּפָּא: וְצָרִיךְ שֶׁיֹּאמַר: ״זֶה גֶּזֶל אָבִי״.

GEMARA With regard to the *halakha* written in the mishna that one who robs his father pays the principal and the additional one-fifth payment to the father's heirs, **Rav Yosef says:** One may **even** put this money **in a charity purse**[HN] if he so chooses. **Rav Pappa says: And** when giving the money **he must say: This** is what was **robbed** from **my father.**

אַמַּאי? נִמְחֲלֵיהּ לְנַפְשֵׁיהּ! מִי לָא תְּנַן: מָחַל לוֹ עַל הַקֶּרֶן וְלֹא מָחַל לוֹ עַל הַחוֹמֶשׁ? אַלְמָא בַּר מְחִילָה הוּא!

§ The Gemara questions the mishna's ruling that one who robs his father must return the stolen item to others even if he is the sole heir. **Why** must he do this? **Let him forgive** the debt **to himself;** as the heir, to whom payment is due, he should be able to forgive it. **Didn't we learn** in a mishna (103a) that in the case of a robber who took a false oath claiming to be innocent and later admitted his liability: If the owner **forgave him concerning the principal, but did not forgive him concerning the** additional **one-fifth** payment, he need not pursue him to repay the remaining debt. **Apparently,** even the principal **is subject to forgiveness,** so why doesn't he forgive the obligation to himself?

אָמַר רַבִּי יוֹחָנָן, לָא קַשְׁיָא: הָא רַבִּי יוֹסֵי הַגְּלִילִי, הָא רַבִּי עֲקִיבָא;

Rabbi Yoḥanan said: This is **not difficult. That** mishna is in accordance with the opinion of **Rabbi Yosei HaGelili,** who says that this obligation can be forgiven, while **this** mishna, ruling that a son who robbed his father and is his sole heir cannot forgive the obligation to himself, is in accordance with the opinion of **Rabbi Akiva,** who holds that this obligation cannot be forgiven.

NOTES

In his life and in his death – בְּחַיָּיו וּבְמוֹתוֹ: The Rid writes that this vow does not in fact prohibit the property after the death of the father, as he cannot create a prohibition that will survive him using this terminology. Nevertheless, the Sages ruled that the son should not directly violate the vow by deriving benefit from the late father's property since the prohibition stated in the vow could instead be circumvented. By contrast, had the father made a more limited *konam* vow prohibiting specific items of his such that the wording of the vow is centered not on his ownership but on the items themselves, then the vow would remain fully in effect even after his death and the Sages would not have suggested a way for the son to circumvent it.

Does not inherit from him – לֹא יִירָשֶׁנּוּ: Early commentaries explain that this does not mean that the son literally does not inherit his father's property, as the *halakhot* of inheritance are dictated by the Torah and the father cannot override them. Rather, it means that once the father rendered his property as that from which benefit is prohibited for the son, this is akin to the son inheriting, for example, meat cooked with milk, from which a Jew may not derive benefit.

And if he does not have – וְאִם אֵין לוֹ: Rashi explains this to mean that he, the son, has no other income or way to subsist. The *Sefer HaNer* and Rambam's Commentary on the Mishna explain this to mean that he, the father, has no other heirs than the son for whom he had rendered the items prohibited.

And the creditors come and are repaid – וּבַעֲלֵי חוֹב בָּאִים וְנִפְרָעִים: The Rashba explains, based on the Rambam (see *Hilkhot Nedarim* 5:8), that the mishna allows the son who was prohibited from deriving benefit from his father's property to give it to his sons or pay his debts with that property as long as he declares that the property given is that which his father had prohibited to him. The declaration indicates that he is not giving property that belongs to him, but only empowering another to take that which does not belong to him.

By contrast, the Meiri holds that having one's loan paid off by the father's estate is not considered deriving benefit, as the son abrogates his right to the inheritance and the creditors collect from this money on their own, without any involvement of the son. Even if the son physically hands them the money it is not considered a significant act of giving from which he derives benefit. The *Beit Yosef* also rules accordingly (*Yoreh De'a* 223).

In a charity purse – לְאַרְנְקִי שֶׁל צְדָקָה: According to the Ra'avad, the novelty of this statement is that one should not say that this stolen item should not be accepted by a charity even if it cannot be returned to the owner. According to Rashi, the novelty is that if the father has no other heirs the son must still remove the stolen item from his possession, even by giving it to charity.

Some commentaries understand Rav Yosef's statement to apply not to the clause teaching to whom the son returns the item he stole but to the one teaching that if the son does not have money he may collect from charity, and the charity will then take the stolen item in exchange (*Shita Mekubbetzet*, citing *Ge'onim*). The Ra'avad suggests that in light of this explanation, the same *halakha* would apply to money forbidden to the son as a result of the father's vow. The son may take money from charity and have the charity collect the money that was prohibited to him.

HALAKHA

In his life and in his death – בְּחַיָּיו וּבְמוֹתוֹ: If a father vowed to prohibit his son from deriving benefit from his property, specifying that this restriction will be in effect during his life and after his death, then when he dies his son does not inherit from him. Even though in principle the son has a share in the estate as his father's heir, he is prohibited to derive benefit from his father (Rambam *Sefer Hafla'a*, *Hilkhot Nedarim* 5:6 and *Kesef Mishne* there; *Shulḥan Arukh*, *Yoreh De'a* 216:7, 223:2).

And he returns it to his sons, etc. – וְיַחֲזִיר לְבָנָיו וכו׳: A son who is prohibited by vow from deriving benefit from his father's estate is permitted to give his portion of the estate to his brothers or sons, or, according to some commentaries, to his father's brothers (*Taz*, citing *Tur*). According to the *Taz* he may not do so *ab initio*, but if he did, it takes effect after the fact.

The son may not give the money directly to these other relatives, but may only show them where the money is located, and they then take it on their own (*Beit Yosef*, citing Ran). The Beit Yosef also cites other authorities who hold that he may give them the money directly. He may also use the money to pay back loans or to pay his wife's marriage contract in the event that he divorces her, and he must declare that the money came from his father's estate from which he was prohibited to derive benefit. According to the *Shakh*, the permission to pay back loans from this money applies only to a loan by oral agreement or other debts in which his liability is not clear (*Shulḥan Arukh*, *Yoreh De'a* 223:4).

Even in a charity purse – אֲפִילּוּ לְאַרְנְקִי שֶׁל צְדָקָה: If a son robs his father and takes an oath denying it, and then his father dies leaving him as the only heir, he must remove the stolen item from his possession and give it to his own children, to his creditor, or to charity, provided that he informs the recipient that this money should have been given as restitution for an item he stole from his father. The *Sma* rules that he may borrow from others before giving it to charity, letting the creditor collect his due from the charity coffers. The Rema, citing the *Tur*, holds that if the robber has no brothers he should give the stolen item to his father's brothers (Rambam *Sefer Nezikin*, *Hilkhot Gezeila VaAveda* 8:3; *Shulḥan Arukh*, *Ḥoshen Mishpat* 367:5).

HALAKHA

Established it as a loan for him and then died, etc. – **זְקָפוֹ עָלָיו בְּמִלְוָה וּמֵת וכו׳**: If one robbed a convert without heirs, took a false oath that he did not rob him, and then admitted that he did rob him, and the convert established the robbery payment as a loan but then died, even though the robber retains the value of the stolen item due to its having become a standard loan debt, he nevertheless must remove the stolen item itself from his possession. According to the *Tur* and the *Sma* he must give the value of the stolen item to charity. This is in accordance with Rabbi Akiva's opinion, which is followed in his disputes with other individual Sages (Rambam *Sefer Nezikin, Hilkhot Gezeila VaAveda* 8:4–5; *Shulḥan Arukh, Ḥoshen Mishpat* 367:6).

דְּתַנְיָא: ״וְאִם אֵין לָאִישׁ גֹּאֵל לְהָשִׁיב הָאָשָׁם״ – וְכִי יֵשׁ אָדָם בְּיִשְׂרָאֵל שֶׁאֵין לוֹ גּוֹאֲלִים? אֶלָּא בְּגָזֶל הַגֵּר הַכָּתוּב מְדַבֵּר.

Rabbi Yoḥanan explains: **As it is taught** in a *baraita* (*Tosefta* 10:16) that the verse states with regard to one who steals from one who then died: **"But if the man has no kinsman** to whom **restitution may be made for the guilt,** the restitution for guilt that is made shall be the Lord's, even the priest's" (Numbers 5:8). The *baraita* asks: **But is there** any **Jewish person who has no kinsmen?** Since every Jew descends from Jacob our forefather, all Jews have relatives to inherit from them. **Rather,** it must be that **the verse is speaking of robbery of a convert** who never married or had children as a Jew, and in any case is no longer legally related to his gentile family; he has no heirs. In this situation the Torah instructs one who robbed from a now-deceased convert to return the stolen item to a priest.

הֲרֵי שֶׁגָּזַל הַגֵּר וְנִשְׁבַּע לוֹ, וְשָׁמַע שֶׁמֵּת הַגֵּר, וְהָיָה מַעֲלֶה כַּסְפּוֹ וַאֲשָׁמוֹ לִירוּשָׁלַיִם, וּפָגַע בְּאוֹתוֹ הַגֵּר וּזְקָפוֹ עָלָיו בְּמִלְוֶה, וּמֵת – זָכָה הַלָּה בְּמַה שֶּׁבְּיָדוֹ, דִּבְרֵי רַבִּי יוֹסֵי הַגְּלִילִי; רַבִּי עֲקִיבָא אוֹמֵר: אֵין לוֹ תַּקָּנָה עַד שֶׁיּוֹצִיא גְּזֵילוֹ מִתַּחַת יָדוֹ;

The *baraita* continues: In the case of one **who robbed a convert and took** a false **oath to him** saying that he did not rob him, **and** then **heard that the convert died; and he was bringing his money,** for the principal and the additional one-fifth payment, **and his guilt-offering up to Jerusalem** to pay his debt to the priests and sacrifice his offering, **and he encountered that same convert,** who in fact had not died; **and,** instead of having the robber pay the money right away the convert **established it as a loan for** the robber, **and** then the convert **died,**[H] leaving his property ownerless, as he had no heirs; **this** robber **acquires** all **that is in his possession,** as it is now a loan, not money to pay back the theft; this is **the statement of Rabbi Yosei HaGelili. Rabbi Akiva says:** The robber **has no remedy until he will remove his stolen item from his possession.**

לְרַבִּי יוֹסֵי הַגְּלִילִי, לָא שְׁנָא לְנַפְשֵׁיהּ לָא שְׁנָא לַאֲחֵרִים – מָצֵי מָחֵיל, וּלְרַבִּי עֲקִיבָא, לָא שְׁנָא לַאֲחֵרִים וְלָא שְׁנָא לְנַפְשֵׁיהּ – לָא מָצֵי מָחֵיל;

Rabbi Yoḥanan explains their respective opinions. **According to** the opinion of **Rabbi Yosei HaGelili,** there **is no difference** if the one to whom payment is due forgives the return of a stolen item **to himself,** such as in this case of a convert who died or in the case of the mishna where a son robbed his father who then died, and there **is no difference** if he forgives the return of a stolen item **to others.** In either case, he **can forgive** payment. **And according to** the opinion of **Rabbi Akiva,** there **is no difference** if the one to whom payment is due forgives the return of a stolen item **to others** and there **is no difference** if he forgives the return of a stolen item **to himself.** In either case, he **cannot forgive** payment.

וּלְרַבִּי יוֹסֵי, הוּא הַדִּין דַּאֲפִילּוּ לֹא זְקָפוֹ בְּמִלְוֶה, וְהַאי דְּקָתָנֵי זְקָפוֹ עָלָיו בְּמִלְוֶה – לְהוֹדִיעֲךָ כֹּחוֹ דְּרַבִּי עֲקִיבָא, דַּאֲפִילּוּ זְקָפָן עָלָיו בְּמִלְוֶה, אֵין לוֹ תַּקָּנָה עַד שֶׁיּוֹצִיא גְּזֵילָה מִתַּחַת יָדוֹ.

Rabbi Yoḥanan continues his analysis: **And according to** the opinion of **Rabbi Yosei** HaGelili, **the same is true,** i.e., the *halakha* would also be, **that** no liability would remain in the case of the convert **even had he not established** the robbery debt **as a loan,** as the robber could forgive the obligation to himself once the convert died. **And** the fact **that** the *baraita* **teaches** its *halakha* in a case where he **established it as a loan for** the robber **is to convey to you the far-reaching nature of** the opinion of **Rabbi Akiva: That even** if he **established it as a loan for him,** in which case it could be considered as though the robber had returned the stolen item and now has a standard loan debt, nevertheless, the robber **has no remedy until he will remove his stolen item from his possession,** so as to not benefit from his act of robbery.

מַתְקִיף לָהּ רַב שֵׁשֶׁת: אִי הָכִי, לְרַבִּי יוֹסֵי הַגְּלִילִי – לַשְׁמְעִינַן לְנַפְשֵׁיהּ, וְכָל שֶׁכֵּן לַאֲחֵרִים, לְרַבִּי עֲקִיבָא – לַשְׁמְעִינַן לַאֲחֵרִים דְּלָא מָצֵי מָחֵיל, וְכָל שֶׁכֵּן לְנַפְשֵׁיהּ דְּלָא מָצֵי מָחֵיל!

Rav Sheshet objects to this interpretation of the *baraita*: **If so,** then **according to** the opinion of **Rabbi Yosei HaGelili, let** the mishna on 103a, which indicates that one can forgive the principal payment of a robbery, **teach us** instead that the robbery victim can forgive the obligation **to himself, and** it would be understood that **all the more so** one can forgive the obligation **to others.** And **according to** the opinion of **Rabbi Akiva,** which Rabbi Yoḥanan explains to be the opinion stated in the mishna here, **let it teach us that one cannot forgive** the obligation **to others, and** it would be understood **all the more so** with regard to the robber, **that** he **cannot forgive** the obligation **to himself.**

אֶלָּא אֲמַר רַב שֵׁשֶׁת: הָא וְהָא רַבִּי יוֹסֵי הַגְּלִילִי; כִּי קָאָמַר רַבִּי יוֹסֵי הַגְּלִילִי דְּמָצֵי מָחֵיל – לַאֲחֵרִים, אֲבָל לְנַפְשֵׁיהּ לָא מָצֵי מָחֵיל. אֶלָּא אַמַּאי זָכָה הַלָּה בְּמַה שֶּׁבְּיָדוֹ? מִשּׁוּם דְּזַקְפָן עָלָיו בְּמִלְוֶה.

Rather, Rav Sheshet said: That mishna and this mishna are both in accordance with the opinion of Rabbi Yosei HaGelili. When Rabbi Yosei HaGelili is saying that one can forgive the return of a stolen item, he meant specifically forgiving the obligation to others, but he cannot forgive the obligation to himself. The Gemara asks: But if that is the *halakha*, why did this one who robbed a convert who subsequently died acquire all that is in his possession? Because the convert established it as a loan for him, and henceforth it is no longer considered stolen property, but a standard loan debt.

רָבָא אֲמַר: הָא וְהָא רַבִּי עֲקִיבָא; כִּי אָמַר רַבִּי עֲקִיבָא דְּלָא מָצֵי מָחֵיל – לְנַפְשֵׁיהּ, אֲבָל לַאֲחֵרִים מָצֵי מָחֵיל.

The Gemara offers a different explanation. Rava said: That mishna and this mishna are both in accordance with the opinion of Rabbi Akiva. When Rabbi Akiva says that he cannot forgive the return of a stolen item he meant specifically forgiving the obligation to himself, as in the case of the convert, but he can forgive the obligation to others.

Perek **IX**
Daf **109** Amud **b**

מִכְּלָל דְּרַבִּי יוֹסֵי הַגְּלִילִי סָבַר אֲפִילּוּ לְנַפְשֵׁיהּ נַמִי מָצֵי מָחֵיל? אֶלָּא גֶּזֶל הַגֵּר דְּקָאָמַר רַחֲמָנָא נְתִינָה לַכֹּהֲנִים הֵיכִי מַשְׁכַּחַתְּ לָהּ?

The Gemara questions Rava's explanation: By inference does it follow that Rabbi Yosei HaGelili holds that he can forgive the return of the stolen item even to himself? But if so, payment for robbery of a convert who dies without heirs, about which the Merciful One says that it requires giving repayment to the priests, how can you find these circumstances if in every case where one robs a convert and the convert dies the robber can forgive the return of the item to himself?

אֲמַר רָבָא: הָכָא בְּמַאי עָסְקִינַן – כְּשֶׁגָּזַל אֶת הַגֵּר וְנִשְׁבַּע לוֹ, וּמֵת הַגֵּר, וְהוֹדָה לְאַחַר מִיתָה, דִּבְעִידָּנָא דְּאוֹדֵי קְנָאוֹ הַשֵּׁם וּנְתָנוֹ לַכֹּהֲנִים.

Rava said: With what are we dealing here? With a case where one robbed the convert and took an oath to him that he did not rob him, and then the convert died, and the robber admitted his false oath after the convert's death,[H] such that at the time that he admitted[N] to it, the Name, i.e., God, acquired the principal and the additional one-fifth payment and gave it to the priests. Once the right to the payment is transferred to the priests the robber can no longer forgive it. By contrast, if he admitted his false oath while the convert was still alive and then the convert dies, the convert can forgive the obligation to himself, since he already took ownership of it.

בָּעֵי רָבִינָא: גָּזֶל הַגִּיּוֹרֶת, מַהוּ? "אִישׁ" אָמַר רַחֲמָנָא – וְלֹא אִשָּׁה, אוֹ דִּלְמָא אוֹרְחֵיהּ דִּקְרָא הוּא?

§ Ravina raises a dilemma: With regard to payment for robbery of a female convert, what is the *halakha*? The Merciful One states in the Torah: "But if the man has no kinsman" (Numbers 5:8), indicating that the *halakha* applies to a male convert, but not to a woman, i.e., a female convert; if she dies after being robbed, payment is not given to the priests. Or perhaps it is the manner of the verse to employ masculine wording, but the *halakha* applies in the case of a female convert as well?

אֲמַר לֵיהּ רַב אַהֲרֹן לְרָבִינָא: תָּא שְׁמַע, דְּתַנְיָא: "אִישׁ" – אֵין לִי אֶלָּא אִישׁ, אִשָּׁה מִנַּיִן? כְּשֶׁהוּא אוֹמֵר: "הַמּוּשָׁב" – הֲרֵי כָּאן שְׁנַיִם,

Rav Aharon said to Ravina: Come and hear a solution to your dilemma, as it is taught in a *baraita* that the verse states in its entirety: "But if the man has no kinsman to whom restitution may be made for the guilt, the restitution for guilt that is made shall be the Lord's, even the priest's; besides the ram of the atonement, whereby atonement shall be made for him." I have derived only that it is referring to a man; from where is it derived that this applies equally to a woman? When it states: "The restitution for guilt that is made," there are two instances of the phrase "that is made" here, as the verse mentions making restitution twice, to include a female convert in this *halakha*.

HALAKHA

Where one robbed…and admitted it after the convert's death – כְּשֶׁגָּזַל...וְהוֹדָה לְאַחַר מִיתָה: If one robbed a convert who had no heirs, took an oath that he did not rob him, and after the convert died admitted that he had robbed him, he is liable to pay the principal and the additional one-fifth payment to the priests of the priestly watch when he brings his guilt-offering. Through this, he achieves atonement (Rambam *Sefer Nezikin, Hilkhot Gezeila VaAveda* 8:5).

NOTES

That at the time that he admitted, etc. – דִּבְעִידָּנָא דְּאוֹדֵי וכו׳: Rashi explains that if the robber admits to his false oath while the convert is alive, the obligation to pay for the robbery is converted into a standard debt, which the convert has the ability to forgive. The Ra'avad challenges this explanation, and writes that if the robber admits to the false oath while the convert is alive, the money is henceforth considered like any other property of the convert's.

When the robber admits to taking a false oath after the convert's death, this debt is considered never to have been owed to the convert, as at the time of the death, there was no debt, rather an obligation to return the stolen item to the robbery victim. In this case, it is now impossible, because he is dead. Since the money of the debt has no owner, God, the owner of all things, acquires it and bestows it as a gift to the priests.

אִם כֵּן מַה תַּלְמוּד לוֹמַר ״אִישׁ״? אִישׁ – אַתָּה צָרִיךְ לַחֲזוֹר אַחֲרָיו אִם יֵשׁ לוֹ גּוֹאֲלִים אִם לָאו, קָטָן – אִי אַתָּה צָרִיךְ לַחֲזוֹר אַחֲרָיו, בְּיָדוּעַ שֶׁאֵין לוֹ גּוֹאֲלִין.

The *baraita* continues: **If so, what** is the meaning when **the verse states** specifically **"man"?** The *baraita* explains: To pay a convert who is **a man, you need to investigate**[H] **concerning him** to determine **if he has a kinsman or not,** but to pay a convert who is **a minor you do not need to investigate concerning him. It is known that he has no kinsman,** since as a convert he has no kin among his birth family, and as a minor he does not have children.

תָּנוּ רַבָּנַן: ״לַה׳ לַכֹּהֵן״ – קְנָאוֹ הַשֵּׁם וּנְתָנוֹ לַכֹּהֵן שֶׁבְּאוֹתוֹ מִשְׁמָר. אַתָּה אוֹמֵר: לַכֹּהֵן שֶׁבְּאוֹתוֹ מִשְׁמָר, אוֹ אֵינוֹ אֶלָּא לְכָל כֹּהֵן שֶׁיִּרְצֶה? כְּשֶׁהוּא אוֹמֵר: ״מִלְּבַד אֵיל הַכִּפֻּרִים אֲשֶׁר יְכַפֶּר בּוֹ עָלָיו״, הֲרֵי לַכֹּהֵן שֶׁבְּאוֹתוֹ מִשְׁמָר הַכָּתוּב מְדַבֵּר.

§ With regard to the payment to priests in the case of one who robbed a convert who then died without heirs, **the Sages taught:** The verse states: "Restitution for guilt that is made **shall be the Lord's, even the priest's"** (Numbers 5:8), teaching that **the Name,** i.e., God, **acquired it and gave it to the priest who is in that priestly watch.**[B] **Do you say** that it is given only **to the priest who is on that priestly watch? Or** perhaps that is **not** the case, and **rather** he may give it **to any priest that he wishes? When it says** in that verse: **"Besides the ram of the atonement, whereby atonement shall be made for him,"** this teaches that **the verse speaks of** giving it **to the priest who is on that priestly watch.** Just as the ram that the robber brings is given only to the priest on duty who sacrifices it, so too, the money is also given only to the priest on duty.

תָּנוּ רַבָּנַן: הֲרֵי שֶׁהָיָה גּוֹזֵל כֹּהֵן, מִנַּיִן שֶׁלֹּא יֹאמַר: הוֹאִיל וְיוֹצֵא לַכֹּהֲנִים, וַהֲרֵי הוּא תַּחַת יָדִי, יְהֵא שֶׁלִּי? וְדִין הוּא: אִי בְּשֶׁל אֲחֵרִים הוּא זוֹכֶה, בְּשֶׁל עַצְמוֹ לֹא כָּל שֶׁכֵּן!

Concerning this payment, **the Sages taught:** In a case **where** the one who **robs** the convert **was a priest, from where** is it derived **that he shall not say: Since** the payment usually **is removed** from the robber and given **to the priests and it is** now **in my possession, it should be mine. And** there is **a logical derivation** to support this reasoning, as follows: **If** a priest **has the right to acquire** the payment **belonging to others** who stole from a convert, then with regard to payment **belonging to himself,** which is already in his possession, is it **not all the more so** that he should keep it?

רַבִּי נָתָן אוֹמֵר בְּלָשׁוֹן אַחֵר: וּמַה דָּבָר שֶׁאֵין לוֹ חֵלֶק בּוֹ עַד שֶׁיִּכָּנֵס בִּרְשׁוּתוֹ, כְּשֶׁיִּכָּנֵס לִרְשׁוּתוֹ אֵינוֹ יָכוֹל לְהוֹצִיאוֹ מִיָּדוֹ, דָּבָר שֶׁיֵּשׁ לוֹ חֵלֶק בּוֹ עַד שֶׁלֹּא יִכָּנֵס בִּרְשׁוּתוֹ, מִשֶּׁנִּכְנָס לִרְשׁוּתוֹ אֵינוֹ דִּין דְּאֵין אַחֵר יָכוֹל לְהוֹצִיאוֹ מִיָּדוֹ?

The *baraita* continues: **Rabbi Natan states** this logical inference **with different wording: And just as** with regard to **a matter in which** a priest **has no portion**[N] **until it enters his possession,** e.g., *teruma,* which can be given to any priest, **once it enters his possession** another priest **cannot remove it from his possession;** so too, with regard to **a matter in which** a priest **has a portion** even **before it enters his possession,** e.g., an item stolen from a convert, in which he has a portion as one of the priests on the priestly watch, **isn't it logical that another** priest **cannot remove it from his possession** once it is in his possession?

לֹא, אִם אָמַרְתָּ בְּדָבָר שֶׁאֵין לוֹ חֵלֶק בּוֹ, שֶׁכְּשֵׁם שֶׁאֵין לוֹ חֵלֶק בּוֹ כָּךְ אֵין לַאֲחֵרִים חֵלֶק בּוֹ, תֹּאמַר בְּגֶזֶל – שֶׁכְּשֵׁם שֶׁיֵּשׁ לוֹ חֵלֶק בּוֹ כָּךְ יֵשׁ לַאֲחֵרִים חֵלֶק בּוֹ? אֶלָּא גְּזֵילוֹ יוֹצֵא מִתַּחַת יָדוֹ וּמִתְחַלֵּק לְכָל אֶחָיו הַכֹּהֲנִים.

The *baraita* continues, countering that this logical inference is not correct: **No, if you said** this **concerning a matter in which** a priest **has no portion,** where the reason why once it enters his possession another priest cannot remove it from his possession is **that just as he has no portion in it, so too, others have no portion in it; would you say** the same **concerning** an item **robbed** from a convert? As there it could be said **that just as** the priest who robbed him **has a portion in it** as one of the priests on the priestly watch, **so too, other** priests on that watch **have a portion in it. Rather,** the *halakha* is that **the item he stole is removed from his possession and is distributed**[H] **to all of his brethren, the priests.**

וְהָכְתִיב: ״וְאִישׁ אֶת קֳדָשָׁיו לוֹ יִהְיוּ״! הָכָא בְּמַאי עָסְקִינַן – בְּכֹהֵן טָמֵא.

The Gemara raises an objection: **But isn't it written: "And every man's hallowed things**[N] **shall be his;** whatsoever any man gives to the priest, it shall be his" (Numbers 5:10), indicating that a priest is not required to give to the other priests the offerings he sacrifices? Therefore, just as he has the right to the flesh of the guilt-offering that he brings to atone for robbing the convert, shouldn't he also have the right to the payment? The Gemara answers: **With what are we dealing here,** in this case? We are dealing **with a ritually impure priest,** who is unfit to sacrifice the guilt-offering and therefore does not have rights to the flesh of the offering. In this case, he will not be able to keep the payment for himself.

HALAKHA

To pay a man you need to investigate, etc. – **אִישׁ אַתָּה צָרִיךְ לַחֲזוֹר וכו׳**: The reason the Torah specifies the word "man" in the context of robbery from a convert who then died is to teach that if the convert was an adult, the robber must investigate whether he left heirs who can receive the payment. If the convert was a minor, the presumption is that there are no heirs (Rambam *Sefer Nezikin, Hilkhot Gezeila VaAveda* 8:7).

The item he stole is removed from his possession and is distributed, etc. – **גְּזֵילוֹ יוֹצֵא מִתַּחַת יָדוֹ וּמִתְחַלֵּק וכו׳**: If a priest robs a convert and takes an oath that he did not do it, and then the convert dies without heirs, the priest is not entitled to keep the stolen item in his possession, but must give it to the priests of the priestly watch serving on the day he brings his guilt-offering (Rambam *Sefer Nezikin, Hilkhot Gezeila VaAveda* 8:9).

BACKGROUND

Priestly watch – **מִשְׁמָר**: The priests who served in the Temple were divided into twenty-four groups, called priestly watches. Each watch served for one week at a time. In this manner, each watch performed the Temple service for approximately two weeks every year. Each watch received the priestly gifts that were contributed to the Temple during their week of Temple service. The watches were divided into extended patrilineal families.

The priests were originally divided into watches in the time of King David. However, during the Second Temple period, many of the Jews who had been exiled to Babylonia after the destruction of the First Temple remained in Babylonia. Therefore, those priestly families who returned to Eretz Yisrael had to be divided again into twenty-four watches.

During the pilgrimage Festivals, the members of all the priestly watches ascended to the Temple and performed the Temple service together.

NOTES

And just as with regard to a matter in which a priest has no portion, etc. – **וּמַה דָּבָר שֶׁאֵין לוֹ חֵלֶק בּוֹ וכו׳**: Rashi offers two interpretations. First, he explains that this refers to a priest's personal offering, which a priest may bring at any time. He keeps the entire priestly portion of the meat for himself, without sharing it with the members of the priestly watch. Second, he explains that it refers to priestly gifts, such as *teruma*, the portion separated from all produce for priests, and *ḥalla*, the portion separated from dough for priests, to which no individual priest has a claim until the owner gives it to a specific priest and after which no other priest has the right to it. This second explanation also seems to be the explanation of *Tosafot* and the Rid. The Gemara suggests that all the more so, payment for the robbery of a deceased convert, in which each priest of the priestly watch does have a claim from the outset, may not be removed from the priest of the watch who had it in his possession.

The Ra'avad, following Rashi's first interpretation, explains the logic as follows: If with regard to an offering brought by a priest to the Temple during the shift of a different priestly watch, the priest who brought the offering keeps it himself, all the more so with regard to a matter in which a priest does have a claim from the outset, such as the payment for the robbery of a deceased convert, no one can take it from the priest who is in possession of it.

And every man's hallowed things, etc. – **וְאִישׁ אֶת קֳדָשָׁיו וכו׳**: The Sages explicate this verse to mean that a priest may bring his personal offerings at any time and is entitled to the sacrificial animal's flesh and hide. If so, just as the guilt-offering that a priest sacrifices after having taken the false oath belongs to him, so should the payment for the robbery of the convert, as they are juxtaposed in the verse (Rashi; see Ra'avad).

אִי בְּכֹהֵן טָמֵא, דָּבָר שֶׁיֵּשׁ לוֹ חֵלֶק בּוֹ? מִי אִית לֵיהּ?! אֶלָּא אָתְיָא "לַכֹּהֵן" "לַכֹּהֵן" מִשְּׂדֵה אֲחוּזָּה;

The Gemara asks: If the *baraita* states its ruling specifically **with regard to an impure priest,** how can it describe the payment as **a matter in which** the priest **has a portion? Does he have** a portion in it? Therefore, the *baraita* must not be referring to an impure priest. **Rather,** there is another reason why he has no right to the payment. This *halakha* is **derived** through a verbal analogy between the phrase **"even the priest's [*lakohen*]"** (Numbers 5:8) written in this context, and the phrase **"to the priest [*lakohen*]"** (Leviticus 27:21) **from** the verse stated concerning **an ancestral field,**[N] which, if consecrated and then redeemed by another does not revert to its original owner in the Jubilee Year, but is given to the priests, as the *baraita* will now explain.

דְּתַנְיָא: "אֲחֻזָּתוֹ" – מָה תַּלְמוּד לוֹמַר? מִנַּיִן לְשָׂדֶה הַיּוֹצְאָה לַכֹּהֲנִים בַּיּוֹבֵל וּגְאָלָהּ אֶחָד מִן הַכֹּהֲנִים, מִנַּיִן שֶׁלֹּא יֹאמַר: הוֹאִיל וְיוֹצְאָה לַכֹּהֲנִים בַּיּוֹבֵל וַהֲרֵי הִיא תַּחַת יָדִי, תְּהֵא שֶׁלִּי?

As it is taught in a *baraita* that the verse states: "But the field, when it goes out in the Jubilee, shall be holy unto the Lord, as a field dedicated; the possession thereof shall be to the priest" (Leviticus 27:21). The *baraita* asks: **What** is the meaning when **the verse states** the term: **"The possession thereof"? From where** is it derived **that** with regard to **a field that goes out to the priests in the Jubilee** Year **and one of the priests redeemed it** before the Jubilee Year, **from where** is it derived **that** a priest **shall not say: Since** a field that is redeemed by another **goes out to the priests in the Jubilee** Year, **and** the field that I redeemed **is** now **in my possession, it should be mine,** and not be given to the priests in general?

וְדִין הוּא, בְּשֶׁל אֲחֵרִים אֲנִי זוֹכֶה, בְּשֶׁל עַצְמִי לֹא כׇּל שֶׁכֵּן!

The *baraita* continues: **And** there is **a logical derivation** to support this reasoning, as follows: If **I acquire** the field **belonging to others,** who consecrated it and it was then redeemed, then with regard to a field **belonging to me,** which is already in my possession, is it **not all the more so** that I should keep it?

תַּלְמוּד לוֹמַר: "כִּשְׂדֵה הַחֵרֶם לַכֹּהֵן תִּהְיֶה אֲחֻזָּתוֹ", אֲחוּזָּה שֶׁלּוֹ וְאֵין זוֹ שֶׁלּוֹ, הָא כֵּיצַד? יוֹצְאָה מִתַּחַת יָדוֹ וּמִתְחַלֶּקֶת לְכׇל אֶחָיו הַכֹּהֲנִים.

The *baraita* continues, countering that this logical inference is not correct. **The verse states: "As a field dedicated; the possession thereof shall be to the priest"** (Leviticus 27:21), indicating that a field of which the priest has **possession** from his ancestors **is his, but this** field that he redeemed **is not his. How so? It is removed from his possession and is distributed to all of his brethren,the priests.**[H]

תָּנוּ רַבָּנַן: מִנַּיִן לְכֹהֵן שֶׁבָּא וּמַקְרִיב קׇרְבְּנוֹתָיו בְּכׇל עֵת וּבְכׇל שָׁעָה שֶׁיִּרְצֶה? תַּלְמוּד לוֹמַר: "וּבָא בְּכׇל אַוַּת נַפְשׁוֹ...וְשֵׁרֵת",

§ The Gemara records another *baraita* concerning the rights of a priest to offerings he sacrifices. **The Sages taught** (*Tosefta, Menahot* 13:17): **From where** is it derived **that a priest** may **come and sacrifice his offerings**[H] **at any time and at any hour that he wishes** and does not have to wait for his priestly watch to serve in the Temple? **The verse states:** "And if a Levite comes from any of your gates out of all Israel, where he sojourns, **and comes with all the desire of his soul** unto the place that the Lord shall choose; **then he shall minister** in the name of the Lord his God" (Deuteronomy 18:6–7).

וּמִנַּיִן שֶׁעֲבוֹדָתָהּ וְעוֹרָהּ שֶׁלּוֹ? תַּלְמוּד לוֹמַר: "וְאִישׁ אֶת קֳדָשָׁיו לוֹ יִהְיוּ", הָא כֵּיצַד? אִם הָיָה בַּעַל מוּם – נוֹתְנָהּ לְכֹהֵן שֶׁבְּאוֹתוֹ מִשְׁמָר, וַעֲבוֹדָתָהּ וְעוֹרָהּ שֶׁלּוֹ.

The *baraita* continues: **And from where** is it derived **that the performance of** the offering's **service,** i.e., eating the meat of the animal he sacrifices, **and** the offering's **hide, belong to him? The verse states: "And every man's hallowed things shall be his"** (Numbers 5:10). **How so? If** this priest **was blemished,**[H] **he gives** his offering **to** another **priest that is on the same priestly watch** as him to sacrifice it, **but the performance of its service and its hide belong to him.**[N]

NOTES

From an ancestral field – **מִשְּׂדֵה אֲחוּזָּה**: The Gemara applies the principle of this case to the distribution of money among priests, but as far as the guilt-offering itself goes, it stands to reason that the priest who committed the robbery brings it himself and is entitled to it (Rid).

The performance of its service and its hide belong to him – **עֲבוֹדָתָהּ וְעוֹרָהּ שֶׁלּוֹ**: Rashi explains that since he is fit to eat the offering it is considered his. Therefore, the flesh and hide are his. Rashi also quotes an alternative version of the text, reading: Its service and hide are for the members of the priestly watch. The Rambam's ruling accords with this latter version of the text.

HALAKHA

Is distributed to all his brethren the priests – **וּמִתְחַלֶּקֶת לְכׇל אֶחָיו הַכֹּהֲנִים**: If one consecrates a field and a priest redeems it from the Temple treasury of consecrated property and is in possession of it when the Jubilee Year arrives, that priest has no additional right to this field, but shares in it equally with all his priestly brethren (Rambam *Sefer Hafla'a, Hilkhot Arakhin VaHaramim* 4:23).

A priest may come and sacrifice his offerings, etc. – **כֹּהֵן שֶׁבָּא וּמַקְרִיב קׇרְבְּנוֹתָיו וכו׳**: A priest who is required to bring an offering may offer it any day he wishes. Even if it is a sin-offering or guilt-offering he may offer it himself, keep the hide, and eat the meat. He is allowed to give the animal to another priest to offer, in which case the priest who offers it is entitled to the hide and the flesh (Rambam *Sefer Avoda, Hilkhot Kelei HaMikdash* 4:7).

If this priest was blemished – **אִם הָיָה בַּעַל מוּם**: If the priest bringing his offering has a physical blemish that disqualifies him from performing the Temple service, he gives the offering to the members of the priestly watch currently serving and the hide belongs to them, in accordance with the variant reading of the text quoted in Rashi (Rambam *Sefer Avoda, Hilkhot Kelei HaMikdash* 4:8).

וְאִם הָיָה זָקֵן אוֹ חוֹלֶה – נוֹתְנָהּ לְכָל כֹּהֵן שֶׁיִּרְצֶה, וַעֲבוֹדָתָהּ וְעוֹרָהּ לְאַנְשֵׁי מִשְׁמָר.

The *baraita* continues: **And if he was old or sick,**[H] so that he cannot perform the Temple service or eat from the offering, **he gives it to any priest he wishes** to sacrifice it, even to one not on his priestly watch, **and performance of its service and its hide** are given **to the members of the priestly watch.**

הַאי זָקֵן אוֹ חוֹלֶה הֵיכִי דָּמֵי? אִי דְּמָצֵי עָבֵיד עֲבוֹדָה – עֲבוֹדָתָהּ וְעוֹרָהּ נַמִי תֶּיהֱוֵי דִּידֵיהּ, וְאִי דְּלָא מָצֵי עָבֵיד עֲבוֹדָה – שָׁלִיחַ הֵיכִי מְשַׁוֵּי?

The Gemara clarifies: **What are the circumstances of this old or sick** priest? **If** he is in a condition **that he is able to perform** the Temple **service,** then **performance of its service and its hide should be his as well,** as the priest that sacrificed it was acting as his agent. **And if** he is in a condition **that he is not able to perform** the Temple **service, how can he appoint an agent?**[N] The *baraita* stated that he may give it to any priest he wishes, indicating that he chooses which priest he will appoint as his agent.

אֲמַר רַב פַּפָּא: שֶׁיָּכוֹל לַעֲשׂוֹת עַל יְדֵי הַדְּחָק; עֲבוֹדָה, דְּכִי עָבֵיד לַיהּ עַל יְדֵי הַדְּחָק – עֲבוֹדָה הִיא וּמְשַׁוֵּי שָׁלִיחַ; אֲכִילָה, דְּכִי אָכֵיל עַל יְדֵי הַדְּחָק אֲכִילָה גַּסָּה הִיא, וַאֲכִילָה גַּסָּה לָאו כְּלוּם הוּא – מִשּׁוּם הָכִי עֲבוֹדָתָהּ וְעוֹרָהּ לְאַנְשֵׁי מִשְׁמָר.

Rav Pappa said: The *baraita* is referring to a case **where he is able to do** it **with difficulty.** With regard to the Temple **service, where** the *halakha* is that if **he performs it with difficulty**[N] **it is** still considered performance of the Temple **service,** he is therefore able to **appoint an agent** to do it for him. With regard to **eating** the offering, **where** the *halakha* says that **if he eats** it **with difficulty it is excessive eating,**[HBN] **and excessive eating is nothing,** i.e., he does not thereby fulfill the mitzva to eat the sacrificial portion, he is not able to appoint an agent to eat it for him. **Due to that** reason, **performance of its service and its hide** are given **to the members of the priestly watch.**

אָמַר רַב שֵׁשֶׁת: אִם הָיָה כֹּהֵן טָמֵא, בְּקָרְבַּן צִבּוּר – נוֹתְנָהּ לְכָל מִי שֶׁיִּרְצֶה, וַעֲבוֹדָתָהּ וְעוֹרָהּ לְאַנְשֵׁי מִשְׁמָר. הֵיכִי דָּמֵי? אִי דְּאִיכָּא טְהוֹרִים, טְמֵאִים מִי מָצוּ עָבְדִי? וְאִי דְּלֵיכָּא טְהוֹרִים, עֲבוֹדָתָהּ וְעוֹרָהּ לְאַנְשֵׁי מִשְׁמָר? הָא טְמֵאִים נִינְהוּ וְלָא מָצוּ אָכְלִי!

Rav Sheshet says: If a priest of the priestly watch **was ritually impure,**[N] then **with regard to a communal offering**[H] **he gives it to any** priest **he wishes, and performance of its service and its hide** are given **to the members of the priestly watch.** The Gemara asks: **What are the circumstances** where this *halakha* applies? **If there are ritually pure** priests available, then **can impure ones perform** the Temple service, and by extension appoint an agent to perform it in their stead? **And if there are no ritually pure** priests there, as all members of the priestly watch are impure, is the **performance of its service and its hide** given **to the members of the priestly watch?** Even though communal offerings are sacrificed in such a circumstance, the priests **are impure and are not able** to **eat** the offering, even though they may sacrifice it.

אֲמַר רָבָא, אֵימָא: לְבַעֲלֵי מוּמִין טְהוֹרִין שֶׁבְּאוֹתוֹ מִשְׁמָר.

Rava said in explanation: **Say** that they are given **to blemished** but **ritually pure** priests **who are on that priestly watch.** Even though blemished priests are disqualified from performing the Temple service and therefore the offering must be sacrificed by impure priests, the blemished priests are permitted to eat the sacrifice, as they are ritually pure.

HALAKHA

If he was old or sick, etc. – **אִם הָיָה זָקֵן אוֹ חוֹלֶה**: An elderly or sick priest who can perform the Temple service only by forcing himself may give his offering to any priest he chooses, and the hide belongs to the members of the watch. If he is completely unable to perform the Temple service, then the offering itself belongs to the members of the priestly watch and he cannot dictate to whom to give it (Rambam *Sefer Avoda*, *Hilkhot Kelei HaMikdash* 4:8).

Excessive eating – **אֲכִילָה גַּסָּה**: If priests have only a small amount of consecrated flesh to eat, they should eat unconsecrated food or partake of *teruma* with it, in order that the eating of the sacrificial flesh should satiate them. If they have abundant consecrated flesh they may not eat unconsecrated food or partake of *teruma* with it, lest their consumption of the sacrificial flesh be gluttonous, excessive eating (Rambam *Sefer Avoda*, *Hilkhot Ma'aseh HaKorbanot* 10:11).

A priest who was ritually impure with regard to a communal offering – **כֹּהֵן טָמֵא בְּקָרְבַּן צִבּוּר**: If all the other members of the priestly watch were ritually impure, the flesh of the communal sacrifices is eaten by ritually pure but blemished priests of that priestly watch. The offering is sacrificed by the impure members of the watch, and they also keep the hide (Rambam *Sefer Avoda*, *Hilkhot Kelei HaMikdash* 4:9).

BACKGROUND

Excessive eating – **אֲכִילָה גַּסָּה**: Usually this term is used to refer to abnormally gluttonous eating, without regard to etiquette or appropriate quantities consumed and where one mindlessly follows his craving. The halakhic meaning of the term is eating despite being fully satiated. This eating is done not out of desire but with effort, and is an unpleasant experience. With regard to certain *halakhot*, consuming food in this manner is not considered eating.

NOTES

How can he appoint an agent – **שָׁלִיחַ הֵיכִי מְשַׁוֵּי**: This question requires an explanation, for even if he is not capable of performing the Temple service due to his frailty, why should he not be able to appoint an agent to perform the service? Additionally, there is no requirement that an Israelite bringing an offering be healthy enough to sacrifice it, so why should the *halakha* be different with regard to a priest? Moreover, the halakhic consensus elsewhere (see *Kiddushin* 23b) is that when priests sacrifice offerings they act as agents of God, not of the owners of the offerings.

In light of this, the later commentaries explain that the Gemara here does not refer to agency in the technical, legal sense. A priest has the right to sacrifice his own offering, but this right can be transferred to another priest only when the priest who is bringing the offering is himself capable of sacrificing it. Otherwise, it is like the offering of any Jew, which is sacrificed by any member of the priestly watch (*Noda BiYehuda*; *Darkhei David*).

Performs it with difficulty – **עָבֵיד לֵיהּ עַל יְדֵי הַדְּחָק**: *Tosafot* note that as far as Torah law is concerned there is no upper age limit on priests performing the Temple service. As long as a priest has no disqualifying blemish he may continue to serve in the Temple his whole life. By rabbinic law, a priest whose hands tremble due to his old age may not perform the Temple service.

Excessive eating [*akhila gassa*] – **אֲכִילָה גַּסָּה**: Eating is considered excessive when the person recoils from the thought of eating the food (Rashi) and must force himself to eat it. This consumption is not even considered eating, but merely a physical act of forcing food down one's throat. See *Tosafot*, who point out that the term *akhila gassa* can also mean gluttonous eating, performed not for the sake of Heaven.

If a priest was ritually impure, etc. – **אִם הָיָה כֹּהֵן טָמֵא וכו׳**: The Rid explains that this refers to an instance where a ritually impure priest was the winner in the lottery drawn to determine who will perform a particular sacrificial rite.

אָמַר רַב אַשִׁי: אִם הָיָה כֹּהֵן גָּדוֹל אוֹנֵן – נוֹתְנָהּ לְכָל כֹּהֵן שֶׁיִּרְצֶה, וַעֲבוֹדָתָהּ וְעוֹרָהּ לְאַנְשֵׁי מִשְׁמָר. מַאי קָא מַשְׁמַע לָן? תָּנֵינָא: כֹּהֵן גָּדוֹל מַקְרִיב אוֹנֵן, וְאֵינוֹ אוֹכֵל, וְאֵינוֹ חוֹלֵק לֶאֱכוֹל לָעֶרֶב!

Rav Ashi says: If a High Priest was an acute mourner,[H] i.e., one whose immediate relative died on that day but had yet to be buried, and he had an offering to sacrifice on his own behalf, **he gives** the offering **to any priest that he wishes** to sacrifice it, **and performance of its service and its hide** are given **to the members of the priestly watch.** The Gemara asks: **What is** Rav Ashi's statement **teaching us? We** already **learned** in a *baraita* (*Tosefta, Zevaḥim* 11:3): **A High Priest may sacrifice** an offering even when he is **an acute mourner,**[H] **but he does not eat** it during that day while he is an acute mourner **and does not** receive **a portion** of the sacrifice **to eat at night**[N] after his acute mourning is finished. It follows from this *baraita* that since he sacrifices it by himself he is able to appoint another priest in his stead, and since he may not eat it, it is given to the priestly watch to eat. What, then, was the novelty of Rav Ashi's statement?

סָלְקָא דַּעְתָּךְ אָמִינָא, כִּי חַס רַחֲמָנָא עֲלֵיהּ דְּכֹהֵן גָּדוֹל – לְקָרוֹבֵי הוּא, אֲבָל לְשַׁוּוֹיֵי שָׁלִיחַ לָא מָצֵי מְשַׁוֵּי, קָא מַשְׁמַע לָן.

The Gemara answers: It might **enter your mind to say** that **when the Merciful One had compassion on the High Priest,** permitting him to continue serving in the Temple even while in a state of acute mourning, it was for **him to sacrifice; but** with regard **to appointing an agent, he is not able** to **appoint** one. Therefore, Rav Ashi **teaches us** that he is able to appoint an agent, since he himself is permitted to perform the Temple service.

מתני׳ הַגּוֹזֵל אֶת הַגֵּר וְנִשְׁבַּע לוֹ וּמֵת – הֲרֵי זֶה מְשַׁלֵּם קֶרֶן וְחוֹמֶשׁ לַכֹּהֲנִים וְאָשָׁם לַמִּזְבֵּחַ, שֶׁנֶּאֱמַר: ״וְאִם אֵין לָאִישׁ גּוֹאֵל לְהָשִׁיב הָאָשָׁם אֵלָיו הָאָשָׁם הַמּוּשָׁב לַה׳ לַכֹּהֵן מִלְּבַד אֵיל הַכִּפֻּרִים אֲשֶׁר יְכַפֶּר בּוֹ עָלָיו״.

MISHNA With regard to **one who robs a convert and takes** a false **oath** denying having done so, and then the convert **dies,** the robber, in order to achieve repentance, **pays the principal,** i.e., the stolen item or, if it is no longer extant, its monetary value, **and** an additional **one-fifth** of its value **to the priests,**[H] **and** presents **a guilt-offering to the altar, as it is stated: "But if the man has no kinsman to whom restitution may be made for the guilt, the restitution for guilt that is made shall be the Lord's, even the priest's; besides the ram of the atonement, whereby atonement shall be made for him"** (Numbers 5:8).

הָיָה מַעֲלֶה אֶת הַכֶּסֶף וְאֶת הָאָשָׁם וּמֵת – הַכֶּסֶף יִנָּתֵן לְבָנָיו, וְהָאָשָׁם יִרְעֶה עַד שֶׁיִּסְתָּאֵב, וְיִמָּכֵר וְיִפְּלוּ דָּמָיו לִנְדָבָה. נָתַן הַכֶּסֶף לְאַנְשֵׁי מִשְׁמָר וּמֵת – אֵין הַיּוֹרְשִׁין יְכוֹלִין לְהוֹצִיא מִיָּדָם, שֶׁנֶּאֱמַר: ״וְאִישׁ אֲשֶׁר יִתֵּן לַכֹּהֵן לוֹ יִהְיֶה״.

The mishna continues: If the robber **was bringing the money and the guilt-offering up** to Jerusalem **and he died**[H] before paying the priests and bringing his offering, **the money shall be given to** the robber's **children,**[N] **and the** animal designated for the **guilt-offering shall graze until it becomes blemished** and consequently disqualified from being sacrificed. **And** the animal **shall** then **be sold and the money** received **for it shall be allocated for** communal gift offerings. If the robber **gave the money to the members of the priestly watch**[H] and then **died** before they sacrificed his guilt-offering, **the heirs cannot remove** the money **from** the priests' **possession, as it is stated:** "And every man's hallowed things shall be his; **whatsoever any man gives to the priest, it shall be his"** (Numbers 5:10).

NOTES

And does not receive a portion to eat at night – וְאֵינוֹ חוֹלֵק לֶאֱכוֹל לָעֶרֶב: Rashi writes that even though by Torah law acute mourning applies only for the day of death and not the night following, regardless of whether the burial had occurred, nevertheless, by rabbinic law, a priest in a state of acute mourning is prohibited from eating any consecrated food until after the burial.

The money shall be given to the robber's children – הַכֶּסֶף יִנָּתֵן לְבָנָיו: The robber was the owner of the money at the time of his death, having assumed ownership from the convert, and therefore the money is subject to the *halakhot* of inheritance. The fact that the robber had been obligated to bring the money to the priests does not indicate that he was not the owner, but rather that he was required to atone for his sin. Once he is dead, there is no more atonement to seek (Rashi).

HALAKHA

A High Priest was an acute mourner – הָיָה כֹּהֵן גָּדוֹל אוֹנֵן: If a High Priest was an acute mourner, whose immediate relative had died that day but had not yet been buried, and he had an offering to sacrifice on his own behalf, he gives it to any priest he wishes, and its flesh and its hide are given to the members of that priestly watch (Rambam *Sefer Avoda, Hilkhot Kelei HaMikdash* 4:10).

A High Priest may sacrifice when he is an acute mourner – כֹּהֵן גָּדוֹל מַקְרִיב אוֹנֵן: A High Priest may perform the Temple service when in a state of acute mourning. Nevertheless, he may not eat from the consecrated offerings and may not even take a portion to save and eat in the evening, after the end of the period of acute mourning (Rambam *Sefer Avoda, Hilkhot Biat HaMikdash* 2:6, 8).

Pays the principal and one-fifth of its value to the priests – מְשַׁלֵּם קֶרֶן וְחוֹמֶשׁ לַכֹּהֲנִים: If one robs a convert and takes a false oath denying it, and does not admit his sin before the convert dies leaving no heirs, the robber, wishing to repent, must pay the principal and an additional one-fifth of the value of the stolen item to the priests of the priestly watch on duty. Only after giving this payment to the priests does he bring his guilt-offering to achieve atonement (Rambam *Sefer Nezikin, Hilkhot Gezeila VaAveda* 8:5).

If the robber was bringing the money and the guilt-offering up and he died – הָיָה מַעֲלֶה אֶת הַכֶּסֶף וְאֶת הָאָשָׁם וּמֵת: If one robbed a convert and was obligated to pay the principal and the additional one-fifth payment to the priests, and he designated money for this purpose and designated an animal for the accompanying guilt-offering, but then died before bringing it to the Temple, the robber's children inherit the money and the animal designated for the guilt-offering is left to pasture until it develops a blemish, which invalidates it to be sacrificed as an offering (Rambam *Sefer Nezikin, Hilkhot Gezeila VaAveda* 8:10).

If he gave the money to the members of the priestly watch, etc. – נָתַן הַכֶּסֶף לְאַנְשֵׁי מִשְׁמָר וכו׳: If the robber had already given the payment for the robbery to members of the priestly watch but died before bringing his offering to achieve atonement, the robber's heirs cannot remove the money from the possession of the priests (Rambam *Sefer Nezikin, Hilkhot Gezeila VaAveda* 8:11).

נָתַן הַכֶּסֶף לִיהוֹיָרִיב וְאָשָׁם לִידַעְיָה – יָצָא; אָשָׁם לִיהוֹיָרִיב וְכֶסֶף לִידַעְיָה, אִם קַיָּים הָאָשָׁם – יַקְרִיבוּהוּ בְּנֵי יְדַעְיָה, וְאִם לֹא – יַחֲזִיר וְיָבִיא אָשָׁם אַחֵר, שֶׁהַמֵּבִיא גְּזֵילוֹ עַד שֶׁלֹּא הֵבִיא אֲשָׁמוֹ – יָצָא, הֵבִיא אֲשָׁמוֹ עַד שֶׁלֹּא הֵבִיא גְּזֵילוֹ – לֹא יָצָא.

The mishna continues: If the robber **gave the money to** the priestly watch of **Joiarib**[NH] **and** then gave the **guilt-offering to** the priestly watch of **Jedaiah**, the following priestly watch, to sacrifice on his behalf, he has **fulfilled** his obligation. By contrast, if he first gave the **guilt-offering to** the priestly watch of **Joiarib and** then gave the **money to** the priestly watch of **Jedaiah**, **if** the animal designated for **the guilt-offering** is **extant**, then **members of** the priestly watch of **Jedaiah**, who received the money, **should sacrifice it.**[N] **But if** it is **no** longer extant because the priestly watch of Joiarib had already sacrificed it, he **should return and bring another guilt-offering; for one who brings his stolen item** to the priests **before** he **brings his guilt-offering** has **fulfilled** his obligation, but one who **brings his guilt-offering before** he **brings his stolen item**[H] has **not fulfilled** his obligation.

נָתַן אֶת הַקֶּרֶן וְלֹא נָתַן אֶת הַחוֹמֶשׁ – אֵין הַחוֹמֶשׁ מְעַכֵּב.

Although he cannot sacrifice the offering before paying the principal, if **he gave the principal but did not** yet **give the** additional **one-fifth** payment, the lack of having given **the** additional **one-fifth** payment **does not preclude** sacrificing the offering.

גמ׳ תָּנוּ רַבָּנַן: ״אָשָׁם״ – זֶה קֶרֶן, ״הַמּוּשָׁב״ – זֶה חוֹמֶשׁ. אוֹ אֵינוֹ, אֶלָּא ״אָשָׁם״ זֶה אַיִל?

GEMARA **The Sages taught** in explanation of the verse cited in the mishna: "But if the man has no kinsman…the restitution for guilt that is made shall be the Lord's, even the priest's" (Numbers 5:8): With regard to the word **"guilt," this** is referring to the **principal**, i.e., the stolen item itself or its equivalent value; **"the restitution…that is made," this** is referring to the additional **one-fifth** payment. **Or** perhaps this is **not** the proper interpretation of the verse. **Rather,** it should be interpreted: **"Guilt," this** is referring to the **ram** of the guilt-offering.

וּלְמַאי נָפְקָא מִינָּהּ – לְאַפּוּקֵי מִדְּרָבָא, דְּאָמַר רָבָא: גֶּזֶל הַגֵּר שֶׁהֶחֱזִירוֹ בַּלַּיְלָה – לֹא יָצָא, הֶחֱזִירוֹ חֲצָאִין – לֹא יָצָא, מַאי טַעְמָא? אָשָׁם קַרְיֵיהּ רַחֲמָנָא.

Before continuing the *baraita* the Gemara interrupts to clarify: **And for what purpose** does the *baraita* distinguish between the two interpretations of guilt, as in any event, both the principal and the guilt-offering must be brought? The Gemara explains: **To exclude that which Rava** holds, **as Rava says:** With regard to the **stolen item of a convert that** the robber **returned at night,**[NH] the robber **did not fulfill** his obligation. And similarly, if **he returned it to him in halves,** he **did not fulfill** his obligation. **What is the reason? The Merciful One labeled** the stolen item with the term **"guilt,"** teaching that just as a guilt-offering cannot be offered at night or in halves, so too, the stolen item cannot be returned at night or in halves.

כְּשֶׁהוּא אוֹמֵר: ״מִלְּבַד אֵיל הַכִּפֻּרִים״, הֲוֵי אוֹמֵר: ״אָשָׁם״ – זֶה קֶרֶן.

The *baraita* continues: **When it says** in that verse: **"Besides the ram of the atonement"** (Numbers 5:8), referring to the offering, **you must say** concerning the word **"guilt"** written earlier in the verse that **this** is referring to the **principal.**

תַּנְיָא אִידָךְ: ״אָשָׁם״ – זֶה קֶרֶן, ״הַמּוּשָׁב״ – זֶה חוֹמֶשׁ. אוֹ אֵינוֹ, אֶלָּא ״אָשָׁם״ זֶה חוֹמֶשׁ? לְמַאי נָפְקָא מִינָּהּ – לְאַפּוּקֵי מִמַּתְנִיתִין, דִּתְנַן: נָתַן לוֹ אֶת הַקֶּרֶן וְלֹא נָתַן לוֹ אֶת הַחוֹמֶשׁ – אֵין הַחוֹמֶשׁ מְעַכֵּב; אַדְּרַבָּה, חוֹמֶשׁ מְעַכֵּב.

It is taught in **another** *baraita*: With regard to the word **"guilt," this** is referring to the **principal; "the restitution…that is made," this** is referring to the additional **one-fifth** payment. **Or** perhaps this is **not** the proper interpretation of the verse. **Rather,** it should be interpreted: **"Guilt," this** is referring to the additional **one-fifth** payment. Before continuing the *baraita*, the Gemara interrupts to clarify: **For what purpose** does the *baraita* distinguish between the two interpretations? The Gemara explains: **To exclude** that which **the mishna** teaches, **as we learned** in the mishna: If he **gave him the principal but did not** yet **give him the** additional **one-fifth** payment, the lack of having given **the** additional **one-fifth** payment **does not preclude** sacrificing the offering. If "guilt" is referring to the additional one-fifth payment, then, **on the contrary,** it would follow that the lack of having given the additional **one-fifth** payment **precludes** sacrificing the offering.

כְּשֶׁהוּא אוֹמֵר: ״וְהֵשִׁיב אֶת אֲשָׁמוֹ בְּרֹאשׁוֹ וַחֲמִישִׁתוֹ״, הֲוֵי אוֹמֵר: ״אָשָׁם״ – זֶה קֶרֶן.

The *baraita* continues: **When it says** in the previous verse: **"And he shall make restitution for his guilt in full, and add unto it the fifth part thereof"** (Numbers 5:7), **you must say** concerning the word **"guilt"** that **this** is referring to the **principal.**

NOTES

To Joiarib – לִיהוֹיָרִיב: Joiarib was the first in the order of priestly watches, followed by Jedaiah (see I Chronicles 24:7–19). Rashi explains that they were chosen as examples in this mishna because they are the first two.

Members of Jedaiah should sacrifice it – יַקְרִיבוּהוּ בְּנֵי יְדַעְיָה: Rashi explains, according to the Gemara's clarification (110b), that since the members of Joiarib acted counter to *halakha* when they accepted the guilt-offering before the robber gave the money, they should transfer the offering to the members of Jedaiah.

That the robber returned at night, etc. – שֶׁהֶחֱזִירוֹ בַּלַּיְלָה וכו׳: The Meiri adds that another reason to return the stolen item during the daytime is in order to publicize that he has done so.

HALAKHA

If the robber gave the money to Joiarib, etc. – נָתַן הַכֶּסֶף לִיהוֹיָרִיב וכו׳: If one who robbed a convert gave the payment for the robbery to members of one priestly watch and gave the guilt-offering to members of the priestly watch presently on duty, the priests who received the money should give it to the priests on duty, since priests have no right to robbery money they receive while not on their watch, and it can be forcibly removed from their possession (Rambam *Sefer Nezikin*, *Hilkhot Gezeila VaAveda* 8:12).

Brings his guilt-offering before he brings his stolen item – הֵבִיא אֲשָׁמוֹ עַד שֶׁלֹּא הֵבִיא גְּזֵילוֹ: A robber's guilt-offering should not be sacrificed before the robber returns the stolen item or its monetary value, along with an additional one-fifth payment, to the robbery victim or to the priests in the case of robbery of a convert who died without heirs. Despite this, if the guilt-offering has already been sacrificed, the lack of having paid the additional one-fifth does not preclude its validity, but he is obligated to give the additional one-fifth payment later (Rambam *Sefer Nezikin*, *Hilkhot Gezeila VaAveda* 8:13).

The stolen item of a convert that the robber returned at night – גֶּזֶל הַגֵּר שֶׁהֶחֱזִירוֹ בַּלַּיְלָה: One who robbed a convert who died without heirs does not fulfill the obligation to return the stolen item if he returns it at night (Rambam *Sefer Nezikin*, *Hilkhot Gezeila VaAveda* 8:6).

תניא אידך: "אשם" – זה קרן, "המושב" – זה חומש, ובגזל הגר הכתוב מדבר. או אינו, אלא "המושב" זה כפל, ובגניבת הגר הכתוב מדבר? כשהוא אומר: "והשיב את אשמו בראשו וחמישתו", הרי בממון המשתלם בראש הכתוב מדבר.

It is taught in another *baraita*: With regard to the word **"guilt," this** is referring to the **principal; "the restitution…that is made," this** is referring to the additional **one-fifth** payment, **and the verse is speaking of robbery of a convert. Or** perhaps this is **not** the proper interpretation of the verse. **Rather,** it should be interpreted: **"The restitution…that is made," this** is referring to **double payment** that a thief must pay, **and the verse is speaking of theft from a convert. When it says** in the previous verse: **"And he shall make restitution for his guilt in full,** and add unto it **the fifth part thereof"** (Numbers 5:7), **the verse is speaking of money that is paid** exactly **according to the principal,** and not double payment.

גופא, אמר רבא: גזל הגר שהחזירו בלילה – לא יצא, החזירוהו חצאין – לא יצא; מאי טעמא? אשם קרייה רחמנא.

§ Having quoted Rava's statement, the Gemara returns to discuss **the matter itself. Rava says:** With regard to the **stolen item of a convert that** the robber **returned at night,** the robber **did not fulfill** his obligation. And similarly, if **he returned it to him** in **halves,** he **did not fulfill** his obligation. **What is the reason? The Merciful One labeled** the stolen item with the term **"guilt,"** teaching that just as a guilt-offering cannot be offered at night or in halves, so too, the stolen item cannot be returned at night or in halves.

ואמר רבא: גזל הגר שאין בו שוה פרוטה לכל כהן וכהן – לא יצא ידי חובתו; מאי טעמא? דכתיב: "האשם המושב", עד שיהא השבה לכל כהן וכהן.

And Rava says: With regard to the **stolen item of a convert that does not have the value of one** *peruta*[H] **for each and every priest**[N] on the priestly watch, the robber **did not fulfill his obligation** by giving it to the priestly watch. **What is the reason? As it is written: "The restitution for guilt that is made,"** meaning that the robber has not fulfilled his obligation to return the stolen item **until there will be** halakhically significant **restitution made to each and every priest,** minimally one *peruta*. If the stolen item was of less value than can be distributed with each priest in the watch receiving at least one *peruta*, the robber must add to the payment so that each priest receives one *peruta*.

בעי רבא: אין בו למשמרת יהויריב ויש בו

Based on this *halakha*, **Rava raises a dilemma:** If the stolen item **does not have** the value of one *peruta* **for** each priest on **the priestly watch of Joiarib,** which had many priests, **but it has**

HALAKHA

That does not have the value of one *peruta*, etc. – שאין בו שוה פרוטה וכו׳: One who robbed a convert who died without heirs does not fulfill his obligation to return the stolen item to the priests if it is not of sufficient value for each priest of the priestly watch to receive the value of at least one *peruta* (Rambam *Sefer Nezikin, Hilkhot Gezeila VaAveda* 8:7).

NOTES

The value of one *peruta* for each and every priest – שוה פרוטה לכל כהן וכהן: Rashi explains that if the stolen item lacks the value of one *peruta* for each priest in the watch, the robber must add from his own property until each priest receives at least that value. By contrast, the Meiri explains that such additions would be considered separate, independent gifts, and that there is no way for this robber to fulfill the mitzva of restitution.

Perek **IX**
Daf **110** Amud **b**

למשמרת ידעיה מהו?

the value of one *peruta* **for** each priest on the **priestly watch of Jedaiah,** which had fewer priests, **what is the** *halakha*?

היכי דמי? אילימא דיהביה לידעיה במשמרת ידעיה, הא אית ביה!

The Gemara asks: **What are the circumstances** with regard to which Rava raised his dilemma? **If we say** that the dilemma is raised in a case **where he gave** the money **to** the priestly watch of **Jedaiah, during** the time of the Temple service of the **priestly watch of Jedaiah,** there would be no dilemma. **There is in** this payment enough value for each priest to receive one *peruta*.

לא צריכא, דיהביה לידעיה במשמרתו דיהויריב, מאי? מי אמרינן: כיון דלאו משמרתו הוא – ולא כלום הוא, או דלמא כיון דלא חזי ליה, מעיקרא לידעיה קאי? תיקו.

The Gemara explains: **No,** it is **necessary** to raise the dilemma in a case **where he gave it to** the **Jedaiah** priestly watch **during** the time of the Temple service of the **priestly watch of Joiarib;** in that case, **what** is the *halakha*? The Gemara explains the two possibilities: **Do we say** that **since it is not** during Jedaiah's **priestly watch, it is nothing,** i.e., it is not a fulfillment of the mitzva to return the stolen item? **Or perhaps** we say that **since it was not fit for** the Joiarib priestly watch, as it was of insufficient value, **from the outset it stands** ready **for** the **Jedaiah** priestly watch, and by giving it to them he fulfilled the mitzva? The Gemara comments: The question **shall stand** unresolved.

בָּעֵי רָבָא: כֹּהֲנִים, מַהוּ שֶׁיַּחְלְקוּ גֶּזֶל הַגֵּר כְּנֶגֶד גֶּזֶל הַגֵּר?

Rava raises another **dilemma:** With regard to **priests, what is the** *halakha* concerning **whether they may divide** among themselves the restitution for **robbery**[N] **of a convert,** with some priests taking a larger share **in exchange for** taking a smaller share in the restitution for another **robbery of a convert?** In other words, can the priests arrange that one priest or several priests will receive the restitution for one robbery and another priest or several priests will receive the restitution for a different robbery another time?

מִי אָמְרִינַן: אָשָׁם קָרְיֵיהּ רַחֲמָנָא, מָה אָשָׁם אֵין חוֹלְקִין אָשָׁם כְּנֶגֶד אָשָׁם, אַף גֶּזֶל אֵין חוֹלְקִין גֶּזֶל הַגֵּר כְּנֶגֶד גֶּזֶל הַגֵּר. אוֹ דִּלְמָא גֶּזֶל הַגֵּר מָמוֹנָא הוּא?

He explains the two possibilities: **Do we say** that **the Merciful One labeled** the stolen item with the term **"guilt,"** and therefore, **just as** with **a guilt-offering** the priests **may not divide** portions of **a guilt-offering,**[H] with some priests taking a larger share **in exchange for** taking a smaller share in other portions of **a guilt-offering,** but rather all priests of the watch share in the sacrificial flesh, **so too** with the restitution for **robbery:** The priests **may not divide** the restitution for **robbery of a convert,** with some priests taking a larger share **in exchange for** taking a smaller share in the restitution for another **robbery of a convert? Or perhaps** the restitution for **robbery of a convert** paid to priests is not in fact an offering, but it **is monetary restitution,** and monetary restitution may be divided in this manner among the priests?

הֲדַר פַּשְׁטָהּ: אָשָׁם קָרְיֵיהּ רַחֲמָנָא. רַב אַחָא בְּרֵיהּ דְּרָבָא מַתְנֵי לַהּ בְּהֶדְיָא, אָמַר רָבָא: כֹּהֲנִים אֵין חוֹלְקִין גֶּזֶל הַגֵּר כְּנֶגֶד גֶּזֶל הַגֵּר, מַאי טַעֲמָא? אָשָׁם קָרְיֵיהּ רַחֲמָנָא.

Rava **then resolves it** himself: **The Merciful One labeled** the stolen item with the term **"guilt,"** so it may not be divided in this manner. **Rav Aḥa, son of Rava, teaches it explicitly** as a ruling, and not as a dilemma and solution, that **Rava says: Priests may not divide** the restitution for **robbery of a convert**[H] with some priests taking a larger share **in exchange for** taking a smaller share in the restitution for another **robbery of a convert. What is the reason? The Merciful One labeled** the stolen item with the term **"guilt."**

בָּעֵי רָבָא: כֹּהֲנִים בְּגֶזֶל הַגֵּר, יוֹרְשִׁין הָווּ אוֹ מְקַבְּלֵי מַתָּנוֹת הָווּ?

§ **Rava raises a dilemma:** What is the status of **priests with regard to** the restitution for **robbery of a convert? Are they** considered **heirs** of the convert **or are they recipients of gifts?**

לְמַאי נָפְקָא מִינָּהּ – כְּגוֹן שֶׁגָּזַל חָמֵץ שֶׁעָבַר עָלָיו הַפֶּסַח; אִי אָמְרַתְּ יוֹרְשִׁין הָווּ – הַיְינוּ הַאי דְּיָרְתֵי מוֹרִית, וְאִי אָמְרַתְּ מְקַבְּלֵי מַתָּנוֹת הָווּ – מַתָּנָה קָאָמַר רַחֲמָנָא דְּנֵיתִיב לְהוּ, וְהָא לָא קָא יָהֵיב לְהוּ מִידֵּי, דְּעַפְרָא בְּעָלְמָא הוּא.

The Gemara asks: **What is the** practical **difference?** The Gemara answers: The difference would be in a case **where one robbed** a convert of **leavened bread,**[H] and then **Passover elapsed over it,**[N] rendering it an item from which one is prohibited to derive benefit and therefore valueless. **If you say** that the priests **are heirs, this is what they inherit:** Only that which the robber **bequeaths**[N] to them, and the priests receive the valueless leavened bread as is. **And if you say** that **they are recipients of gifts,** it is **a gift that the Merciful One is saying that** the robber **should give to them, and this** robber **is not giving them anything, for it is merely dust.** Therefore, the robber should have to pay the priests what the value of the bread had been at the time of the robbery.

רַב זְעֵירָא בָּעֵי הָכִי: אֲפִילּוּ אִם תִּימְצֵי לוֹמַר מְקַבְּלֵי מַתָּנָה הָווּ, הָא לָא אִיבַּעְיָא לַן דְּהַהִיא מַתָּנָה אָמַר רַחֲמָנָא דְּנֵיתִיב לְהוּ,

Rav Zeira raises the dilemma like this: Even if you say that **they are recipients of gifts, this** question, i.e., whether a robber of leavened bread over which Passover then elapsed fulfills the mitzva to return the stolen item even in this devalued state, **is not our dilemma,** as this is certainly a fulfillment of the obligation. **For this** stolen item is the **gift** with regard to which **the Merciful One states** in the Torah **that** the robber **should give** it **to** the priests.

NOTES

What is the *halakha* concerning whether they may divide the restitution for robbery, etc. – מַהוּ שֶׁיַּחְלְקוּ גֶּזֶל וכו׳: The Rosh explains the dilemma as follows: Since the restitution for the robbery is entirely the priests' personal property once it is given to them and has no sanctity, they should be able to divide it in any manner they see fit. Or perhaps, since the Torah describes this restitution with the same term used to describe a guilt-offering, it should carry the same stricture as offerings with regard to division.

Leavened bread and Passover elapsed over it – חָמֵץ שֶׁעָבַר עָלָיו הַפֶּסַח: Many commentaries point out that the standard version of the text, which reads: Leavened bread over which Passover has elapsed, is incorrect, as the Gemara must be referring to where he stole the bread before Passover while it still had value; otherwise he would be entirely exempt (see *Tosafot*; Gra; *Baḥ*).

This is what they inherit, that which he bequeaths – הַיְינוּ הַאי דְּיָרְתֵי מוֹרִית: If the convert were still alive the robber could return the leavened bread to him as is and say: That which is yours is before you, notwithstanding its current prohibition; therefore, the priests, who are considered to be the heirs of the convert with regard to the robbery, should also be required to accept the leavened bread as is (Rashi).

HALAKHA

May not divide a guilt-offering, etc. – אֵין חוֹלְקִין אָשָׁם וכו׳: All the priests of a priestly watch must divide all the offerings brought to them during their watch. They may not divide offerings such that one group receives a certain offering while another group receives a different one. They may not do so even within one type of offering, such as exchanging a grain-offering for a grain-offering, or even exchanging a grain-offering brought in a pan for a grain-offering brought in a pan or the like; nor a bird offering for a bird offering, a sin-offering for a sin-offering, the breast and thigh for the breast and thigh (Rambam *Sefer Avoda, Hilkhot Ma'aseh HaKorbanot* 10:15–16).

May not divide restitution for robbery of a convert – אֵין חוֹלְקִין גֶּזֶל הַגֵּר: The priests who receive payment for robbery of a convert may not divide it, giving one payment for some priests and the next for others (Rambam *Sefer Nezikin, Hilkhot Gezeila VaAveda* 8:6).

Where one robbed a convert of leavened bread, etc. – שֶׁגָּזַל חָמֵץ וכו׳: If one robbed leavened bread from a convert and took a false oath denying it, and then the convert died without heirs, and then Passover elapsed, the robber must give the priests the value of the leavened bread at the time of the robbery, since payment for robbery of a convert is considered a priestly gift, in accordance with Rava's ruling (Rambam *Sefer Nezikin, Hilkhot Gezeila VaAveda* 8:8).

אֶלָּא כִּי קָמִבַּעְיָא לָן – כְּגוֹן שֶׁנָּפְלוּ לוֹ עֶשֶׂר בְּהֵמוֹת בְּגֶזֶל הַגֵּר, מְחַיְּיבִי לְאַפְרוֹשֵׁי מִינַּיְיהוּ מַעֲשֵׂר אוֹ לָא?

Rav Zeira continues: **Rather, when we have a dilemma** whether the priests are considered as heirs or as recipients of gifts, the practical difference arises in a case **where ten animals**[H] **came into** the priest's possession **for** payment of **robbery of a convert.** The dilemma is: **Are they obligated to separate tithe from them, or not?**

יוֹרְשִׁין הָווּ, דְּאָמַר מָר: קָנוּ בִּתְפִיסַת הַבַּיִת – חַיָּיבִין, אוֹ דִּלְמָא מְקַבְּלֵי מַתָּנוֹת הָווּ, וּתְנַן: הַלּוֹקֵחַ וְהַנִּיתָּן לוֹ בְּמַתָּנָה – פָּטוּר מִמַּעֲשַׂר בְּהֵמָה, מַאי?

The Gemara explains the two possibilities: Perhaps **they are heirs,** in which case they will be obligated, **for the Master said** in a mishna (*Bekhorot* 56b) that if heirs **acquired** animals **in the** jointly **held** property **of the estate,** i.e., the heirs jointly owned the animals as the inheritance had yet to be divided, **they are obligated** to separate tithes from animals born to those animals, and the same will apply to the priests. **Or perhaps they are recipients of gifts, and we learned** in a mishna (*Bekhorot* 55b): **One who purchases** an animal **or one who** has an animal **given to him as a gift is exempt from** the obligation to separate the **animal tithe,**[H] and the same will apply to the priests. **What is** the *halakha* in this case?

תָּא שְׁמַע: עֶשְׂרִים וְאַרְבַּע מַתְּנוֹת כְּהוּנָּה נִיתְּנוּ לְאַהֲרֹן וּלְבָנָיו, וְכוּלָּן נִיתְּנוּ בִּכְלָל וּפְרָט וּכְלָל וּבְרִית מֶלַח,

The Gemara answers: **Come** and **hear** a resolution to this dilemma from a *baraita* (*Tosefta, Ḥalla* 2:7–10): **Twenty-four priestly gifts**[H] **were given to Aaron and to his sons, and all of them were given with** a derivation from **a generalization, and a detail, and a generalization; and with a covenant of salt.** The verses in the book of Numbers, chapter 18, detail the gifts of the priesthood. The first verse (18:8) is written in general terms, followed by verses listing the actual gifts (9–18), followed by a final verse written in general terms. The method of interpreting verses written in this manner is one of the thirteen hermeneutical principles. Additionally, the phrase: "Covenant of salt," is written in the final verse (18:19), and is referring to all of the gifts of the priesthood.

כָּל הַמְקַיְּימָן – כְּאִילּוּ מְקַיֵּים כְּלָל וּפְרָט וּכְלָל וּבְרִית מֶלַח, כָּל הָעוֹבֵר עֲלֵיהֶם – כְּאִילּוּ עוֹבֵר עַל כְּלָל וּפְרָט וּכְלָל וּבְרִית מֶלַח;

This serves to teach that **anyone who fulfills** the mitzva of giving the gifts of the priesthood is considered **as if he fulfills** the entire Torah, which is interpreted using the principle of a **generalization,**[N] **and a detail, and a generalization; and** as if he has brought all of the offerings, concerning which there is a **covenant of salt. And anyone who violates** the mitzva of giving the gifts of the priesthood is considered **as if he violates** the entire Torah, which is interpreted using the principle of **a generalization, and a detail, and a generalization; and** as if he has not brought all of the offerings, concerning which there is **a covenant of salt.**

וְאֵלּוּ הֵן: עֶשֶׂר בַּמִּקְדָּשׁ, וְאַרְבַּע בִּירוּשָׁלַיִם, וְעֶשֶׂר בַּגְּבוּלִים; עֶשֶׂר בַּמִּקְדָּשׁ: חַטָּאת בְּהֵמָה, וְחַטָּאת הָעוֹף, וְאָשָׁם וַדַּאי, וְאָשָׁם תָּלוּי, וְזִבְחֵי שַׁלְמֵי צִבּוּר, וְלוֹג שֶׁמֶן שֶׁל מְצוֹרָע, וּמוֹתַר הָעוֹמֶר, וּשְׁתֵּי הַלֶּחֶם, וְלֶחֶם הַפָּנִים, וּשְׁיָרֵי מְנָחוֹת.

The *baraita* continues: **And these are** the twenty-four gifts: There are **ten in the Temple,**[H] **and four in Jerusalem, and ten in the boundaries** of Eretz Yisrael. The **ten** gifts that the priests consume only **in the Temple** are **an animal sin-offering; and a bird sin-offering; and a definite guilt-offering; and a provisional guilt-offering; and communal peace-offerings,** i.e., lambs offered on *Shavuot*; **and a** *log* **of oil** that accompanies the guilt-offering **of a** recovered **leper; and the surplus of the** *omer*, i.e., what remains of the measure of barley brought as a communal offering on the sixteenth of Nisan; **and the two loaves,** i.e., the public offering of two loaves from the new wheat offered on *Shavuot*; **and the shewbread; and the leftovers of grain-offerings,** after the priests have offered the required handful.

HALAKHA

Ten animals – עֶשֶׂר בְּהֵמוֹת: A priest to whom ten animals that had been robbed from a convert are paid is exempt from separating animal tithe from them, as payment for robbery of a convert is considered a gift to the priests (Rambam *Sefer Korbanot, Hilkhot Bekhorot* 6:13).

Animal tithe – מַעֲשַׂר בְּהֵמָה: One is exempt from separating animal tithe for lambs he purchases, receives as gifts, or inherits from his father, even if he receives them in the same year as their birth. Siblings who purchase animals with inheritance money are required to tithe the animals born afterward, counter to the conclusion of this Gemara (Rambam *Sefer Korbanot, Hilkhot Bekhorot* 6:10 and *Leḥem Mishne* there).

Twenty-four priestly gifts – עֶשְׂרִים וְאַרְבַּע מַתְּנוֹת כְּהוּנָּה: Twenty-four gifts are given to priests as part of Aaron's covenant, all explicitly mentioned in the Torah. Any priest who does not admit to the validity of the sacrificial rite (see *Menaḥot* 18b) has no portion in the priesthood and is not given any of the gifts (Rambam *Sefer Zera'im, Hilkhot Bikkurim* 1:1).

Ten in the Temple – עֶשֶׂר בַּמִּקְדָּשׁ: The Sages classified the twenty-four priestly gifts into categories, as follows: Ten of the gifts were consumed in the Temple. They are animal sin-offerings; bird sin-offerings; guilt-offerings; provisional guilt-offerings; communal peace-offerings; the leper's *log* of oil; the public offering of two loaves from the new wheat offered on *Shavuot*; the shewbread; leftovers from grain-offerings; and the surplus of the *omer*. Four gifts were consumed anywhere in Jerusalem: Firstborn animals; first fruits; the portions separated from the thanks-offering and the nazirite's ram; and hides of sacred offerings. Ten gifts were given anywhere within Eretz Yisrael: *Teruma*; *teruma* of the tithe; *ḥalla*; the first of the sheared wool; the gift portions of non-sacrificial, slaughtered animals; money given for the redemption of a firstborn son; the sheep or goat given as redemption of the firstborn donkey; dedicated fields; consecrated ancestral fields; and payment for robbery of a convert who died without heirs (Rambam *Sefer Zera'im, Hilkhot Bikkurim* 1:12–15).

NOTES

As if he fulfills a generalization, etc. – כְּאִילּוּ מְקַיֵּים כְּלָל וכו׳: The listing of the priestly gifts in the Torah is preceded by a generalization: "And the Lord spoke unto Aaron: And I, behold, have given you the charge of My heave-offerings; even of all the hallowed things of the children of Israel unto you have I given them for a consecrated portion, and to your sons, as a portion forever" (Numbers 18:8). Over the following ten verses, the Torah lists the various gifts, and then concludes with another generalization: "All the heave-offerings of the holy things, which the children of Israel offer unto the Lord, have I given you, and your sons and your daughters with you, as a portion forever" (Numbers 18:19). It then states: "It is an everlasting covenant of salt before the Lord unto you and to your seed with you" (Numbers 18:19).

וְאַרְבַּע בִּירוּשָׁלַיִם: הַבְּכוֹרָה, וְהַבִּיכּוּרִים, וְהַמּוּרָם מִן הַתּוֹדָה וְאֵיל נָזִיר, וְעוֹרוֹת קָדָשִׁים.

The *baraita* continues: **And the four** gifts that the priests consume anywhere **in Jerusalem: The firstborn**[N] of kosher animals; **and the first fruits; and the** portions **separated** for the priests **from the thanks-offering**[N] **and the nazirite's ram; and hides of consecrated** animals.[N]

וַעֲשָׂרָה בַּגְּבוּלִין: תְּרוּמָה, וּתְרוּמַת מַעֲשֵׂר, וְחַלָּה, וְרֵאשִׁית הַגֵּז, וְהַמַּתָּנוֹת, וּפִדְיוֹן הַבֵּן, וּפִדְיוֹן פֶּטֶר חֲמוֹר, וּשְׂדֵה אֲחוּזָּה, וּשְׂדֵה חֲרָמִים, וְגֶזֶל הַגֵּר.

The *baraita* continues: **And ten** gifts that the priests consume anywhere **in the boundaries** of Eretz Yisrael: ***Teruma***, i.e., the portion of the produce designated for the priest; **and *teruma* of the tithe,** which the Levite separates from the tithe he receives and gives to a priest; **and *ḥalla***, i.e., the portion of dough of the five main grains designated for the priest; **and the first of the sheared** wool; **and the gifts** of non-sacrificial, slaughtered animals, namely, the right foreleg, the cheeks, and the maw; **and** money given for the **redemption of the** firstborn **son; and** a sheep or goat given as **redemption of the firstborn donkey; and** a consecrated **ancestral field** the priests receive in the Jubilee Year; **and a dedicated field;** and payment for **robbery of a convert** who died without heirs.

וְקָא קָרֵי מִיהַת מַתָּנָה, שְׁמַע מִינָּהּ: מְקַבְּלֵי מַתָּנוֹת הָווּ, שְׁמַע מִינָּהּ.

The Gemara infers from the wording of the *baraita*: **And this** *baraita*, **in any event, labels** the payment for robbery of a convert **a gift.** The Gemara suggests: **Conclude from** this *baraita* that the priests who receive it **are** considered **recipients of gifts,** and not heirs. The Gemara affirms: **Conclude from it** that this is so.

״נָתַן אֶת הַכֶּסֶף לְאַנְשֵׁי מִשְׁמָר״ [וכו׳]. אֲמַר אַבַּיֵי, שְׁמַע מִינָּהּ: כֶּסֶף מְכַפֵּר מֶחֱצָה. דְּאִי לָא מְכַפֵּר, הֲוָה אָמִינָא מַהְדַּר לְיוֹרְשִׁין, מַאי טַעֲמָא? אַדַּעְתָּא דְּהָכִי לָא יְהַב לֵיהּ.

§ The mishna teaches: If he **gave the money to the members of the priestly watch** and then died before they sacrificed his guilt-offering, the heirs cannot remove the money from the priests' possession. **Abaye said: Learn from** this mishna that **monetary restitution** for the robbery **atones for half**[N] of the sin, **for if** it **does not atone** at all, and atonement is not achieved until the guilt-offering is sacrificed, **I would say** that in the case of robbery of a convert, if the guilt-offering is not brought the priest **returns** the money **to the robber's heirs. What is the reason** I would say this? Because **he did not give** the money **to** the priests **with this intention** of giving the money and not achieving atonement at all, and it would be a mistaken transaction.

אֶלָּא מֵעַתָּה, חַטָּאת שֶׁמֵּתוּ בְּעָלֶיהָ תֵּיפוֹק לְחוּלִּין, דְּאַדַּעְתָּא דְּהָכִי לָא אַפְרְשָׁהּ! אָמְרִי: חַטָּאת שֶׁמֵּתוּ בְּעָלֶיהָ, הִלְכְתָא גְּמִירִי לָהּ דִּלְמִיתָה אָזְלָא.

The Gemara asks: **If that is so,** it would follow that **a sin-offering whose owners have died,** leaving no one to bring the offering, **should be transferred to non-sacred status,** as the robber **did not separate** the animal as an offering **with this intention** of its not being sacrificed to atone for his sin. The Sages **say** in response: In the case of **a sin-offering whose owners have died,**[H] the Sages **learned this *halakha* through tradition**[N] **that** the animal **is left to die.**

אֶלָּא מֵעַתָּה, אָשָׁם שֶׁמֵּתוּ בְּעָלָיו לִיפּוֹק לְחוּלִּין, דְּאַדַּעְתָּא דְּהָכִי לָא אַפְרְשֵׁיהּ! אָשָׁם נַמִי הִלְכְתָא גְּמִירִי לָהּ: כָּל שֶׁבְּחַטָּאת מֵתָה – בְּאָשָׁם רוֹעֶה.

The Gemara asks: **If that is so, a guilt-offering whose owner has died**[H] **should be transferred to non-sacred status,** as the owner **did not separate** the animal as an offering **with this intention** of it not being sacrificed to atone for his sin. The Gemara answers: With regard to **a guilt-offering,** the Sages **also learned this *halakha* through tradition: Any** occurrence **that,** if it occurs **with regard to a sin-offering** the animal is placed in isolation for it to **die,** if it occurs **with regard to a guilt-offering** the animal is left to **graze** until it develops a blemish precluding its use as an offering, at which point it can be redeemed.

אֶלָּא מֵעַתָּה, יְבָמָה שֶׁנָּפְלָה לִפְנֵי מוּכֵּה שְׁחִין תֵּיפּוֹק בְּלָא חֲלִיצָה, דְּאַדַּעְתָּא דְּהָכִי לָא קִדְּשָׁה עַצְמָהּ! הָתָם אֲנַן סָהֲדֵי

The Gemara asks: **If that is so,** then in the case of **a woman whose husband died childless [*yevama*], who happened before** her late husband's brother who was **afflicted with boils**[H] to enter levirate marriage with him, **should go out** free to marry **without** being required to perform **the ritual through which the *yavam* frees the *yevama* of her levirate bonds [*ḥalitza*]. For she did not betroth herself** to this man's deceased brother **with this intention** of having a levirate bond with a man afflicted with boils. The Gemara answers: **There, it is clear to us**

NOTES

Firstborn – הַבְּכוֹרָה: This refers to an unblemished firstborn animal brought as an offering, whose meat is eaten by the priests anywhere in Jerusalem. A blemished firstborn animal, even though it is given to a priest, can be consumed anywhere.

The portions separated from the thanks-offering – הַמּוּרָם מִן הַתּוֹדָה: The breast and thigh of a thanks-offering are given to the priests, along with four of the forty loaves that are brought with the thanks-offering.

Hides of consecrated animals – עוֹרוֹת קָדָשִׁים: This refers to the hides of offerings of the most sacred order, which are given to the priests who sacrifice them, but not to hides of offerings of lesser sanctity, which belong to the owners of the offerings. Even though these hides result from the offering, they are not counted in the category of gifts in the Temple, since they may be taken out of the Temple to any location (Rashi). The Rashba writes that the hides are divided among the priests who are fit to eat sacrificial offerings, and those priests are located in Jerusalem.

Monetary restitution atones for half – כֶּסֶף מְכַפֵּר מֶחֱצָה: *Tosafot* derive from here that the priest cannot forgive this payment since it is not a monetary debt, but its purpose is to atone.

Learned this *halakha* through tradition – הִלְכְתָא גְּמִירִי לָהּ: There is a principle in halakhic tradition (see *Nazir* 57b) that the regular methods of legal inference and reasoning, such as *a fortiori* inferences, are not applied to those laws that are described as *halakha* transmitted to Moses from Sinai. These *halakhot* stand alone and cannot serve as a source to prove anything about other *halakhot* (Ra'avad).

HALAKHA

A sin-offering whose owners have died – חַטָּאת שֶׁמֵּתוּ בְּעָלֶיהָ: A sin-offering whose owners have died must be placed in isolation to allow it to die. This is a *halakha* transmitted to Moses from Sinai (Rambam *Sefer Avoda, Hilkhot Pesulei HaMukdashin* 4:1).

A guilt-offering whose owner has died – אָשָׁם שֶׁמֵּתוּ בְּעָלָיו: A definite guilt-offering whose owner has died must be left to graze until it develops a blemish, at which point it can be sold, with its proceeds allocated to purchase communal gift-offerings (Rambam *Sefer Avoda, Hilkhot Pesulei HaMukdashin* 4:14).

A *yevama* who happened before a man afflicted with boils – יְבָמָה שֶׁנָּפְלָה לִפְנֵי מוּכֵּה שְׁחִין: If a woman's husband dies childless, leaving her with the mitzva to enter into levirate marriage with his brother, and the brother is afflicted with boils or any other defect, he performs *ḥalitza*, which releases her from any levirate bond (Rambam *Sefer Nashim, Hilkhot Yibbum VaḤalitza* 2:14; *Shulḥan Arukh, Even HaEzer* 165:4).

דְּמֵינַח נִיחָא לָהּ בְּכָל דְּהוּ, כְּרֵישׁ לָקִישׁ. דְּאָמַר רֵישׁ לָקִישׁ: טַב לְמֵיתַב טַן דּוּ מִלְּמֵיתַב אַרְמְלוּ.

that it is satisfactory for her to have **any** kind of marital arrangement, and even had she taken into consideration the possibility of entering a levirate bond with this *yavam* who is afflicted with boils she still would have accepted betrothal to her husband. This is **in accordance with** the statement of **Reish Lakish, as Reish Lakish says** that women have a saying: **It is better to sit** as **two bodies** [*tan du*],[L] i.e., to be married, **than to sit** lonely like **a widow.**

״נָתַן אֶת הַכֶּסֶף לִיהוֹיָרִיב״ וכו׳. תָּנוּ רַבָּנַן: נָתַן אָשָׁם לִיהוֹיָרִיב וְכֶסֶף לִידַעְיָה – יַחֲזִיר כֶּסֶף אֵצֶל אָשָׁם, דִּבְרֵי רַבִּי יְהוּדָה, וַחֲכָמִים אוֹמְרִים: יַחֲזִיר אָשָׁם אֵצֶל כֶּסֶף.

§ The mishna teaches: If the robber **gave the money to** the priestly watch of **Joiarib** and then gave the guilt-offering to the priestly watch of Jedaiah, the following priestly watch, to sacrifice on his behalf, he has fulfilled his obligation. By contrast, if he first gave the guilt-offering to the priestly watch of Joiarib and then gave the money to the priestly watch of Jedaiah, if the guilt-offering is extant, then members of the priestly watch of Jedaiah, who received the money, should sacrifice it. The Gemara quotes a *baraita* that records a dispute between *tanna'im* concerning this case. **The Sages taught** (*Tosefta* 10:18): If the robber **gave the guilt-offering to** the priestly watch of **Joiarib and** then gave **the money to** the priestly watch of **Jedaiah,** they **should return the money** to be **with the guilt-offering,**[H] i.e., with the priestly watch of Joiarib; this is **the statement of Rabbi Yehuda. And the Rabbis say** the opposite: They **should return the guilt-offering** to be **with the money,** and the priestly watch of Jedaiah will sacrifice it.

הֵיכִי דָּמֵי? אִילֵימָא דְּיָהֵיב לֵיהּ אָשָׁם לִיהוֹיָרִיב בְּמִשְׁמַרְתּוֹ דִּיהוֹיָרִיב, וְכֶסֶף לִידַעְיָה בְּמִשְׁמַרְתּוֹ דִּידַעְיָה, זֶה זָכָה בְּשֶׁלּוֹ וְזֶה זָכָה בְּשֶׁלּוֹ!

The Gemara asks: **What are the circumstances** of this dispute? **If we say that he gave the guilt-offering to** the priestly watch of **Joiarib during the priestly watch of Joiarib and the money to** the priestly watch of **Jedaiah during the priestly watch of Jedaiah,** then **this** one **acquired that which belongs to it and that** one **acquired that which belongs to it.** Why would the court remove what was given lawfully to the priestly watch?

אָמַר רָבָא: הָכָא בְּמַאי עָסְקִינַן – דְּיָהֵיב אָשָׁם לִיהוֹיָרִיב בְּמִשְׁמַרְתּוֹ דִּיהוֹיָרִיב, וְכֶסֶף לִידַעְיָה בְּמִשְׁמַרְתּוֹ דִּיהוֹיָרִיב; רַבִּי יְהוּדָה סָבַר: כֵּיוָן דְּלָאו מִשְׁמֶרֶת דִּידַעְיָה הִיא – לִידַעְיָה קָנְסִינַן לֵיהּ, הִלְכָּךְ יַחֲזִיר כֶּסֶף אֵצֶל אָשָׁם; וְרַבָּנַן סָבְרִי: שֶׁלֹּא כַּדִּין הוּא עֲבוּד בְּנֵי יְהוֹיָרִיב דְּקִיבְּלוּ אָשָׁם מִקַּמֵּי כֶּסֶף, הִלְכָּךְ לְדִידְהוּ קָנְסִינַן לְהוּ, וְיַחֲזוֹר אָשָׁם אֵצֶל כֶּסֶף.

Rava said: With what are we dealing here? We are dealing with a case **where he gave the guilt-offering to** the priestly watch of **Joiarib during the priestly watch of Joiarib and the money to** the priestly watch of **Jedaiah** also **during the priestly watch of Joiarib,** and the dispute is as follows: **Rabbi Yehuda holds** that **since this is not the priestly watch of Jedaiah, we penalize Jedaiah; therefore,** the priestly watch of Jedaiah must **return the money** in their possession **to be with the guilt-offering** held by the Joiarib watch. **And the Rabbis hold** that **the members of** the priestly watch of **Joiarib acted unlawfully when they accepted the guilt-offering before** the robber paid **the money,** since payment for the robbery must be given before the guilt-offering can be offered. **Therefore, we penalize them, and the guilt-offering** in their possession **returns** to be **with the money** held by the Jedaiah watch.

תַּנְיָא, אָמַר רַבִּי: לְדִבְרֵי רַבִּי יְהוּדָה, אִם קָדְמוּ בְּנֵי יְהוֹיָרִיב וְהִקְרִיבוּ אֶת הָאָשָׁם – יַחֲזוֹר וְיָבִיא אָשָׁם אַחֵר, וְיַקְרִיבוּהוּ בְּנֵי יְדַעְיָה, וְזָכוּ הַלָּלוּ בְּמַה שֶּׁבְּיָדָן.

It is taught in a *baraita* on this topic (*Tosefta* 10:18): **Rabbi** Yehuda HaNasi **says: According to the statement of Rabbi Yehuda,** that if during the Joiarib watch the robber gave the guilt-offering to the Joiarib watch and the money to the Jedaiah watch, the money should return to the priestly watch of Joiarib, **if the members of** the priestly watch of **Joiarib went first and sacrificed the guilt-offering** before receiving the money from the priestly watch of Jedaiah, then the robber **should go back and bring another guilt-offering, and the members of** the priestly watch of **Jedaiah,** who are already in possession of the money, **should offer it, and those** members of the priestly watch of Joiarib **acquired that** offering **that is in their possession.**

אָמְרִי: לְמַאי חָזֵי? אָשָׁם פָּסוּל הוּא! אָמַר רָבָא: לְעוֹרוֹ.

The Sages **say: For what** purpose is that offering **useful? It is a disqualified guilt-offering,** since it was sacrificed before the payment for the robbery was given, and had to be entirely burned on the altar. **Rava said:** The *baraita* is referring **to** acquiring **its hide,** which the members of the priestly watch of Joiarib keep.

LANGUAGE

Two bodies [*tan du*] – **טַן דּוּ**: The source of this expression is from the Middle Persian tan dō, literally two bodies, with the sense of: Together. A related term appears in Zoroastrian ritual texts in the term tan ēw, which means one body, and has the sense of being alone.

HALAKHA

Should return the money to be with the guilt-offering – **יַחֲזִיר כֶּסֶף אֵצֶל אָשָׁם**: If the robber gives the payment for robbery of the convert to one priestly watch, and gives the guilt-offering to a different priestly watch, which is performing the Temple service at that time, he should retrieve the money from the priestly watch to whom he had given it and pay it to those who are in possession of the guilt-offering. The *halakha* is in accordance with the opinion of Rabbi Yehuda, as evidenced by the fact that Rabbi Yehuda HaNasi and the Gemara discuss his opinion (Rambam *Sefer Nezikin*, *Hilkhot Gezeila VaAveda* 8:12).

HALAKHA

The first burnt-offering – עוֹלָה רִאשׁוֹנָה: It is prohibited for the priests to sacrifice any offerings before the daily offering of the morning is sacrificed (Rambam *Sefer Avoda, Hilkhot Temidin UMusafin* 1:3).

תַּנְיָא, אָמַר רַבִּי: לְדִבְרֵי רַבִּי יְהוּדָה, אִם קַיָּים אָשָׁם – יַחֲזִיר אָשָׁם אֵצֶל כֶּסֶף.

It is taught in a *baraita* that **Rabbi** Yehuda HaNasi **says: According to the statement of Rabbi Yehuda, if the guilt-offering is** still **extant,** i.e., if the priestly watch of Joiarib did not already sacrifice it, then the priestly watch of Joiarib **should return the guilt-offering** to be **with the money,** and the priestly watch of Jedaiah will sacrifice it.

וְהָא רַבִּי יְהוּדָה, יַחֲזִיר כֶּסֶף אֵצֶל אָשָׁם אִית לֵיהּ! הָכָא בְּמַאי עָסְקִינַן – כְּגוֹן דִּנְפַק מִשְׁמַרְתּוֹ דִּיהוֹיָרִיב וְלֹא תָּבְעוּ, וְהָא קָא מַשְׁמַע לָן, דְּאַחוּלֵי אַחִילוּ גַּבַּיְיהוּ.

The Gemara questions this: **But Rabbi Yehuda holds** that they should **return** the **money** to be **with the guilt-offering.** The Gemara explains: **With what are we dealing here?** With a case **where** it happened **that the priestly watch of Joiarib exited** at the close of their Temple service **and they did not demand** the money from the priestly watch of Jedaiah. **And this** statement of Rabbi Yehuda HaNasi **teaches us this: That** by doing so, the members of the priestly watch of Joiarib **waived** their rights to the money **in favor of** the priestly watch of Jedaiah. Consequently, they are required to give the guilt-offering to the priestly watch of Jedaiah to sacrifice.

תַּנְיָא אִידָךְ, אָמַר רַבִּי: לְדִבְרֵי רַבִּי יְהוּדָה, אִם קַיָּים אָשָׁם – יַחֲזוֹר כֶּסֶף אֵצֶל אָשָׁם. פְּשִׁיטָא, הָכִי אִית לֵיהּ!

It is taught in **another** *baraita* that **Rabbi** Yehuda HaNasi **says: According to the statement of Rabbi Yehuda, if the guilt-offering is** still **extant,** i.e., if the priestly watch of Joiarib did not already sacrifice it, **the money** must **return** to be **with the guilt-offering.** The Gemara asks: Isn't that **obvious? This is** what Rabbi Yehuda **holds** explicitly; what novelty did Rabbi Yehuda HaNasi teach?

הָכָא בְּמַאי עָסְקִינַן – כְּגוֹן דִּנְפֵיק מִשְׁמַרְתָּם דְּהָנֵי וּדְהָנֵי וְלֹא תָּבְעוּ, מַהוּ דְּתֵימָא אַחוּלֵי גַּבֵּי הֲדָדֵי, קָא מַשְׁמַע לָן דְּאָמְרִינַן: כֵּיוָן דְּלָא תָּבְעִי לַהַדְרוּ בְּרֵישָׁא.

The Gemara explains: **With what are we dealing here?** With a case **where** it happened **that the priestly watch of these and of those,** i.e., both Joiarib and Jedaiah, **exited** at the end of their Temple service, **and they did not demand** of the other the item in possession of the other watch. **Lest you say that they waived** their rights **in favor of each other,** so that the money stays in possession of the Jedaiah watch, Rabbi Yehuda HaNasi **teaches us that we say: Since** the Jedaiah watch **did not demand** the guilt-offering from the Joiarib watch after the latter exited, **let them go back to the first,** standard scenario, returning the money to Joiarib to be with the guilt-offering.

״שֶׁהַמֵּבִיא גְּזֵילוֹ עַד שֶׁלֹּא הֵבִיא אֲשָׁמוֹ״ [וכו׳]. מְנָהָנֵי מִילֵּי? אֲמַר רָבָא, דְּאָמַר קְרָא: ״הָאָשָׁם הַמּוּשָׁב לַה׳ לַכֹּהֵן מִלְּבַד אֵיל הַכִּפֻּרִים אֲשֶׁר יְכַפֶּר בּוֹ״, מִכְּלָל דְּכֶסֶף בְּרֵישָׁא.

§ The mishna teaches: **For one who brings his stolen item** to the priests **before he brings his guilt-offering** has fulfilled his obligation, but one who brings his guilt-offering before he brings his stolen item has not fulfilled his obligation. The Gemara asks: **From where are these matters** derived? **Rava said:** This is **as the verse states:** "But if the man has no kinsman to whom restitution may be made for the guilt, **the restitution for guilt that is made shall be the Lord's, even the priest's; besides the ram of the atonement, whereby atonement shall be made for him**" (Numbers 5:8). Learn **by inference that the money** must be returned **first,** before the guilt-offering is brought.

אֲמַר הַהוּא מֵרַבָּנַן לְרָבָא: אֶלָּא מֵעַתָּה, ״מִלְּבַד עֹלַת הַבֹּקֶר״ הָכִי נַמִי מִכְּלָל דְּמוּסָפִין בְּרֵישָׁא?

Having understood that the inference is that the wording "besides the ram of the atonement" indicates that the ram must be brought after the money is given, **one of the Sages said to Rava: If that is so,** then in a different verse, which states concerning the additional offerings sacrificed on the first day of Passover: "You shall offer these **besides the burnt-offering of the morning,** which is for a continual burnt-offering" (Numbers 28:23), **so too** should one learn **by inference that the additional offerings** are brought **first,** before the morning burnt-offering?

וְהָתַנְיָא: מִנַּיִן שֶׁלֹּא יְהֵא דָּבָר קוֹדֵם לְתָמִיד שֶׁל שַׁחַר? תַּלְמוּד לוֹמַר: ״וְעָרַךְ עָלֶיהָ הָעֹלָה״, וְאָמַר רָבָא: ״הָעוֹלָה״ – עוֹלָה רִאשׁוֹנָה!

But isn't it taught in a *baraita*: **From where** is it derived **that no** sacrifice **shall precede the daily morning offering? The verse states:** "And the fire on the altar shall be kept burning on it, it shall not be extinguished; and the priest shall kindle wood upon it every morning, and **he shall prepare the burnt-offering upon it** and shall cause the fats of the peace-offerings to go up in smoke upon it" (Leviticus 6:5). **And Rava says: "The burnt-offering,"** with the definite article, is referring to **the first burnt-offering,**[H] i.e., the daily morning offering, which is first both chronologically and in terms of importance.

אֲמַר לֵיהּ: אֲנָא מֵ״אֲשֶׁר יְכַפֶּר בּוֹ״ נָפְקָא לֵיהּ, וַעֲדַיִין לֹא כִּיפֵּר.

Rava **said to him:** I do not hold that the *tanna* derives this *halakha* from the wording of: "Besides the ram of the atonement," but **I** hold that the *tanna* **derives it from** the phrase in the same verse: **"Whereby atonement shall be made for him"** (Numbers 5:8), which is written in the future tense, indicating that he will achieve atonement in the future by bringing the ram of atonement, **but** as of now, when he is giving payment for the robbery, the offering **did not yet atone** for his sin.

״נָתַן לוֹ אֶת הַקֶּרֶן״ וכו׳. תָּנוּ רַבָּנַן: מִנַּיִן שֶׁאִם הֵבִיא מְעִילָתוֹ וְלֹא הֵבִיא אֲשָׁמוֹ, אֲשָׁמוֹ וְלֹא הֵבִיא מְעִילָתוֹ, שֶׁלֹּא יָצָא?

§ The mishna teaches: If **he gave the principal to him** but did not yet give the additional one-fifth payment, his not giving it does not preclude sacrificing the offering. The Gemara now clarifies the source of this *halakha*. **The Sages taught** in a *baraita* on the topic of the guilt-offering brought by one who misuses consecrated property, which is accompanied by repayment of the value of the item and an additional fifth of its value: **From where** is it derived **that if he brought his** payment for his benefit from **misuse** of consecrated property **but did not bring his guilt-offering,**[H] or if he brought **his guilt-offering but did not bring his** payment for his benefit from **misuse**[H] of consecrated property, **that he did not fulfill** his obligation?

תַּלְמוּד לוֹמַר: ״בְּאֵיל הָאָשָׁם וְנִסְלַח לוֹ״.

The *baraita* continues: **The verse states: "With the ram of the guilt-offering [*ha'asham*], and he shall be forgiven"** (Leviticus 5:16). The *baraita* interprets the phrase: "The ram of the guilt-offering," to be referring to two entities: The ram, i.e., the offering, and the payment, represented by the words "the guilt-offering"; this teaches that forgiveness and atonement are achieved only after both the ram of the guilt-offering is sacrificed and the restitution of the monetary payment is given.

וּמִנַּיִן שֶׁאִם הֵבִיא אֲשָׁמוֹ עַד שֶׁלֹּא הֵבִיא מְעִילָתוֹ, שֶׁלֹּא יָצָא? תַּלְמוּד לוֹמַר: ״בְּאֵיל הָאָשָׁם״, הָאָשָׁם בִּכְבָר.

The *baraita* continues: **And from where** is it derived **that if he brought his guilt-offering before bringing his** payment for his benefit from **misuse** of consecrated property **that he did not fulfill** his obligation? **The verse states: "With the ram of the guilt-offering,"** indicating that **the guilt-offering was already** brought.

יָכוֹל כְּשֵׁם שֶׁאַיִל וְאָשָׁם מְעַכְּבִים, כָּךְ חוֹמֶשׁ מְעַכֵּב? תַּלְמוּד לוֹמַר: ״בְּאֵיל הָאָשָׁם וְנִסְלַח לוֹ״, אַיִל וְאָשָׁם מְעַכְּבִים בְּהֶקְדֵּשׁ, וְאֵין חוֹמֶשׁ מְעַכֵּב.

The *baraita* continues: One **might** have thought that **just as the ram and guilt-offering,** i.e., payment, **preclude** his achieving atonement, **so too,** payment of the additional **one-fifth** of the value **precludes** his achieving it. Therefore, **the verse states: "With the ram of the guilt-offering, and he shall be forgiven,"** which teaches that **the ram and guilt-offering,** i.e., payment, **preclude** his achieving atonement **with regard to consecrated** property, **but** the payment of the additional **one-fifth does not preclude** his achieving it.

וְיִלָּמֵד הֶקְדֵּשׁ מֵהֶדְיוֹט וְהֶדְיוֹט מֵהֶקְדֵּשׁ;

The Gemara clarifies: **And let** the *halakha* of misuse of **consecrated** property **be learned from** the *halakha* of **common** money, i.e., payment for robbery of a convert who died without heirs, **and let** the *halakha* of **common** money be learned **from** the *halakha* of misuse of **consecrated** property.

הֶקְדֵּשׁ מֵהֶדְיוֹט – מָה ״אָשָׁם״ דְּהָתָם קֶרֶן, אַף ״אָשָׁם״ דְּהָכָא קֶרֶן, וְהֶדְיוֹט מֵהֶקְדֵּשׁ – מַה הֶקְדֵּשׁ אֵין חוֹמֶשׁ מְעַכֵּב, אַף הֶדְיוֹט נַמִי אֵין חוֹמֶשׁ מְעַכֵּב.

In what manner? The *halakha* of misuse of **consecrated** property can be learned **from** the *halakha* of **common** money as follows: **Just as** the word **"guilt" that is** written **there,** in the context of robbery of a convert, is referring to the **principal,** i.e., the payment itself, **so too,** the word **"guilt" that is** written **here,** in the context of misuse of consecrated property, is referring to the **principal. And** the *halakha* of **common** money can be learned **from** the *halakha* of misuse of **consecrated** property as follows: **Just as** with regard to the *halakha* of misuse of **consecrated** property the additional **one-fifth** payment **does not preclude** his achieving atonement, **so too,** with regard to the *halakha* of **common** money **as well,** the additional **one-fifth** payment **does not preclude** his achieving atonement.

הדרן עלך הגוזל עצים

HALAKHA

He brought his payment for misuse of consecrated property but did not bring his guilt-offering, etc. – **הֵבִיא מְעִילָתוֹ וְלֹא הֵבִיא אֲשָׁמוֹ וכו׳**: One who unwittingly misuses consecrated property must pay the value of the benefit derived plus an additional one-fifth, and must bring a ram having the value of two *sela* and offer it as a guilt-offering, thereby achieving atonement. The payment of the principal and the bringing of the guilt-offering both preclude the achievement of atonement, but the paying of the additional one-fifth does not (Rambam *Sefer Avoda, Hilkhot Me'ila* 1:3–4).

He brought his guilt-offering but did not bring his payment for misuse – **אֲשָׁמוֹ וְלֹא הֵבִיא מְעִילָתוֹ**: One who misuses consecrated property and brings the guilt-offering before paying the monetary value of the benefit derived has not fulfilled his obligation to bring the guilt-offering (Rambam *Sefer Avoda, Hilkhot Me'ila* 1:5).

Summary of **Perek IX**

When a stolen item undergoes an irreversible change while in the possession of the robber, he becomes its owner and is henceforth liable to return only the monetary value it possessed at the time of the robbery. The Gemara concludes, contrary to the opinion of several Sages, that the robber is obligated to return only the stolen item or its monetary value, but is not obligated to give the owner the profits that he accrued while using it during the time it was in his possession.

If during the time the robber possessed the stolen item it underwent a change that is not physically evident, but that reduced or negated its value, such as leavened bread stolen before Passover over which Passover elapsed, rendering it prohibited for any Jew to derive benefit from it, or stolen coins that are taken out of circulation by the government while in the robber's possession, the robber nevertheless fulfills his obligation if he returns the item as is. If the robber is unable to return it, he pays the monetary value of the stolen item at the time of the robbery.

The Gemara rules that skilled workers hired to manufacture or repair an item who ruin it or diverge from the owner's stated desire are considered akin to robbers. Consequently, they acquire the item and incur liability to pay the owner the monetary value of the raw materials he gave to them, at the time that he gave them.

One who robs another person, denies it, and takes a false oath to that effect does not achieve atonement for this sin until he returns the stolen item to the owner, even if that requires great effort. To ease this burden and encourage repentance, the Sages instituted an ordinance whereby a repentant robber may return the stolen item to the owner via an agent of the court or of the owner.

The robber is also obligated to give the owner an additional one-fifth of the value of the stolen item. Failure to pay the additional amount does not preclude atonement, but failure to give the principal does. This one-fifth payment liability is imposed on account of the robber taking a false oath denying culpability. If he subsequently takes additional false oaths denying culpability, he is liable for an additional one-fifth payment for each false oath. Additionally, the robber must bring a guilt-offering, but he cannot achieve atonement by means of the guilt-offering until he has paid the principal to the owner.

If a robber does not remember from whom he robbed and several parties claim to have been the robbery victim, he fulfills his obligation to Heaven only when he pays each of them.

If one robs a convert who then dies without heirs, the robber must pay the value of the stolen item and an additional one-fifth to the priests whose priestly watch is performing the Temple service at the time he ascends to Jerusalem to pay restitution, and only thereafter may he bring his guilt-offering and achieve atonement. He should give both the money and the guilt-offering to the priests serving at that time, but if he gave the money to the priests serving at that time and the guilt-offering to the following priestly watch, he still fulfills his obligation and achieves atonement. By contrast, if he first gave the guilt-offering to the priests serving at that time and then gave the money to the subsequent priestly watch, he does not fulfill his obligation and does not achieve atonement until he returns and gives the money and the guilt-offering in the proper order.

Image **Credits**

All images are copyright © Koren Publishers Jerusalem Ltd., except:

p217 © TruthBeethoven; **p223** right image © Courtesy of Dr. David and Jemima Jeselsohn, Zurich; **p233** © brightasafig; **p238** © Sippel2707; **p245** bottom left © Pseudoanas; **p245** top right image © H. Zell; **p245** middle right image © CTHOE; **p245** bottom right image © H. Zell; **p246** © SERGZEL; **p263** © David Haberlah.

My Notes

My Notes

My Notes

תלמוד בבלי

— מהדורת נאה —

בבא קמא חלק ז

Steinsaltz Center

ירושלים

KOREN

se note that the number ranges that appear at the bottom of each daf of the Vilna pages
ate the corresponding pages of the Koren Talmud Bavli translation and commentary.

תלמוד בבלי

הוצאת קורֵן ירושלים

— מהדורת נאה —

מסכת בבא קמא
דף צג: עד דף קיא.

COMMENTARY BY
Rabbi Adin Even-Israel
Steinsaltz

EDITOR-IN-CHIEF
Rabbi Dr Tzvi Hersh Weinreb

EXECUTIVE EDITOR
Rabbi Joshua Schreier

STEINSALTZ CENTER
KOREN PUBLISHERS JERUSALEM

עין משפט
נר מצוה

א א מיי' פ"ב מהלכות גזילה הלכה יב סמג לאוין סי' קנו קנז טור ש"ע ח"מ סי' שם סעיף ה:
ב ב מיי' שם הל' ז ועי' בהשגות ובמ"מ סמג שם טוש"ע ח"מ סי' שסב סעיף ח:
ג ג מיי' שם טוש"ע שם סעיף ז:
ד ד מיי' שם הלכה א טוש"ע שם סעיף א וסי' שם סעיף ה וסי' שנג סעיף א:
ה ה ו מיי' שם הל' יב סמג שם טוש"ע ח"מ סי' שם סעיף ו:
ו ז מיי' פ"י מהלכות בכורים הלכה ו סמג עשין קמג טוש"ע י"ד סי' שלג סעיף ג:
ז ח מיי' פ"ב מהלכות גזילה ואבידה הל' יב סמג עשין קנז טוש"ע ח"מ סי' שם סעיף ו וע"ש:

הגוזל *עצים ועשאן כלים, צמר ועשאן בגדים – *[א]משלם כשעת הגזלה. [ב]גזל פרה מעוברת וילדה, רחל טעונה וגזזה – משלם דמי פרה העומדת לילד, ודמי רחל העומדת ליגזז. *[ג]גזל פרה ונתעברה אצלו וילדה, רחל ונטענה אצלו וגזזה – משלם כשעת הגזלה. [ד]זה הכלל: *כל הגזלנים משלמין כשעת הגזלה.§ **גמ'** אמרי: עצים ועשאן כלים – אין, שיפן – לא. צמר ועשאן בגדים – אין, ליבנן – לא; ורמינהי: [ה]גזל עצים ושיפן, אבנים וסיתתן, צמר וליבנן, פשתן ונקהו – משלם כשעת הגזלה! אמר אביי: תנא דידן קתני שינוי דרבנן דהדרא, וכל שכן שינוי דאורייתא; עצים ועשאן כלים – בעצים משופין, ומאי נינהו? נסרים, דשינוי דהדר לברייתא הוא, דאי בעי משליף להו. צמר ועשאן בגדים – בצמר טווי, דשינוי דהדר לברייתא הוא, דאי בעי סתר ליה, וכל שכן שינוי דאורייתא; ותנא ברא, שינוי דאורייתא קתני, ושינוי דרבנן לא קתני. רב אשי אמר: [ו]תנא דידן נמי שינוי דאורייתא קתני; עצים ועשאן כלים – בוכאני, דהיינו שיפן. צמר ועשאן בגדים – נמטי, דהיינו שינוי דלא הדר. וליבון מי הוי שינוי? ורמינהי: *[ז]לא הספיק ליתנו לו עד שצבעו – פטור, לבנו ולא צבעו – חייב! אמר אביי, לא קשיא: הא רבי שמעון, הא רבנן; דתניא: גזזו, טוואו וארגו – אין מצטרף, לבנו – רבי שמעון אומר: אין מצטרף, וחכמים אומרים: מצטרף. רבא אמר: הא והא רבי שמעון, ולא קשיא: [ח]הא דנפציה נפוצי, הא דסרקיה סרוקי. רבי חייא בר אבין אמר: הא דחווריה חוורי, הא דכבריה כברויי. השתא (א) יש לומר צבע לרבי שמעון לא הוי שינוי, ליבון הוי שינוי? דתניא: *גזז ראשון ראשון וצבעו, ראשון ראשון וטוואו, ראשון ראשון וארגו – אין מצטרף. רבי שמעון בן יהודה אומר משום ר' שמעון: צבעו – מצטרף! אמר אביי, לא קשיא: הא רבנן אליבא דר"ש, הא ר"ש בן יהודה אליבא דר"ש. רבא אמר: לעולם לא פליגי רבנן עליה דרבי שמעון בן יהודה, ושאני צבע, הואיל ויכול להעבירו ע"י צפון, וכי קתני התם: לא הספיק ליתנו לו עד שצבעו – פטור, ואוקימנא כדברי הכל – בקלא אילן, דלא עבר. אמר אביי: ר' שמעון בן יהודה ובית שמאי ור' אליעזר בן יעקב ור"ש בן אלעזר ורבי ישמעאל, כולהו סבירא להו: שינוי במקומו עומד. רבי שמעון בן יהודה, הא דאמרן. ב"ש מאי היא? דתני': *נתן לה חטין באתננה ועשאן סולת, זיתים – ועשאן שמן, ענבים – ועשאן יין, תני חדא: אסור, ותניא אידך: מותר; ואמר רב יוסף, תני גוריון דמאספורק

הגוזל עצים. תנא דידן תנא שינוי דרבנן. וא"ת: ולרבא, דאית ליה אפילו שינוי החוזר לברייתו הוי דאורייתא, כדפי' ב"מרובה" (לעיל דף סה: ושם) היכי משני מתניתין? כדאביי לא מצי לשנויי, וכרב אשי נמי לא, דרב אשי מוקי לה דוקא בשינוי שאין חוזר! ויש לומר: דהוה משני דמתני' לרבותא נקט עצים משופים ועשאן כלים, לאשמועינן דאפי' שינוי החוזר לברייתו קני. וברייתא קמשמע לן דשינוי בעלמא הוי שינוי, אף על פי שאין שם כלי עליהן.

עצים ועשאן כלים בוכני. דוקא שיפוי כי האי, שנעשה בכך בוכני מועיל, דחשיב שינוי מעשה. וכן (ב) עבדיה נסרים נמי מהני. אבל שיפוי שאין משתנה שמו בכך – לא מהני. וכן אמרינן לקמן (דף צו.): גזל דיקלא וקטליה – לא קני, דיקלא ועבדיה גושי – לא קני, דגושי דדיקלא מקרי. אבל גושי ועבדינהו כשורי – קני, מעיקרא גושי והשתא כשורי.

לא הספיק ליתנו לו עד שצבעו. פירשתי ב"מרובה" (לעיל דף סו.).

טוואו וארגו. וא"ת: ארגו תיפוק ליה משום טוויה! וי"ל: מאי אריגה – תיכי, דכה"ג מפרש בסוף מכילתין (דף קיט:). **הא** דחווריה חוורי והא דכווריה כוורויי. ותרוייהו אליבא דכ"ע, דחווריה חוורי – אפילו לר"ש לא הוי שינוי, וכווריה כוורויי – אפי' לרבנן הוי שינוי. ורבא לא רצה לתרץ כן, דקסבר כווריה כוורויי לא מקרי ליבון אלא לביעה. והא דלא נקט רבי חייא בר אבין הא דנפציה נפוצי הא דכווריה כוורויי, דהא בנפיצה אפילו ר"ש מודה דלא הוי שינוי, כדמוכח במילתיה דרבא – יש לומר: אורחא דמילתא נקט כל חד וחד, דקודם סירוק עושין ניפוץ, ואין משהין זה אחר זה, אלא מיד מסרקין. וקודם כווריה עושין חיוורי. והשתא נפוצי וחיוורי לכ"ע לא הוי שינוי, ובכוורי לכולי עלמא הוי שינוי, ובסירוק פליגי. וי"ס שכתוב בהן במילתיה דרבי חייא בר אבין: "הא והא רבנן". ולגיר' זו צריך לומר דחיוורי נמי פליגי כמו בסרוקי. ותימה: למה לא העמיד תרוייהו ככ"ע, והא – דנפליה נפולי, והא – דכווריה כוורויי? ושמא קסבר רבי חייא בר אבין בדנפולי נמי פליגי.

השתא צבעו לר"ש לא הוי שינוי. לרבא, דשני: הא והא כר"ש, הוי מצי למיפרך מלבנו אצבע.

בקלא אילן דלא עבר. והא דמפליג בין ליבון לצביעה, בצביעה גופא הו"מ לפלוגי בין עוברת לשאין עוברת, אלא דעדיפא ליה לאיפלוגי בין קלא אילן לליבון, דתרוייהו לא הדרי לברייתן. ולרבא, לרבי שמעון עדיף ליבון דלא הדר מצבע דהדר. ורבנן עדיף להו צבע, אע"ג דהדרא – לפי שהוא שינוי מרובה, מליבון, שהוא שינוי מועט אע"ג דלא הדר.

רבי שמעון בן יהודה הא דאמרן. תימה: הא בטוואו וארגו מודה, ולא פליג אלא בצבעו, משום דלא חשיב ליה שינוי, לפי שלא נשתנה גוף הנמר! וי"ל: דלאו דוקא אמרו דבר אחד, אלא כלומר בשיטה אחת הן. וכה"ג איכא בכמה דוכתי.

הגוזל עצים. משלם כשעת הגזילה. דמי עצים וצמר, ואין חייב להחזיר לו כלים, דקני בשינוי. ודמי רחל הטעונה ליגזז. והעודף ששוה עכשיו הולד והגיזה יותר – שלו הוא, דקנינהו בשינוי. **גמ'** שפוי שייף בעצים, וסתיתה באבנים, ושניהן לשון תיקון, שמתקנן ומחליקן. ונקהו. מן הנעורת. משלם כשעת הגזלה. ומתניתין אמאי נקט כלים ובגדים? הא אינו חוקקם עד שישפם תחלה. וכן צמר, מלבנו תחילה, ואחרי כן טוווהו, ומשעת שפוי וליבון קנה מיד, ולמה לי כולי האי? ה"ג: אמר אביי תנא דידן תני שינוי דרבנן. עצים ועשאן כלים – בעצים משופים, ומאי נינהו כו'. וכ"ש שינוי דאורייתא. כלומר, להכי נקט כלים, לאשמועינן דהני עצים דקתני – בנסרים משופים עסקינן, ועשאן תיבות וקתדראות, דהוי שינוי קל שחוזר לברייתו, דאי בעי משליף ומנתק הנסרים זו מזו והרי הן נסרים כבתחילה, ואפי' הכי קני. וכ"ש עצים ושיפן, דהוי שינוי גמור, ומדאורייתא קני, כדאמר ב"מרובה" (לעיל דף סו.): שינוי קונה – כתיבא ותניא, "והשיב את הגזלה", מה תלמוד לומר "אשר גזל"? אם כעין שגזל – יחזיר, ואם לאו – דמי בעלמא בעי לשלומי. צמר ועשאן בגדים. להכי לא נקט ליבנו, דלא תבעי' למר וליבנו, דשינוי שאין חוזר הוא, אלא אפילו גזל צמר טווי וארגו, דהדר לברייתו, דאי בעי סתר לה והוי חוטין כמעיקרא – אפי' הכי קני. נמי שינוי דאורייתא. דלא הדר, קתני דקני, אבל שינוי דרבנן – לא קני. ודקשיא לך: משיפוי וליבון הוא דקנה, וכלים ובגדים למה לי? הכי נמי קאמר. כלים בוכאני. לכתוש, דהיינו שיפן, וליכא חקיקה. בגדים נמטי = פלטי"ר בלע"ז, דאין מלבנים אותו הצמר. אבל היכא דלבנן – קני"ש. נמטי. אין הצמר חוזר עוד לברייתו להיות כל נימא ונימא בפני עצמה. לא הספיק ליתנו. לראשית הגז לכהן, עד שצבעו. פטור. דקנייה בשינוי, ודמים נמי לא משלם – דלאו גזל גמור הוא, דלא מטא לידיה. אין מצטרף. דתנן בשחיטת חולין: חמש רחלות גוזזות כל אחת מנה ופרס – חייבות בראשית הגז. וראשית הגז מהו? הגוזז רחל, לאחר שגוזזה נותן מן הגיזה לכהן לפי מה שירצה, ובלבד שתהא נתינה חשובה. וקתני דאם גזז אחת *ולבעה, וכן שניה, וכן שלישית – אין מצטרפות למנה ופרס להתחייב, דקננהו בשינוי. נפציה. ביד, ירפי"ר בלע"ז. ולא הוי שינוי כולי האי. סרקיה. במסרק. דכבריה. בגפרית, להתלבן יפה. גזז ראשון ראשון וצבעו. לבד, או שגזז ראשון ראשון וטוואו, וכל שעה כשהוא גוזז היה משנהו. צפון = סיו"ן. אבל ליבון לא הדר לברייתו. קלא אילן. דומה לתכלת. במקומו עומד. אין זו מרשות בעלים הראשונים, ואפילו נשתנה. אסור. למזבח. מאספורק

הגהות הב"ח
(א) גמ' השתא (יש לומר). תא"מ ונ"ב התוס' לא גרסי ליה: (ב) תוס' ד"ה עצים וכו' וכן כשורא ועבדיה נסרים:

מסורת הש"ס
לעיל סו. [תמורה ו.]
[לקמן לה:]
[פסחים לב. לקמן קג. מג.]
לעיל סו. [לקמן לד: קלה.]
[עי' תוספות לעיל ס לא]
[נ"ל וטוואה מסכי']
לעיל סה: תמורה ל.

199–201

דְּמֵאַסְפּוּרַק: בֵּית שַׁמַּאי אוֹסְרִין, וּב"ה מַתִּירִין. מַאי טַעֲמֵיהּ דְּבֵית שַׁמַּאי? אָמַר קְרָא: °"גַּם שְׁנֵיהֶם" — לְרַבּוֹת שִׁינּוּיֵיהֶם. וּבֵית הִלֵּל? אָמַר קְרָא: "הֵם" — וְלֹא שִׁינּוּיֵיהֶם. וּבֵית שַׁמַּאי, הָא כְּתִיב "הֵם"! הַהוּא מִיבָּעֵי לֵיהּ: "הֵם" — וְלֹא וְלָדוֹתֵיהֶם. וּבֵית הִלֵּל? תַּרְתֵּי שָׁמְעַתְּ מִינַּהּ: "הֵם" — וְלֹא שִׁינּוּיֵיהֶם, "הֵם" — וְלֹא וְלָדוֹתֵיהֶם. וּבֵית הִלֵּל נַמִי, הָכְתִיב "גַּם"! "גַּם" לְב"ה קַשְׁיָא. רַבִּי אֱלִיעֶזֶר בֶּן יַעֲקֹב מַאי הִיא? דְּתַנְיָא, *ר' אֱלִיעֶזֶר בֶּן יַעֲקֹב אוֹמֵר: הֲרֵי שֶׁגָּזַל סְאָה שֶׁל חִטִּין, טְחָנָהּ, לָשָׁהּ וַאֲפָאָהּ וְהִפְרִישׁ מִמֶּנָּה חַלָּה, כֵּיצַד מְבָרֵךְ? [א]אֵין זֶה מְבָרֵךְ אֶלָּא מְנָאֵץ, וְעַל זֶה נֶאֱמַר: °"בּוֹצֵעַ בֵּרֵךְ נִאֵץ ה'". ר' שִׁמְעוֹן בֶּן אֶלְעָזָר מַאי הִיא? דְּתַנְיָא, כְּלָל זֶה אָמַר ר' שִׁמְעוֹן בֶּן אֶלְעָזָר: כָּל שֶׁבַח שֶׁהִשְׁבִּיחַ גַּזְלָן — יָדוֹ עַל הָעֶלְיוֹנָה, רָצָה — נוֹטֵל שִׁבְחוֹ, רָצָה — אוֹמֵר לוֹ "הֲרֵי שֶׁלְּךָ לְפָנֶיךָ". מַאי קָאָמַר? אָמַר רַב שֵׁשֶׁת, ה"ק: [ב]הִשְׁבִּיחָהּ — נוֹטֵל שִׁבְחוֹ, כָּחַשׁ — אוֹמֵר לוֹ "הֲרֵי שֶׁלְּךָ לְפָנֶיךָ", דְּשִׁינּוּי בִּמְקוֹמוֹ עוֹמֵד. אִי הָכִי, אֲפִילּוּ הִשְׁבִּיחַ נַמִי! אָמְרִי: [ג]מִפְּנֵי תַּקָּנַת הַשָּׁבִים. ר' יִשְׁמָעֵאל מַאי הִיא? דְּתַנְיָא:* [ד]מִצְוַת פֵּאָה לְהַפְרִישׁ מִן הַקָּמָה, לֹא הִפְרִישׁ מִן הַקָּמָה — מַפְרִישׁ מִן הָעוֹמָרִים, לֹא הִפְרִישׁ מִן הָעוֹמָרִים — מַפְרִישׁ מִן הַכְּרִי עַד שֶׁלֹּא מֵרְחוֹ, מֵרְחוֹ — מְעַשֵּׂר וְנוֹתֵן לוֹ; מִשּׁוּם ר' יִשְׁמָעֵאל אָמְרוּ: [ה]אַף מַפְרִישׁ מִן הָעִיסָּה וְנוֹתֵן לוֹ. א"ל רַב פַּפָּא לְאַבָּיֵי: אִיכְפַּל כָּל הָנֵי תַּנָּאֵי לְאַשְׁמוֹעִינַן כְּב"ש? א"ל, הָכִי קָאָמְרִי: *לֹא נֶחְלְקוּ בֵּית שַׁמַּאי וּב"ה בְּדָבָר זֶה. אָמַר רָבָא: מִמַּאי? דִּלְמָא עַד כָּאן לָא קָאָמַר רַבִּי שִׁמְעוֹן בֶּן יְהוּדָה הָתָם — אֶלָּא בְּצֶבַע, הוֹאִיל וְיָכוֹל לְהַעֲבִירוֹ עַל יְדֵי צָפוֹן; וְעַד כָּאן לָא קָאָמְרִי ב"ש הָתָם — אֶלָּא לְגָבוֹהַּ, מִשּׁוּם דְּאִימְאִיס; וְעַד כָּאן לָא קָאָמַר ר' אֱלִיעֶזֶר בֶּן יַעֲקֹב הָתָם — אֶלָּא לְעִנְיַן בְּרָכָה, מִשּׁוּם *דַּהֲוָה לֵיהּ מִצְוָה הַבָּאָה בַּעֲבֵירָה; וְעַד כָּאן לָא קָאָמַר ר"ש בֶּן אֶלְעָזָר הָתָם — אֶלָּא בְּהַכְחָשָׁה דְּהָדַר; וְעַד כָּאן לָא קָאָמַר ר' יִשְׁמָעֵאל הָתָם — אֶלָּא לְעִנְיַן פֵּאָה, מִשּׁוּם דִּכְתִיב °"תַּעֲזוֹב" יְתֵירָא! וְכִי תֵּימָא, לִיגְמַר מִינֵּיהּ — מַתְּנוֹת עֲנִיִּים שָׁאנֵי, כִּדְבָעֵי ר' יוֹנָתָן; דְּבָעֵי ר' יוֹנָתָן: מַאי טַעְמָא דְּר' יִשְׁמָעֵאל? מִשּׁוּם דְּקָסָבַר שִׁינּוּי אֵינוֹ קוֹנֶה, אוֹ דִּלְמָא בְּעָלְמָא קָסָבַר שִׁינּוּי קוֹנֶה, וְהָכָא מִשּׁוּם דִּכְתִיב "תַּעֲזוֹב" יְתֵירָא? וְאִם תִּמְצֵי לוֹמַר, טַעְמָא דְּר' יִשְׁמָעֵאל מִשּׁוּם דְּקָסָבַר שִׁינּוּי אֵינוֹ קוֹנֶה, "תַּעֲזוֹב" יְתֵירָא דִּכְתַב רַחֲמָנָא לָמָּה לִי? וְתוּ, לְרַבָּנַן "תַּעֲזוֹב" יְתֵירָא דִּכְתַב רַחֲמָנָא לָמָּה לִי? מִבְּעֵי לֵיהּ לְכִדְתַנְיָא: *הַמַּפְקִיר כַּרְמוֹ, וְהִשְׁכִּים לַבֹּקֶר וּבְצָרוֹ — חַיָּיב בְּפֶרֶט וּבְעוֹלֵלוֹת וּבְשִׁכְחָה וּבְפֵאָה, וּפָטוּר מִן הַמַּעֲשֵׂר. אָמַר רַב יְהוּדָה אָמַר שְׁמוּאֵל: הֲלָכָה כְּרַבִּי שִׁמְעוֹן בֶּן אֶלְעָזָר. וּמִי אָמַר שְׁמוּאֵל הָכִי? *וְהָאָמַר שְׁמוּאֵל: אֵין שָׁמִין לֹא לְגַנָּב וְלֹא לְגַזְלָן אֶלָּא לְנִזָּקִין! בִּשְׁלָמָא לְרָבָא, דְּאָמַר: כִּי קָאָמַר ר' שִׁמְעוֹן בֶּן אֶלְעָזָר הָתָם בְּהַכְחָשָׁה דְּהָדַר — לָא קַשְׁיָא, כִּי קָאָמַר הֲלָכָה כְּרַבִּי שִׁמְעוֹן בֶּן אֶלְעָזָר דְּשִׁינּוּי בִּמְקוֹמוֹ עוֹמֵד — בְּהַכְחָשָׁה דְּהָדַר, וְכִי קָאָמַר שְׁמוּאֵל הָתָם: אֵין שָׁמִין לֹא לְגַנָּב וְלֹא לְגַזְלָן אֶלָּא לְנִזָּקִין — בְּהַכְחָשָׁה דְּלָא הָדַר; אֶלָּא לְאַבָּיֵי, דְּאָמַר: כִּי קָאָמַר רשב"א — בְּהַכְחָשָׁה דְּלָא הָדַר קָאָמַר, מַאי אִיכָּא לְמֵימַר? אַבָּיֵי מַתְנֵי הָכִי, אָמַר רַב יְהוּדָה אָמַר שְׁמוּאֵל:
אָמְרוּ

רש"י

מֵאַסְפּוּרַק. שֵׁם מָקוֹם. **בּוֹצֵעַ בֵּרֵךְ.** גּוֹזֵל וּמְבָרֵךְ. בּוֹצֵעַ = כְּמוֹ "כָּל בּוֹצֵעַ בָּצַע" (משלי א). **מַאי קָאָמַר.** אַיְּירֵי בְּשִׁבְחָה, וְקָתָנֵי: "הֲרֵי שֶׁלְּךָ לְפָנֶיךָ", וְהַאי לִישָּׁנָא לָא שַׁיָּיךְ לְמֵימַר אֶלָּא בְּדָבָר שֶׁכִּיחֵשׁ מִקַּדְמוּתוֹ, שֶׁאָמַר לוֹ: טְלֶנּוּ כְּמוֹת שֶׁהוּא כָּחוּשׁ. **מִצְוַת פֵּאָה לְהַפְרִישׁ מִן הַקָּמָה.** דִּכְתִיב: "לֹא תְכַלֶּה פְּאַת שָׂדְךָ לִקְצוֹר" (ויקרא יט). **מֵרְחוֹ.** מַחֲלִיק אֶת הַכְּרִי בְּרַחַת. וּמִירוּחַ הָוֵי גְּמַר מְלָאכָה לְמַעֲשֵׂר, הִלְכָּךְ מְעַשֵּׂר כָּל מַעַשְׂרוֹתָיו תְּחִלָּה, וְאַחַר כָּךְ נוֹתֵן לוֹ פֵּאָה, כְּדֵי שֶׁלֹּא יַפְסִיד עָנִי. שֶׁאִילּוּ הָיָה נוֹתְנוֹ קוֹדֶם מֵירוּחַ, אַע"פ שֶׁעָנִי מְמָרֵחַ לֶקֶט שִׁכְחָה וּפֵאָה הַרְבֵּה וְעוֹשֶׂה מֵהֶן כְּרִי — פָּטוּר מִן הַמַּעֲשֵׂר, שֶׁהֲרֵי הֶפְקֵר הוּא, אֲבָל עֲכָשָׁיו שֶׁנִּתְמָרֵחַ בְּיַד בַּעַל הַבַּיִת — נִתְחַיֵּיב בְּמַעֲשֵׂר, דְּהָכִי אָמְרִינַן בְּמַסֶּכֶת בְּרָכוֹת (דף מ:): לֶקֶט שִׁכְחָה וּפֵאָה שֶׁעֲשָׂאָן בַּגּוֹרֶן הוּקְבְּעוּ. **אַף מַפְרִישׁ מִן הָעִיסָּה** פֵּאָה, אִם לֹא נְתָנָהּ כְּבָר. וְאִילּוּ לְת"ק, מִן הָעִיסָּה — לֹא, דְּקַנְיָיהּ בְּשִׁינּוּי, וְהָוֵי מָמוֹן שֶׁאֵין לוֹ תּוֹבְעִים. דְּעַד הַשְׁתָּא דִּישָׁהּ לָאו שִׁינּוּי הוּא, דְּאוֹכֶל הוּא כְּמוֹ שֶׁהָיָה. **אִיכְפַּל תַּנָּאֵי.** טָרְחוּ וְעָמְלוּ וְנִתְקַבְּלוּ לְכָךְ. **בְּהַכְחָשָׁה דַּהֲדַר.** מַפְטִמוֹ וְחוֹזֵר לְקַדְמוּתוֹ. **תַּעֲזוֹב יְתֵירָא.** בִּ"קְדוֹשִׁים תִּהְיוּ" כְּתִיב: "לֹא תְכַלֶּה פְּאַת שָׂדְךָ לִקְצוֹר", וּבְ"שׁוֹר אוֹ כֶשֶׂב" כְּתִיב: "לֹא תְכַלֶּה פְּאַת שָׂדְךָ בְּקוּצְרֶךָ", תְּרֵי קְרָאֵי "תַּעֲזוֹב אוֹתוֹ" לָמָּה לִי? שְׁמַע מִינָּהּ לְאַתּוֹיֵי שִׁינּוּי דְּלָא קָנֵי הָכָא. **תַּעֲזוֹב יְתֵירָא לָמָּה לִי.** הָא בְּעָלְמָא נַמִי לָא קָנֵי שִׁינּוּי! ה"ג וְתוּ לְרַבָּנַן תַּעֲזוֹב יְתֵירָא לָמָּה לִי. **הַמַּפְקִיר וְהִשְׁכִּים לַבֹּקֶר.** קוֹדֶם שֶׁיָּבֹאוּ עֲנִיִּים לְבָצְרָהּ, שֶׁיִּזְכּוּ בַּהֶפְקֵר אִם הָיוּ קוֹדְמִין. פֶּרֶט — בַּכֶּרֶם, וְלֶקֶט — בַּקָּמָה. **חַיָּיב בְּפֶרֶט כו'.** דְּאַע"ג דְּהֶפְקֵר פָּטוּר מִכּוּלָּם, דִּכְתִיב "אַרְצְךָ" "שָׂדְךָ" וְ"כַרְמְךָ", מֵהַנֵּי "תַּעֲזוֹב" יְתֵירָא לְמַעוּטֵי כִּי הַאי גַּוְונָא דְּלָא הָוֵי הֶפְקֵר לִפְטוֹר, וְאַע"ג שֶׁפָּטוּר מִן הַמַּעֲשֵׂר וּבְכָל הָנֵי כְּתִיב "תַּעֲזוֹב" יְתֵירָא: בִּקְדוֹשִׁים כְּתִיב: "כַּרְמְךָ לֹא תְעוֹלֵל וּפֶרֶט" כו', וּבְמִשְׁנֵה תוֹרָה (כד) כְּתִיב: "כִּי תִבְצוֹר כַּרְמְךָ לֹא תְעוֹלֵל" וְכֵן "לֹא תְפָאֵר אַחֲרֶיךָ" דְּהַיְינוּ פֶּרֶט. תְּפָאֵר = אישקודיי"ר. וּפֵאָה נַמִי מֵהָכָא מַשְׁמַע, דְּתָנָא דְּבֵי ר' יִשְׁמָעֵאל (חולין דף קלא.): שֶׁלֹּא תִּטּוֹל תִּפְאַרְתּוֹ מִמֶּנּוּ. שִׁכְחָה כְּתִיב בְּמִשְׁנֵה תוֹרָה (שם): "לֹא תָשׁוּב לְקַחְתּוֹ" וגו'. וּבְאִילָּן כְּתִיב: "לֹא תְפָאֵר אַחֲרֶיךָ", וְאָמַר מָר בְּפֶרֶק י' דְּחוּלִּין (שם): "אַחֲרֶיךָ" — זוֹ שִׁכְחָה. וְלָא בָּעֵי לְמִיהְדַּר וּמִכְתַּב בְּאִילָן "לַגֵּר לַיָּתוֹם", אֶלָּא "לֹא תְפָאֵר אַחֲרֶיךָ" וַאֲנָא יָדַעְנָא דְּלַעֲנִיִּים הוּא כִּדְאַשְׁכַּחַן בָּעֳמָרִים. אֲבָל בְּמַעֲשֵׂר לָא כְּתִיב "תַּעֲזוֹב" יְתֵירָא. **אֵין שָׁמִין.** בְּפֶרֶק רִאשׁוֹן (דף יא.) גַּבֵּי בְּעָלִים מְטַפְּלִין בִּנְבֵלָה, אָמַר שְׁמוּאֵל דְּלִנְזָקִין הוּא דְּשָׁמִין אֶת הַנְּבֵלָה לַנִּיזָּק, וּמוֹסִיף עָלֶיהָ מַזִּיק עַד שֶׁמַּשְׁלִים לוֹ נִזְקוֹ. אֲבָל גַּנָּב וְגַזְלָן שֶׁנָּטְלוּ בְּהֵמָה וּמֵתָה אוֹ כָּחֲשָׁה — אֵין שָׁמִין אֶת הַנְּבֵלָה, אֶלָּא שֶׁלָּהֶם תְּהֵא, וְהֵם יְשַׁלְּמוּ בְּהֵמָה מַעֲלְיָא. אַלְמָא: שִׁינּוּי קָנֵי. **פְּלוּגְתָּא** דְּאַבַּיֵי וְרָבָא לְעֵיל בִּשְׁמַעְתִּין. **בְּהַכְחָשָׁה דְּלָא הָדַר.** כְּגוֹן מֵתָה אוֹ נִשְׁבְּרָה רַגְלָהּ.
אָמְרוּ

תוספות

וְאָפָאָה (והרים) [והפריש] ממנה חלה. משעת גלגול מתחייב בחלה. אלא רבותא קמ"ל, דאע"פ שעשה כל השינויים הללו אין אלא מנאץ. א"נ, משום דהיכא דאין תחילתו עיסה אין מתחייב בחלה עד אחר אפייה, נקטה הכי.

לא הפריש מן הקמה יפריש מן העומרים. אביי לטעמי', דאמר בריש תמורה (ד' ו. ושם ד"ה אמר): כל דאמר רחמנא לא תעביד, אי עביד — מהני. ומפרש התם דטעמא דיפריש מן העומרים — משום "תעזוב" יתירא, דבלא "תעזוב" יתירא לא היה מיחייב, דכיון דעבר על "לא תכלה" הוה אמינא דאהני ופטור. ולהכי אצטריך אביי בשמעתין ע"כ לר' ישמעאל למימר שינוי במקומה עומדת. אבל לרבא, דאמר התם: כל דאמר רחמנא לא תעביד, כי עביד לא מהני — בלא "תעזוב" יתירא מפריש מן העומרין, ולא מבעי ליה "תעזוב" יתירא אלא למפקיר כרמו, או לרבי ישמעאל אי שינוי קונה אצטריך, דמפריש מן העיסה. ואם תאמר: לאביי, דאצטריך "תעזוב" יתירא לחייב מן העומרים, מפקיר כרמו מנליה דחייב בפאה? וי"ל: דתרתי ש"מ. וכן צ"ל לרבא אליבא דרבי ישמעאל, אי סבר רבי ישמעאל דשינוי קונה, ודריש "תעזוב" יתירא לחייב מן העיסה, אם כן המפקיר כרמו מנליה? דמשמע דההיא דרשה אתיא ככ"ע, מדדייק בפרק "בא סימן" (נדה ד' נא. ושם ד"ה מין) דהא דתנן התם: כל שחייב בפאה חייב במעשר — היינו כל מין שחייב בפאה חייב במעשר, דאי לאו הכי, הרי מפקיר כרמו דחייב בפאה ופטור מן המעשר. ומאי ראיה היא? דלמא מתני' כרבי ישמעאל, דמוקי "תעזוב" יתירא לחייב מן העיסה, ולא מייתי למדרש שיתחייב בפאה! אלא ודאי ליכא דפליג אההוא תנא דמפקיר כרמו, ותרתי ש"מ כדפרישית.

מרחו מעשר ונותן לו. ואפילו למאן דאית ליה ברירה, כל זמן שלא הפריש פאה ולא בררה — היה הכל שלו, ונתחייב הכל במעשר, ושוב לא יפטר. ואם תאמר: תרומה נמי, לתני שתורם ונותן לו! ואין לומר דתרומה בלאו הכי יפריש העני, וכל פאה חייבת בתרומה. חדא: דא"כ מקדים מעשר לתרומה גדולה, ועוד, דתנן במסכת תרומות בפ"ק (מ"ה): אין תורמין מן הלקט ומן השכחה כו'. ונראה לפרש: משום דתרומה דבר קל לתרום לא חש להזכיר. ויש מפרשים דלהכי אין תורם — משום דבגורן רגילין לתרום, *כדתנן במסכת מעשר (פ"ג): מלא פירות ממורחין בשדה, מכונסין — אסורים משום גזל, מפוזרין — מותרין משום גזל. בין כך ובין כך חייבין במעשר ופטורין מן התרומה, לפי שאי אפשר לגורן שתעקר אלא אם כן ניטלה תרומה גדולה.
ותנן

עין משפט נר מצוה

ח א מיי' פ"א מהל' ברכות הל' יט ועי"ש בכ"מ סמג עשין כז טוש"ע א"ח סי' קנו סעיף א:

ט ב ג מיי' פ"ב מהל' גזילה ואבידה הל' ב ועיין בהשגות ובמ"מ סמג עשין עג טוש"ע ח"מ סי' שסב סעי' ב:

י ד ה מיי' פ"א מהל' מתנות עניים הל' א והלכה ב:

מסורת הש"ס

תורה אור — דברים כג; תהלים י; ויקרא יט וכג

סנהדרין ו: [ע"ש]

ת. מכות טז: תמורה ו.

מב. קלה. סוכה טו. יבמות כח.]

[ברכות מז: וש"נ]

ת. נדרים מז: חולין תמורה ו. נדה נח.

לעיל יח.

גליון הש"ס

גמ' גם לב"ה קשיא. עיין לעיל דף נד ע"א תוספות ד"ה חמור: **שם** והפריש ממנה חלה. עיין ברכות דף מה ע"א תוס' ד"ה אכל טבל:

[וכדתני בירושלמי במס' מעשרות פ"ג כצ"ל וכן הגיה מהרש"א בסנהדרין פח. ד"ה מרחו]

אָמְרוּ הֲלָכָה כְּרַבִּי שִׁמְעוֹן בֶּן אֶלְעָזָר. וְלֵיהּ לָא סְבִירָא לֵיהּ. א"ר חִיָּיא בַּר אַבָּא אָמַר רַבִּי יוֹחָנָן: דְּבַר תּוֹרָה — גְּזֵילָה הַנִּשְׁתַּנֵּית חוֹזֶרֶת בְּעֵינֶיהָ, *שֶׁנֶּאֱמַר: °"וְהֵשִׁיב אֶת הַגְּזֵלָה אֲשֶׁר גָּזָל", מִכָּל מָקוֹם; וְאִם תֹּאמַר: מִשְׁנָתֵנוּ! אמִשּׁוּם תַּקָּנַת הַשָּׁבִים. וּמִי אָמַר ר' יוֹחָנָן הָכִי? *וְהָאָמַר רַבִּי יוֹחָנָן: הֲלָכָה כִּסְתָם מִשְׁנָה, וּתְנַן: *לֹא הִסְפִּיק לִיתְּנוֹ לוֹ עַד שֶׁצְּבָעוֹ — פָּטוּר! אֲמַר לְהוּ הַהוּא מִדְּרַבָּנַן וְרַבִּי יַעֲקֹב שְׁמֵיהּ: לְדִידִי מִפָּרְשָׁא לִי מִינֵּיהּ דְּרַבִּי יוֹחָנָן — כְּגוֹן שֶׁגָּזַל עֵצִים מְשׁוּפִּין וַעֲשָׂאָן כֵּלִים, בדַּהֲוָה לֵיהּ שִׁינּוּי הַחוֹזֵר לִבְרִיָּיתוֹ.§ *תָּנוּ רַבָּנַן: גהַגַּזְלָנִין דוּמַלְוֵי בְּרִבִּית שֶׁהֶחֱזִירוּ — אֵין מְקַבְּלִין מֵהֶן, וְהַמְקַבֵּל מֵהֶן — אֵין רוּחַ חֲכָמִים נוֹחָה הֵימֶנּוּ. אָמַר רַבִּי יוֹחָנָן: בִּימֵי רַבִּי נִשְׁנֵית מִשְׁנָה זוֹ; דְּתַנְיָא: מַעֲשֶׂה בְּאָדָם אֶחָד שֶׁבִּקֵּשׁ לַעֲשׂוֹת תְּשׁוּבָה, א"ל אִשְׁתּוֹ: רֵיקָה, אִם אַתָּה עוֹשֶׂה תְּשׁוּבָה, אֲפִילּוּ אַבְנֵט אֵינוֹ שֶׁלָּךְ! וְנִמְנַע וְלֹא עָשָׂה תְּשׁוּבָה. בְּאוֹתָהּ שָׁעָה אָמְרוּ: הַגַּזְלָנִין וּמַלְוֵי רִבִּיּוֹת שֶׁהֶחֱזִירוּ — אֵין מְקַבְּלִין מֵהֶם, וְהַמְקַבֵּל מֵהֶם — אֵין רוּחַ חֲכָמִים נוֹחָה הֵימֶנּוּ. מֵיתִיבֵי: *הִנִּיחַ לָהֶם אֲבִיהֶם מָעוֹת שֶׁל רִבִּית, אע"פ שֶׁהֵן יוֹדְעִין שֶׁהֵן רִבִּית — אֵין חַיָּיבִין לְהַחֲזִיר; אִינְהוּ הוּא דְּלָא, הָא אֲבִיהֶם חַיָּיב לְהַחֲזִיר! בְּדִין הוּא דַּאֲבִיהֶם נַמִי אֵינוֹ חַיָּיב לְהַחֲזִיר, וְהָא דְּקָתָנֵי בְּדִידְהוּ — *מִשּׁוּם דְּקָא בָּעֵי לְמִתְנֵי סֵיפָא: הִנִּיחַ לָהֶם אֲבִיהֶם פָּרָה וְטַלִּית וְכָל דָּבָר הַמְסוּיָּים חַיָּיבִין לְהַחֲזִיר מִפְּנֵי כְבוֹד אֲבִיהֶם — תְּנָא רֵישָׁא נַמִי בְּדִידְהוּ. וּמִפְּנֵי כְבוֹד אֲבִיהֶם חַיָּיבִין לְהַחֲזִיר? אִקְרִי כָּאן °"וְנָשִׂיא בְעַמְּךָ לֹא תָאֹר", *הבְּעוֹשֶׂה מַעֲשֵׂה עַמְּךָ! *כִּדְאָמַר רַב פִּנְחָס: בְּשֶׁעָשָׂה תְּשׁוּבָה, הָכָא נַמִי בְּשֶׁעָשָׂה תְּשׁוּבָה. אִי עָשָׂה תְּשׁוּבָה, מַאי בָּעֵי גַּבֵּיהּ? אִיבָּעֵי לֵיהּ לְאַהֲדוּרֵי! שֶׁלֹּא הִסְפִּיק לְהַחֲזִיר עַד שֶׁמֵּת. תָּא שְׁמַע: *הַגַּזְלָנִים וּמַלְוֵי בְּרִבִּית, אע"פ שֶׁגָּבוּ — מַחֲזִירִין; גַּזְלָנִין מַאי "שֶׁגָּבוּ" אִיכָּא? אִי גְּזוּל — גְּזוּל, וְאִי לָא גְּזוּל — לָא גְּזוּל! אֶלָּא אֵימָא: הַגַּזְלָנִין, וּמַאי נִיהוּ? מַלְוֵי רִבִּיּוֹת, אע"פ שֶׁגָּבוּ — מַחֲזִירִין! אָמְרִי: מַחֲזִירִין וְאֵין מְקַבְּלִין מֵהֶם. אֶלָּא לָמָּה מַחֲזִירִין? לָצֵאת יְדֵי שָׁמַיִם. ת"ש: *ההָרוֹעִים, וְהַגַּבָּאִין, וְהַמּוֹכְסִין — תְּשׁוּבָתָן קָשָׁה, וּמַחֲזִירִין לַמַּכִּירִין! אָמְרִי: מַחֲזִירִין וְאֵין מְקַבְּלִין מֵהֶם. וְאֶלָּא לָמָּה מַחֲזִירִין? לָצֵאת יְדֵי שָׁמַיִם. אִי הָכִי, אַמַּאי תְּשׁוּבָתָן קָשָׁה? וְעוֹד, אֵימָא סֵיפָא: *ווְשֶׁאֵין מַכִּירִין — יַעֲשֶׂה בָּהֶן צָרְכֵי צִיבּוּר, וְאָמַר רַב חִסְדָּא: זבּוֹרוֹת, שִׁיחִין וּמְעָרוֹת! אֶלָּא, לָא קַשְׁיָא: כָּאן קוֹדֶם תַּקָּנָה, כָּאן לְאַחַר תַּקָּנָה. וְהָשְׁתָּא דְּאָמַר רַב נַחְמָן: חבְּשֶׁאֵין גְּזֵילָה קַיֶּימֶת, אֲפִילּוּ תֵּימָא אִידִי וְאִידִי לְאַחַר תַּקָּנָה, וְלָא קַשְׁיָא: כָּאן

רש"י

אָמְרוּ הֲלָכָה כְּרַבִּי שִׁמְעוֹן בֶּן אֶלְעָזָר. כְּלוֹמַר, הָכִי קָאָמַר שְׁמוּאֵל: יֵשׁ שֶׁאוֹמֵר הֲלָכָה כְּרַבִּי שִׁמְעוֹן בֶּן אֶלְעָזָר. וְלֵיהּ לָא סְבִירָא לֵיהּ. הַנִּשְׁתַּנֵּית. אע"פ שֶׁנִּשְׁתַּנָּה — חוֹזֶרֶת בְּעֵינֶיהָ כְּמוֹת שֶׁהִיא עַכְשָׁיו, וַאֲפִי' הִשְׁבִּיחָה, דְּשִׁינּוּי לָא קָנֵי. וְא"ת מִשְׁנָתֵנוּ. דְּקָתָנֵי דְּלָא מְשַׁלֵּם כֵּלִים אֶלָּא דְּמֵי עֵצִים, אַלְמָא קָנֵי בְּשִׁינּוּי. עַד שֶׁצְּבָעוֹ פָּטוּר. לְגַמְרֵי. וְהָכָא תַּקָּנַת הַשָּׁבִים לֵיכָּא, וַאֲפִי' הָכִי קָנֵי בְּשִׁינּוּי! מַתְנִיתִין מוֹקֵי לָהּ רַבִּי יוֹחָנָן בְּגוֹזֵל עֵצִים מְשׁוּפִּים כו'. מִשּׁוּם הָכִי קָאָמַר רַבִּי יוֹחָנָן דְּטַעְמָא מִשּׁוּם תַּקָּנַת הַשָּׁבִים הוּא, דְּשִׁינּוּי כִּי הַאי לָאו שִׁינּוּי הוּא. אֵין רוּחַ חֲכָמִים נוֹחָה הֵימֶנּוּ. אֵין רוּחַ חָכְמָה וַחֲסִידוּת בְּקִרְבּוֹ. אֵין חַיָּיבִין לְהַחֲזִיר. דִּכְתִיב: "וְהֵשִׁיב אֶת הַגְּזֵלָה אֲשֶׁר גָּזָל" וְהָנֵי לָא גְּזוּל מִידֵּי, דְּקַנִּינְהוּ בְּשִׁינּוּי רְשׁוּת, וְקָסָבַר: רְשׁוּת (א) יוֹרֵשׁ כִּרְשׁוּת לוֹקֵחַ דָּמֵי. הַמְסוּיָּים. דָּבָר הַנִּיכָּר לָרַבִּים: זוֹ הִיא שֶׁגָּזַל פְּלוֹנִי וְהִנִּיחָהּ לְיוֹרְשָׁיו. בְּעוֹשֶׂה מַעֲשֵׂה עַמְּךָ. וְזֶה לֹא עָשָׂה מַעֲשֶׂה עַמּוֹ, וְאֵינָן חַיָּיבִין בִּכְבוֹדוֹ. רַב פִּנְחָס. בְּ"חוֹמֶר בַּקּוֹדֶשׁ" (חגיגה כו.). וְאִי לָא גְּזוּל לָא גְּזוּל. וְאַמַּאי קָרֵי לְהוּ גַּזְלָנִין? אע"פ שֶׁגָּבוּ. וְכָל שֶׁכֵּן לֹא גָּבוּ, דְּמַקַּרְעִינָא שְׁטָרָא. הָרוֹעִים. גַּזְלָנִים הֵם, לִרְעוֹת בְּהֵמוֹת בִּשְׂדוֹת אֲחֵרִים. גַּבָּאִים. שֶׁל מֶלֶךְ, לִגְבּוֹת כֶּסֶף גּוּלְגָּלְתָּא וְאַרְנוֹנָא, וְשָׁקְלֵי טְפֵי. תְּשׁוּבָתָם קָשָׁה. שֶׁגָּזְלוּ הָרַבִּים, וְאֵין יוֹדְעִים לְמִי לְהַחֲזִיר. וּמַחֲזִירִין לַמַּכִּירִין. לְמִי שֶׁמַּכִּיר שֶׁלּוֹ שֶׁגְּזָלוּהוּ. בּוֹרוֹת שִׁיחִין וּמְעָרוֹת. לְהַכְנִיס בָּהֶן מַיִם לִשְׁתּוֹת, דַּהֲוֵי דָּבָר הַצָּרִיךְ לַכֹּל, וְיֵהָנוּ מֵהֶן הַנִּגְזָלִים. אַלְמָא אַהֲדוּרֵי בָּעֵי. קוֹדֶם תַּקָּנָה. שֶׁבִּימֵי רַבִּי נִשְׁנֵית מִשְׁנָה זוֹ דִּמְחַיֵּיב לְמֶהְדַּר. גְּזֵילָה

תוספות

ותנן לא הספיק ליתנו לו כו'. תימה: דלא מייתי מתני' דבהמה והזקינה עבדים והזקינו — דמשלם כשעת הגזילה, לקמן (דף צו:)! ואפי' ר"מ לא פליג אלא בעבדים. דליכא למימר דלדבריהם דרבנן קאמר להו, כדבעי למימר לקמן (דף צה.), דהא ר"מ אית ליה דשינוי קונה גבי נותן צמר לצבע (לקמן ק:)! ועוד, הא קתני: גזל מטבע ונסדק משלם כשעת הגזילה (לקמן צו:)! וי"ל: דכל הני הוי מלי למימר דהוה סתם ואח"כ מחלוקת, דפליגי לקמן (ק:) ר"מ ור"י בצבעו לו אדום וצבעו שחור. ואע"ג דטעמא דר' יהודה לא משום דסבר שינוי אין קונה, כמו שאפרש לקמן, (ב) מ"מ היינו יכולים לדחות כן. אבל ההיא דלא הספיק ליתנו — אין לדחות, דאפי' הוי סתם בחדא מסכת ומחלוקת במסכת אחריתי, אית ליה לר' יוחנן הלכה כסתם משנה.

בימי רבי נשנית משנה זו. אור"ת: דלא לפניו ולא לאחריו, אלא לדורו דוקא תקן משום מעשה שהיה, ולא לדורות הבאין. דהא מעשים בכל יום שמקבלים מן הגזלנים ודנין דיני גזילות, כי ההוא דגזל פדנא דתורא לקמן (דף צו:), וההוא גרשא דגנב סיפרא (לקמן דף קטו.), וההוא רעיא דבפ"ק דב"מ (דף ה.), ונסכא דרבי אבא (ב"ב דף לג:). ואמר נמי ב"איזהו נשך" (ב"מ דף סא:) דרבית קצוצה יוצאה בדיינין. ולכך לא פריך לקמן אלא מברייתות דהוה שונה ר' חייא שהיה תלמידו של רבי, ולא הקשה ממתני' דקתני: משלם כשעת הגזילה — לפי שהמשניות היו קודם רבי, אלא שרבי סדרם. אבל ברייתות היה שונה ר' חייא מה שהיה מוסיף רבי על המשניות. ור"י אומר: דממתני' לא ה"מ למפרך, דלא תקן רבי דאין מקבלים אלא מאותן בני אדם שרוב עסקם ומחייתם בכך, והיו יזונים בגזל ורבית ומתפרנסים בכך כל ימיהם, כדקתני: הגזלנין ומלוי ברבית, דמשמע שאומנותם בכך, וכן רועים, וכל הנהו דמייתי. אבל ממתניתין לא פריך, שלא עשו תקנה תלקבל מאדם שגוזל ומלוה ברבית באקראי בעלמא. אבל אין לפרש דלהכי לא פריך ממתני' — משום דרבי לא תיקן אלא באותם שעשו תשובה, וברייתא דמוכח מינה מיירי בעבד תשובה, מדקתני: וחייבים להחזיר מפני כבוד אביהם. מכ"מ ההיא דגזלנים ומלוי ברבית לא משמע דאיירי בעבדי תשובה. ועוד שכל אדם יכול להערים שיעשה תשובה ויחזור מעצמו ולא יקבלו ממנו. וכן ההיא ד"כל הכלים" (שבת דף קכג:) דאמר ר' חנינא: בימי נחמיה בן חכליה נשנית משנה זו. וההיא דסוף "אלו מציאות" (ב"מ דף לג:) דקאמר: בימי רבי נשנית משנה זו — הכל מפרש ר"ת דלא נשנית אלא להווא דרא, וכן ההיא דהוריות (דף יג:). ואין להאריך.

הא אביהם חייב להחזיר. ואם תאמר: לצאת ידי שמים קאמר! ויש לומר: דדייק מדנקט לשון "חייבין". דהוה ליה למימר "אין מחזירין" דהוה משמע: הא אביהן — מחזיר, לצאת ידי שמים. **אי** עשה תשובה כו'. וא"ת: ולימא כגון שלא קיבלו ממנו, דאין מקבלין מהם! וי"ל: דאם החזיר ולא קיבלו ממנו — לא מחייבין בנים להחזיר מפני כבוד אביהן, דתו ליכא גנאי. א"נ: בדבר המסוים, ומקבלין מהן מפני כבודו. ומשני: בשלא הספיק להחזיר עד שמת, לפיכך חייבים בנים להחזיר מפני כבוד אביהן, ומקבלין מהן, דלא שייכא תקנה גבי בנים. ועי"ל: מאי בעי גביה — דאיבעי ליה למוכרו או להוציא מתחת ידו, ומדלא חשש לכבודו — א"כ אמאי חייבין בנים להחזיר? וכן צ"ל ב"איזהו נשך" (ב"מ דף סב. ושם ד"ה תנאי), דשם לא יתכן לפרש בע"א. דפריך מהא ברייתא למ"ד רבית קצוצה אין יוצאה בדיינין, דמשמע: הא אביהן חייב להחזיר, ומשני כי הכא. ופריך: אי עבד תשובה מאי בעי גביה? ומאי קושיא? אי רבית קצוצה אין יוצאה בדיינין — אין חייב להחזירה אפילו לצאת ידי שמים. כדמוכח התם, דפריך מההיא דמייתי בסמוך: הגזלנים ומלוי רביות אע"פ שגבו מחזירין, ומשני: תנאי היא, ולא משני בבא לצאת ידי שמים, כדמשני הכא בסמוך. דכיון דדרשינן למיתה ניתן ולא להשבון, או למורא ניתן ולא להשבון — אפי' לצאת ידי שמים לא מחייב. ולא כפי' ריב"ן שפירש: למורא ניתן (ג) — הירא את ה' והחרד מיראתו, ולא להשבון — על פי ב"ד. אלא צ"ל דהכי פריך: מאי בעי גביה — דכיון דלא חשש למוכרה ולהוציאה או להחזירה מפני כבודו, תו לא מחייבי בנים משום כבוד אביהן. **לצאת** ידי שמים. בפרק "איזהו נשך" לא ה"מ לשנויי הכי למ"ד רבית קצוצה אינה יוצאה בדיינין, דלדידיה אפי' לצאת ידי שמים לא מחייב, כדפרישית. וסוגיא דהכא כמ"ד רבית קצוצה יוצאה בדיינין, אלא דתיקנו דאין מקבלין מדרבנן. ולא שייך לשנויי הכא: תנאי היא כדמשני התם, דהנהו תנאי דהתם קדמו.
כאן

עין משפט נר מצוה

יא א מיי' פ"ב מהל' גזלה ואבדה הלכה ב ועיין בהשגות ובמ"מ סמג עשין עג טוש"ע ח"מ סי' שסב סעי' ב:
יב ב מיי' שם הל' י סמג שם טוש"ע ח"מ סי' שם סעי' ה:
יג ג מיי' פ"א מהל' גזלה ואבידה הלכה יג ופ"ד מהל' מלוה ולוה הלכה ה סמג לאוין קנג ועשין עג טוש"ע ח"מ סי' שסו סעי' א:
יד ד מיי' פ"ד מהל' מלוה ולוה הלכה ה סמג לאוין קנג טוש"ע י"ד סי' קסא סעי' ז:
טו ה ו ז טוש"ע ח"מ סי' שסו סעיף ב:
טז ח מיי' פ"א מהל' גזלה ואבדה הל' יג סמג עשין עג טוש"ע ח"מ סי' שסו סעיף א:

הגהות הב"ח

(א) רש"י ד"ה אין חייבין וכו' וקסבר רשות. נ"ב ע"ל בפ' בתרא ריש דף קיב: (ב) תוס' ד"ה ותנן וכו' שאפרש לקמן. נ"ב בדף לה ע"ב בד"ה בשבח לפי פר"ת: (ג) ד"ה אי עשה וכו' כפי' ריב"ן שפירש למורא ניתן לירא את ה' שיש לו להחזיר מיראתו:

ב"מ [מח:] סב. יבמות כב: סנהדרין פה. [ב"ב ד. מכות ח:]

גליון הש"ס

רש"י ד"ה אין רוח חכמים כו' אין רוח חכמה. עי' תוי"ט פ"ג משנה י' דאבות:

מסורת הש"ס

לעיל סז.
[שבת מו. וש"נ]
[חולין קלז. לעיל סו.]
[תוס' שביעית פ"ח]
ב"מ סב. [תוס' ספ"ה] לקמן קיב.
[שבת ל. וש"נ נדרים וש"נ]
שמות כב
חגיגה כו.
ב"מ סב.
[תוספתא דב"מ פ"ה]
ביצה כט. ע"ש

כָּאן בִּגְזֵילָה קַיֶּימֶת. כָּאן בְּשֶׁאֵין גְּזֵילָה קַיֶּימֶת. וְהָא אַבְנֵט, דִּגְזֵילָה קַיֶּימֶת הִיא! מַאי אַבְנֵט? דְּמֵי אַבְנֵט. וְכָל הֵיכָא דִּגְזֵילָה קַיֶּימֶת, לָא עֲבוּד רַבָּנַן תַּקַּנְתָּא? וַהֲרֵי מְרִישׁ דִּגְזֵילָה קַיֶּימֶת הִיא, וּתְנַן: *עַל הַמְּרִישׁ הַגָּזוּל שֶׁבְּנָאוֹ בַּבִּירָה — שֶׁיִּטּוֹל דָּמָיו, מִפְּנֵי תַּקָּנַת הַשָּׁבִים! שָׁאנֵי הָתָם, דְּכֵיוָן דְּאִיכָּא פְּסֵידָא דְבִירָה, שַׁוְיוּהָ רַבָּנַן כִּדְלֵיתָא.§ "גָּזַל פָּרָה מְעוּבֶּרֶת וְיָלְדָה" וכו'.§ *תָּנוּ רַבָּנַן: הַגּוֹזֵל רָחֵל (א) וּגְזָזָהּ, פָּרָה וְיָלְדָה — מְשַׁלֵּם אוֹתָהּ וְאֶת גִּיזּוֹתֶיהָ וְאֶת וְלָדוֹתֶיהָ, דִּבְרֵי רַבִּי מֵאִיר; *ר' יְהוּדָה אוֹמֵר: גְּזֵילָה חוֹזֶרֶת בְּעֵינֶיהָ; רַבִּי שִׁמְעוֹן אוֹמֵר: רוֹאִין אוֹתָהּ כְּאִילּוּ הִיא שׁוּמָא אֶצְלוֹ בְּכֶסֶף. אִיבַּעְיָא לְהוּ: מַאי טַעְמֵיהּ דְּרַבִּי מֵאִיר? (ב) מִשּׁוּם דְּקָסָבַר שִׁינּוּי בִּמְקוֹמוֹ עוֹמֵד, אוֹ דִּילְמָא בְּעָלְמָא שִׁינּוּי קוֹנֶה, וְהָכָא קְנָסָא הוּא דְּקָא קָנֵיס? לְמַאי נָפְקָא מִינָּהּ — לְהֵיכָא דְּכָחֲשָׁא מִכְחַשׁ. תָּא שְׁמַע: *גָּזַל בְּהֵמָה וְהִזְקִינָה, עֲבָדִים וְהִזְקִינוּ — מְשַׁלֵּם כִּשְׁעַת הַגְּזֵילָה. רַבִּי מֵאִיר אוֹמֵר: בַּעֲבָדִים — אוֹמֵר לוֹ "הֲרֵי שֶׁלְּךָ לְפָנֶיךָ". וְאִילּוּ בְּהֵמָה — כִּשְׁעַת הַגְּזֵילָה; וְאִי סָלְקָא דַּעְתָּךְ סָבַר רַבִּי מֵאִיר שִׁינּוּי בִּמְקוֹמוֹ עוֹמֵד, אֲפִי' בְּהֵמָה נַמִי! אֶלָּא לָאו ש"מ: קָסָבַר ר' מֵאִיר שִׁינּוּי קוֹנֶה, וְהָכָא קְנָסָא הוּא דְּקָא קָנֵיס. אָמְרִי, רַבִּי מֵאִיר לְדִבְרֵיהֶם דְּרַבָּנַן קָאָמַר לְהוּ: לְדִידִי שִׁינּוּי אֵין קוֹנֶה, וַאֲפִילּוּ בְּהֵמָה נַמִי, אֶלָּא לְדִידְכוּ דְּאָמְרִיתוּ שִׁינּוּי קוֹנֶה, אוֹדוּ לִי מִיהַת בְּעַבְדָּא דִּכְמִקַּרְקְעֵי דָּמֵי, *וְקַרְקַע אֵינָהּ נִגְזֶלֶת! וְאָמְרֵי לֵיהּ רַבָּנַן: לָא, עַבְדָּא כִּמְטַלְטְלֵי דָּמֵי. ת"ש: *לִצְבּוֹעַ לוֹ אָדוֹם וּצְבָעוֹ שָׁחוֹר, שָׁחוֹר וּצְבָעוֹ אָדוֹם — ר' מֵאִיר אוֹמֵר: נוֹתֵן לוֹ דְּמֵי צַמְרוֹ; דְּמֵי צַמְרוֹ אִין, דְּמֵי צַמְרוֹ וְשִׁבְחוֹ לָא; וְאִי סָלְקָא דַּעְתָּךְ סָבַר רַבִּי מֵאִיר שִׁינּוּי אֵין קוֹנֶה, דְּמֵי צַמְרוֹ וְשִׁבְחוֹ בָּעֵי לְמֵיתַב לֵיהּ! אֶלָּא לָאו ש"מ: קָסָבַר ר"מ שִׁינּוּי קוֹנֶה, וְהָכָא קְנָסָא הוּא דְּקָא קָנֵיס, שְׁמַע מִינָּהּ. אִיכָּא דְּאָמְרִי: הָא לָא אִיבַּעְיָא לָן, מִדְּאַפֵּיךְ רַב וְתָנֵי: גָּזַל *פָּרָה וְהִזְקִינָה, עֲבָדִים וְהִזְקִינוּ — מְשַׁלֵּם כִּשְׁעַת הַגְּזֵילָה, דִּבְרֵי רַבִּי מֵאִיר, וַחֲכָמִים אוֹמְרִים: בַּעֲבָדִים אוֹמֵר לוֹ "הֲרֵי שֶׁלְּךָ לְפָנֶיךָ", וַדַּאי לְרַבִּי מֵאִיר שִׁינּוּי קוֹנֶה, וְהָכָא קְנָסָא הוּא דְּקָא קָנֵיס לֵיהּ. כִּי קָא אִיבַּעְיָא לָן — הָכִי אִיבַּעְיָא לָן: כִּי קָא קָנֵיס בְּמֵזִיד, אֲבָל בְּשׁוֹגֵג לָא קָנֵיס, אוֹ דִּילְמָא אֲפִי' בְּשׁוֹגֵג נַמִי קָנֵיס? תָּא שְׁמַע: *חֲמִשָּׁה גּוֹבִין מִן הַמְּחוֹרָרִין, וְאֵלּוּ הֵן: [א]פֵּירוֹת, [ב]וְשֶׁבַח פֵּירוֹת, [ג]וְהַמְקַבֵּל עָלָיו לָזוּן בֶּן אִשְׁתּוֹ וּבַת אִשְׁתּוֹ, וְגֵט חוֹב שֶׁאֵין בּוֹ אַחֲרָיוּת, וּכְתוּבַּת אִשָּׁה שֶׁאֵין בָּהּ אַחֲרָיוּת; מַאן שָׁמְעַתְּ לֵיהּ דְּאָמַר *אַחֲרָיוּת לָאו טָעוּת סוֹפֵר הוּא? רַבִּי מֵאִיר, וְקָתָנֵי: פֵּירוֹת וְשֶׁבַח פֵּירוֹת; שֶׁבַח פֵּירוֹת הֵיכִי דָּמֵי? [ד]כְּגוֹן שֶׁגָּזַל שָׂדֶה מֵחֲבֵירוֹ וּמְכָרָהּ לְאַחֵר וְהִשְׁבִּיחָהּ, וַהֲרֵי הִיא יוֹצְאָה מִתַּחַת יָדוֹ, כְּשֶׁהוּא גּוֹבֶה —

גּוֹבֶה

גְּזֵילָה קַיֶּימֶת. חַיָּיב לְהַחֲזִירָהּ. וְהָא אַבְנֵט דִּגְזֵילָה קַיֶּימֶת הוּא. וְעָלָיו נִשְׁנֵית תַּקָּנָה שֶׁבִּימֵי רַבִּי שֶׁלֹּא לְהַחֲזִירוֹ. וְעַל הַמְּרִישׁ. מַסֶּכֶת גִּיטִּין. מְרִישׁ = קוֹרָה. מִשּׁוּם פְּסֵידָא דְבִירָה שָׁוְיוּהָ רַבָּנַן כִּדְלֵיתָא. וּמִיהוּ דְּמֵי בָּעֵי לְאַהֲדוּרֵי, הוֹאִיל וּגְזֵילָה קַיֶּימֶת בַּבִּירָה. מְשַׁלֵּם אוֹתָהּ וְאֶת (ג) גִּיזּוֹתֶיהָ. כָּל מַה שֶּׁנָּטַל מִמֶּנָּה, וּמַה שֶּׁהִשְׁבִּיחָה. גְּזֵילָה חוֹזֶרֶת בְּעֵינֶיהָ. כְּמוֹת שֶׁהִיא עַכְשָׁיו רֵיקָנִית יַחֲזִירֶנָּה, וַהֲדַר מְשַׁלֵּם דְּמֵי גִיזּוֹת וְעוּבָּר כְּמוֹ שֶׁהָיָה בִּשְׁעַת הַגְּזֵילָה. וְלֹא שֶׁבַח הַגִּיזָּה שֶׁהִשְׁבִּיחָה אֶצְלוֹ, וְלֹא שֶׁבַח הַוָּלָד, דְּלָא קָנֵיס רַבִּי יְהוּדָה. אֲבָל דָּמִים שֶׁבִּשְׁעַת הַגְּזֵילָה — מְשַׁלֵּם, דְּלֵיכָּא לְמַאן דְּאָמַר כָּל הַגַּזְלָנִים בְּלִיר מִשְּׁעַת הַגְּזֵילָה יְשַׁלְּמוּ. רוֹאִים אוֹתָהּ כְּאִילּוּ הִיא שׁוּמָא אֶצְלוֹ בְּכֶסֶף. מִשְּׁעַת הַגְּזֵילָה, וּמְשַׁלֵּם דָּמִים כִּשְׁעַת הַגְּזֵילָה. וּלְקַמָּן מְפָרֵשׁ בְּמַאי פְּלִיגִי ר' יְהוּדָה וְר"ש. קְנָסָא קָנֵיס. שֶׁלֹּא יְהֵא חוֹטֵא נִשְׂכָּר בַּגְּזֵילָה לִיטּוֹל אֶת הַשֶּׁבַח. וְנָפְקָא מִינָּהּ. לְהֵיכָא דְּלֹא הִשְׁבִּיחָה אֶלָּא כָּחֲשָׁה: אִי אָמְרַתְּ טַעְמָא מִשּׁוּם דְּשִׁינּוּי בִּמְקוֹמוֹ עוֹמֵד — כָּחֲשָׁה נַמִי הָדַר כִּדְאִיתָא הַשְׁתָּא. וְאִי טַעְמָא מִשּׁוּם קְנָס' הוּא, וְשִׁינּוּי קָנֵי — מְשַׁלֵּם כִּדְמֵעִיקָּר' (הֵיכָא דְּלֵיכָּא קְנָסָא. ה"נ אִיכָּא שִׁינּוּי, וּמְשַׁלֵּם כִּמְעִיקָּרָא). וְהִזְקִינָה. דְּאִשְׁתַּנֵּי לִגְרִיעוּתָא, וְהַיְינוּ כָּחֲשָׁה. בַּעֲבָדִים אוֹמֵר לוֹ הֲרֵי שֶׁלְּךָ לְפָנֶיךָ. דְּעַבְדָּא כִּמְקַרְקְעֵי דָּמֵי, וְקַרְקַע הָדְרָא בְּעֵינָהּ וְאֵינָהּ נִגְזֶלֶת לִקְנוֹת לַגַּזְלָן בְּשִׁינּוּי וְלִהְיוֹת בִּרְשׁוּתוֹ. דְּמֵי צַמְרוֹ. כִּדְמֵעִיקָּרָא, וְאַף עַל פִּי דְּמֵהָשְׁתָּא שָׁוֵי טְפֵי לַצְּרִיכִים לֶמֶר אָדוֹם. וְהָכָא קְנָסָא קָא קָנֵיס. בְּמַתְנִי'. וּבְלֶבַע, דְּלָאו גַּזְלָן הוּא וְלָאו חוֹטֵא הוּא — לָא קָנֵיס, דְּהָא שׁוֹגֵג הוּא. מִדְּאַפֵּיךְ רַב. לְקַמָּן בְּפִרְקִין (דף צו:). בְּשׁוֹגֵג. כְּגוֹן לוֹקֵחַ שֶׁלְּקָחָהּ מִגַּזְלָן וְהִשְׁבִּיחָהּ, וְלֹא יָדַע שֶׁהִיא גְּזוּלָה. מִן הַמְּחוֹרָרִין. מִנְּכָסִים בְּנֵי חוֹרִין וְלֹא מִנְּכָסִים מְשׁוּעְבָּדִים. פֵּירוֹת וְשֶׁבַח פֵּירוֹת. תְּנַן בְּמַסֶּכֶת גִּיטִּין (דף מח:): אֵין מוֹצִיאִין לַאֲכִילַת פֵּירוֹת וּלְשֶׁבַח קַרְקָעוֹת מִנְּכָסִים מְשׁוּעְבָּדִים, מִפְּנֵי תִּקּוּן הָעוֹלָם — הֶפְסֵד לָקוֹחוֹת. אֲכִילַת פֵּירוֹת וּשְׁבַח קַרְקָעוֹ' מְפָרֵשׁ לְהוּ בִּ"שְׁנַיִם אוֹחֲזִין" (ב"מ ד' יד:). גֵּט חוֹב. שְׁטַר חוֹב. שֶׁאֵין בּוֹ אַחֲרָיוּת. שֶׁלֹּא שִׁיעְבֵּד לוֹ לֹוֶה בִּשְׁעַת הַלְוָאָה אֶת נְכָסָיו, וְלֹא כָּתַב לוֹ: כָּל נְכָסַי אַחֲרָאִין לָךְ לִפְרוֹעַ מִלְוֶה זֶה. לָאו טָעוּת סוֹפֵר הוּא. וְאֵינוֹ גּוֹבֶה מִנְּכָסִי' מְשׁוּעְבָּדִים. וְלֹא אָמְרִינַן: אֵין לְךָ אָדָם הַמַּלְוֶה מְעוֹתָיו בְּלֹא שִׁעְבּוּד נִכְסֵי לֹוֶה, וְהַסּוֹפֵר טָעָה וְלֹא כָּתַב בּוֹ אַחֲרָיוּת. אֶלָּא דַּוְקָא אָזְלִינַן בָּתַר שְׁטָר. רַבִּי מֵאִיר. בִּ"שְׁנַיִם אוֹחֲזִין" (שם דף יג:): מָצָא שִׁטְרֵי חוֹב אֵין בָּהֶן אַחֲרָיוּת נְכָסִים — יַחֲזִיר, לְפִי שֶׁאֵין ב"ד נִפְרָעִין מֵהֶן. כְּשֶׁהוּא גּוֹבֶה. הַלּוֹקֵחַ חוֹזֵר עַל הַגַּזְלָן, שֶׁהַנִּגְזָל בָּא וְנוֹטֵל שָׂדֵהוּ כְּמוֹת שֶׁהוּא, וְהַלּוֹקֵחַ חוֹזֵר עַל הַגַּזְלָן שֶׁמְּכָרָהּ לוֹ בְּאַחֲרָיוּת.

גּוֹבֶה

כאן בגזילה קיימת. תימה: רועים מאי גזלה קיימת איכא? וי"ל: דאיירי ברועה בהמה של אחרים, וגנב מהן גיזה וחלב. ולאו משום דחשוד להרעות בשדות של אחרים, דכיון שאין הבהמה שלו אין אדם חוטא ולא לו, כדאמר בפרק קמא דבבא מציעא (דף ה:).

*__משלם__ דמי פרה העומדת לילד. (ד) וכל שבח שמשעת גזלה עד שתלד [א] — לגזלן.

חמשה גובין מן המחוררים. אע"ג דתנא מניא — תנא ושייר הנך דתנן ב"הניזקין" (גיטין דף מח: ושם נ:): אין מוציאין למזון האשה והבנות מנכסים משועבדים, מפני תיקון העולם. והתם נמי שייר המקבל עליו לזון בן אשתו ובת אשתו, וגט חוב שאין בו אחריות. ומהכא קשה לשמואל, דאמר בפ"ק דב"מ (דף יג.), אומר היה ר"מ: שטר חוב שאין בו אחריות נכסים — אין גובה לא מנכסים משועבדים ולא מבני חורין. והכא משמע דגבי מבני חורין. ומיהו, בלאו הכי איתותב שמואל התם מברייתא אחריתי. ויש לדחות: דשמואל הוה מפרש שאין בו אחריות — היינו שמפורש שלא קבל עליו אחריות, והא דמוקי לה הכא כר"מ משום דלכאורה כוותיה אתיא.

מאן שמעת ליה דאמר אחריות לאו טעות סופר כו'. וא"ת: [ב] בלאו האי טעמא ה"מ למפרך: מאן שמעת ליה דקנים — ר"מ, וש"מ דבשוגג קנים. ואז לא הוה צריך לאתויי ברייתא, אלא מתני' ד"הניזקין" (גיטין דף מח: ושם) דאין מוציאין לאכילת פירות! וי"ל: דמכח זה לא ה"מ לאוכוחי דאתיא כר"מ, דהא רבי יהודה נמי מצינן למימר דקנים, לרב זביד דאמר דלרבי יהודה שבח שעל גבי הגזילה הוי דנגזל אע"ג דנשתנית ע"י, כגון נטענה או נתעברה אצל גזלן. והאי שבח שהשביח הלוקח היינו נמי שבח שעל גבי הגזלה, ויקנוס בו ר' יהודה כמו בההיא דלקמן (ע"ב) לרב זביד. ואע"ג דכי נוקי לה נמי כרבי יהודה אכתי מצי לאוכוחי, דהשתא ר' יהודה, דלא קנים ליה כולי האי — קנים בשבח זה שע"ג קרקע, ר"מ דקנים טפי — לא כ"ש. מכל מקום טפי ניחא ליה לאוכוחי מר' מאיר גופיה. ר"י.

*__דאתא__ בעל ארעא ושקיל ארעא ושבחא ש"מ בשוגג נמי קנים. ה"מ לשנויי דשבח היתר על היציאה מיירי, דההוא לא הוה קנס, דכיון דקרקע אין נגזלת — ברשותיה דמריה אשבחיה, ולא דמי למטלטלי. ואפילו לשמואל, דאמר בפ"ק דב"מ (דף יד: ושם) דלוקח מגזלן לית ליה שבחא — איכא לאוקמי כגון שקנו מידו, כדאמר התם. אלא דבלאו הכי משני שפיר. [ג] אבל ליכא למימר דסתם שבח משמע הכל, בין כנגד היציאה בין מה שיתר על היציאה. דהא התם גבי פלוגתא דרב ושמואל במוכר שדה לחבירו ונמצאת שאינה שלו, דפליגי אם יש לו שבח אם לאו — היינו ע"כ בשבח היתר על היציאה, דיציאה למה לא יטול מן הנגזל? מי גרע מיורד בשדה חבירו שלא ברשות? ועוד, דעדיפא מיניה משנינן בפ' "מי שמת" (ב"ב דף קנז:): מאי שבח — חצי שבח. ומיהו המקשה ודאי ס"ד דטריף כל השבח אף שכנגד היציאה. ולפי סברתו הא דתניא בפ"ק דב"מ (דף טו.): אם השבח יותר על היציאה נוטל השבח מבעל הקרקע והיציאה מב"ח, ואוקמינן בגזול וגזל — לא אתיא כר' מאיר, דלר"מ אפי' יציאה מנגזל לית ליה, משום דקנים. א"כ יש לחלק: דהתם איירי בלא ידע שהיא גזולה — דבשוגג כי האי לא קנים.

דילמא

מסורת הש"ס

סו: גיטין נה. [עדיות פ"ז מ"ט]

ב"מ מג: ע"ש

תוס' ע"ז ז. ד"ה ר"מ]

לקמן לו: ב"מ ק:

רש"ל מוחק זה

[סוכה ל: לא.]

לקמן ק: וש"נ

גי' רש"ל בהמה

כתובות נה:

[שם וב"ב קסט:]

עין משפט נר מצוה

יז א מיי' פ"ט מהל' גזילה הל' ז ופכ"א מהלכות מלוה הלכה א סמג עשין עג טוש"ע ח"מ סי' שעב סעי' א:

[שייך למתני' בדף לג:]

יח ב מיי' וסמג שם טור ש"ע ח"מ שעג סעי' א וסי' קטו סעי' א:

יט ג מיי' פכ"ג מהל' אישות הלכ' יח סמג עשין מח טוש"ע אה"ע סי' קיד סעיף ד:

כ ד מיי' פ"ט מהלכות גזילה ואבידה הלכה ו סמג עשין עג טוש"ע ח"מ סי' שעג סעיף א:

הגהות הב"ח

(א) גמ' ת"ר הגוזל רחל וגזזה וילדה כצ"ל ותיבת פרה נמחק: (ב) שם משום דקסבר שינוי במקומו עומד. בע"ז מז ע"א משמע דילדה לא מקרי שינוי כלל. (והשאר חסר): (ג) רש"י ד"ה משלם אותה ואת גיזותיה ואת ולדותיה כל כו' כצ"ל: (ד) תוד"ה משלם כו' וכל שבח. וכ"כ האשר"י וע"ש שהאריך:

הגהות הגר"א

[א] תוס' ד"ה משלם כו' לגזלן (רשום קו על תיבת לגזלן). נ"ב לנגזל כצ"ל דלא כרא"ש: [ב] ד"ה מאן כו' וא"ת כו'. נ"ב אבל להרמב"ם ניחא דס"ל דוקא לאחר יאוש לר"י וקרקע אין לה יאוש דר"י ס"ל דשינוי אינו קונה כאן וכמש"ל ק"ב ב וח"ש ת"ש לצבוע כו' ואזלי לשיטתייהו (ועבהגר"א סימן שנ"ד ס"ק א'): [ג] ד"ה דאתא כו' אבל ליכא למימר כו'. נ"ב אבל הרי"ף והרמב"ם מפרשים הכל בשבחא דממילא וניחא דסתם שבח משמע כל השבח ולכן לא פריך לר"י משום דלדידיה לא קני אלא לאחר יאוש בשבחא דממילא כנ"ל:

שייך לע"ב

כא א מיי' פ"ט מהל' גזילה ואבידה הל' ו ז וע"ש וסמג עשין עג טוש"ע ח"מ סימן שע"ג ס"א ובהג"ה:
כב ב ג ד מיי' פ"ב מהל' גזילה ואבידה הל' ו סמג עשין עג טוש"ע ח"מ סי' שסב סעי' ב וסעי' ז:
כג ה מיי' פ"ג מהל' נחלות הל' ד סמג עשין לו טוש"ע ח"מ סי' רעח סעיף ו:
כד ו מיי' פכ"א מהל' מלוה ולוה הל' ז וע"ש סמג עשין לד טוש"ע ח"מ סי' קטו סעיף ה:
כה ז מיי' שם הלכה א טוש"ע שם סעי' א:

גּוֹבֶה אֶת הַקֶּרֶן מִנְּכָסִים מְשׁוּעְבָּדִים וְאֶת הַשֶּׁבַח מִנְּכָסִים בְּנֵי חוֹרִין, דְּאָתָא בַּעַל אַרְעָא וְשָׁקֵיל (א) אַרְעֵיהּ וְשִׁבְחֵיהּ. מַאי לָאו בְּעַם הָאָרֶץ, דְּלָא יָדַע דְּקַרְקַע נִגְזֶלֶת אוֹ אֵינָהּ נִגְזֶלֶת, וַאֲפִי' הָכִי קָאָתֵי בַּעַל קַרְקַע וְשָׁקֵיל לְאַרְעָא וְשִׁבְחָהּ? וּשְׁמַע מִינַּהּ: בְּשׁוֹגֵג נַמִי קָנֵים. אָמְרִי: [א]לָא, בְּלוֹקֵחַ תַּלְמִיד חָכָם וְיָדַע. תָּא שְׁמַע: *לִצְבּוֹעַ לוֹ אָדוֹם וּצְבָעוֹ שָׁחוֹר, שָׁחוֹר וּצְבָעוֹ אָדוֹם — ר' מֵאִיר אוֹמֵר: נוֹתֵן לוֹ דְּמֵי צַמְרוֹ; דְּמֵי צַמְרוֹ — אִין, דְּמֵי צַמְרוֹ וְשִׁבְחוֹ — לָא; וְאִי סָלְקָא דַּעְתָּךְ בְּשׁוֹגֵג נַמִי קָנֵים, דְּמֵי צַמְרוֹ וְשִׁבְחוֹ בָּעֵי לְמֵיתְבָא לֵיהּ! אֶלָּא לָאו שְׁמַע מִינַּהּ: בְּמֵזִיד קָנֵים, בְּשׁוֹגֵג לָא קָנֵים, שְׁמַע מִינַּהּ. § רַבִּי יְהוּדָה אוֹמֵר: גְּזֵילָה חוֹזֶרֶת בְּעֵינֶיהָ; ר"ש אוֹמֵר: רוֹאִין אוֹתָהּ כְּאִילּוּ הִיא שׁוּמָא אֶצְלוֹ בְּכֶסֶף. *מַאי בֵּינַיְיהוּ? אָמַר רַב זְבִיד: בְּשֶׁבַח שֶׁעַל גַּבֵּי גְזֵילָה קָמִיפַּלְגִי, ר' יְהוּדָה סָבַר: דְּנִגְזָל הָוֵי, וְר"ש סָבַר: דְּגַזְלָן הָוֵי. רַב פָּפָּא אָמַר: דְּכ"ע — [ב]שֶׁבַח שֶׁעַל גַּבֵּי גְזֵילָה דְּגַזְלָן הָוֵי, וְהָכָא — לְמֶחֱצָה, לִשְׁלִישׁ וְלִרְבִיעַ קָמִיפַּלְגִי; רַבִּי יְהוּדָה סָבַר: שֶׁבַח שֶׁעַל גַּבֵּי גְזֵילָה [ג]כּוּלֵּיהּ דְּגַזְלָן הָוֵי, וְרַבִּי שִׁמְעוֹן סָבַר: לְמֶחֱצָה, לִשְׁלִישׁ וְלִרְבִיעַ הוּא דְּשָׁקֵיל גַּזְלָן. תְּנַן: *גָּזַל פָּרָה וְנִתְעַבְּרָה אֶצְלוֹ וְיָלְדָה, רָחֵל וְנִטְעֲנָה אֶצְלוֹ וּגְזָזָהּ — מְשַׁלֵּם כִּשְׁעַת הַגְּזֵילָה; יָלְדָה — אִין, לָא יָלְדָה — הָדְרָא בְּעֵינָא. בִּשְׁלָמָא לְרַב זְבִיד דְּאָמַר: שֶׁבַח שֶׁעַל גַּבֵּי גְזֵילָה דְּנִגְזָל הָוֵי לְר' יְהוּדָה, הָא מַנִּי? רַבִּי יְהוּדָה הִיא. אֶלָּא לְרַב פָּפָּא דְּאָמַר דְּגַזְלָן הָוֵי, הָא מַנִּי? לָא רַבִּי יְהוּדָה וְלָא ר"ש! אָמַר לָךְ רַב פָּפָּא: הוּא הַדִּין [ד]אֲפִילּוּ לֹא יָלְדָה נַמִי — כִּשְׁעַת הַגְּזֵילָה הוּא דִּמְשַׁלֵּם, וְהָא דְּקָתָנֵי יָלְדָה — אַיְּידֵי דְּנָסֵיב רֵישָׁא יָלְדָה, נְסֵיב סֵיפָא נַמִי יָלְדָה. תַּנְיָא כְּוָותֵיהּ דְּרַב פָּפָּא, ר' שִׁמְעוֹן אוֹמֵר: רוֹאִין אוֹתָהּ כְּאִילּוּ הִיא שׁוּמָא אֶצְלוֹ בְּכֶסֶף לְמֶחֱצָה, לִשְׁלִישׁ וְלִרְבִיעַ. אָמַר רַב אַשִׁי: כִּי הֲוֵינַן בֵּי רַב כָּהֲנָא, אִיבַּעְיָא לָן: לְר' שִׁמְעוֹן דְּאָמַר: לְמֶחֱצָה, לִשְׁלִישׁ וְלִרְבִיעַ הוּא דְּשָׁקֵיל גַּזְלָן, כִּי מְסַלְּקִינַן לֵיהּ — בִּדְמֵי מְסַלְּקִינַן לֵיהּ, אוֹ דִילְמָא מִבִּשְׂרָא שָׁקוֹל? וּפַשְׁטָנָא מֵהָא *דְּאָמַר רַב נַחְמָן אָמַר שְׁמוּאֵל: שְׁלֹשָׁה שָׁמִין לָהֶן הַשֶּׁבַח וּמַעֲלִין אוֹתָן בְּדָמִים, וְאֵלּוּ הֵן: [ה]בְּכוֹר לַפָּשׁוּט, וּבַעַל חוֹב לַלּוֹקֵחַ, [ו]וּבַעַל חוֹב לַיְּתוֹמִים. אֲמַר לֵיהּ רָבִינָא לְרַב אַשִׁי, מִי אֲמַר שְׁמוּאֵל: בַּעַל חוֹב לַלּוֹקֵחַ יָהֵיב לֵיהּ שֶׁבַח? *וְהָאָמַר שְׁמוּאֵל: [ז]בַּעַל חוֹב גּוֹבֶה אֶת הַשֶּׁבַח! א"ל, לָא קַשְׁיָא: כָּאן בְּשֶׁבַח הַמַּגִּיעַ לִכְתֵפַיִם, וְכָאן בְּשֶׁבַח שֶׁאֵין מַגִּיעַ לִכְתֵפַיִם. אֲמַר לֵיהּ: *וְהָא מַעֲשִׂים בְּכָל יוֹם, וְקָא מַגְבֵּי שְׁמוּאֵל אֲפִי' שֶׁבַח הַמַּגִּיעַ לִכְתֵפַיִם! אֲמַר לֵיהּ, לָא קַשְׁיָא: הָא

רש"י

גּוֹבֶה מִנְּכָסִים מְשׁוּעְבָּדִים. שֶׁהוּא קָדַם, וְהָוְיָא כְּמִלְוֶה בִּשְׁטָר, שֶׁהֲרֵי כָּתַב לוֹ בִּשְׁטַר הַמְּכִירָה שֶׁאִם יִטְרְפוּהָ מִמֶּנּוּ יַחֲזוֹר וְיִגְבֶּה מִנְּכָסָיו. קָנֵים. דְּלֶהְדַּר שֶׁבַח לַנִּגְזָל. צְבָעוֹ. שׁוֹגֵג חֲשִׁיב לֵיהּ, דְּאִיכָּא אִינָשֵׁי טוּבָא דְּלָא יָדְעִי דְּאָסוּר לְשַׁנּוֹת בְּדִבּוּר שֶׁל בַּעַל הַבַּיִת. בְּשֶׁבַח שֶׁעַל גַּבֵּי גְזֵילָה. כְּגוֹן שֶׁהִשְׁבִּיחָהּ אֶצְלוֹ וַעֲדַיִין לֹא נְטָלָהּ הֵימֶנּוּ, כְּגוֹן (ב) רֵיקָנִית וְנִתְעַבְּרָה, אוֹ טְעוּנָה גִּיזָּה. דְּרַבִּי יְהוּדָה סָבַר דְּנִגְזָל הָוֵי. וְהָכִי קָאָמַר רַבִּי יְהוּדָה: גְּזֵלָה חוֹזֶרֶת בְּעֵינֶיהָ לִבְעָלֶיהָ, בֵּין לְשֶׁבַח בֵּין לִגְרִיעוּתָא כְּמוֹ שֶׁהָיְתָה בִּשְׁעַת תְּבִיעָה בְּבֵ"ד הִיא חוֹזֶרֶת. וְהֵיכָא דְּגָרְעָה, כְּגוֹן גְּזָזָהּ וְיָלְדָה — מְשַׁלֵּם פְּחָתָהּ וַדַּאי, דַּהֲדַר קָתָּבַע לֵיהּ נִגְזָל דְּמֵי גִּזִּיזָה וְעוּבָּר שֶׁגָּזַל מִמֶּנּוּ. וּפְלִיגָא אַדְּר' מֵאִיר, דְּאָמַר: כּוּלֵּיהּ שְׁבָחָא יָהֵיב לֵיהּ. וְאַע"ג דְּקָנָה גִּיזָּה וְוָלָד בְּשִׁינּוּי — חָזֵינָא לֵיהּ כְּמַאן דְּכוּלֵּיהּ שְׁבָחָא אַכַּתֵּי עֲלָהּ, כְּמִי שֶׁלֹּא נִגְזְזָה, וּמְשַׁלֵּם כּוּלָּהּ מִשּׁוּם קְנָסָא, וְקָאָמַר לֵיהּ רַבִּי יְהוּדָה: כִּדְאִיתָא הַשְׁתָּא הָדְרָא, וְאִי הֲדַר תָּבַע נַמִי מִינֵּיהּ גִּיזָּה וְוָלָד — יָהֵיב לֵיהּ דְּמֵי דְּמֵעִיקָּר', דְּקָנָה גִּיזָּה וְוָלָד בְּשִׁינּוּי. וְהֵיכָא דַּעֲדַיִין כָּל הַשֶּׁבַח עָלֶיהָ — חוֹזֶרֶת כְּמוֹת שֶׁהִיא. וְאָתָא ר"ש לְמֵימַר: אֲפִילּוּ שְׁבָחָא עֲלֵיהּ נוֹטְלוֹ גַּזְלָן, דְּשִׁינּוּי קוֹנֶה, וְלֹא יְשַׁלֵּם אֶלָּא דָּמִים רִאשׁוֹנִים כְּאִילּוּ הִיא שׁוּמָא אֶצְלוֹ בְּכֶסֶף. דְּכ"ע שֶׁבַח גְּזֵילָה דְּגַזְלָן הָוֵי. וּ"בְעֵינֶיהָ" דְּקָאָמַר ר' יְהוּדָה — כִּדְמֵעִיקָּרָא קָאָמַר. לְמֶחֱצָה לִשְׁלִישׁ כו'. כְּדֶרֶךְ מִנְהַג הַמְּדִינָה לִמְקַבְּלֵי בְּהֵמוֹת לְהַשְׁבִּיחָן לִזְמַן גָּדוֹל כָּזֶה. לֹא ר' יְהוּדָה וְלֹא ר"ש. וְכ"ש דְּכְר"מ לָא מִתּוֹקְמָא, דְּקָתָנֵי רֵישָׁא: גָּזַל פָּרָה מְעוּבֶּרֶת וְיָלְדָה, רָחֵל טְעוּנָה וּגְזָזָהּ — מְשַׁלֵּם דְּמֵי פָּרָה הָעוֹמֶדֶת לֵילֵד כו', וּלְר"מ מְשַׁלֵּם גִּיזּוֹת וּוְלָדוֹת כִּדְהַשְׁתָּא. אַיְּידֵי דְּנָסֵיב רֵישָׁא יָלְדָה. לְאַשְׁמוּעִינַן דְּלָא מְשַׁלֵּם גִּיזּוֹת וּוְלָדוֹת כִּדְהַשְׁתָּא, אֶלָּא דְּמֵי פָּרָה הָעוֹמֶדֶת לֵילֵד — נָקַט נַמִי סֵיפָא יָלְדָה. בְּכוֹר לַפָּשׁוּט. שֶׁהִשְׁבִּיחוּ אֶת הַנְּכָסִים קוֹדֶם חֲלוּקָה, וּבִשְׁעַת חֲלוּקָה נוֹטֵל הַבְּכוֹר פִּי שְׁנַיִם בַּקַּרְקָעוֹת — צָרִיךְ לְהַחֲזִיר לַפָּשׁוּט רְבִיעַ הַשֶּׁבַח שֶׁל חֵלֶק בְּכוֹרָה בְּמָעוֹת, שֶׁאֵין לוֹ לִיטּוֹל פִּי שְׁנַיִם בַּמֶּה שֶׁהִשְׁבִּיחַ זֶה, וְאִם הִשְׁבִּיחַ בְּי"ב זוּז, כְּשֶׁנָּטַל זֶה פִּי שְׁנַיִם בַּקַּרְקַע — נוֹטֵל מִן הַשֶּׁבַח ח' זוּזִים — צָרִיךְ לְהַחֲזִיר לוֹ ב' זוּזִים, וּמַעֲלֶה לוֹ בְּדָמִים. וְאֵין נוֹתֵן לוֹ מִן הַקַּרְקַע, אֶלָּא אִם רָצָה מְסַלְּקוֹ בְּדָמִים וְנוֹתֵן לוֹ שְׁנֵי זוּזִים, וְאֵין יָכוֹל לוֹמַר לוֹ הַפָּשׁוּט: תֵּן לִי קַרְקַע כָּזֶה שָׁוֶה ב' זוּזִים. וּבַעַל חוֹב לַלּוֹקֵחַ. ב"ח הַטּוֹרֵף לָקוֹחוֹת בִּשְׁבִיל חוֹב שֶׁיֵּשׁ לוֹ עַל הַמּוֹכֵר, אֵין לוֹ כֹּחַ בַּמֶּה שֶׁהִשְׁבִּיחַ לוֹקֵחַ. וּמְסַלְּקוֹ ב"ח בְּדָמִים, וְנוֹתֵן לוֹ דְּמֵי שִׁבְחוֹ, וְאֵין נוֹתֵן לוֹ קַרְקַע בְּשִׁיעוּר שִׁבְחוֹ. וּב"ח לַיְּתוֹמִים. ב"ח שֶׁיּוֹרֵד לְנִכְסֵי יְתוֹמִים בִּשְׁבִיל חוֹב אֲבִיהֶן, אֵין לוֹ בַּמֶּה שֶׁהִשְׁבִּיחוּ נְכָסִים לְאַחַר מִיתַת אֲבִיהֶן כְּלוּם, וּמַעֲלֶה לָהֶן לְשִׁבְחָן בְּדָמִים, וְנוֹתֵן מָעוֹת אִם יִרְצֶה. גּוֹבֶה אֶת הַשֶּׁבַח. וְאֵינוֹ מַחֲזִיר לַלּוֹקֵחַ כְּלוּם. הַמַּגִּיעַ לִכְתֵפַיִם. כְּגוֹן תְּבוּאָה שֶׁגָּדְלָה כָּל צָרְכָּהּ — נוֹתְנָהּ לַלּוֹקֵחַ, אוֹ דָּמֶיהָ. לא

תוספות

דילמא בלוקח ת"ח דידע. וא"ת: ואמאי גובה שבח מנכסים בני חורין? דבפ"ק דב"מ (דף טו:) איפליגו בהכיר בה שאין שלו ולקחה, אם מעות מתנה או פקדון, אבל לכ"ע אין לו שבח! וי"ל: דהתם שלא באחריות, והכא באחריות. דבאחריות לא שייך למימר לא מתנה ולא פקדון.

בשבח שעל גבי גזילה קמפלגי דרבי יהודה סבר דנגזל הוי. אבל שבח שלא ע"ג גזילה — הוי דגזלן, או משום דהוי שינוי גמור, או משום תקנת השבים. ואם גזל עצים ועשאן כלים, או אפי' נסרים ועשאן כלים, דהוי שינוי דהדר — שמא מודה ר' יהודה דמשלם כשעת הגזילה, אף על גב דהוי שבח שע"ג הגזילה, דכיון דטרח בהאי שינוי — שייך ביה תקנת השבים. ואף על גב דגבי נתן לצבוע לו אדום וצבעו שחור קאמר רבי יהודה דאם השבח יתר על היציאה כו' — התם דלא נחת בתורת גזילה לא שייך תקנת השבים. וכן צ"ל לרב פפא ע"כ דאמר לרבי יהודה שבח שעל גבי גזילה דגזלן הוי — דהיינו משום תקנת השבים, דהא ס"ל בההיא דלצבוע לו אדום שינוי לא קני, ובההיא לא שייך תקנת השבים כדפי'. [א] והשתא הוי סברא הפוכה דר' יהודה מדר"מ, דבצבע לר"מ שינוי קונה, ובגזלן אין קונה משום דקנים. ולרבי יהודה, בצבע שינוי לא קני, ובגזלן קני, משום תקנת השבים. ור"ת מפרש: דאין אנו צריכים לר' יהודה טעמא דתקנת השבים, אלא סברא דר"י — שינוי קונה. ולרב זביד שבח שלא ע"ג גזילה דלא הדרא הוי דגזלן, אבל שבח שע"ג גזילה, דשינוי דהדר הוא ולא קני — הוי דנגזל. ולרב פפא, אפי' דע"ג גזילה, דשינוי דהדר הוא — קני, והוי דגזלן. והא דלא קני בצבע — לפי שאין מתכוין לקנותו. וכן נראה, דלא צריכי השתא לאוקמא ר"י כב"ש, וא"ש נמי דלא חשיב ר' יהודה לעיל (דף צג:) בהדי הני תנאי דסברי שינוי אין קונה, כי היכי דחשיב ר"ש דלביעא.

מני לא ר' יהודה ולא ר"ש. וא"ת: לעולם ר"ש היא לרב פפא, ונימא הכי: ילדה — אין, לא ילדה — לא, אלא הוי למחצה לשליש ולרביע! וי"ל: דלר"ש אפילו ילדה קאמר דלמחצה ושליש ורביע קשקיל גזלן, דקאי אר"מ דאיירי בילדה.

לר"ש כי מסלק כו'. לא בעי לר' יהודה, כיון דמתקנת השבים מוקמי' לה כולה שבחא ביד גזלן פשיטא דמגופיה שקיל (ג).

שלשה שמין להן השבח. אע"ג דקתני ג' — תנא ושייר *גזלן, ושייר נמי אריס, שאם בא לסלקו מאריסותו — מסלקו מן השבח בדמים.

שבח המגיע לכתפים. כאן פ"ה: כגון תבואה שגדלה כל צרכה. ושאין מגיע לכתפים — שצריכה לקרקע. וקשה, דאם כן לפירושו גבי ב"ח אפי' מתבואה שאין צריכה לקרקע, כדאמר: והא מעשים בכל יום וקמגבי שמואל אפי' בשבח המגיע לכתפים. ובפרק "נערה שנתפתתה" (כתובות דף נ:) משמע דלא גבי ב"ח אלא ממידי דצריכא לקרקע, גבי הא דקאמר: זיל הב ליה מתמרי דעל בודיא. דפריך: לא יהא אלא ב"ח, וכה"ג מי הוי שקיל? אלא: דחזו לבודיא קאמינא. סוף סוף כל העומד ליגזז כגזוז דמי! וי"ל: דשבח המגיע לכתפים קורא דבר שסופו ליתלש ולישא בכתפים, אפי' כגון פגין או בוסר דצריכי לארעא. ור"ת מפרש: דשבח המגיע לכתפים — כגון דבר הבא בטורח. וב"חזקת הבתים" (ב"ב דף מב: ושם ד"ה שבח) מפורש. הא

הגהות הב"ח

(א) גמ' ארעא ושבחא כו' לארעא ושבחא כו' למיתב ליה: (ב) רש"י ד"ה בשבח כו' כגון שגזלה ריקנית כצ"ל: (ג) תוס' סד"ה לר"ש כו' דמגופיה שקיל. עי' באשר"י כתב בהיפך:

הגהות הגר"א

[א] תד"ה בשבח כו' והשתא הוי סברא כו'. נ"ב אבל להרמב"ם ניחא הלוי' לשיטתייהו כנ"ל:

[עי' מ"ש על הגליון תוס' יבמות ג: ד"ה למעוטי]

[לקמן ק: וש"נ]
[ברי"ף וברא"ש במאי קמיפלגי]
לעיל לג:
ב"מ קי:
שם יד: טו. [קי: נב.]
[סוכה מח. כתובות נ: ב"מ טו: קטנ:]

לא יהא לך פרעון אלא מזה. ואי נמי הוו ליה זוזי ללוקח – לא מצי מסלק ליה. מה שהשביח מכר. ושקיל לוקח מחצה או שליש או רביע, וכן יורש. אי נמי כוליה שבחא, כמתניתין, מפני תקנת השבים. כדאמרן לעיל בשמעתא קמייתא. כל זכות שתבא לידו. וכי היכי דגזלן אי אשבח הוה שקיל מחצה או שליש או רביע, הכי נמי כי אשבח לוקח, שקיל מחצה או שליש או רביע, ואליבא דר"ש. וקטליה. קצצו. לא קני. לשלומי דמי, אלא יהיב ליה דיקלא גופיה, דליכא שנוי השם למקנייה. גובי. בלע"ז טרינקיי"ש. קצוצייתא = קורות. הוצי. שנתקן עלה מן השדרה. חופיא. אסקוב"א, שבו מכבדים את הבית. וחולק כל הוצא לשנים, דתו לא הדרא. שרשורא. חבל. *התיומת. כך אומר האמצעי העליון תיומת היא. מאי

הא דמסיק ביה כשיעור ארעא ושבחא, הא דלא מסיק ביה אלא כשיעור ארעא. אמר ליה, *הניחא למאן דאמר: אי אית ליה זוזי ללוקח לא מצי מסלק ליה לבעל חוב – שפיר. אלא למ"ד: אי אית ליה זוזי ללוקח [א]מצי מסלק ליה לבעל חוב, לימא ליה: אי הוו לי זוזי הוה מסלקינא לך מכוליה ארעא, השתא הב לי גריוא דארעא שיעור שבחאי! אמר ליה: הכא במאי עסקינן – [ב]כגון דשויה ניהליה אפותיקי, *דאמר ליה: לא יהא לך פרעון אלא מזה.§ אמר רבא: [ג]גזל והשביח ומכר, וגזל והשביח והוריש – מה שהשביח מכר, מה שהשביח הוריש.§ בעי רבא: השביח לוקח, מהו? בתר דבעיא [ד]הדר פשטה: מה מכר ראשון לשני? כל זכות שתבא לידו.§ בעי רבא: השביח גוי, מהו? א"ל רב אחא מדפתי לרבינא: [ה]תקנתא לגוי ניקו ונעבוד? אמר ליה: לא צריכא, כגון דזבניה לישראל. סוף הבא מחמת גוי הרי הוא כגוי! לא צריכא, כגון דגזל ישראל וזבנה ניהליה והשביחה גוי, והדר גוי וזבנה לישראל, מאי? מי אמרינן: כיון דמעיקרא ישראל והדר ישראל – עבדי רבנן תקנתא, או דלמא כיון דאיכא גוי באמצע – לא עבדו ליה רבנן תקנתא? [ו]תיקו.§ אמר רב פפא: [ז]האי מאן דגזל דיקלא מחבריה וקטליה, אע"ג דשדיא מארעא לארעא דידיה – לא קני, מאי טעמא? מעיקרא דיקלא מיקרי והשתא נמי דיקלא מיקרי; [ח]דיקלא ועביד *גובי – לא קני, השתא מיהת גובי דדיקלא מיקרי; [ט]גובי ועבדינהו כשורי – קני; כשורי [י]רברבי ועבדינהו כשורי זוטרי – לא קני, [כ]עבדינהו קצוצייתא – קני. אמר רבא: [ל]האי מאן דגזל לוליבא ועבדינהו הוצי – קני, דמעיקרא לוליבא מיקרי והשתא הוצי; הוצי ועבדינהו חופיא – קני, מעיקרא הוצי והשתא חופיא; חופיא ועבדיה שרשורא – לא קני, מאי טעמא? דהדר סתר ליה והוי חופיא. *בעי רב פפא: נחלקה התיומת, מהו? תא שמע, דאמר רבי מתון אמר רבי יהושע בן לוי: ניטלה התיומת – פסול; מאי

הא דמסיק ביה שיעור ארעא ושבחא. פירוש: הא דקאמר שמואל ב"ח גובה את השבח, דכיון דמסיק ביה שיעור ארעא ושבחא – גובה את השבח בחנם מן הלקוחות. ונראה דגם מיתמי גבי ב"ח השבח בחנם, ואין נותן דמים, כמו מן הלקוחות. ואע"ג דאין להם על מי לחזור, והוי כמו מתנה דלא גבי מינה ב"ח שבחא, כדמשמע בפ"ק דב"מ (דף טו. ושם ד"ה ב"ח) דדוקא מלקוחות גובה, לפי שכתב לו מוכר ללוקח: "אנא איקום ואשפי ואדכי ואמריק זביני אלין אינון ועמליהון ושבחיהון", אבל מתנה דלא כתב ליה הכי ואין לו על מי לחזור – לא, מכל מקום גובה מן היתומים, משום דכרעיה דאבוהון נינהו, כדמוכח בפרק "יש בכור" (בכורות דף נב.). דתנן: אין הבכור נוטל בראוי ולא בשבח, ולא האשה בכתובתה, ולא הבנות במזונותיהם. ופריך בגמרא: והאמר שמואל ב"ח גובה את השבח! ומשני: מקולי כתובה שנו כאן. ומזונות בנות נמי – תנאי כתובה ככתובה דמי. והתם משבח יתומים מיירי, דאי משבח לקוחות – א"כ מאי איריא דלא טרפי בנות משבח? והא מגוף הקרקע נמי לא טרפי, דאין מוציאין למזון האשה והבנות מנכסים משועבדים! אלא בשבח יתומים מיירי. ודוקא כתובת אשה ומזונות דקילי – לא גבי משבח, אבל שאר ב"ח – גבי. ובקונטרס פירש התם: מזון הבנות – כגון נשא אשה ופסק לזון בתה ה' שנים. ולפירושו אין ראיה, דמלי מיירי שפיר בשבח לקוחות. אבל לא נהירא, דא"כ ה"ל למיתני: ולא בת אשתו למזונות. ועוד: דלא שייך בהו תנאי כתובה. והא דאמר ב"המקבל" (ב"מ דף קי.): יתומים אומרים אנו השבחנו, ואין השבח שלך. משמע דלא גבי משבח יתומים! התם מיירי בשעשה אפותיקי, ואמרי: אנו השבחנו, ותן לנו יציאה כדין היורד לתוך שדה חבירו שלא ברשות. וכן מוקי לה במסקנא בעשאו אפותיקי. וגם בתחילה משמע דמיירי בעשאו אפותיקי, דקאמר: על היתומים להביא ראיה, מ"ט – ארעא כיון דלגוביינא קיימא כמאן דגביא דמיא. ואי לא מיירי דשויה אפותיקי – אמאי הויא בחזקת ב"ח ויתמי נייתו ראיה? אדרבה, ארעא בחזקת יתמי קיימא, דאי בעי מסלקי ליה בזוזי, ועל ב"ח להביא ראיה! אלא ודאי בעשאוהו אפותיקי איירי, וגרע כחו של בעל חוב טפי במה שעשה לו הלוה אפותיקי, דהויא כאחת משדותיו דמשלם יציאה למי שמשבית. ואילו לא עשאו אפותיקי היה גובה הכל מן היתומים בלא פריעת יציאה כמו מלקוחות, כדפירשתי. והשתא מצינו למימר דבלקוחות נמי, אם עשאה אפותיקי יש לו לשלם ללוקח היציאה, אפי' מסיק ביה שיעור ארעא ושבחא. ולמסקנא דמוקי לה הכא בעשאה אפותיקי – לא נחלק עוד בין מסיק ביה שיעור ארעא ולא מסיק, ובטל במסקנא אותו חילוק. דכיון שעשאו אפותיקי משלם יציאה, אע"ג דמסיק שיעור ארעא ושבחא. ומיהו, יש לחלק: דבלקוחות, כיון שיש להם על מי לחזור, היכא דמסיק שיעור ארעא ושבחא – אינו פורע יציאה, אפי' עשאה אפותיקי, דמשום דעשה אפותיקי לא יגרע כח ב"ח בכך, כיון שיש ללוקח על מי לחזור. דדוחק לומר דמסקנא דמוקי לה בעשאה אפותיקי לא צריך למה שהיה מחלק בין מסיק ביה שיעור ארעא ללא מסיק, שהרי כל אלו דברי רב אשי שהיה משיב לרבינא. דבכל הספרים כתוב: אמר ליה הא דמסיק ביה שיעור ארעא כו', א"ל הכא במאי עסקינן דשויה ניהליה אפותיקי. ואין דומה שהיה חוזר מדבריו הראשונים. ומיהו, אור"י לפי הספרים שכתוב בהן: אמר ליה כאן בשבח המגיע לכתפים כאן כו' – אותו תירוץ ודאי לא קאי. ומיהו ברוב הספרים גרסינן: וכי תימא כאן בשבח המגיע לכתפים כו'. **הניחא** למאן דאמר כו'. פלוגתא היא בפרק "מי שהיה נשוי" (כתובות דף נא: ושם) גבי ההוא גברא דהוו מסקי ביה אלפא זוזי. ומאן דאית ליה דלא מצי מסלק ליה היינו רמי בר חמא דסבר התם למימר דהיינו מתניתין. **כל** זכות שתבא לידו. [א] אע"ג דבפ"ק דב"מ (דף טו: ושם) משמע דאפי' לרב, דאמר: יש לו שבח בשלא הכיר בה שאינו שלו ולקחה, היינו מגזלן, אבל נגזל לא יהיב שבח – היינו בקרקע שאין נגזלת, דגזלן גופיה לית ליה שבח. אבל הכא במטלטלין שיש שבח לגזלן מפני תקנת השבים, גם ללוקח ממנו יש לו. **דגזל** דיקלא וקטליה. אע"ג דגזל בהמה וקטלה קני – התם הוי שינוי דמינכר טפי. **נחלקה** התיומת כו'. מלא ר"י בתשובת הגאונים: (א) ניטלה התיומת – אותו הועא העליון בראש הלולב שאין הועא למעלה הימנה, והוא כשני הוצין דבוקין זה בזה, ונקראין תיומת. וכן משמע מתוך ה"ג שרולים לפרש כן. ולדבריהם לא ימצא לנו לולב כשר, כי בטורח נמצאין אותן שיש להם תיומת כזה אפי' אחד בה' מאות. ויש לומר: שאף לדבריהם אין פסול אלא שהיה מתחילה כענין זה, ונחלק, שנשתנה מברייתו. ובקונטרס פירש: נחלקה תיומת – שני עלים עליונים אמצעיים שבהם כלה השדרה, נחלקה זה מזה ונסדקה השדרה עד העלין של מטה מהן. ומתוך פירושו משמע שנסדק השדרה כל כך שנראה העלין העליונים חלוקין ומפוזרין זה מזה. ועוד אור"י: דיש מפרשים שכל עלי הלולב כפולין כל אחד לשנים, ויש בראש הלולב בסוף השדרה ב' עלין יוצאין ממנה שכל אחד כפול לשנים כשאר עלי הלולב, ואותם שנים עלין היוצאין מראש השדרה נקראין תיומת, ואהנהו בעי: נחלקה התיומת מהו? אם נחלקו זה מזה, דהיינו קצת מן השדרה. ומיהו, אין רוב הלולבין נמצאין כענין זה. ומכל מקום יש לומר דבעי דאי משתכח כה"ג תיומת ונחלקה, מהו? **ניטלה** התיומת פסול. נראה לר"י דהא דאמר נקטם ראשו פסול – היינו שנקטמו הרבה מן העלין. תדע דאין לך נקטם יותר מבניטלת התיומת, ומשמע דוקא ניטלה אבל נקטם כשר. ועוד אר"י: דמאי למימר דניטלה אצטריכא ליה, דס"ד דהוי הדר טפי כשניטלה כולה יותר מנקטם.

ועבדיה

כו א ב מיי' פכ"א מהלכות מלוה ולוה הל' ז סמג עשין צ טוש"ע ח"מ סימן קטו סעיף ב:
כז ג ד מיי' פ"ב מהל' גזילה הלכה ד ועיין בהשגות ובמ"מ סמג עשין עג טוש"ע ח"מ סימן שסב סעיף ד:
כח ה מיי' שם הלכה ה טוש"ע שם סעיף ה:
כט ו מיי' שם טוש"ע שם סעי' ו:
ל ז ח ט מיי' שם הלכה יד סמג שם טוש"ע ח"מ סימן שם סעיף ח:
[ב"מ סו:]
לא י כ מיי' שם טוש"ע שם סעיף ט:
לב ל מיי' שם טוש"ע שם סעי' י:

הגהות הב"ח
(א) תוס' ד"ה נחלקה וכו' בתשובות הגאונים נחלקה התיומת:

הגהות הגר"א
[א] תוד"ה כל כו' אע"ג כו'. נ"ב ורי"ף תירץ דשם בשבחא דממילא וכאן מחמת הוצאה ועי' (אולי צ"ל ומתורץ) בזה קושית המ"מ על הרמב"ם מגמ' דכאן וכן ההיא דס"פ המפקיד (ועי' בהגר"א ריש סי' שנ"ד):

[ב"מ טו: קי: ע"ש ועיין תוספות ב"מ לה. ד"ה הניחא]
[בסוכה פי' רש"י פירוש אחר]
פי' חוליות
סוכה לב.

מַאי לָאו הוּא הַדִּין לְנֶחְלְקָה? לָא, נִיטְּלָה שָׁאנֵי, דְּהָא חָסֵר לָהּ. אִיכָּא דְּאָמְרִי: ת"ש, דְּא"ר מָתוּן א"ר יְהוֹשֻׁעַ בֶּן לֵוִי: [א]נֶחְלְקָה הַתִּיוֹמֶת – נַעֲשָׂה כְּמִי שֶׁנִּטְּלָה וּפָסוּל, ש"מ. אָמַר רַב פַּפָּא: [ב]הַאי מַאן דִּגְזַל עַפְרָא מֵחַבְרֵיהּ וַעֲבְדֵיהּ לְבֵינְתָא – לָא קָנֵי, מַאי טַעְמָא? [ג]דְּהָדַר מְשַׁוֵּי לֵיהּ עַפְרָא; [ד]לְבֵינְתָא וַעֲבְדֵיהּ עַפְרָא – קָנֵי. מַאי אָמְרַתְּ? דִּלְמָא הָדַר וְעָבֵיד לֵיהּ לְבֵינְתָא – הַאי לְבֵינְתָא אַחֲרִיתִי הוּא, וּפָנִים חֲדָשׁוֹת בָּאוּ לְכָאן. וְאָמַר רַב פַּפָּא: [ה]הַאי מַאן דִּגְזַל נַסְכָא מֵחַבְרֵיהּ וְעָבֵיד זוּזֵי – לָא קָנֵי, מַאי טַעְמָא? הָדַר עָבֵיד לְהוּ נַסְכָא; [ו]זוּזֵי וַעֲבְדִינְהוּ נַסְכָא – קָנֵי. (א) מַאי אָמְרַתְּ? הָדַר עָבֵיד לְהוּ זוּזֵי – פָּנִים חֲדָשׁוֹת בָּאוּ לְכָאן; [ז]שְׁחִימֵי וַעֲבְדִינְהוּ חֲדַתֵּי – לָא קָנֵי, [ח]חֲדַתֵּי וַעֲבְדִינְהוּ שְׁחִימֵי – קָנֵי. מַאי אָמְרַתְּ? הָדַר עָבֵיד לְהוּ חֲדַתֵּי – *מֵידַע יְדִיעַ שִׁיחֲמַיְיהוּ. § "זֶה הַכְּלָל: כָּל הַגַּזְלָנִין מְשַׁלְּמִין כִּשְׁעַת הַגְּזֵלָה". § (*זֶה הַכְּלָל) לְאֵתוֹיֵי מַאי? לְאֵתוֹיֵי הָא *דְּאָמַר ר' אֶלְעָא: גָּנַב טָלֶה וְנַעֲשָׂה אַיִל, עֵגֶל וְנַעֲשָׂה שׁוֹר – נַעֲשָׂה שִׁינּוּי בְּיָדוֹ וּקְנָאוֹ, טָבַח וּמָכַר – שֶׁלּוֹ הוּא טוֹבֵחַ, שֶׁלּוֹ הוּא מוֹכֵר. הַהוּא גַּבְרָא [ט]דִּגְזַל פַּדְנָא דְּתוֹרֵי מֵחַבְרֵיהּ, אֲזַל כְּרַב בְּהוּ כְּרָבָא, זְרַע בְּהוּ זַרְעָא, לְסוֹף אַהַדְרִינְהוּ לְמָרֵיהּ. אֲתָא לְקַמֵּיהּ דְּרַב נַחְמָן, אֲמַר לְהוּ: זִילוּ שׁוּמוּ שְׁבָחָא דְּאַשְׁבַּח. אֲמַר לֵיהּ רָבָא: תּוֹרֵי אַשְׁבַּח, אַרְעָא לָא אַשְׁבַּח? אֲמַר: מִי קָאָמִינָא נְשַׁיְּימוּ כּוּלֵּיהּ? פַּלְגָא קָאָמִינָא. א"ל: [ט]סוֹף סוֹף גְּזֵילָה הוּא, וְקָא הָדְרָה בְּעֵינָא, דִּתְנַן: *כָּל הַגַּזְלָנִין מְשַׁלְּמִין כִּשְׁעַת הַגְּזֵלָה! אֲמַר לֵיהּ, לָא אָמֵינָא לָךְ: כִּי יָתֵיבְנָא בְּדִינָא לָא תֵּימָא לִי מִידֵּי, דְּאָמַר הוּנָא חַבְרִין עֲלַאי: אֲנָא וְשָׁבוּר מַלְכָּא אַחֵי בְּדִינָא? הַאי אֱינָשׁ גַּזְלָנָא עַתִּיקָא הוּא [י]וּבָעֵינָא דְּאִיקְנְסֵיהּ. § **מתני'** *[כ]גָּזַל בְּהֵמָה וְהִזְקִינָה, עֲבָדִים וְהִזְקִינוּ – מְשַׁלֵּם כִּשְׁעַת הַגְּזֵלָה; רַבִּי מֵאִיר אוֹמֵר: [ל]בַּעֲבָדִים – אוֹמֵר לוֹ "הֲרֵי שֶׁלְּךָ לְפָנֶיךָ". [מ]גָּזַל מַטְבֵּעַ וְנִסְדַּק, פֵּירוֹת וְהִרְקִיבוּ, יַיִן וְהֶחְמִיץ – מְשַׁלֵּם כִּשְׁעַת הַגְּזֵלָה. *[נ]מַטְבֵּעַ וְנִפְסַל, תְּרוּמָה וְנִטְמֵאת, *חָמֵץ וְעָבַר עָלָיו הַפֶּסַח, בְּהֵמָה וְנִתְעַבְּדָה בָּהּ עֲבֵירָה, אוֹ *שֶׁנִּפְסְלָה מֵעַל גַּבֵּי הַמִּזְבֵּחַ, אוֹ שֶׁהָיְתָה יוֹצְאָה לִיסָּקֵל – אוֹמֵר לוֹ "הֲרֵי שֶׁלְּךָ לְפָנֶיךָ". § **גמ'** אָמַר רַב פַּפָּא: לֹא הִזְקִינָה – הִזְקִינָה מַמָּשׁ, אֶלָּא אֲפִי' כָּחֲשָׁה. וְהָא אֲנַן הִזְקִינָה תְּנַן! (ב) כָּחֲשָׁה כְּגוֹן הִזְקִינָה, [ס]דְּלָא הָדַר בָּרְיָא. אֲמַר לֵיהּ מָר קַשִּׁישָׁא בְּרֵיהּ דְּרַב חִסְדָּא לְרַב אַשִׁי, הָכִי קָאָמְרִי מִשְּׁמֵיהּ דְּרַבִּי יוֹחָנָן: אֲפִילּוּ גָּנַב טָלֶה וְנַעֲשָׂה אַיִל, עֵגֶל וְנַעֲשָׂה שׁוֹר – נַעֲשָׂה שִׁינּוּי בְּיָדוֹ וּקְנָאוֹ, טָבַח וּמָכַר – שֶׁלּוֹ הוּא טוֹבֵחַ, שֶׁלּוֹ הוּא מוֹכֵר. אֲמַר לֵיהּ, לָאו אָמֵינָא לָךְ: לָא תַּחֲלִיף גַּבְרֵי? הַהוּא מִשְּׁמֵיהּ דְּרַבִּי אֶלְעָא אִיתְּמַר. § "רַבִּי מֵאִיר אוֹמֵר: בַּעֲבָדִים – אוֹמֵר לוֹ הֲרֵי שֶׁלְּךָ לְפָנֶיךָ". § אָמַר רַב חֲנִינָא בַּר אַבְדִּימִי אָמַר רַב: הֲלָכָה כְּרַבִּי מֵאִיר. וְרַב שָׁבֵיק רַבָּנַן וְעָבֵיד כְּרַבִּי מֵאִיר? אָמְרִי: *מִשּׁוּם דִּבְרַיְיתָא אִיפְּכָא תַּנְיָא. וְרַב שָׁבֵיק מַתְנִיתִין וְעָבֵיד כְּבָרַיְיתָא? רַב, מַתְנִיתִין נַמִי אִיפְּכָא תָּנֵי. וּמַאי (ג) טַעְמֵיהּ דְּרַב דְּאַפֵּיךְ מַתְנִי' מִקַּמֵּי דְּבָרַיְיתָא? אַדְּרַבָּה, נֵיפוֹךְ לְבָרַיְיתָא מִקַּמֵּי מַתְנִיתִין! אָמְרִי: רַב נַמִי מַתְנִיתִין אִיפְּכָא אַתְנְיֵיהּ. וְאִי בָּעֵית אֵימָא: כִּי לָא אַפֵּיךְ – חֲדָא מִקַּמֵּי חֲדָא, *חֲדָא מִקַּמֵּי תַּרְתֵּי אַפֵּיךְ; דְּתַנְיָא: *[ע]הַמַּחֲלִיף פָּרָה בַּחֲמוֹר וְיָלְדָה, וְכֵן הַמּוֹכֵר שִׁפְחָתוֹ וְיָלְדָה, זֶה אוֹמֵר "בִּרְשׁוּתִי יָלְדָה" וְהַלָּה שׁוֹתֵק – זָכָה בָּהּ. [פ]זֶה אוֹמֵר "אֵינִי יוֹדֵעַ" וְזֶה אוֹמֵר "אֵינִי יוֹדֵעַ" – יַחֲלוֹקוּ. [צ]זֶה אוֹמֵר "בִּרְשׁוּתִי" וְזֶה אוֹמֵר "בִּרְשׁוּתִי" – יִשָּׁבַע הַמּוֹכֵר שֶׁבִּרְשׁוּתוֹ יָלְדָה, לְפִי *[ק]שֶׁכָּל הַנִּשְׁבָּעִין שֶׁבַּתּוֹרָה נִשְׁבָּעִין וְלֹא מְשַׁלְּמִין, דִּבְרֵי ר' מֵאִיר; וַחֲכָמִים אוֹמְרִים: [ר]אֵין נִשְׁבָּעִין לֹא עַל הָעֲבָדִים וְלֹא עַל הַקַּרְקָעוֹת. הַאי הֲלָכָה כְּר' מֵאִיר, הֲלָכָה כְּרַבָּנַן מִבְּעֵי לֵיהּ! הָכִי קָאָמַר: לְמַאי דְּאַפְּכִיתוּ וְתָנֵיתוּ, הֲלָכָה כְּרַבִּי מֵאִיר.

וּמִי

מאי לאו ה"ה לנחלקה. וכיון דלענין פסול מפסלא, לענין מקנה נמי שינוי הוא, וקני. **פנים חדשות באו לכאן.** לא זו היא לבינה הראשונה, אלא זו לבינה אחרת, שהוצרך תיקון וגיבול בפני עצמה, ומשונה היא (ד) מהראשונים, דאי אפשר לצמצם או גדולה או קטנה. **נסכא** = פלטא של כסף. **הדר עביד להו נסכא.** אם ירצה, ושינוי החוזר לברייתו הוא. והכא ליכא למימר פנים חדשות – דאין אדם מקפיד על רבועה ותקונה, אלא שתהא חתיכה בעלמא. **שחימי.** שחורין, כעין ישנים. **ועבדיה חדתי.** שליבנה. **לא קני.** שסופן לחזור ליושנן. **נעשה שינוי בידו וקנאו.** *לכך דאם טבח ומכר – שלו הוא טובח ושלו הוא מוכר, ואין משלם אלא כפל. **פדנא.** תרגום של צמד בקר. ופדן ארם על שם ששני ארמים היו, ארם נהריים וארם צובה. **כרבא.** חרישה. **דאמר הונא חברין עלאי דאנא ושבור מלכא.** שמואל אחי בדינא. **מתני' בעבדים אומר לו הרי שלך לפניך.** דכקרקע דמי, וברשותיה דמריה קיימי. **גזל מטבע ונסדק.** שינוי הניכר הוא (ה). **ונעבדה בה עבירה.** נרבעת או נעבדה פסולה לקרבן, כדתניא ב"שור שנגח ארבעה וחמשה" (לעיל דף מ:). **שנפסלה מעל גבי המזבח.** במום (ו) שאין ניכר, כדוקין שבעין. **פטורין.** דכל בהמות לאו למזבח קיימי. **גמ' אלא אפילו כחשה.** דלא הוי שינוי כולי האי, דלא אישתני כולי גופה. **איפכא תניא.** רבי מאיר אומר: כשעת הגזלה, וחכמים אומרים: בעבדים אומר לו "הרי שלך לפניך", וקאמר רב: הלכה כר' מאיר דמתניתין, דהיינו רבנן דברייתא. **איפכא אתנייה.** לתלמידיו. **ואב"א כי לא מפכינא.** מתני' מקמי ברייתא. **חדא מקמי חדא.** אבל חדא משנה מקמי תרתי ברייתא – מפיך. והכא תרתי איכא; חדא – הא דאמרן לעיל ברייתא איפכא תניא, ואידך – הא דתניא כו'. **המחליף כו'.** להכי נקט מחליף גבי בהמה ולא תנא מוכר, כדנקט בשפחה – דבהמה אינה נקנית בכסף עד שימשוך, וכי משך – דבר הנראה לעינים הוא אם ילדה אם לאו, ואין כאן ספק. אבל בחליפין מתוקמא כגון שלא משך בעל החמור את הפרה, אלא בעל הפרה משך את החמור, ונקנית הפרה אל בעל החמור במשיכת החמור בכל מקום שהיא, כדתנן קדושין (ד' כח.): כל הנעשה דמים באחר, כיון שזכה זה – נתחייב זה בחליפיו, ולא ידעינן השתא אי כבר ילדה פרה בשעת משיכת החמור, וברשות מוכר ילדה, או לאחר משיכת החמור וברשות לוקח [ילדה]. **וכן המוכר שפחתו.** עבד כנעני נקנה בכסף, ואע"ג שאין לפנינו בשעת מתן מעות. **והלה שותק.** ברי ושמא ברי עדיף. **ישבע המוכר.** דאיכא הודאה במקצת, ואיכא שבועה דאורייתא, (ז) דקטע לידיה, דאם קתבע ליה האי לוקח "שפחה שלימה יש לי בידך עם ולדה", וזה אומר "אין, שפחה שלימה יש לך בידי אבל לא ולדה", דמודה ליה במקצת, ומשום "הילך" לא מפטר, דהא קטע ידה ולאו "הילך" הוא. והכי מוקי לה ב"השואל". **נשבעין ולא משלמין.** מי שמשביעים אותו ישבע ויפטר, דכתיב (שמות כב): "ולקח בעליו ולא ישלם" – מי שעליו לשלם הוא נשבע, ולא נשבע התובע ויטול. **אין נשבעין.** וברשות מוכר תעמוד עד שיביא לוקח ראיה. אלמא: לרבנן עבדא כמקרקעי דמי. **אין נשבעין על הקרקעות.** בפרק "הזהב" (ב"מ דף נו.). **אי הכי.** דמתניתין נמי בעינן למיתנא איפכא, "הלכה כרבנן" מבעי ליה!

פטור

ועבדיה זוזי לא קני. דוקא עבדיה זוזי, אבל עשה מן הנסכא כלי כגון כוס של כסף – קני, אע"ג דהדר עביד ליה נסכא, דלא גרע מנסרים ועשאן כלים. אבל זוזי ולבינה – אין תורת חשיבות עליהן כ"כ.

המחליף פרה בחמור. אורחא דמילתא נקט, שדרך להחליף פרה בחמור ולמכור שפחה בדמים. אבל אין לפרש דלא מצי למינקט המוכר פרה וילדה, לפי שאין פרה נקנית בכסף אלא במשיכה, ובשעת משיכה רואה אם ילדה אם לאו, אבל שפחה נקנית בכסף, דעבדים הוקשו לקרקעות. דהא רבי מאיר קתני לה, ורבי מאיר לא מקיש, דהא קאמר דנשבעים על העבדים, ועל הקרקעות אית ליה דאין נשבעין, כדמוכח בשבועות (דף מג. ושם) גבי יש דברים שהן כקרקע ואינן כקרקע. וכיון דלא מקיש לענין שבועה – ה"ה לענין קנין, דהא מייתי ראיה הכא משבועה אגזל. ומיהו, קצת יש לחלק, דלענין גזל ושבועה נראה לגמרא להשוות, דתרווייהו נפקי על ידי כלל ופרט: גזל – לקמן בפ' בתרא (דף קיז:), ושבועות – בפרק ["שבועת הדיינים"] (שבועות דף מג:).

והלה שותק זכה בה. למ"ד* דברי ושמא ברי עדיף – ניחא. ולמאן דאמר לא ברי עדיף – אור"י: שהוא מפרש דשתיקה כהודאה דמיא, ולא כאומר "איני יודע".

ומי

עין משפט נר מצוה

לג א מיי' פ"ח מהל' לולב הלכה ד סמג עשין מד טוש"ע א"ח סימן תרמה סעיף ג:

לד ב ג מיי' פ"ב מהל' גזילה ואבידה הל' יא סמג עשין עג טוש"ע ח"מ סימן שס סעיף ה:

לה ד מיי' שם הלכה יב טוש"ע שם סעיף ו:

לו ה מיי' שם הלכה יא טוש"ע שם סעיף ה:

לז ו מיי' שם הלכה יב טוש"ע שם סעיף ו:

לח ז ח מיי' שם הלכה יג טוש"ע שם סעיף ז:

לט ט י מיי' שם פ"ג הלכה ו סמג שם טוש"ע ח"מ סימן שסג סעיף ג:

מ כ ל נ ס מיי' שם הלכה ד טוש"ע שם סעיף א:

מא ע מיי' פ"כ מהל' מכירה הלכה י סמג עשין פב טוש"ע ח"מ סימן רכג סעיף א:

מב פ צ מיי' שם הלכה יא וע"ש טוש"ע שם סעיף ב:

ברא"ש איתא פנים חדשות באו לכאן

[לקמן קיח.]

מג ק מיי' פ"א מהלכות טוען ונטען הלכה ד סמג עשין פה טוש"ע ח"מ סימן פט סעיף א:

מד ר מיי' שם פ"ה הלכה א ופ"כ מהל' מכירה הלכה י סמג עשין לה טוש"ע ח"מ סימן לה סעיף א:

ויוון נגו

הגהות הב"ח

(א) גמ' נסכא קני (מאי אמרת) תא"מ ונ"ב ס"א וכי תימא וכן בסמוך: (ב) שם והא אנן הזקינה תנן אמרי כחשה כעין הזקינה כצ"ל: (ג) שם איפכא תני ומאי (טעמיה) תז"מ ונ"ב ס"א דוחקיה: (ד) רש"י ד"ה פנים וכו' ומשונה היא מהראשונה: (ה) ד"ה גזל וכו' הניכר הוא וקנייה בשינוי הס"ד ואח"כ מ"ה והחמיץ נמי נשתנה ריחו וטעמו ולא מצי למימר ליה הרי שלך לפניך הס"ד: (ו) ד"ה שנפסלה וכו' במום אע"פ שניכר בדוקין שבעין פטור דכל: (ז) ד"ה ישבע וכו' דאורייתא כגון דקטע לידה לאם וקתבע:

מסורת הש"ס

עיין בספר פני יהושע

גי' רש"ל כל

לעיל סה:

[לעיל לג: וש"נ]

ב"מ ק: [לעיל לה.]

לעיל סו. לקמן קה.

[עיין תוספות לקמן דף ... ד"ה הגורס]

ב"מ ק.

[שבועות מד: וש"נ]

גליון הש"ס

גמ' האי מאן דגזל נ[סכא] מחבריה עיין מנחות קז ע"א תוס' ד"ה ... **שם** דגזל פדנא ויקח בקר (ש"א יא) ... מתורגם פדנא ... **שם** משום דבר[ייתא] איפכא תניא. עיין ... קמא ע"ב תוספות ... וריה"א: **שם** חדא ... תרתי אפיך. עיין יומא נו ע"ב תוספות ד"ה ...

מה א ב ג מיי' פ"ג מהלכות גזילה ואבידה הלכה ז סמג עשין פג ולאוין קנג טוש"ע ח"מ סימן שסג סעיף ד:
מו ד ה מיי' פ"ו מהל' מלוה ולוה הלכה ב סמג שם טוש"ע י"ד סימן קסו סעיף א:
מז ו ז מיי' פ"ג מהל' גזילה ואבידה הלכה ח סמג עשין עג טוש"ע ח"מ סימן שסג סעיף ה:
מח ח ט מיי' שם הל' ד טוש"ע שם סעיף א:

תורה אור

וּמִי אָמַר רַב עַבְדָּא כִּמְקַרְקְעֵי דָּמֵי? וְהָאָמַר *רַב דָּנִיֵּאל בַּר רַב קְטִינָא אָמַר רַב: אהַתּוֹקֵף בְּעַבְדּוֹ שֶׁל חֲבֵירוֹ וְעָשָׂה בּוֹ מְלָאכָה — פָּטוּר. וְאִי ס"ד עַבְדָּא כִּמְקַרְקְעֵי דָּמֵי, אַמַּאי פָּטוּר? בִּרְשׁוּתָא דְּמָרֵיהּ קָאֵי! הָכָא בְּמַאי עָסְקִינַן — בשֶׁלֹּא בִּשְׁעַת מְלָאכָה; כִּי הָא *דִּשְׁלַח לֵיהּ רַבִּי אַבָּא לְמָרִי בַּר מָר, בְּעֵי מִינֵּיהּ מֵרַב הוּנָא: הַדָּר בַּחֲצַר חֲבֵירוֹ שֶׁלֹּא מִדַּעְתּוֹ, צָרִיךְ לְהַעֲלוֹת לוֹ שָׂכָר אוֹ אֵין צָרִיךְ לְהַעֲלוֹת לוֹ שָׂכָר? וְשָׁלְחוּ לֵיהּ: אֵינוֹ צָרִיךְ לְהַעֲלוֹת לוֹ שָׂכָר. הָכִי הַשְׁתָּא?! בִּשְׁלָמָא הָתָם, בֵּין לְמ"ד בֵּיתָא מִיתְּבָא יָתֵיב — נִיחָא לֵיהּ, בֵּין לְמ"ד °"וּשְׁאִיָּה יוּכַּת שַׁעַר" — נִיחָא לֵיהּ, אֶלָּא הָכָא מִי נִיחָא לֵיהּ דְּנִכְחוֹשׁ עַבְדֵּיהּ? אָמְרִי: ה"נ נִיחָא לֵיהּ, גדְּלָא לִיסְתְּרִי עַבְדֵּיהּ. *בֵּי רַב יוֹסֵף בַּר חָמָא הֲווּ תָּקֵיף עַבְדֵי דְּאֶינָשֵׁי דְּמַסֵּיק בְּהוּ זוּזֵי וְעָבְדִי בְּהוּ מְלָאכָה, א"ל *רַבָּה בְּרֵיהּ: מ"ט עָבֵיד מָר הָכִי? א"ל, דְּאָמַר רַב נַחְמָן: עַבְדָּא — נְהוּם כְּרֵיסֵיהּ לָא שָׁוֵי. אֲמַר לֵיהּ: אֵימָא דְּאָמַר רַב נַחְמָן, כְּגוֹן דָּארוּ עַבְדֵּיהּ דְּמַרְקִיד בֵּי כוּבֵי, כּוּלְּהוּ עַבְדֵי מֵעֲבַד עָבְדִי? א"ל: אֲנָא כְּרַב דָּנִיֵּאל סְבִירָא לִי, דְּאָמַר רַב דָּנִיֵּאל בַּר רַב קְטִינָא אָמַר רַב: הַתּוֹקֵף בְּעַבְדּוֹ שֶׁל חֲבֵירוֹ וְעָשָׂה בּוֹ מְלָאכָה — פָּטוּר, אַלְמָא נִיחָא לֵיהּ דְּלָא לִיסְתְּרִי עַבְדֵּיהּ. אֲמַר לֵיהּ: הָנֵי מִילֵּי הֵיכָא דדְּלָא מַסֵּיק בְּהוּ זוּזֵי, מָר כֵּיוָן דְּמַסֵּיק בְּהוּ זוּזֵי מִיחְזֵי כְּרִבִּית, דְּאָמַר רַב יוֹסֵף בַּר מַנְיוּמֵי אָמַר רַב נַחְמָן: אַף עַל פִּי שֶׁאָמְרוּ הַדָּר בַּחֲצַר חֲבֵירוֹ שֶׁלֹּא מִדַּעְתּוֹ א"צ לְהַעֲלוֹת לוֹ שָׂכָר, ההִלְוָהוּ וְדָר בַּחֲצַר חֲבֵירוֹ — צָרִיךְ לְהַעֲלוֹת לוֹ שָׂכָר! א"ל: הָדַרִי בִּי.§ אִיתְּמַר: הַתּוֹקֵף סְפִינָתוֹ שֶׁל חֲבֵירוֹ וְעָשָׂה בָּהּ מְלָאכָה, אָמַר רַב: רָצָה — שְׂכָרָהּ נוֹטֵל, רָצָה — פְּחָתָהּ נוֹטֵל; וּשְׁמוּאֵל אָמַר: אֵינוֹ נוֹטֵל אֶלָּא פְּחָתָהּ. אָמַר רַב פַּפָּא: לָא פְּלִיגִי, והָא דַּעֲבִידָא לְאַגְרָא, הָא דְּלָא עֲבִידָא לְאַגְרָא. וְאִיבָּעֵית אֵימָא: הָא וְהָא דַּעֲבִידָא לְאַגְרָא, זהָא דְּנָחֵית לֵיהּ אַדַּעְתָּא דְּאַגְרָא, וְהָא דְּנָחֵית לֵיהּ אַדַּעְתָּא דְּגַזְלָנוּתָא.§ "גָּזַל מַטְבֵּעַ וְנִסְדַּק" [וכו']§ אָמַר רַב הוּנָא: נִסְדַּק — נִסְדַּק מַמָּשׁ, נִפְסַל — פְּסָלַתּוּ מַלְכוּת; וְרַב יְהוּדָה אָמַר: פְּסָלַתּוּ מַלְכוּת נַמִי חהַיְינוּ נִסְדַּק. אֶלָּא ה"ד נִפְסַל? טשֶׁפְּסָלַתּוּ מְדִינָה זוֹ וְיוֹצְאָה בִּמְדִינָה אַחֶרֶת. א"ל רַב חִסְדָּא לְרַב הוּנָא: לְדִידָךְ דְּאָמְרַתְּ נִפְסַל — פְּסָלַתּוּ מַלְכוּת, הֲרֵי פֵּירוֹת וְהִרְקִיבוּ, יַיִן וְהֶחְמִיץ, דְּכִי פְּסָלַתּוּ מַלְכוּת דָּמֵי, וְקָתָנֵי: מְשַׁלֵּם כִּשְׁעַת הַגְּזֵילָה! א"ל: הָתָם נִשְׁתַּנָּה טַעֲמוֹ וְרֵיחוֹ, הָכָא לֹא נִשְׁתַּנָּה. א"ל *רָבָא לְרַב יְהוּדָה: לְדִידָךְ דְּאָמְרַתְּ פְּסָלַתּוּ מַלְכוּת נַמִי הַיְינוּ נִסְדַּק, הֲרֵי תְּרוּמָה וְנִטְמֵאת דְּכִי פְּסָלַתּוּ מַלְכוּת דָּמֵי, וְקָתָנֵי: אוֹמֵר לוֹ "הֲרֵי שֶׁלְּךָ לְפָנֶיךָ"! א"ל: הָתָם לָא מִינְכָּר הֶיזֵּיקָהּ, הָכָא מִינְכָּר הֶיזֵּיקָהּ. אִיתְּמַר: הַמַּלְוֶה אֶת חֲבֵירוֹ עַל הַמַּטְבֵּעַ וְנִפְסְלָה הַמַּטְבֵּעַ, רַב אָמַר: נוֹתֵן

ישעיה כד

רש"ל
[ב"מ סד:]
גיל כא. [ע"ש] ב"מ סד:
מ שם [וע"ש ברש"י ותוס']
דלא נפיק לגמרי כצ"ל
רבא דהא משמת רב ה טלל רבא כמבואר קדושין עב:

רש"י

פטור. מלשלם לבעליו שכרו. **שלא בשעת מלאכה.** בשעה [שאינו רגיל] לעשות מלאכה, או שאין עכשיו לבעליו מלאכה לעשות, דזה נהנה וזה אין חסר הוא – ופטור. **כדשלח ליה כו' הדר בחצר חבירו.** ומוקמינא לה בפ"ב (דף כא.) בחצר דלא קיימא לאגרא. **ביתא מיתבא יתיב.** זה הדר בתוכה ההנה לבית זה שהוא מיושב בדיורין. **יתיב.** אין חרב, לפי שהדר בתוכה טס ומשפיץ סדקיה תמיד. **ושאיה יוכת שער.** שד הוא ושמו שאיה, מכתת שערים וכותלי בית שאין אדם דר בתוכה. **דלא נסתרי.** שלא ילמד דרכי הבטלה. **פחתה.** אם נשברה או נתקלקלה, ודמי פחתה יתירין על שכרה – נוטל דמי פחתה. **עביד לאגרא.** מסתמא כי נחית לה אדעתא דאגרא נחית, הלכך לאו בתורת גזלן דיינינן ליה, ונותן שכרה על כרחו, אם רבין הן על דמי פחתה. **הא דלא עבידא לאגרא.** לא יהיב ליה אלא פחתה. **נחת לה אדעתא דאגרא.** רצה שכרה נוטל, ואם פחתה יתר על שכרה – נוטל דמי פחתה, דהא ע"כ שקלה, וגזל הוא. **נחית לה אדעתא דגזלנותא.** אפי' שכרה גדול מפחתה לא יהיב אלא פחתה, דכל הגזלנין משלמין כשעת הגזלה. **פסלתו מלכות.** המלך גזר שלא יצא לא במדינה זו ולא במדינה אחרת. **היינו נסדק.** דכיון דלא *נסדק לגמרי – היזק גמור הוא, ומשלם כשעת הגזלה. **אלא היכי דמי נפסל.** דקתני מתניתין "הרי שלך לפניך" – כגון שפסלתו מדינה זו, בני מדינה פסלוהו מעצמן. **ויוצא במדינה אחרת.** שיכול לומר לו: לך להוציאו שם. **תרומה לא מינכר היזיקה.** לא נשתנה מראיתה משאר חטים. **הכא מינכרא היזיקה.** שאין צורה זו דומה לצורה של כל היוצאים עכשיו, וכשגזלה הימנו היו כל צורות המדינות שוות לה. **המלוה את חבירו.** שוה פרגמטיא. **על המטבע.** שקצץ לו מעות. **נותן**

תוספות

ומי אמר רב עבדא כמקרקעי דמי והאמר רב דניאל בר רב קטינא כו'. ואם היה כמקרקעי דמי, אפי' נחת ליה בתורת גזלנות — לא נפק מרשותיה דמריה, דהוי כקרקע דאין נגזלת. ומשלם אגרא היכא דקאי לאגרא, כמו ספינה דלקמן, היכא דלא נחת ליה בתורת גזלנות.

הלוהו ודר בחצירו. כולה סוגיא דהכא כלישנא קמא ד"איזהו נשך" (ב"מ דף סד: ושם). וא"ע: היאך הלוה מותר לעשות שום טובה למלוה? אפי' דברים שהיה עושה לו בלא הלואה, ואפילו דברים שאין רגילות ליטול מהן שכר יהא אסור, דומיא דחצר דלא קיימא לאגרא, וכ"ש דברים שאין רגילות להשאיל בחנם, כגון להשאיל סוסו שיהא אסור אפי' הוא כ"כ אוהבו שבלאו הכי היה משאילו. וא"כ יותר מדאי יש לו ליזהר ללוה שלא יעשה למלוה שום הנאה! וי"ל: דדוקא מילי דפרהסיא והוושא טובא, כגון לדור בחצירו ולתקוף בעבדו. אבל להשאיל לו כליו או אפי' סוסו, כיון דבלאו הכי משאילו — מותר. ודיקא נמי, דנקט במתני' חצירו, ולא נקט: לא ישכיר לו כליו או בהמתו בפחות. ועוד: שמא י"ל דכל היכא דקודם הלואה היו אוהבים זה את זה, שהיו משאילין חצר זה לזה אם היו צריכין — מותר להשאיל אף לאחר הלואה. ומתני' ד"איזהו נשך" (שם) — בסתם בני אדם, שאין רגילות שיהא עושה לוה למלוה אותה הנאה בלא הלואה. דומיא דהקדמת שלום שאין אסור אלא באותו שלא היה רגיל להקדים לו מקודם לכן. ומיהו, אפילו דבר שהיה משאילו בלאו הכי, כגון חצר דלא קיימא לאגרא, אם נכנס שלא מדעת חבירו — חייב, אע"פ שאם לא הלוה לו לא היה חייב לתת לו שכר, כדמשמע הכא. ולפי זה ההיא ד"איזהו נשך" (שם) איירי דוקא בחצר דקיימא לאגרא, דהתם איירי מדעתו, כדקאמר: לא ישכור הימנו בפחות, אבל בלא קיימא לאגרא — היה מותר, כיון דברשותו נכנס, וגם בלא הלואה היה מניח לו לדור בחנם. והאי דקאמר התם עלה דמילתא דהכא: מאי קמ"ל? תנינא! ומשני: מהו דתימא ה"מ חצר דקיימא לאגרא כו', קמ"ל — לא בעי למימר: קמ"ל דמתניתין איירי אפילו בדלא קיימא לאגרא. דמתניתין ודאי לא מיירי אלא דוקא בדקיימא לאגרא, כיון דמיירי מדעתו. אלא ה"פ: קמ"ל דאפי' לא קיימא לאגרא אסור, היכא דלא הוי מדעתו. ופירוש זה דחוק, דהפשט משמע דאמתניתין קאי, וקמ"ל דמתני' איירי אפי' בדלא קיימא לאגרא, אע"ג דאיירי שנכנס מדעתו.

נ"ל רבא

המלוה את חבירו על המטבע. פ"ה: הלוה לחבירו שום פרקמטיא על המטבע, שקצץ לו במעות — נותן לו מעות שיוצאין בשעת פרעון, דהא קבל עליו לתת מטבע. ודוקא הלוהו פרקמטיא, אבל הלוהו מעות — מה שהלוהו משלם לו, עכ"ל הקונטרס. ולפירושו נראה דאם הלוהו מעות נמי, וקצץ לו שישלם לו מעות — דמשלם מטבע היוצא באותה שעה, דמעות שנפסלו לאו מטבע נינהו. ולא נקט בקונטרס פרקמטיא אלא משום דכשמלוה אדם מעותיו אין רגילין להזכיר דבר, אבל כשמוכר פרקמטיא, אפי' אמר סתם: כך וכך מעות תתן — צריך לשלם לו מטבע היוצא. וקשה לפירושו, דה"ל למימר: המוכר לחבירו על המטבע, או ה"ל למינקט: הקיף. ועוד: כיון דמעות פרקמטיא זוקף עליו במלוה — אין סברא כלל לחלק בין הלוהו מעות לפרקמטיא שמכר במעות. ונראה לפרש: דאין חילוק בין מכר לו פרקמטיא בין הלוהו מעות, ומיירי כשהתנה עמו ע"מ שישלם לו מעות, וכיון שפירש לו כך — סתמא דמילתא לכך פירש, שאם יפסל — יתן לו מטבע היוצא, דאותו שנפסל אין שמו מטבע. ושמואל סבר: דכיון שיוצא במישן — שם מטבע עליו. ועוד אור"י, די"ל: כגון שהלוהו סאה חטין, ואמר לו: או תחזור לי סאה, או כך וכך מעות. ואילו במעות לחודייהו קצב — היה משלם לו מטבע שנפסל, אבל הכא שלא זקף עליו במלוה גמורה, שיכול לפרוע לו חטין אם ירצה — נותן לו מטבע היוצא באותה שעה. ולכל הפירושים, אם הלוהו מעות סתם — מעות שהלוה לו יפרע

עין משפט
נר מצוה

מט א ב מיי׳ פ״ד מהלכות מלוה ולוה הלכה יב סמג לאוין קסג טוש״ע ח״מ סימן עד סעיף ז וטוש״ע י״ד סימן קסה:

נ ג מיי׳ פ״ד מהלכות מעשר שני הלכה י סמג עשין קלו טוש״ע י״ד סי׳ שלא סעיף קלח:

נא ד מיי׳ שם הל׳ יד:

נב ה ו מיי׳ פ״ד מהל׳ מלוה ולוה הלכה יח סמג לאוין קסג טוש״ע י״ד סימן קסה:

מסורת הש״ס

נוֹתֵן לוֹ מַטְבֵּעַ הַיּוֹצֵא בְּאוֹתָהּ שָׁעָה. וּשְׁמוּאֵל אָמַר: ^א^יָכוֹל לוֹמַר לוֹ ״לֵךְ הוֹצִיאוֹ בְּמֵישָׁן״. אָמַר רַב נַחְמָן: ^ב^מִסְתַּבְּרָא מִילְּתֵיהּ דִּשְׁמוּאֵל — דְּאִית לֵיהּ אוֹרְחָא לְמֵיזַל לְמֵישָׁן, אֲבָל לֵית לֵיהּ אוֹרְחָא — לָא. אֵיתִיבֵיהּ רָבָא לְרַב נַחְמָן: *^ג^אֵין מְחַלְּלִין עַל הַמָּעוֹת שֶׁאֵינָם יוֹצְאוֹת, כֵּיצַד? הָיוּ לוֹ מָעוֹת כּוֹזְבִיּוֹת, יְרוּשַׁלְמִיּוֹת, אוֹ שֶׁל מְלָכִים הָרִאשׁוֹנִים — אֵין מְחַלְּלִין; הָא שֶׁל אַחֲרוֹנִים דּוּמְיָא דְּרִאשׁוֹנִים — מְחַלְּלִין! א״ל: הָכָא בְּמַאי עָסְקִינַן — כְּשֶׁאֵין מַלְכֻיּוֹת מַקְפִּידוֹת זוֹ עַל זוֹ. אֶלָּא כִּי אָמַר שְׁמוּאֵל — כְּשֶׁמַּלְכֻיּוֹת מַקְפִּידוֹת זוֹ עַל זוֹ? הֵיכִי מָצֵי מַמְטֵי לְהוּ? (א) דְּמַמְטֵי לָהּ ע״י הַדְּחָק, דְּלָא בָּחֲשִׁי, וְאִי מַשְׁכְּחִי קָפְדִי. ת״ש: ^ד^אֵין מְחַלְּלִין עַל מָעוֹת שֶׁל כָּאן וְהֵן בְּבָבֶל, וְשֶׁל בָּבֶל וְהֵן כָּאן. שֶׁל בָּבֶל וְהֵן בְּבָבֶל — מְחַלְּלִין; קָתָנֵי מִיהַת: אֵין מְחַלְּלִין עַל מָעוֹת שֶׁל כָּאן וְהֵן בְּבָבֶל, אע״ג דְּסוֹפוֹ לְמֵיסַק לְהָתָם! הָכָא בְּמַאי עָסְקִינַן — כְּשֶׁמַּלְכֻיּוֹת מַקְפִּידוֹת זוֹ עַל זוֹ. אִי הָכִי, שֶׁל בָּבֶל וְהֵן בְּבָבֶל לְמַאי חֲזוּ? חֲזוּ דְּזָבֵין בְּהוּ בְּהֵמָה וּמַסֵּיק לִירוּשָׁלַיִם. וְהָתַנְיָא: הִתְקִינוּ שֶׁיְּהוּ (ב) הַמָּעוֹת יוֹצְאוֹת בִּירוּשָׁלַיִם מִפְּנֵי כָּךְ! א״ר זֵירָא, לָא קַשְׁיָא: כָּאן בִּזְמַן שֶׁיַּד יִשְׂרָאֵל תַּקִּיפָה עַל אוּמּוֹת הָעוֹלָם, כָּאן בִּזְמַן שֶׁיַּד אוּמּוֹת הָעוֹלָם תַּקִּיפָה עַל עַצְמָן. ת״ר: אֵיזֶהוּ מַטְבֵּעַ שֶׁל יְרוּשָׁלַיִם? דָּוִד וּשְׁלֹמֹה מִצַּד אֶחָד, וִירוּשָׁלַיִם עִיר הַקּוֹדֶשׁ מִצַּד אַחֵר; וְאֵיזֶהוּ מַטְבֵּעַ שֶׁל אַבְרָהָם אָבִינוּ? זָקֵן וּזְקֵנָה מִצַּד אֶחָד, וּבָחוּר וּבְתוּלָה מִצַּד אַחֵר. בְּעָא מִינֵּיהּ רָבָא מֵרַב חִסְדָּא: הַמַּלְוֶה אֶת חֲבֵירוֹ עַל הַמַּטְבֵּעַ, וְהוֹסִיפוּ עָלָיו, מַהוּ? אָמַר לוֹ: ^ה^נוֹתֵן לוֹ מַטְבֵּעַ הַיּוֹצֵא בְּאוֹתָהּ שָׁעָה. א״ל: וַאֲפִילּוּ כִּי נָפְיָא? א״ל: אִין. א״ל: אֲפִי׳ כִּי תַּרְטְיָא? א״ל: אִין. וְהָא קָא זַיְילִין פֵּירֵי! אָמַר רַב אַשִׁי: ^ו^חָזֵינַן, אִי מֵחֲמַת טִיבְעָא זִיל — מְנַכֵּינַן לֵיהּ, וְאִי

רש״י

נוֹתֵן לוֹ מַטְבֵּעַ הַיּוֹצֵא. בִּשְׁעַת פֵּרָעוֹן, דְּהָא קִיבֵּל עָלָיו לָתֵת לוֹ מַטְבֵּעַ, וְהַאי לָאו מַטְבֵּעַ הוּא. וְדַוְקָא הִלְוָהוּ פְּרַגְמַטְיָא, אֲבָל הִלְוָהוּ מָעוֹת — אֶת שֶׁהִלְוָהוּ מְשַׁלֵּם לוֹ. עַל מָעוֹת שֶׁאֵין יוֹצְאוֹת. כְּלָל בִּירוּשָׁלַיִם, דְּלָאו כֶּסֶף צוּרָה קָרֵינָא בֵּיהּ. כּוֹזְבִיּוֹת. מַטְבֵּעַ שֶׁל בֶּן כּוֹזִיבָא וִירוּשַׁלְמִיּוֹת הָווּ. וְה״ג: כּוֹזְבִיּוֹת יְרוּשַׁלְמִיּוֹת אוֹ שֶׁל מְלָכִים הָרִאשׁוֹנִים. וְכוֹזְבִיּוֹת וִירוּשַׁלְמִיּוֹת לָא נָפְקֵי כְּלָל. ל״א: כּוֹזְבִיּוֹת — שֶׁל כְּזִיב. וְה״ג: כּוֹזְבִיּוֹת, אוֹ יְרוּשַׁלְמִיּוֹת, אוֹ שֶׁל מְלָכִים הָרִאשׁוֹנִים. **הָא שֶׁל אַחֲרוֹנִים.** דְּנָפְקֵי בִּמְדִינָה אַחֶרֶת, וְדוּמְיָא דְּרִאשׁוֹנִים הוּא בְּכָךְ דְּאֵין יוֹצְאוֹת כָּאן בִּמְקוֹמוֹ שֶׁל בַּעַל הַבַּיִת, שֶׁנִּפְסְלוּ בְּכָאן. מְחַלְּלִין. וְאַף עַל גַּב דְּלֵית לֵיהּ אוֹרְחָא לְהָתָם בְּמָקוֹם שֶׁיּוֹצְאִין, שֶׁהֲרֵי בִּירוּשָׁלַיִם צָרִיךְ לֵילֵךְ וּלְהוֹצִיאָן. וְקַשְׁיָא לְרַב נַחְמָן אַלִּיבָּא דִּשְׁמוּאֵל, דְּאָמַר: אֲבָל לֵית לֵיהּ אוֹרְחָא לְמֵישָׁן — לָא. **אֶלָּא כִּי אָמַר.** רַב נַחְמָן אַלִּיבָּא דִּשְׁמוּאֵל דְּכִי לֵית לֵיהּ אוֹרְחָא לְמֵישָׁן לָא. כְּשֶׁמַּלְכֻיּוֹת מַקְפִּידוֹת. בִּתְמִיָּה. אִי הָכִי, כִּי אִית לֵיהּ אוֹרְחָא לְמֵישָׁן הֵיכִי מָצֵי מַמְטֵי לְהוּ? הָא כִּי בָּדְקִי לְהוּ בְּנֵי מְדִינָה זוֹ וּמַשְׁכְּחִי לֵיהּ אוֹתָן מָעוֹת, מַפְסְדֵי לֵיהּ! וּמְשַׁנֵּי: **דְּלָא בָּחְשֵׁי.** שֶׁאֵין מַקְפִּידִין כָּל כָּךְ שֶׁיְּהוּ בּוֹדְקִין וּמְחַפְּשִׂין עַל דָּבָר זֶה, וְאִי אַשְׁכְּחִי — קָפְדִי. הִלְכָּךְ, אִית לֵיהּ אוֹרְחָא — שֶׁנִּצְרַךְ לֵילֵךְ שָׁם — יְקַבְּלֵם, וְיוֹצִיא לְשָׁם בִּסְחוֹרָה. וְאִי לָאו — הוֹאִיל וְאֵין יָכוֹל לְהַרְאוֹתָם בְּכָאן בְּפַרְהֶסְיָא לִבְנֵי מֵישָׁן הַבָּאִים כָּאן, אִם רוֹצֶה — לֹא יְקַבְּלֵם. **אֵין מְחַלְּלִין עַל מָעוֹת שֶׁל כָּאן וְהֵן בְּבָבֶל.** אֵין מְחַלְּלִין מַעֲשֵׂר שֵׁנִי עַל מָעוֹת שֶׁל כָּאן, יְרוּשָׁלַיִם, וְהַמָּעוֹת וְהַבְּעָלִים בְּבָבֶל — הוֹאִיל וְאֵינָן יוֹצְאוֹת מִיָּד בְּמָקוֹם שֶׁהֵן שָׁם, דְּבָעֵינַן ״צָרוּר״ בְּיָדְךָ וְלֵיכָּא. וְלֹא עַל שֶׁל בָּבֶל וְהֵן בְּכָאן, בִּירוּשָׁלַיִם. וְהַפֵּירוֹת לָא שָׁנֵי לָן כְּלָל, הֵיכָא דְּאִיתְנְהוּ יָכוֹל לְחַלְּלָן וְהֵן [וּ]הוֹן לִירוּשָׁלַיִם. קָתָנֵי מִיהַת: אֵין מְחַלְּלִין עַל הַמָּעוֹת שֶׁל כָּאן וְהֵן בְּבָבֶל. אַלְמָא: אע״ג דְּאִית לֵיהּ אוֹרְחָא לְמֵישָׁן, כְּגוֹן הָכָא, דְּסוֹפוֹ לַעֲלוֹת כָּאן וּלְהוֹצִיאָן — וַאפ״ה לָא קָרֵי לְהוּ מָעוֹת הַיּוֹצְאוֹת. מַקְפִּידוֹת זוֹ עַל זוֹ. יָתֵר מִדַּאי, דְּבָחְשֵׁי וּבָדְקִי, הִלְכָּךְ מְסוּכָּנוֹת הֵן שֶׁל בָּבֶל בְּמַלְכוּת יְרוּשָׁלַיִם, דְּמַקְפֶּדֶת וּבָחְשֵׁי טְפֵי. **לְמַאי חֲזֵי.** הָא לָא מָצֵי לְאַמְטוּיִינְהוּ (ג) לְהָכָא. **וְהָתַנְיָא** הִתְקִינוּ כו׳. וְאַמַּאי תָּנֵי לְעֵיל: וְלֹא עַל שֶׁל בָּבֶל וְהֵן כָּאן? דָּוִד וּשְׁלֹמֹה. כָּתוּב מִצַּד אֶחָד, וּמִצַּד שֵׁנִי כָּתוּב: יְרוּשָׁלַיִם עִיר הַקֹּדֶשׁ. בָּחוּר וּבְתוּלָה. יִצְחָק וְרִבְקָה. זָקֵן וּזְקֵינָה. אַבְרָהָם וְשָׂרָה. וְהוֹסִיפוּ עֲלֵיהֶן מַהוּ. אַלִּיבָּא דְּרַב, דְּאוֹמֵר: נוֹתֵן לוֹ מַטְבֵּעַ שֶׁל אוֹתָהּ שָׁעָה, הֵיכָא דְּהוֹסִיפוּ עָלָיו מַאי אָמַר רַב? **בְּאוֹתָהּ שָׁעָה.** בִּשְׁעַת פֵּרָעוֹן. **כִּי תַּרְטְיָא.** סֶלַע גָּדוֹל בְּמִדָּה מַחֲזֶקֶת רוֹבַע. **וְהָא** קָזַיְילִין **פֵּירוֹת.** לְגַבֵּי מַטְבֵּעַ זוֹ, נִמְצָא שֶׁמִּשְׁתַּכֵּר זֶה בַּתּוֹסֶפֶת, וְאֵינָהּ דּוֹמָה לָרִאשׁוֹנִים, וְהָוֵי רִבִּית! מֵחֲמַת

פ״ק דתוספתא דמעשר שני

תוספות

יפרע לו, אפי׳ שנפסל. ואם תאמר: ומ״ש מגזלן, דתניא: גזל מטבע ונפסל — אומר לו הרי שלך לפניך. משמע משום דישנו בעין, אבל ליתנהו בעין — משלם כשעת הגזילה. והכא גבי הלואה, אפי׳ איתנהו בעין — כי ליתנהו דמי, דמלוה להוצאה ניתנה! וי״ל: דיש לחלק בין הלואה לגזילה; דמטבע שנפסל חשיב כהוזל, וכמעיקרא שוין ד׳ ולבסוף שוין זוזא. גבי גזלן אמרינן דכי ליתנהו בעין — דמשלם כדמעיקרא, אבל גבי הלואה היכא דהוזל — משלם כי זולא דהשתא, כדאמרינן ב״איזהו נשך״ (ב״מ דף עה.): מלוה אדם כור חטין, הוזלו — נותן חטין, הוקרו — נותן דמיהן. ומטבע שנפסל ודאי הוי כהוזל. ונראה דרב ושמואל סברי כרב הונא דלעיל, דלרב יהודה דחשיב מטבע שנפסל כנסדק — גבי הלואה לא מצי פטר נפשיה במטבע שנפסל. אבל לרב הונא, דלא חשיב ליה כנסדק — מצי פטר ליה נפשיה בנפסל. אע״פ דרב הונא מדמה מטבע שנפסל לתרומה ונטמאת וחמץ שעבר עליו הפסח, והא פשיטא דאין לוה יכול לשלם תרומה טמאה תחת תרומה טהורה, וחמץ אסור בתשלומין היתר — לא דמי לגמרי, דמטבע שנפסל דמי להוזל, והנהו לא דמו להוזל. ומכל מקום, כשהוא בעין — יכול לומר ״הרי שלך לפניך״, וכשאינו בעין, אפי׳ בהוזל — משלם כדמעיקרא.

*__אי__ **הכי של בבל והן בבבל למאי חזי.** קצת משמע דלא פריך אלא לרב נחמן, דאוקי מילתא דשמואל דוקא בדאית ליה אורחא למישן, מדפריך: א״ה של בבל כו׳, משמע דאי לאו דאוקמא כשמלכיות מקפידות — לא הוה קשה ולא מידי. וקשה לר״י: דבלאו רב נחמן צריך ע״כ לאוקמי ברייתא בתרייתא כשמלכיות מקפידות, דלא תיקשי מינה לשמואל דחשיב ליה מטבע אפילו לית ליה אורחא למישן אי ליתא לדרב נחמן. והכא קתני דאין מחללין על מעות של כאן והן בבבל, ואע״ג דאית ליה אורחא לירושלים! ותקשי נמי עלה דברייתא בתרייתא מההיא דלעיל דשל מלכים אחרונים מחללין, אע״ג דאין יוצאות שם במקום שעומד, לפי שיוצאת במקום אחר. והכא קתני דעל מעות של כאן והן בבבל אין מחללין, אע״ג דיוצאות בירושלים! אלא התם איירי כשאין מלכיות מקפידות אם נראות מטבע של מלך האחד במדינתו של זה, הלכך [באים] בני מלכיות אחרת כאן ומוכרין בהמתם במטבע שלהם, ויכול הוא להוציאם בירושלים לבני שאר מדינות הבאות לכאן. והכא איירי במקפידות. ונראה לר״י: דודאי אי לאו מילתיה דרב נחמן הוה א״ש הכל, ולא הוה צריך לאוקמא ברייתא בתרייתא כשהמלכיות מקפידות, דלא קשה מיניה לשמואל ולא לההיא ברייתא דלעיל. דיש לחלק בין מעות של כאן והן בבבל, להנהו דלעיל דאיירי במטבע שנפסל במקום אחד ויוצא במקום אחר. דהתם ודאי חשוב מטבע, דקודם שנפסלה היה שם חשוב מטבע, ועדיין מטבע קיים לבני אותו מקום עצמו שנפסל שם, שיכולין להוציאו במקום אחר. אבל של כאן והן בבבל — לא היה עליו שם מטבע בבבל מעולם, ולכך אין מחללין אע״ג דאית ליה אורחא לירושלים. אבל לרב נחמן, דאוקי מילתא דשמואל דוקא בדאית ליה אורחא למישן, אבל כי לית ליה אורחא למישן — לא חשיב מטבע מטעם שהיה כבר מטבע באותו מקום ועדיין יכול להוציא במישן, ולא תלי אלא באית ליה אורחא להתם — א״כ יש לו מטבע שהיה כבר במקום זה כמו מטבע של מקום אחר שלא בא מעולם כאן, א״כ של כאן והן בבבל נמי לישויה ליה מטבע, דהא אית ליה אורחא לירושלים!

דזבין בהו בהמה ומסיק לירושלים. ואם תאמר: והתניא בפרק ״האיש מקדש״ (קדושין דף נה:): אין לוקחין בהמה במעות מעשר שני! ויש לומר: דפלוגתא היא בפרק ״לולב הגזול״ (סוכה דף מ:), דתניא: אחד שביעית ואחד מעשר שני מתחללין על בהמה חיה, דברי ר״מ. וחכמים אומרים: על שחוטין — מחללין, על חיין — אין מחללין. ולר״מ אפי׳ לכתחילה שרי, כדמוכח בתוספתא דהתם, דקתני בהדיא: מחללין. והא דקתני בסוכה מתחללין — משום רבנן, דאפי׳ בדיעבד אין מתחללין. ועוד י״ל: דבשמעתין, כיון דאי אפשר בענין אחר, שאין יכול להעלות המעות בירושלים — שרי למיזבן בהו בהמה לכולי עלמא. וטעמא דאין לוקחין בהמה ממעות מעשר שני, פירש בקונטרס בקדושין (דף נה:) — משום כחשא. ואין הטעם בשביל כן, אלא כדמפרש בסוכה (דף מ:), דאמר התם: מחלוקת בזכרים, אבל בנקבות, דברי הכל בשחוטין — מתחללין, ועל חיין — אין מתחללין, שמא יגדל מהם עדרים. ובזכרים פליגי אי גזרינן זכרים אטו נקבות, אי לא. וכן מפרש בירושלמי דמסכת מעשר שני דטעמא דאסור לקנות זכרים — גזירה אטו נקבות. **שיהו** כל המעות יוצאות בירושלים. טעמא מפרש במסכת שקלים (דף ח), דתקנו משום שקלים שהיו מביאין לירושלים מכל המקומות.

מטבע של אברהם אבינו זקן וזקינה מצד אחד. בבראשית רבה דריש: ״ואגדלה שמך״ שיצא לו מוניטי״ן בעולם. ומהו מוניטי״ן — זקן וזקינה מכאן, בחור ובתולה מכאן. ונראה: לא שהיה בו צורת זקן וזקינה מכאן בחור ובתולה מכאן, דאסור לעשות צורת אדם. אלא כך היה כתוב, מצד אחד זקן וזקינה ומצד אחר בחור ובתולה. וכן פירש בקונטרס גבי דוד ושלמה וירושלים עיר הקודש, שכך היה כתוב במטבע*.

עיין במפרשי ש״ס מה שכתבו בדיבור זה

[ועי׳ תוספות ע״ז נב: דינרי ובכתוב׳ ג. דינרא]

הגהות הב״ח

(א) גמ׳ דממטי להו (דממטי לה ע״י הדחק) תא״מ ונ״ב רש״י לא גרים ליה: (ב) שם התקינו שיהיו כל המעות: (ג) רש״י ד״ה למאי וכו׳ לאמטויינהו להתם הס״ד:

עד

מחמת תרעא. שבאו גשמים, ונמצאו רוב תבואות בעולם, והוזלו הפירות. לענין נסכא. אם בא להתיכן ולעשות מהן גרוטאות – יש יותר מן הראשונים, והוי רבית. עבדו עובדא. באדם שהלוה את חבירו על המטבע, והוסיפו עליו, והלכו אצל אגרדימוס סוחר ישמעאל והיה לו מן הראשונה ומן השניה, ומצאו בא' של מטבע שניה י' מן הראשונה, ונתן לו שמנה. אמר רבה גרסינן בכולהו. הזורק מטבע של חבירו בים. אע"ג שאין יכול ליטלו. פטור. כדמפרש ואזיל: דלא שקליה בידיה, אלא דאדייה – שהיתה ביד בעלים והכהו זה תחת ידו וניתזה לים. הואיל וצלולים הן וקא חזו ליה, אמר ליה, הא מנח קמך ואינה אבודה. ואי משום דבעי למיתב זוזא לבר אמורא למיטש ולמישקליה – גרמא הוא, שגורם להפסידו אותו שכר, וגרמא בנזקין פטור. אבל עכורין. בשעת התזה, דהוה ליה מעשה בידים – אבוד הוא, ואין זה גורם, אלא ממש, דהא ממש התיזו. היה לו מעות בקיסטרא. מקום, והוא רחוק מאד ויש בו סכנת דרכים, ואין שיירות מצויות שם. אין מחללין. אלמא אבוד חשיב ליה בים הגדול. השף. אשפריי"ר בלע"ז, שפחת את הצורה. בקורנסא. מרטי"ל בלע"ז. וטרשיה. עשאן כאבן חלקה, לשון טרשים. בשופינא. לימ"א בלע"ז, של נפחים. חסורי חסריה. וממש הוא, ולא גרמא. טעמא דרבה בכולהו משום גרמא בנזקין הוא, ופטור. על אזנו וחרשו. אלמא: אף על גב דלא חסריה, כיון דעשה מעשה בגופו – לאו גרמא קחשיב ליה, אלא ממש. והכא נמי, כיון דמחייה בקורנסיה ופחתיה, *ועל ככה חסרו דמים – מעשה הוא. רבה לטעמיה. הלכך, גבי עבד נמי חסרון הוא. [וכנגד אזנו פטור – משום דהכי לא הוי ליה למיחש, והאי ודאי גרמא הוא]. הצורם. אשקרניי"ר בלע"ז, פוגם. במי חטאת. שקל כנגדן משקולות. ופרה וכל מעשיה נפסלים במלאכה.

[מע"ש פ' א משנה ב] [ירושלמי פ"ב דמע"ש] לעיל נח. קדושין כד: לעיל פו. [קדושין סו.] גיטין נג. לעיל ע. רש"ל לעיל נג:

תורה אור

ואי מחמת תרעא זיל לא מנכינן ליה. והא קא שבח לענין נסכא! אלא, [א]כי הא דרב פפא ורב הונא בריה דרב יהושע עבדי עובדא בזוזי דאגרדמים טייעא עד י' בתמניא. אמר רבה: [ב]הזורק מטבע של חבירו לים הגדול – פטור; מאי טעמא? אמר: הא מנח קמך, אי בעית שקליה. והני מילי בצלולין, דקא חזי ליה, אבל עכורין דלא קחזי ליה – לא; והני מילי דאדייה אדויי, אבל שקליה בידיה – מיגזל גזליה, השבה בעי מיעבד. מתיב רבא: *[ג]אין מחללין על מעות שאינן ברשותו, *כיצד? היו לו מעות בקסטרא או בהר המלך, או שנפל כיסו לים הגדול – אין מחללין! אמר רבה: שאני לענין מעשר, דבעינן מצוי בידך, דרחמנא אמר:

(דברים יד) "וצרת הכסף בידך", וליכא. ואמר רבה: [ד]השף מטבע של חבירו – פטור; מאי טעמא? דהא לא עבד ולא מידי. וה"מ דמחייה בקורנסא וטרשיה, אבל שייפא בשופינא – חסורי חסריה. מתיב רבא: *הכהו על עינו וסמאה, על אזנו וחרשו – עבד יוצא בהן לחירות; כנגד עינו ואינו רואה, כנגד אזנו ואינו שומע – אין עבד יוצא בהן לחירות! רבה לטעמיה, *דאמר רבה: חרשו לאביו – נהרג, שאי אפשר לחרישה בלא חבורה, דטפתא דדמא נפלת ליה (א) באוניה. ואמר רבה: [ה]הצורם אוזן פרתו של חבירו – פטור; מאי טעמא? פרה כדקיימא קיימא, דלא עבד ולא מידי, *וכולהו שוורים לאו לגבי מזבח קיימי. מתיב רבא: *העושה מלאכה במי חטאת ובפרת חטאת – פטור מדיני אדם וחייב בדיני שמים; מלאכה הוא דלא מינכר היזיקה, אבל צורם דמינכר היזיקה, הכי נמי דמחייב בדיני אדם! אמרי: הוא הדין דאפילו צורם פטור, והא קא משמע לן, דאפילו מלאכה דלא מינכר היזיקה – חייב בדיני שמים. *ואמר רבה: השורף [ו]שטרו של חבירו – פטור;

מנא

דאמר ליה: ניירא קלאי מינך. מתקיף לה רמי בר חמא: היכי דמי? אי

עד י' בתמניא. פי' בקונטרס: ונותן לו שמונה. ולפירושו חשיב ממעלה למטה, כלומר י"ב או י"א בתמניא, עד י' בתמניא א] — יהיב ליה תמניא. אבל הא תשעה מן הראשונים בתמניא בשניים — יהיב ליה ט' מן השניים תחת ט' של ראשונים, או י' בי'. ור"ח פי': עד י' בתמניא — ויהיב ליה י'. ולפירושו הוי מלמטה למעלה.

עכורין וצלולין. לאו דוקא, אלא אפי' עכורין, אי מלי בר אמוראה למשקלינהו, הוו כצלולין. ואפי' צלולין, אי לא מלי למשקלינהו — חייב. והא דנקט צלולין ועכורין — משום דסתם צלולין מלי שקיל להו בר אמוראה, וסתם עכורין לא מלי שקיל בר אמוראה.

וה"מ דאדייה אדויי. משמע הכא דלא חשיב הגבהה כי אדייה אדויי בלא נטילה בידו, אע"פ שעומד באויר למעלה מג' קודם שיפול לגמרי. וכן ב"הניזקין" (גיטין דף נט:) גבי עני המנקף בראש הזית. וקשה: דבפ"ק דב"מ (דף ט. ושם*) אמר גבי טלית שראשו אחד על העמוד וראשו אחד מונח ע"ג קרקע, שאם הגביה אדם ראשו המונח ע"ג קרקע ונתק ראש שע"ג העמוד להביאו אצלו, שהוא קונה מטעם הגבהה. ואי משיכה קאמר התם — אמאי נקט ראשו אחד ע"ג העמוד? אלמא חשיב הגבהה הואיל ומביאו על האויר למעלה מג'! וי"ל: דהתם חשיבא הגבהה טפי, לפי שראשו אחד אוחז בידו. א"נ: התם איירי כגון שידו כ"כ גבוהה, כשינתקנו לא יפול ראשו לארץ אלא יהא מוגבה ג' מעל הארץ. וא"ת: דבסוף "שילוח הקן" (חולין דף קמא:) משמע דכי טריף אקן ומתגבהי יונים דחשיבא הגבהה לקנות, אע"פ שאין תופסס בידו! וי"ל: דדוקא הכא וב"הניזקין" לא חשיבא הגבהה — דאיכא תרתי לגריעותא; דלא תפסס, וגם אין מגביה אלא משפיל. אבל יונים דמתגבהי — חשיבא הגבהה. אבל אם היו נופלין למטה ע"י טריפת הקן — לא היה קונה, כיון שאין תפוס בידו כלל. ולפי' זה הו"מ לפלוגי הכא באדייה אדויי בין דרך ירידה לדרך עלייה, אלא דניחא ליה לפלוגי בדרך ירידה גופיה, בין אדייה אדויי בין שקליה בידיה. אי נמי: אין חילוק בין דרך ירידה לדרך עליה, דאפילו דרך עליה לא קני הכא באדייה אדויי — לפי שאין דרך הגבהה בזה העניין. אבל ביונים, שהן בעלי חיים — דרך הגבהה בכך, כמו קורא לה והיא באה, או הכישה במקל ורצתה לפניו, דחשיב משיכה אף על פי שהלכה מאיליה. ומיהו, אם היו היונים יורדים ע"י טריפת הקן — לא חשיב הגבהה, אלא עלייתם דוקא.

השף מטבע של חבירו פטור. נראה דרבה סבר: פסלתו מלכות לא הוי כנסדק. דאי הוי כנסדק — אם כן כ"ש דשף מטבע הוי כנסדק, והרי חסריה טובא, ואמאי פטור? **מתיב** רבא הכהו על עינו וסמאה על אזנו וחרשה עבד יוצא בהן לחירות. ואמאי? והא לא חסריה, דאין בו פגם וחסרון! אלא, כיון שקלקלו — חייב, אע"פ שאין בו שום פגם וחסרון. והואיל וכן הוא ה"נ ליחייב! ומשני: רבה לטעמיה כו', ויש שם חסרון — טיפתא דדמא דנפלה באזניה, וכיון דיש חסרון באותו קלקול — חייב על כל הקלקול, כמו בשפייה דחייב בכל הקלקול. דליחייביה על מה שחסריה לא היה צריך רבה להשמיענו דחייב. וא"ת: ואמאי עבד יוצא בהן לחירות? הא בעינן מומין שבגלוי, דומיא דשן ועין, ובחרשו היכי הוי בגלוי? וי"ל: נהי שאין ניכר בו כלום כשהוא ישן או עומד במקום אחד ושותק, מכ"מ כיון דלפי מנהגו שמתנהג והולך ניכר שהוא חרש — חשיב מום שבגלוי. ועי"ל: דאין צריך שיהא קלקול בגלוי, אלא שהאבר שיש בו קלקול יהא בגלוי.

הצורם אוזן פרתו של חבירו פטור. והא דתנן לעיל (דף נו:): גזל בהמה ונתעבדה בה עבירה, או שנפסלה מעל גבי המזבח — אומר לו "הרי שלך לפניך", ונפסלה — היינו שנפל בה מום, דאי נרבעה — היינו שנעבדה בה עבירה. ומשמע דוקא שנפסלה מאיליה, אבל הטיל בה מום בידים — חייב! וי"ל: דמתני' איירי בבהמה קדושה, דודאי לגבי מזבח קיימא. **הא** קמ"ל דאפי' מלאכה דלא מינכר היזיקה. תימה: דבפרק "הניזקין" (גיטין דף נג. ושם*) פריך מהכא למ"ד היזק שאין ניכר שמיה היזק, דעושה מלאכה במי חטאת ובפרת חטאת פטור, ואי שמיה היזק — אמאי פטור? ומאי קושיא? הא אפי' בצורם אוזן דמינכר פטור, משום דסתם שוורים לאו לגבי מזבח קיימי! וא"ל דהתם פריך מפרת חטאת, דפרה אדומה דדמיה יקרים פשיטא דלגבי מזבח קיימא, והכא בשמעתין פריך לרבה ממי חטאת, דסתם מים לאו למי חטאת קיימי, דקודם קידושן דוקא פסלה בהן מלאכה, כדתנן במסכת פרה (פ"ד מ"ד): ומים המלאכה פוסלת בהן עד שיטילו את אפר לתוכן. ותניא נמי בספרי: יכול אף משיקדשו בכלי — תלמוד לומר "למי נדה", וכבר הם מי נדה. דע"כ בגיטין (דף נג. ושם) ממי חטאת נמי פריך, מדמשני התם: מי חטאת ששקל בהן משקלות! וי"ל: דכיון דנקט מלאכה לרבותא, כדקאמר הכא דאפי' מלאכה דלא מינכר היזיקה חייב בדיני שמים — א"כ דייק שפיר התם דהיזק שאין ניכר לא שמיה היזק. דאי שמיה היזק — אין כאן שום רבותא במאי דנקט מלאכה, כיון דבכל מקום חשיב שאינו ניכר כניכר. ועוד יש לומר: דרבה סבר דהיזק שאין ניכר לא שמיה היזק, אבל למ"ד שמיה היזק — כ"ש דמחייב בצורם, דמינכר טפי. ורבא דפריך בשמעתין לרבה סבר בצורם הוי מינכר היזיקה, וחייב אפי' למ"ד היזק שאין ניכר לא שמיה היזק. כדאמר: מלאכה דלא מינכר היזיקו, אבל צורם דמינכר היזיקו — הכי נמי דמחייב. וא"ת: והיאך יכול אדם לפסול פרתו של חבירו? והא בעינן "עובד" דומיא ד"עבד", דניחא ליה! ויש לומר: הני מילי בנעשית המלאכה ממילא, אבל בעושה המלאכה בידים — לא בעיא אלא שיהא ניחא ליה לעושה. וכן בהכשר, דבעינן "יותן" דומיא ד"כי יתן".

נבתוב

נג א מיי' פ"ד מהלכות מלוה הלכה יב סמג לאוין קסג טוש"ע יו"ד סימן קסה:
נד ב מיי' פ"ז מהלכות חובל ומזיק הלכה יא סמג עשין ע טוש"ע ח"מ סימן שפו סעיף א וסעיף ג בהג"ה:
נה ג מיי' פ"ד מהלכות מעשר שני הלכה יא סמג עשין קלו טוש"ע י"ד סי' שלא סעיף קלח:
נו ד מיי' פ"ז מהלכות חובל ומזיק הלכה יא סמג עשין קע טוש"ע ח"מ סימן שפו סעיף א ועיין שם בסעיף ג בהג"ה:
נז ה מיי' שם הל' יא:
נח ו מיי' שם הלכה ט סמג שם טור ש"ע שם סעיף ב [רב אלפס כאן ובסוף פ"ב דף יג:]:

[ד"ה הואיל]

הגהות הב"ח
(א) גמרא נפלת ליה באודניה:

הגהות מהר"ב רנשבורג
א] תוס' ד"ה עד י' וכו' עד עשר בתמניא יהיב ליה תמניא. עיין בים של שלמה בפירקין סי' טו ובשו"ת מהר"א ששון ר"ס קנג בביאור דבריהם:

[ד"ה בדיני]

אִי דְּאִיכָּא סָהֲדֵי דְּיָדְעִי מַאי הֲוָה בִּשְׁטָרָא — לִיכְתְּבוּ לֵיהּ שְׁטָרָא מְעַלְּיָא, וְאִי דְּלֵיכָּא סָהֲדֵי — אֲנַן מְנָא יָדְעִינַן? אָמַר רָבָא: *[א]תְּהֵא בְּמַאֲמִינוֹ. אָמַר רַב דִּימִי בַּר חֲנִינָא: הָא דְּרַבָּה — מַחֲלוֹקֶת ר"ש וְרַבָּנַן הִיא; לְר"ש דְּאָמַר: *דָּבָר הַגּוֹרֵם לְמָמוֹן כְּמָמוֹן דָּמֵי — מְחַיֵּיב, לְרַבָּנַן דְּאָמְרִי: דָּבָר הַגּוֹרֵם לְמָמוֹן לָאו כְּמָמוֹן דָּמֵי — לָא מְחַיֵּיב. מַתְקִיף לָהּ רַב הוּנָא בְּרֵיהּ דְּרַב יְהוֹשֻׁעַ: אֵימַר דְּשָׁמְעַתְּ לֵיהּ לְרַבִּי שִׁמְעוֹן דָּבָר הַגּוֹרֵם לְמָמוֹן כְּמָמוֹן דָּמֵי — בְּדָבָר שֶׁעִיקָּרוֹ מָמוֹן, כִּדְרַבָּה, דְּאָמַר רַבָּה: גָּזַל חָמֵץ לִפְנֵי הַפֶּסַח, וּבָא אַחֵר וּשְׂרָפוֹ בַּמּוֹעֵד — פָּטוּר, שֶׁהַכֹּל מְצוּוִּים עָלָיו לְבַעֲרוֹ. לְאַחַר הַפֶּסַח — מַחֲלוֹקֶת ר' שִׁמְעוֹן וְרַבָּנַן, לְרַבִּי שִׁמְעוֹן דְּאָמַר: דָּבָר הַגּוֹרֵם לְמָמוֹן כְּמָמוֹן דָּמֵי — [ב]חַיָּיב, לְרַבָּנַן דְּאָמְרִי: דָּבָר הַגּוֹרֵם לְמָמוֹן לָאו כְּמָמוֹן דָּמֵי — פָּטוּר. בְּדָבָר שֶׁאֵין עִיקָּרוֹ מָמוֹן מִי אָמְרִינַן? *אָמַר אַמֵימָר: מַאן דְּדָאֵין דִּינָא דְּגַרְמֵי — מַגְבֵּי בֵּיהּ דְּמֵי שְׁטָרָא מְעַלְּיָא, וּמַאן דְּלָא דָּאֵין דִּינָא דְּגַרְמֵי — מַגְבֵּי בֵּיהּ דְּמֵי נְיָירָא בְּעָלְמָא. הֲוָה עוּבְדָּא, וְכַפְיֵיהּ רַפְרָם לְרַב אַשִׁי, [ג]וְאַגְבֵּי בֵּיהּ כִּי כְּשׁוּרָא לְצַלְמָא.§ "חָמֵץ וְעָבַר עָלָיו הַפֶּסַח — אוֹמֵר לוֹ הֲרֵי שֶׁלְּךָ לְפָנֶיךָ".§ מַאן תַּנָּא: אוֹמְרִין בְּאִיסּוּרֵי הֲנָאָה "הֲרֵי שֶׁלְּךָ לְפָנֶיךָ"? אָמַר רַב חִסְדָּא: ר' יַעֲקֹב הִיא, דְּתַנְיָא: *שׁוֹר שֶׁהֵמִית, עַד שֶׁלֹּא נִגְמַר דִּינוֹ, מְכָרוֹ — מָכוּר, הִקְדִּישׁוֹ — מוּקְדָּשׁ, שְׁחָטוֹ — בְּשָׂרוֹ מוּתָּר, הֶחֱזִירוֹ שׁוֹמֵר לִבְעָלָיו — מוּחְזָר; מִשֶּׁנִּגְמַר דִּינוֹ, מְכָרוֹ — אֵינוֹ מָכוּר, הִקְדִּישׁוֹ — אֵינוֹ מוּקְדָּשׁ, שְׁחָטוֹ — בְּשָׂרוֹ אָסוּר, הֶחֱזִירוֹ שׁוֹמֵר לִבְעָלָיו — אֵינוֹ מוּחְזָר. רַבִּי יַעֲקֹב אוֹמֵר: *אַף מִשֶּׁנִּגְמַר דִּינוֹ, הֶחֱזִירוֹ שׁוֹמֵר לִבְעָלָיו — מוּחְזָר; מַאי לָאו בְּהָא קָמִיפַּלְגִי, דְּרַבִּי יַעֲקֹב סָבַר: אוֹמְרִין בְּאִיסּוּרֵי הֲנָאָה "הֲרֵי שֶׁלְּךָ לְפָנֶיךָ", וְרַבָּנַן סָבְרִי: אֵין אוֹמְרִין בְּאִיסּוּרֵי הֲנָאָה "הֲרֵי שֶׁלְּךָ לְפָנֶיךָ"? א"ל רַבָּה: לָא, דְּכוּלֵּי עָלְמָא — אָמְרִינַן בְּאִיסּוּרֵי הֲנָאָה "הֲרֵי שֶׁלְּךָ לְפָנֶיךָ", דְּאִם כֵּן, נִפְלְגוּ בְּחָמֵץ בְּפֶסַח. אֶלָּא אָמַר רַבָּה: הָכָא בְּגוֹמְרִין דִּינוֹ שֶׁל שׁוֹר שֶׁלֹּא בְּפָנָיו קָא מִיפַּלְגִי, רַבָּנַן סָבְרִי: אֵין גּוֹמְרִין דִּינוֹ שֶׁל שׁוֹר שֶׁלֹּא בְּפָנָיו, דְּאָמַר לֵיהּ: אִי אַיְיתִיתֵיהּ נִיהֲלַיהּ הֲוָה מַעֲרִיקְנָא לֵיהּ לְאַגְמָא, הַשְׁתָּא מְסַרְתֵּיהּ בְּיַד מַאן דְּלָא מָצֵינָא לְאִישְׁתַּעוּיֵי דִּינָא בַּהֲדֵיהּ; וְר' יַעֲקֹב סָבַר: גּוֹמְרִין דִּינוֹ שֶׁל שׁוֹר שֶׁלֹּא בְּפָנָיו, דְּאָמַר לֵיהּ: מַאי עֲבַדִי לֵיהּ? סוֹף סוֹף הֲוָה גָּמְרִי לֵיהּ דִּינָא שֶׁלֹּא בְּפָנָיו. אַשְׁכְּחֵיהּ רַב חִסְדָּא לְרַבָּה בַּר שְׁמוּאֵל, א"ל: תָּנֵית מִידֵּי בְּאִיסּוּרֵי הֲנָאָה? אָמַר לֵיהּ: אִין, תְּנֵינָא: *°"וְהֵשִׁיב אֶת הַגְּזֵלָה" — מַה תַּלְמוּד לוֹמַר "אֲשֶׁר גָּזָל"? יַחֲזִיר כְּעֵין שֶׁגָּזַל. מִכָּאן אָמְרוּ: גָּזַל מַטְבֵּעַ וְנִפְסַל, פֵּירוֹת וְהִרְקִיבוּ, יַיִן [א] *וְהֶחְמִיץ, תְּרוּמָה וְנִטְמֵאת, חָמֵץ וְעָבַר עָלָיו הַפֶּסַח, בְּהֵמָה וְנֶעֶבְדָה בָּהּ עֲבֵירָה, וְשׁוֹר עַד שֶׁלֹּא נִגְמַר דִּינוֹ — אוֹמֵר לוֹ "הֲרֵי שֶׁלְּךָ לְפָנֶיךָ". מַאן שָׁמְעַתְּ לֵיהּ דְּאָמַר: עַד שֶׁלֹּא נִגְמַר דִּינוֹ אִין, מִשֶּׁנִּגְמַר דִּינוֹ לָא — רַבָּנַן, וְקָתָנֵי: חָמֵץ וְעָבַר עָלָיו הַפֶּסַח — אוֹמֵר לוֹ "הֲרֵי שֶׁלְּךָ לְפָנֶיךָ". א"ל: *אִי מַשְׁכַּחַתְּ לְהוּ, לָא תֵּימָא לְהוּ וְלָא מִידֵּי.§ פֵּירוֹת וְהִרְקִיבוּ — אוֹמֵר לוֹ "הֲרֵי שֶׁלְּךָ לְפָנֶיךָ".§ וְהָתְנַן: פֵּירוֹת וְהִרְקִיבוּ — מְשַׁלֵּם כִּשְׁעַת הַגְּזֵילָה! אָמַר רַב פָּפָּא: [ד]כָּאן שֶׁהִרְקִיבוּ כּוּלָּן, כָּאן שֶׁהִרְקִיבוּ מִקְצָתָן.§

מתני' [ה]נָתַן לָאוּמָּנִין לְתַקֵּן וְקִלְקְלוּ — חַיָּיבִין לְשַׁלֵּם. נָתַן לְחָרָשׁ שִׁידָּה תֵּיבָה וּמִגְדָּל לְתַקֵּן וְקִלְקֵל — חַיָּיב לְשַׁלֵּם. [ו]וְהַבַּנַּאי שֶׁקִּיבֵּל עָלָיו לִסְתּוֹר אֶת הַכּוֹתֶל, וְשִׁיבֵּר הָאֲבָנִים אוֹ שֶׁהִזִּיקָן — חַיָּיב לְשַׁלֵּם; הָיָה סוֹתֵר מִצַּד זֶה וְנָפַל מִצַּד אַחֵר — פָּטוּר, וְאִם מֵחֲמַת הַמַּכָּה — חַיָּיב.§

גמ' אָמַר רַב אַסִּי: לֹא שָׁנוּ אֶלָּא שֶׁנָּתַן לְחָרָשׁ שִׁידָּה תֵּיבָה וּמִגְדָּל לִנְעוֹץ בָּהֶן מַסְמֵר, וְנָעַץ בָּהֶן מַסְמֵר וְשִׁיבְּרָן. אֲבָל נָתַן לְחָרָשׁ עֵצִים לַעֲשׂוֹת שִׁידָּה תֵּיבָה וּמִגְדָּל, וְעָשָׂה מֵהֶן שִׁידָּה תֵּיבָה וּמִגְדָּל וְשִׁיבְּרָן — פָּטוּר; מַאי טַעְמָא? אוּמָּן קוֹנֶה בְּשֶׁבַח כְּלִי. תְּנַן: נָתַן לָאוּמָּנִין וְקִלְקְלוּ — חַיָּיבִין לְשַׁלֵּם; מַאי לָאו [ז]דְּיָהֵיב לְהוּ עֵצִים? לָא, שִׁידָּה תֵּיבָה וּמִגְדָּל. הָא מִדְּקָתָנֵי סֵיפָא שִׁידָּה תֵּיבָה וּמִגְדָּל, מִכְּלָל דְּרֵישָׁא עֵצִים! אָמְרִי: פֵּרוּשֵׁי קָא מְפָרֵשׁ לָהּ: כֵּיצַד נָתַן לָאוּמָּנִין לְתַקֵּן וְקִלְקְלוּ חַיָּיבִין לְשַׁלֵּם? כְּגוֹן שֶׁנָּתַן לְחָרָשׁ שִׁידָּה תֵּיבָה וּמִגְדָּל. וְהָכִי נַמִי מִסְתַּבְּרָא דְּ"כֵיצַד" קָתָנֵי, דְּאִי סָלְקָא דַּעְתָּךְ רֵישָׁא עֵצִים, הַשְׁתָּא אַשְׁמְעִינַן עֵצִים חַיָּיבִין לְשַׁלֵּם, וְלָא אָמְרִינַן אוּמָּן קוֹנֶה בְּשֶׁבַח כֵּלִים, שִׁידָּה תֵּיבָה וּמִגְדָּל מִבַּעְיָא? אִי מִשּׁוּם הָא לָא אִירְיָא, תְּנָא סֵיפָא לְגַלּוּיֵי רֵישָׁא; שֶׁלֹּא תֹּאמַר רֵישָׁא שִׁידָּה תֵּיבָה וּמִגְדָּל, אֲבָל עֵצִים לָא — תְּנָא סֵיפָא שִׁידָּה תֵּיבָה וּמִגְדָּל, מִכְּלָל דְּרֵישָׁא עֵצִים, וְאפ"ה חַיָּיב לְשַׁלֵּם. לֵימָא מְסַיֵּיעַ לֵיהּ: *הַנּוֹתֵן צֶמֶר לַצַּבָּע

וְהִקְדִּיחוֹ

רש"י

מְנָא יָדְעִינַן. מַאי הֲוֵי כְּתִיב בֵּיהּ, וּמַאי בָּעֵי לְמֵיתְבֵּי? וְלָא אִצְטְרִיךְ לֵיהּ לְמֵימַר דְּפָטוּר. בְּמַאֲמִינוֹ. *בַּעַל הַשְּׁטָר לַשּׂוֹרֵף בְּכָל מַה שֶּׁאוֹמֵר שֶׁכָּךְ הָיָה כָּתוּב בֵּיהּ, וְאַפ"ה פָּטוּר. דְּר"ש. בְּפֶרֶק "מְרוּבֶּה" (לעיל דף עד:) גַּבֵּי קָדָשִׁים שֶׁחַיָּיב בְּאַחֲרָיוּתָן כו'. בַּמּוֹעֵד. בִּזְמַן בִּיעוּרוֹ — בּוֹ' שָׁעוֹת, וְדִכְוָותָהּ בִּפְסָחִים (דף י:): לֹא בָּדַק בְּתוֹךְ הַמּוֹעֵד יִבְדּוֹק לְאַחַר הַמּוֹעֵד. לְר"ש חַיָּיב. הַאי שֶׁשְּׂרָפוֹ לְשַׁלֵּם לַגַּזְלָן דְּמֵיהֶם, דְּדָבָר הַגּוֹרֵם לְמָמוֹן הוּא, שֶׁאִם הָיָה בְּעֵין הָיָה מַחֲזִירוֹ גַּזְלָן לִבְעָלָיו וּפָטוּר, דִּתְנַן לְעֵיל (דף צו:): גָּזַל חָמֵץ וְעָבַר עָלָיו הַפֶּסַח – אוֹמֵר לוֹ "הֲרֵי שֶׁלְּךָ לְפָנֶיךָ". וְעַכְשָׁיו שֶׁאֵין בְּעֵין — יַחֲזִיר דָּמִים לִבְעָלָיו. וּבְחָמֵץ בְּפֶסַח הוּא דְּאָמְרִינַן הָכִי, מִשּׁוּם דְּעִיקָּרוֹ, כְּלוֹמַר בִּתְחִלָּתוֹ — מָמוֹן הָוֵי, וְעַכְשָׁיו אע"פ שֶׁאֵינוֹ שָׁוֶה לִכְלוּם גּוֹרֵם לְמָמוֹן הוּא. אֲבָל בִּשְׁטָרֵי, דְּמֵעוֹלָם לֹא הָיָה גּוּפוֹ מָמוֹן — מִי שָׁמְעַתְּ לֵיהּ? מַאן דְּדָאֵין דִּינָא דְּגַרְמֵי. ר"מ הִיא (בְּ"הַגּוֹזֵל בַּתְרָא") [לְקַמָּן (דף ק.)]. מַגְבֵּי לֵיהּ. מִן הַשּׂוֹרֵף כָּל הַשְּׁטָר, שֶׁהֲרֵי גָּרַם לוֹ לְהַפְסִיד. וְאַכְפְּיֵיהּ רַפְרָם לְרַב אַשִׁי. שֶׁשָּׂרַף שְׁטַר חֲבֵירוֹ בְּיַלְדוּתוֹ. וְאַגְבֵּי מִינֵּיהּ. גּוּבַיְינָא מְעַלְּיָא כָּל מַה שֶּׁכָּתוּב בַּשְּׁטָר. כִּי כְּשׁוּרָא לְצַלְמָא. פֵּרָעוֹן גָּמוּר מִן הָעִידִּית, כְּקוֹרָה זוֹ הַנִּבְחֶרֶת מִשְּׁאָר קוֹרוֹת לְתַקֵּן בָּהּ צוּרָה וּדְיוֹקְנָאוֹת. שׁוֹר שֶׁהֵמִית. אֶת הָאָדָם, וּמְכָרוֹ עַד שֶׁלֹּא נִגְמַר דִּינוֹ. מָכוּר. וְלֹא יִסָּקֵל, דְּבָעֵינַן מִיתָה וְהַעֲמָדָה בַּדִּין שֶׁיִּהְיוּ שָׁוִין כְּאֶחָד, בְּפֶרֶק "שׁוֹר שֶׁנָּגַח ד' וְה'" (א). הֶחֱזִירוֹ שׁוֹמֵר לִבְעָלָיו מוּחְזָר. וּפָטוּר שׁוֹמֵר. דְּכ"ע אוֹמְרִים בְּאִיסּוּרֵי הֲנָאָה כו'. וּמַתְנִיתִין דְּחָמֵץ בְּפֶסַח — אֲפִי' לְרַבָּנַן. דְּאִם כֵּן. דִּלְרַבָּנַן אֵין אוֹמְרִים, אַדְּמִפַּלְגִי בְּשׁוֹר לְגַבֵּי שׁוֹמֵר — לִיפְלְגוּ נַמִי לְגַבֵּי גָּזַל חָמֵץ וְעָבַר עָלָיו הַפֶּסַח. (ב) אֲבָל הָכָא בְּשׁוֹר שֶׁהֵמִית הוּא דְּקָאָמַר אֵין מוּחְזָר — מִשּׁוּם דְּאָמַר לֵיהּ: הַאי אִיסּוּר הֲנָאָה לָאו אִיסּוּר דְּאָתֵי עֲלֵיהּ מִמֵּילָא הוּא, כְּגוֹן חָמֵץ בְּפֶסַח, אֶלָּא אַתְּ קְטַלְתֵּיהּ עֲדָיִים שֶׁהֲבֵאתוֹ לְב"ד, דְּאִי הֲוָה גַּבָּאי — הֲוָה מַעֲרִיקְנָא לֵיהּ לְאַגְמָא כו'. אֲבָל סֵיפָא דְּמַתְנִיתִין — וַדַּאי רַבִּי יַעֲקֹב הִיא וְלֹא רַבָּנַן, דְּקָתָנֵי: אוֹ שֶׁהָיְתָה יוֹצְאָה לִיסָּקֵל, אוֹמֵר לוֹ "הֲרֵי שֶׁלְּךָ לְפָנֶיךָ". אַשְׁכְּחֵיהּ רַב חִסְדָּא כו'. רַב חִסְדָּא מְהַדַּר אַמַּתְנִי' דְּלֶיהֱוֵי בָּהּ פְּלוּגְתָּא אַחָמֵץ בְּפֶסַח, לְאוֹקְמָא לְמִילְּתֵיהּ דְּטַעְמָא דְּרַבָּנַן מִשּׁוּם דְּאֵין אוֹמְרִים בְּאִיסּוּרֵי הֲנָאָה "הֲרֵי שֶׁלְּךָ לְפָנֶיךָ". אִי מַשְׁכַּחַתְּ לְהוּ. לִבְנֵי הַיְשִׁיבָה. לָא תֵּימָא לְהוּ וְלָא מִידֵּי. מִשּׁוּם דְּחָדוּ, דְּמַשְׁכְּחִי תְּיוּבְתָּא לְמִילְּתִי. שִׁידָּה. אַרְגָּז שֶׁל עֲגָלָה הָעֲשׂוּיָה לְמֶרְכַּב נָשִׁים.

וְהִקְדִּיחוֹ

תוספות

נכתוב ליה שטרא. לא שייך הכא "מפיסה ולא מפי כתבם", ולא בההיא דתנן ב"גט פשוט" (ב"ב דף קסח.): מי שנמחק שטר חובו — דעדים החתומים על השטר נעשה כמי שנחקרה עדותן בב"ד, והוי כאילו אמרי הני עדים: ראינוס שנחקרו עדותן בב"ד. ובפ"ב דכתובות (דף כ.*) הארכתי*.

פרושי קמפרש כיצד כו'. תימה דלא פריך: אי הכי "חייבין" תרי זימני למ"ל? כדפריך בפרק קמא דסנהדרין (דף ג. ושם*) "אי הכי שלשה שלשה למה לי". ובכמה מקומות דייק, ובכמה מקומות לא דייק*.

הכא

עין משפט נר מצוה

נט א מיי' פ"ז מהל' חובל ומזיק הלכה ט סמג עשין קע טוש"ע ח"מ סימן שפו סעיף ב:

[ד"ה ור"י]

[ועיין תוספות ב"ב קע: ד"ה אין]

[ד"ה ועוד]

[ועיין תוספות בכורות לח: ד"ה א"כ]

ס ב מיי' פ"ג מהלכות גזילה הלכה ד סמג עשין עג טוש"ע ח"מ סימן שסג סעיף ב.

סא ג מיי' פ"ז מהל' חובל ומזיק הלכה ט סמג עשין ע טוש"ע ח"מ סימן שפו סעיף ב [פ"ב אלפס כאן ובסוף פ"ב דף יג:]:

סב ד מיי' פ"ג מהל' גזילה הלכה ד סמג עשין עג טוש"ע ח"מ סי' שסג סעיף א:

סג ה מיי' פ"י מהל' שכירות הלכה ד סמג עשין פ"ט טוש"ע ח"מ סימן שו סעיף ב:

סד ו מיי' פ"ו מהלכות חובל ומזיק הל' יא סמג עשין פט טוש"ע ח"מ שס בהג"ה וסי' שפד סעיף ג:

סה ז מיי' פ"י מהלכות שכירות הלכה ד סמג עשין פט טוש"ע ח"מ סימן שו סעיף ב:

הגהות הב"ח

(א) רש"י ד"ה מכור וכו' מיתה והעמדה בדין וכו' בפרק שור שנגח. נ"ב סוף דף מד ופ"ק דף יג: (ב) ד"ה דאם כן וכו' הפסח הס"ד ואח"כ מה"ד אלא הכא:

הגהות הגר"א

[א] גמ' יין והחמיץ. רשום קו על תיבת והחמיץ וכ"ב והקרים:

מסורת הש"ס

ביש"ש גרס השורף השטר

[ב"מ לה.]

[לעיל עא: לקמן פסחים ה: וש"נ]

כתובות פו. [לקמן ק

[לעיל מד:]

לעיל [מה.] עא: [לז.]

[לעיל סו. וש"נ]

[גי' ס' ת"ח בשם ה ונתנסך וע"ש

[ערכין יא. לט:]

לקמן ק:

תורה אור

ויקרא ה

והקדיחו יורה — נותן לו דמי צמרו; דמי צמרו — אין, דמי צמרו ושבחו — לא. לאו שהקדיחו לאחר נפילה, דאיכא שבחא, ושמע מינה: אומן קונה בשבח כלי? אמר שמואל: הכא במאי עסקינן — כגון שהקדיחו בשעת נפילה, דליכא שבחא. אבל הקדיחו לאחר נפילה מאי, נותן לו דמי צמרו ושבחו? לימא, שמואל לית ליה דרב אסי? אמר לך שמואל: הכא במאי עסקינן — כגון דצמר וסמנין דבעל הבית, וצבע אגר ידיה הוא דשקיל. אי הכי, נותן לו דמי צמרו וסמנין מיבעי ליה! אלא, שמואל דחויי קא מדחי ליה. תא שמע: *[א]הנותן טליתו לאומן, גמרו והודיעו — אפילו מכאן ועד עשרה ימים אינו עובר עליו משום °"לא תלין", נתנה לו בחצי היום — כיון ששקעה עליו החמה עובר עליו משום "בל תלין"; ואי ס"ד אומן קונה בשבח כלי, אמאי עובר משום "בל תלין"? אמר רב מרי בריה דרב כהנא: בגרדא דסרבלא, דליכא שבחא. סוף סוף למאי יהבה נהליה? לרכוכי, כיון דרכביה היינו שבחא! לא צריכא, דאגריה לביטשי, ביטשא ביטשא במעתא, דהיינו שכירות. ולמאי דסליק אדעתין מעיקרא דלא אגריה לביטשי, מסייע ליה לרב ששת. דבעו מיניה מרב ששת: *קבלנות, עובר עליו משום "בל תלין" או אינו עובר? ואמר להו רב ששת: [ב]עובר. לימא, דרב ששת פליגא אדרב אסי? אמר שמואל בר אחא: בשליחא דאיגרתא. לימא כתנאי: "עשה לי שירים, נזמין וטבעות ואקדש לך", כיון שעשאן — מקודשת, דברי רבי מאיר. וחכמים אומרים: [ג]אינה מקודשת עד שיגיע ממון לידה; מאי ממון? אילימא אותו ממון, מכלל דר"מ סבר אותו ממון לא? אלא במאי מקדשא? אלא, פשיטא מאי ממון? [ד]ממון אחר. וסברוה, דכולי עלמא — [ה]ישנה לשכירות מתחילה ועד סוף, ודכולי עלמא — [ו]המקדש במלוה אינה מקודשת; מאי לאו באומן קונה בשבח כלי קמיפלגי, דר"מ סבר: אומן קונה בשבח כלי, ורבנן סברי: [ז]אין אומן קונה בשבח כלי? לא, דכולי עלמא — אין אומן קונה בשבח כלי, אלא הכא בישנה לשכירות מתחילה ועד סוף קא מיפלגי, רבי מאיר סבר: אין לשכירות אלא לבסוף, ורבנן סברי: יש לשכירות מתחילה ועד סוף. ואי בעית אימא: דכולי עלמא — ישנה לשכירות מתחילה ועד סוף, והכא במקדש במלוה קמיפלגי, דרבי מאיר סבר: המקדש במלוה — מקודשת, ורבנן סברי: *המקדש במלוה — אינה מקודשת.

רבא

רש"י

והקדיחו יורה. נתקלקל הצבע מעצמו. **לאחר נפילה.** לאחר שקלט הצבע ונעשה שבח בצמר. **לימא שמואל לית ליה דרב אסי.** הואיל ומהדר לאוקמי בהכי מתניתין, ומהשתא לא עבדינן כרב אסי, דהא קיימא לן כשמואל בדיני. **אמר לך.** הא מתניתין דמשמע דאי הקדיח לאחר נפילה יהיב ליה נמי דמי שבחיה — כגון שצמר וסממנין דבעל הבית, דהא ליכא למימר אומן קונה בשבח כלי, דסממנין הוא דמשבחי ליה, והצבע — שכיר בעלמא הוא. ודאי אומן שהסממנין שלו — קונה בשבח כלי, ואין משלם אלא דמי צמרו. **דחויי מדחי ליה.** כלומר: ממתניתין לא תסייעיה. ולא משום דנשמע מינה דשמואל פליג אדרב אסי. **אמאי עובר.** הא זכויי קא מזכן ליה ניהליה, ולא שכירות היא. **בגרדא דסרבלא** = פלוקי"ר, בגדים. **לבטושי** = פלארא"ש בלע"ז. ושכרו לדרכה, והתנה עמו סכום הדריכות, כל דריכה במעה, דשכיר יום הוא, ולא קבלן דליקני בשבחא. **ולמאי דסליק אדעתא מעיקרא דלא אגריה למנין בטשי.** וקבלנות הוא, וקתני: עובר. **מסייע ליה לרב ששת.** לא גרסינן "נימא". **נימא פליגא דרב ששת אדרב אסי.** דמדקאמר עובר — קסבר: אין אומן קונה בשבח כלי, ולא זביני ניהו. וכיון דלא קני בשבחא, היכא דנתן לו עצים לעשות מהן תיבה ועשאה, ושיברה — משלם תיבה? **בשליחא דאיגרתא.** דקבלנות היא, שלא שכרו ליום, אלא להוליך לו אגרת למקום פלוני — בההיא קאמר רב ששת דעובר, דליכא שבחא דליקני. **עשה לי שירים.** למידין משלי, אקדש לך בשכר פעולתך. **ישנה לשכירות מתחילה ועד סוף.** כיון שעלה שכרו לפרוטה נתחייבה לו מיד פרוטה, והויא ליה מלוה גבה. ואי לאו דאומן קונה בשבח כלי, משום שכירות לא לימא ר"מ דמתקדש, דהמקדש במלוה אינה מקודשת, דמלוה להוצאה ניתנה ואינה בעין. אלא משום דקסבר אומן קונה בשבח כלי, וכי יהיב (א) לה ניהליה — מקדשה בשבחא [מה] דאית ליה בגויה, אף על פי שלא נתן לה ממון אחר. ורבנן סברי: לא קני, ואינה מקודשת עד שיגיע ממון אחר לידה. **אינה לשכירות אלא לבסוף.** כי מהדר להו ניהלה. הלכך, לאו מלוה הוא.

תוספות

הכא במאי עסקינן בצמר וסמנין דבעל הבית. הו"מ למפרך: מאי דוחקיה לאוקמי בצמר וסממנין דבעל הבית ודוקא בשעת נפילה? לוקמה בסממנין דפועל, ואפילו לאחר נפילה! אלא משום דאית ליה עדיפות למיפרך.

דאגריה לביטשי. פי' בקונטרס: שהתנה עמו סכום הדריכות, כל דריכה במעה, דשכיר יום הוא ולא קבלן דליקני בשבחא. תימה: מה ר"ל? דמ"מ הרי קבלן הוא ולא שכיר יום! וב"המקבל" (ב"מ דף קיב. ושם*) פירשה בע"א: דאגריה לבטשי — כשבא לבית הגרדי בוטשין ברגלים בתוך הכלי במים. ומיהו לא בקבלנות עסקינן אלא בשכירות, בין ישבית בין לא ישבית — שכרו לפי מנין בטישות, כך וכך בטישות בכך וכך מעות. עכ"ל. וי"מ: דכי אגריה לבטשי עובר משום "בל תלין" — אביטשא קמייתא, דבההיא ליכא שבחא. וא"ת: אמאי לא תירץ דבשכיר יום עסקינן? ויש לומר: משום דקתני: וגמר והודיעו, ובשכיר יום מאי הודעה שייכא?

בשליחא דאגרתא. ההוא דלעיל לא מצי לאוקמי בשליחא דאיגרתא, דהא בהדיא קתני: הנותן טליתו. אבל בענין דרב ששת דהכא — ה"מ לאוקמי דאגריה לביטשא. וא"ת: והיכי מוקי לה בשליחא דאגרתא? והא בהדיא ב"המקבל" (שם) פירש בעייתו, דמספקא ליה אי אומן קונה בשבח כלי אי לא. דקאמר, בעו מיניה מרב ששת: קבלן עובר ב"בל תלין" או אין עובר? אומן קונה בשבח כלי ואין עובר, או אין אומן קונה בשבח כלי ועובר? וי"ל: שהם שאלו סתם, וגמרא הוא שמפרש שאילתו כן, שסבור שבזה מסתפק. וכן אורחיה דגמרא לעיל בריש פ"ב (דף יט.), ובכמה מקומות. ואין להאריך*.

אלא במאי מקדשא. אור"י: דסברא הוא שאין מקודשת במה שמוחל לה שכרו. אפי' לא יהא אומן קונה בשבח כלי, אלא מלוה יש לו עליה והוא מוחל לה — אין מקודשת, שאין דעתה להתקדש עד שיבאו השיראים והנזמים לידה. ועוד אור"י, ונראה לו עיקר: שאפי' שניהם רוצים שיחולו קודם הגעת ממון לידה — אינה מקודשת, אע"פ שמתחייבת לו ראשון ראשון לפי שישנה לשכירות מתחילה ועד סוף, כיון שאין יכול לתובעה בדין שכרו עד שיגיע הממון לידה, ואין חשוב כנותן לה כלום בתחילתו עד שתבא שעה שיכול לתובעה בדין.

ואיבעית אימא דכ"ע ישנה לשכירות מתחילה ועד סוף. דאי אינה אלא בסוף, (ב) כיון שנגמרה כל המלאכה, שאין מתחייב שכרו אלא הכל יחד, ואז מוחל לה בתורת קדושין — לא חשיב מלוה. ואין לדקדק מכאן דכן הלכה דישנה לשכירות מתחילה ועד סוף, כיון דלא מצי למימר בע"א. אבל יש להביא ראיה מפ"ק דע"ז (דף יט: ושם*) גבי הגיע לכיפה שמעמידין בה ע"ז — אסור לבנותה. וקאמר בגמרא: אם בנה — שכרו מותר, ומפרש טעמא: משום דישנה לשכירות מתחילה ועד סוף, אימת מיתסרא — במכוש אחרון, מכוש אחרון לית בה שוה פרוטה. וליכא דפליג התם, משמע דהכי הלכתא. ואע"ג דקיי"ל דשכירות אין משתלמת אלא לבסוף, אפי' למ"ד ישנה — מודה דאין משתלמת אלא לבסוף, כדנפקא לן ב"איזהו נשך" (ב"מ דף סה. ושם) מדכתיב "כשכיר שנה בשנה" — שכירות של שנה זו אין משתלמת אלא לשנה אחרת. והא דאמר נמי דפועל יכול לחזור בו אפי' בחצי היום — הוי אפי' למ"ד אינה אלא לבסוף, דכשחוזר בו ואין רוצה לפעול יותר — אז הוא הסוף. ולא נ"מ בפלוגתא דישנה לשכירות ואין לשכירות אלא לענין הך דשמעתא, אי הויא מלוה אי לאו, ולענין ההיא דע"ז.

רבי מאיר סבר המקדש במלוה. מקודשת. ותימה: בפרק ב' דקדושין (דף מז.) אמר רבי שמעון בן אלעזר משום רבי מאיר: מלוה הרי היא כפקדון, ואם לא נשתייר הימנו כלום — אינה מקודשת, משום דאין בעין! ואין סברא לומר דמה שהחזיר לה הנזמים חשיב כמלוה בעין, כיון דאין אומן קונה בשבח כלי. ועוד: דאם כן אמאי אין מקודשת לרבי מאיר ללישנא דלעיל?

אימא

עין משפט נר מצוה

סו א ב מיי' פי"א מהלכות שכירות הלכה ג סמג לאוין קפא טוש"ע ח"מ סימן שלט סעיף ו:

סז ג ד מיי' פ"ה מהל' אישות הלכה כ סמג עשין מח טוש"ע אה"ע סימן כח סעיף טו ובהג"ה שם:

סח ה מיי' שם הלכה כ סמג שם טוש"ע אה"ע שם:

סט ו מיי' וסמג שם טוש"ע שם סעי' ז:

ע ז מיי' פ"י מהלכות שכירות הלכה ד ועי' בהשגות ובמ"מ סמג עשין פט טוש"ע ח"מ סימן שו סעיף ב [רב אלפס ב"מ פ"ט דף קלד ועיין בטוש"ע אה"ע סימן כח סעיף טו בהג"ה]:

הגהות הב"ח

(א) רש"י ד"ה ישנה וכו' וכי יהיב להו ניהלה מקדשה: (ב) תוס' ד"ה ואיבעית אימא וכו' אלא בסוף כיון שאין מתחייב שכרו אלא הכל ביחד כשנגמרה כל המלאכה ואז מוחל כצ"ל:

תורה אור: ויקרא יט

מסורת הש"ס: ב"מ קיב. | ג"ז שם | קדושין מח. | [קדושין ו: וש"נ]

[ד"ה אומן] | [ועיין תוספות נדה לד: ד"ה כי] | [ד"ה אלמא]

רָבָא אָמַר: דְּכ"ע יֶשְׁנָהּ לִשְׂכִירוּת מִתְּחִילָּה וְעַד סוֹף, וּדְכוּלֵּי עָלְמָא — הַמְקַדֵּשׁ בְּמִלְוֶה אֵינָהּ מְקוּדֶּשֶׁת, וּדְכוּלֵּי עָלְמָא — אֵין אוּמָּן קוֹנֶה בְּשֶׁבַח כְּלִי. אֶלָּא הָכָא בְּמַאי עָסְקִינַן — כְּגוֹן שֶׁהוֹסִיף לָהּ נוֹפֶךְ מִשֶּׁלּוֹ, רַבִּי מֵאִיר סָבַר: *מִלְוֶה וּפְרוּטָה — [א]דַּעְתָּהּ אַפְּרוּטָה, וְרַבָּנַן סָבְרִי: מִלְוֶה וּפְרוּטָה — דַּעְתָּהּ אַמִּלְוֶה. וּבִפְלוּגְתָּא דְּהָנֵי תַּנָּאֵי; *דְּתַנְיָא: "בִּשְׂכַר שֶׁעָשִׂיתִי עִמָּךְ" — אֵינָהּ מְקוּדֶּשֶׁת, "בִּשְׂכַר שֶׁאֶעֱשֶׂה עִמָּךְ" — מְקוּדֶּשֶׁת; רַבִּי נָתָן אוֹמֵר: "בִּשְׂכַר שֶׁאֶעֱשֶׂה עִמָּךְ" — אֵינָהּ מְקוּדֶּשֶׁת, וְכָל שֶׁכֵּן "בִּשְׂכַר שֶׁעָשִׂיתִי עִמָּךְ"; וְרַבִּי יְהוּדָה הַנָּשִׂיא אוֹמֵר, בֶּאֱמֶת אָמְרוּ: [ב]בֵּין "בִּשְׂכַר שֶׁעָשִׂיתִי עִמָּךְ" וּבֵין "בִּשְׂכַר שֶׁאֶעֱשֶׂה עִמָּךְ" — אֵינָהּ מְקוּדֶּשֶׁת, וְאִם הוֹסִיף לָהּ נוֹפֶךְ מִשֶּׁלּוֹ — מְקוּדֶּשֶׁת; (מַאי אִיכָּא) בֵּין ת"ק לְרַבִּי נָתָן — אִיכָּא בֵּינַיְיהוּ שְׂכִירוּת, בֵּין רַבִּי נָתָן לְר' יְהוּדָה הַנָּשִׂיא — אִיכָּא בֵּינַיְיהוּ מִלְוֶה וּפְרוּטָה. אָמַר שְׁמוּאֵל: טַבָּח אוּמָּן שֶׁקִּלְקֵל — חַיָּיב לְשַׁלֵּם, מַזִּיק הוּא, פּוֹשֵׁעַ הוּא, נַעֲשָׂה כְּאוֹמֵר לוֹ "שְׁחוֹט לִי מִכָּאן" וְשָׁחַט לוֹ מִכָּאן. לָמָּה לֵיהּ לְמֵימַר "מַזִּיק הוּא, פּוֹשֵׁעַ הוּא"? אִי אָמַר "מַזִּיק הוּא", הֲוָה אָמִינָא: הָנֵי מִילֵּי הֵיכָא דְּקָא עָבֵיד בְּשָׂכָר, אֲבָל הֵיכָא דְּקָא עָבֵיד בְּחִנָּם — לָא, קמ"ל: פּוֹשֵׁעַ הוּא. אֵיתִיבֵיהּ רַב חָמָא בַּר גּוּרְיָא לִשְׁמוּאֵל: [ג]הַנּוֹתֵן בְּהֵמָה לְטַבָּח וְנִיבְּלָהּ, אוּמָּן — פָּטוּר, הֶדְיוֹט — חַיָּיב, [ד]וְאִם נוֹתֵן שָׂכָר, בֵּין הֶדְיוֹט בֵּין אוּמָּן — חַיָּיב! אֲמַר לֵיהּ: לֵעֲבַר מוֹחָךְ! אֲתָא הַהוּא מֵרַבָּנַן קָא מוֹתִיב לֵיהּ, א"ל: הָשְׁתָּא שָׁקַלְתְּ מַאי דִּשְׁקַל חַבְרָךְ, קָאָמֵינָא לְכוּ אֲנָא רַבִּי מֵאִיר, וְקָאָמְרִיתוּ לִי רַבָּנַן. אַמַּאי לָא דָּיְיקַתְּ מִילַּי? שֶׁאֲנִי אוֹמֵר: מַזִּיק הוּא, פּוֹשֵׁעַ הוּא, נַעֲשָׂה כְּאוֹמֵר לוֹ שְׁחוֹט לִי מִכָּאן וְשָׁחַט לוֹ מִכָּאן. מַאן אִית לֵיהּ הַאי סְבָרָא — רַבִּי מֵאִיר, דְּאָמַר: מִבָּעֵי לֵיהּ לְמִירְמֵי אַנַּפְשֵׁיהּ. הֵי רַבִּי מֵאִיר? אִילֵימָא [הָא] רַבִּי מֵאִיר, (קל"ן סִימָן) דִּתְנַן: *קְשָׁרוֹ בְּעָלָיו בְּמוֹסֵירָה וְנָעַל בְּפָנָיו כָּרָאוּי, וְיָצָא וְהִזִּיק, בֵּין תָּם בֵּין מוּעָד — חַיָּיב, דִּבְרֵי רַבִּי מֵאִיר; הָתָם בִּקְרָאֵי פְּלִיגֵי! אֶלָּא הָא רַבִּי מֵאִיר, דִּתְנַן: *לִצְבּוֹעַ לוֹ אָדוֹם וּצְבָעוֹ שָׁחוֹר, שָׁחוֹר וּצְבָעוֹ אָדוֹם — רַבִּי מֵאִיר אוֹמֵר: נוֹתֵן לוֹ דְּמֵי צַמְרוֹ; הָתָם בְּיָדַיִם קָלָאוֹ מִינֵּיהּ! אֶלָּא הָא רַבִּי מֵאִיר, *דִּתְנַן: *נִשְׁבְּרָה כַּדּוֹ וְלֹא סִילְּקָהּ, נָפְלָה גְּמַלּוֹ וְלֹא הֶעֱמִידָהּ — רַבִּי מֵאִיר אוֹמֵר: חַיָּיב בְּנִזְקָן, וַחֲכָמִים אוֹמְרִים: פָּטוּר מִדִּינֵי אָדָם וְחַיָּיב בְּדִינֵי שָׁמַיִם, וְקַיְימָא לָן, *דִּבְנִתְקַל פּוֹשֵׁעַ הוּא פְּלִיגֵי. אָמַר רַבָּה בַּר בַּר חָנָה אָמַר רַבִּי יוֹחָנָן: טַבָּח אוּמָּן שֶׁקִּלְקֵל — חַיָּיב, וַאֲפִילּוּ הוּא אוּמָּן כְּטַבָּחֵי צִיפּוֹרִי. וּמִי אָמַר רַבִּי יוֹחָנָן הָכִי? וְהָאָמַר רַבָּה בַּר בַּר חָנָה: עוּבְדָא הֲוָה קַמֵּיהּ דְּרַבִּי יוֹחָנָן בִּכְנִישְׁתָּא דְּמָעוֹן, וַאֲמַר לֵיהּ: זִיל [ה]אַיְיתִי רְאָיָה דִּמְמַחֵית לְתַרְנְגוֹלִים וְאִפְטְרָךְ! לָא קַשְׁיָא: [ו]כָּאן בְּחִנָּם, כָּאן בְּשָׂכָר; כִּי הָא דְּאָמַר רַבִּי זֵירָא: הָרוֹצֶה שֶׁיִּתְחַיֵּיב לוֹ טַבָּח, יַקְדִּים לוֹ דִּינָר. מֵיתִיבֵי: *[ז]הַמּוֹלִיךְ חִטִּים לִטְחוֹן, וְלֹא לְתָתָן, וַעֲשָׂאָן סוּבִּין אוֹ מוּרְסָן, קֶמַח לַנַּחְתּוֹם וַעֲשָׂאוֹ פַּת נִיפּוֹלִין, בְּהֵמָה לְטַבָּח וְנִיבְּלָהּ — חַיָּיב, מִפְּנֵי שֶׁהוּא כְּנוֹשֵׂא שָׂכָר! אֵימָא: מִפְּנֵי שֶׁהוּא נוֹשֵׂא שָׂכָר. הַהוּא [ח]מַגְרוֹמְתָּא דַּאֲתַאי לְקַמֵּיהּ דְּרַב, טַרְפֵיהּ, [ט]וּפַטְרֵיהּ לְטַבָּח מִלְּשַׁלּוּמֵי דָּמֵי; פַּגְעוּ בֵּיהּ רַב כָּהֲנָא וְרַב אַסִּי בְּהַהוּא גַּבְרָא, אֲמַרוּ לֵיהּ: עָבֵיד בָּךְ רַב תַּרְתֵּי. מַאי תַּרְתֵּי? אִילֵימָא תַּרְתֵּי לְגְרִיעוּתָא, דְּאִיבָּעֵי לֵיהּ לְאַכְשׁוּרֵי *כְּר' יוֹסֵי בְּר' יְהוּדָה וְטָרְפָהּ כְּרַבָּנַן, וְאִי נַמִּי כְּרַבָּנַן, דְּאִיבָּעֵי לֵיהּ חִיּוּבָא לְטַבָּחָא, וּמִי שָׁרֵי לְמֵימַר כִּי הַאי גַּוְונָא? וְהָתַנְיָא: *[י]לִכְשֶׁיֵּצֵא, לֹא יֹאמַר: "אֲנִי מְזַכֶּה וַחֲבֵירַי מְחַיְּיבִין, אֲבָל מָה אֶעֱשֶׂה שֶׁחֲבֵירַי רַבּוּ עָלַי", וְעַל זֶה נֶאֱמַר: °"הוֹלֵךְ רָכִיל מְגַלֶּה סּוֹד"! אֶלָּא תַּרְתֵּי לְמַעַלְיוּתָא, דְּלָא אוֹכְלָךְ סְפֵק אִיסּוּרָא, וּמְנָעָךְ מִסְּפֵק גְּזֵילָה. אִיתְּמַר: [כ]הַמַּרְאֶה דִּינָר לְשׁוּלְחָנִי וְנִמְצָא רַע, תָּנֵי חֲדָא: אוּמָּן — פָּטוּר, הֶדְיוֹט — חַיָּיב, וְתַנְיָא אִידָךְ: בֵּין אוּמָּן בֵּין הֶדְיוֹט — חַיָּיב! אָמַר רַב פָּפָּא: [ל]כִּי תַנְיָא אוּמָּן פָּטוּר — כְּגוֹן דַּנְכוּ וְאִיסּוּר, דְּלָא צְרִיכֵי לְמִיגְמַר כְּלָל. אֶלָּא בְּמַאי טָעוּ? טָעוּ בְּסִיכְתָּא חֲדַתָּא, [א]דְּהַהִיא שַׁעְתָּא דִּנְפַק מִתּוּתֵי סִיכְתָּא. הַהִיא אִיתְּתָא דְּאַחֲזְיָא דִּינָרָא לְרַבִּי חִיָּיא, אָמַר לָהּ: מְעַלְּיָא הוּא. לְמָחָר אֲתַאי לְקַמֵּיהּ וְאָמְרָה לֵיהּ: אַחֲזִיתֵיהּ וְאָמְרוּ לִי בִּישָׁא הוּא, וְלָא קָא נָפֵיק לִי. אֲמַר לֵיהּ לְרַב: זִיל חַלְּפֵיהּ נִיהֲלָהּ, וּכְתוֹב אַפִּנְקָסִי: "דֵּין עֵסֶק בִּישׁ". וּמַאי שְׁנָא דַּנְכוּ וְאִיסּוּר דְּפָטִירִי, מִשּׁוּם דְּלָא צְרִיכֵי לְמִיגְמַר? רַבִּי חִיָּיא נַמִּי לָאו לְמִיגְמַר קָא בָּעֵי! רַבִּי חִיָּיא *לִפְנִים מִשּׁוּרַת הַדִּין הוּא דַּעֲבַד; *כִּדְתָנֵי רַב יוֹסֵף: °"וְהוֹדַעְתָּ לָהֶם" — זֶה בֵּית

רבא אמר דכ"ע כו' ודכ"ע אין אומן קונה בשבח כלי ה"ג. מלוה ופרוטה. כי יהיב לה פרוטה מדידיה. דעתה אפרוטה. ומיקדשא. להכי נקט פרוטה, דקדושי אשה דיו להו בכך. בשכר שעשיתי עמך. התקדשי לי. אינה מקודשת. הואיל וכבר החזירו לה, והוא מלוה גבה. בשכר שאעשה עמך מקודשת. דאינה לשכירות אלא לבסוף, וכי מהדר להו ניהלה — מיקדשא ליה בשכרו. בשכר שאעשה עמך אינה מקודשת. דקסבר ר' נתן: ישנה לשכירות מתחילה ועד סוף, וכל פרוטה ופרוטה הוה ליה מלוה. וכל שכן שעשיתי. דמיום שהחזירו לה נזקף שכרו עליה במלוה. ואם הוסיף כו' מקודשת. דקסבר: מלוה ופרוטה — דעתה אפרוטה. ואילו לרבי נתן, אע"ג דהוסיף לה — אינה מקודשת, דדעתה אמלוה. טבח אומן שקלקל חייב. וכ"ש הדיוט, דלא היה לו לשוחטה, הואיל ואינו בקי. דקעביד בשכר. דמזיק חייב באונסין, דאדם מועד לעולם בין שוגג בין מזיד. מדקרי ליה מזיק לחייבו באונס — ש"מ: (א) באותו שכר קאמר. וקמ"ל דפושע הוא, דלא חשיב ליה אונס אלא פשיעה, דהוה ליה למירמיה אנפשיה שמא תפרכס הבהמה ויזהר בה. אומן פטור. דאנוס הוא. לעבר מוחך. כמו מים עכורים. קא מותיב ליה. הא מילתא. התם בקראי פליגי. וגזירת הכתוב הוא, בפ' "שור שנגח ארבעה וחמשה" (ב). בידים קלאו מיניה. שנתכוון לשנות. לטחון. אדם הממונה על כך ועליו ללותתן במים וכותשן במכתשת להסיר הקליפה החיצונה, כדי שתהא סולת נקיה. סובין. גסין ממורסן. ניפולי. נשבר ונופל כשאוחזין אותו. כנושא שכר. אף זה חייב כנושא שכר, ואף על פי שאין נושא, אלמא פשיעה היא ולא אונס, דאי אונס אפי' נושא נמי חייב. מגרומתא. שחט מתוך אחת הטבעות והגרים חוץ בין טבעת לטבעת, ושייר מלא החוט על פני רובה. ורבי יוסי ברבי יהודה מכשר ליה במלא החוט על פני רובה, ורבנן בעו על פני כולה, ב"הכל שוחטין" (חולין דף יח.). בההוא גברא. בעל הבהמה. לכשיצא כו'. בדיין קמיירי, בסנהדרין. דלא אוכלך ספק איסורא. דמספקא ליה הלכתא כמאן, אי כרבנן דאסרי, אי כרבי יוסי ברבי יהודה דמכשר. ומנעך מספק גזילה. דאי כשרה היא — הוי טבח פטור. המראה דינר. לדעת אם טוב הוא ויקבלנו מחבירו. דנכי ואיסור. שולחנין אומנין היו. טעו בסיכתא חדתי. שנפסל המטבע והעמידו צורה אחרת, ועדיין לא היו בקיאין בה. סיכתא. קוי"ן בלע"ז. רב שומר גנזיו של רבי חייא דודו הוה. דין עסק ביש. סחורה רעה היא, שעל עסקי חנם אני מפסיד, שלא היה לי לראותה.

אימא מפני שהוא נושא שכר. אבל בחנם פטור. אף על גב דאדם מועד לעולם, באונס כי האי לא מחייב אדם המזיק, כדפרישית בריש "המניח" (לעיל דף כז: ושם*).

מנעך מספק איסורא. אור"ת: דמשום הכי קרי ליה ספק איסורא — משום דרב פסיק בפ"ק דחולין (דף יח.) כרבי יוסי בר' יהודה בטבעת הגדולה, והיה רב מחמיר עליו לפי שהיה עם הארץ, שלא יבא להקל בשאר טבעות. כדאשכחן בפרק קמא דחולין (דף טו.) גבי מבשל בשבת, כי מורי [*רבא] לתלמידיו — מורי להו כר"מ, וכי דריש להו בפירקא — דריש כר' יהודה משום עמי הארץ. ולהכי קרי ליה ספק גזילה ולא ודאי גזילה, דאותו האיש ששחט לעם הארץ — ה"ל לאסוקי אדעתיה שיחמירו עליו. ור"י מפרש דההיא עובדא בשאר טבעות הוה, ורב דקאמר בפרק קמא דחולין (דף יח:): ואין הלכה כמותו בשאר טבעות — משום דמספקא ליה אי הלכה כמותו אי לאו.

ותניא אידך בין אומן בין הדיוט חייב. לא שייך הכא לשנויי: כאן בשכר כאן בחנם, כדמשני גבי שחיטה. דבהכרת מטבע צריך בקיאות גדול, ולית ליה למיחזי אם אין בקי כדנכו ואיסור.

לפנים

[ד"ה ושמואל]

עא א מיי' פ"ה מהל' איסות הלכה טז סמג עשין מח טוש"ע אה"ע סי' כח סעיף יד:

עב ב מיי' שם הלכה כ טוש"ע שם סעי' טו:

[נ"ל רב]

עג ג ד מיי' פ"י מהל' שכירות הלכה ה סמג עשין פט טוש"ע ח"מ סימן שו סעיף ד:

עד ה מיי' שם טוש"ע שם סעי' ז:

עה ו ז מיי' שם טוש"ע שם סעי' ד:

עו ח ט טוש"ע שם סעיף ה:

עז י מיי' פכ"ב מהל' סנהדרין הלכה ז סמג לאוין ט טוש"ע ח"מ סימן יט סעיף א:

עח כ ל מיי' פ"י מהל' שכירות הלכה ה סמג עשין פט טוש"ע ח"מ סימן שו סעיף ו:

הגהות הב"ח

(א) רש"י ד"ה דקעביד וכו' ש"מ בעושה בשכר קאמר: (ב) ד"ה התם וכו' בפ' שור שנגח. נ"ב סוף דף מה:

הגהות מהר"ב רנשבורג

א] גמ' דההיא שעתא דנפק מתותי סיכתא. עיין שיטה מקובצת:

[קדושין מו. מח: סנהדרין יט:]

קדושין מח.

רש"ל מ"ז

יתרון י: וש"נ

[ג"ל דתניא]

לעיל מח: נה:

לעיל כח: ב"מ

[לעיל כט.]

ב"ב לג: [תוספתא]

[חולין יח.]

סנהדרין כט.

מש"י יא

[כתובות ז. וש"נ]

ב"מ ל: שמות יח

תורה אור

בֵּית חַיֵּיהֶם, "אֶת הַדֶּרֶךְ" — זוֹ גְּמִילוּת חֲסָדִים, "יֵלְכוּ" — זוֹ בִּיקּוּר חוֹלִים, "בָּהּ" — זוֹ קְבוּרָה, "אֶת הַמַּעֲשֶׂה" — זֶה הַדִּין, "אֲשֶׁר יַעֲשׂוּן" — זוֹ לִפְנִים מִשּׁוּרַת הַדִּין. רֵישׁ לָקִישׁ אַחֲוֵי לֵיהּ דִּינָרָא לְרַבִּי אֶלְעָזָר. אֲמַר: מְעַלְּיָא הוּא. אֲמַר לֵיהּ: [א]חֲזִי, דַּעֲלָךְ קָא סָמְכֵינָא. א"ל: כִּי סָמְכַתְּ עֲלַי מַאי לְמֵימְרָא, דְּאִי מִשְׁתַּכַּח בִּישָׁא בָּעֵינָא לְאִיחְלוּפֵי לָךְ? וְהָא אַתְּ הוּא דְּאָמְרַתְּ: רַבִּי מֵאִיר הוּא *דְּדָאֵין דִּינָא דְּגַרְמֵי, מַאי לָאו ר' מֵאִיר וְלָא סְבִירָא לָן כְּוָותֵיהּ? א"ל: לָא, ר' מֵאִיר [ב]וּסְבִירָא לָן כְּוָותֵיהּ. הֵי רַבִּי מֵאִיר? אִילֵימָא רַבִּי מֵאִיר (ד' ל' מ' פ' סִימָן) דִּתְנַן: *[ג]דָּן אֶת הַדִּין, זִיכָּה אֶת הַחַיָּיב, חִיֵּיב אֶת הַזַּכַּאי, טִמֵּא אֶת הַטָּהוֹר, טִיהֵר אֶת הַטָּמֵא — מַה שֶּׁעָשָׂה עָשׂוּי וִישַׁלֵּם מִבֵּיתוֹ; הָא אִיתְּמַר עֲלַהּ, אָמַר רַבִּי אֶלְעָא אָמַר רַב: [ד]וְהוּא שֶׁנָּטַל וְנָתַן בַּיָּד! אֶלָּא הָא ר' מֵאִיר, דִּתְנַן: לִצְבּוֹעַ לוֹ אָדוֹם וּצְבָעוֹ שָׁחוֹר, שָׁחוֹר וּצְבָעוֹ אָדוֹם — ר' מֵאִיר אוֹמֵר: נוֹתֵן לוֹ דְּמֵי צַמְרוֹ; הָתָם קָא עָבֵיד בְּיָדַיִם! אֶלָּא הָא ר' מֵאִיר, דִּתְנַן: *הַמְסַכֵּךְ גַּפְנוֹ עַל גַּבֵּי תְּבוּאָתוֹ שֶׁל חֲבֵירוֹ — הֲרֵי זֶה קִידֵּשׁ וְחַיָּיב; הָתָם נַמִי קָא עָבֵיד בְּיָדַיִם! אֶלָּא הָא ר"מ, דְּתַנְיָא: *[ה]מְחִיצַת הַכֶּרֶם שֶׁנִּפְרְצָה — אוֹמֵר

בֵּית חַיֵּיהֶם. *תַּלְמוּד תּוֹרָה. בִּיקּוּר חוֹלִים וּקְבוּרָה. פָּרְכִינַן בְּ"אֵלּוּ מְצִיאוֹת": הַיְינוּ גְּמִילוּת חֲסָדִים! וּמוֹקֵי לָהּ בִּיקּוּר חוֹלִים – בְּבֶן גִּילוֹ, וְנוֹטֵל אֶחָד מִשִּׁשִּׁים בְּחָלְיוֹ. וּקְבוּרָה – בְּזָקֵן וְאֵינוֹ לְפִי כְּבוֹדוֹ, וַאֲפִילּוּ הָכִי חַיָּיב. שֶׁנָּשָׂא וְנָתַן בַּיָּד. וְזִיכָּה אֶת הַחַיָּיב. שֶׁהָיָה לוֹ מַשְׁכּוֹן לַמַּלְוֶה מִמֶּנּוּ, וְנָטַל דַּיָּין לַמַּשְׁכּוֹן וְהֶחֱזִירוֹ לַלֹּוֶה. וְחִיֵּיב אֶת הַזַּכַּאי – נָטַל בַּיָּד מָמוֹן מִן הַנִּתְבָּע וְשִׁילֵּם לַתּוֹבֵעַ. וְטִימֵּא אֶת הַטָּהוֹר – נָטַל שֶׁרֶץ בְּיָדַיִם וּזְרָקוֹ עָלֶיהָ לְטַמְּאוֹ וַדַּאי, לְהַחֲזִיק דְּבָרָיו. וְטִיהֵר אֶת הַטָּמֵא – נָטַל הַדַּיָּין לְפֵירוֹת טְמֵאִים וְעֵרְבָן עִם שְׁאָר פֵּירוֹת הָאִישׁ הַשּׁוֹאֲלוֹ, וַהֲוָה לֵיהּ עוֹשֶׂה מַעֲשֶׂה בְּיָדַיִם, וּמַזִּיק. וְהָכִי מְפָרֵשׁ בְּסַנְהֶדְרִין בְּפֶרֶק "אֶחָד דִּינֵי מָמוֹנוֹת" (דף לג.). קִידֵּשׁ. אָסַר אֶת הַתְּבוּאָה. מְחִיצַת הַכֶּרֶם. קַיְימָא לָן: הָיָה גָּדֵר בֵּינְתַיִים – זֶה סוֹמֵךְ זְרָעִים לַגָּדֵר מִכָּאן, וְזֶה סוֹמֵךְ גְּפָנִים לַגָּדֵר מִכָּאן, בְּ"לֹא יַחְפּוֹר" (ב"ב דף כו.).

גְּדוֹר

לפנים משורת הדין עבד כדתני [רב יוסף] והודעת להם וגו'. והך ברייתא מייתי נמי בפרק "אלו מציאות" (ב"מ דף ל:) גבי זקן ואינו לפי כבודו, ורבי ישמעאל בר' יוסי — לפנים משורת הדין עבד, כדתני כו'. אבל בסוף פרק "האומנים" (שם דף פג.) גבי רבה בר רב הונא דשקלינהו לגלימייהו דהנהו שקולאי — לא מייתי לה, אלא מייתי "למען תלך בדרך טובים". ומפ' הר"י מאורליינ"ש דלא שייך לפנים משורת הדין אלא בדבר שאחרים חייבין וזה פטור, כמו רבי חייא דהכא, ור' ישמעאל ברבי יוסי ב"אלו מציאות" (שם דף ל:). אבל בההיא דרבה בר רב הונא — אין חילוק בינו לבין אחרים. ואין נראה, דבפרק "אלו מציאות" (שם דף כד: ושם*) אמר דעבד לפנים משורת הדין גבי הא [דאבוה] דשמואל אשכחינהו להנך חמרי במדברא, אהדרינהו למרייהו לבתר תריסר ירחי שתא, ובההיא פטרי כ"ע. וי"ל: דבהנהו שקולאי לא שייך לפנים משורת הדין, כיון שעשו לו היזק גדול בפשיעה, ששיברו לו חבית של יין. **אחוי** דינר לר' אלעזר. אכתי הוה צריך למיגמר, דאי לא הוה צריך למיגמר — לא היה מחויב, כדמשמע גבי ר' חייא, דעבד לפנים משורת הדין. והא דקאמר (*מר) "חזי דעלך קסמכינא", אפילו לא אמר הוה מחייב, כמו ר' חייא דאע"ג דלא אמרה ליה הוה מחייב אי לאו משום דלא הוה צריך למילף. ורב אלפס כתב דלעולם לא מחייב עד שיאמרו לו.

טימא את הטהור. אע"ג דאמר ב"הניזקין" (גיטין דף נג:): המטמא והמדמע והמנסך בשוגג — פטור, הכא אית ליה לחיובי, אע"ג דשוגג הוא, מההיא טעמא דמחייב התם במזיד, למ"ד היזק שאין ניכר לא שמיה היזק, כדי שלא יהא כל אחד ואחד הולך ומטמא טהרותיו של חבירו — הכא נמי חייב, כדי שידקדק בדין יפה. ולמ"ד נמי שמיה היזק, ושוגג פטור כדי שיודיעו — הכא חייב, דליכא למיחש להכי, דאפילו טיהר את הטמא ועירבו עם פירותיו — ליכא למיחש שמא אח"כ לא יודיעו שהן טמאים, דכיון שדיין זה חכם ובעל הוראה — ודאי יודיענו.

טיהר את הטמא מה שעשה עשוי וישלם מביתו. א"א לייתב טיהר את הטמא בשום ענין אלא כשעירבו עם פירותיו, כדמפרש במסקנא בפ' "אחד דיני ממונות" (סנהדרין דף לג: ושם*) ובפרק "עד כמה" (בכורות דף כח: ושם). דאם הן בעין — לא מה שעשה עשוי, ולא ישלם מביתו שייך בהן. והא דלא מפרש הכי אלא כי מוקי לה כשנשא ונתן ביד — לאו משום דמעיקרא לאו בהכי עסקינן, אלא דמעיקרא לא איירי כשעירבן חכם, אלא הבעלים. אבל במסקנא קאמר שהחכם בעצמו עירבן. ובבכורות, שבא לייתב "וישלם מביתו" בטיהר את הטמא כשערבו עם פירותיו — איירי כשעירב עם פירות מועטים. ובסנהדרין שבא לייתב "מה שעשה עשוי" — איירי כשעירבו עם פירות מרובים, ונתבטלו הטמאים ברוב. דתרוייהו ליכא לאוקמי בענין אחד, דפשיטא דבמקום מה שעשה עשוי שהוא טהור — לא שייך ישלם מביתו. וא"ת: למאי דבעי לאוקמי כר"מ, היכי מתבטלים הטמאים ברוב? והא ס"ל לר"מ ב"הניזקין" (גיטין דף נד:) גבי אגוזי פרך ורימוני באדן נפלו ונתפצעו אפילו שוגג לא יעלו! וי"ל דשוגג כי האי, שעשה ע"פ חכם — לא קניס ר' מאיר. א"נ, התם דוקא שנתפצעו אחר הנפילה, שנאסרו בתחילת תערובתן — קאמר ר' מאיר דלא יעלו, אבל אם נתפצעו קודם שנתערבו — מודה ר"מ דשרי. א"נ, בהך מילתא דוקא דדאין דינא דגרמי אתיא כר"מ. ותימה: מאי בעי לאתויי מהכא דר' מאיר (א) דדאין דינא דגרמי, ואמאי מוקי לה נמי כשנשא ונתן ביד? בלא נשא ונתן ביד חייב, אפילו לרבנן דלא דייני דינא דגרמי, כיון דבאמירה בעלמא קם דינא, כדמוכח בפרק "אחד דיני ממונות" (סנהדרין דף לג. ושם*). דקאמר: אי אמרת בשלמא טעה בדבר משנה אין חוזר, אלמא קם דינא — היינו דקמפחד ר"ט. אלא אי אמרת חוזר — לימא ליה: כיון דאילו הואי פרה [קמן] הוה הדרא, השתא נמי דיינך לאו דינא, ולאו כלום עבדת. והתם ע"כ אתי כרבנן, דלר"מ דדאין דינא דגרמי, אע"ג דאילו הואי קמן הוה הדר — היה לו להתחייב כמו מראה דינר לשולחני דחייב, אע"ג דאילו הוה קמן הוה מהדר ליה! וי"ל: דלעולם ההיא סוגיא כר"מ. ולא דמי למראה דינר לשולחני, דכיון שהראהו לשולחני — שוב לא היה לו להראותו לאחר. אבל גבי פרה, כשאסרה לו חכם זה — לא היה לו למהר להאכילה לכלבים או לערבם עם פירות, והיה לו לישאל עדיין לחכם אחר. ומיהו, קשה מטיהר (ב) הטמא, אמאי מחייב חכם אפילו לר"מ במה שעירבו בעל הבית עם פירות? נימא כיון דאילו לא עירבו הוה הדר — השתא נמי לאו כלום עבד! וכן ברישא דהך דדן את הדין בפ' "עד כמה" (בכורות דף כח.), דתנן: מי שאינו מומחה וראה את הבכור ונשחט על פיו — הרי זה יקבר, וישלם מביתו. ואמאי? נימא: כיון דאילו לא נשחט היה מותר — השתא נמי לאו כלום עבד! וע"ק: דע"כ סוגיא דהכא ודבכורות דלא כרב חסדא, דהא משמע דאליבא דר"מ ניחא ליה בלא נשא ונתן ביד, אלא כרב ששת. וא"כ, כיון, דמה שעשה עשוי משום דאיירי דטעה בשיקול הדעת כדמוקי לה רב ששת בריש סנהדרין (דף ו.), למה נתחייב הדיין לרבנן במאי דנגע ביה שרץ? הלא בלאו הכי מה שעשה עשוי! ועוד, היכא דקם דינא, למה לא יתחייב אפילו לרבנן דלא דייני דינא דגרמי? מ"ש מכהנים שפיגלו במקדש דמזידין חייבין בין לר"מ בין לרבנן, אע"ג דבדבור בעלמא מיפסל, ולא חשיב דינא דגרמי? ונראה לפרש: דכל היכא דקם דינא אפילו בדבור — חשיב כמעשה ולא כגרמא, ומחייב אפילו לרבנן. אבל היכא דאילו הוה קמן הוה הדר, כגון מראה דינר וכגון טעה בדבר משנה — לר"מ חייב ולרבנן פטור, דהא ודאי גרמא הוא מה שהאכילו אחרי כן על פיו או מה שעירבו עם פירותיו. וסוגיא דסנהדרין כרבנן. והא דבעי הכא לאוכוחי דר"מ (ג) דאין דינא דגרמי — מטיהר את הטמא דייק דחייב חכם במה שעירבם בעל הבית עם פירותיו, ומחייב את הזכאי — דחייב חכם אמאי דשילם זכאי אחר כך. אבל טימא את הטהור וזיכה את החייב, דבדבורו של חכם מה שעשה עשוי — חייב לשלם אפילו לרבנן דלא דייני דינא דגרמי. וכן בפרק "עד כמה" (בכורות דף כח:) דקאמר: לימא תנן סתמא כר"מ — משום טיהר את הטמא וחייב את הזכאי קאמר, ולא משום טימא את הטהור וזיכה את החייב. והא דמפרש התם לשנויי מתני' כרבנן: טימא את הטהור — דנגע בה שרץ, זיכה את החייב — שהיה לו משכון ונטלו הימנו, אגב אחרינא מפרש להו. א"נ, סוגיא דהתם כרב חסדא ומפרש האמת. ורישא, דמי שאין מומחה וראה את הבכור ונשחט על פיו — לאו דוקא, אלא הוא עצמו שחטו. ול"ע: לרבנן, מ"ש דפטרי בשורף שטרות חבירו מטימא הטהור וכהנים שפיגלו, דלא חשיב דינא דגרמי? דמה לי אם גורם לו הפסד ע"י ששורף שטרותיו, ומה לי ע"י דיבורו? ול"ל: דדיבור חשיב כמעשה והוי מזיק בגוף הממון בידים, אבל בשורף שטר — אינו נוגע בגוף הממון, ונייהא בעלמא הוא דקלי מיניה, ואין (ד) אלא גרס בעלמא. ועוד י"ל: דסוגיא דהכא ודבכורות דלא כרב ששת אלא כרב חסדא, דלא קם דינא בדיבורי' בעלמא, ואיירי בנשא ונתן ביד כדמוקי התם רב חסדא. אלא דס"ד דגמ' דנשא ונתן בעלי דינין, ודמי דאיירי בנשא ונתן ביד הדיין עצמו. **שאני** התם דבידים עביד. תימה: ודקארי לה מאי קארי להו? וי"ל: משום דאין האמר משתנה מיד כשנותן בסממנים, דאין קולט הצבע מיד עד ב' ימים או ג', וגרמא בעלמא הוא. ודומה למסכך גפנו, שאין מזיק עד אחר זמן. ובתרוייהו משני: בידים קעביד. ומ"מ, מסכך גפנו לא מזיק כל כך בידים כמו בגמר לצבע, לפיכך הביאה אחר כך. **מחיצת** הכרם שנפרצה כו'. אור"ת: שאין (ה) משנה בשום מקום, אלא ברייתא היא. ומ"מ דייק דאתיא כר"מ ◎מכח ההיא משנה דהמסכך דלעיל, דפליגי התם בסיפא ר' יוסי ור"ש, ואמרי: אין אדם אוסר דבר שאין שלו, וא"כ ברייתא דמחיצת הכרם כר' יוסי ור"ש לא אתיא, אלא כת"ק דידהו, דהיינו כר"מ, דסתם משנה ר"מ היא. וא"ת: ומאן תנא דפליג אדר"מ בדינא דגרמי? דרבי יוסי ור"ש לא פליגי אלא משום דאין אדם אוסר דבר שאין שלו, ורבנן דפליגי אדר"ש בדבר הגורם לממון — ליכא למימר דיש חילוקין, כדפרישית ב"מרובה" (לעיל דף עא:*)! וי"ל: דההוא תנא דפרק "המניח" (לעיל דף לג:) דקתני: שחטו ונתנו במתנה — מה שעשה עשוי, פליג אר"מ, דמשמע דיש לפטור יותר בשורף שטרותיו מבשחטו. ולמאן דדאין דינא דגרמי אמר לעיל דמגבי ביה דמי שטרא מעליא.

אומר

מסורת הש"ס

כפ' אלו מציאו' דף ל: פי' רש"י בית חייהם ללמוד להן אומנות להתפרנס בו וחוקות ותורות כתיבי ברישא דקרא

[לעיל לח: כתובות פו.]

סנהדרין ו. לג. לקמן קיז: בכורות כח:

כלאים פ"ז מ"ד וה' יבמות פג.

ב"ב ב. [וש"נ]

עין משפט נר מצוה

עט א מיי' פ"י מהל' שכירות הלכה ה סמג עשין פט טוש"ע ח"מ סי' שו סעיף ו:

פ ב מיי' פ"ז מהל' חובל ומזיק הלכה יא ועיין בהשגות ובמ"מ סמג עשין ע טוש"ע ח"מ סי' שפו סעיף א:

פא ג ד מיי' פ"ו מהלכות סנהדרין הלכה ד סמג עשין לו טוש"ע ח"מ סי' כה סעיף ד:

פב ה מיי' פ"ז מהל' כלאים הלכה יז סמג לאוין רפ טוש"ע י"ד סי' רצו סעיף מז:

[ד"ה לפנים]

[ד"ה שעירבן]

[ד"ה הטמא]

[ד"ה וסבר]

הגהות הב"ח

(א) תום' ד"ה טיהר וכו' דר"מ היא דדאין וכו': (ב) בא"ד מיהו קשה מטיהר את הטמא כצ"ל: (ג) בא"ד והא דבעי הכא לאוכוחי דר"מ דדאין וכו': (ד) בא"ד ואין זה אלא גרס: (ה) ד"ה מחיצת וכו' שאין זה משנה:

גליון הש"ס

תום' ד"ה מחיצת וכו' מכח ההיא משנה דהמסכך. עי' לקמן דף קטז ע"ב תוס' ד"ה ל"ל הב':

עין משפט נר מצוה

פג א ב מיי' פ"י מהל' שכירות הלכה ד ועיין בהשגות ובמ"מ סמג עשין פט טוש"ע ח"מ סי' שו סעיף ג:

מסורת הש"ס

אומֵר לוֹ "גְּדוֹר, נִפְרְצָה — אומֵר לוֹ "גְּדוֹר", נִתְיָאֵשׁ מִמֶּנָּה וְלֹא גְּדָרָהּ — ה"ז קִידֵּשׁ וְחַיָּיב בְּאַחֲרָיוּתוֹ.§

מתני' *[א]הַנּוֹתֵן צֶמֶר לַצַּבָּע וְהִקְדִּיחוֹ יוֹרָה — נוֹתֵן לוֹ דְּמֵי צַמְרוֹ. צְבָעוֹ כָּאוּר, אִם הַשֶּׁבַח יָתֵר עַל הַיְּצִיאָה — נוֹתֵן לוֹ אֶת הַיְּצִיאָה, וְאִם הַיְּצִיאָה יְתֵירָה עַל הַשֶּׁבַח — נוֹתֵן לוֹ אֶת הַשֶּׁבַח. *לִצְבּוֹעַ לוֹ אָדוֹם וּצְבָעוֹ שָׁחוֹר, שָׁחוֹר וּצְבָעוֹ אָדוֹם — רַבִּי מֵאִיר אוֹמֵר: נוֹתֵן לוֹ דְּמֵי צַמְרוֹ; ר' יְהוּדָה אוֹמֵר: [ב]אִם הַשֶּׁבַח יָתֵר עַל הַיְּצִיאָה — נוֹתֵן לוֹ אֶת הַיְּצִיאָה, וְאִם הַיְּצִיאָה יְתֵירָה עַל הַשֶּׁבַח — נוֹתֵן לוֹ אֶת הַשֶּׁבַח.§

גמ' מַאי כָּאוּר? אָמַר ר"נ אָמַר רַבָּה בַּר בַּר חָנָה: כְּלַבּוּם. מַאי כְּלַבּוּם? אָמַר רַבָּה בַּר שְׁמוּאֵל:

כַּפְרָא

רש"י

גְּדוֹר. שֶׁלֹּא יוֹסִיף הַתְּבוּאָה אֶחָד מִמָּאתַיִם בְּעוֹד הַמְּחִיצָּה פְּרוּצָה, וְתֵאָסֵר. **נִתְיָאֵשׁ וְלֹא גְּדָרָהּ.** וּבְתוֹךְ כָּךְ הוֹצִיא הַזֶּרַע אֶחָד מִן הַמָּאתַיִם שֶׁהָיוּ בָּהּ בְּהֶיתֵּר. א] **הֲרֵי זֶה קִידֵּשׁ.** וְאֵין בָּטֵל אֶלָּא בְּאֶחָד וּמָאתַיִם, וְכָאן יֵשׁ קנ"ט מִן הַהֶיתֵּר וְחַד בְּאִיסּוּר. **מתני'** וְהִקְדִּיחוֹ יוֹרָה. שֶׁרְפָתּוּ יוֹרָה. שֶׁהִרְתִּיחוֹ יוֹתֵר מִדַּאי. **נוֹתֵן לוֹ דְּמֵי צַמְרוֹ.** וְהָכָא לֵיכָּא שְׁבָחָא כְּלָל, דְּהָא נִשְׂרַף לְגַמְרֵי, וְלֵיכָּא לְמֵימַר אִם הַשֶּׁבַח יוֹתֵר. **צְבָעוֹ כָּאוּר.** כְּמוֹ כָּעוּר. בַּגְּמָ' מְפָרֵשׁ שֶׁצְּבָעוֹ בִּשְׁיָרֵי צֶבַע, וּמַזִּיק בְּכַוָּונָה הוּא, לְפִיכָךְ יָדוֹ עַל הַתַּחְתּוֹנָה דִּבְרֵי הַכֹּל. **וְאִם הַשֶּׁבַח.** שֶׁהִשְׁבִּיחַ הַצֶּמֶר, יָתֵר עַל הַיְּצִיאָה שֶׁל צַבָּע. **נוֹתֵן לוֹ.** לַצַּבָּע אֶת הַיְּצִיאָה, וְלֹא שָׂכָר שָׁלֵם, וּמְקַבֵּל צַמְרוֹ. וּדְמֵי צַמְרוֹ לֹא קָאָמַר דְּיָהֵיב, דְּלִקְנֵי אִיהוּ שְׁבָחָא דְּצֶמֶר, דְּהָא בַּצֶּבַע שֶׁהִתְנָה עִמּוֹ צְבָעוֹ, וְלֵיכָּא שִׁנּוּיָא דְּנִקְנְיֵיהּ. **לִצְבּוֹעַ לוֹ אָדוֹם כו'.** קָנֵי בְּשִׁינּוּי לְר"מ, וְלָא יָהֵיב לֵיהּ אֶלָּא דְּמֵי צַמְרוֹ, אֲבָל לֹא דְּמֵי שִׁבְחוֹ. אוֹ זֶה יִתֵּן שְׂכָרוֹ מִשָּׁלֵם וְיִקַּח הַצֶּמֶר. **ר' יְהוּדָה אוֹמֵר כו'.** דְּקָנֵיס לֵיהּ לְהַאי דְּשִׁינָּה, לִהְיוֹת יָדוֹ עַל הַתַּחְתּוֹנָה, וְלָא נִתְהֲנֵי מִשְּׁבָחָא. וְאַגְּרָא נַמִּי כּוּלֵּיהּ לָא יִשְׁקוֹל אֶלָּא יְצִיאָה. וְאִם יְצִיאָה יְתֵירָה עַל הַשֶּׁבַח – יִתֵּן לוֹ אֶת הַשֶּׁבַח שֶׁהִשְׁבִּיחַ אֶת הַצֶּמֶר, וְאִם יִרְצֶה לָתֵת אֶת שְׂכָרוֹ, כְּגוֹן שֶׁהַשֶּׁבַח יוֹתֵר עַל הַשָּׂכָר – יִתֵּן שְׂכָרוֹ. **גמ'**

כַּפְרָא

תוספות

אומר לו גדור. פי': לבעל הכרם, דהוא המזיק. דד' אמות שאמרו להרחיק הוא בשביל עבודת הכרם. כדתנן ב"לא יחפור" (ב"ב דף כו. ושם): לא יטע אדם אילן סמוך לשדה חבירו אא"כ הרחיק ממנו ד' אמות, אחד גפנים ואחד כל אילן. ומפרש בגמ': ד' אמות שאמרו — כנגד עבודת הכרם. ואפילו ר' יוסי דאמר התם על הניזק להרחיק את עצמו — הא א"ר אשי התם: מודה ר"י בגירי דיליה, והכא גירי דבעל כרם הם, דאסדינן ליה שלא יביא מחרישתו בשדה חבירו, לפיכך צריך לעשות כותל או להרחיק ארבע אמות. והא דנקט "אומרין לו גדור" ולא נקט "חייב לגדור", נראה לר"י: לפי שצריך להתרות בו, ואם לא התרו בו לגדור — אין חייב באחריותו. ולהכי נקט נמי תרי זימני "נפרצה אומר לו גדור", דאף פעם שנית דנפרצה צריך להתרות בו, ואם לא התרו בו לגדור — אין חייב באחריותו, שאין סבור להיות חייב לגדור כל שעה שנפרצה. ונפרצה פעם שלישית מספקא לר"י אם צריך להתרות בו בכל פעם, או שמא סגי בתרי זימני. ור"ת מפרש: דלהכי נקט תרי זימני — לאשמועינן שאם יש תוספת מאתים בין מה שהוסיף כשנפרצה ראשונה ובין מה שהוסיף כשנפרצה שניה — דאין מצטרפין לאסור, דקמא קמא בטלה. ודוקא [ספ"ז דכלאים] כשיש הפסק בינתיים, אבל בעלמא כלאים נאסרין במאתים, *ולא [ד"ה כי] אמרינן כל פורתא כשהוא גדל מתבטל. והא דאמר בפ' בתרא דע"ז (דף עג. ושם*): המערה יין נסך מחבית לבור אפילו כל היום כולו, קמא קמא בטל — מפרש ר"ת בדפסיק פסוקי, אבל אם מערה בלא הפסק — אסור, מידי דהוה אכלאים הנאסרין בתוספת מאתים לפי שגדל בלא הפסק. [ד"ה שמא] והא דאמר ב"במה אשה" (שבת דף סה: ושם*): שמואל עביד לבנתיה מקוואות ביומי ניסן כו' שמא ירבו הנוטפים על הזוחלים — היינו שמא ירבה בלא הפסק. וכן בפרק "הנודר מן הירק" (נדרים דף נז:) גבי בצל שעקרו בשביעית ונטעו בשמינית ורבו גידוליו על עיקרו — מותר, ולא אמרינן קמא קמא בטיל, לפי שגדל בלא הפסק. ורבי יוחנן גופיה, דקאמר בפרק בתרא דע"ז (דף עג. ושם) ראשון ראשון בטל, אית ליה התם בנדרים דגידולי היתר מעלין את האיסור. ור"י בן רבינו מאיר פירש בתוספתא בנדרים דבצל וכלאים, וגבי נוטפין דווסתן בכך ליגדל מעט מעט — לא בטיל קמא קמא כמו ביין נסך, דהתם לא שייך למימר הכי. אבל קשה, דאמר בפ' "הערל" (יבמות דף פב: ושם*): נתן סאה ונטל סאה — עד רובו. [ד"ה אמר] וברובו מיהא מיפסל, ולא אמר קמא קמא בטיל! וי"ל: דהתם במי פירות איירי, דהחמירו טפי. וא"ת: אי במי פירות איירי — היכי מדמה לה לתרומה דרבנן? דמי פירות דפסולין דאורייתא, כדמשמע בפרק "כיסוי הדם" (חולין דף פד. ושם) מדכתיב "מים" יתירא, והיאך יהיו כשרים במקוה על מקוה דאורייתא? וי"ל בדוחק: דאע"ג דמיפסלי מדאורייתא — מקוה על מקוה כשרים להטביל בהם מחטין וצינוריות, דאין צריכין ארבעים סאה מדאורייתא אלא מדרבנן. ומיהו, אכתי קשה מהא דמסיק רב דימי בפרק שלישי דבכורות (דף כב. ושם*) [ד"ה יתיב] גבי הלוקח ציר מעם הארץ משיקו במים והוא טהור: אי רובא מיא נינהו — סלקא להו השקה, ואי רובא ציר נינהו — לא בעי השקה, דמים בטלים בציר. ומסיק: לא שנו אלא לטבל בו פיתו, אבל לקדירה — לא, דמצא מין את מינו וניעור. אלמא, התם אע"ג שהיו כבר מבוטלות — חוזרות וניעור בתוך הקדירה, וכל שכן דלא אמרינן קמא קמא בטיל! וי"ל: דהתם חומרא הוא שהחמירו גבי טומאה, דלאו בדפסיק פסוקי — לא נעלה. ואע"ג דבכמה דברים איסור חמור מטומאה, כדאמרינן בפרק "כיסוי הדם" (חולין דף פו: ושם): אם אמרו ספק טומאה לטהר, יאמרו ספק איסור להתיר — התם החמירו חכמים בטומאה יותר. ואין ראיה משמעתא בתרייתא דנדה (דף עא: ושם) דמחלק גבי דם תבוסה בין פסק ללא פסק — דשאני דם תבוסה דרבנן, ויש להקל בו יותר. [ד"ה רואין] ומהא דאמר בפ' "כיסוי הדם" (חולין דף פז. ושם*) ובפרק "התערובת" (זבחים דף עז: ושם*) גבי הא דתנן: דם שנתערב במים, אם יש (א) מראית דם בו — כשר. וקאמר בגמ': לא שנו אלא כשנפלו מים לתוך דם, אבל דם שנתערב במים ראשון ראשון בטל — התם בלא שינויא אתי שפיר, דהתם נמי דה היינו טעמא, דכיון שנדחה שוב אין נראה, שכן הוא הדין בכל דבר הקרב. ואפילו למ"ד אין דיחוי בבעלי חיים — בשחוטין יש דיחוי. וכן מוכח בפרק "כיסוי הדם" (חולין דף פז: ושם) דטעמא משום דיחוי הוא, דמסיק בתר הכי: ולענין כיסוי — אין בו דיחוי, דאין דיחוי אלא מצות מכלל דלענין דם הוי טעמא משום דיחוי. ואין להקשות מהא דאמר בפרק "נוטל" (שבת דף קמב.): סאה תרומה שנפלה למאה של חולין ולא הספיק להעלותה עד שנפלה אחרת — לא תעלה, ולא אמרינן ראשון ראשון בטל, אע"ג דנפל ע"י הפסק — דהתם צריך להרים. ובענין אחר אין ק' סאה שנפלה בהן מתירין, ולא שייך התם ראשון ראשון בטל. **נתייאש** ממנה ולא גדרה. דוקא נתייאש, אבל אם לא נתייאש, ועוסק כל שעה לגדור, אע"פ שהוסיף מאתים — מותר, כדתנן במס' כלאים (פ"ה מ"ו): הרואה ירק בתוך כרמו, ואמר: כשאגיע שם אלקטנו — מותר. לכשאחזור שם אלקטנו, והוסיף מאתים — אסור. אלמא: כשהוא מחזר אחר לקיטתו כל שעה, אפילו הוסיף מאתים — מותר. וטעמא י"ל, משום דכתיב "לא תזרע כרמך", משמע זריעה דניחא ליה. **חייב** באחריותו. אע"ג דהיזק שאין ניכר לא שמיה היזק, נראה לר"י דהא חשיב היזק ניכר, שהרי ניכר שהוא כלאים, כשרואה הגפנים בשדה. אבל מטמא טהרות חבירו, אע"פ שרואין השרץ על הטהרות — לא חשיב היזק ניכר, דמי יודע אם הוכשרו? אבל אין לומר: הכא נמי הוי היזק שאין ניכר, וקנסוהו כמו במטמא, שלא יהא כל אחד הולך ומטמא טהרותיו של חבירו — דהכא ליכא למיחש, כיון שבעל כרם נמי מפסיד. ועוד: *אי קנס הוא — במזיד דוקא היה לו להתחייב. **אם** השבח יתר על היציאה. מפרש בירושלמי: מהו השבח יתר על היציאה? בר נש דיהיב לחבריה חמש מנוי למר וחמש מנוי סממנין, ועשרה מנוי אגרא, ואמר ליה: זיל צבעיה סומקי, ואזל וצבעיה אוכם. א"ל: אילו צבעתיה סומקא — הוה שוה עשרים וחמש מנוי, השתא דצבעתיה אוכם — לית הוא שוי אלא עשרים מנוי. את אבדך דידך, ואנא לא אבדנא דידי. עד כאן לשון הירושלמי בפירקא. ואור"י דהכי *פי' דרבי יהודה לפי הירושלמי: אם השבח שהושבח הצמר יותר על ט"ו מנים, והיתר על ט"ו [א] מנים קרי שבח יתר על הוצאה, והוצאה קרי עשרה מנים של שכר הצבע, שמוציא הצבע וטורח ויהיה בשכרו י' מנים. דהשתא אם השבח על ט"ו מנים יותר מי' מנים, שהם יציאה — נותן לו היציאה דהיינו י' מנים, ולא יתן לו יותר. ואם היציאה יתירה על השבח, שלא הושבח על ט"ו מנים אלא ד' או ה' — יתן לו השבח מה שהושבח על ט"ו, ואין נותן לו כל י' מנים שהתנה עמו, דא"ל: את אפסדת דידך, ואנא לא אפסדנא דידי. ויש ליתן טעם לדברי הירושלמי למה לא יהיה כאן הדין כמו *בנוטע שלא ברשות — דנעשה כאן כאילו כן התנה עמו. א"נ, קנסא הוא משום דשינה ממה שצוה לו. ומיהו, "אם השבח יתר על היציאה" דתנן גבי צבע כעור — לא הוי פירוש כי ההיא דירושלמי, כי איך יהיה השבח של צבע כעור יותר משבח של צבע גמור? וגבי כסא כעור דגמרא — אפשר ודאי שיהא טוב מן הנאה, כגון שהנאה אין חזק כמו הכעור, ע"י כך דמי הכעור יתירה על הנאה. ואין לשון ירושלמי משמע כפי' ר"י, שהרי משמע שבא לפרש מהו אם השבח יתר על היציאה, ולדברי ר"י הוא מפרש היציאה יתירה על השבח. והר"ר אלחנן פי' בע"א, ולא מצאתי כתוב*.

הא

הגהות הב"ח

(א) תוס' ד"ה אומר וכו' אם יש בו מראית דם כשר:

הגהות הגר"א

[א] תוס' ד"ה אם כו' ט"ו מנים קרי שבח (יתר על הוצאה) תא"מ (וכן מחקו רש"ל):

גליון הש"ס

תוס' ד"ה חייב וכו' אי קנס הוא במזיד דוקא. ק"ל הא הברייתא מוקמינן כר"מ ור"מ הא סבור כדרבנן קנסו שוגג אטו מזיד וא"כ י"ל דסבר כת"ק דר"ע דמקיים כלאים לא הוי לאורייתא וההיא דמסכך גפנו י"ל במזיד דהרי תוס' לא הקדימו קושייתם אההיא דהמסכך (לעיל) [ל"ל] כו' דנתייאש משמע אף בשכח וא"כ קשה כנ"ל והיינו מרויחים בזה קושית תוס' ד"ה מחילת כרם די"ל דמוכח דהברייתא כר"מ מלקינים גם בשוגג:

הגהות מהר"ב רנשבורג

א] רש"י ד"ה הרי זה קידש וכו' ומאתים וכאן כו'. עיין רש"י ותוס' בחולין דף לט ע"ב ד"ה לא במאה ובשבת דף קמב ע"א בתוס' ד"ה שנפלה ודוק היטב:

כ' מהרנ"ש ז"ל בקצרה הר"י בא לפרש התיבות אם השבח יתר על ההוצאה ומציין תחלה אם השבח ומפ' והיתר על ט"ו מנים קרי שבח ואח"כ מציין יתר על ההוצאה ומפ' והוצאה קרי ובזה א"ש לשון התוס' וא"ל למחוק תיבות יתר על היציאה שמחק מהרש"ל. העתק מחילופי גרסאות

לעיל לח:

[לעיל לה. לה: לקמן ב"מ עח. קיז: ע"ז ו: ז. בתוס' ד"ה ר"מ]

כתובות פ. ב"מ קו:

עיין בהגהות הרא"ה

מסורת הש"ס

עין משפט נר מצוה

כַּפְרָא דוּדֵי.§ תָּנוּ רַבָּנַן: הַנּוֹתֵן עֵצִים לְחָרָשׁ לַעֲשׂוֹת מֵהֶן כִּסֵּא וְעָשָׂה מֵהֶן סַפְסָל, סַפְסָל וְעָשָׂה מֵהֶן כִּסֵּא — ר' מֵאִיר אוֹמֵר: נוֹתֵן לוֹ דְּמֵי עֵצָיו; רַבִּי יְהוּדָה אוֹמֵר: [א]אִם הַשֶּׁבַח יָתֵר עַל הַיְצִיאָה — נוֹתֵן לוֹ אֶת הַיְצִיאָה, וְאִם הַיְצִיאָה יְתֵירָה עַל הַשֶּׁבַח — נוֹתֵן לוֹ אֶת הַשֶּׁבַח; וּמוֹדֶה רַבִּי מֵאִיר: [ב]אִם נָתַן עֵצִים לְחָרָשׁ לַעֲשׂוֹת מֵהֶן כִּסֵּא נָאֶה וְעָשָׂה מֵהֶן כִּסֵּא כָּעוּר, סַפְסָל נָאֶה וְעָשָׂה סַפְסָל כָּעוּר, אִם הַשֶּׁבַח יָתֵר עַל הַיְצִיאָה — נוֹתֵן לוֹ דְּמֵי הַיְצִיאָה, וְאִם הַיְצִיאָה יְתֵירָה עַל הַשֶּׁבַח — נוֹתֵן לוֹ דְּמֵי הַשֶּׁבַח.§ [ג]אִיבַּעְיָא לְהוּ: יֵשׁ שֶׁבַח סַמָּנִין עַל הַצֶּמֶר, אוֹ אֵין שֶׁבַח סַמָּנִין עַל הַצֶּמֶר? הֵיכִי דָּמֵי? אִילֵימָא דִּגְזַל סַמָּנִין וְדַקִּינְהוּ וּתְרַנְהוּ וְצָבַע בָּהֶן, תֵּיפוֹק לֵיהּ מִשּׁוּם דְּקַנִּינְהוּ בְּשִׁינּוּי! לָא צְרִיכָא, דִּגְזַל סַמָּנִין שְׁרוּיִין וּצְבַע בְּהוּ, מַאי? יֵשׁ שֶׁבַח סַמָּנִין עַל גַּבֵּי צֶמֶר, דְּאָמַר לֵיהּ: הַב לִי סַמָּנַאי דִּשְׁקַלְתִּינְהוּ, אוֹ דִלְמָא אֵין שֶׁבַח סַמָּנִין עַל גַּבֵּי הַצֶּמֶר, דְּא"ל: לֵית לָךְ גַּבַּאי וְלָא מִידֵּי? אָמְרִי: וְאִי אֵין שֶׁבַח סַמָּנִין עַל גַּבֵּי צֶמֶר, מִי מָצֵי אָמַר לֵיהּ לֵית לָךְ גַּבַּאי וְלָא מִידֵּי? נֵימָא לֵיהּ: הַב לִי סַמָּנַאי דְּאַפְסַדְתִּינְהוּ! אֶלָּא לְהַךְ גִּיסָא: אֵין שֶׁבַח סַמָּנִין עַל גַּבֵּי הַצֶּמֶר וּבָעֵי שַׁלּוּמֵי לֵיהּ, אוֹ דִלְמָא יֵשׁ שֶׁבַח סַמָּנִין עַל גַּבֵּי צֶמֶר, וְא"ל: הָא מַנְחִי קַמָּךְ, שְׁקַלִינְהוּ? שְׁקַלִינְהוּ?! בְּמַאי שָׁקְלֵיהּ, בְּצָפוֹן? צָפוֹן עֲבוּרֵי מִיעֲבַר, הֲשָׁבָה לָא עָבֵיד! [ד]אֶלָּא הב"ע — כְּגוֹן דִּגְזַל צֶמֶר וְסַמָּנִין דְּחַד, וּצְבָעֵיהּ לְהַהוּא צֶמֶר בְּהָנָךְ סַמָּנִין, וְקָא מַהֲדַר לֵיהּ נִיהֲלֵיהּ לַצֶּמֶר; יֵשׁ שֶׁבַח סַמָּנִין ע"ג הַצֶּמֶר, וְקָא מַהֲדַר לֵיהּ סַמָּנִין וְצֶמֶר, אוֹ דִלְמָא אֵין שֶׁבַח סַמָּנִין עַל גַּבֵּי צֶמֶר, וְצֶמֶר מַהֲדַר לֵיהּ, סַמָּנִין לָא מַהֲדַר לֵיהּ? אָמְרִי: תֵּיפוֹק לֵיהּ דְּאִייַּקַר לֵיהּ נִיהֲלֵיהּ בְּדָמֵי! לָא צְרִיכָא, דְּזַל צִיבְעָא. וְאִיבָּעֵית אֵימָא: כְּגוֹן שֶׁצָּבַע בְּהוּ קוֹפָא. רָבִינָא אָמַר: הָכָא בְּמַאי עָסְקִינַן — כְּגוֹן דְּצֶמֶר דְּחַד וְסַמָּנִין דְּחַד, וְקָאָתֵי קוֹף וּצְבָעֵיהּ לְהַהוּא צֶמֶר בְּהָנָךְ סַמָּנִין; יֵשׁ שֶׁבַח סַמָּנִין עַל גַּבֵּי צֶמֶר, דְּאָמַר לֵיהּ: הַב לִי סַמָּנַאי דְּגַבָּךְ נִינְהוּ. אוֹ דִלְמָא אֵין שֶׁבַח סַמָּנִין עַל גַּבֵּי צֶמֶר, וְאָמַר לֵיהּ: לֵית לָךְ גַּבַּאי כְּלוּם? תָּא שְׁמַע: *[ה]בֶּגֶד שֶׁצְּבָעוֹ בִּקְלִיפֵּי עָרְלָה — יִדָּלֵק; אַלְמָא חֲזוּתָא מִילְּתָא הִיא. אָמַר רָבָא: *הֲנָאָה הַנִּרְאָה לָעֵינַיִם אָסְרָה תּוֹרָה, דְּתַנְיָא: °"עֲרֵלִים לֹא יֵאָכֵל" — *אֵין לִי אֶלָּא אִיסּוּר אֲכִילָה, [ו]מִנַּיִן שֶׁלֹּא יֵהָנֶה מִמֶּנּוּ, וְלֹא יִצְבַּע [בּוֹ] וְלֹא יַדְלִיק בּוֹ אֶת הַנֵּר? תַּלְמוּד לוֹמַר: °"וַעֲרַלְתֶּם עָרְלָתוֹ אֶת פִּרְיוֹ עֲרֵלִים לֹא יֵאָכֵל", לְרַבּוֹת אֶת כּוּלָּם. תָּא שְׁמַע: [ז]בֶּגֶד שֶׁצְּבָעוֹ בִּקְלִיפֵּי שְׁבִיעִית — יִדָּלֵק. שָׁאנֵי הָתָם, דְּאָמַר קְרָא: °"תִּהְיֶה", בַּהֲוָיָתָהּ תְּהֵא.

רָבָא

רש"י

כַּפְרָא דוּדֵי. קִינַּח בּוֹ אֶת הַיּוֹרָה. כְּלוֹמַר: בִּשְׁיָרֵי צֶבַע שֶׁנִּשְׁתַּיְּירוּ בַּיּוֹרָה צְבָעוֹ. כּוּפְרָא = לְשׁוֹן קִינּוּחַ, *כְּמוֹ בְּלִיתָא דִּפְרָסָא לְמִכְפְּרֵיהּ, בְּ"הַכֹּל שׁוֹחֲטִין" (חולין דף ח.). נוֹתֵן לוֹ דְּמֵי עֵצָיו. דְּקַנְיֵיהּ בְּשִׁינּוּי. אֲבָל נָתַן עֵצִים כו', דְּלָא שִׁינָּה וְלָא קָנֵי – יָדוֹ עַל הַתַּחְתּוֹנָה. יֵשׁ שֶׁבַח כו'. כְּלוֹמַר: חֲזוּתָא מִילְּתָא הִיא, אוֹ לָאו מִילְּתָא. וּתְרַנְהוּ. שְׁרָאָן בַּמַּיִם כְּדַרְכָּן. וְצָבַע בָּהֶן. צֶמֶר שֶׁלּוֹ. מִבַּעְיָא לָן: יֵשׁ שֶׁבַח סַמָּנִין עַל הַצֶּמֶר, דַּחֲזוּתָא מִילְּתָא הִיא, וְאָמַר לֵיהּ: הַב לִי סַמָּנַאי דִּשְׁקַלְתִּינְהוּ כו', כִּדְבָעֵינָא לְמֵימַר קַמָּן. אָמְרִי וְאִי אֵין שֶׁבַח כו' מִי מָצֵי אָמַר לֵיהּ לֵית לָךְ גַּבַּאי וְלָא מִידֵּי. בִּתְמִיָּה, נְהִי נַמִּי דַּחֲזוּתָא לָאו מִילְּתָא הִיא – לֵימָא לֵיהּ: הַב לִי סַמָּנַאי דְּאַפְסַדְתִּינְהוּ! צָפוֹן. שוו"ן. וְקָא מַהֲדַר לֵיהּ. לַצֶּמֶר כְּשֶׁהוּא צָבוּעַ, מַאי? יֵשׁ שֶׁבַח סַמָּנִים עַל גַּבֵּי צֶמֶר. דַּחֲזוּתָא מִילְּתָא הִיא, וְקָמַהֲדַר לֵיהּ צֶמֶר וְקָמַהֲדַר לֵיהּ סַמָּנִים, כְּלוֹמַר: בְּהַךְ הֲשָׁבָה דְּצֶמֶר קָמַהֲדַר (א). דְּזוּל צִיבְעָא. צֶמֶר צָבוּעַ הוּזַל בָּעוֹלָם, וְאֵין (ב) מַגִּיעִין שֶׁבַח לִדְמֵי סַמָּנִים. וְאָמַר לֵיהּ נִגְזָל: ⊕אֲנִי הָיִיתִי מוֹכֵר סַמָּנִים, אוֹ הָיִיתִי צוֹבֵעַ בֶּגֶד, וְעַכְשָׁיו הִפְסַדְתַּנִי, דְּהָא לֹא הִשְׁבִּיחוּ בַּצֶּמֶר. א"נ דְּצָבַע בְּהוּ קוֹפָא. גָּזַל קוֹף וְסַמָּנִים וְצָבַע אֶת הַקּוֹף וּמַחֲזִירוֹ לוֹ, דְּלָא אִייַּקַּר לֵיהּ. *וְאָמְרֵי לָהּ: קוּפָּה שֶׁל נְצָרִים. כְּגוֹן דְּצֶמֶר דְּחַד וְסַמָּנִין דְּחַד כו'. וְלָאו לְעִנְיַן גַּזְלָן קָבָעֵי לָהּ, דְּאֵין כָּאן גָּזֵל. בִּקְלִיפֵּי עָרְלָה. קְלִיפֵּי אֱגוֹזִים אוֹ שְׁאָר פֵּירוֹת. אֲבָל קְלִיפַּת הָעֵץ – לֹא, דְּאֵין עָרְלָה אֶלָּא בְּפֵירוֹת. הַנִּרְאָה לָעֵינַיִם. מַרְאֶה בְּעָלְמָא, אע"פ שֶׁאֵין בּוֹ מַמָּשׁ, כְּגוֹן נֵר וָצֶבַע. שְׁבִיעִית. אָסוּר לַעֲשׂוֹת סְחוֹרָה בְּפֵירוֹתֶיהָ. וּקְלִיפֵּי פֵּירוֹת קָאָמַר, וְלֹא קְלִיפֵּי עָלִים, דְּעָלִים אֵין שְׁבִיעִית חָלָה עֲלֵיהֶן, כִּדְלְקַמָּן, דִּסְתָם עָלִים לְהַסָּקָה נִיתְּנוּ.

רְבִיעִית

תוספות

הא מנחי קמך שקלינהו. ומ"מ אגרא בעי למיתב למישקל להו, דכיון דאתי לידיה — בעי למיעבד השבה, כדאמר לעיל (דף לח.) גבי זורק מטבע לים. דזל ציבעא. ומכל מקום איירי דגזל סממנים שרויין, דאי דקינהו ושרנהו — קננהו בשינוי. דצבע בהו קופא. פירש בקונטרס: שגזל קוף וסממנים שרויין, וצבע את הקוף. ותימה: דאם כן אפסדיה בידים, וכה"ג היזק ניכר הוא, ומחייב! ונראה לפרש: דצבע בהו קופא — כלומר בגריעות ובכיעור כעין קוף, שהוא מכוער. או דלמא אין שבח של סממנין על גבי צמר. תימה: הרי נהנה, שאמרו מעולה בדמים יותר, וישלם מה שנהנה. כמו אכלה* מלידי רחבה דפ"ב (דף יט:), *וירדה לגינה ד"הכונס" (לעיל דף נה:), ובפרק "אלו נערות" (כתובות דף ל: ושם) אמר: תחב לו חבירו משקין של אחרים בבית הבליעה — דמשלם מה שנהנה! ויש לחלק, דהנאה דהכא אין באה ע"י מעשיו, ולא ע"י מעשה בהמתו. ובתחב לו חבירו, אע"פ שאין זה ע"י מעשיו — מכל מקום נהנה גופו. אי נמי, הנאה דהכא לא חשיבא הנאה, שאין ⊕אלא נוי בעלמא יותר.

מנין שלא יהנה ממנו. בפרק "כל שעה" (פסחים דף כב: ושם ד"ה מנין) פריך: אמאי לא נפקא לן איסור הנאה מ"לא יאכל"?

ולא יצבע בו ולא ידליק בו הנר. אע"ג דאסר שאר הנאות, אצטריך לרבויי צביעה והדלקה, צביעה — משום דחזותא בעלמא הוא, והדלקה — משום שכלה האיסור בשעת הדלקה. ואם תאמר: והא בפרק "כל שעה" (שם דף כו:) שרינן עצים להדלקה למאן דאמר אין שבח עצים בפת, ולא משכחי עצים דאיסורא אלא כעין כסא ושרשיפא! ויש לומר: דשמן הוי בעין בשעה שהוא דולק, אבל עצים נעשים גחלת, והשלהבת אין באה אלא מן הגחלת. ואם תאמר: ומ"ש דהכא מצריכין קרא להדלקה, וגבי תרומה טמאה מצריכין קרא להתיר, כדדרשינן: שלך תהא, להסיקה תחת תבשילך? וי"ל: משום דס"ד דנילף תרומה ממעשר הקל, דאמרה תורה "לא בערתי ממנו בטמא", כדאמר ב"במה מדליקין" (שבת דף כה.). ור"ת מפרש: דאיצטריך קרא הכא לאסור צביעה והדלקה שלא כדרך הנאתו, כגון צביעה דתאנים ורמונים, ודברים דלאו אורחייהו. והדלקה איצטריך לשמן שאין עומד להדלקה כלל. והיינו דפרק "כל שעה" (פסחים דף כה:) דהוה *שייף לברתיה *בגוהרקי דערלה, וקאמר: מידי דרך הנאה קעבידנא — התם לא הוה דרך הנאה כלל. וקשה לפי': דהא בעי למפשט מהכא דחזותא מילתא היא, ודחי דשאני הכא דגלי קרא, משמע דלא אתא קרא למיסר שלא כדרך הנאה, אלא למיסר אע"ג דליכא אלא חזותא בעלמא. וא"ת: אם כן, תיפשוט לאידך גיסא: מדאיצטריך למיסר — שמע מינה דחזותא לאו מילתא היא! ויש לומר: דאיכא למילף מהכא דחשיב כאילו הוא בעין. ותימה: לרבי יהושע, דגמר בערלה "פרי" מ"פרי" מבכורים בפרק "העור והרוטב" (חולין דף קכ: ושם), וסבר דאין סופגין את הארבעים על הערלה אלא על היוצא מן הזיתים ומן הענבים, אבל היוצא משאר פירות — מותר, היאך יאסר לצבוע במשקיהן מן התורה, וכל שכן במים שנישורו בהם הקליפין? ויש לומר: דלא איצטריך קרא אלא שלא יצבע בזיתים וענבים ויוצא מהם, או בממשות של עפרורית הקליפין הנטחנין. ומיהו, לא יצבע דקתני בברייתא — איירי שפיר בכל עניני צביעה דערלה ומשקיהן בכל ענין, ומדרבנן. ומיהו, קרא לא אתיא אלא כדפרישית. אי נמי, יש לומר: דפרי דערלה דוקא גמר פרי מפרי דביכורים, ולהכי אימעוט משקה דידהו. אבל שומר לפרי, דאיתרבו מ"את פריו" — את הטפל לפריו, לא אמעיט משקה דידהו, וליכא למעוטי מפרי דביכורים, דביכורים ליתנהו בשומר לפרי כלל. ואע"ג דהוי השתא טפל חמור מן העיקר — יש ליתן טעם שלא יקשה מזה על שמעתא דריש "איזהו מקומן" (זבחים דף מח:). אבל אין לומר דאף על גב דליכא מלקות ביוצא משאר פירות, עשה ד"ערלתם ערלתו" איכא, דהא אכל מאי דכתיב "וערלתם" קאי "לא יאכל" דכתיב בתר הכי. ועוד: אם היה במשקה דשאר פירות דערלה איסור עשה — אם כן מנא ליה שלא יצבע בו? הא איצטריך לאסור המשקין בשתיה ובהנאה כשהן בעין! ואין להקשות: כיון דאיתרבי שומר לפרי, דלא חזי לאכילה — אם כן על כרחך מיתסרא ערלה בהנאה, ולמאי איצטריך קרא שלא יהנה? דהא איכא שומרין טובא דחזו לאכילה.

רבא

מסורת הש"ס

רש"י זבחים כה. ד"ה כפורי זהב

תורה אור

מפירוש הערוך. רש"ל

ערלה פ"ג מ"א

[מעילה כ.]

ויקרא יט

שם

שם כה

פי' מוסף

עין משפט נר מצוה

פד א ב מיי' פ"י מהל' שכירות הלכה ד סמג עשין פט טוש"ע ח"מ סי' שו סעיף ג:

פה ג ד מיי' פ"ג מהל' גזילה ואבידה הלכה י טוש"ע ח"מ סי' שסג סעיף יא:

פו ה מיי' פט"ז מהלכות מאכלות אסורות הלכה כ:

פז ו מיי' שם פ"י הלכה ט סמג לאוין קמד טוש"ע י"ד סי' רלד סעיף א:

פח ז מיי' פ"ו מהלכות שמיטין הלכה ב:

[נ"ל מתוך הרחבה]

[נ"ל ונפלה לגינה]

פסחים כב: קדושין נו: [ע"ש]

פי' בוסר זיתים קטנים משום רפואה. רש"ל בשם רש"י

גליון הש"ס

רש"י ד"ה דזול וכו' אני הייתי מוכר סמנים. לפ"ז דזול ליבעא היינו דלמר לבוע הוזל אבל הסמנים עצמן לא הוזלו ותמוה לי דלמאי צריכי לזה ואמאי ל"א בפשיטות דהוזלו סמנים ואף דגם אלו מכרן לא היה מוכרן ביוקר מ"מ כיון דאין שבח סמני' ולא מקרי השבה הוי כנאבד הגזילה דמשלם כשעת הגזילה וצ"ע. ובאמת ק"ל גם על הגמרא למאי צריך לאוקמא דגזל צבע וסמנים לחד לוקי כדמעיקרא דגזל סמנים שרויים וצבע צמר שלו והוזל הרבה עד שהצמר עם הצבע שעליו אין עולים לדמי הצבע כשהיה בעידן הגזילה ואי יש סמנים מהדר ליה הסמנים ואומר הרי שלך לפניך ואי דבמאי נשקליה יאמר באמת החזק לך גם בצמרי ואי אין שבח סמנים לא הוי השבה על הסמנים וצריך לשלם כדמעיקרא וצע"ג: תוס' ד"ה או וכו' אלא נוי בעלמא יותר. עיין ש"ך סי' שנא סק"ב:

הגהות הב"ח

(א) רש"י ד"ה יש שבח וכו' (ב) צ"ל סמנים הס"ד: ד"ה דזול וכו' ואין מגיע השבח:

עין משפט
נר מצוה

פט א ב מיי' פ"ד מהלכות טומאת מת הלכה יד:
צ ג מיי' שם הלכה יג:
צא ד מיי' שם פ"ב הלכה יג:
צב ה מיי' פ"ז מהלכות שמיטין הלכה יג:
צג ו מיי' פ"ה שם הלכה יא:

רָבָא רָמֵי, תְּנַן: בֶּגֶד שֶׁצְּבָעוֹ בִּקְלִיפֵּי עָרְלָה — יִדָּלֵק; אַלְמָא חֲזוּתָא מִילְּתָא הִיא. וּרְמִינְהִי: *[א]רְבִיעִית דָּם שֶׁנִּבְלְעָה בְּבַיִת — הַבַּיִת טָמֵא, וְאָמְרִי לָהּ: הַבַּיִת טָהוֹר. וְלָא פְּלִיגִי, [ב]הָא בְּכֵלִים דַּהֲווּ מֵעִיקָּרָא, הָא בְּכֵלִים דְּאָתוּ לְבַסּוֹף; [ג]נִבְלְעָה בִּכְסוּת, רוֹאִין, אִם מִתְכַּבֶּסֶת הַכְּסוּת וְיוֹצֵא מִמֶּנָּה רְבִיעִית דָּם — (א) טְמֵאָה, וְאִם לָאו — טְהוֹרָה! אָמַר רַב כָּהֲנָא: מִקּוּלֵּי רְבִיעִיּוֹת שָׁנוּ כָּאן, בְּדַם תְּבוּסָה [ד]דְּרַבָּנַן.§ רָבָא רָמֵי, *תְּנַן: [ה]מִמִּין הַצּוֹבְעִין — סְפִיחֵי סָטִים וְקוֹצָה, יֵשׁ לָהֶן שְׁבִיעִית וְלִדְמֵיהֶן שְׁבִיעִית, יֵשׁ לָהֶן בִּיעוּר וְלִדְמֵיהֶן בִּיעוּר; אַלְמָא, עֵצִים יֵשׁ בָּהֶן מִשּׁוּם קְדוּשַּׁת שְׁבִיעִית. וּרְמִינְהִי: *עֲלֵי קָנִים וַעֲלֵי גְפָנִים שֶׁגִּיבְּבָן בַּחֲבָא עַל פְּנֵי הַשָּׂדֶה, [ו]לִקְטָן לַאֲכִילָה — יֵשׁ בָּהֶן מִשּׁוּם קְדוּשַּׁת שְׁבִיעִית, לְעֵצִים — אֵין בָּהֶן מִשּׁוּם קְדוּשַּׁת שְׁבִיעִית! וּמְשַׁנֵּי, אָמַר קְרָא: °"לְאָכְלָה", בְּמִי שֶׁהֲנָאָתוֹ וּבִיעוּרוֹ שָׁוִין, יָצְאוּ עֵצִים שֶׁהֲנָאָתָן אַחַר בִּיעוּרָן. וְהָא אִיכָּא עֵצִים דְּמַשְׁחָן, דַּהֲנָאָתָן וּבִיעוּרָן שָׁוִין! אָמַר רָבָא:

סְתָם

תורה אור: ויקרא כה

רש"י

רביעית דם. מטמאה באהל, דכתיב: "על כל נפשות מת לא יבא" (ויקרא כא) ודם הוא הנפש, וקים להו לרבנן דברביעית דם חי. נבלעה בקרקע הבית טמא. כלים שבבית, דבית לא מקבל טומאה, דקרקע היא. בכלים. דהוו בבית קודם שנבלעה, שהיתה בעין והאהיל הבית עליה ועל הכלים, ונטמאו. לבסוף. לאחר שנבלעה. אם מתכבסת הכסות ויוצא הימנה [רביעית דם]. שבתחילה נבלעה בו יותר מרביעית, והכנים הכסות לבית — הבית (ב) טמאה. ויוצא הימנה רביעית דם. שאם יתנו מים במדה — ימלאו רביעית יותר. ואם לאו טהור. הבית. שלא האהיל על רביעית, שכבר חסר בהבלעו בכסות. אבל הכסות טמא, שתחלת נגיעה ברביעית מלוגמס נטמאה. וקתני מיהת: ואם לאו — טהור, אע"ג דחזותא דרביעית איכא, שהדם שנשאר בבגד שאי אפשר לסוחטו נראה לנו בבגד. אלמא: חזותא לאו מילתא היא. מקולי רביעיות. של דם קל, כגון דם תבוסה (ג) שאינו מטמא באהל אלא מדרבנן. דם תבוסה. הרוג שיצא ממנו רביעית דם בחייו ובמותו, ספק כולה בחייו ספק כולה במותו, בפ' "תינוקת" (נדה דף עא.). ספיחי סטים וקוצה. סטים = קרוג"א בלע"ז. כרכום קוצה = *גווד"א בלע"ז. להכי נקט ספיחי, דבשביעית ליכא אלא ספיחים. יש להן ולדמיהן שביעית. שאין עושין מהן סחורה, דרחמנא אמר "לאכלה" ולא לסחורה, ואסור לצבוע בהן דהיינו סחורה, אבל מותרים הן להסיקן קודם זמן הביעור, דהיינו דומיא דלאכלה. יש להן ביעור. כשמגיע זמן הביעור חייב לבערן, כדכתיב: "ולבהמתך ולחיה" וגו' (ויקרא כה) כלה לחיה מן השדה כלה לבהמתך שבביתך, והני ספיחי עץ בעלמא נינהו. בחבא. לעשות מהן מחבואה, אוצר לימות החורף. אין בהן משום קדושת שביעית. והנה מהן אף לאחר זמן הביעור. שהנאתן וביעורן שוה. דבר שבשעת הנאתו כלה מן העולם. יצאו עצים. שלאחר ביעורן שנעשים גחלים הוא דהויא עיקר הנאתן. אבל מיני צבעים — בשעת רתיחת היורה כלה השורש וקולט הצבע, נתנאו הנאתן וביעורן שוה, הלכך חיילא עלייהו שביעית. והא איכא עצים דמשחן. שמאירין כנר אבוקה לנושאן בידו, והנאתן וביעורן שוה — תיחול עלייהו שביעית.

סתם

תוספות

רבא רמי תנן בגד שצבעו בקליפי ערלה כו'. תימה: דהא רבא שני לעיל: שאני ערלה דכתיב קראי, ומהתם לא ילפינן. ואם כן מאי פריך מערלה אטומאה? ונראה כספרים דגר' לעיל "רבה". ואי גרס "רבא" — יש לומר דדיחוי הוא. רואין אם מתכבסת הכסות ויוצא ממנה רביעית דם. פירש בקונטרס: שאם יתנו מים במדה — ימלאו רביעית יותר. וקשה לפי': אפילו אם לא ימלאו רביעית אמאי טהורה? דאי אפשר לעולם אם לא ישתייר בבגד מן המים! אלא י"ל כדאמר בתוספתא בפ' ד' דאהלות: רביעית דם שנבלעה בכסות כיצד משערין אותה? מביא מים במדה ומכבס בה, ומביא מים אחרים ונותן לתוכן רביעית דם, אם היה מראיהן שוה — טמאה, ואם לאו — טהורה. והשתא אין מזיק כלום מה שמשתייר מן המים בבגד, דכשם שנשתייר מן המים — כך נשתייר מן הדם, שמכ"מ היה הכל מעורב יחד מה שיצא ומה שנשתייר, ומראה אחד הן כאילו יצא הכל. וטהורה וטמאה דקתני היינו לענין אם טמאה את הבית שתנתן בו, אבל כסות עצמה — טמאה היא, שנבלע בה רביעית דם מתחילה, כדפי' בקונטרס. ומיהו קשה: דאין סברא שיסייע הדם שמשתייר בבגד, כיון שאין יכול לצאת בכיבוס זה! ומיהו, אין לחוש כל כך אם תולין הדבר להחמיר. ועוד מצינן לפרש: שאומדין כמה נשתייר מן המים הראשונים בבגד, ומביא מים אחרים כמדת הראשון, רק שיחסר מהן כשיעור שנבלע מהן בבגד. אבל יש תימה: דמי יכול לכוין זהו? ועוד קשה: דמאי צריך למדידת מים הראשונים? בלא מדידת מים הראשונים יכול הוא לדעת אם יש רביעית דם במה שיצא ע"י כיבוס, שיסחוט לתוך כלי כל מה שיצא מן הכסות, וימדוד כמה יש בין מים לדם, ויביא רביעית דם מעלמא ויוסיף עליו מים עד שיהא בין מים ובין דם כשיעור מים ודם שיצאו מן הכסות, ואם מראיהן שוה — טמאה! ונראה לפרש: דלא נקט מים במדה אלא משום שאם ימלאו יותר מן המדה שנתנו רביעית — שלא יצטרכו להביא מים אחרים, דודאי יצא מן הכסות רביעית דם. אבל אם אין רביעית דם יותר — אז יביא רביעית דם ותוסיף עליו מים, עד שיהא בין מים ודם כמדת הראשונה אחר שתכבס בה הכסות, ואם מראיהן שוה — טמאה, ואם לאו — טהורה. ומיהו קשה, דהא קתני בתוספתא ברישא: ומביא מים אחרים, ואחר כך קתני: ונותן לתוכו רביעית דם. ואם לאו טהורה. אע"פ שעל ידי הדחק היה יוצא מהן רביעית דם, כגון על ידי היסק התנור או על ידי צפון, כיון דבסתם כיבוס אין יכול לצאת רביעית דם — טהורה, לר"ל משום דדם תבוסה דרבנן, ולר' יוחנן משום שאין דרך להקפיד עליה כשאין יכול לצאת בכיבוס סתם. כך צ"ל במסכת נדה בפרק "האשה" (דף סב: ושם*) מתוך הסוגיא, ואין צריך להביאה כאן. מקולי רביעיות שנו כאן. הך סוגיא מסיק רב כהנא בנדה אליבא דר"ל. וה"נ דוקא לר"ל צריך האי שינויא, דלר' יוחנן לא קשה מידי מערלה אטומאה, דלדידיה בקפידא תליא מילתא. ומ"מ, צבעו בקליפי ערלה ידלק, דלא שייך להתירו מטעם דאין מקפיד, דנהנה הוא בצבע וניחא ליה. ספיחי סטים וקוצה. מה שפי' בקונטרס כאן משום דבשביעית אין זורעין, ואין בה אלא ספיחים — אין מיושב הכא טעמא אלא הכא, אבל גבי מעשר ופאה דקאמר: כל שהוא אוכל ונשמר כו', אוכל — למעוטי ספיחי סטים וקוצה, אין מיושב למה נקט ספיחים. ע"כ נראה כמו שפי' בפסחים (דף נא: ושם*): דלהכי נקט ספיחים — לפי שאין דרך ללקטן בשנה שנזרעים, אלא לבסוף ד' או ה' שנים, שהשרשים מתפשטים בארץ ומשביחין ושורש שלהן עיקר. ממין הצובעין. רישא דמתניתין הכי איתא במס' שביעית (פ"ז מ"א): כלל גדול אמרו: כל שהוא מאכל אדם ומאכל בהמה וממין הצובעין כו'. ולדמיהן ביעור. כגון שלקט מתחילה לאכילה, דיכול למוכרן. ויש לשניהם ביעור — להן ולדמיהן, דפרי עצמו לעולם אסור, כדנפקא לן מ"קודש תהיה לכם" (בע"ז דף נד:). שהנאתן אחר ביעורן. כשנעשית גחלת. אע"ג דזימנין הנאתן וביעורן שוה, כגון להתחמם כנגדו או לבשל — מכ"מ עיקרו לא קיימא להכי, אלא לאחר שנעשית גחלת, כגון להסיק תנור לאפות. אבל צבע — הנאתן וביעורן שוה, דהנאתן כשלובשן — ואז הוא כלה ומתבער הצבע מיום אל יום. ובקונטרס פי': דבשעת רתיחת היורה כלה השורש וקולט הצבע. ואין נראה, דהא אמרן דלענין שביעית חזותא מילתא היא, ולא הוי ביעורו בקליטת הצבע. והאיכא עצים דמשחן. לפי' הקונטרס דפי': עצים שמאירים בהן כמו נר, צ"ל הא דמתרץ עצים להסקה ניתנו, כלומר אף עצים דמשחן. דאין לפרש: סתם שאר עצים להסקה ניתנו, והנך דמשחן בטלים לגבייהו. דהא בסוכה (דף מ. ושם*) משמע דלולב נוהג בו שביעית משום דהנאתו וביעורו שוה, שראוי לכבד בו הבית, ולא אמר דבטל לגבי שאר עצים, וה"נ עצים דמשחן. אלא צ"ל דסתם עצים דמשחן נמי להסקה הן עומדין, ולא דמי ללולב דסתמו עומד לכבד בו את הבית. ור"ח פירש: והא איכא עצים דמשחן — שמחממין בו, כגון במדורה שעשויה להתחמם, דהנאתן וביעורן שוה, דבשעת ביעורן מתחמם כנגדן. פי' משחן — כמו "תמרי משחנן" כתובות (דף י:), וכן "טעולה *או שחונה" ביומא (דף נג:). ומשני רבא: סתם עצים להסקה ניתנו. פי': להסקת תנור ניתנו, דהוי הנאתן אחר ביעורן, הלכך — אפילו להתחמם מותר, דלא חל עליהם שם שביעית. ואע"ג דחשיב הכא עצים דמשחן הנאתן וביעורן שוה, מכ"מ לענין עצי איסור לא היו אוסרין רבנן אפילו להתחמם כנגדן או להאיר בהן אלא דוקא בשרשיפא, כדדרשינן בפרק "כל שעה" (פסחים דף כו: ושם*) דהנאה מיהא אינה מתחלת עד לאחר שמתחיל האיסור להיות כלה — הלכך לא אסרי רבנן אלא בשרשיפא. אבל הנאתו וביעורו שוה קרינן ביה, דעדיין האיסור קיים כשנהנה ממנו. וא"ת: בפ"ק דנדה (דף ח. ושם*) דקאמר: אי קטפא פירא הוי — אית ביה שביעית, ואי לאו פירי הוי — לית ביה שביעית, ואמאי? אי הנאתו וביעורו שוה — הלא אפילו לא הוי פירא יהא אסור בשביעית. ואי אין הנאה וביעורו שוה — אפילו הוי פירא יהא מותר! ותו, אמאי קמפלגי בין קטפא דפירא לקטפא דגווזא? ונראה, ודאי קטפא הוי הנאתו וביעורו שוה, ואפילו הכי אי לא הוי פירא — בטיל לגבי עץ, והרי הוא כאילו הוא בתוך העלין ולא יצא לחוץ. אבל אי הוי פירא — חשיב באפי נפשיה, ולא בטיל לגבי עץ, ואית ביה קדושת שביעית.

ה"ג

הגהות הב"ח

(א) גמ' ויוצא ממנה רביעית דם טמא ואם לאו טהור כצ"ל: (ב) רש"י ד"ה אם וכו' הבית טמא: (ג) ד"ה מקולי כו' כגון דם תבוסה דקי"ל שאינו כצ"ל:

מסורת הש"ס

נדה סב: תוספות פ"ג
שביעית פ"ז מ"א
סוכה מ.
הוא אחד ממיני רש"ל בשם הרמב"ם
[ד"ה אם]
ד"ה כל
[ד"ה יצאו]
צ"ל אם
[ד"ה מכלל]
[ד"ה מאן]

סתם עצים להסקה ניתנו. ולא להאיר. הלכך עצים נינהו, ומעיקרא לא חל עלייהו שביעית. אבל ספיחי סטים – סתמן לצביעה הלכך חל עלייהו קדושה ואסירי לאחר הביעור אף להיסק. ועצי קנים וגפנים יש שאוכלין אותן ויש שמסיקין אותן, הלכך בתר מחשבת לקיטה אזלינן. **תנאי היא.** איכא למאן דאמר סתם עצים להסקה ניתנו, ולא חיילא שביעית אפילו אעצים דמשחן. ואיכא למאן דלית ליה, ואעצים דמשחן מיהא חיילא. **לתוך המשרה.** אין שורין פשתן ביין של שביעית, וכן אין מכבסין בגדים, דהוי סחורה. **מי שהנאתו וביעורו שוה.** הנאה שהיא בשעה שהוא כלה מן העולם – אתה יכול ליהנות מפירות שביעית קודם זמן הביעור. *__יצאו משרה וכבוסה.__ שמשעה שמטילין פשתן או בגד ביין נתקלקל ונבער, והנאתו אינו אלא עד שלשה ימים וד', עד שיהא הפשתן שרוי, וכן הבגד. והיינו תנאי, דרבנן סברי: סתם פירות לאכילה, וחיילא עלייהו קדושת שביעית, כדאמרן לעיל דכל דבר שהנאתו וביעורו שוה חיילא. הלכך אפילו לקטן למשרה וכביסה – לא מהניא מחשבה לאפקועי איסורן למיהוי כעצי קנים שלקטן לעצים דמשתרו, דהתם סתמייהו להכי ולהכי, אבל פירות – סתמן לאכילה, ומשעת יצירתן חייל קדושתן, ותו לא מהני מחשבה לאפקועי, ואסורין למשרה וכביסה, דאין נהנין בקדושת שביעית אלא הנאה הדומה לאכילה. וגבי עצים נמי, סתם עצים להסקה ניתנו, ולא חיילא אפילו אעצים דמשחן. ור' יוסי סבר: לא אמרינן סתם פירות לאכילה ניתנו, ומהניא בהו מחשבה כעצי קנים וגפנים, דהיכא דליקטן למשרה – הוי דבר שהנאתו אחר ביעורו, ולא חל עלייהו שביעית. כך מצאתי, ויש לשונות אחרים, וזו שמעתי והגון. **למלוגמא.** אלנפסט"ר. **אינה שוה בכל אדם.** אינה צריכה אלא לחולים. **לזלף.** שמזלפין יין בבית. והאי נמי אין שוה בכל אדם, שא"צ זילוף אלא אדם מעונג ומעודן. **אפיקטויזין.** ווסי"ט, להקיא. **איכא נמי משרה וכביסה.** והכא לא נקט אלא דבר שאין שוה בכל אדם. **מלוה בשטר אין נפרעין מהן.** לפני אידיהן, מפני ששמחה היא לו, ואזיל ומודה לגוייס ביום חגם. ורבנן סברי: אסור לפורען וליפרע מהן כלל. **ואיבעית אימא.** הך סתמא ודאי עיקר הוא, דקתני לה התם בב"מ (עו.) גבי הלכתא פסיקתא. דהא לא שייכא התם, ולא תני אלא משום פיסוק הלכה, שפסקה התנא עם כל החוזר בו, שלא נחלק אדם עליהן.
ליקח

[מסורת הש"ס: א] לג. סוכה מ. נדרים סב:] · סוכה מ. · [מכות יג. וש"נ] · ברש"י במס' סוכה שכתב פי' אחר · ע"ז ו: · [סוכה יח.] · [ברכות ט. וש"נ] · [יבמות מב:] · לעיל ק: [וש"נ] · ב"מ עו. [ע"ז ז.]]

*סתם עצים להסקה הן עומדין. אמר רב כהנא: ועצים להסקה תנאי היא; דתניא: *אאין מוסרין פירות שביעית לא למשרה ולא לכבוסה, ור' יוסי אומר: נותנין פירות שביעית לתוך המשרה ולתוך הכבוסה. מאי טעמא דרבנן? אמר קרא: °"לאכלה" — ולא למשרה, "לאכלה" — ולא לכבוסה; ורבי יוסי אומר, אמר קרא: "לכם", *"לכל צרכיכם". ורבנן נמי, הכתיב "לכם"! "לכם" דומיא ד"לאכלה" — במי שהנאתו וביעורו שוין, *יצאו משרה וכבוסה שהנאתן אחר ביעורן. ור"י נמי, הכתיב "לאכלה"! אמר לך: ההוא מיבעי ליה לכדתניא, דתניא: "לאכלה" ולא למלוגמא; אתה אומר: "לאכלה" ולא למלוגמא, או אינו אלא "לאכלה" ולא לכבוסה? כשהוא אומר: "לכם" — הרי כבוסה אמור, הא מה אני מקיים "לאכלה"? "לאכלה" — ולא למלוגמא. ומה ראית לרבות הכבוסה ולהוציא את המלוגמא? מרבה אני את הכבוסה ששוה בכל אדם, ומוציא אני את המלוגמא שאינו שוה בכל אדם. כמאן אזלא הא דתניא: ב"לאכלה" — ולא למלוגמא, "לאכלה" — ולא לזילוף, "לאכלה" — ולא לעשות ממנה אפיקטויזין, כמאן? כר' יוסי, דאי כרבנן — גאיכא נמי משרה וכבוסה.§ "רבי יהודה אומר: אם השבח" כו'. (סימן סבן) *יתיב רב יוסף אחורי דרבי אבא קמיה דרב הונא, ויתיב רב הונא וקאמר: הלכה כרבי יהושע בן קרחה והלכה כרבי יהודה. *אהדרינהו רב יוסף לאפיה, אמר: בשלמא רבי יהושע בן קרחה אצטריך, סלקא דעתך אמינא *יחיד ורבים הלכה כרבים, קמ"ל הלכה כיחיד. ר' יהושע בן קרחה מאי היא? דתניא, רבי יהושע בן קרחה אומר: דמלוה בשטר אין נפרעין מהן, מלוה על פה נפרעין מהן, מפני שהוא כמציל מידם. אלא הלכה כר' יהודה למה לי? מחלוקת ואחר כך סתם היא, *ומחלוקת ואח"כ סתם הלכה כסתם! מחלוקת בבבא קמא: *לצבוע לו אדום וצבעו שחור, שחור וצבעו אדום — רבי מאיר אומר: נותן לו דמי צמרו, רבי יהודה אומר: אם השבח יתר על היציאה — נותן לו את היציאה, ואם היציאה יתירה על השבח — נותן לו את השבח; וסתם בבבא מציעא, דתנן: *כל המשנה — ידו על התחתונה, הוכל החוזר בו — ידו על התחתונה. ורב הונא? אצטריך, סלקא דעתך אמינא אין סדר למשנה, וסתם ואחר כך מחלוקת היא. ורב יוסף? אי הכי, כל מחלוקת ואח"כ סתמא, נימא: אין סדר למשנה, וסתם ואח"כ מחלוקת היא. ורב הונא? כי לא אמרינן אין סדר למשנה — בחדא מסכתא, אבל בתרי מסכתות אמרינן. ורב יוסף? כולה נזיקין חדא מסכתא היא. ואיבעית אימא, משום דקתני לה גבי הלכתא פסיקתא: כל המשנה — ידו על התחתונה, וכל החוזר בו — ידו על התחתונה.§ תנו רבנן: הנותן מעות לשלוחו
ליקח

[תורה אור: ויקרא כה]

ה"ג בקונטרס במס' סוכה (דף מ. ושם*): אמר רב כהנא ועצים דהסקה תנאי היא כו'. וכן עיקר פי': כל עצים בשביעית הויא פלוגתא דתנאי אי אית בהו קדושת שביעית. דכיון דטעמא דשרינא להו היינו משום דהנאתן אחר ביעורן, אם כן לרבי יוסי דלית ליה דרשה דהנאתו וביעורו שוה לענין פירות שביעית — ה"נ לא דריש לה לענין דלא לחול קדושת שביעית. ואם תאמר: לר' יוסי היאך מותרין עצים בארץ ישראל להסיק בהן תנור? והלא יש בהן איסור שביעית לאחר הביעור! וי"ל: דבטלי בשאר עצים דשאר שנים. ועוד י"ל לפי גירסת הספרים: ועצים דהסקה תנאי היא. פירוש: עצים שיש בהם קדושת שביעית, כגון לולב דהנאתו וביעורו שוה, דסתמיה קאי לכבד בו את הבית, אם מותר להסיקו, דהוי הנאה לאחר ביעורו או לא. דתניא: אין מוכרין פירות שביעית כו' — הרי לרבנן אסור להסיקו, מידי דהוי אמשרה וכביסה, ולר' יוסי מותר. אבל שאר עצים — לדברי הכל אין בהן קדושת שביעית. אבל הטעם אין מיושב, דכי היכי דר' יוסי דריש "לכם" לכל צרכיכם אפירות שביעית, ולא בעי "לכם" דומיא ד"לאכלה" — הכי נמי לענין לחול קדושת שביעית על כל דבר שהוא "לכם", דמ"ש, דהא כוליה חד קרא הוא "והיתה שבת הארץ לכם לאכלה" וגו'. **אין** סדר למשנה. דפעמים היה שונה שלא על הסדר, ושמא תחילה שנה ב"מ ואחר כך ב"ק. אבל ודאי אח"כ סדרן רבי על הסדר, כדייק בריש (פרק) שבועות (דף ג:): מכדי תנא ממכות קסליק כו'*. **גבי** הלכתא פסיקתא. תימה: אמאי קרי לה הלכתא פסיקתא להדיא ד"כל החוזר בו ידו על התחתונה"? הא בפרק "האומנין" (ב"מ דף עז:) מוקמינן לה כיחידאה, כרבי דוסא, ורבנן פליגי עליה. ומוכח התם דרב לא סבר לה כרבי דוסא בההוא ד"כל החוזר בו"! וי"ל: דהכא סבר כאיבעית אימא דהתם, דאמר: כל החוזר בו ידו על התחתונה — לאתויי כדקתני. וי"מ: דקתני לה בלשון הלכתא פסיקתא, דלישנא ד"כל החוזר" ו"כל המשנה" — משמע לפסוק הלכתא*. **הנותן** מעות לשלוחו. נראה דמיירי שנותן למחצית שכר, אם פחתו — פחתו לו, ואם הותירו — הותירו לאמצע. מכאן יש להביא ראיה, אם אדם נותן מעות לחבירו למחצית שכר, ואמר: ע"מ שלא תלווה אלא על משכונות של כסף וזהב, ותשמרם בקרקע, ואם תשנה יהא ברשותך לחייב בכל דבר, ואם פחתו פחתו לך — שאין זה רבית. דהא הכא, אם שינה מדעתו, אמר: אם פחתו פחתו לו, אפ"ה, אם הותירו — הותירו לאמצע. ולא הוי רבית, כיון דאם לא היה משנה דעתו — לא היו כולן ברשותו אלא השכר, וההפסד לאמצע, כדין פלגא מלוה ופלגא פקדון.
הא

[ד"ה ועצים] · [ועי"ע תוס' ריש ב"מ וריש ב"ב] · [ועי' תוס' מנחות סו. ד"ה זכר]

עין משפט נר מצוה

צד א ב ג מיי' פ"ה מהל' שמיטין הלכה י:

צה ד מיי' פ"ט מהלכות ע"ז הלכה א סמג לאוין מה טוש"ע י"ד סי' קמח סעיף א:

צו ה מיי' פ"ח מהלכות מכירה הלכה ב סמג עשין פב טוש"ע ח"מ סי' קל סעי' י יא:

גליון הש"ס

גמ' יצאו משרה וכבוסה. עיין ברכות דף יב ע"ב תוס' ד"ה ולאו:

צז א מיי' פ"א מהלכות שלוחין הלכה ה ופ"ה הלכה ב סמג עשין קעד טוש"ע ח"מ סי' קפג סעיף ה וסי' קעו סעיף יא וע"ש:
צח ב מיי' פ"ג מהל' ערכין הלכה יד סמג עשין קלא:
צט ג מיי' שם פ"ו הלכה ג סמג עשין קלב:
ק ד מיי' שם פ"ג הלכה יד:
קא ה מיי' פ"ב מהלכות שלוחין הלכה ה סמג עשין פב טוש"ע ח"מ סי' קפד סעי' ב:

ליקח לו חטין — ולקח מהם שעורין, שעורין — ולקח מהם חטין, תניא חדא: אם פחתו — פחתו לו, ואם הותירו — הותירו לו, ותני חדא: [א]אם פחתו — פחתו לו, ואם הותירו — הותירו לאמצע. אמר רבי יוחנן: לא קשיא; הא — ר"מ, והא — רבי יהודה. הא ר"מ דאמר שינוי קונה, והא רבי יהודה דאמר שינוי אינו קונה. מתקיף לה ר' אלעזר: ממאי? דלמא עד כאן לא קאמר ר"מ — אלא במידי דחזי ליה לגופיה, אבל לסחורה — לא אמר! אלא א"ר אלעזר: הא והא ר' מאיר, ולא קשיא: כאן — לאכילה, כאן — לסחורה. *מחכו עלה במערבא, לר' יוחנן אליבא דר' יהודה: וכי מי הודיעו לבעל חטין שיקנה חטין לבעל מעות? מתקיף לה רב שמואל בר ססרטי: אי הכי, אפילו חטין וחטין נמי לא! אמר רבי אבהו: שאני חטין וחטין, דשליחותיה קא עביד, וכי בעל הבית דמי. תדע, דתנן: *[ב]אחד המקדיש נכסיו ואחד המעריך את עצמו, אין לו בכסות אשתו, ולא בכסות בניו, ולא בצבע שצבע לשמן, ולא בסנדלים חדשים שלקחן לשמן; ואמאי? לימא הכא נמי: מי הודיעו לצבע שיקנה צבעו לאשה? אלא לאו משום דאמרינן [דשליחותיה קא עביד, וכיד אשתו דמי? הכא נמי] — שליחותיה קא עביד, וכיד בעה"ב דמי. א"ר אבא: לא, כל המקדיש נכסיו אין דעתו על כסות אשתו ובניו. מתקיף לה רבי זירא: וכי דעתו של אדם על תפיליו? *ותנן: [ג]המקדיש נכסיו — מעלין לו תפילין! א"ל אביי: אין, דעתו של אדם על תפילין — המקדיש נכסיו סבר: *מצוה קא עבידנא. ואין דעתו של אדם על כסות אשתו ובניו — משום איבה. מתקיף לה רב אושעיא: והלא חייבי ערכין שנו כאן, *ותנן: [ד]חייבי ערכין ממשכנין אותן; וכי דעתו של אדם על עצמו למשכנו?! אלא אמר רבי אבא: כל המקדיש נכסיו — נעשה כמי שהקנה להן כסות אשתו ובניו מעיקרא. תנו רבנן: הלוקח שדה בשם חבירו — אין כופין אותו למכור, ואם אמר לו "על מנת" — כופין אותו למכור. מאי קאמר? אמר רב ששת, ה"ק: הלוקח שדה מחבירו בשם ריש גלותא — אין כופין אותו ריש גלותא למכור, ואם אמר "על מנת" — כופין את ריש גלותא למכור. אמר מר: הלוקח שדה בשם ריש גלותא — אין כופין אותו ריש גלותא למכור; מכלל דמקנא קניא ליה. לימא פליגא דבני מערבא, דאמרי: וכי מי הודיעו לבעל חטין שיקנה חטין לבעל הבית? אי משום הא לא קשיא, כגון דאודעיה לבעל שדה, ואודעינהו לסהדי. אלא אימא סיפא: "על מנת" — כופין אותו ריש גלותא למכור, אמאי? ולימא ריש גלותא: לא יקרייכו בעינא, ולא זילותייכו בעינא! אלא אמר אביי, [ה]ה"ק: הלוקח שדה בשם חבירו (ריש גלותא) — אין

רש"י

ליקח בהן חטין. למחצית שכר. [הא ר"מ]. קמייתא ר"מ [דאמר] שינוי קונה, בתרייתא ר' יהודה [דאמר] שינוי אינו קונה. ומיהו אם פחתו — פחתו לו, דלאו לעוותיה שדריה. לגופיה. צמר ללבוש וספסל להשתמש. אבל לסחורה. בכל מידי דאיכא רווחא ניחא ליה, וכי הותירו — לאו שינוי הוא. מי הודיעו. למוכר החטין שלצורך בעל המעות הן, שיקנה לו, דקתני: הותירו לאמצע? בשלמא לר' אלעזר אליבא דר"מ, דאמר בכל דהו ניחא ליה — לאו משנה הוא, ושליחותיה דבעל הבית קעביד, וקני בעל מעות מחצית השכר. אלא לר' יוחנן, דאמר משנה הוא, ולא הוי שליחות, ומיהו שינוי לא קני — קשיא, דממאן קבעי למקניי? הא לא קננהו בעל מעות מעולם? אין לו. לגזבר, לא בכסות אשתו למשכנו בשביל הערך. וכן לגבי מקדיש, לא הוו בכלל נכסים להקדישו. לשמן. דאשתו ובניו. חדשים. רבותא נקט. מעלין לו תפילין. ולוה המעות, ויתן בשבילם להקדש. מעלין. שמין. אמר ליה אביי אין. ודאי דעתו של אדם על תפילין להקדישן, דסבר: האי נמי מצוה קעבידנא, דיהיבנא להקדש. והלא חייבי ערכין שנו כאן. דקתני: המעריך את עצמו. ממשכנין. בעל כרחו. אלמא: לאו משום דעתו הוא. הלוקח שדה מחבירו בשם ריש גלותא. שאמר לו למוכר: לצורך ריש גלותא אני לוקחה, ונתכוון להטיל אימה, שלא יבאו עליה עסיקין. וכתב המוכר שטר המכירה בשם ריש גלותא. אין כופין ריש גלותא. לחזור ולכתוב שטר מכירה שהוא מכרה ללוקח. ואם אומר לו לוקח למוכר: על מנת שיכתוב לי ריש גלותא בשמו לשמי שטר אחר — כופין ריש גלותא למכור. לא יקרייכו. שעשיתם אותי ראש, להטיל אימה. ולא זילותייכו. שאתם באים לעשות אותי למוכר שדות. הכי קאמר: הלוקח שדה בשם חבירו ריש גלותא

אין

תוספות

הא רבי יהודה דאמר שינוי אין קונה. הלכך, אם הותירו — לאמצע, שכך נותן לו למחצית שכר. ואם פחתו — פחתו לו, דמצי אמר ליה: לא היה לך לשנות מדעתי, ואת הוא דפשעת. מי הודיעו לבעל חטין שיקנה חטין לבעל מעות. אם נפרש דמהאי טעמא אין קונה אותו המשלח, אבל לוקח, דהיינו שליח, קנה להו — איכא למפרך נמי לר' אלעזר: אמאי לא אוקי נמי הא והא כרבי יהודה, כאן לאכילה כאן לסחורה; ההיא דקתני: אם פחתו פחתו לו ואם הותירו הותירו לו — היינו לאכילה, דקפיד, ולא שליחותיה קעביד, הלכך לא קני להו לבעל המעות כלל, משום טעמא דמי הודיעו לבעל חטין. וההיא דקתני: אם הותירו הותירו לאמצע — לסחורה, דלא קפיד, ושליחותיה קעביד, הלכך קני להו בעל המעות, ואם הותירו — הותירו לאמצע. ומיהו, אם פחתו — פחתו לו, דאמר ליה: לתקוני שדרתיך ולא לעוותי. ומיהו אין קושיא כ"כ לר"א כמו לר' יוחנן, הלכך לא פריך אלא לר' יוחנן. ואם נפרש: מי הודיעו לבעל חטין שיקנה חטין לבעל מעות, הרי בעל מעות לא קנה, ושליח נמי לא קנה, שלא נתכוון לקנות לעצמו וחוזר המקח כמו מקח טעות — אז ליכא למפרך לר' אלעזר, דלא מצי לאוקמי תרוייהו כרבי יהודה, דכיון דשינוי לא קני לרבי יהודה — אם כן אמאי אם פחתו פחתו לו אפילו לאכילה? הא כיון דמקפיד, ולא שליחותיה קעביד, ואיכא למימר מי הודיעו לבעל חטין שיקנה חטין לבעל מעות — אם כן חוזר המקח, ואם כן אמאי אם פחתו לו, ואם הותירו הותירו לו, דמשמע שקונה אותו השליח?

שאני חטין וחטין דשליחותיה קעביד תדע דתנן כו'. תימה: אמאי איצטריך לאתויי מהא דחון? והלא מגופא דברייתא משמע הכי, דדוקא נקט ליקח בהן חטין ולקח בהן שעורים, הא חטין וחטין — משמע דפשיטא דאם הותירו — הותירו לאמצע! וה"נ משמע דתירוצא דרבי אלעזר למתרך: כאן לסחורה — משמע משום דלסחורה לא קפיד, והוי כחטין וחטין, והותירו — הותירו לאמצע! וי"ל: דברייתא מצינן לאוקמי כגון שהודיעו שהוא קונה לבעל המעות. והא דפריך מי הודיעו — בעי למימר דמסתמא איירי הברייתא בכל ענין, אפילו לא הודיעו. והא פריך רב שמואל: אי הכי אפילו חטין וחטין נמי, אי איירי שלא הודיעו! אלא ע"כ איירי כשהודיעו. ומשני: שאני חטין וחטין דשליחותיה קעביד, דתנן כו'. והשתא ודאי צריך להביא מהא דתנן, דמגופא דברייתא ליכא למשמע מידי, דאיכא לאוקמי כשהודיעו. וא"ת: מאי מוכח טפי מהא דתנן? הא איכא לאוקמא נמי כשהודיעו לצבע דהאי צמר דאשתו היא! ונראה דלא דמי, דלעיל ודאי איכא למימר הוא מודיע כדי שיקנה לבעל המעות, אבל הכא למה יש להודיעו? הלא דעתו ליתן לאחר כך, ומן ההקדש לא מסיק אדעתיה. מי הודיעו לצבע שיקנה צבע לאשה. תימה: מאי פריך? תינח אם יש שבח סממנין על גבי צמר, אבל אם אין שבח סממנין על גבי הצמר — מה לנו לחוש אם אין הצבע מקנה צבעו לאשה? וי"ל דהכי פריך: כיון דאין הצבע מקנה צבעו לאשה, ויכול הצבע לתבוע שבח מן האשה. דאע"ג דאין שבח סממנים ע"ג הצמר מ"מ היא נהנית ממעשה ידיו, וצריכה ליתן לו שכר. וכיון דיכול ליקח שכר מאשה — א"כ מעות שקיבל מבעל האשה הן הקדש, דאינן שכירות, כיון שהאשה חייבת שכירות. ולפי מה שפירשתי לעיל, דכיון דלא הודיעו לבעל חטין שיקנה חטין לבעל המעות חוזר המקח ע"כ לא פריך הכא אלא ממעות שקיבל הצבע שיהיו הקדש — אפילו אם יש שבח סממנין על גבי הצמר לא קנתה האשה, והבעל נמי לא קנה, וחוזר הצבע לצבע בכ"מ שהוא, ואין לו להקדש בצבע כלום. אלא המעות שקיבל הצבע, כיון שחוזרין לבעל — יהו הקדש, והצבע יחזור ויתבע השכירות מן האשה. ואמאי קתני: אין לו לבעל בכסות אשתו, משמע שבחנם בא לה! אין דעתו של אדם על כסות אשתו. הלכך אין דעתו להקדיש אותן מעות שנתן לצבע, שלא יחזור ויתבע מן האשה. ולפי האי טעמא הוה ליה למפרך: תינח הקדש דתלוי בדעתו, וכיון שאין רוצה להקדיש — לא הוי הקדש. אלא ערכין, כיון שהעריך עצמו — מה מועיל שאין דעתו עליהם? מ"מ בע"כ נערך מכל מה שיש לו! אלא משום דאית ליה פירכא אחריתי לא חש למפרך.

כגון

מסורת הש"ס

[סנהדרין יז: וש"נ]
כתובות נד. ערכין כד
ב"ב קנא. ערכין כג:
[ערכין כז.]
שם כא. לעיל מ.
ברא"ש אינו

גליון הש"ס

גמ' מחכו עלה במע[רבא]. ביצה דף לח ע"ב ש[ם] דף כו ע"א: שם ל[?] המקדיש. עי' נדרים ד[ף] ע"ב:

אין כופין את המוכר למכור זימנא אחריתי, ואם אמר לו "על מנת" — כופין את המוכר למכור. אמר מר: הלוקח שדה בשם חבירו — אין כופין את המוכר למכור זימנא אחריתי. פשיטא! מהו דתימא מצי א"ל: מידע ידעת דאנא לנפשאי שקילנא, ופנחיא בעלמא הוא דקבעינא, וזוזי בכדי לא שדינא, אלא אדעתא דכתב ליה שטרא אחרינא — קא משמע לן דאמר ליה: ענינא עבדי לך בהדי ההוא דזבנת ליה בשמיה, ויכתוב לך שטרא אחרינא. ואם אמר לו "על מנת" — כופין את המוכר למכור. פשיטא! [א]לא צריכא, דאמר להו לסהדי קמיה דידיה: חזו דשטרא אחרינא קא בעינא; מהו דתימא, מצי א"ל: אמינא שטרא מהיאך דקא שקלת בשמיה קאמרת, קא משמע לן דאמר ליה: להכי טרחי ואמרי להו לעדים קמך, דמינך הוא דקא בעינא. רב כהנא יהב זוזא אכיתנא, לסוף אייקר כיתנא, זבניה מרוותיה דכיתנא. אתא לקמיה דרב, א"ל: מה אעביד, איזיל אישקיל זוזאי? א"ל: אי כי קא זבני אמרי "האי כיתנא דכהנא הוא" — זיל שקול, ואי לא — לא תשקול. כמאן? כבני מערבא, דאמרי: מי הודיעו לבעל חטין שיקנה חטין לבעל מעות? אטו מי יהיב רב כהנא ארבע ושקיל תמני? כיתנא ממילא הוא דאייקר, מיגזל גזלוה, ותנן: *כל הגזלנין משלמין כשעת הגזלה! אמרי: התם אמנה הואי, ולא משכיה רב כהנא לכיתנא. ורב לטעמיה, *דאמר רב: [ב]עושין אמנה בפירות, ואין עושין אמנה בדמים.§

מתני׳ *[ג]הגוזל את חבירו שוה פרוטה ונשבע לו — יוליכנו אחריו (א) למדי. [ד]לא יתן לא לבנו ולא לשלוחו, [ה]אבל נותן לשליח בית דין. [ו]ואם מת — יחזיר ליורשיו. [ז]נתן לו את הקרן ולא נתן לו את החומש, *מחל לו על הקרן ולא מחל לו על החומש, מחל לו על זה ועל זה *חוץ מפחות שוה פרוטה בקרן — [ח]אינו צריך לילך אחריו. [ט]נתן לו את החומש ולא נתן לו את הקרן, מחל לו על החומש ולא מחל לו על הקרן, מחל לו על זה ועל זה חוץ משוה פרוטה בקרן — [י]צריך לילך אחריו. *נתן לו את הקרן ונשבע לו על החומש — הרי

רש"י

אין כופין את המוכר. לחזור ולכתוב שטר מכירה אחר ללוקח, שהיה לו להתנות ולהודיעו: כתוב שטרי בשם ריש גלותא, שאם יבאו עסיקין אראה להם שהוא של ריש גלותא. וכתוב לי שטר אחר בשמי, שלא יבאו היום או למחר יורשי ראש גולה לתובעה ממני. ופנחיא בעלמא הוא דבעינא. כלומר: להנאה נתכוונתי. פנחיא = לשון חוזק. וחבירו ב"האשה [שלום]" ביבמות (דף קטו:): לפנחיא שבקיה, גבי מצא כלי וכתוב עליו קו"ף – קרבן, מ"ם – מעשר, תי"ו – תרומה. ענינא = תנאי. דאמר להו לוקח לסהדי קמי מוכר חזו כו׳. ובהדי מוכר גופיה לא אתני. אמינא שטרא אחרינא מהיאך כו׳. אני הייתי סובר שאתה אומר לעדים: בעינא דנכתוב לי שטרא אחרינא ריש גלותא. זבניה מרוותא דכיתנא. על מנת ליתן דמיהן שהן לוקחין לרב כהנא. לא תשקול. משום רבית. כמאן כבני מערבא. בתמיה; כלומר דאמרינן: מי הודיען ללוקחין שיקנו מעותיהן לרב כהנא, לפיכך לא זכה בהן? אטו. מאי איכפת לן בהקנאתן? וכי רב כהנא עתיד ליטול מעות היה ויטול רבית שנתן לו ד׳ ויטול ח׳? והלא פשתנו היה נוטל, וכל מקום שהיה שם שלו היה. ואלו שמכרוהו גזלוהו מיניה, ומשלמים כל דמיו ביוקר כשעת הגזלה, ובשעת הגזלה כבר הוקר! אמנה הואי. שנתן להם מעות באמנה, ולא היה להם פשתן כשקבלו דמים, והתנו עמו כשער הזול ליתן לו כל השנה בשער זה. דתנן, ב"מ (דף עב:): יצא השער – פוסקין, אע"פ שאין לזה יש לזה. ורב. דאסר ליה למשקל זוזי. לטעמיה דא"ר. ב"איזהו נשך" (ב"מ סג.): עושין אמנה ליתן מעות על השער של זול של עכשיו. בפירות. לקבל פירות בשער היוקר. ואין עושין אמנה בדמים. כשבא לשער היוקר לקבל פירותיו – אסור ליתן לו מוכר דמים של עכשיו, דמיחזי כרבית, דיהיב ליה תרתי סלעים ושקיל ארבע. מתני׳ ונשבע לו. על שקר, והודה. יוליכנו אחריו אפילו למדי. דאין לו כפרה עד שיחזיר לנגזל עצמו, דכתיב: "לאשר הוא לו" וגו׳ (ויקרא ה), וגבי נשבע לשקר כתיב. לא יתן לא לבנו. של נגזל להוליכו לנגזל, שאם יאנסוהו – חייב להחזיר, דלא הוי השבה עד דמטי לידיה, כדאמרן. לשליח ב"ד. תקנתא הוא דעבוד רבנן מפני תקנת השבים, שלא נחייב לזה להוציא מנה בהוצאת הדרך. ואם מת. נגזל, יחזיר גזלן ליורשיו דנגזל. ולא נתן לו את החומש. או שמחל לו נגזל על הקרן לאחר שהודה לו, ולא מחל לו על החומש, או שמחל לו על זה ועל זה כו׳. נתן לו את הקרן. לאחר שנשבע והודה, ונתחייב קרן וחומש – נשבע לו שבועה שניה על החומש שנתנו לו, והודה. הרי

תוספות

כגון דאודעינהו לדידיה ואודעינהו נמי לסהדי. תימה: אם כן אמאי צריך לדחוק את ריש גלותא שיכתוב לו שטר! יכתבו לו עדים, כיון שיודעין שהוא קונה לעצמו! וי"ל: כגון דלא בעו עדים למיכתב ליה שטרא אחרינא. יהב זוזי אכיתנא. השתא ס"ד דאיירי דמשך נמי, ופקדון בעלמא הוא דהוי גביה. כמאן כבני מערבא דאמרי מי הודיעו לבעל חטין כו׳. כלומר: ומשום הכי, אי לאו דאודעיה ללוקח — כי קמזבין דהאי כיתנא דכהנא הוא, נמצא דכהנא לא קני להנהו מעות, דאינהו לאו אדעתא דהכי יהבו ליה מעותיו, ואי שקיל כהנא מידי דמרוותייהו — ה"ל כאילו מדידהו יהבו ליה, ומחזי כרבית. התם אמנה הוא. פי׳ בקונטרס: שנתן להם המעות באמנה, ולא היה להם פשתן כשקבלו המעות. וקשה: דאם כן היכי מסיק רב לטעמיה? והא בכה"ג אפילו רבי ינאי מודה דאסור לקבל המעות, כיון שלא היה לו פירות באותה שעה שהוא פוסק עמו, דהא דאמר ר׳ ינאי: מה לי הן מה לי דמיהן — היינו דוקא כשיש לו פירות באותה שעה שהוא פוסק עמו, ורב אפילו בכה"ג אוסר לקבל מעות, אלא פירות דוקא. דהא בפרק "איזהו נשך" (ב"מ דף סג. ושם) מייתי דרבי ינאי אברייתא דרבי אושעיא דהיה נושה בחבירו מנה והלך על גורנו, ואמר לו: תן לי מעות שאני רוצה ליקח בהן חטין, אמר ליה: חטין יש לי כו׳, עד: וכולן, יש לו — מותר, אין לו — אסור. וקאמר התם: ש"מ איתא לר׳ ינאי דאמר: מה לי הן מה לי דמיהן. משמע דר׳ ינאי דוקא כי יש לו מותר, ובכה"ג פליג רב! ומיהו, יש ליישב פי׳ הקונטרס: דהתם דוקא דאיירי בהלואה, לא שרי רבי ינאי אלא כשיש לו פירות דוקא, אבל זביני אמר התם דפוסקין על שער שבשוק אפילו אין לו, והיינו אמנה בפירות. ומה שפירש בקונטרס [התם] דרבי ינאי מתיר דמיהן — שאין מעות ממש, אלא דוקא פירות, דומיא דההיא דברייתא: יין דמי חטים, וכן יין דמי שמן, שמן דמי יין, דלא מחזי כרבית, אבל מעות אסור — אין נראה, דהכא בשמעתין מוכחא דאפילו זוזי מותר לקבל. והלכה כרבי ינאי, כדמוכח התם. הגוזל מחבירו שוה פרוטה ונשבע כו׳. כגון שנשבע מעצמו. דאין ב"ד משביעין אלא בטענת שתי כסף והודאה שוה פרוטה. ואפילו *בשבועה עצמו מיחייב חומש, כדמוכח בשילהי פירקין. ובמס׳ שבועות (דף לו:) תני נמי: שבועת הפקדון נוהגת באנשים ובנשים, בפני ב"ד ושלא בפני ב"ד [מפי עצמו]. א"נ: מיירי בטוענו שתי כסף והודה לו שוה פרוטה*. אבל נותן לשליח ב"ד. פי׳ הקונטרס: מפני תקנת השבים, שלא נחייבנו להוציא מנה בהוצאת הדרך. משמע מתוך פירושו דנותנו לשליח ב"ד, והוא שומרו בידו עד שיבא הנגזל. ואין נראה; חדא, דלישנא לא משמע הכי, דאמאי נקט שליח ב"ד? הל"ל: אם יש ב"ד שם — נותן לב"ד. ועוד, דאמר בגמ׳ (דף קד.): שליח ב"ד פסיקא ליה מילתא, ל"ש עשאו גזלן להוליך לנגזל. ועוד: אמאי קאמר בגמ׳ דלא מיתוקמא מתני׳ כר׳ טרפון? והא בפרק "המפקיד" (ב"מ דף לז: ושם) פריך אמילתא דר׳ טרפון: ושקלי ליה כולהו ואזלי! ומשני: תני ויניח. וע"כ ביד בית דין קאמר, כי הא דר׳ אלעזר בר צדוק דמסיק אליבא דר׳ טרפון. ועוד: בגמ׳ אמאי איצטריך לאתויי דרבי אלעזר? ממתניתין ה"מ לאתויי!? ע"כ נראה דמתני׳ איירי לענין אחריות הדרך, דמיפטר כשיתן לשליח ב"ד, ויש לו כפרה מיד, ואין צריך לו להמתין עד שיגיע ליד הנגזל כיון שקבלו שליח ב"ד. אבל בתקנתא זו לא איירי מתניתין כלל. ואם מת יחזיר לבניו. נראה דאתא לאשמועינן דאפילו ליורשים יוליך למדי. א"נ: אתא למימר דאין חילוק בין שהנגזל קיים בין שהוא מת לענין קרן חומש ואשם, כי היכי דיש חילוק בגזלן בין הוא לבניו, דבניו אין משלמין חומש ואשם על גזל אביהם, קמ"ל דלענין נגזל אין חילוק.

מניח

עין משפט נר מצוה

קב א מיי׳ פ"ב מהלכות שלוחין ושותפין הלכה ה סמג עשין פב טוש"ע ח"מ סי׳ קפד סעיף ב:

קג ב טוש"ע י"ד סי׳ קעה סעיף ו:

קד ג מיי׳ פ"ז מהלכות גזילה הלכה ט סמג עשין עג טוש"ע ח"מ סי׳ שסז סעיף א:

קה ד ה מיי׳ שם הלכה י טוש"ע שם סעיף ב:

קו ו מיי׳ שם פ"ח הל"א טוש"ע שם סעיף ד:

קז ז ח מיי׳ שם פ"ז הל׳ יא סמג שם טוש"ע שם סעיף ג:

קח ט מיי׳ שם טוש"ע שם סעיף ב:

[ד"ה דאמר]

הגהות הב"ח

(א) במשנה אחריו אפילו למדי:

[נ"ל בשבועת עצמו]

ונשבע על השתי כסף ואח"כ הודה על פרוטה יתר על הפרוטה שהודה כבר כ"ש דאיירי שטענו ב׳ כסף והודה הכל וכפר פרוטה אחת ונשבע אח"כ על הפרוטה שכפר. העתק מחילופי גרסאות

מסורת הש"ס

קף לג: לו: ב"מ מג. פסחים לב.

ב"מ סג.

שם נה.

[לקמן קט.]

תוס׳ לקמן קד: ד"ה חוץ

[ע׳ תוס׳ לקמן קד: ד"ה נתן]

אהֲרֵי זֶה מְשַׁלֵּם חוֹמֶשׁ עַל חוֹמֶשׁ עַד שֶׁיִּתְמַעֵט הַקֶּרֶן מִשָּׁוֶה פְּרוּטָה. בוְכֵן בְּפִקָּדוֹן, שֶׁנֶּאֱמַר: °"(אוֹ) בְּפִקָּדוֹן אוֹ בִתְשׂוּמֶת יָד אוֹ בְגָזֵל אוֹ עָשַׁק אֶת עֲמִיתוֹ, אוֹ מָצָא אֲבֵידָה וְכִחֶשׁ בָּהּ וְנִשְׁבַּע עַל שָׁקֶר" — גהֲרֵי זֶה מְשַׁלֵּם קֶרֶן וְחוֹמֶשׁ וְאָשָׁם.§

גמ' נִשְׁבַּע לוֹ — אִין, דלֹא נִשְׁבַּע לוֹ — לָא, מַנִּי? לָא רַבִּי טַרְפוֹן וְלָא רַבִּי עֲקִיבָא. *דְּתַנְיָא: גָּזַל אֶחָד מֵחֲמִשָּׁה וְאֵינוֹ יוֹדֵעַ (א) אֵיזֶה מֵהֶן, וְכָל אֶחָד אוֹמֵר "אוֹתִי גָּזַל" — מַנִּיחַ גְּזֵילָה בֵּינֵיהֶם וּמִסְתַּלֵּק, דִּבְרֵי רַבִּי טַרְפוֹן; ר"ע אוֹמֵר: הלֹא זוֹ דֶּרֶךְ מוֹצִיאָתוֹ מִידֵי עֲבֵירָה, עַד שֶׁיְּשַׁלֵּם גְּזֵילָה לְכָל אֶחָד [וְאֶחָד] מַנִּי? אִי ר"ט — אע"ג דְּאִשְׁתַּבַּע, אָמַר: מַנִּיחַ גְּזֵילָה בֵּינֵיהֶם וּמִסְתַּלֵּק, אִי רַבִּי עֲקִיבָא — אע"ג דְּלָא אִשְׁתַּבַּע, אָמַר: עַד שֶׁיְּשַׁלֵּם גְּזֵילָה לְכָל אֶחָד וְאֶחָד! לְעוֹלָם רַבִּי עֲקִיבָא הִיא, וְכִי קָאָמַר רַבִּי עֲקִיבָא עַד שֶׁיְּשַׁלֵּם גְּזֵילָה לְכָל אֶחָד וְאֶחָד, הֵיכָא דְּאִשְׁתַּבַּע הוּא דְּקָאָמַר; מַאי טַעֲמָא? דְּאָמַר קְרָא: °"לַאֲשֶׁר הוּא לוֹ יִתְּנֶנּוּ בְּיוֹם אַשְׁמָתוֹ". וְרַבִּי טַרְפוֹן? אע"ג דְּאִשְׁתַּבַּע עֲבוּד רַבָּנַן תַּקַּנְתָּא; דְּתַנְיָא, ר' אֶלְעָזָר בְּרַבִּי צָדוֹק אוֹמֵר: °ותַּקָּנָה גְּדוֹלָה הִתְקִינוּ, שֶׁאִם הָיְתָה הוֹצָאָה יְתֵירָה עַל הַקֶּרֶן — מְשַׁלֵּם קֶרֶן וְחוֹמֶשׁ לְבֵית דִּין, וּמֵבִיא אֲשָׁמוֹ וּמִתְכַּפֵּר לוֹ. וְר' עֲקִיבָא? כִּי עֲבוּד רַבָּנַן תַּקַּנְתָּא — הֵיכָא דְּיָדַע לְמַאן גַּזְלֵיהּ, דְּקָא מַהֲדַר לֵיהּ מָמוֹנָא לְמָרֵיהּ. (ב) גָּזַל אֶחָד מֵחֲמִשָּׁה, דְּלָא יָדַע לְמַאן גַּזְלֵיהּ, דְּלָא הָדַר מָמוֹנָא לְמָרֵיהּ — לָא עֲבוּד רַבָּנַן תַּקַּנְתָּא. מְתִיב רַב הוּנָא בַּר יְהוּדָה: *א"ר שִׁמְעוֹן בֶּן אֶלְעָזָר: לֹא נֶחְלְקוּ רַבִּי טַרְפוֹן וְרַבִּי עֲקִיבָא עַל שֶׁלָּקַח אֶחָד מֵחֲמִשָּׁה וְאֵינוֹ יוֹדֵעַ מֵאֵיזֶה מֵהֶן לָקַח, זשֶׁמַּנִּיחַ דְּמֵי מִקָּח בֵּינֵיהֶם וּמִסְתַּלֵּק. עַל מָה נֶחְלְקוּ? שֶׁגָּזַל אֶחָד מֵחֲמִשָּׁה בְּנֵי אָדָם וְאֵינוֹ יוֹדֵעַ מֵאֵיזֶה מֵהֶן גָּזַל, שֶׁר' טַרְפוֹן אוֹמֵר: מַנִּיחַ דְּמֵי גְּזֵילָה בֵּינֵיהֶם וּמִסְתַּלֵּק, וְרַבִּי עֲקִיבָא אוֹמֵר: אֵין לוֹ תַּקָּנָה עַד שֶׁיְּשַׁלֵּם גְּזֵילָה לְכָל אֶחָד וְאֶחָד; וְאִי סָלְקָא דַּעְתָּךְ דְּאִשְׁתַּבַּע, חמַה לִּי לָקַח מַה לִּי גָּזַל? וְעוֹד מְתִיב רָבָא: מַעֲשֶׂה בְּחָסִיד אֶחָד שֶׁלָּקַח מִשְּׁנֵי בְּנֵי אָדָם וְלֹא הָיָה יוֹדֵעַ מֵאֵיזֶה מֵהֶן לָקַח, וּבָא לִפְנֵי רַבִּי טַרְפוֹן, אָמַר לוֹ: הַנַּח דְּמֵי מִקָּחֲךָ בֵּינֵיהֶם וְהִסְתַּלֵּק. בָּא לִפְנֵי רַבִּי עֲקִיבָא, אָמַר לוֹ: טאֵין לְךָ תַּקָּנָה עַד שֶׁתְּשַׁלֵּם לְכָל אֶחָד וְאֶחָד; וְאִי סָלְקָא דַּעְתָּךְ דְּמִישְׁתַּבַּע, חָסִיד מִי מִשְׁתַּבַּע בְּשִׁיקְרָא? וְכִי תֵּימָא, דְּמִשְׁתַּבַּע וַהֲדַר הֲוֵי חָסִיד, וְהָא *כָּל הֵיכָא דְּאָמְרִינַן "מַעֲשֶׂה בְּחָסִיד אֶחָד" — אוֹ רַבִּי יְהוּדָה בֶּן בָּבָא אוֹ רַבִּי יְהוּדָה בְּרַבִּי אִילְעַאי, וְרַבִּי יְהוּדָה בֶּן בָּבָא וְרַבִּי יְהוּדָה בְּרַבִּי אֶילְעַאי חֲסִידִים דְּמֵעִיקָּרָא הֲווּ! אֶלָּא לְעוֹלָם ר' טַרְפוֹן הִיא, וּמוֹדֶה ר' טַרְפוֹן הֵיכָא דְּאִשְׁתַּבַּע, מַאי טַעֲמָא? דְּאָמַר קְרָא: "לַאֲשֶׁר הוּא לוֹ יִתְּנֶנּוּ בְּיוֹם אַשְׁמָתוֹ". וְרַבִּי עֲקִיבָא, (דְּאָמַר) יאע"ג דְּלָא מִישְׁתַּבַּע — קָנֵיס. וְר' טַרְפוֹן, מִכְּדֵי הֵיכָא דְּמִישְׁתַּבַּע לָא סַגְיָא דְּלָא הוֹדָה, מַאי אִירְיָא וְנִשְׁבַּע? אֲפִילּוּ בְּלֹא שְׁבוּעָה נַמִי! דְּתַנְיָא: *מוֹדֶה רַבִּי טַרְפוֹן, כבְּאוֹמֵר לִשְׁנַיִם "גָּזַלְתִּי אֶחָד מִכֶּם מָנֶה וְאֵינִי יוֹדֵעַ אֵיזֶה מִכֶּם" — נוֹתֵן לָזֶה מָנֶה וְלָזֶה מָנֶה,

שֶׁכְּבָר

הֲרֵי זֶה מְשַׁלֵּם חוֹמֶשׁ עַל חוֹמֶשׁ. חוּמְשׁוֹ שֶׁל חוֹמֶשׁ, דְּחוֹמֶשׁ רִאשׁוֹן נַעֲשָׂה קֶרֶן. עַד שֶׁיִּתְמַעֵט כו'. שֶׁאִם חָזַר וְנָתַן לוֹ חוֹמֶשׁ רִאשׁוֹן וְנִשְׁבַּע עַל הַשֵּׁנִי וְהוֹדָה — מְשַׁלֵּם חוּמְשׁוֹ וְחוּמְשׁוֹ שֶׁל חוֹמֶשׁ שֵׁנִי, וְכֵן לְעוֹלָם, עַד שֶׁיִּתְמַעֵט הַקֶּרֶן שֶׁל חוֹמֶשׁ, שֶׁלֹּא יִכְפּוֹר לוֹ שָׁוֶה פְּרוּטָה. תורה אור או עָשַׁק אֶת עֲמִיתוֹ. שְׂכַר שָׂכִיר. תְּשׂוּמֶת יָד. הַלְוָאָה. גמ' לֹא נִשְׁבַּע. לָא בָּעֵי לְהוֹלִיךְ אַחֲרָיו עַד דְּמָטֵי לִידֵיהּ. עַד שֶׁיְּשַׁלֵּם לְכָל אֶחָד. דַּהֲשָׁבָה לִידֵיהּ בָּעֵינַן, וְלָא סַגֵּי בְּמַנִּיחַ לְפָנָיו, לוֹמַר: מִי שֶׁהוּא שֶׁלּוֹ יִטְּלֶנָּה. מַנִּיחַ גְּזֵילָה. וְלָא בָּעֵי לְאַמְטוּיֵי לִידֵיהּ, וְסַגֵּי בְּמַנִּיחַ לְפָנָיו, שֶׁהֲרֵי הַבְּעָלִים שָׁם הוּא. לְעוֹלָם רַבִּי עֲקִיבָא. כְּר"ע מֵעִיקָּרָא מְהַדְּרִינַן לְאוֹקְמֵי מִשּׁוּם דְּכוּלְּהוּ תַּנָּאֵי סְתִימְתָּאָה אַלִּיבָּא דְּר"ע סָתַם, כִּדְאָמַר בְּ"אֵלּוּ הֵן הַנֶּחֱנָקִין" (סנהדרין דף פו.). עֲבוּד רַבָּנַן תַּקַּנְתָּא. תַּקָּנַת הַשָּׁבִים. וְהָכָא דְּמִסְתַּפְּקָא לֵיהּ — תִּסְגֵּי לְהוּ בְּמַנִּיחַ, כִּדְתַנְיָא. עֲבוּד תַּקָּנוֹת גַּבֵּי גּוֹזֵל וְנִשְׁבָּע וְהוֹדָה וְאֵין הַנִּגְזָל כָּאן, דְּאַע"פ דִּכְתִיב: "לַאֲשֶׁר הוּא לוֹ" — תַּקּוּן רַבָּנַן דְּנִתְבֵיהּ לִשְׁלִיחַ בֵּית דִּין, וִיהֵא תַּחַת יָדָם, עַד שֶׁיָּבֹא נִגְזָל וְיִטְּלֶנּוּ. דְּקָא מַהֲדַר מָמוֹנָא לְמָרֵיהּ. לְאַחַר זְמַן יַחֲזִירֶנּוּ בֵּית דִּין. לֹא נֶחְלְקוּ עַל שֶׁלָּקַח. דְּכֵיוָן דְּלֵיכָּא אִיסּוּרָא סַגֵּי לֵיהּ בְּהָכִי, דְּלָא כְּתִיב "לַאֲשֶׁר הוּא לוֹ" אֶלָּא בְּמָקוֹם שֶׁחָטָא, דְּבָעֵי כַּפָּרָה. מַה לִּי לוֹקֵחַ כו'. הֲרֵי נִשְׁבַּע לַשֶּׁקֶר, וְאַשְּׁבוּעַת שֶׁקֶר כְּתִיב: "לַאֲשֶׁר הוּא לוֹ", בֵּין אַגָּזֵל בֵּין אַתְּשׂוּמֶת יָד דִּבְהֶיתֵּר אֲתָא לִידֵיהּ. תַּנָּא דְּחָסִיד אֶחָד פָּלֵיג אַדְּר' שִׁמְעוֹן בֶּן אֶלְעָזָר. רַבִּי טַרְפוֹן הִיא. מַתְנִי' דְּקָתָנֵי נִשְׁבַּע. דְּאִי ר"ע — אֲפִילּוּ לֹא נִשְׁבַּע נַמִי. וְר' טַרְפוֹן מִכְּדֵי כו'. אַמַּתְנִיתִין פָּרֵיךְ, דְּאָמַר: נִשְׁבַּע — אִין, לֹא נִשְׁבַּע — לָא, וְאוֹקִימְנָא כְּר' טַרְפוֹן. לָא סַגְיָא דְּלָא הוֹדָה דְּכַפָּרָה וְאָשָׁם דִּקְרָא אַהוֹדָה כְּתִיב, דִּכְתִיב בְּגֶזֶל הַגֵּר: "וְהִתְוַדּוּ אֶת חַטָּאתָם" וגו' (במדבר ה).

שֶׁכְּבָר

מניח גזילה ביניהם ומסתלק. בפרק "המפקיד" (ב"מ לז:) מוקי לה דלאו דוקא ביניהם, דשקלי להו כולהו ואזלי, אלא יניח עד שיתברר הדבר מי הם הבעלים. **דברי** רבי טרפון. ואפילו לרב הונא ולרב יהודה דאמרי ב"הגוזל בתרא" (לקמן דף קיח.) גבי "מנה לי בידך" והלה אומר "איני יודע" חייב, דשמא וברי ברי עדיף, ומפקינן ממונא — הכא מודו דאין צריך לשלם לכל אחד, דהא לדידיה נמי ברי שארבעה משקרין, שבודאי לא גזל אלא האחד, הלכך ברי דידהו לא חשיב לגבי שמא דידיה, לאפוקי ממונא. ואפילו רב נחמן ורבי יוחנן דאמרי התם פטור, דלאו ברי עדיף, אלא מוקמינן ממונא בחזקת מריה — מצו סברי הכא אפילו כרבי עקיבא. דאמר: עד שישלם גזילה לכל אחד ואחד. דהכא מיהא מנה מודה דאית ליה לשלומי, אבל התם לא מודי מידי. **לעולם** ר"ע. משום הכי מוקי פלוגתייהו בנשבע וכר"ע, ולא מוקי לה בשלא נשבע ותיתי כר' טרפון — משום דבכל דוכתא מהדרי לאוקמי מתני' כר' עקיבא, כדאשכחן בסוף "השוכר את האומנין" (ב"מ דף פב.) דפריך: אי הכי קמה לה מתני' דלא כרבי עקיבא.

*__ורבי__ טרפון אע"ג דנשבע עבוד רבנן תקנתא כו'. תימה: דמשמע הא אין הוצאת הדרך יתירה — מוליכה אחריו למדי. ואמאי? והאמר ר' טרפון: מניח גזילה ביניהם ומסתלק! וכ"ת ה' בני אדם היינו הוצאה מרובה על הקרן — הא בשנים נמי קתני לקמן בברייתא דחסיד! ושמא הש"ס אכתי לא שמיע ליה. ומיהו, תימה: כיון דמודה ר"א היכא דאין הוצאה יתירה — אמאי קאמר ר"ע היא? כר' טרפון נמי אתיא, דאפילו למאן דמוקי לה כר"ע — לא מיתוקמא מתניתין אלא באין הוצאה יתירה! וי"ל: דמתני' איירי אפילו בהוצאה יתירה, שצריך להוליך עד מדי כשאינו מוצא ב"ד עד מדי, אע"ג דלא שכיח. ולא נקט מתניתין מדי אלא לפרושי דאפילו בהוצאה יתירה איירי, וצריך להוליך עד מדי או עד מקום ב"ד אם יש קרוב יותר, אע"ג דהוצאה יתירה עד שם. ומש"ה מתוקמא כר"ע ולא כר' טרפון, דלר' טרפון אפילו כי אין מוצא ב"ד — לעולם אין צריך לעשות הוצאה יתירה על הקרן, אלא מניח בידו עד שמוצא ב"ד במקום קרוב. וא"ת: מנלן דס"ל הכי לר' טרפון? דלמא כשאין ב"ד — מודה! וי"ל: דסברא הוא, דאי הוה מצריך הולכה למדי כשאין ב"ד — כ"ש בגזל אחד מחמשה דלא הוי סגי במסירה לב"ד, כיון דלא הדר ממונא למריה, אלא עד שישלם לכל אחד ואחד. והוה מצי ר"א בן צדוק לאשמועינן רבותא, שאם הוצאה יתירה עד ב"ד דמניח בידו. אלא אתא לאשמועינן כשב"ד קרוב — טוב יותר להניח בידם. ועוד י"ל: דודאי מדלא תני תקנתא במתני' — שמע מינה דליכא תקנתא כלל בנשבע, הלכך דוקא מוקי לה כר"ע ולא כר' טרפון, דאית ליה תקנתא. ור"ע לית ליה תקנתא אפילו בגזל מאחד היכא דנשבע. והא דקאמר ר"ע: כי עבוד רבנן תקנתא היכא דידע כו' — לדבריו דר' טרפון קאמר, כלומר: לדידי לית ליה תקנתא כלל בנשבע, אלא אפילו לדידך דאית לך דרבי אלעזר בר' צדוק אפילו בנשבע, אכתי איכא למימר הני מילי היכא דידע למאן גזל. **כל** היכא דנשבע לא סגי דלאו הודה. וכיון שהודה — מסתמא בא לצאת ידי שמים כיון שלא תבעוהו. וה"נ צריך להוליכו למדי, כי היכי דצריך ליתן מנה לכל אחד ואחד.

שכבר

קט א מיי' פ"ז מהל' גזילה הלכה יב סמג עשין עג:
קי ב מיי' שם הלכה יג סמג שם:
קיא ג מיי' שם הלכה א ב ופרק א מהלכות שבועות הלכה ח ט סמג לאוין רמ:
קיב ד מיי' פ"ז מהל' גזילה הלכה א סמג עשין עג טוש"ע ח"מ סי' שסז סעיף א:
קיג ה מיי' שם פ"ד הלכה ט סמג שם טוש"ע ח"מ סי' שסה סעיף א:
קיד ו מיי' שם פ"ז הלכה י סמג שם טוש"ע ח"מ סי' שסז סעיף ב:
קטו ז מיי' פ"כ מהלכות מכירה הלכה ב סמג עשין פב טוש"ע ח"מ סי' רכב סעיף ב:
קטז ח מיי' שם הלכה ג טוש"ע שם סעיף ג:
[עיין במפרשי ש"ס מה שכתבו בדיבור זה]
קיז ט מיי' שם טוש"ע שם סעיף ב:
קיח י מיי' פ"ד מהל' גזילה הלכה ט סמג עשין עג טוש"ע ח"מ סי' שסה סעיף א:
קיט כ מיי' שם הלכה י טוש"ע שם סעיף ב:

ויקרא ה

יבמות קיח: ב"מ לז דתנן]

שם

יבמות קיח: [ה דיבמות פי"ד]

[תמורה טו:]

רס"ל מ"ז

ב"מ לז:

הגהות הב"ח

(א) גמ' ואינו יודע מאיזה וכו' לא זו הדרך: (ב) שם ממונא למריה אבל גזל:

גליון הש"ס

גמ' תקנה גדולה התקינו. עי' שבועות ד' מה מ"א תוס' ד"ה גדולות:

שֶׁכְּבָר הוֹדָה מִפִּי עַצְמוֹ! אֶלָּא אָמַר רָבָא: שָׁאנֵי מַתְנִי', דְּכֵיוָן דִּידַע לְמַאן גַּזְלֵיהּ וְאוֹדֵי לֵיהּ, כֵּיוָן דְּאֶפְשָׁר לְאַהֲדוּרֵי מָמוֹנָא לְמָרֵיהּ הֲוָה לֵיהּ כְּמַאן דְּאָמַר לֵיהּ "יְהִיוּ לִי בְּיָדְךָ". הִלְכָּךְ: נִשְׁבַּע, אע"ג דְּקָאָמַר לֵיהּ "יְהִיוּ לִי בְּיָדְךָ", כֵּיוָן דְּבָעֵי כַּפָּרָה – לָא סַגִּי עַד דְּמָטֵי לִידֵיהּ; [א]הָא לָא אִישְׁתַּבַּע – הָוֵי גַּבֵּיהּ פִּקָּדוֹן עַד דְּאָתֵי וְשָׁקֵיל לֵיהּ.§ "לֹא יִתֵּן לֹא לִבְנוֹ וְלֹא לִשְׁלוּחוֹ".§ אִיתְּמַר: שָׁלִיחַ שֶׁעֲשָׂאוֹ בְּעֵדִים, רַב חִסְדָּא אָמַר: [ב]הָוֵי שָׁלִיחַ, רַבָּה אָמַר: לָא הָוֵי שָׁלִיחַ. רַב חִסְדָּא אָמַר הָוֵי שָׁלִיחַ; לְהָכִי טָרְחִי וְאוֹקְמֵיהּ בְּעֵדִים – דְּלֵיקוּ בִּרְשׁוּתֵיהּ. רַבָּה אָמַר לָא הָוֵי שָׁלִיחַ; ה"ק: אִינִישׁ מְהֵימְנָא הוּא, אִי סָמְכַתְּ – סְמוֹךְ, אִי בָּעֵית לְשַׁדּוּרֵיהּ בִּידֵיהּ – שַׁדַּר בִּידֵיהּ. תְּנַן: *[ג]הַשּׁוֹאֵל אֶת הַפָּרָה, וְשִׁילְּחָהּ בְּיַד בְּנוֹ בְּיַד עַבְדּוֹ בְּיַד שְׁלוּחוֹ, אוֹ בְּיַד בְּנוֹ בְּיַד עַבְדּוֹ בְּיַד שְׁלוּחוֹ שֶׁל שׁוֹאֵל, וּמֵתָה – פָּטוּר; הַאי שְׁלוּחוֹ הֵיכִי דָּמֵי? אִי דְּלָא עָשָׂה בְּעֵדִים, מְנָא יָדְעִינַן? אֶלָּא דְּעָשָׂה בְּעֵדִים, וְקָתָנֵי דְּפָטוּר, קַשְׁיָא לְרַב חִסְדָּא! כִּדְאָמַר רַב חִסְדָּא: בִּשְׂכִירוֹ וּלְקִיטוֹ, הָכָא נַמִי בִּשְׂכִירוֹ וּלְקִיטוֹ. תְּנַן: *לֹא יִתֵּן לֹא לִבְנוֹ וְלֹא לִשְׁלוּחוֹ; הַאי שְׁלוּחוֹ הֵיכִי דָּמֵי? אִי דְּלָא עֲשָׂאוֹ בְּעֵדִים, מְנָא יָדְעִינַן? אֶלָּא לָאו דַּעֲשָׂאוֹ בְּעֵדִים! תַּרְגְּמָא רַב חִסְדָּא: בִּשְׂכִירוֹ וּלְקִיטוֹ. אֲבָל שָׁלִיחַ שֶׁעֲשָׂאוֹ בְּעֵדִים, מַאי? הָכִי נַמִי דְּהָוֵי שָׁלִיחַ? אַדְּתָנֵי סֵיפָא: אֲבָל נוֹתֵן הוּא לִשְׁלִיחַ בֵּית דִּין, לִפְלוֹג וְלִיתְנֵי בְּדִידֵיהּ: (א) שָׁלִיחַ שֶׁעֲשָׂאוֹ בְּעֵדִים הָכִי נַמִי דְּהָוֵי שָׁלִיחַ! אָמְרִי: לָא פְּסִיקָא לֵיהּ; שְׁלִיחַ ב"ד, לָא שְׁנָא עֲשָׂאוֹ נִגְזָל וְלָא שְׁנָא עֲשָׂאוֹ גַּזְלָן הָוֵי שָׁלִיחַ – פְּסִיקָא לֵיהּ. שָׁלִיחַ שֶׁעֲשָׂאוֹ בְּעֵדִים, דְּכִי עֲשָׂאוֹ נִגְזָל הוּא דְּהָוֵי שָׁלִיחַ, עֲשָׂאוֹ גַּזְלָן לָא הָוֵי שָׁלִיחַ – לָא פְּסִיקָא לֵיהּ; וּלְאַפּוּקֵי מֵהַאי תַּנָּא, דְּתַנְיָא, רַבִּי שִׁמְעוֹן בֶּן אֶלְעָזָר אוֹמֵר: שְׁלִיחַ בֵּית דִּין שֶׁעֲשָׂאוֹ נִגְזָל וְלֹא עֲשָׂאוֹ גַּזְלָן, אוֹ עֲשָׂאוֹ גַּזְלָן וְשָׁלַח הַלָּה וְנָטַל אֶת שֶׁלּוֹ מִיָּדוֹ – פָּטוּר. רַבִּי יוֹחָנָן וְרַבִּי אֶלְעָזָר דְּאָמְרִי תַּרְוַיְיהוּ: שָׁלִיחַ שֶׁעֲשָׂאוֹ בְּעֵדִים הָוֵי שָׁלִיחַ, וְא"ת: מִשְׁנָתֵנוּ! [ד]בְּמַמְצִיא לוֹ שָׁלִיחַ, דְּאָמַר לֵיהּ: אִית לִי זוּזֵי גַּבֵּי פְּלָנְיָא וְלָא קָא מְשַׁדַּר לְהוּ, אִיתְחֲזֵי לֵיהּ, דִּלְמָא אִינִישׁ הוּא דְּלָא מַשְׁכַּח לְשַׁדּוּרֵי לֵיהּ; א"נ, כִּדְרַב חִסְדָּא: בִּשְׂכִירוֹ וּלְקִיטוֹ. א"ר יְהוּדָה אָמַר שְׁמוּאֵל: אֵין

רש"י

שכבר הודה מפי עצמו. ובא לצאת ידי שמים. ואע"ג דבי דינא לא מצו מחייבי ליה, אלא מניח לפניהם – מיהו ידי עונש אין יוצא עד שישלם לשניהם, דהא לאו לבעלים אהדריה כו'. אלא אמר רבא. מתני' דברי הכל היא. ולא דמיא לאין יודע, דהתם בין נשבע בין לא נשבע הוא דפליגי ר' טרפון ור"ע לענין דינא, דר' טרפון לא מחייב להחזיר ליד הנגזל, ור"ע מחייב אע"ג דלא נשבע. והאי דפרכת לעיל: ואי ר"ע אע"ג דלא אשתבע – לאו פירכא היא, דהתם דין הוא דאע"ג דלא משתבע דיחזיר לכל אחד, שהרי אין יודע למי גזל, ולא נפיק ידי שמים כלל. אבל הכא במתני', דידע למאן גזל ומודי ליה – משעת הודאה דמזומן הוא להשיב הוי גביה כפקדון. הלכך, נשבע תחילה קודם הודאה אע"ג כו'. שליח שעשאו בעדים. ראובן שיש לו מעות ביד שמעון, ומינה שליח בעדים לקבלם הימנו, ונתנם לו. הוי שליח. ואם נאנסו בדרך – פטור בעל הבית שנתנם לו. פטור. דלא קמה ברשות שואל להתחייב באונסים עד שיאמר לו מפיו לשלחה לו ביד בנו כו'. מנא ידעינן. דשלוחו הוא, דקרי ליה מתני' שלוחו(ב)? לקיטו. שלקטו אצלו לדור עמו בביתו לגוותא בעלמא. לשון מורי. ושכירו. נשכר עמו ליום ולחדש ולשנה ולשבת. לישנא אחרינא: לקיטו = לוקט תבואתו. ולאפוקי מהאי תנא. הא מתניתין דאוקימנא שליח ב"ד אפילו עשאו גזלן ולא נגזל הוה שליח, והוי באחריותו דנגזל – לאפוקי מהאי תנא. שליח ב"ד. דמשמע מתני' דמשנתן לו נפטר גזלן – כשעשאו נגזל קאמר, ולא כשעשאו גזלן. ושלח הלה ונטל שלו. מיד השליח. פטור. מאונס הדרך. טעמא דנטל הנגזל, הא נאנסו מן השליח הראשון – חייב. וא"ת משנתנו. דקתני: לא יתן לשלוחו, ואי דלא עשאו בעדים מנא ידעינן – [לא] תוקמא כשעשאו בעדים, אלא בממציא לו שליח – ביקש מחבירו שימציא לו לגזלן את עצמו, לומר לו: אם תרצה לשלח כלום לפלוני – שלח בידי. בדיוקני

תוספות

שכבר הודה מפי עצמו. מהאי לישנא דייק ב"המפקיד" (ב"מ דף לז:), וגם מחמת פירכא אחריתי, מוקי לה בבא לצאת ידי שמים. ותימה: א"כ ההוא מעשה דחסיד אחד, אמאי אמר ליה רבי טרפון "הנח דמי מקחך ביניהם"? הא כיון דחסיד הוה, מסתמא היה בא לצאת ידי שמים! וי"ל: דלכתחילה בא עמו לדין אם הוא חייב מן הדין, ושוב מה שעשה עשה. א"נ, אפילו לצאת ידי שמים אין חייב לר' טרפון אלא בגזל, אבל בפקדון ומקח דלא עשה איסורא — לא. וכן משמע ב"המפקיד" (שם דף לז. ושם*) דכי רמי התם גזל אגזל, משני: הכא בבא לצאת ידי שמים. ולעיל מיניה כי רמי פקדון אפקדון — לא בעי לשנויי הכי. ואין להאריך כאן בסוגיא דהתם. אמר רבא שאני מתני' כו'. לפי הספרים דל"ג אלא משמע דאתא רבא לתרולי פירכא דפרכינן לר' טרפון, ולעולם רבי טרפון היא. וקאמר: כיון דאודי ליה כמ"ד "יהא בידך" דמי, א"כ מסתמא מיירי כשהודה בפניו, דאם לא כן אמאי הוי כמ"ד "יהא בידך", וכיון דבהודאה (ג) מיירי מתניתין, אכתי תקשה: אמאי לא מוקי מתני' נמי כר"ע? ואע"ג דקניס ר"ע אפילו היכא דלא נשבע — ה"מ דלא הדר ממונא למריה, אבל במתני' היכא דלא נשבע והודה לו בפניו — הדר ממונא למריה, דכיון דהודה לו בפניו — מה לי תופס בידו מ"ל נתן ביד ב"ד? הלכך לא יקנוס ר"ע! וי"ל: דסברת גמרא היה: כיון דקניס ר"ע — בכל מקום קניס, כיון דעבד איסורא, ולא יחלק. ומיהו, אין נראה דמיירי הכא בשהודה בפניו, דא"כ אפילו נשבע נמי אין צריך להוליכו אחריו למדי, ויכול להביא כפרה. דכיון דהודה לו בפניו והניחו בידו והלך — הרי הוא כהפקידו בידו, ואמאי יהא צריך להוליכו אחריו? אלא ודאי מיירי כשהודה שלא בפניו אלא בפני עדים, והשתא א"ש דלא מתוקמא מתני' כר"ע, דלא מהדר ממונא למריה כיון שלא נתן ביד ב"ד. ולפי מה שפי' בקונטרס "אלא אמר רבא" — א"ש, דרבא לא בא לתרץ פירכא, (ד) אלא טעמא דמתני' מפרש בכה"ג דמצי לאוקמי בין כר"ע בין כרבי טרפון. שליח שעשאו כו'. לכאורה נראה דאיירי כגון דלא אמר לו (ה) "שלח לי על ידו", רק עדים מעידים שעשאו שליח. אבל אם היה אומר "שלח לי על ידו" — פשיטא דהוי שליח, דהא תנן ב"השואל" (ב"מ דף צח: ושם) אמר ליה השואל: "שלח לי ביד בני ביד עבדי ביד שלוחי, או ביד בנך או ביד עבדך או ביד שלוחך", ושלחה — חייב. ומ"ל א"ל בפניו "שלח", ומ"ל אמר ליה שלא בפניו "שלח". *ומיהו, לקמן לא משמע הכי, דבעי לשמואל מאי תקנתיה — הו"ל ששלח ליה "שלח לי ע"י זה", דאז הוי שליח. לכך נ"ל: דבכל ענין שלא בפניו לא הוי שליח, עד שיאמר לו בפניו "שלח לי על ידו", כההיא ד"השואל" דאיירי בפניו, וכן מוכיח מתוך הקונטרס. רבה אמר לא הוי שליח. יש מקשים דרבה אדרבה, דהכא קאמר רבה דלא הוי שליח, ובפ' "המוכר את הספינה" (ב"ב דף פו:) אמרינן, רבה ורב יוסף דאמרי תרוייהו: הכא בחנוני מוכר ללוחית עסקינן, ואזדא ר' יהודה לטעמיה דאמר לאתויי שדריה. הרי לרבה אליבא דר' יהודה הוי שליח! וי"ל: דשאני התם, דכיון שנתן לו פונדיון ולוה לו להביא באיסר שמן — הוי כאילו א"ל בהדיא "שלח לי על ידו", ופטור. ולפי מה שפירשתי דדוקא שאמר ליה בפניו, אית לן למימר דכיון דנתן הפונדיון הוי כאילו אמר ליה בפניו "שלח", הלכך אמר לר' יהודה לאתויי שדריה. הכי קא"ל איניש מהימנא הוא. תימה: אמאי חייב הוא מן הדין באחריות אונס הדרך? והא אין יכול לומר "אין רצוני שיהא פקדוני ביד אחר", כיון דתפיס ליה באיניש מהימנא! וי"ל: דנראה דאפילו הוא עצמו הביאו בדרך ונאנס חייב, דפשיעה הוא עושה שמוליכו בדרך במקום פלוני שיש בו סכנה, ובע"כ חייב לשמור עד שיחזירנו לו בישוב במקום שהפקידו אצלו. כדאמרינן לקמן (דף קיח.) (ו) בהמפקיד אצל חבירו בישוב לא יחזיר לו במדבר, משמע דבעל כרחו חייב לשמור עד שיחזירנו בישוב במקום שהפקידו, ולאו כל כמיניה להחזיר לו במדבר במקום סכנה. אי דלא עשאו בעדים מנא ידעינן. כלומר: היכי מסר לו משאיל, כיון דלא ידע אי האי שליח של שואל הוא? בשכירו ולקיטו. תימה: אמאי לא אמר רב חסדא נמי אהא? ועוד תימה: אמאי לא פריך ליה מעיקרא ממתני' והדר הוה ליה למפרך מההיא דפ' "השואל"? אין

עין משפט נר מצוה

קכ א מיי' פ"ז מהל' גזילה הלכה ט סמג עשין עג טוש"ע ח"מ סי' שסז סעיף א:

קכא ב מיי' שם הלכה י ופ"ג מהלכות שלוחין ושותפין הלכה ה סמג עשין עב טוש"ע ח"מ סי' שסז סעיף ב וסי' קכא סעיף א וסעיף ב וסי' קכב סעיף א וע"ש:

[ד"ה התם]

קכב ג מיי' פ"ג מהל' שאלה ופקדון הלכה א סמג עשין פב טוש"ע ח"מ סי' שמ סעיף ה:

קכג ד (מיי' שם) טוש"ע ח"מ סי' קכא סעיף ב:

ב"מ נח:

לעיל קג.

וכב"מ פ' השואל כתבו להיפך ע"ש

הגהות הב"ח

(א) גמ' לפלוג וליתני בדידיה כד"א בשליח שלא עשאו בעדים אבל שליח שעשאו בעדים: (ב) רש"י ד"ה מנא ידעינן וכו' שלוחו הס"ד ואח"כ מ"ה שכירו נשכר וכו' ולשבת לקיטו שלקטו וכו' לשון מורי לישנא אחרינא כצ"ל: (ג) תוס' ד"ה אמר וכו' וכיון דבהודאה בפניו מיירי: (ד) בא"ד לא בא לתרץ פירכא דפרכי' לר"ט אלא טעמא: (ה) ד"ה שליח וכו' כגון דלא אמר לו אמור לפלוני ישלח לי על ידך רק עדים מעידים שעשאו שליח להביא לו אבל אם היה אומר לו אמור לפלוני ישלח לי על ידך פשיטא דהוי: (ו) ד"ה הכי וכו' דהמפקיד אצל חבירו:

[א]אין מְשַׁלְּחִין מָעוֹת בִּדְיוֹקָנִי, וַאֲפִילּוּ עֵדִים חֲתוּמִים עָלֶיהָ; וְרַבִּי יוֹחָנָן אָמַר: אִם עֵדִים חֲתוּמִים עָלֶיהָ — מְשַׁלְּחִין. אָמְרִי: לִשְׁמוּאֵל מַאי תַּקַּנְתָּא? כִּי הָא דְּרַבִּי אַבָּא הֲוֵי מַסֵּיק זוּזֵי בִּדְרַב יוֹסֵף בַּר חָמָא, א"ל לְרַב סָפְרָא: בַּהֲדֵי דְּאָתֵית אַיְיתִינְהוּ נִיהֲלִי. כִּי אֲזַל לְהָתָם, אֲמַר לֵיהּ רָבָא בְּרֵיהּ: מִי כְּתַב לָךְ "הִתְקַבַּלְתִּי"? א"ל: לָא. אִי הָכִי, זִיל בְּרֵישָׁא וְיִכְתּוֹב לָךְ "הִתְקַבַּלְתִּי". לַסּוֹף אֲמַר לֵיהּ: אִי כְּתַב לָךְ נַמִי "הִתְקַבַּלְתִּי" [ב]לָאו כְּלוּם הוּא, דִּלְמָא אַדְּאָתֵית שָׁכֵיב רַבִּי אַבָּא וְנָפְלוּ זוּזֵי קַמֵּי יַתְמֵי, וְ"הִתְקַבַּלְתִּי" דְּרַבִּי אַבָּא לָאו כְּלוּם הוּא. א"ל: וְאֶלָּא מַאי תַּקַּנְתָּא? [ג]זִיל נַקְנֵינְהוּ לָךְ אַגַּב אַרְעָא, וְתָא אַתְּ כְּתוֹב לָן "הִתְקַבַּלְתִּי". [ד]כִּי *הָא דְּרַב פַּפָּא הֲוָה מַסֵּיק תְּרֵיסַר אַלְפֵי זוּזֵי בֵּי חוֹזַאי, אַקְנִינְהוּ נִיהֲלֵיהּ לְרַב שְׁמוּאֵל בַּר אַבָּא אַגַּב אַסִּיפָּא דְּבֵיתֵיהּ. כִּי אֲתָא, נְפַק לְאַפֵּיהּ עַד תָּוָאךְ. § "נָתַן לוֹ אֶת הַקֶּרֶן" וכו'. § אַלְמָא חוֹמֶשׁ מָמוֹנָא הוּא, וְאִם מָיֵית — מְשַׁלְּמִי לֵיהּ יוֹרְשִׁין. וּתְנַן נַמִי: נָתַן אֶת הַקֶּרֶן וְנִשְׁבַּע עַל הַחוֹמֶשׁ — הֲרֵי מוֹסִיף חוֹמֶשׁ עַל חוֹמֶשׁ; אַלְמָא חוּמְשָׁא מָמוֹנָא הוּא. וְתַנְיָא נַמִי הָכִי: הַגּוֹזֵל אֶת חֲבֵירוֹ, וְנִשְׁבַּע לוֹ וּמֵת — [ה]יוֹרְשִׁין מְשַׁלְּמִים קֶרֶן וְחוֹמֶשׁ [ו]וּפְטוּרִין מִן הָאָשָׁם. וְיוֹרְשִׁין בְּנֵי שַׁלּוּמֵי חוּמְשָׁא דַּאֲבוּהוֹן הָווּ, (אַלְמָא חוֹמֶשׁ מָמוֹנָא הוּא וּבָעֵי שַׁלּוּמֵי יוֹרְשִׁין)? וּרְמִינְהוּ: עֲדַיִין אֲנִי אוֹמֵר: אֵימָתַי אֵינוֹ מְשַׁלֵּם חוֹמֶשׁ עַל גֶּזֶל אָבִיו — בִּזְמַן שֶׁלֹּא נִשְׁבַּע לֹא הוּא וְלֹא אָבִיו; הוּא וְלֹא אָבִיו, אָבִיו וְלֹא הוּא, הוּא וְאָבִיו [ז]מִנַּיִן? ת"ל: °"אֲשֶׁר גָּזָל" וַ"אֲשֶׁר עָשָׁק", וְהוּא לֹא גָּזַל וְלֹא עָשַׁק! אָמַר רַב נַחְמָן, לָא קַשְׁיָא: כָּאן שֶׁהוֹדָה, כָּאן שֶׁלֹּא הוֹדָה. אִי לֹא הוֹדָה, קֶרֶן נַמִי לֹא מְשַׁלֵּם! וְכִי תֵּימָא הָכִי נַמִי דְּלָא מְשַׁלֵּם, וְהָא מִדְּקָא מַהֲדַר אַחוֹמֶשׁ, לְמֵימְרָא דְּקֶרֶן מְשַׁלֵּם! וְעוֹד תַּנְיָא: וַעֲדַיִין אֲנִי אוֹמֵר: אֵימָתַי הוּא מְשַׁלֵּם קֶרֶן עַל גֶּזֶל אָבִיו — בִּזְמַן שֶׁנִּשְׁבַּע הוּא וְאָבִיו; אָבִיו וְלֹא הוּא, הוּא וְלֹא אָבִיו, לֹא הוּא וְלֹא אָבִיו מִנַּיִן? ת"ל: גְּזֵילָה וְעוֹשֶׁק אֲבֵידָה וּפִקָּדוֹן יֵשׁ תַּלְמוּד; וְיָתֵיב רַב הוּנָא וְקָאָמַר לְהָא שְׁמַעְתָּא, א"ל: רַבָּה בְּרֵיהּ: "יֵשׁ תַּלְמוּד" קָאָמַר מָר, אוֹ "יְשַׁתַּלְּמוּ" קָאָמַר מָר? א"ל: "יֵשׁ תַּלְמוּד" קָאָמִינָא, וּמֵרִיבּוּיָא דִּקְרָאֵי אָמְרִי! אֶלָּא מַאי "לֹא הוֹדָה" — [ח]לֹא הוֹדָה אָבִיו וְהוֹדָה בְּנוֹ. וְנִחַיַּיב בְּנוֹ חוֹמֶשׁ אַשְּׁבוּעָה דִּידֵיהּ! אָמְרִי: [ט]בְּשֶׁאֵין גְּזֵילָה קַיֶּימֶת. אִי בְּשֶׁאֵין גְּזֵילָה קַיֶּימֶת, אֲפִילּוּ קֶרֶן נַמִי לָא מְשַׁלֵּם! לָא צְרִיכָא, דְּאִיכָּא אַחֲרָיוּת. (א) וְכִי אִיכָּא אַחֲרָיוּת נְכָסִים מַאי הָוֵי? מִלְוֶה עַל פֶּה הִיא, *וּמִלְוֶה עַל פֶּה אֵינוֹ גּוֹבֶה לֹא מִן הַיּוֹרְשִׁין [י]וְלֹא מִן הַלָּקוֹחוֹת! אָמְרִי: בְּשֶׁעָמַד

רש"י

בִּדְיוֹקָנִי. מָסַר לוֹ בַּעַל הַפִּקָּדוֹן לַשָּׁלִיחַ סִימָנִין, וְכָתַב לוֹ חוֹתָמוֹ בְּאִגֶּרֶת, וּמְסָרָהּ לוֹ, וְאָמַר לוֹ: לֵךְ *וְהִתְרָאֶה לִפְלוֹנִי וְיִתֵּן לְךָ מָעוֹת שֶׁיֵּשׁ לִי בְּיָדוֹ (ב). [נ"ל והראה] אִי כְּתַב לָךְ. ר' אַבָּא. הִתְקַבַּלְתִּי. מָעוֹתַי קִבַּלְתִּים שֶׁל רַב סַפְרָא. אַדְּאָתֵית. בְּעוֹד שֶׁתִּהְיֶה בַּדֶּרֶךְ בְּשׁוּבְךָ אֶצְלֵנוּ. שָׁכֵיב רַבִּי אַבָּא. דְּזָקֵן הוּא, וּכְבָר בָּטֵל שְׁלִיחוּתוֹ קוֹדֶם שֶׁתְּקַבְּלֵם, וְאִי הָווּ אֲנָסֵי לְהוּ מִינָּךְ בְּאוֹרְחָא — תָּבְעֵי לָן יַתְמֵי. נַקְנֵינְהוּ נִיהֲלָךְ אַגַּב אַרְעָא. וְיִהְיוּ שֶׁלְּךָ בְּכָל מָקוֹם שֶׁהֵן, דְּקַיְימָא לָן קִדּוּשִׁין (דף כו.): נְכָסִים שֶׁאֵין לָהֶם אַחֲרָיוּת נִקְנִין עִם נְכָסִים שֶׁיֵּשׁ לָהֶן אַחֲרָיוּת. אַסִּיפָּא דְּבֵיתֵיהּ. מִפְתַּן בֵּיתוֹ, דִּמְחוּבָּר לַקַּרְקַע הוּא, וּכְקַרְקַע הוּא. כָּךְ שָׁמַעְתִּי. ל"א: סִיפָא דְּבֵיתֵיהּ = סוֹף בַּיִת, הִקְנָה לוֹ זָוִית אַחַת. נְפַק לְאַפֵּיהּ עַד תָּוָךְ = הָלַךְ לִקְרָאתוֹ עַד תָּוָךְ, שֵׁם מָקוֹם, שֶׁהָיָה שָׂמֵחַ שֶׁהֵבִיא לוֹ מְעוֹתָיו. אַלְמָא חוּמְשָׁא מָמוֹנָא הוּא. מִדְּאִיצְטְרִיךְ לֵיהּ לְמִתְנֵי: א"צ לֵילֵךְ אַחֲרָיו — אַלְמָא מָמוֹנָא הוּא גַּבֵּיהּ. וְאִי מָיֵית. גַּזְלָן, מְשַׁלְּמִי יוֹרְשִׁין. וְעוֹד, מִדְּקָתָנֵי: הֲרֵי זֶה מוֹסִיף חוֹמֶשׁ עַל חוֹמֶשׁ — ש"מ מָמוֹנָא כַּפְרֵיהּ. וּפְטוּרִין מִן הָאָשָׁם. דְּהָא מֵתוּ בְּעָלָיו. דְּאִם הִפְרִישׁוֹ בְּחַיָּיו הָיָה טָעוּן [רְעִיָּה], וְכִי לֹא הִפְרִישׁוֹ — פְּטוּרִין, דְּאָשָׁם כַּפָּרָה הוּא, וְלָאו מָמוֹנָא, וְאֵין כַּפָּרָה לַמֵּתִים. עֲדַיִין אֲנִי אוֹמֵר. רֵישָׁא בְּתוֹרַת כֹּהֲנִים: "אֲשֶׁר גָּזָל" — עַל גְּזֵילוֹ הוּא מוֹסִיף חוֹמֶשׁ, וְלֹא עַל גְּזֵילַת אָבִיו. כָּאן שֶׁהוֹדָה. אָבִיו בְּחַיָּיו אַחַר שֶׁנִּשְׁבַּע, וְנִתְחַיֵּיב לוֹ חוּמְשָׁא — מְשַׁלְּמִי יוֹרְשִׁין. וּבָרַיְיתָא בְּת"כ — בְּשֶׁלֹּא הוֹדָה. וְקס"ד הַשְׁתָּא בְּלֹא הוֹדָה לֹא אָב וְלֹא בֵּן. ה"ג: וְיָתֵיב רַב הוּנָא. יֵשׁ תַּלְמוּד קָאָמַר מָר. וְתַנָּא מִקְּרָא מַיְיתֵי לָהּ, מִדִּכְתִיב כָּל הָנֵי רִיבּוּיָא הוּא, שֶׁהַבֵּן חַיָּיב לְשַׁלֵּם. אוֹ "יְשַׁתַּלְּמוּ" קָאָמַר מָר, וּמִסְּבָרָא הוּא מְשַׁלֵּם, וְלָא מִקְּרָאֵי? לֹא הוֹדָה אָבִיו וְהוֹדָה בְּנוֹ. קֶרֶן מְשַׁלֵּם, אֲבָל חוֹמֶשׁ — לֹא, דְּמַעֲטֵיהּ קְרָא מֵחוֹמֶשׁ עַל גֶּזֶל אָבִיו. וְנִחַיַּיב (ג) חוֹמֶשׁ אַשְּׁבוּעֲתָא דִּידֵיהּ. דְּקָתָנֵי נִשְׁבַּע הוּא וְאָבִיו לִפְטוּרָא, דְּכֵיוָן דְּבֵן נִשְׁבַּע וְהוֹדָה — אַמַּאי פָּטוּר? בְּשֶׁאֵין גְּזֵילָה קַיֶּימֶת. דְּלָאו עֲלֵיהּ רַמְיָא לְשַׁלּוּמֵי, דִּתְנַן (לקמן דף קיא:): הַגּוֹזֵל וּמַאֲכִיל אֶת בָּנָיו — פְּטוּרִים מִלְּשַׁלֵּם. הִלְכָּךְ אִי כָּפַר — כְּפִירַת דְּבָרִים בְּעָלְמָא הִיא, וּשְׁבוּעַת בִּטּוּי הוּא, דְּלֵיכָּא חוֹמֶשׁ. לָא צְרִיכָא דְּאִיכָּא אַחֲרָיוּת נְכָסִים. וְאָמְרִינַן לְקַמָּן (שם) דְּאִם הִנִּיחַ אֲבִיהֶן אַחֲרָיוּת נְכָסִים קַרְקָעוֹת — חַיָּיבִים לְהַחֲזִיר מִפְּנֵי כְּבוֹד אֲבִיהֶן. וְכִי אִיכָּא אַחֲרָיוּת נְכָסִים מַאי הָוֵי כו'. ל"ג, חֲדָא: דְּהָא תָּנֵי הָתָם דְּמִשּׁוּם כְּבוֹד אֲבִיהֶם חַיָּיבִים לְהַחֲזִיר, וְעוֹד

תוספות

אין משלחין מעות בדיוקני אפילו עדים חתומים עליה. פי': אם אמר לסופר "כתוב לפלוני שישלח לי מעות ע"י פלוני", ואחר כך חתם בדיוקני שלו, ואפילו עדים חתומים עליה שהיא דיוקני שלו — אינו מועיל. אבל אם היו חתומים על זה שאמר ליה לשלוח על ידו — אז הוי שליח. אי נמי, אם כתב בכתב ידו "שלח על ידי פלוני". וא"ת: ואמאי לא מהני דיוקני דידיה? והא אמרינן ב"השולח" (גיטין דף לו.) וב"המגרש" (שם דף פז:) דמר חתים כוורא, ומר חתים מכותא! וי"ל: דהני מילי בשמות חכמים דפקיעי, אבל אינים אחרינא — לא. ולפי מאי שפירשנו לעיל — אפילו כתב בכתב ידו וחתם בדיוקני אין מועיל, כל זמן שלא אמר ליה בפניו. **ורבי** יוחנן אמר אם עדים חתומים עליו שולחין. וה"ה לרבי יוחנן בלא דיוקני, בשליח שעשאו בעדים, כדאמר רבי יוחנן לעיל דהוי שליח. והכא אתא לאשמועינן דדיוקני בלא עדים לא מהני ולא מידי. ונראה דהלכתא כרב חסדא דשליח שעשאו בעדים הוי שליח, דהא ר' יוחנן ור' אלעזר קיימי כוותיה. ואע"ג דשמואל קאי כרבה — קי"ל דרב ור' יוחנן — הלכה כר' יוחנן, וה"ה דלגבי שמואל הלכה כר' יוחנן. **אגב** אסיפא דביתיה. ומה שכותבין בהרשאה "והקניתי לו ד' אמות בחצרי" — לאו דוקא, דהא אמרינן בפ"ק דקדושין (דף כו: ושם) דקרקע כל שהו חייב בפאה כו' וקונין עמה נכסים שאין להם אחריות. ומה שכותבין הרשאה אפילו אותם שאין להם קרקע — י"מ משום דהודאת בעל דין כמאה עדים דמי. וקשה: דבפרק "חזקת הבתים" (ב"ב דף מד: ושם) דפריך: וליחוש דילמא אקני ליה מטלטלי אגב מקרקעי! ומשני: לא צריכא, דאמרי עדים "ידענא ביה בהאי גברא דלא הוה ליה ארעא מעולם". ובפרק "מי שמת" (שם דף קיט.) גבי עובדא דאיסור גיורא, דקאמר: במאי ליקני רב מרי בריה להנהו זוזי? אי דליקני ליה איסור גיורא אגב קרקע — לית ליה קרקע! וי"ל: דההוא דאיסור גיורא מעיקרא ודאי לא אסיק אדעתיה טעמא דהודאה, אבל במסקנא קאמר: אדהכי נפק אודיתא מבי איסור. והיא ד"ת"ה" כיון שאין אלא חששא בעלמא דלמא אקני ליה, כיון דלית ליה ארעא — לא חיישינן. והיא דפ' "הזהב" (ב"מ דף מו. ושם*) גבי היה עומד בגורן, דפריך: וליקני ליה אגב ארעא! ומשני: דלית ליה ארעא — התם מדאורייתא בעינן דאית ליה ארעא, דאי לית ליה ארעא — לא היו קרוין מעותיו מדאורייתא שיוכל לפדות בהן פירות מעשר שני. אבל לענין לגבות, כיון שהודה שיש לו והקנה לו אגב קרקע — למה לא יגבה? [עי' תוס' כתובות נד: ד"ה אע"פ וב"ב מד: ד"ה דלא]: *חוץ מפחות שוה פרוטה בקרן. תימה: אמאי איצטריך למיתני הא? כיון דברישא תנן שוה פרוטה, משמע: אבל פחות לא!*. **נתן** לו את הקרן ונשבע לו על החומש. הוא הדין אם לא נתן לו את הקרן ונשבע אתרוייהו, אקרן ואחומש — היה מוסיף חומש על חומש, אלא אורחא דמילתא נקט, דאקרן אין נשבעין שני פעמים. והוא הדין אם נשבע על החומש דיוליכנו אחריו למדי, דכיון שנשבע עליו — נעשה כגזלן. **יש** תלמוד קאמינא ומריבויא דקראי. תימה: אמאי איצטריך קרא לקרן? דאמאי לא ישלם קרן כיון דאיכא אחריות נכסים ועמד בדין, דהכי מוקמינן לה בסמוך! **מלוה** על פה היא ואין גובה לא מן היורשים ולא מן הלקוחות. למ"ד שיעבודא לאו דאורייתא פריך, דהכא משמע דמדאורייתא גובין מיורשין. ומההיא ברייתא ד"הגוזל ומאכיל" (לקמן דף קיא:): אם הניח להם אביהם אחריות נכסים חייבים לשלם — ליכא למפרך ליה מידי, דאיהו מוקי ליה מדרבנן, כדי שלא תנעול דלת בפני לוין, כדפסיק רב פפא בפרק "גט פשוט" (ב"ב דף קעו. שם). ומיהו, לרב ושמואל, דאמרי: מלוה ע"פ אין גובה לא מן היורשין ולא מן הלקוחות ואפילו מדרבנן, כדמוכח ב"ת"ה" (שם דף מב.) ובסוף "מי שמת" (שם דף קנז.), איכא לאקשויי מההיא ברייתא דלקמן. ואיכא למימר דאינהו מוקמי לה בשעמד בדין. ומה שהקשה בקונט': דהך העמדה בדין מאי מהני? הרי כפר ונשבע, דהא אוקימנא לעיל בשלא הודה אביו והודה בנו! י"ל: בעמד בדין לאחר שבועה ע"י עדים, דלא מיחייב האב חומש, כדתנן לקמן במתניתין, דהיכא דאיכא עדים — לא מיחייב חומש.

עין משפט נר מצוה

קכד א מיי' פ"א מהל' שלוחין ושותפין הלכה א סמג עשין עב טוש"ע ח"מ סי' קכא סעיף ג:
קכה ב ג ד (מיי' שם) טוש"ע ח"מ סי' קכב סעיף א:
קכו ה מיי' פ"ז מהלכות גזילה ואבידה הלכה ד:
קכז ו מיי' שם הלכה ו:
קכח ז מיי' שם הלכה ג:
קכט ח מיי' שם הלכה ה ו:
קל ט מיי' שם הלכה ד:
קלא י מיי' פי"א מהלכות מלוה ולוה הלכה ד סמג עשין צד טוש"ע ח"מ סי' קיא סעיף א:

הגהות הב"ח

(א) גמ' דאיכא אחריות נכסים וכי: (ב) רש"י ד"ה בדיוקני וכו' בידו הס"ד ואח"כ מה"ד מי כתב לך: (ג) ד"ה ונחייב בנו חומש:

מסורת הש"ס

[נ"ל והראה]
ב"מ מו. ב"ב עז: [ט] קנ: [ע"ש] [ועי' בתוס' עז: ד"ה רב פפא]
רש"ל מ"ז
[ד"ה ונקנינהו]
[קידושין יג: ב"ב מב. קנז. קעה. ערכין ו: ז. כ. בכורות מח:]
[שייך למתני' לעיל קג.]
[התוי"ט כתב ייסוב לזה ע"ש]

תורה אור

ויקרא ה

אמר

אמר רבא גזל שלש אגודות בג' פרוטות והוזלו ועמדו על שתים חייב להחזיר לו אחרת. פי': אם ישנה בעין מחזיר אותה, ואם לאו — משלם ליה שוה פרוטה כמו שהיתה שוה בשעת הגזילה. והוא הדין באחת שגזלה והוזלה, שמחזיר לו אגודה או דמיה. אלא רבותא נקט, דאפילו בשלשה, דקיים מצות השבה בתרתי — אפ"ה חייב להחזיר לו אחת. אע"ג דמהאי "ותנא תונא" דמייתי לא משמע מינה אלא היכא דגזל אחת והוזלה, דהיא דמיא לגזל חמץ ועבר עליו הפסח — ההיא רבותא דג' קאמר רבא מסברא. ומדנקט והוזלו — משמע דפשיטא ליה דאם גזל ג' אגודות שוות שתי פרוטות והחזיר לו ב' מהן — דלא מיחייב להחזיר לו שלישית, כיון דמעיקרא בשעת גזלה לא הוי ממונא, ולשמא תייקר לא חיישינן.

ה"ג: בעי רבא גזל ב' אגודות בפרוטה והחזיר אחת מהן מהו? מי אמרי' השתא מיהא ליכא גזילה גביה, או דלמא הא לא אהדר גזילה. ול"ג הא דגרס בספרים: הוקרו ועמדה כו'. **מצות** השבה אין כאן. נראה דלא בעי למיפשט אלא דלא מעכב מצות השבה, ומצות השבה מיהא לא קיים. **מצות** גילוח אין כאן. ומעכב מלשתות יין ומלטמא למתים כאילו לא גילח. כלומר: כמ"ד גילוח מעכב, ד"אחר ישתה הנזיר יין" — אחר כולם. א"נ, לענין מצוה קאמר — דלא קיים מצות גילוח, ואליבא דכ"ע. דפלוגתא היא בנזיר בפ' "ג' מינין" (דף מו.). **הרי** אמרו חבית שנקבה וסתמוה שמרים כו'. מה שפירש בקונטרס: חבית שנתנה ע"פ ארובה ומגלת על העלייה — אין נראה. דההיא משנה דמייתי בסמוך חבית שנקבה היא במס' כלים בפ"י (מ"ו), דמשמע דמיירי להציל מה שבתוכה אם היא באהל המת. דאי הוה מיירי ע"פ ארובה — הי"ל לשנותה במס' אהלות. ועוד: דלשון הצלה לא הוה משמע הכי, דה"ל למימר "מגלת". ונראה לפרש דאיירי בחבית המוקפת צמיד פתיל, שאין טומאה נכנסת בה באהל המת, ונקבה בכונס משקה, דהכי הויא שיעורא, כדאמר במס' כלים (פ"ט מ"ח) וסתמוה שמרים — מצלת על כל מה שבתוכה. והא דאמר בסוף "המצניע" (שבת דף צו.): ולענין צמיד פתיל עד שיפחת רובו — היינו בסתומה, שאם נקבה וסתמה — הוי שם כלי עליה עד שיפחות רובה, דאז לא מהני לה סתימה, דהוי כאוכלים שגיבלן בטיט כיון דאין שם כלי עליו. ולא כמו שפי' בקונטרס ב"המצניע": ולענין צמיד פתיל עד שיפחת רובו — דכלי חרס המוקף צמיד פתיל אין טומאה נכנסת דרך נקביו עד שיפחת רובו, כדמוכח במסכת כלים בפרק "שלשה" דשיעורו בכונס משקה. וכן משמע בההיא שמביא התם בקונטרס: נתנה קדירה ע"פ ארובה, דאמר ב"ש: הכל טמאים בכונס משקה, ואפילו ב"ה לא מטהרי אלא עלייה, אבל קדירה — טמאה, אלמא טומאה נכנסת בתוכו בכונס משקה. **אגף** חציה. תימה: היכי דמיא הך בעיא להנך בעיות דלעיל? דכיון דגף — אין כאן נקב, ולמה לא תועיל הסתימה? דמ"ל אם לא נקבה מעולם אלא כך, ומ"ל שאגף חליה? [ועוד] תימה: דהכא אמר בסתמוה שמרים שמה סתימה, ובספ"ק דיבמות (דף טו:) אמרינן: חבית של זיתים מגולגלים, ב"ש אומרים: אין צריכה לינקב, ומודים שאם נקבה וסתמוה שמרים — שהיא טהורה! וי"ל: דהתם ודאי לענין הכשר — מסתמא לא ניחא להו לבעלים במה שיוצא ממנה, כיון שנקבה אף על פי שסתמוה שמרים — לאו סתימה מעלייתא היא, אבל לענין להציל מטומאה — הויא סתימה מעלייתא.

בְּשֶׁעָמַד בַּדִּין. אִי בְּשֶׁעָמַד בַּדִּין אֲפִילּוּ חוֹמֶשׁ נַמִי מְשַׁלֵּם! אָמַר רַב הוּנָא בְּרֵיהּ דְּרַב יְהוֹשֻׁעַ: לְפִי [א]שֶׁאֵין מְשַׁלְּמִין חוֹמֶשׁ עַל כְּפִירַת שִׁעְבּוּד קַרְקָעוֹת. רָבָא אָמַר: הָכָא בְּמַאי עָסְקִינַן — כְּגוֹן שֶׁהָיְתָה דִּיסַקַּיָּא שֶׁל אָבִיו מוּפְקֶדֶת בְּיַד אֲחֵרִים, קֶרֶן מְשַׁלֵּם — דְּהָא אִיתֵיהּ, חוֹמֶשׁ לָא מְשַׁלֵּם — דְּכִי אִישְׁתַּבַּע בְּקוּשְׁטָא אִישְׁתַּבַּע, דְּהָא לָא הֲוָה יָדַע. § "חוּץ מִפָּחוֹת שָׁוֶה פְּרוּטָה בְּקֶרֶן" כו'. § אָמַר רַב פַּפָּא: לֹא שָׁנוּ אֶלָּא שֶׁאֵין גְּזֵילָה קַיֶּימֶת, אֲבָל גְּזֵילָה קַיֶּימֶת — צָרִיךְ לֵילֵךְ אַחֲרָיו, חָיְישִׁינַן שֶׁמָּא תִּיַּיקֵּר. אִיכָּא דְּאָמְרִי, אָמַר רַב פַּפָּא: [ב]לָא שְׁנָא גְּזֵילָה קַיֶּימֶת, וְלָא שְׁנָא שֶׁאֵין גְּזֵילָה קַיֶּימֶת — אֵינוֹ צָרִיךְ לֵילֵךְ אַחֲרָיו, לְשֶׁמָּא תִּיַּיקֵּר לָא חָיְישִׁינַן. אָמַר רָבָא: [ג]גָּזַל שָׁלֹשׁ אֲגוּדּוֹת בְּשָׁלֹשׁ פְּרוּטוֹת וְהוּזְלוּ וְעָמְדוּ עַל שְׁתַּיִם, אִם הֶחֱזִיר לוֹ שְׁתַּיִם — חַיָּיב לְהַחֲזִיר לוֹ אַחֶרֶת. וְתָנָא תּוּנָא: *גָּזַל חָמֵץ וְעָבַר עָלָיו הַפֶּסַח — אוֹמֵר לוֹ "הֲרֵי שֶׁלְּךָ לְפָנֶיךָ"; טַעֲמָא דְּאִיתֵיהּ בְּעֵינֵיהּ, הָא לֵיתֵיהּ בְּעֵינֵיהּ, אע"ג דְּהָשְׁתָּא לָאו מָמוֹנָא, (א) כֵּיוָן דְּמֵעִיקָּרָא מָמוֹנָא הוּא — בָּעֵי שַׁלּוּמֵי. הָכָא נַמִי, אַף עַל גַּב דְּהָשְׁתָּא לֹא שָׁוֶה פְּרוּטָה, [כֵּיוָן דְּמֵעִיקָּרָא הֲוֵי שָׁוֶה פְּרוּטָה] — בָּעֵי שַׁלּוּמֵי. בָּעֵי רָבָא: גָּזַל שְׁתֵּי אֲגוּדּוֹת בִּפְרוּטָה וְהֶחֱזִיר לוֹ אַחַת מֵהֶן, מַהוּ? מִי אָמְרִינַן הָשְׁתָּא לֵיכָּא גְּזֵילָה, (ב) אוֹ דִּלְמָא הָא לָא הֲדַר גְּזֵילָה דְּהָוֵאי גַּבֵּיהּ? [ד]הֲדַר פְּשָׁטָהּ: גְּזֵילָה אֵין כָּאן, הֲשָׁבָה אֵין כָּאן. אִי גְּזֵילָה אֵין כָּאן, הֲשָׁבָה יֵשׁ כָּאן! [ה]הָכִי קָאָמַר: אַף עַל פִּי שֶׁגְּזֵילָה אֵין כָּאן, מִצְוַת הֲשָׁבָה אֵין כָּאן. *וְאָמַר רָבָא, הֲרֵי אָמְרוּ: [ו]נָזִיר שֶׁגִּילַּח וְשִׁיֵּיר שְׁתֵּי שְׂעָרוֹת — לֹא עָשָׂה וְלֹא כְלוּם. בָּעֵי רָבָא: גִּילַּח אַחַת וְנָשְׁרָה אַחַת, מַהוּ? [ז]אֲמַר לֵיהּ רַב אַחָא מִדִּיפְתִּי לְרָבִינָא: נָזִיר שֶׁגִּילַּח אַחַת אַחַת קָא מִבַּעְיָא לֵיהּ לְרָבָא?! אֲמַר לֵיהּ: לָא צְרִיכָא, כְּגוֹן שֶׁנָּשַׁר אַחַת מֵהֶן וְגִילַּח אַחַת; מִי אָמְרִינַן: הָשְׁתָּא מִיהַת הָא לֵיכָּא שִׁיעוּר, אוֹ דִּלְמָא הָא לָאו גִּילּוּחַ הוּא, דְּמֵעִיקָּרָא הָא שִׁיֵּיר שְׁתֵּי שְׂעָרוֹת, וְהָשְׁתָּא כִּי גִּילַּח לָא הֲוֵי ב' שְׂעָרוֹת? הֲדַר פְּשָׁטָהּ: שֵׂעָר אֵין כָּאן, גִּילּוּחַ אֵין כָּאן. אִי שֵׂעָר אֵין כָּאן, גִּילּוּחַ יֵשׁ כָּאן! הָכִי קָאָמַר: אע"פ שֶׁשֵּׂעָר אֵין כָּאן, [ח]מִצְוַת גִּילּוּחַ אֵין כָּאן. וְאָמַר רָבָא, הֲרֵי אָמְרוּ: [ט]חָבִית שֶׁנִּיקְּבָה וּסְתָמוּהָ שְׁמָרִים — הִצִּילוּהָ. [י]בָּעֵי רָבָא: אָגַף חֶצְיָהּ, מַהוּ? א"ל רַב יֵימָר לְרַב אַשִׁי: לָאו מִשְׁנָתֵנוּ הִיא זוֹ? דִּתְנַן: *חָבִית שֶׁנִּיקְּבָה וּסְתָמוּהָ שְׁמָרִים — הִצִּילוּהָ, [כ]פְּקָקָהּ בִּזְמוֹרָה — עַד שֶׁיְּמָרֵחַ, [ל]הָיוּ בָּהּ שְׁתַּיִם — עַד שֶׁיְּמָרֵחַ מִן הַצְּדָדִים וּבֵין זְמוֹרָה לַחֲבֶירְתָּהּ; טַעֲמָא דְּמָרַח, הָא לֹא מָרַח לֹא, אַמַּאי? וְתֶיהֱוֵי כִּי אָגַף חֶצְיָהּ! אָמְרִי: הָכִי הָשְׁתָּא?! הָתָם אִי לָא מָרַח לָא קָאֵי, אָגַף חֶצְיָהּ — בְּמִידֵי דְּקָאֵי קָאֵי. וְאָמַר רָבָא, הֲרֵי אָמְרוּ: *גָּזַל חָמֵץ וְעָבַר עָלָיו הַפֶּסַח — אוֹמֵר לוֹ "הֲרֵי שֶׁלְּךָ לְפָנֶיךָ". בָּעֵי רָבָא:

נִשְׁבַּע

וְעוֹד, דְּקָמַשְׁנֵי לֵיהּ: כְּשֶׁעָמַד בַּדִּין קוֹדֶם מִיתָתוֹ, וְהַךְ הַעֲמָדָה מַאי מְהַנְּיָא? הֲרֵי כָּפַר וְנִשְׁבַּע וְלֹא הוֹדָה, דְּהָא אוֹקְמִינַן דְּלֹא הוֹדָה אָב וְהוֹדָה בְּנוֹ! וְעוֹד: דְּקָמְשַׁנֵּי כְּשֶׁעָמַד בַּדִּין, מִכְּלָל דְּעַד הָשְׁתָּא בְּשֶׁלֹּא עָמַד בַּדִּין, וְהָא "נִשְׁבַּע הוּא וְאָבִיו" קָתָנֵי, מִכְּלָל דְּבְבֵ"ד הֲוָה! הִלְכָּךְ ל"ג לֵיהּ. וְה"ג: אִי הָכִי, חוֹמֶשׁ נַמִי מְשַׁלֵּם! א"ר הוּנָא כו'. אִי הָכִי מָמוֹן גָּמוּר הוּא, וְחוֹמֶשׁ נַמִי לְשַׁלֵּם. לְפִי שֶׁאֵין מְשַׁלְּמִין חוֹמֶשׁ עַל כְּפִירַת שִׁעְבּוּד קַרְקָעוֹת. דְּחוֹמֶשׁ אַמַּאי קָאָתֵי — אַשְּׁבוּעָתָא, לָאו שְׁבוּעָה הִיא, דְּקַיְ"ל שְׁבוּעוֹת (דף מב:): אֵין נִשְׁבָּעִין עַל הַקַּרְקָעוֹת. וְהַאי בֵּן, כִּי אִישְׁתַּבַּע — כָּפַר לָהּ שִׁעְבּוּד הַקַּרְקָעוֹת, דְּאִי לָאו מִשּׁוּם אַחֲרָיוּת נְכָסִים — לָאו עֲלֵיהּ רַמְיָא לְשַׁלּוּמֵי. רָבָא אָמַר. לְעוֹלָם בִּגְזֵילָה קַיֶּימֶת. וּדְקַשְׁיָא לָךְ: וּלְחַיֵּיב הַבֵּן חוֹמֶשׁ עַל שְׁבוּעַת עַצְמוֹ כֵּיוָן דְּהוֹדָה — הָכָא כְּשֶׁהָיְתָה דִּסְקַיָּא שֶׁמָּמוֹן אָבִיו נָתוּן בָּהּ מוּפְקֶדֶת בְּיַד אֲחֵרִים, וּגְזֵילָה זוֹ בְּתוֹכָהּ, דְּכִי אִשְׁתַּבַּע הַאי — בְּקוּשְׁטָא אִשְׁתַּבַּע. (*וְלָא תֵּימָא בְּשִׁיקְרָא אִשְׁתַּבַּע כִּדְסָבְרַתְּ לְעֵיל) וּתְנַן בְּמַסֶּ' שְׁבוּעוֹת (דף לו:): וְחַיָּיבִים עַל זְדוֹן הַשְּׁבוּעָה וְעַל שִׁגְגָתָהּ עִם זְדוֹן הַפִּקָּדוֹן, וְאֵין חַיָּיבִין עַל שִׁגְגָתָהּ גְּרֵידָתָא, כִּי הָכָא דְּלֵיכָּא אֲנָסֵיהּ. לֹא שָׁנוּ אֶלָּא שֶׁאֵין. אוֹתָהּ חֲצִי פְּרוּטָה קַיֶּימֶת מִן הַגְּזֵילָה עַצְמָהּ, וַחֲצִי פְּרוּטָה הוּא דְּמִחַיֵּיב לֵיהּ, וְלָאו מָמוֹנָא אִיכָּא. אֲבָל אִם קַיֶּימֶת הִיא מִן הַגְּזֵילָה עַצְמָהּ — צָרִיךְ לֵילֵךְ. חָיְישִׁינַן שֶׁמָּא תִּיַּיקֵּר. וְתַעֲמוֹד עַל הַפְּרוּטָה. חַיָּיב לְהַחֲזִיר לוֹ. אֲגוּדָּה אַחֶרֶת. וְאע"פ דְּהָשְׁתָּא לָא שָׁוְיָא פְּרוּטָה, כֵּיוָן דְּבִשְׁעַת גְּזֵילָה הָוֵי שָׁוֶה פְּרוּטָה — בָּעֵי לְאַהֲדוּרֵיהּ וּלְהוֹלִיכָהּ אַחֲרָיו. וְתַנָּא תּוּנָא. תַּנָּא דִּידָן סַיְּיעוֹ. שֶׁגִּילֵּחַ. אַחַת מֵהַשְּׁתַּיִם שֶׁשִּׁיֵּיר. וְנָשְׁרָה הַשְּׁנִיָּה מַהוּ. הָוֵי גִּילּוּחַ, אוֹ לָא? אֲמַר לֵיהּ רַב אַחָא לְרָבִינָא נָזִיר שֶׁגִּילֵּחַ. כָּל הַשְּׂעָרוֹת אַחַת אַחַת קָמִבַּעְיָא לֵיהּ? בִּתְמִיָּה. כְּלוֹמַר: הָא וַדַּאי גִּילּוּחַ הָוֵי, כֵּיוָן שֶׁבְּשָׁעָה שֶׁבָּא לְגַלֵּחַ הַאי שִׁיּוּר הֲוָה בֵּיהּ שִׁיעוּר גִּילּוּחַ, וְגִילֵּחַ אַחַת, וְאע"פ דְּנָשְׁרָה שְׁנִיָּה — גִּילּוּחַ הוּא. שֶׁנָּשְׁרָה אַחַת. שֶׁכְּשֶׁבָּא לְגַלֵּחַ אֵין כָּאן שִׁיעוּר גִּילּוּחַ. ה"ג: מִי אָמְרִינַן הָשְׁתָּא מִיהָא לֵיכָּא שִׁיעוּר. חָבִית שֶׁנִּיקְּבָה וּסְתָמוּהָ שְׁמָרִים. וּנְתָנוּהָ ע"פ אֲרוּבָּה, (ג) וּמְמָרַחַת יָפֶה סְבִיבוֹתֶיהָ, וְטוּמְאָה בַּבַּיִת — מַצֶּלֶת עַל הָעֲלִיָּיה כּוּלָּהּ מִלָּבֹא בָּהּ שׁוּם טוּמְאָה, דִּסְתִימַת שְׁמָרִים סְתִימָה הִיא, וְלָא שָׁלְטָה בֵּיהּ טוּמְאָה, בְּמַסֶּכֶת כֵּלִים בְּפֶרֶק (ד) "וְאֵלּוּ מַצִּילִין". **אָגַף** = לְשׁוֹן מְגוּפָה. אָגַף חֶלְיָיהּ — הָיָה בָּהּ תַּחְתֶּיהָ שִׁיעוּר נֶקֶב לְטַמֵּא, וּכְלִי הַמְקַבֵּל טוּמְאָה אֵינוֹ חוֹצֵץ בִּפְנֵי הַטּוּמְאָה, וְאָגַף בְּטִיט חֶלְיָיהּ, מַהוּ? מִי אָמְרִינַן הָשְׁתָּא מִיהָא לֵיכָּא שִׁיעוּר נֶקֶב, אוֹ דִּלְמָא הָא לֹא סָתַם שִׁיעוּר סְתִימָה. פְּקָקָהּ בִּזְמוֹרָה. וְאֵין שָׁם שְׁמָרִים. עַד שֶׁיְּמָרֵחַ. בְּטִיט מִן הַצְּדָדִין שֶׁל זְמוֹרָה, לְסוֹתְמוֹ הֵיטֵב.

נִשְׁבַּע

ס"א ל"ג
לעיל צו:
נזיר מב.
כלים פ"י מ"ו
לעיל צו:

קלב א מיי' פ"ח מהל' גזילה ואבידה הלכ' יד ופ"ז מהל' שבועות הלכה ג ד סמג לאוין רה ועשין עג:
קלג ב מיי' פ"ד מהל' גזילה ואבידה הלכה יא סמג עשין עג טור ש"ע ח"מ סי' שסז סעיף ג:
קלד ג מיי' שם פ"א הלכה ו סמג שם טוש"ע ח"מ סי' שם סעיף ג:
קלה ד ה מיי' שם טוש"ע שם סעיף ד:
קלו ו מיי' פ"ח מהלכות נזירות הלכה ו:
קלז ז ח מיי' שם הלכ' ז:
קלח ט י כ ל מיי' פכ"ב מהלכות טומאת מת הלכה ח:

הגהות הב"ח

(א) גמ' דהשתא לאו ממונא הוא כיון: (ב) שם ליכא גזילה גביה או דלמא: (ג) רש"י ד"ה חבית וכו' וממרחת יפה וכו' בפ' אלו כלים מגילין:

ושמואל

עין משפט
נר מצוה

קלט א מיי' פ"ח מהל' שבועות הלכה ח:
קמ ב ג מיי' שם הלכה ט:
קמא ד ה ו ז מיי' שם הלכ' י' והלכ' יא:
קמב ח מיי' שם פ"י הלכה ה:
קמג ט מיי' פ"ג מהל' גזילה הלכה יד סמג עשין עג טוש"ע ח"מ סי' רלד סעיף א [רב אלפס כאן ובב"מ פ"א דף סג. ובפ"ג דף עט.]:
קמד י מיי' פ"ב מהל' טוען ונטען הלכה ב סמג עשין לה טוש"ע ח"מ סי' לב סעיף ב:
קמה כ ל מ טוש"ע שם סעיף ד עיין בב"י:

נִשְׁבַּע עָלָיו מַהוּ? מִי אָמְרִינַן: כֵּיוָן דְּאִי מִיגְּנַב בָּעֵי שַׁלּוּמֵי לֵיהּ — מָמוֹנָא קָא כָּפַר לֵיהּ. אוֹ דִּלְמָא הַשְׁתָּא מִיהַת הָא מַנַּח, וְעַפְרָא בְּעָלְמָא הוּא, וְלָא כָּפַר לֵיהּ מָמוֹנָא? מִילְּתָא דְּאִיבַּעְיָא לֵיהּ לְרָבָא, פְּשִׁיטָא לֵיהּ לְרַבָּה; דְּאָמַר רַבָּה: א"שׁוֹרִי גָּנַבְתָּ", וְהוּא אוֹמֵר "לֹא גָּנַבְתִּי". "מַה טִּיבוֹ אֶצְלְךָ"? "שׁוֹמֵר חִנָּם אֲנִי עָלָיו" — חַיָּיב, שֶׁהֲרֵי פָּטַר עַצְמוֹ מִגְּנֵיבָה וַאֲבֵידָה. ב"שׁוֹמֵר שָׂכָר אֲנִי עָלָיו" — חַיָּיב, שֶׁהֲרֵי פָּטַר עַצְמוֹ מִשְּׁבוּרָה וּמֵתָה, ג"שׁוֹאֵל אֲנִי עָלָיו" — חַיָּיב, שֶׁהֲרֵי פָּטַר עַצְמוֹ מִמֵּיתָה מֵחֲמַת מְלָאכָה; אַלְמָא, אע"ג דְּהָא קָאֵים, כֵּיוָן דְּאִי מִיגְּנִיב מָמוֹנָא קָא כָּפַר, הַשְׁתָּא נַמִי מָמוֹנָא קָא כָּפַר — הָכָא נַמִי, אַף עַל גַּב דְּעַפְרָא בְּעָלְמָא הוּא, כֵּיוָן דְּאִי מִיגְּנִיב בָּעֵי שַׁלּוּמֵי לֵיהּ מָמוֹנָא מְעַלְּיָא, הַשְׁתָּא נַמִי מָמוֹנָא קָא כָּפַר לֵיהּ. יָתֵיב (א) רָבָא וְקָאָמַר לְהָא שְׁמַעְתָּא, אֵיתִיבֵיהּ רַב עַמְרָם לְרָבָא: °"וְכִחֵשׁ בָּהּ" — פְּרָט לְמוֹדֶה בְּעִיקָּר, כֵּיצַד? "שׁוֹרִי גָּנַבְתָּ", וְהוּא אוֹמֵר "לֹא גָּנַבְתִּי". "מַה טִּיבוֹ אֶצְלְךָ"? "אַתָּה מְכַרְתּוֹ לִי, אַתָּה נְתַתּוֹ לִי בְּמַתָּנָה, אָבִיךָ מְכָרוֹ לִי, אָבִיךָ נְתָנוֹ לִי בְּמַתָּנָה, אַחַר פָּרָתִי רָץ, מֵאֵלָיו בָּא אֶצְלִי, תּוֹעֶה בַּדֶּרֶךְ מְצָאתִיו, שׁוֹמֵר חִנָּם אֲנִי עָלָיו, שׁוֹמֵר שָׂכָר אֲנִי עָלָיו, שׁוֹאֵל אֲנִי עָלָיו", וְנִשְׁבַּע וְהוֹדָה, יָכוֹל יְהֵא חַיָּיב? תַּלְמוּד לוֹמַר: "וְכִחֵשׁ בָּהּ" — דפְּרָט לְמוֹדֶה בְּעִיקָּר! א"ל: תְּדוּרָא! כִּי תַּנְיָא הַהִיא — הדְּקָאָמַר לֵיהּ "הֵילָךְ", כִּי קָאָמֵינָא — דְּקַיְימָא בַּאֲגַם. "אַתָּה מְכַרְתּוֹ לִי", מַאי מוֹדֶה בְּעִיקָּר אִיכָּא? לָא צְרִיכָא, דְּא"ל: ו"לֹא נָתַתִּי לְךָ דְּמֵי, שְׁקִיל תּוֹרָךְ וְזִיל. "אַתָּה נְתַתּוֹ לִי, אָבִיךָ נְתָנוֹ לִי", מַאי מוֹדֶה בְּעִיקָּר אִיכָּא? דְּאָמַר לֵיהּ: עַל מְנָת דַּעֲבֵידְנָא לָךְ נַיְיח דְּנַפְשָׁא, וְלָא עֲבַדִי לָךְ, שְׁקִיל תּוֹרָךְ וְזִיל. "תּוֹעֶה בַּדֶּרֶךְ מְצָאתִיו", לֵימָא: אִיבָּעֵי לָךְ לְאַהֲדוּרֵיהּ לִי! אָמַר אֲבוּהּ דִּשְׁמוּאֵל: זבְּאוֹמֵר: "שְׁבוּעָה, אֲבֵידָה מָצָאתִי, וְלֹא הָיִיתִי יוֹדֵעַ שֶׁהִיא שֶׁלְּךָ שֶׁאַחֲזִירֶנָּה לְךָ". תַּנְיָא: אָמַר בֶּן עַזַּאי, ג' שְׁבוּעוֹת הֵן: הִכִּיר בָּהּ וְלֹא בְּמוֹצְאָהּ, בְּמוֹצְאָהּ וְלֹא בָּהּ, לֹא בָּהּ וְלֹא בְּמוֹצְאָהּ. לֹא בָּהּ וְלֹא בְּמוֹצְאָהּ, קוּשְׁטָא אִשְׁתַּבַּע! אֵימָא: בָּהּ וּבְמוֹצְאָהּ. לְמַאי הִלְכְתָא? רַב אַמִי אָמַר רַבִּי חֲנִינָא: לִפְטוּר, וּשְׁמוּאֵל אָמַר: לְחִיּוּב. וּבִפְלוּגְתָּא דְּהָנֵי תַּנָּאֵי, דְּתַנְיָא: *ח הַמַּשְׁבִּיעַ עֵד אֶחָד — פָּטוּר, וְרַבִּי אֶלְעָזָר בְּר' שִׁמְעוֹן מְחַיֵּיב; בְּמַאי קָא מִיפַּלְגִי, מָר סָבַר: *דָּבָר הַגּוֹרֵם לְמָמוֹן כְּמָמוֹן דָּמֵי, וּמָר סָבַר: לָאו כְּמָמוֹן דָּמֵי. אָמַר רַב שֵׁשֶׁת: טהַכּוֹפֵר בְּפִקָּדוֹן — נַעֲשָׂה עָלָיו גַּזְלָן וְחַיָּיב בְּאוֹנָסִין. וְתָנָא תּוּנָא: "וְכִחֵשׁ בָּהּ" — לָמַדְנוּ עוֹנֶשׁ, אַזְהָרָה מִנַּיִן? תַּלְמוּד לוֹמַר: °"לֹא תְכַחֲשׁוּ"; מַאי לָאו לְעוֹנֶשׁ מָמוֹן? לָא, לְעוֹנֶשׁ שְׁבוּעָה. הָא מִדְּקָתָנֵי סֵיפָא (ב) וְאִישְׁתַּבַּע, מִכְּלָל דְּרֵישָׁא דְּלָא אִישְׁתַּבַּע! דְּקָתָנֵי סֵיפָא: "וְנִשְׁבַּע עַל שָׁקֶר" — לָמַדְנוּ עוֹנֶשׁ, אַזְהָרָה מִנַּיִן? ת"ל: "לֹא תְשַׁקְּרוּ"; וּמִדְּסֵיפָא דְּאִישְׁתַּבַּע, רֵישָׁא דְּלָא אִישְׁתַּבַּע! אָמְרִי: אִידִי וְאִידִי דְּאִישְׁתַּבַּע, כָּאן שֶׁהוֹדָה, כָּאן שֶׁבָּאוּ עֵדִים; אָתוּ עֵדִים — חַיָּיב בְּאוֹנָסִין, אוֹדוּיֵי אוֹדֵי — חַיָּיב בְּקֶרֶן וְחוֹמֶשׁ וְאָשָׁם. § מְתִיב רָמִי בַּר חָמָא: *וְשֶׁכְּנֶגְדּוֹ חָשׁוּד עַל הַשְּׁבוּעָה, כֵּיצַד? יאֶחָד שְׁבוּעַת הָעֵדוּת וְאֶחָד שְׁבוּעַת הַפִּקָּדוֹן, וַאֲפִילּוּ שְׁבוּעַת שָׁוְא; וְאִם אִיתָא, כבִּכְפִירָה הוּא דְּאִיפְּסֵיל לֵיהּ! אָמְרִי: להָכָא בְּמַאי עָסְקִינַן — דְּקָאֵי בַּאֲגַם, דְּלָאו כְּפִירָה הוּא, דְּסָבַר: אֶשְׁתַּמִּיטְנָא לֵיהּ אַדְּאָזֵילְנָא וּמַיְיתִינָא לֵיהּ; תֵּדַע, *דְּאָמַר רַב אִידִי בַּר אָבִין: מהַכּוֹפֵר בְּמִלְוֶה כָּשֵׁר לְעֵדוּת,

בְּפִקָּדוֹן

ושמואל אמר לחיוב. תימה: היכי מ"ל לחיוב? דאם כן הויא ברייתא "זו ואין צ"ל זו". **מאי** לאו עונש דממון. תימה: בממון מה שייך לומר לא ענש אלא א"כ הזהיר? דבשלמא בעונש שבועה דהיינו קרבן — שייך, דבפסח ומילה ליכא קרבן משום דלית בהו לאו, אע"ג דאיכא כרת. **כאן** שהודה כאן שבאו עדים. ואיצטריך שתי אזהרות משום דעונשן אין שוין, דבהודה — שייך חומש ואשם, ובעדים לא שייך אלא חיוב עונשין. ומיהו, תימה: אמאי קאמר ברישא מ"וכחש" עונש שמענו, ובסיפא אומר מ"ונשבע על שקר"? דכיון דלא איירי אלא לאחר שבועה — תרוייהו ה"ל למימר מ"ונשבע על שקר"! **אחד** שבועת העדות ואחד שבועת הפקדון. וא"ת: אמאי לא חשיב שבועת מלוה? וי"ל: משום דשבועה במלוה לא כתיב, אלא מפקדון אתיא.

איתיביה

נִשְׁבַּע עָלָיו. לְאַחַר שֶׁנֶּחֱסַר נִשְׁבַּע שֶׁאֵין אֶצְלוֹ וְלֹא גְּזָלוֹ מִמֶּנּוּ. מַהוּ. מִי אָמְרִינַן: הָא מַנַּח, וְיָכוֹל לִפְטוֹר בּוֹ אֶת עַצְמוֹ, וְאִשְׁתַּכַּח דְּלָאו מִידֵּי כָּפְרֵיהּ? שׁוֹמֵר חִנָּם אֲנִי עָלָיו. וְנִשְׁבַּע וְהוֹדָה. חַיָּיב. קָרְבַּן שְׁבוּעָה, אע"פ שֶׁהוֹדָה קוֹדֶם שְׁבוּעָה בְּגוּף הַמָּמוֹן. שֶׁהֲרֵי פָּטַר עַצְמוֹ. בִּשְׁבוּעָה. מִגְּנֵיבָה וַאֲבֵידָה. שֶׁאִם הָיָה נִגְנָב מִמֶּנּוּ מִשְּׁבוּעָה וְאֵילָךְ – הָיָה נִפְטָר בְּדִבְרֵי שֶׁקֶר, שֶׁהֲרֵי הוּא עַצְמוֹ גְּנָבוֹ, וְחַיָּיב בְּכָל אוֹנָסִין עַד שֶׁיַּחֲזִירֶנּוּ. שׁוֹאֵל פָּטוּר בְּמֵתָה מֵחֲמַת מְלָאכָה, וּמִכְחַשׁ בְּשָׂכָר מֵחֲמַת מְלָאכָה, דִּלְמֶעְבַּד מְלָאכָה שַׁיְילֵיהּ וְלָאו לְאוֹקְמֵיהּ בְּכִילְתָּא. אע"ג דְּהָא קָאֵים. וּמוֹדֶה לֵיהּ בְּגוּפֵיהּ, וְהַשְׁתָּא אִיהוּ לָא כָּפַר מִידֵּי, אפ"ה, כֵּיוָן דְּשֶׁמָּא סוֹף הַשְּׁבוּעָה לָבֹא לִידֵי כְּפִירַת מָמוֹן – חַיָּיב. הָכָא נַמִי. אע"ג דִּכְפִירָה דְּחָמֵץ כְּהוֹדָאָה הוּא, דְּהָא עַפְרָא בְּעָלְמָא הוּא, כֵּיוָן דְּשֶׁמָּא יֹאבַד וְיִתְחַיֵּיב לוֹ מָמוֹן, וְנִמְצָא שֶׁמּוֹעִיל לוֹ שְׁבוּעָה זוֹ לְהִפָּטֵר – חַיָּיב. אַתָּה מְכַרְתּוֹ. לְקַמָּן פָּרֵיךְ: מַאי מוֹדֶה בְּעִיקָּר אִיכָּא. תּוֹעֶה בַּדֶּרֶךְ מְצָאתִיו. וַהֲבֵיאוֹתִיו לַבַּיִת. *תְּדוּרָא = אֵין לֵב. הֵילָךְ. וְלֵיכָּא לְמֵימַר אִילּוּ מִיגְּנִיב, דְּהָא קַמֵּיהּ קָאֵי וְשָׁקֵיל לֵיהּ. אִיבָּעְיָא לָךְ לְאַהֲדוּרֵיהּ נִיהֲלִי. כְּשֶׁמְּצָאתוֹ לֹא הָיָה לְךָ לְאוֹסְפוֹ אֶל בֵּיתְךָ, שֶׁהֲרֵי מַכִּיר הָיִיתָ בּוֹ. וְאֵין לְךָ גַּנָּב גָּדוֹל מִזֶּה. שָׁלֹשׁ שְׁבוּעוֹת הֵן. בְּעֵדוּת אֲבֵידָה, שֶׁהִשְׁבִּיעַ אֶת הָעֵד "אִם רָאִיתָ אֶת אֲבֵידָתִי", וְאָמַר "לָאו", וְאַחַר כָּךְ הוֹדָה. הִכִּיר בָּהּ וְלֹא בְּמוֹצְאָהּ. הָאֲבֵידָה – שֶׁאָמַר שֶׁרָאָה אוֹתָהּ מְהַלֶּכֶת בִּרְשׁוּת אַחֶרֶת, וְאֵינוֹ יוֹדֵעַ מִי הוּא. אוֹ הוֹדָה שֶׁהִכִּיר בְּמוֹצְאָהּ וְלֹא בָּהּ, וְהָיָה לוֹ לוֹמַר: אִישׁ פְּלוֹנִי מָצָא אֲבֵידָה וְאֵינִי יוֹדֵעַ אִם שֶׁלְּךָ הוּא. וּבְעֵד אֶחָד קַמַּיְירֵי. לִפְטוּר. עַל כּוּלָּן פָּטוּר הָעֵד. הַמַּשְׁבִּיעַ עֵד אֶחָד. וְכָפַר, וְאָמַר: שְׁבוּעָה שֶׁאֵינִי יוֹדֵעַ לְךָ עֵדוּת. פָּטוּר. הָעֵד מִקָּרְבַּן שְׁבוּעַת הָעֵדוּת, דְּהָא אִי הֲוָה מַסְהִיד לֵיהּ – לָא הֲוָה מְחַיֵּיב לְהֵיסַךְ אֶלָּא שְׁבוּעָה. וְאַע"ג דְּאִיכָּא לְמֵימַר דִּלְמָא לָא מִשְׁתַּבַּע — גּוֹרֵם לְמָמוֹן פָּטוּר, וְהָנֵי נַמִי גּוֹרֵם לְמָמוֹן נִינְהוּ. בָּהּ וְלֹא בְּמוֹצְאָהּ. אִי הֲוָה מַסְהִיד לֵיהּ: רְאִיתִיהָ שֶׁנִּמְצָא בְּזָוִית פְּלוֹנִי וְאֵינִי יוֹדֵעַ מִי מְצָאָהּ — הָיָה מְחַזֵּר בְּאוֹתָהּ שְׁכוּנָה עַד שֶׁיּוֹדִיעוּהוּ, *וְכ"ש בְּמוֹצְאָהּ וְלֹא בָּהּ. [וּמִיהוּ, מָמוֹן מַמָּשׁ לֹא מַפְסְדוֹ, דְּאִי נַמִי אַסְהִידוּ לֵיהּ רָאִינוּ שֶׁמְּצָאָהּ פְּלוֹנִי זֶה — הָיָה יָכוֹל לוֹמַר: נֶאֶנְסָה מִמֶּנִּי, וּפוֹטֵר עַצְמוֹ מִשְּׁבוּעָה]. הַכּוֹפֵר בְּפִקָּדוֹן. וּבָאוּ עֵדִים. נַעֲשָׂה עָלָיו גַּזְלָן. מִשְּׁעַת כְּפִירָה, וְאַע"פ שֶׁלֹּא נִשְׁבַּע. וּמִכָּאן וְאֵילָךְ אֵין לוֹ דִּין דְּשׁוֹמֵר חִנָּם, אֶלָּא חַיָּיב בְּאוֹנָסִים אִם יֶאֱנַס. וְכִחֵשׁ בָּהּ לָמַדְנוּ לְעוֹנֶשׁ. דִּכְתִיב בַּתְרֵיהּ: "וְהֵשִׁיב אֶת הַגְּזֵלָה" — אַלְמָא קָמָה לֵיהּ בִּרְשׁוּתֵיהּ מִשְּׁעַת "וְכִחֵשׁ" עַד דְּעָבֵיד הֲשָׁבָה, וְזֶהוּ עוֹנְשׁוֹ. ה"ג: מַאי לָאו עוֹנֶשׁ כְּפִירָה. כְּלוֹמַר: עוֹנֶשׁ דְּמַאי? לָאו דְּאִיעֲנִישׁ אַכְּפִירָה, אַף עַל גַּב דְּלָא אִשְׁתַּבַּע. לֹא עוֹנֶשׁ שְׁבוּעָה. הַאי עוֹנֶשׁ דְּעַנְשֵׁיהּ קְרָא לְהִתְחַיֵּיב בְּאוֹנָסִין – מִשּׁוּם שְׁבוּעַת שֶׁקֶר הִיא, אֲבָל אִי לָא אִשְׁתַּבַּע – לָא. וְנִשְׁבַּע עַל שֶׁקֶר לָמַדְנוּ לְעוֹנֶשׁ. דִּכְתִיב בַּתְרֵיהּ חוֹמֶשׁ וְאָשָׁם. ת"ל לֹא תְשַׁקְּרוּ. דְּהַיְינוּ אַזְהָרַת שְׁבוּעַת שֶׁקֶר, דִּסְמִיךְ לֵיהּ "לֹא תִשָּׁבְעוּ בִשְׁמִי לַשָּׁקֶר", וּמִ"לֹּא תְשַׁקְּרוּ" נָפְקָא לָן דִּבִשְׁבוּעַת כְּפִירַת מָמוֹן מִשְׁתָּעֵי, כִּדְכְתִיב "אִישׁ בַּעֲמִיתוֹ" כְּמוֹ "וְכִחֵשׁ בַּעֲמִיתוֹ" בְּפִקָּדוֹן. כָּאן שֶׁהוֹדָה. בְּסֵיפָא – כְּשֶׁהוֹדָה שֶׁיֵּשׁ חוֹמֶשׁ וְאָשָׁם. וְשֶׁכְּנֶגְדּוֹ חָשׁוּד. בְּמַסֶּכֶת שְׁבוּעוֹת (דף מד:) גַּבֵּי וְאֵלּוּ נִשְׁבָּעִין וְנוֹטְלִין, דְּזֶה אֶחָד מֵהֶן: מִי שֶׁהָיָה לוֹ חֲבֵירוֹ חַיָּיב שְׁבוּעָה, וְהוּא חָשׁוּד עַל הַשְּׁבוּעָה, שֶׁנִּמְצָא שַׁקְרָן בִּשְׁבוּעָתוֹ — שֶׁכְּנֶגְדּוֹ נִשְׁבָּע וְנוֹטֵל. אֶחָד. שֶׁנֶּחְשַׁד עַל שְׁבוּעַת הָעֵדוּת. וְאֶחָד. *שֶׁנִּשְׁבַּע עַל שְׁבוּעַת הַפִּקָּדוֹן, שֶׁרְאִינוּהוּ שֶׁנִּשְׁבַּע לַשֶּׁקֶר. וַאֲפִילּוּ לֹא נֶחְשַׁד אֶלָּא לִשְׁבוּעַת שָׁוְא שֶׁאֵין בָּהּ כְּפִירַת מָמוֹן, וְרַע לַשָּׁמַיִם הוּא וְלֹא רַע לַבְּרִיּוֹת – נִפְסָל לִשְׁבוּעַת מָמוֹן. וְאִם אִיתָא. לְרַב שֵׁשֶׁת, דְּמִשְּׁעַת כְּפִירָתוֹ נַעֲשָׂה גַּזְלָן – לָמָּה לִי לְמִתְנְיֵיהּ גַּבֵּי הָנָךְ, דְּמַשְׁמַע דְּלָא אִפְסִיל עַד שְׁעַת שְׁבוּעָה, כִּי הָנָךְ? הָא מִשְּׁעַת כְּפִירָה אִפְסִיל לֵיהּ מִשּׁוּם דַּהֲוֵי גַּזְלָן! דְּקָאֵי בַּאֲגַם. וְכִי אָמַר רַב שֵׁשֶׁת – כְּגוֹן דְּאָמְרֵי סָהֲדֵי דְּכִי כָּפַר לֵיהּ בִּידֵיהּ נָקֵט לֵיהּ. (תֵּדַע) דְּהֵיכָא דְּאִיכָּא לְמֵימַר לְאִשְׁתַּמּוֹטֵי אִיכַּוֵּין עַד דְּמַיְיתֵי לֵיהּ — לָא מִפְסִיל בְּלֹא שְׁבוּעָה. דְּאָמַר רַב אִידִי הַכּוֹפֵר בְּמִלְוֶה. וְלֹא נִשְׁבַּע, וּבָאוּ עֵדִים — כָּשֵׁר לְעֵדוּת, דְּמִלְוֶה לְהוֹצָאָה נִיתְּנָה וְאֵינָהּ עַכְשָׁיו בְּיָדוֹ, וְרוֹצֶה לִדְחוֹתוֹ עַד שֶׁתַּשִּׂיג יָדוֹ.

בְּפִקָּדוֹן

תורה אור: ויקרא ה

מסורת הש"ס: ס"א תדורא מקומות; פי' רש"י בב"מ כ; פרש"י כריתות יח: וב כה:] — שבועות לב. — [לעיל עה: לה: פס וש"נ] — ס"א כ"ש בה וכמו — שבועות מד. — שבועות מ: ב"מ [ע"ש] — נ"ל שנתחלף — רש"ל מוחק זה

הגהות הב"ח
(א) גמ' יתיב רבה וקאמר וכו' רב עמרם לרבה: (ב) שם מדקתני סיפא דאישתבע:

בפקדון פסול לעדות. והאמר אילפא: שבועה קונה; שבועה היא דקניא, אבל כפירה לא קניא! הכא נמי דקיימא באגם. ואיבעית אימא: מאי שבועה קונה — כדרב הונא, דאמר רב הונא אמר רב: [א]"מנה לי בידך", והלה אומר: "אין לך בידי", ונשבע, ואח"כ באו עדים — פטור, שנאמר: (שמות כב) "ולקח בעליו ולא ישלם" — כיון שקבלו הבעלים שבועה, שוב אין משלם ממון. גופא, אמר רב הונא אמר רב: "מנה לי בידך", והלה אומר "אין לך בידי כלום", ונשבע ובאו עדים — פטור, שנאמר: "ולקח בעליו ולא ישלם", כיון שקבלו בעלים שבועה, שוב אין משלמין ממון. אמר רבא: מסתברא מילתיה דרב במלוה, דלהוצאה ניתנה, אבל פקדון — ברשותיה דמריה קאי; והאלהים! אמר רב אפילו בפקדון, דכי כתיב קרא — בפקדון כתיב. יתיב רב נחמן וקאמר להא שמעתא. איתיביה רב אחא בר מניומי לרב נחמן: "היכן פקדוני"? א"ל: "אבד", "משביעך אני", ואמר: "אמן", והעדים מעידים אותו שאכלו — משלם את הקרן. הודה מעצמו — משלם קרן וחומש ואשם! א"ל רב נחמן: הכא במאי עסקינן — כגון דנשבע חוץ לב"ד. א"ל: אי הכי, אימא סיפא: "היכן פקדוני"? אמר לו: "נגנב", "משביעך אני", ואמר: "אמן", והעדים מעידים אותו שגנבו — משלם תשלומי כפל, הודה מעצמו — משלם קרן וחומש ואשם; ואי סלקא דעתך חוץ לב"ד, מי איכא כפל? א"ל: יכילנא לשנויי לך: רישא חוץ לבית דין, וסיפא בבית דין, *מיהו שינויא דחיקא לא משנינן לך; אידי ואידי בבית דין, ולא קשיא: כאן בקפץ, כאן בשלא קפץ. א"ל רמי בר חמא לרב נחמן: מכדי דרב [ב]לא סבירא לך, משכוני נפשך אדרב למה לך? אמר ליה: לפרושה לדרב, דרב הכי מתרץ לה למתניתין. והא רב קרא קאמר! אמרי: קרא, *[ג]לכל הנשבעין שבתורה נשבעין ולא משלמין הוא דאתא, "ולקח בעליו ולא ישלם" — מי שעליו לשלם הוא נשבע. מתיב רב המנונא: *[ד]השביע עליו חמשה פעמים, בין בפני ב"ד ובין שלא בפני בית דין, וכפר עליו — חייב על כל אחת ואחת, ואמר ר' שמעון: מה טעם? הואיל ויכול לחזור ולהודות; והכא קפץ לא מצית אמרת — "השביע עליו" קתני, חוץ לב"ד לא מצית אמרת — "בפני ב"ד" קתני! הוא מותיב לה, והוא מפרק לה: לצדדין קתני; השביע עליו חוץ לבית דין, ובב"ד קפץ. מתיב רבא: *בעל הבית שטען טענת גנב בפקדון, ונשבע והודה ובאו עדים, אם עד שלא באו עדים הודה — משלם קרן וחומש ואשם, ואם משבאו עדים הודה — משלם תשלומי כפל ואשם; והכא חוץ לב"ד וקפץ לא מצית אמרת — "כפל" קתני! אלא אמר רבא: כל הודה, לא שנא טוען טענת אבד ולא שנא טוען טענת גנב (נמי) — לא אמר רב, דהא כתיב "והתודה", דבעי שלומי קרן וחומש; טוען טענת גנב ובאו עדים — נמי לא אמר רב, דהא כתיב תשלומי כפל; כי קאמר (א) — כגון שטוען טענת אבד, ונשבע ולא הודה ובאו עדים. אזל רב גמדא ואמרה לשמעתא קמיה דרב אשי. אמר ליה: השתא ומה רב המנונא תלמידיה דרב, וידע דאמר רב הודה וקמותיב הודה, ואת אמרת: הודה לא אמר רב?! אמר ליה רב אחא סבא לרב אשי, רב המנונא הכי קא קשיא ליה: אי

בפקדון פסול לעדות. ומוקמינן לה בריש "שנים אוחזין" כגון דאמרי סהדי דההיא שעתא דכפר ליה נקיט בידיה, ומפסיל אף ע"ג דלא אשתבע, דאי באשתבע — מה לי מלוה מה לי פקדון. שבועה קונה. קס"ד להתחייב באונסים משעה שנשבע לשקר קאמר. ואיבעית אימא שבועה קונה. דקאמר אילפא — לגמרי קאמר, דתו לא משלם, כדרב הונא. דלהוצאה ניתנה. ובעיא תשלומין, ואיכא למימר דבשבועה איפטר ליה מתשלומין, כדכתיב: "ולא ישלם". אבל פקדון ברשותיה דמריה קאי. ואין כאן "ולא ישלם" — דהא כל היכא דאיתיה — דמריה הוא. בפקדון כתיב. גבי שומר שכר. להא שמעתא. דרב הונא. משלם את הקרן. וכפל לא, דאין כפל אלא בטוען נגנב. וחומש ואשם נמי לא שייכי אלא כשהודה, דכתיב בגזל הגר "והתוודו". הודה מעצמו. לאחר שבועה. קתני מיהא רישא משלם קרן על ידי עדים, וקשיא לרב דאמר: כיון שנשבע לא ישלם אפי' באו עדים. ומסיפא לא פריך, דבהודה לא קאמר רב, דהא כתיב "והשיב את הגזלה" ובנשבע והודה משתעי קרא. חוץ לב"ד. לא אלימא שבועה לאפקועי ממונא. כאן בקפץ. ברישא דקתני משלם — כשקפץ זה והשביעו קודם שחייבוהו בית דין. וכי קאמר רב — בלא קפץ, והדיינין השביעוהו, וקנייה אותה שבועה, דקרא בשבועת הדיינין כתיב. ואע"ג דסיפא לא מתוקמא בקפץ, דקתני כפל, וכפל לא איתי' אלא בשבועת הדיינין — מ"מ רישא בקפץ. וניחא ליה לאוקמי בתרי גווני ובחד דוכתא, ולא לאוקמי בשני מקומות. וסיפא לא קשיא ליה לרב, דאע"ג דקתני משלם כפל לאחר שבועה, וכל שכן קרן — דמודה רב בטוען טענת גנב, כדלקמן בשמעתין, דשבועה דקא מחייב ליה כפל לא מקנייה ליה קרנא. משכוני נפשך. לבא במקומו, לתרץ קושיות ולהעמיד דבריו. נשבעין ולא משלמין. הנתבע ישבע ויפטר, ולא ישבע התובע ליטול. חייב על כל אחת ואחת. חומש ואשם. הואיל ויכול לחזור ולהודות. ונמצא דבכולן כופר ממון. השביע עליו קתני. ומדלא תני "השביעו" — שמע מינה על ידי דיינין הטיל עליו שבועה וקיבל על כרחו. וקתני: יכול לחזור ולהודות, אלמא: אכתי ממונא אית ליה גביה. לצדדין קתני השביעו עליו חוץ לב"ד. דאע"ג דחייבוהו ב"ד שבועה, כיון דמחוץ לב"ד השביעו — לא קנייה. ובפני ב"ד דקתני — לא אהשביע עליו קאי. אם עד שלא באו עדים הודה משלם קרן וחומש ואשם. ולא כפל, דאין משלם קנס על פי עצמו. משלם כפל ואשם. אבל חומש לא, דחומשו עולה לו בכפלו, כדאמרינן בפרק "מרובה" (לעיל דף סה.). אלמא: בין נשבע ובאו עדים בין נשבע והודה — חייב. אלא אמר רבא. לא תשנייה לתיובתיה דרב המנונא לצדדין, דיכול לחזור ולהודות — לאו תיובתא הוא לרב הונא, דכיון דהודה לא קאמר רב, דכל הודה לא שנא טוען טענת גנב ונשבע והודה, ולא שנא טוען טענת אבד ונשבע והודה — לא אמר רב דפטור. דהא כתיב והתודה. בגזל הגר כתיב (במדבר ה), ובנשבע, דהא קרן וחומש כתיב. וטוען טענת גנב ובאו עדים נמי לא אמר רב. דכפל כי כתיב בהכי כתיב בנשבע ובאו עדים, כדאמר בפרק "מרובה". אמרה לשמעתא. להא דרבא, דאמר: כל הודה לא אמר רב. רב המנונא תלמידו דרב הוה. דקיימא לן: אמרי בי רב — רב המנונא, בפ"ק דסנהדרין (דף יז:). ואי לאו דידע דאפילו בהודה פטר רב — לא הוה מותיב ליה מהואיל דיכול לחזור ולהודות.
אי

איתיביה רב אחא בר מניומי. פי' בקונט' דלא פריך אלא מרישא והעדים מעידין כו', ולא מסיפא. ואין נראה, דהא רבא מקשה לקמן בהדיא מ"הודה", דאכתי לא מחלק בין הודה לעדות, עד דמתרץ לקמן הכי. וא"ת: א"כ אמאי לא פריך נמי מסיפא? ונראה: דהא ודאי פשיטא דלא אמר בטוען טענת גנב ונשבע ובאו עדים שיהא פטור — דא"כ לא משכחת כפל דכתיב באורייתא. אבל בהודה ס"ד דרב פוטר. ואע"ג דבשבועה והודאה כתיב חומש — רב הוה מוקי לקרא בקפץ ונשבע, דחומש ואשם מחייב אף אשבועות עצמו. אבל בנשבע ע"פ ב"ד והודה — בעי למימר רב דפטור, דאשבועת ב"ד כתיב "ולקח בעליו ולא ישלם".
כאן שקפץ. תימה: אם כן אמאי נקט ברישא טוען טענת אבד? אפי' בטוען טענת גנב, ה"מ למנקט דלא מחייב כפל, כיון שקפץ!
קפץ לא מצית אמרת דהשביע עליו קתני. ותימה: דלעיל קתני "משביעך אני" ומוקי לה בקפץ! ויש לומר: ד"השביע עליו" משמע ע"י ב"ד, אבל "משביעך אני" — משמע שקפץ והשביעו.
ולישני

קמו א ב מיי' פ"ב מהל' טוען ונטען הלכה יא סמג עשין צה טוש"ע ח"מ סי' פז סעיף כט וסעיף ל [ודלא כרב] [רב אלפס כאן ובשבועות סוף פ"ז דף שיט]:
קמז ג מיי' פ"א שם הלכה ד סמג שם טוש"ע ח"מ סי' פט סעיף א:
קמח ד מיי' פ"ז מהל' שבועות הלכה ט סמג לאוין רמח:

הגהות הב"ח
(א) גמ' כי קאמר רב כגון שטוען:

גליון הש"ס
גמ' אמר רבא מסתברא מילתיה דרב. גיטין דף יג ע"ב וש"נ: שם הודה מעצמו. עיין לקמן דף קח ע"א תוס' ד"ה ובאו עדים:

[לעיל סג:] לקמן קח: שבועות מט.
[לעיל מג. כתובות מב:]
שבועות מה.
שם לו:
לעיל סה. שבועות לז:

אִי אָמְרַתְּ בִּשְׁלָמָא: נִשְׁבַּע כִּי אָתוּ עֵדִים מִיחַיַּיב, אַמְטוּ לְהָכִי מְחַיְּיבִינַן לֵיהּ קָרְבָּן אַשְּׁבוּעָה בַּתְרַיְיתָא, הוֹאִיל וְיָכוֹל לַחֲזוֹר וּלְהוֹדוֹת. אֶלָּא אִי אָמְרַתְּ: כִּי אָתוּ עֵדִים פָּטוּר, מִי אִיכָּא מִידֵּי דְּאִילּוּ אָתֵי סָהֲדֵי וּמְסַהֲדֵי בֵּיהּ פָּטוּר, וַאֲנַן נֵיקוּ נִיחַיְּיבֵיהּ קָרְבָּן אַשְּׁבוּעָה, הוֹאִיל וְיָכוֹל לַחֲזוֹר וּלְהוֹדוֹת? הָשְׁתָּא מִיהַת (א) לָא אוֹדֵי! § *אָמַר רַבִּי חִיָּיא בַּר אַבָּא א"ר יוֹחָנָן: אהַטּוֹעֵן טַעֲנַת גַּנָּב בְּפִקָּדוֹן — מְשַׁלֵּם תַּשְׁלוּמֵי כֶפֶל, טָבַח וּמָכַר — מְשַׁלֵּם תַּשְׁלוּמֵי אַרְבָּעָה וַחֲמִשָּׁה; הוֹאִיל וְגַנָּב מְשַׁלֵּם תַּשְׁלוּמֵי כֶפֶל, וְטוֹעֵן טַעֲנַת גַּנָּב מְשַׁלֵּם תַּשְׁלוּמֵי כֶפֶל, מַה גַּנָּב שֶׁהוּא מְשַׁלֵּם כֶּפֶל — טָבַח וּמָכַר מְשַׁלֵּם תַּשְׁלוּמֵי אַרְבָּעָה וַחֲמִשָּׁה, אַף טוֹעֵן טַעֲנַת גַּנָּב בְּפִקָּדוֹן כְּשֶׁהוּא מְשַׁלֵּם תַּשְׁלוּמֵי כֶפֶל — טָבַח וּמָכַר מְשַׁלֵּם תַּשְׁלוּמֵי אַרְבָּעָה וַחֲמִשָּׁה. מַה לְּגַנָּב שֶׁכֵּן מְשַׁלֵּם תַּשְׁלוּמֵי כֶפֶל שֶׁלֹּא בִּשְׁבוּעָה, תֹּאמַר בְּטוֹעֵן טַעֲנַת גַּנָּב — שֶׁאֵין מְשַׁלֵּם תַּשְׁלוּמֵי כֶפֶל באֶלָּא בִּשְׁבוּעָה! אָמְרִי: הֶיקֵּישָׁא הִיא, *וְאֵין מְשִׁיבִין עַל הֶיקֵּישָׁא. הָנִיחָא לְמ"ד: חַד בְּגַנָּב וְחַד בְּטוֹעֵן טַעֲנַת גַּנָּב — שַׁפִּיר. אֶלָּא לְמ"ד: הַאי "אִם יִמָּצֵא הַגַּנָּב" וְ"אִם לֹא יִמָּצֵא" תַּרְוַיְיהוּ בְּטוֹעֵן טַעֲנַת גַּנָּב, מַאי אִיכָּא לְמֵימַר? אָמְרִי: "גַּנָּב" "הַגַּנָּב". אֵיתִיבֵיהּ רַבִּי חִיָּיא בַּר אַבָּא לְר' יוֹחָנָן: "הֵיכָן שׁוֹרִי?" "נִגְנַב", "מַשְׁבִּיעֲךָ אֲנִי", וְאָמַר: "אָמֵן", וְהָעֵדִים מְעִידִים אוֹתוֹ *שֶׁאֲכָלוֹ — מְשַׁלֵּם תַּשְׁלוּמֵי כֶפֶל. וְהָא הָכָא דְּאִי אֶפְשָׁר לִכְזַיִת בָּשָׂר בְּלֹא שְׁחִיטָה, וְקָתָנֵי: מְשַׁלֵּם תַּשְׁלוּמֵי כֶפֶל; תַּשְׁלוּמֵי כֶפֶל — אִין, תַּשְׁלוּמֵי ד' וְה' — לָא! הָכָא בְּמַאי עָסְקִינַן — כְּגוֹן שֶׁאֲכָלוֹ נְבֵילָה. וְלִישְׁנֵי לֵיהּ: כְּגוֹן שֶׁאֲכָלוֹ טְרֵיפָה! כְּר"מ, דְּאָמַר: *שְׁחִיטָה שֶׁאֵינָהּ רְאוּיָה שְׁמָהּ שְׁחִיטָה. וְלִישְׁנֵי לֵיהּ: בְּבֶן פְּקוּעָה! כְּר"מ, דְּאָמַר: *בֶּן פְּקוּעָה טָעוּן שְׁחִיטָה. וְלִישְׁנֵי לֵיהּ: כְּגוֹן שֶׁעָמַד בַּדִּין, וְאָמְרוּ לוֹ: "צֵא תֵּן לוֹ". דְּהָא אָמַר רָבָא: "צֵא תֵּן לוֹ", טָבַח וּמָכַר — פָּטוּר, מַאי טַעְמָא? כֵּיוָן דְּפַסְקֵיהּ לְמִילְּתֵיהּ וְטָבַח וּמָכַר הָוֵי גַּזְלָן, וְגַזְלָן לֹא מְשַׁלֵּם תַּשְׁלוּמֵי אַרְבָּעָה וַחֲמִשָּׁה; "חַיָּיב אַתָּה לִיתֵּן לוֹ", וְטָבַח וּמָכַר — חַיָּיב, מַאי טַעְמָא? כָּל כַּמָּה דְּלָא פְּסִיקָא לֵיהּ מִילְּתָא, אַכַּתִּי גַּנָּב הוּא! אָמְרִי: וְלִיטַעֲמִיךְ, לִישְׁנֵי לֵיהּ: בְּשׁוּתָּף שֶׁטָּבַח שֶׁלֹּא מִדַּעַת חֲבֵירוֹ! אֶלָּא, *חֲדָא מִתְּרֵי וּתְלָתָא נָקַט. *וְאָמַר רַבִּי חִיָּיא בַּר אַבָּא א"ר יוֹחָנָן: הַטּוֹעֵן טַעֲנַת גַּנָּב בַּאֲבֵידָה — מְשַׁלֵּם תַּשְׁלוּמֵי כֶפֶל; מַאי טַעְמָא? דִּכְתִיב: °"עַל כָּל אֲבֵדָה אֲשֶׁר יֹאמַר". [שמות כב] אֵיתִיבֵיהּ רַבִּי אַבָּא בַּר מֶמֶל לְרַבִּי חִיָּיא בַּר אַבָּא: °"כִּי יִתֵּן אִישׁ" [שם] — גאֵין נְתִינַת קָטָן כְּלוּם; וְאֵין לִי אֶלָּא שֶׁנְּתָנוֹ כְּשֶׁהוּא קָטָן וּתְבָעוֹ כְּשֶׁהוּא קָטָן, דנְתָנוֹ כְּשֶׁהוּא קָטָן וּתְבָעוֹ כְּשֶׁהוּא גָּדוֹל מִנַּיִן? ת"ל: °"עַד הָאֱלֹהִים יָבֹא דְּבַר שְׁנֵיהֶם" [שם] — עַד שֶׁתְּהֵא נְתִינָה וּתְבִיעָה שָׁוִין כְּאֶחָד; וְאִם אִיתָא, תֶּיהֱוֵי נַמִי כַּאֲבֵידָה! א"ל: הָכָא בְּמַאי עָסְקִינַן — כְּגוֹן שֶׁאֲכָלוֹ כְּשֶׁהוּא קָטָן. אֲבָל כְּשֶׁהוּא גָּדוֹל, מַאי? הָכִי נַמִי דִּמְשַׁלֵּם? אִי הָכִי, אַדְּתָנָא: עַד שֶׁתְּהֵא נְתִינָה וּתְבִיעָה שָׁוִין כְּאֶחָד, לִיתְנֵי: עַד שֶׁתְּהֵא אֲכִילָה וּתְבִיעָה שָׁוִין כְּאֶחָד! א"ל, תְּנֵי: עַד שֶׁתְּהֵא אֲכִילָה וּתְבִיעָה שָׁוִין כְּאֶחָד. רַב אַשִׁי אָמַר: לָא דָּמֵי, אֲבֵידָה קָא אָתְיָא מִכֹּחַ בֶּן דַּעַת, וְהָא לָא אָתְיָא מִכֹּחַ בֶּן דַּעַת. וְאָמַר ר' חִיָּיא בַּר אַבָּא א"ר יוֹחָנָן: הַטּוֹעֵן טַעֲנַת גַּנָּב בְּפִקָּדוֹן — אֵינוֹ חַיָּיב עַד שֶׁיִּכְפּוֹר בְּמִקְצָת וְיוֹדֶה בְּמִקְצָת; מַאי טַעְמָא? דְּאָמַר קְרָא: °"כִּי הוּא זֶה". [שם] א] וּפְלִיגָא דְּר' חִיָּיא בַּר יוֹסֵף, דְּאָמַר ר' חִיָּיא בַּר יוֹסֵף:

עירוב

תורה אור

אִי אָמְרַתְּ בִּשְׁלָמָא אִי אָתוּ עֵדִים. אַחַר שְׁבוּעָה קַמַּיְיתָא מִחַיַּיב לְשַׁלּוּמֵי קַרְנָא — אִשְׁתַּכַּח דַּאֲכַתִּי מָמוֹנָא הוּא גַּבֵּיהּ, וְאַמְטוּ לְהָכִי מְחַיְּיבִינַן לֵיהּ קָרְבַּן שְׁבוּעָה אַשְּׁבוּעָה שְׁנִיָּה. דְּמִשּׁוּם דְּאֵין שְׁבוּעָה חָלָה עַל שְׁבוּעָה לָא תִּפְטְרֵיהּ, דְּהוֹאִיל וְיָכוֹל לַחֲזוֹר וּלְהוֹדוֹת בֵּין זוֹ לָזוֹ — נִמְצָא דְּכָל אַחַת שְׁבוּעַת כְּפִירָה בִּפְנֵי עַצְמָהּ הִיא. הָשְׁתָּא מִיהַת הָא לָא אוֹדֵי. בֵּין זוֹ לָזוֹ, וְאִשְׁתַּכַּח דִּכְפִירַת דְּבָרִים בְּעָלְמָא הוּא, וְלָאו מָמוֹנָא הוּא גַּבֵּיהּ, שֶׁהֲרֵי אֵין יָכוֹל לְהוֹצִיאוֹ בְּעֵדִים. טוֹעֵן טַעֲנַת גַּנָּב אֵינוֹ מְשַׁלֵּם כֶּפֶל עַד שֶׁיִּשָּׁבַע וְאַחַר כָּךְ יָבֹאוּ עֵדִים, כִּדְיָלְפִינַן בִּ"מְרוּבָּה". הֶיקֵּישָׁא הוּא. דְּאִיתְקַשׁ גַּנָּב וְטוֹעֵן טַעֲנַת גַּנָּב, דִּסְמִיכִי קְרָאֵי אַהֲדָדֵי; "אִם יִמָּצֵא הַגַּנָּב" — הֲרֵי גַּנָּב, וְ"אִם לֹא יִמָּצֵא הַגַּנָּב" כְּמוֹ שֶׁאָמַר אֶלָּא הוּא עַצְמוֹ גְּנָבוֹ — הַיְינוּ טוֹעֵן טַעֲנַת גַּנָּב וְנִמְצָא שֶׁהוּא גְּנָבוֹ. אֶלָּא לְמַאן דְּאָמַר. בְּפֶרֶק "מְרוּבָּה" (דף סג:). תַּרְוַיְיהוּ בְּטוֹעֵן טַעֲנַת גַּנָּב. דְּגַנָּב עַצְמוֹ נָפְקָא לָן מֵ"אִם הִמָּצֵא (ב) בְיָדוֹ" דִּכְתִיב בְּפָרָשָׁה אַחֲרִיתִי, הֵיכִי אִיתְקוּשׁ? גַּנָּב הַגַּנָּב. מֵרִבּוּיָא דְּהֵ"א דְּאִתְרַבַּאי בְּטוֹעֵן טַעֲנַת גַּנָּב [יָלְפִינַן לָהּ כָּל דִּינֵי גְּנֵיבָה, לְרַבּוֹת] תַּשְׁלוּמֵי [כֶפֶל] וד' וְה'. מְשַׁלֵּם תַּשְׁלוּמֵי כֶפֶל. דְּטוֹעֵן טַעֲנַת גַּנָּב. וְלִישְׁנֵי לֵיהּ כְּגוֹן שֶׁאֲכָלוֹ טְרֵיפָה. דְּאִיכָּא ר"ש דְּפָטַר בְּהַשּׁוֹחֵט וְנִמְצֵאת טְרֵיפָה מִתַּשְׁלוּמֵי ד' וְה', לְעֵיל (דף ע.)! וּמְשַׁנֵּי: רַבִּי יוֹחָנָן כְּר"מ ס"ל, דְּאָמַר: שְׁחִיטָה שֶׁאֵינָהּ רְאוּיָה לַאֲכִילָה, הוֹאִיל וְנִשְׁחֲטָה כְּהִלְכָתָהּ — שְׁמָהּ שְׁחִיטָה. וְלִישְׁנֵי לֵיהּ בְּגוֹנֵב בֶּן פְּקוּעָה. שֶׁנִּמְצָא בִּמְעֵי אִמּוֹ, וּפָקְעָה לְאַחַר שְׁחִיטָה, וְהוֹצִיאוּהוּ. דְּאִיכָּא לְמַאן דְּמַכְשַׁר לֵיהּ בְּלֹא שְׁחִיטָה בְּפֶ' "בְּהֵמָה הַמַּקְשָׁה" (חולין דף עד:), דִּתְנַן, ר"ש שְׁזוּרִי אוֹמֵר: אֲפִילּוּ הוּא בֶּן חָמֵשׁ שָׁנִים וְחוֹרֵשׁ בַּשָּׂדֶה — שְׁחִיטַת אִמּוֹ מְטַהַרְתּוֹ. כְּר"מ. בִּשְׁחִיטַת חוּלִּין, דִּתְנַן: הַשּׁוֹחֵט אֶת הַבְּהֵמָה וּמָצָא בָּהּ בֶּן ט' חַי כו'. וְלִישְׁנֵי לֵיהּ כְּגוֹן שֶׁעָמַד בַּדִּין. קוֹדֶם לָכֵן, וְאָמַר "נִגְנַב" וְנִשְׁבַּע, וּבָאוּ עֵדִים שֶׁגְּנָבוֹ הוּא עַצְמוֹ, וְחִיְּיבוּהוּ ב"ד וְאָמְרוּ: צֵא תֵּן לוֹ קֶרֶן וְכֶפֶל, וְאַחַ"כ שְׁחָטוֹ וַאֲכָלוֹ (וְחָזַר וְנִשְׁבַּע עָלָיו), דִּמְשַׁלֵּם כֶּפֶל אַשְּׁבוּעָה קַמַּיְיתָא, וּפָטוּר מִטְּבִיחָה כִּדְרָבָא כו'. בְּשׁוּתָּף שֶׁטָּבַח. שׁוּתָּפִין שֶׁגְּנָבוּ וְטָבְחוּ הָאֶחָד שֶׁלֹּא מִדַּעַת חֲבֵירוֹ, אָמְרִינַן בְּפֶרֶק "מְרוּבָּה" (לעיל ד' עח:) שֶׁפָּטוּר מִד' וְה', דַּ"חֲמִשָּׁה בָקָר" אָמַר רַחֲמָנָא וְלֹא חֲמִשָּׁה חֲצָאֵי בָקָר, ◎וְהָכָא לָא קָרֵינָא "וּטְבָחוֹ" כּוּלּוֹ בְּחִיּוּבָא, דְּעַל הַחֲצִי שֶׁל חֲבֵירוֹ הֲוָה טוֹבֵחַ וּמוֹכֵר אַחַר הַגַּנָּב דְּפָטוּר. אֲבָל לְדַעַת חֲבֵירוֹ — מְשַׁלְּמִין שְׁנֵיהֶם, דִּשְׁלוּחוֹ הוּא, וְאָמְרִינַן: "תַּחַת" — לְרַבּוֹת אֶת הַשָּׁלִיחַ. עַל כָּל אֲבֵדָה. וגו' יְשַׁלֵּם שְׁנַיִם. אֵין נְתִינַת קָטָן כְּלוּם. דִּכְתִיב "אִישׁ" — פְּרָט לְקָטָן, דְּאֵין נִשְׁבָּעִין עַל טַעֲנַת נְתִינָתוֹ, וְאֵין בָּאִין לִידֵי כֶפֶל עַל יָדוֹ, דְּהָכָא כֶּפֶל כְּתִיב. אֵין לִי אֶלָּא כְּשֶׁנְּתָנוֹ כְּשֶׁהוּא קָטָן וּתְבָעוֹ כְּשֶׁהוּא קָטָן. דְּאִיכָּא לְמֵימַר דְּהַאי "אִישׁ" אַהַשְׁתָּא קָאֵי, וְה"ק: כִּי יִתֵּן מִי שֶׁהוּא עַכְשָׁיו אִישׁ בִּשְׁעַת טַעֲנָה — פְּרָט לִנְתִינַת מִי שֶׁהוּא עֲדַיִין קָטָן. אֲבָל אִי הָוֵי עַכְשָׁיו אִישׁ — לָא מְמַעֵט לֵיהּ. נְתָנוֹ כְּשֶׁהוּא קָטָן וּתְבָעוֹ כְּשֶׁהוּא גָּדוֹל מִנַּיִן. דְּפָטוּר. ת"ל יָבֹא דְּבַר שְׁנֵיהֶם. אִיתְקוּשׁ נְתִינָה וְהַעֲמָדָה בַּדִּין לַהֲדָדֵי, דִּבְתַרְוַיְיהוּ בָּעֵינַן אִישׁ. תֶּהֱוֵי נַמִי כַּאֲבֵידָה. דְּלֵיכָּא נְתִינָה, וְהָוֵי טַעֲנָה לְהַשְׁבִּיעַ וּלְהִתְחַיֵּיב כֶּפֶל. וְכִי תְּבָעוֹ כְּשֶׁהוּא גָּדוֹל — לִיחַיְּיבֵיהּ לְהָאֵיךְ שְׁבוּעָה וּכְפֵילָא, אע"ג דִּנְתִינָה לֵיכָּא. שֶׁאֲכָלוֹ. בַּעַל הַבַּיִת לַפִּקָּדוֹן בְּעוֹד שֶׁהַמַּפְקִיד קָטָן, דְּלֹא יָרַד פִּקָּדוֹן זֶה לְתוֹרַת טַעֲנָה מֵעוֹלָם. אֲבָל אֲבֵידָה — מִכִּי מָטָא לִידֵיהּ דְּהַאי אִיחַיַּיב לֵיהּ, שֶׁהֲרֵי יֵשׁ לָהּ בְּעָלִים בְּנֵי טַעֲנְתָּא. הָכִי נַמִי דִּמְשַׁלֵּם. דְּמִשֶּׁהִגְדִּיל קָטָן וְנַעֲשָׂה בַּר טַעֲנָה — נִתְחַיֵּיב זֶה לָבֹא עִמּוֹ לַדִּין, וְאע"ג דִּנְתִינָה לָא הֲוַאי. דְּאָמַר קְרָא כִּי הוּא זֶה. הַיְינוּ הוֹדָה בְּמִקְצָת, וּבְפָרָשַׁת טוֹעֵן טַעֲנַת גַּנָּב כְּתִיב.

עירוב

ולישני ליה כגון שעמד בדין ואמרו ליה צא תן לו. והשתא צריך להוסיף על הברייתא ולפרש הכי: היכן שורי? א"ל: נגנב. משביעך אני ואמר אמן, ואח"כ באו עדים ואמרו שיש בידו, ועמד בדין וא"ל: צא ותן לו, ואח"כ טבחו, והעדים מעידים אותו שאכלו — משלם תשלומי כפל. ואף ע"ג דהשתא צריך להוסיף על הברייתא ולפרש בדוחק — ניחא ליה לגמרא לאוקמי הכי מלאוקמי כשאכלו נבלה, שזה נראה לו דוחק יותר.

אבל אכלו כשהוא גדול מאי הכי נמי דמשלם כו'. משמע אם נשבע ובאו עדים שאכלו — משלם תשלומי כפל. ותימה: אמאי בעי שבועה מעיקרא כשאמר נגנב? יהא נאמן במגו, דאי בעי אמר "החזרתיו לך כשהייתי קטן", יהא נמי נאמן לומר נגנב בלא שבועה! וי"ל: דהכא מיירי שטוען זה הקטן כשהגדיל: נתתי לך פקדון כשהייתי קטן, ויודע אני שיש בידך עכשיו. דהשתא לא שייך למימר *מגו דהאכלתיו כשהיה קטן — דא"כ הוה כפר במה שאמר ליה עדיין ישנה בידך, ואין זה מגו, כדאמר לקמן דאין מעיז פניו לומר להד"ס.

הא לא אתי מכח בן דעת. ואליבא דרב אשי, דאמר: אין יכול להשביע כלל כל מה שהפקידו בקטנותו, אפילו הפקדון בעין. אבל לשינויא קמא — יכול להשביעו כשהוא בעין.

עין משפט נר מצוה

קמט א ב מיי' פ"ד מהלכות גניבה הלכה א סמג עשין עא טוח"מ סי' שנג:

קנ ג מיי' פ"ה מהל' טוען ונטען הלכה י ופ"ב מהל' שכירות הל' ז ועיין בהשגות ובמ"מ ופ"ד מהל' גניבה הל' ט סמג עשין פט טוש"ע ח"מ סי' צו סעיף א:

קנא ד מיי' פ"ד מהל' גניבה הלכה ט טוח"מ סי' שנג:

הגהות הב"ח

(א) גמ' מיהת הא לא אודי: (ב) רש"י ד"ה תרוייהו וכו' המצא תמצא בידו:

גליון הש"ס

רש"י ד"ה בשותף וכו' והכא לא קרינא וטבחו כולו. לא ידעתי אמאי נקיט רש"י תרתי הא בטעם אחד סגי כלמפורש בפ' מרובה דף עח ע"ב ואולי יש להגיה א"נ:

הגהות מהר"ב רנשבורג

א] גמ' ופליגא דר' חייא בר יוסף. כאן נרשם אות ה' מסימני עין משפט. מציין עליו מיי' פ"ב מהלכות שכירות הלכה ח וע"ש בהה"מ:

[יומא ווו: יבמות מח: סוטה ח. זבחים י: ל. לד: מנחות פט: כריתות ג:]

מסורת הש"ס

לעיל סב: סג:

רש"ל

[לעיל סג: מנחות פב

לקמן קח: [ע"ש] מט. [ע"ש]

[עי' בשבועות ... ד"ה והעדים]

[חולין פה.]

[שם עד:]

לעיל סח: [דומה לזה עז: יז.]

לעיל ז. סג. רש"ל מ"ז

[סנהדרין ג:] שמות כב

*עִירוּב פָּרָשִׁיּוֹת כָּתוּב כָּאן, וְכִי כְּתִיב °"כִּי הוּא זֶה" — אמִּלְוֶה הוּא דִּכְתִיב. וּמַאי שְׁנָא מִלְוֶה? כִּדְרַבָּה, *דְּאָמַר רַבָּה: מִפְּנֵי מָה אָמְרָה תּוֹרָה מוֹדֶה בְּמִקְצָת הַטַּעֲנָה יִשָּׁבַע? חֲזָקָה אֵין אָדָם מֵעִיז פָּנָיו בִּפְנֵי בַעַל חוֹבוֹ; וְהַאי בְּכוּלֵּי בָּעֵי דְּנִכְפְּרֵיהּ, וְהַאי דְּלָא כָּפְרֵיהּ — מִשּׁוּם דְּאֵין אָדָם מֵעִיז פָּנָיו; וּבְכוּלֵּי בָּעֵי דְּלוֹדֵי לֵיהּ, וְהַאי דְּכָפַר לֵיהּ בְּמִקְצָת — סָבַר: אִי מוֹדֵינָא לֵיהּ בְּכוּלֵּיהּ תָּבַע לִי בְּכוּלֵּיהּ, אִישְׁתַּמִּיט לִי מִיהָא הָשְׁתָּא אַדְּהָווּ לִי זוּזֵי וּפָרַעְנָא; הִלְכָּךְ רָמָא רַחֲמָנָא שְׁבוּעָה עִילָּוֵיהּ כִּי הֵיכִי דְּלוֹדֵי לֵיהּ בְּכוּלֵּיהּ. וְגַבֵּי מִלְוֶה הוּא דְּאִיכָּא לְמֵימַר הָכִי, אֲבָל גַּבֵּי פִּקָּדוֹן מֵעִיז וּמֵעִיז. *תָּנֵי רָמִי בַּר חָמָא: אַרְבָּעָה שׁוֹמְרִין צְרִיכִין

שבועות מב: ב"מ ג. ה: כתובות יח. גיטין נא:

ב"מ ה: לח.

עִירוּב פָּרָשִׁיּוֹת. פָּסוּק שֶׁהוּא מִפָּרָשָׁה אַחֶרֶת נִתְעָרֵב בְּזוֹ, שֶׁאֵינוֹ מְקוֹמוֹ. דְּהַאי "כִּי הוּא זֶה" בְּ"אִם כֶּסֶף תַּלְוֶה" הֲוָה לֵיהּ לְמִכְתְּבֵיהּ, דְּהָתָם קָאֵי. דְּאִילּוּ בְּהַךְ פָּרָשָׁתָא דְּפִקָּדוֹן — בְּלָא הוֹדָאָה בְּמִקְצָת מְחַיֵּיב. וּמַאי שְׁנָא מִלְוֶה. דְּעָקְרִינַן לִקְרָא מִדּוּכְתֵּיהּ וּמוֹקְמִינַן לֵיהּ עֲלָהּ. כִּדְרַבָּה דְּאָמַר רַבָּה. אֵין אָדָם מֵעִיז פָּנָיו בִּפְנֵי זֶה שֶׁעוֹשֶׂה לוֹ טוֹבָה. הִלְכָּךְ, הֵיכָא דְּכָפַר הַכֹּל — פָּטוּר מִשְּׁבוּעָה, דְּאִי לָאו קוּשְׁטָא קָאָמַר — לָא הֲוָה מָצֵי לְמִכְפַּר בֵּיהּ. וְהֵיכָא דְּמוֹדֶה מִקְצָת — בְּכוּלָּהּ בָּעֵי לְמִכְפְּרֵיהּ, וְהָא דְּלָא כָּפְרֵיהּ — מִשּׁוּם דְּאֵין אָדָם מֵעִיז. אֲבָל בְּפִקָּדוֹן, דְּאֵין כָּאן טוֹבָה. מֵעִיז וּמֵעִיז. הִלְכָּךְ, אֲפִי' כָּפַר בְּכוּלֵּיהּ — רַמְיָא רַחֲמָנָא שְׁבוּעָה עֲלֵיהּ.

קנב א מיי' פ"א מהל' טוען ונטען הל' א סמג עשין צה טוש"ע ח"מ סי' פז סעיף א:

עירוב פרשיות כתוב כאן וכי כתיב כי הוא זה אמלוה הוא דכתיב. פי' בקונט': דפסוק זה ד"כי הוא זה" מפרשה אחרת, דב"ואם כסף תלוה את עמי" הוה ליה למיכתב, דהתם קאי. דאי בהך פרשתא דפקדון — בלא הודאה במקצת נמי מחייב. וטעמא דעקרינן ליה מדוכתא — כדמסיק: ומ"ש מלוה — כדרבה דאין אדם מעיז פניו, לכן כופר הכל פטור. אבל בפקדון שלא עשה לו טובה — מעיז ומעיז. הלכך, אפי' כופר הכל חייב. וקשה: דבריש סנהדרין (דף ג: ושם) משמע דאפילו למ"ד עירוב פרשיות כתוב כאן לא עקרינן ליה לגמרי מפקדון, לענין שלשה ומומחין! ומיהו, יש לדחות: דלענין מודה מקצת, דאיכא טעמא — עקרינן ליה מפקדון לגמרי. אבל לענין שלשה ומומחין, דליכא טעמא — קאי אתרוייהו. אבל קשה, דבפרק "השואל" (ב"מ דף צז:) גבי הא דמוקי מתניתין דהתם כשיש עסק שבועה ביניהם, ומוקי רישא בתרתי וסיפא בתלת, משמע דלא מחייב שבועה אלא א"כ יש חדא דקמודה, והתם כרבי חייא בר יוסף, מדקאמר בתר הכי ולרמי בר חמא. אלמא דלא מחייב רבי חייא בר יוסף בלא הודאה מקצת — אלמא לא עקר לגמרי "כי הוא זה" מפקדון. ועוד: דבכמה משניות משמע דלא מתחייב בפקדון אלא במודה במקצת, כי ההיא דשבועות (דף מג.) ד"סלע הלויתני עליו ושתים היה שוה", וכן ההיא דמנורה בת עשרה ליטרין (שם), וההיא ד"עשר גפנות טעונות מסרתי לך" (שם דף מג:), וב"הניזקין" (גיטין דף נא. ושם) גבי "שני כיסין קשורים מלאת לי", דמחייבינן מודה מקצת ופטרינן כופר הכל, אע"ג שלא עשה לו שום טובה. ובפרק שני דכתובות (דף יח. ושם) וב"שבועת הדיינים" (שבועות דף מב.) פטרינן "מנה לאביך בידי והאכלתיו פרס", במגו דאי בעי כופר הכל, משום דבגנו מעיז. ולפירוש הקונטרס אדרבה, כופר הכל ה"ל לחיובי התם. וכן בפ"ק דב"מ (דף ד:) בשמעתא דהילך גבי סלעין דנרין! ומפרש ר"ת דה"ק: דכי כתיב "כי הוא זה" — אמלוה נמי הוא דכתיב, דבעינן הודאה בהדי שבועה דכפירה, והכי נמי בעינן הודאה בהדי שבועה דנאנסו, אבל כפירה לא בעינן בההיא דנאנסו. ובאותו ענין דקאי "כי הוא זה" אמלוה — קאי נמי אפקדון, וכי היכי דמלוה מחייב אשתי פרות לחוד, חדא דהודאה וחדא דכפירה — מחייב נמי אפקדון אשתי פרות, חדא דהודאה וחדא דנאנסו. אבל רבי חייא בר אבא ורמי בר חמא בעו שלש פרות, חדא דהודאה וחדא דכפירה וחדא דנאנסו, ד"כי הוא זה" אפקדון דוקא כתיב, ולא אמלוה. והא דבעיא כפירה והודאה במלוה — שמא ב"מה מצינו" ילפינן מפקדון. אע"ג דלענין שלשה ומומחין לא ילפינן מלוה מפקדון במסכת סנהדרין (דף ג: ושם) למאן דלית ליה עירוב פרשיות, לענין מודה מקצת מסתבר למילף טפי. והוא הדין דבפקדון מחייב בכפירה והודאה לחוד בלא נאנסו, אבל בנאנסו בלא "כי הוא זה" — לא מחייב. דהכי משמע ליה פשטיה דקרא לאצרוכי "כי הוא זה" בהדי נאנסו, ולא נאנסו בהדי "כי הוא זה". אבל כופר הכל — פטור לכ"ע בכל מקום, אפילו במקום שיכול להעיז, דגזירת הכתוב הוא "כי הוא זה" דוקא, ולא כופר הכל. והא דקאמר מ"ש מלוה, מפרש ר"ת: מאי טעמא דמלוה, פירוש: [מאי] טעמא דמודה מקצת חייב, ולא מהימן במגו דאי בעי כפר הכל. והוי כי ההוא דסוף "כל הנשבעין" (שבועות דף מח:) גבי נשבעין שלא בטענה, דקאמר: מאי שנא הני, ופירוש — מאי טעמא דהני. ומה שכתוב בספרים "גבי מלוה הוא דאיכא למימר הכי, אבל בפקדון מעיז ומעיז" — לא גרים ליה רבינו תם, ובספרים ישנים ליתא. והא דאמר בסוף "המוכר את הבית" (ב"ב דף ע:) גבי המפקיד אצל חבירו בשטר: אילו אמר נאנסו — לאו שבועה בעי? דמשמע דנאנסו לחוד בלא הודאה כלל מחייב שבועה — אור"ת: דההיא שבועה דרבנן, שנתקנה קודם שבועת היסת, כי הנהו דפרק "הכותב" (כתובות דף פז:) הפוגמת כתובתה, ואינך דסבר רמי בר חמא שבועה דאורייתא, ומסיק: אלא מדרבנן. והא דתנן בפרק "השואל" (ב"מ דף צז:): זה אומר שאולה וזה אומר שכורה — ישבע, ופריך בגמרא: ואמאי? מה שטענו לא הודה לו! והך פירכא ליתא אליבא דרב נחמן, דמוקמא התם מתני' אליביה כשיש עסק שבועה ביניהם, ורישא בתרתי וסיפא בתלת, או רישא בתלת וסיפא בארבע, ויש כאן מה שטענו הודה לו. אלא לרב הונא ורב יהודה פריך, דליכא אלא הך דשאלה ושכירות. ומשני: ע"י גלגול דכדרבה מתה — ההיא שבועה נמי מדרבנן, דמדאורייתא לא מחייב, כיון דאין כאן הודאה. ומיהו, בין לפ"ה ובין לפי' ר"ת קשה מהא דאמרינן בפ' "כל הנשבעין" (שבועות דף מה: ושם) דאם שכרו בלא עדים, מתוך שיכול לומר "לא שכרתיך מעולם" — יכול לומר "שכרתיך ונתתי לך שכרך". ופריך: אלא שבועת שומרים דחייב רחמנא היכי משכחת לה? מתוך שיכול לומר "להד"ם", יכול לומר נאנסו! והשתא לפירוש ר"ת אהייא קאי? אי אההיא דהודאה קאי — אי אמר "לא היו דברים מעולם" א"כ היה כופר הכל, ואין זה מגו, דאל"כ ליפרוך אכל מודה מקצת דליפטר במגו, דאי בעי כופר הכל. ואי אההיא דנאנסו קאי — כי קאמר נמי "להד"ס" מחייב שבועה, כיון דאיכא כפירה והודאה! ולפי' הקונטרס נמי, דליכא הודאה, כי אמר אההיא דנאנסו נמי להד"ס — בעי שבועה, דהא מחייב שבועה בפקדון אכופר הכל! ואי הוה אמרינן דלרבי יוחנן ולרמי בר חמא לא מחייב אפקדון אכפירה והודאה בלא נאנסו — הוה ניחא, דפריך לה התם. אבל לא יתכן כלל, דע"כ על כפירה והודאה לחוד מחייב אפילו אפקדון, כדמוכח במשניות טובא, בההיא ד"סלע הלויתני", ומנורה, ועשר גפנים. ואע"ג דמוקמינן מתניתין ד"השואל" בכמה פרות אע"ג דלא מתני במתני' — הנהו לא מסתבר לאוקמי הכי. וכן בהלואה, דילפינן מפקדון גבי סלעים דנרים, ובשבועות גבי "סלע הלויתיך". ונראה כפירוש ריב"א, דמפרש: כי כתיב "כי הוא זה" אמלוה הוא דכתיב, והלכך בפקדון נמי לא מוקמינן ליה אלא בטענה דשייכא במלוה, דהיינו בכפירה והודאה. אבל טענת נאנסו — לא. והכי קאמר: מאי שנא טענה דשייכא במלוה מטענת נאנסו? ומסיק כדרבה. וגבי מלוה הוא דאיכא למימר הכי — כלומר: בטענה השייכא במלוה, כגון כפירה והודאה דאין מעיז פניו לכפור במידי דידע בה חבריה. אבל בפקדון — כלומר: טענה השייכא בפקדון — כגון נאנסו, דלא ידע ביה חבריה — מעיז ומעיז, ומחייב בלא הודאה. דאם כופר הכל היה פטור — במקצת נמי יפטר, במגו דאי בעי כפר הכל. ומיהו, בטענות כפירה, אפילו במקום שיכול להעיז — פטור, דגזירת הכתוב היא. והשתא ניחא ההיא ד"כל הנשבעין" דקאמר: מתוך שיכול לומר "להד"ס" יכול לומר נאנסו, אע"ג דאין זה מגו לגמרי, דהאי חשוב העזה והאי לא חשוב, דבהאי ידע ובהאי לא ידע — מכל מקום מדמה ליה למגו דלעיל, דההוא נמי לאו מגו הוא, דניחא ליה למימר טפי "שכרתיך ונתתי לך שכרך" דחושבו טועה, משום דטרוד בפועליו ולא כמשקר במזיד, ממאי דנימא "לא שכרתיך מעולם" דליכא למיתלי בטרוד בפועליו. וההיא ד"ח"ה" (ב"ב דף לו.) גבי הנהו עיזי דאכלי חושלי בנהרדעא, דיכול לטעון עד כדי דמיהם, במגו שיכול לומר "לקוחים הן בידי", ובפ"ב דכתובות (דף *יח) גבי "שדה זו של אביך היה ולקחתיו ממנו", דאפילו טענו הבן שהיה של אביו אלא שאין לו עדים מהימן לומר "לקחתיו" במגו שיכול לומר "לא היה של אביך מעולם", אע"ג דבהאי ידע ובהאי לא ידע — לא דמי למידי דכפירה, דלכפור ודאי אינו מעיז במידי דידע ביה חבריה, והנהו דהתם — לאו מידי דכפירה נינהו. ומיהו, ההיא ד"השואל" קשה לפירושו, דמשמע דר' חייא ב"ר יוסף נמי בעי הודאה בהדי נאנסו, דמוקי רישא בתרתי וסיפא בתלתא. אם לא נאמר סוגיא דהתם לא כר' חייא בר אבא ולא כר' חייא ב"ר יוסף. וא"ת: למאן דבעי שלש פרות ליפטריה במגו דאי בעי אמר נאנסו אההיא דכפירה! וי"ל: כגון דההיא דכפירה קמן. וא"ת: דליפטריה במגו, דאי בעי מודה בה, וההיא דטען דמתה בפשיעה יכפור, ובאידך נאנסה, דהשתא ה"ל בההיא דמודה בה הילך, ופטור משבועה! לאו פירכא היא, דאם הילך הוא — א"כ ה"ל כופר הכל, ואין אדם מעיז. אי נמי: כגון דההיא דקיימא קמן עדיפא, ואין רוצה להודות בה. ואין להקשות: יהא נאמן במגו דאי בעי אמר להד"ס נמי אההיא דנאנסו! דבריש "כל הנשבעים" (שבועות דף מה:) משני לה דאפקיד ליה בשטר. חזקה אין אדם מעיז. הכל מפורש בכמה מקומות.

[טו: וכמבואר שם תוס' ד"ה ומודה ר"ן]

עד

קנג א מיי' פ"ד מהלכות גניבה הל' ג טוח"מ סי' שנ שנב:
קנד ב מיי' שם הל' ב:
קנה ג מיי' פ"ו מהל' שאלה ופקדון הל' א סמג עשין פח טוש"ע ח"מ סי' רצו סעיף ח וסי' רצה סעיף ב:

צריכין כפירה במקצת והודאה במקצת, ואלו הן: שומר חנם והשואל, נושא שכר והשוכר. אמר רבא: מאי טעמא דרמי בר חמא? שומר חנם, בהדיא כתיב ביה "כי הוא זה"; שומר שכר, יליף נתינה נתינה משומר חנם; שואל, "וכי ישאל" — וי"ו מוסיף על ענין ראשון; שוכר, אי למ"ד כשומר שכר — היינו שומר שכר, אי למ"ד כשומר חנם — היינו שומר חנם. וא"ר חייא בר יוסף: הטוען טענת גנב בפקדון, אינו חייב עד שישלח בו יד; מאי טעמא? (א) "ונקרב בעל הבית אל האלהים אם לא שלח ידו במלאכת רעהו", מכלל דאי שלח בה יד — מיחייב; למימרא דבשלח בה יד עסקינן. אמר להו ר' חייא בר אבא, הכי א"ר יוחנן: בעומדת על אבוסה שנו. א"ל ר' זירא לר' חייא בר אבא: דוקא בעומדת על אבוסה קאמר, אבל שלח בה יד — קנה, ושבועה לא מהניא ביה כלום. או דלמא אפי' עומדת על אבוסה קאמר? א"ל: זו לא שמעתי, כיוצא בה שמעתי, דא"ר אסי א"ר יוחנן: הטוען טענת אבד ונשבע, וחזר וטען טענת גנב ונשבע, ובאו עדים — פטור; מ"ט, לאו משום דקנה בשבועה ראשונה? א"ל: לא, הואיל ויצא ידי בעלים בשבועה ראשונה. איתמר נמי, א"ר אבין א"ר אילעא א"ר יוחנן: [א]הטוען טענת אבידה בפקדון ונשבע, וחזר וטען טענת גניבה ונשבע, ובאו עדים — פטור, הואיל ויצא ידי בעלים בשבועה ראשונה. אמר רב ששת: [ב]הטוען טענת גנב בפקדון, כיון ששלח בו יד — פטור; מאי טעמא? הכי קאמר רחמנא: "ונקרב בעל הבית אל האלהים אם לא שלח ידו" וגו', הא שלח ידו — פטור. אמר ליה רב נחמן: והלא *[ג]שלש שבועות משביעין אותו: "שבועה שלא פשעתי בה", "שבועה שלא שלחתי בה יד", "שבועה שאינה ברשותי"; מאי לאו "שבועה שלא שלחתי בה יד" דומיא ד"שבועה שאינה ברשותי", מה "שבועה שאינה ברשותי", כי מיגליא מילתא דאיתיה ברשותיה — חייב, אף "שבועה שלא שלחתי בה יד", כי מיגליא מילתא דשלח בה יד — חייב? אמר ליה: לא, "שבועה שלא שלחתי בה יד" דומיא ד"שלא פשעתי בה"; מה "שבועה שלא פשעתי בה", כי מיגליא מילתא דפשע בה — פטור מכפל, אף "שבועה שלא שלחתי בה יד", כי מיגליא מילתא דשלח בה יד — פטור מכפל. בעי רמי בר חמא: ממון המחייבו כפל פוטרו מן החומש, או דלמא שבועה המחייבתו כפל פוטרתו מן החומש? היכי דמי — כגון שטען טענת גנב ונשבע, וחזר וטען טענת אבד ונשבע, ובאו

שמות כב; שם; שם

עד שישלח בו יד. והא דקתני לעיל (דף קו.): והעדים מעידים אותו שגנבו משלם תשלומי כפל — היינו ששלח בו יד. **הואיל** ויצא ידי בעלים בשבועה ראשונה. דאע"ג שהודה שלשקר נשבע — אין חייב מן הדין לישבע פעם שניה שנגנב, כמו שחוזר וטוען, אלא נאמן שלא נשבע לומר שנגנב, במגו דאי בעי אמר באמת נשבעתי, והיה פטור. והא קמ"ל אע"ג שמושבע מפי ב"ד, כגון שטענו בפני ב"ד אחר שלא היו יודעים שנשבע כבר קודם, והשביעוהו עתה — דפטור, כיון שמן הדין לא היה לו לישבע.: **ושלח** בו יד פטור. והא דאמר לעיל: והעדים מעידים אותו שאכלו משלם תשלומי כפל — צ"ל כגון שאכלו לאחר שבועה. ונראה דדוקא קאמר ושלח, דגזירת הכתוב היא, כדקאמר: "אם לא שלח", הא שלח — פטור. אבל כופר בפקדון, אע"ג דאמר רב ששת לעיל: הכופר בפקדון נעשה עליו גזלן — כפל מיהא מחייב, דהא דקאמר נעשה עליו גזלן — היינו להתחייב באונסין. **והלא** שלש שבועות משביעין אותו. וצריך כולהו. דאי נשבע שלא פשעתי — אכתי חיישינן שמא ברשותו הוא, ובאמת נשבע. וכשנשבע שאינה ברשותו — איכא למיחש שמא שלח בה יד, ומתחייב אע"פ שלא פשע ואינה ברשותו*. **מאי** לאו שלא שלחתי כו'. ה"ג ה"מ לאותובי לרבי חייא ב"ר יוסף, ולימא: מאי לאו "[שלא] שלחתי" דומיא ד"לא פשעתי"? ולשנויי: לא, דומיא ד"אין ברשותי". **מה** שבועה שלא פשעתי בה כי מגליא מילתא דפשע בה פטור. דהא מהכא דרשינן טוען טענת גנב, מדכתיב "אם לא ימצא הגנב" אלא הוא עצמו גנבו, וזה שפשע בה לא גנבו. **כגון** שטוען טענת גנב וחזר וטען טענת אבד. ואיפכא לא מצי למימר — דאם כן לא מיחייב כפל, כדאמר לעיל: שכבר יצא ידי בעלים בשבועה ראשונה. והכי פירושו: וחזר וטען טענת אבד, ואומר: מה שנשבעתי שנגנב — לא כי, אלא אבד, והיה לי לישבע שאבד. אבל אין לפרש שאמר: אחר שבועה אבד — שא"כ לא ה"מ למפטר נפשיה באבד, כיון שהיא ברשותו בשעה שנשבע, דאההיא שעה שנשבע לשקר מתחייב באונסין, ולא מחייב אהך שבועה חומש ואשם, דלא הויא כפירת ממון אלא כשבועת ביטוי בעלמא.

ובאו

[ועי' תוס' ב"מ ו. ד"ה שבועה]

צריכין כפירה במקצת והודאה במקצת. קודם שיתחייבו שבועה. ואם נשבעו בלא כפירה והודאה — אין שבועתו של ש"ח כלום, ולא מחייבתו כפל. ודרמי בר חמא פליג אדרבי חייא בר יוסף. פרשה ראשונה נאמרה בש"ח ושניה בשומר שכר. שוכר. פלוגתא דר"מ ורבי יהודה לעיל (דף נז:). אינו חייב. כפל. עד שישלח בה יד. קודם שבועה, כגון שעשה בה מלאכה. ה"ג: דאמר קרא ונקרב בעל הבית אל האלהים אם לא שלח. למימרא. דהאי דכתיב בתריה: "אשר ירשיעון אלהים" וגו'. בששלח בה יד עסקינן. דנמצא רשע דבכך שנשבע לשקר, שהרי שלח בה יד. בעומדת על אבוסה. שלא שלח בה יד, שנו דחייב כפל. אבל שלח בה יד. קודם שבועה — קנאה בתורת גזילה. ושומר חנם אינו נעשה גנב אלא בטענת גנב, וזה קודם שטען טענת גנב קנאה, וקמה ליה ברשותיה שאם מתה ישלמנה, ואשתכח דכי כפר — דידיה קא כפר. או דלמא אפילו עומדת על אבוסה קאמר. וכל שכן כי שלח בה יד, דבהכי קאי קרא, כדאמר ר' חייא בר יוסף. הטוען טענת אבידה ונשבע. ל"ג והודה. פטור. מן הכפל. מ"ט לאו משום דקנה בשבועה ראשונה. להתחייב באונסין, כדרב ששת דאמר לעיל: הכופר בפקדון נעשה עליו גזלן, אפי' בלא שבועה. והיכא דאשתבע — כל שכן דכ"ע מודו. אלמא, כיון דקמה ליה ברשותיה, כי כפר — דידיה קא כפר, ולא מיחייב ליה כפל. וה"ה לשולח בה יד, כיון דפשיטא לן בפ' "המפקיד" (ב"מ מא:) דקמה ליה ברשותיה, תו לא מיחייב עליה כפל. לא. התם לאו משום דקמה ליה ברשותיה הוא, אלא הואיל ויצא שומר זה ידי בעלים בשבועה ראשונה, שמכיח דין ראשון נסתלק מידם — ושבועה אחרונה זו לאו שבועת הדיינים הוא לחייבו כפל, (ב) דכיון דנשבע בתחילה שוב לא היה מחויב שבועה לבעלים. כיון ששלח בה יד. קודם שבועה. ה"ק אם לא שלח. ונקרב בעל הבית. וקיימא לן ב"המפקיד" (שם) דהאי "ונקרב" — לשבועה הוא, וכתיב בתריה "ישלם שנים" אם נמצא רשע. הא שלח יד פטור. מכל הדין הזה. שלש שבועות משביעין. את שומר חנם האומר נגנבה. שבועה שלא פשעתי. בשמירתו, כשנגנבה. דאי פשע בה — חייב, דכתיב: "על כל דבר פשע". שבועה שלא שלחתי בה יד. ליהנות בה קודם לכן. דאם שלח בה יד — קמה ליה ברשותיה, דנעשה גזלן עליה, ומיחייב באונסין, וכ"ש בגניבה ואבידה. כי מגליא מילתא דאיתיה ברשותיה. והוא גנב עליה — מחייב כפל, דהיינו טוען טענת גנב. אף שבועה שלא שלחתי בה יד. כי משתכח שקרן — נמי חייב כפל, משום שבועה שאין ברשותו. כי מגליא מילתא דפשע בה. ונגנבה. פטור מכפל. דהא אינו גנב עליה. אף שבועה דשלח בה יד כי מגליא מילתא דשלח בה יד פטור מכפל. אפילו עדיין היא אצלו. בעי רמי בר חמא. דקיימא לן בפרק "מרובה" (לעיל דף סה:): ממון שאין משתלם בראש, דאיכא כפל בהדיה — אין מוסיף חומש. ולעיל (דף קו.) נמי תנינן לה: אם משבאו עדים הודה — משלם תשלומי כפל ואשם, אבל חומש לא. מאן פטר ליה מחומשא, ממונא או שבועה? והיכי דמי. כלומר, לדברי ר"מ — כגון שטען טענת גנב כו'.

ובאו

ב"מ ו.

הגהות הב"ח

(א) גמ' מאי טעמא דאמר קרא ונקרב: (ב) רש"י ד"ה לא התם וכו' לחייבו כפל ואי קשיא הא דאמרינן לעיל השביע עליו ה' פעמים בין בפני ב"ד בין שלא בפני ב"ד חייב על כל אחת ואחת והכא אמרינן פטור איכא לתרוצי דהתם ולאי חייב דקא בקרבן שבועה קמיירי ולא שני לן בין בפני ב"ד בין שלא בפני ב"ד דסתמא כתיב מכל אשר ישבע עליו לשקר וגו' אבל הכא בכפל קאמר דפטור דהא שבועה בתרייתא לאו שבועת הדיינין היא ואע"פ שנעשית בב"ד שלא היה להם לב"ד להשביעו שהרי כבר נפטר מכפל משבועה ראשונה דטוען טענת אבידה ונשבע לא משלם כפל וכפל לא משלם אלא בשבועת הדיינין דבהכי כתיב ונקרב בעל הבית וגו' לשבועה לשלם שנים ואין דיינין דכיון לנשבע בתחילה שוב לא היה מחויב שבועה לבעלים כצ"ל:

ובאו עדים. דכשנשבע היתה אצלו, לחייב כפל, והדר הודה איהו אבתרייתא. מאי. מיחייב חומש אהך שבועה בתרייתא, או לא? והא איחייב ליה כפילא. עליה דהאי ממון. או דלמא שבועה המחייבתו כפל פוטרתו מן החומש. כגון אי הוה מודה השתא אקמייתא, אחר העדאת עדים – הוה מיפטר מחומש. אבל השתא דאבתרייתא אודי, והך שבועה לא חייבתיה כפילא – תחייביה חומשא. והכא ליכא למימר יצא ידי בעלים בשבועה ראשונה, דכי אמרינן ליה – היכא דאתו סהדי אשבועה שניה, דאמרינן אשבועת חנם לא מחייבי כפילא. אבל היכא דאודי עלה – קיימא לן לעיל (דף קו.): השביע עליו חמשה פעמים כו', דלענין חומש ואשם לא שני ליה בין שבועת עצמו לשבועת דיינין, ובלבד שיכפור ממון. **אמר** לאחד מן השוק. שאין שומר על שורו. משביעך אני. משום הודה מעצמו דסיפא נקט. אבל משום כפל – בלאו שבועה נמי מיחייב. תרי חומשי או תרי כפילי בחד גברא מאי. הכי גרסינן. לקרן אחת. אם כפר וחזר וכפר, וה"ה לתרין כפילי. תבעוהו בעלים לשומר חנם ונשבע. שנגנבה, ונפטר, ואח"כ שילם לפנים משורת הדין. כיון דאטרחיה. שומר לבעלים עד שהביאוהו לבית דין ונשבע, אע"ג דהדר שילם – לא מקנו ליה בעלים לשומר כפילא בשעת תשלומים. שהרי אמרו וכו'. ויכול היה ליפטר בשבועה.

ובאו עדים אקמייתא והודה אבתרייתא, מאי? ממון המחייבתו כפל פוטרו מן החומש, והא איחייב ליה עילויה כפילא, או דלמא: שבועה המחייבתו כפל פוטרתו מן החומש, והא שבועה בתרייתא הואיל דלא קא מחייבא ליה כפילא – תחייביה חומשא? אמר רבא, ת"ש: *אמר לאחד מן השוק: "היכן שורי שגנבת"? והוא אומר: "לא גנבתי", "משביעך אני" ואמר "אמן", והעדים מעידים אותו שגנבו – משלם תשלומי כפל, ואם הודה מעצמו – משלם קרן וחומש ואשם; והא הכא עדים הוא דמחייבי ליה כפילא, הודה מעצמו – אין, אבל הודה אחר עדים – לא; ואי סלקא דעתך שבועה המחייבתו כפל פוטרתו מן החומש, אמאי הודה אחר עדים לא? מכדי הא שבועה לא קא מיחייבא ליה כפילא, תחייביה חומשא! אלא לאו שמע מינה: [א]ממון המחייבו כפל פוטרתו מן החומש, ש"מ. בעי רבינא: חומש וכפילא בתרי גברי, מאי? היכי דמי – כגון שמסר שורו לשני בני אדם וטענו בו טענת גנב, חד נשבע והודה, וחד נשבע ובאו עדים, מאי? מי אמרינן: בחד גברא קפיד רחמנא דלא משלם חומשא וכפילא, (א) האי נשלם כפילא והאי נשלם חומשא. או דלמא: עלויה חד ממונא קפיד רחמנא דלא נשלם עלה חומשא וכפילא, והכא נמי חד ממונא הוא? [ב]תיקו.§ בעי רב פפא: תרי חומשי או תרי כפילי בחד גברא, מאי? היכי דמי – (ב) שטען טענת אבד ונשבע והודה, וחזר וטען טענת אבד ונשבע והודה; אי נמי, כגון שטען טענת גנב ונשבע ובאו עדים, וחזר וטען טענת גנב ונשבע ובאו עדים, מאי? מי אמרינן: [ג]תרי גווני ממונא קאמר רחמנא דלא נשתלמו עילוי חד ממונא, והכא חד גוונא הוא. או דלמא: תרי ממונא אמר רחמנא דלא לשתלמו עילוי חד ממונא, והכא נמי תרי ממונא נינהו? תא שמע, *דאמר רבא: °"וחמישיתו יוסיף עליו" – התורה ריבתה חמישיות הרבה לקרן אחת, [ד]שמע מינה.§ תבעוהו בעלים לשומר ונשבע ושילם, והוכר הגנב, כפל למי? אביי אמר: לבעל הפקדון, רבא אמר: [ה]למי שהפקדון אצלו. אביי אמר לבעל הפקדון, כיון דאטרחיה בשבועה לא מקני ליה כפילא; רבא אמר למי שהפקדון אצלו, כיון דשילם מקני ליה כפילא. וקא מיפלגי בדיוקא דמתניתין, דתנן: *[ו]המפקיד אצל חבירו בהמה או כלים ונגנבו או שאבדו, שילם ולא רצה לישבע, שהרי אמרו שומר חנם נשבע ויוצא, נמצא הגנב – משלם תשלומי כפל, טבח ומכר – משלם תשלומי ארבעה וחמשה, למי הוא משלם? למי שהפקדון אצלו; נשבע ולא רצה לשלם, ונמצא הגנב – משלם תשלומי כפל, טבח ומכר – משלם תשלומי ארבעה וחמשה, למי הוא משלם? לבעל הפקדון. אביי דייק מרישא, רבא דייק מסיפא. אביי דייק מרישא, דקתני: שילם ולא רצה לישבע; טעמא דלא רצה לישבע, הא

ובאו עדים אקמייתא. תימה: דע"כ כשבאו עדים אקמייתא ואומרים: באותה שעה ראינוהו ברשותו, ונמצא שמכחישין גם שבועה שניה שנשבע שאבד, וכשהודה אחר עדים אמאי משלם חומש? הא קתני לעיל *בברייתא ד"היכן פקדוני" כו': הודה מעצמו — משלם קרן וחומש. משמע דוקא הודה מעצמו, אבל אחר עדים — לא! ויש לומר: לעולם בטענת אבד הודה לאחר עדים נמי משלם חומש, כדמשמע בסמוך, דקאמר: מכדי האי שבועה לא מחייבא ליה כפל — תחייביה חומש, אלא שמע מינה ממון המחייבו כפל פוטרו מן החומש. משמע: הא היכא דליכא כפל בהעדאת עדים, כמו בטענת אבד — דמתחייב חומש בהודה אחר עדים. ולעיל לאו דוקא נקט מעצמו, אלא הוא הדין אחר עדים, ואיידי דתנא בסיפא הודה מעצמו גבי טוען טענת גנב — תנא נמי ברישא.

חד [נשבע] והודה וחד [נשבע] ובאו עדים. נראה דוקא נקט מתחילה הודה, דאי מתחילה כפר חד ובאו עדים, ואח"כ הודה חד — הוו עדים קודמין להודאה ומחייבין תרוייהו כפילא, דעדים כשבאו להעיד על שניהם העידו. אבל כשהודה חד קודם, אע"פ שאח"כ באו עדים — יש לומר דפטור. והכי משמע בכולה הך שמעתא, דמודה בקנס ואח"כ באו עדים דפטור.

טען טענת אבד ונשבע והודה וחזר וטען טענת אבד. נראה דל"ג "והודה". דאם הודה — מיד הויא ברשותו להתחייב באונסים משעה שנשבע לשקר, ומה שיחזור ויטעון שוב אבד — אין כופר כלום, ואפי' אמר לאחר שבועה אבד. אלא נראה דלא הודה אלא לאחר שבועה שניה. ומיהו, תימה: מאי קמבעיא ליה לרב פפא? הא מתניתין היא דמייתי לעיל (דף קו.): השביע עליו ה' פעמים, בין בפני ב"ד בין שלא בפני ב"ד, וכפר עליו — חייב על כל אחת ואחת.

וחזר וטען טענת גנב ונשבע. תימה: היאך השביעוהו בית דין, כיון שנפטר בבית דין בשבועה ראשונה? ואפילו חזר וטען שלאחר שבועה ראשונה נגנב — מ"מ למה השביעוהו? והלא משבועה ראשונה שנשבע לשקר חייב באונסים, נמצא שלא כפר כלום במה שטען שנגנב אחר שבועה ראשונה! ואין לומר שבאו לפני בית דין אחר שלא ידעו שכבר נפטר והשביעוהו, וכיון שנשבע על פי בית דין (אע"ג) שלא ידעו מיחייב כפל, והא דאמרינן לעיל שכבר יצא בשבועה ראשונה — היינו שאותו בית דין עצמו השביעוהו וטעו. דאין סברא לחלק כלל. ונראה דמיירי דאמר ליה בעל הפקדון שוב לאחר שנמצא שקרן בשבועה ראשונה: רצוני שתהא עליו שומר חנם כבתחילה, וחזר וטען: לאחר שעשיתני שומר חנם נגנב, ופוטר עצמו, שהרי לא נתחייב באונסין במה שעשאו בפירוש ש"ח. אבל תימה: דא"כ לא הוי חד ממונא, דהשתא הפקידו אצלו פעם שניה, ומה לי לקחו בידו ונתן ולו, ומ"ל שלא לקחו אלא אמר ליה בעודו בידו: תהא עליו שומר חנם? *ותרי כפילי. מחמת שנעשה פסול בשבועה שניה משעה שנמצא שקרן בראשונה — אין לפוטרו, משום דחשוד על השבועה מדרבנן הוא דמיפסל, כדמוכח בשבועות (דף מה.) דקתני ושכנגדו חשוד על השבועה, ומשמע התם דמדרבנן הוא וכיון דמדאורייתא שבועתו שבועה — מחייב כפל. **רבא** אמר למי שהפקדון אצלו. וא"ת: דהכא סבר רבא דאע"ג דאטרחיה לבי דינא — מקני ליה כפילא. ובפרק "המפקיד" (ב"מ דף לה.) גבי ההוא גברא דאפקיד כיפי גבי חבריה, קאמר רבא: שפיר עבד דלא אהדר ליה, הכא אטרחיה לבי דינא התם לא אטרחיה לבי דינא! ויש לומר: דהתם שאני, דאטרחיה לבי דינא ולא פרע ליה מידי, אלא רב נחמן אגבייה לאפדנא מיניה. אבל הכא, אע"ג דאטרחיה לבי דינא קצת, שנשבע לו תחילה — מכל מקום הרי שילם לו לבסוף, ולא אטרח בי דינא, הלכך מקני ליה כפילא.

קו. [ע"ש] שבועות מט.

לעיל סה:

ויקרא ה

ב"מ לג:

שייך קודם ד"ה טען

קנו א מיי' פ"ד מהל' גניבה הל' ו:

קנז ב מיי' שם הל' ז:

מתניתין היא לקמן מע"ל וכן בשבועות ועיין בספר כ"י

קנח ג ד מיי' שם הל' ה [רב אלפס ב"מ פ"ג דף עט.]:

קנט ה מיי' פ"ח מהל' שאלה ופקדון הל' ד טוח"מ סי' רלד וסי' רלה:

קס ו מיי' שם הל' א טוח"מ שם:

הגהות הב"ח

(א) גמ' דלא משלם חומשא וכפילא אבל בתרי גברי האי נשלם כפילא: (ב) שם היכי דמי כגון שטען:

תבעו

הָא נִשְׁבַּע — אע"פ שֶׁשִּׁילֵּם, לְמִי מְשַׁלֵּם? לְבַעַל הַפִּקָּדוֹן. רָבָא דָּיֵיק מִסֵּיפָא: (א) נִשְׁבַּע וְלֹא רָצָה לְשַׁלֵּם; טַעְמָא דְּלֹא רָצָה לְשַׁלֵּם, הָא שִׁילֵּם — אע"פ שֶׁנִּשְׁבַּע, לְמִי מְשַׁלֵּם? לְמִי שֶׁהַפִּקָּדוֹן אֶצְלוֹ. לְאַבַּיֵי קַשְׁיָא סֵיפָא! אָמַר לָךְ אַבַּיֵי, הָכִי קָתָנֵי: נִשְׁבַּע, וְלֹא רָצָה לְשַׁלֵּם קוֹדֶם הַשְּׁבוּעָה אֶלָּא לְאַחַר הַשְּׁבוּעָה, לְמִי מְשַׁלֵּם? לְבַעַל הַפִּקָּדוֹן. לְרָבָא קַשְׁיָא רֵישָׁא! אָמַר לָךְ רָבָא, הָכִי קָתָנֵי: שִׁילֵּם, וְלֹא רָצָה לַעֲמוֹד בִּשְׁבוּעָתוֹ אֶלָּא שִׁילֵּם, לְמִי מְשַׁלֵּם? לְמִי שֶׁהַפִּקָּדוֹן אֶצְלוֹ. תְּבָעוּהוּ בְּעָלִים לַשּׁוֹמֵר וְנִשְׁבַּע, וְהוּכַּר הַגַּנָּב, תְּבָעוֹ שׁוֹמֵר וְהוֹדָה, [א]תְּבָעוּהוּ בְּעָלִים וְכָפַר, וְהֵבִיאוּ עֵדִים, מִי נִפְטָר הַגַּנָּב בְּהוֹדָאַת שׁוֹמֵר אוֹ לֹא נִפְטָר הַגַּנָּב בְּהוֹדָאַת שׁוֹמֵר? אָמַר רָבָא: [ב]אִם בֶּאֱמֶת נִשְׁבַּע — נִפְטָר הַגַּנָּב בְּהוֹדָאַת שׁוֹמֵר, אִם בְּשֶׁקֶר נִשְׁבַּע — לֹא נִפְטָר הַגַּנָּב בְּהוֹדָאַת שׁוֹמֵר. בָּעֵי רָבָא: עָמַד לִישָּׁבַע בְּשֶׁקֶר וְלֹא הִנִּיחוּהוּ, מַהוּ? תֵּיקוּ. רַב כָּהֲנָא מַתְנֵי הָכִי. רַב טַבְיוּמֵי מַתְנֵי,(ג) [ג]בָּעֵי רָבָא: נִשְׁבַּע לַשֶּׁקֶר, מַהוּ? תֵּיקוּ. תְּבָעוּהוּ בְּעָלִים לַשּׁוֹמֵר וְשִׁילֵּם, וְהוּכַּר הַגַּנָּב, [ד]תְּבָעוּהוּ בְּעָלִים וְהוֹדָה, תְּבָעוֹ שׁוֹמֵר וְכָפַר, וְהֵבִיא עֵדִים, נִפְטָר גַּנָּב בְּהוֹדָאַת בְּעָלִים אוֹ לֹא? מִי אָמְרִינַן, מָצֵי אָמַר לֵיהּ שׁוֹמֵר לַבְּעָלִים: אַתּוּן כֵּיוָן דִּשְׁקַלִיתוּ לְכוּ דְּמֵי אִסְתַּלֵּיקְתוּ לְכוּ מֵהָכָא, אוֹ דִלְמָא מָצֵי אָמְרִי לֵיהּ: כִּי הֵיכִי דְּאַתְּ עֲבַדְתְּ לָן מִילְּתָא אֲנַן נַמִי עָבְדִינַן לָךְ, טָרְחִינַן בָּתַר גַּנָּבָא, שָׁקְלִינָא אֲנַן דִּידָן, וּשְׁקוֹל אַתְּ דִּידָךְ? [ה]תֵּיקוּ. *אִתְּמַר: נִגְנְבָה בְּאוֹנֶס וְהוּכַּר הַגַּנָּב, אָמַר אַבַּיֵי: אִם שׁוֹמֵר חִנָּם הוּא — רָצָה עוֹשֶׂה עִמּוֹ דִּין, רָצָה נִשְׁבָּע. אִם שׁוֹמֵר שָׂכָר הוּא — עוֹשֶׂה עִמּוֹ דִּין וְאֵינוֹ נִשְׁבָּע; רָבָא אָמַר: אֶחָד זֶה וְאֶחָד זֶה — [ו]עוֹשֶׂה עִמּוֹ דִּין וְאֵינוֹ נִשְׁבָּע. לֵימָא, פְּלִיגָא אַדְּרַב הוּנָא בַּר אָבִין, דִּשְׁלַח רַב הוּנָא בַּר אָבִין: נִגְנְבָה בְּאוֹנֶס וְהוּכַּר הַגַּנָּב, אִם שׁוֹמֵר חִנָּם הוּא — רָצָה עוֹשֶׂה עִמּוֹ דִּין, רָצָה נִשְׁבָּע, וְאִם שׁוֹמֵר שָׂכָר הוּא — עוֹשֶׂה עִמּוֹ דִּין וְאֵינוֹ נִשְׁבָּע? אָמַר לָךְ רָבָא: הָכָא בְּמַאי עָסְקִינַן — [ז]כְּגוֹן שֶׁקָּדַם וְנִשְׁבַּע. וְהָא רָצָה עוֹשֶׂה עִמּוֹ דִּין, רָצָה נִשְׁבָּע קָאָמַר! הָכִי קָאָמַר: [ח]רָצָה שׁוֹמֵר חִנָּם עוֹמֵד בִּשְׁבוּעָתוֹ, רָצָה עוֹשֶׂה עִמּוֹ דִּין. רַבָּה זוּטֵי בָּעֵי לָהּ הָכִי: [ט]נִגְנְבָה בְּאוֹנֶס, וְהֶחֱזִיר גַּנָּב בְּבֵית שׁוֹמֵר וּמֵתָה בִּפְשִׁיעָה, מַהוּ? מִי אָמְרִינַן: כֵּיוָן דְּנִגְנְבָה בְּאוֹנֶס כַּלְיָא לֵיהּ שְׁמִירָתוֹ, אוֹ דִלְמָא כֵּיוָן דַּהֲדַרָה הֲדַרָה לִשְׁמִירָתוֹ? [י]תֵּיקוּ.§

מתני' "הֵיכָן פִּקְדוֹנִי"? אָמַר לוֹ: "אָבַד", "מַשְׁבִּיעֲךָ אֲנִי" וְאָמַר "אָמֵן", וְהָעֵדִים מְעִידִים אוֹתוֹ שֶׁאֲכָלוֹ — מְשַׁלֵּם קֶרֶן, [הוֹדָה מֵעַצְמוֹ — מְשַׁלֵּם קֶרֶן וְחוֹמֶשׁ וְאָשָׁם]. "הֵיכָן פִּקְדוֹנִי"? אָמַר לוֹ: "נִגְנַב", "מַשְׁבִּיעֲךָ אֲנִי", וְאָמַר "אָמֵן", וְהָעֵדִים מְעִידִים אוֹתוֹ שֶׁגְּנָבוֹ — מְשַׁלֵּם תַּשְׁלוּמֵי כֶפֶל, הוֹדָה מֵעַצְמוֹ — מְשַׁלֵּם קֶרֶן חוֹמֶשׁ וְאָשָׁם. [כ]הַגּוֹזֵל [א] אֶת אָבִיו וְנִשְׁבַּע לוֹ וּמֵת — הֲרֵי זֶה מְשַׁלֵּם קֶרֶן וְחוֹמֶשׁ *וְאָשָׁם לְבָנָיו אוֹ לְאֶחָיו, וְאִם אֵינוֹ רוֹצֶה אוֹ שֶׁאֵין לוֹ — לֹוֶה וּבַעֲלֵי חוֹב בָּאִין וְנִפְרָעִים. *הָאוֹמֵר [ל]לִבְנוֹ "קוֹנָם אִי אַתָּה נֶהֱנֶה מִשֶּׁלִּי", אִם מֵת — יִרָשֶׁנּוּ; בְּחַיָּיו

רש"י

הָא נִשְׁבַּע אע"פ שֶׁשִּׁילֵּם. כֵּיוָן דְּאַטְרְחֵיהּ בִּשְׁבוּעָה, לְמִי מְשַׁלֵּם גַּנָּב כֶּפֶל – לְבַעַל הַפִּקָּדוֹן, כְּטַעְמֵיהּ דְּאַבַּיֵי דִּלְעֵיל. מִי נִפְטָר הַגַּנָּב. מִן הַכֶּפֶל, כִּשְׁאָר מוֹדֶה בִּקְנָס. בְּהוֹדָאָה. שֶׁהוֹדָה לַשּׁוֹמֵר. אוֹ לֹא נִפְטָר. דְּכֵיוָן דְּנִשְׁבַּע שׁוֹמֵר תְּחִילָּה – נִסְתַּלֵּק, וְשׁוּב אֵינָהּ בִּשְׁמִירָתוֹ, וְלָא הָוְיָא הוֹדָאָה. אִם בֶּאֱמֶת נִשְׁבַּע. הַשּׁוֹמֵר, שֶׁטָּעַן נִגְנְבָה בְּאוֹנֶס, וְנִמְצָא כֵּן. נִפְטָר הַגַּנָּב בְּהוֹדָאַת שׁוֹמֵר. דְּכֵיוָן דְּנֶאֱמָן הוּא – אֲנַן סָהֲדֵי דְּאִי הֲוָה מִשְׁתַּכְּחָא בְּהֵמָה נִיחָא לֵיהּ לְמָרֵיהּ דְּתֶיהֱוֵי בִּידֵיהּ דְּהָאֵיךְ. הִלְכָּךְ עַל שׁוֹמֵר זֶה לַחֲזוֹר אַחֲרֶיהָ, וּתְבִיעָתוֹ תְּבִיעָה, וְהוֹדָאַת גַּנָּב הוֹדָאָה. וְאִם נִשְׁבַּע לַשֶּׁקֶר. שֶׁטּוֹעֵן: מֵת אוֹ נִשְׁבַּר אוֹ נִשְׁבָּה אוֹ נִגְנְבָה בְּאוֹנֶס, וּבָא וּמָצָא שֶׁאֵינוֹ כֵּן. דְּכֵיוָן דְּמִגַּלְיָא מִילְּתָא דְּשַׁקְרָן הֲוָה – אֲנַן סָהֲדֵי דְּלָא נִיחָא לֵיהּ לְמָרָהּ דְּלֶיהֱוֵי תּוּ שׁוֹמֵר עֲלָהּ, וּתְבִיעָתוֹ אֵינָהּ תְּבִיעָה. וְלֹא הִנִּיחוּהוּ מַאי. מִדְּלָא נִשְׁבַּע – נֶאֱמָן הוּא עֲדַיִין לַבְּעָלִים. אוֹ דִּלְמָא כֵּיוָן דְּעָמַד לִישָּׁבַע – תּוּ לָא מְהֵימְנִי לֵיהּ (ג) בְּעָלִים? נִשְׁבַּע לַשֶּׁקֶר מַהוּ. מִי אָמְרִינַן: אַכַּתִּי עֲלֵיהּ רַמְיָא, דְּכֵיוָן דְּלַשֶּׁקֶר נִשְׁבַּע סוֹפוֹ לְהִתְחָרֵט וּלְשַׁלֵּם, הִלְכָּךְ תְּבִיעָתוֹ תְּבִיעָה, אוֹ לָא? אִית דְּגָרַס: אִם בֶּאֱמֶת נִשְׁבַּע, דְּלָא פָּשַׁע – לָא נִפְטָר הַגַּנָּב, דְּכֵיוָן דְּבֶאֱמֶת נִשְׁבַּע – אִפַּטַּר לֵיהּ שׁוֹמֵר, וְתוּ לָא רַמְיָא עֲלֵיהּ לְמִתְבָּעֵיהּ לַגַּנָּב. וְאִם לַשֶּׁקֶר נִשְׁבַּע, כְּגוֹן דְּפָשַׁע – נִפְטָר הַגַּנָּב בְּהוֹדָאַת שׁוֹמֵר, דְּאַכַּתִּי עֲלֵיהּ רַמְיָא לְשַׁלּוּמֵי. וְרִאשׁוֹן שָׁמַעְתִּי, וְעִיקָּר הוּא. דְּהָכָא אִיכָּא לְאַקְשׁוּיֵי: א"כ מַאי בָּעֵי רָבָא: עָמַד לִישָּׁבַע לַשֶּׁקֶר וְלֹא הִנִּיחוּהוּ מַהוּ? הַשְׁתָּא נִשְׁבַּע מַמָּשׁ, דְּאִסְתַּלַּק לֵיהּ מִבֵּי דִינָא, דְּתוּ לָא רַמְיָא עֲלֵיהּ לָא שְׁבוּעָה וְלֹא פֵּרָעוֹן עַד שֶׁיָּבֹאוּ עֵדִים שֶׁפָּשַׁע, אָמְרִינַן דְּנִפְטָר הַגַּנָּב, דְּאַכַּתִּי אַשּׁוֹמֵר רַמְיָא לְמִתְבָּעֵיהּ כָּל שֶׁכֵּן הֵיכָא דְּלֹא נִשְׁבַּע, דַּעֲלֵיהּ רַמְיָא לְשַׁלּוּמֵי! אַתְּ עֲבַדְתְּ לָן מִילְּתָא. טוֹבָה, שֶׁשִּׁילַּמְתָּ לְפָנִים מִשּׁוּרַת הַדִּין, הִלְכָּךְ עַל דִּידָן נַמִי רַמְיָא לְמֶיעְבַּד מִילְּתָא דְּטִיבוּתָא – לַאֲהַדּוּרֵי בָּתַר גַּנָּבָא וּלְמִתְבָּעֵיהּ, וּתְבִיעָתָן תְּבִיעָה. נִגְנְבָה בְּאוֹנֶס. בְּלִסְטִים מְזוּיָּן, דְּשׁוֹמֵר שָׂכָר פָּטוּר בּוֹ. וְאַח"כ הוּכַּר הַגַּנָּב, וְיָכוֹל לְכוֹפוֹ וּלְהוֹצִיא מִיָּדוֹ. רָצָה נִשְׁבָּע. וְהַבְּעָלִים יִפָּרְעוּ מִן הַגַּנָּב. עוֹשֶׂה עִמּוֹ דִּין. מְשַׁלֵּם לַבְּעָלִים, וְהוּא יִפָּרַע מִן הַגַּנָּב. וְאִם שׁוֹמֵר שָׂכָר הוּא. אע"ג דְּפָטוּר בְּלִסְטִים מְזוּיָּן, הָכָא הוֹאִיל וְהוּכַּר הַגַּנָּב וְלֹא יַפְסִיד כְּלוּם – עָלָיו לִטְרוֹחַ אַחֲרֶיהָ. לְפִיכָךְ הוּא יְשַׁלֵּם לַבְּעָלִים וְיַחֲזוֹר וְיִפָּרַע מִן הַגַּנָּב. עוֹשֶׂה עִמּוֹ דִּין. יְשַׁלֵּם, דְּמִלְוָה עָלָיו לַחֲזוֹר אַחַר הָאֲבֵידָה. לֵימָא פְּלִיגָא. דְּרָבָא אַדְּרַב הוּנָא בַּר אָבִין. כְּגוֹן שֶׁקָּדַם וְנִשְׁבַּע. קוֹדֶם שֶׁהוּכַּר הַגַּנָּב. **מתני'** מְשַׁלֵּם קֶרֶן. דְּאֵין חוֹמֶשׁ וְאָשָׁם אֶלָּא אִם הוֹדָה, דִּכְתִיב בְּגֶזֶל הַגֵּר בְּפָרָשַׁת נָשֹׂא: "וְהִתְוַדּוּ". (ד) וְאַחַר כָּךְ מֵת אָבִיו. *וְאַחַר מִיתַת הָאָב הוֹדָה. הֲרֵי זֶה מְשַׁלֵּם קֶרֶן וְחוֹמֶשׁ לְבָנָיו. שֶׁל אָבִיו, אוֹ לְאֶחָיו שֶׁל אָבִיו אִם אֵין לוֹ בָּנִים. וְאַף עַל גַּב דְּנָפְלָה יְרוּשָּׁה קַמֵּיהּ דְּהָאֵיךְ – בָּעֵי לְמֶעְבַּד הֲשָׁבָה, וְאֵין מְעַכֵּב אֲפִילּוּ כְּנֶגֶד חֶלְקוֹ. אֵין לוֹ. נְכָסִים כָּל כָּךְ, שֶׁיָּכוֹל לְוַותֵּר עַל חֶלְקוֹ, אוֹ שֶׁאֵין רוֹצֶה לְהַפְסִיד חֶלְקוֹ. לוֶֹה. מֵאֲחֵרִים, וּמֵשִׁיב לְאֶחָיו לְקַיֵּים מִצְוַת הֲשָׁבָה. וּבַעֲלֵי הַחוֹב בָּאִין וְנִפְרָעִין. מִן *הַהֲשָׁבָה אֶת חֶלְקוֹ. כְּגוֹן אִם הָיוּ שְׁנַיִם אַחִין וְהוּא שְׁלִישִׁי – נִפְרָעִים בַּעֲלֵי חוֹבִים מִן (*הַהֲשָׁבָה שְׁלִישׁ הַחוֹב) וְהַשְּׁאָר יִגְבּוּ מִמֶּנּוּ. בְּחַיָּיו

תוספות

תבעו שומר והודה תבעוהו בעלים והביא עדים. משמע דהודה לאחר שאין בעל הדבר, דלא הויא הודאה. ותימה: אמאי לא בעי לענין קרן גופיה בשלא באו עדים, אי הויא הודאה אי לאו, ואמאי נקט "והביא עדים", משמע דלא מבעיא אלא לענין כפל? וי"ל: דמשום דאקרן לא הוי מצי למיפשט הא דפשיט: אם בשקר נשבע לא נפטר הגנב כו'. **ולא** הניחוהו מהו. הקשה בקונט' אהך גירסא דגרסינן "אם באמת נשבע לא נפטר גנב" וכו', דא"כ מאי בעי רבא: עמד לישבע לשקר ולא הניחוהו מהו? השתא נשבע לשקר ממש, דאיסתליק ליה מבי דינא, דתו לא רמיא עליה — כ"ש היכא דלא נשבע, דעליה רמיא לשלומי! ויש מתרצים: דכיון (*דלא הניחוהו לישבע — מחל לו, והרי נפטר נמי שומר כאילו) שומר נשבע באמת, ותו לא רמיא עליה, ולהכי קבעי. ולאו מילתא היא, דמשום דלא הניחוהו לישבע לא מחל לו, ולא מיפטר שומר בהכי. וכן פוסק בה"ג, דאע"פ שמחל לו השבועה לנתבע — בשביל כך לא מחל לו ממון לגמרי. וכל שכן היכא דלא מחל לו שבועה, אלא שלא הניחו לישבע באותה שעה.

נגנבה באונס. נראה דאין שום גניבה קרויה אונס אלא בלסטים מזוין, כדפירש בקונט', וכן מוכח לעיל ב"הכונס" (דף נז.).

לבניו או לאחיו. נראה: לבניו של גזלן או לאחיו של גזלן. כלומר, בתחילה לבניו אם יש לו, דהם קודמים לכל אדם בחלק המגיעו, ונחשב אותו כאילו מת הוא, והרי בניו יורשים חלקו עם אחיו. והם אין באים מכחו אלא מכח אבוה דאבא, כדאמר בסוף "מי שמת" (ב"ב דף קנט.): "תחת אבותיך יהיו בניך". הלכך, אע"פ שאין לאביהן בהן כלום, שהרי יש לו להחזיר גזילה — אפ"ה הם קודמין בחלקו מההוא טעמא דב"ב. או לאחיו — כשאין לו בנים. **לוה** וב"ח באין ונפרעין. נראה לפרש: לוה על הקרקע שלו מאחרים אפי' בלא אפותיקי, דקרקע משועבד לבעל חוב. ואח"כ נותן קרקע שלו לבניו או לאחיו בעבור הגזילה, וכגון שאין הגזילה קיימת, וחוזרים ב"ח ונפרעין מאותה קרקע, אע"ג דיש לו שאר נכסים במה לפרוע. ונראה דאין צריך לומר בשעת נתינתו לבניו או לאחיו "ע"מ שיפרעו בעלי חוב מכם", דבלאו הכי אין יכולין לזכות שלא מדעתו. ואם הגזילה בעין — צריך לפרש שילוה עליה או יעשנה אפותיקי למלוה, ויחזירנה לבניו

עין משפט נר מצוה

קסא א ב ג ד ה מיי' פ"ד מהלכות גניבה הלכה ח טוש"ע ח"מ סי' שנב:

קסב ו ז ח מיי' פ"ח מהל' שאלה ופקדון הלכה ו סמג עשין פח טוש"ע ח"מ סי' רצא סעיף ו:

קסג ט מיי' שם סמג שם:

קסד י מיי' פ"ח מהל' גזילה ואבידה הל' ב סמג עשין עג טוש"ע ח"מ סי' שסז סעיף ה:

רס"ל מ"ז וגורס דכיון דשומר נשבע

קסה ל מיי' פ"ה מהל' נדרים הלכה ו סמג לאוין רמב טוש"ע י"ד סי' רכ"ז סעיף ז וסי' רנג סעיף ב:

הגהות הב"ח

(א) גמ' דייק מסיפא דקתני נשבע: (ב) שם רב טביומי מתני הכי בעי: (ג) רש"י ד"ה ולא הניחוהו וכו' לבעלים הס"ד: (ד) ד"ה ונשבע לו ואח"כ מת אביו:

הגהות הגר"א

[א] מתני' הגוזל כו' לבניו כ"ב גירסת הרמב"ם לאחיו או לבניו ואם אין לו לוה כו' וכ"ל שאין לו אחים ובנים ואלו נעלין אלא שילא מתחת ידו ואף באחיו מחשב עמהם אח"כ וכל זה בגזילה קיימת:

[צריך תיקון ובפרש"י וכן בכרבטרלא ליתא תיבת ואשם]

ס"א מן שליש הירושה

מסורת הש"ס

ה"מ גנו

לעיל סג: קו. שבועות

עיין רש"א ובספר

[נדרים מב. מז.]

ס"א הירושה

תורה אור

בחייו ובמותו — אם מת לא ירשנו, [א]ויחזיר לבניו או לאחיו, [ב]ואם אין לו — לוה ובעלי חוב באים ונפרעים.§ **גמ'** אמר רב יוסף: [ג]אפילו לארנקי של צדקה. אמר רב פפא: [ד]וצריך שיאמר: "זה גזל אבי". אמאי? נמחליה לנפשיה! מי לא תנן: *מחל לו על הקרן ולא מחל לו על החומש? אלמא בר מחילה הוא! אמר רבי יוחנן, לא קשיא: הא רבי יוסי הגלילי, הא רבי עקיבא; דתניא: *°"ואם אין לאיש גואל להשיב האשם" — וכי יש אדם בישראל שאין לו גואלים? אלא בגזל הגר הכתוב מדבר. הרי שגזל הגר ונשבע לו, ושמע שמת הגר, והיה מעלה כספו ואשמו לירושלים, ופגע באותו הגר וזקפו עליו במלוה, ומת — זכה הלה במה שבידו, דברי רבי יוסי הגלילי; ר' עקיבא אומר: [ה]אין לו תקנה עד שיוציא גזילו מתחת ידו; לרבי יוסי הגלילי, לא שנא לנפשיה ל"ש לאחרים — מצי מחיל, ולרבי עקיבא, ל"ש לאחרים ולא שנא לנפשיה — לא מצי מחיל; ולר' יוסי, הוא הדין דאפי' לא זקפו במלוה, והאי דקתני זקפו עליו במלוה — להודיעך כחו דרבי עקיבא, דאפילו זקפן עליו במלוה, אין לו תקנה עד שיוציא גזילה מתחת ידו. מתקיף לה רב ששת: אי הכי, לרבי יוסי הגלילי — לשמעינן לנפשיה, וכל שכן לאחרים, לרבי עקיבא — לשמעינן לאחרים דלא מצי מחיל, וכ"ש לנפשיה דלא מצי מחיל! אלא אמר רב ששת: הא והא רבי יוסי הגלילי; כי קאמר רבי יוסי הגלילי דמצי מחיל — לאחרים, אבל לנפשיה לא מצי מחיל. אלא אמאי זכה הלה במה שבידו? משום דזקפן עליו במלוה. רבא אמר: הא והא רבי עקיבא; כי אמר רבי עקיבא דלא מצי מחיל — לנפשיה, אבל לאחרים מצי מחיל. מכלל

במדבר ה

רש"י

בחייו ובמותו אם מת לא ירשנו*. ואם אין לו. מה יאכל, לוה ואוכל ובעלי חוב באין ונפרעין מן הירושה את חלקו. **גמ'** ואפי' לארנקי של צדקה. אם אינו מוצא יורש לאביו למי ישיב — יתן אותה לארנקי של צדקה, ולא יעכבנו בידו. וצריך שיאמר. כשהוא משיב לארנקי של צדקה: זה גזל אבא. ונמחליה לנפשיה. היכא דאין יורש אלא הוא, וכולה שלו. מי לא תנן מחל לו על הקרן. ולא מקיימא מצות השבה. אלמא: למיפק ידי גזילה בעינן, והא נפקא ליה במחילה. הכא נמי, כיון דירושה קמיה נפלה — נפק ליה מידי גזילה. [לעיל קג.] להשיב האשם. זה קרן של גזילה, כדתניא לקמן בפרקין (דף קי.). גואל. יורש. וכי יש לך אדם בישראל שאין לו גואלים. [סנהדרין סח:] אם אין לו בן או בת או אח — יש לו קרוב עד יעקב אבינו, הקרוב קרוב יורש. **אלא** בגזל הגר. ונשבע לשקר, דכתיב: "למעול מעל בה'". והיה מעלה כספו ואשמו לירושלים. לכהנים, כדכתיב: "האשם המושב לה' לכהן" ואמרינן לקמן בשמעתין: "אשם" — זה קרן. וזקפו עליו. גר במלוה, נפק ליה מתורת גזילה. ולכי מיית גר — הוה ליה האי מוחזק, וזכה מן ההפקר. **לא שנא** לנפשיה. כגון הכא, דמחיל ליה האי גברא גזל הגר לנפשיה, וה"ה גוזל את אביו ונשבע לו, ומת אביו, דמחיל לנפשיה. ול"ש לאחרים. נגזל לגוזל, מצי מחיל. ומתני' דקתני מחל לו על הקרן — רבי יוסי הגלילי היא, ואשמעינן לאחרים וה"ה לנפשיה היכא דנפק מידי גזילה, כגון יורש או גזל הגר. וקס"ד האי זקפו לאו דוקא, כדמפרש ואזיל. לר' עקיבא **לא שנא** כו'. ומתני' דקתני: משלם קרן וחומש לבניו או לאחיו — ר' עקיבא היא, ולאשמועינן לנפשיה דלא מצי מחיל וה"ה לאחרים, דאפילו מחיל ליה נגזל גופיה — לאו מחילה היא. ה"ה **אפי' לא** זקפן. הלכך, יורש את אביו נמי, אע"ג דלא זקפו עליו במלוה ולא יצא מתורת גזילה בחיי אביו, כיון דמת אביו ונפלו נכסים לפניו — מחיל לנפשיה. ולקמן (ע"ב) פריך: א"כ גזל הגר דנפיק לכהנים היכי משכחת לה? **א**"ה. דבלא זקפו נמי קאמר ר' יוסי לנפשיה מצי מחיל, מתני' דמחל לו על הקרן, דאמרת ר' יוסי היא, כיון דאמר לנפשיה מצי מחיל — לשמעי' ביורש את אביו דמחיל לנפשיה, וליתני: פטור, ולוקמה כר' יוסי, וכ"ש דנגזל גופיה לגזלן מצי מחיל. וגבי מחל לו על הקרן, דאוקמיה כר' יוסי — ליתני: אינה מחילה, ולוקמה כרבי עקיבא, דלשמעינן מתני' לרבי עקיבא דלאחרים לא מצי מחיל. ומהתם שמעינן שפיר דכל שכן לנפשיה, דזקפו במלוה היינו אחרים, וקאמר ר' עקיבא דלא מצי מחיל. אבל השתא דאשמועינן לאחרים הויא מחילה ולנפשיה לא הויא מחילה — איכא למימר דדווקא קתני, וחד תנא הוא רישא דמתני' וסיפא. הא והא ר' יוסי. הא דאמר בזקפו במלוה, דכיון דאפקיה גר גופיה דהוה נגזל מתורת גזילה, דהוי כמוחל לאחרים, הוי מחילה, ולכי מיית קנייה האי. הלכך מחל לו על הקרן דמתני' — ר' יוסי היא. דאי לרבי עקיבא — בעי השבה מעלו, כדקתני: אין לו תקנה עד שיוציא גזילה. וסיפא נמי רבי יוסי היא, דמודי רבי יוסי (א) לנפשיה דלא מצי מחיל, כיון דלא אפקיה נגזל מתורת גזילה. **רבא אמר** הא והא רבי עקיבא. דלרבי יוסי לנפשיה נמי מצי מחיל, דזקפו לאו דוקא. וכי אמר רבי עקיבא דלא מצי מחיל — לנפשיה הוא דקאמר, דאע"ג דגר זקפו, כיון דלא מחיל מחילה גמורה — לא נפקא ליה מתורת גזילה. אבל נגזל לגזלן — מודה ר' עקיבא דמחיל. מכלל

תוספות

לבניו או לאחיו ויחזור ויטרפנה מהם ב"ח. אע"ג דאמרינן לעיל (דף יא:): עשה שורו אפותיקי ומכרו אין ב"ח גובה הימנו — היינו דוקא מכרו, דכיון דליכא קלא לא (ב) אפסדינא ללקוחות. ◉ אבל נתנו במתנה, דלא שייך פסידא ללקוחות — ב"ח גובה הימנו, דאין יכול ליתן מה שמשועבד לאחרים. אבל לא עשאו אפותיקי — לא היה ב"ח חוזר וטורף מהם, דכי היכי דמטלטלי דיתמי לא משתעבדי לב"ח — ◉ ה"נ לא משתעבדי מטלטלי דמקבל מתנה לבעל חוב, והוי כאילו נותן להם במתנה, כיון שהוא עצמו אינו יכול לחזור ולטרוף מהן. ומיהו, נראה דלא חשיב הכא מה שמחזיר להן כאילו נתן להם, דאינו נותן להם לשם מתנה אלא סתמא בשתיקה מחזיר להם, ואין דעתו אלא לקיים מצות השבה בעלמא. הלכך לא הויא מתנה, ויכול ב"ח לטרוף מהם. והוא ודאי אינו יכול לחזור וליקח מהן — דאז לא היתה מתקיים השבה כלל אם היה לוקח בעצמו מה שנתן. אבל מה שב"ח נוטל — מתקיימא שפיר מצות השבה, כיון שבעצמו אין נוטל, ומיירי אפי' בלא אפותיקי.

ב"ח באין ונפרעין. אחר מיתה. ואפילו בחייו הוי שרי בכה"ג, כדאמרינן (נדרים דף מג.): המודר הנאה מחבירו ואין לו מה יאכל — ילך אצל חנוני הרגיל אצלו ויאמר לו: איש פלוני מודר הנאה ממני, ואין לו מה יאכל ואיני יודע מה אעשה לו, נותן לו ובא ונוטל מזה. אלא לפי שזה אין רוצה שיהנה ממנו כלל בחייו, ואין יכול לעשות תקנה אלא מדעתו. והא דלא תני הכא "ואם אין רוצה", כדקתני רישא — משום שהרי ודאי [אינו] רוצה. או שמא דוקא אין לו מה יאכל שרי, כדקתני גבי המודר הנאה מחבירו, אבל אם יש לו מה יאכל — אפי' [אינו] רוצה אין לו תקנה בכך. וא"ת: והיאך נפרע ממנו? והא תנן בפרק "אין בין המודר" (שם דף לג.): המודר הנאה מחבירו — שוקל לו שקלו ופורע לו חובו, ופר"ת דדוקא במזונות אשתו, אבל שאר חובות — אסור לפרוע, דודאי קא משתרשי ליה ואסור. וה"נ משתרשי ליה! וי"ל: דלא דמי, דהתם כיון שמתחייב למי שפרע בעבורו, אם יפרע בחנם בעבורו — א"כ מהנהו, ואסור. אבל הכא, מה שבאים ב"ח ונפרעין מן הנכסים — אין זה נהנה מן הנכסים. והיא דהולך אצל חנוני — לא תקשה, דהתם דרך מתנה מיירי, שהחנוני נותן לזה פירות במתנה, וחוזר ומקבל מזה מעות דרך מתנה. אבל הא דאמר בפרק "השותפין" (שם דף מז:*): (ג) "קונם אשתי שאני נהנית לך" כו' לוה וב"ח באין ונפרעין מבעל. בשלמא "קונם שאני נהנה לאשתי" — איכא למימר במזונות אשתו, ואליבא דחנן. אלא "קונם שאני נהנה לך" — משמע שאומר לחבירו, נמצא שהוא פורע חובו! ויש לומר: כגון שלוה הימנו על מנת שלא לפרוע, דהשתא אין נהנה כלום במה שפורע חובו. וא"ת: וכי בשופטני עסקינן שילוה ע"מ שלא לפרוע? וי"ל: שהוא אוהבו, שלא יניח מלפרוע בעבורו. **אלא** אמר רב ששת הא והא ר' יוסי הגלילי. וא"ת: ואמאי לא מוקי מתני' כר' עקיבא, ומודה דלאחרים מצי מחיל, ולנפשיה לא מצי מחיל, ובזקפו עליו במלוה הוא דפליג עליו רבי עקיבא ארבי יוסי, דלא חשיב ליה זקיפה כמו מחילה דאחריני? וי"ל: דרב ששת סבר כיון דמחילה דאחריני מועלת — זקפו נמי מועיל לכ"ע, וכיון דאמר ר' עקיבא דזקפו במלוה אינו מועיל — א"כ ודאי ס"ל דמחילת אחרים נמי אינו מועיל, הלכך לא מתוקמא מתני' כר' עקיבא, דקתני במתניתין: מחל לו את הקרן, משמע דמחילת אחריני מועלת. ורבא דמוקי לה כרבי עקיבא, סבר דזקפו במלוה אינו מועיל כלום לכ"ע, אי לא מצי מחיל לנפשיה. הלכך, רבי יוסי דקאמר זכה הלה במה שבידו — ע"כ משום דסבר דמצי מחיל לנפשיה. הלכך מתני' לא מיתוקמא כוותיה אלא כרבי עקיבא, ומודה רבי עקיבא דלאחריני מצי מחיל. והשתא הא דנקט זקפו במלוה — להודיעך כחו דרבי עקיבא, דאפי' זקפו במלוה לא מצי מחיל לנפשיה, כיון דליכא מחילה דאחריני.

אלא

רש"ל

עין משפט נר מצוה

קטו א ב מיי' פ"ה מהלכות נדרים הל' ו ועיין בכ"מ סמג לאוין רמב טוש"ע יו"ד סי' רכג סעיף ד:

קטז ג ד מיי' פ"ח מהל' גזילה ואבידה הלכה ג סמג עשין עג טוש"ע ח"מ סי' שסו סעיף ה:

קטח ה מיי' שם הלכה ד ה ועיין בהשגות ובמ"מ טוש"ע שם סעי' ו:

הגהות הב"ח

(א) רש"י ד"ה הא והא וכו' דמודי ר' יוסי דלנפשיה לא מצי: (ב) תום' ד"ה לוה וכו' דכיון דליכא קלא לא מפסידינן ללקוחות: (ג) ד"ה ב"ח וכו' בפ' השותפין האומר לאשתו קונם שאני נהנית לך:

גליון הש"ס

תום' ד"ה לוה וכו' אבל נתנו במתנה. עיין כתובות דף מט ע"ב תום' ד"ה הוא ועיין בתשובת הרשב"א סי' תרי"ח דחולק ע"ז: **בא"ד** הכי נמי לא משתעבדי מטלטלי. עיין יבמות לט ע"א תום' ד"ה כתב ובכתובות דף מט ע"ב תום' ד"ה הוא:

מכלל דרבי יוסי הגלילי סבר אפילו לנפשיה נמי מצי מחיל? אלא גזל הגר דקאמר רחמנא נתינה לכהנים היכי משכחת לה? אמר רבא: *הכא במאי עסקינן – אכשגזל את הגר ונשבע לו, ומת הגר, והודה לאחר מיתה, דבעידנא דאודי קנאו השם ונתנו לכהנים. בעי רבינא: גזל הגיורת, מהו? (במדבר ה) "איש" אמר רחמנא – ולא אשה, או דלמא אורחיה דקרא הוא? אמר ליה רב אהרן לרבינא: תא שמע, דתניא: "איש" – אין לי אלא איש, אשה מנין? כשהוא אומר: (שם) "המושב" – הרי כאן שנים, א"כ מה ת"ל "איש"? *באיש – אתה צריך לחזור אחריו אם יש לו גואלים אם לאו, קטן – אי אתה צריך לחזור אחריו, בידוע שאין לו גואלין. *תנו רבנן: (שם) "לה' לכהן" – *קנאו השם גונתנו לכהן שבאותו משמר. אתה אומר: לכהן שבאותו משמר, או אינו אלא לכל כהן שירצה? כשהוא אומר: (שם) "מלבד איל הכפורים אשר יכפר בו עליו", הרי לכהן שבאותו משמר הכתוב מדבר. ת"ר: הרי שהיה גוזל כהן, מנין שלא יאמר: הואיל ויוצא לכהנים, והרי הוא תחת ידי, יהא שלי? ודין הוא: אי בשל אחרים הוא זוכה, בשל עצמו לא כ"ש! רבי נתן אומר בלשון אחר: ומה דבר שאין לו חלק בו עד שיכנס ברשותו, כשיכנס לרשותו אינו יכול להוציאו מידו, דבר שיש לו חלק בו עד שלא יכנס ברשותו, משנכנס לרשותו אינו דין דאין אחר יכול להוציאו מידו? לא, אם אמרת בדבר שאין לו חלק בו, שכשם שאין לו חלק בו כך אין לאחרים חלק בו, תאמר בגזל – שכשם שיש לו חלק בו כך יש לאחרים חלק בו? דאלא גזילו יוצא מתחת ידו ומתחלק לכל אחיו הכהנים. והכתיב: (שם) "ואיש את קדשיו לו יהיו"! הכא במאי עסקינן – בכהן טמא. אי בכהן טמא, דבר שיש לו חלק בו? מי אית ליה?! אלא אתיא "לכהן" "לכהן" משדה אחוזה; דתניא: (ויקרא כז) *"אחוזתו" – מה ת"ל? מנין לשדה היוצאה לכהנים ביובל וגאלה אחד מן הכהנים, מנין שלא יאמר: הואיל ויוצאה לכהנים ביובל והרי היא תחת ידי, תהא שלי? ודין הוא, בשל אחרים אני זוכה, בשל עצמי לא כ"ש! ת"ל: (שם) "כשדה החרם לכהן תהיה אחוזתו", אחוזה שלו ואין זו שלו, הא כיצד? היוצאה מתחת ידו ומתחלקת לכל אחיו הכהנים.§ תנו רבנן: *מנין ולכהן שבא ומקריב קרבנותיו בכל עת ובכל שעה שירצה? תלמוד לומר: (דברים יח) "ובא בכל אות נפשו ושרת", זומניין שעבודתה ועורה שלו? תלמוד לומר: (במדבר ה) "ואיש את קדשיו לו יהיו", הא כיצד? חאם היה בעל מום – נותנה לכהן שבאותו משמר, ועבודתה ועורה שלו. ואם

מכלל דרבי יוסי הגלילי סבר מצי מחיל לנפשיה. אפי' לא זקפו? לרבה פרכינן. קנאו השם. הקב"ה, כדכתיב: "המושב לה' לכהן". קנאו השם ונתנו לכהנים. אבל הודה בחיי הגר – נעשה אצלו כמלוה, וכי מיית גר – מחיל לנפשיה. גזל הגיורת. שגזל אותה, ונשבע, והודה לאחר מיתה. מהו. מי נפיק לכהנים, או זכה בה איהו. איש אמר רחמנא. "אם אין לאיש גואל". הרי כאן שנים. תרי השבות כתיב, "להשיב" "המושב". לישנא אחרינא: תרי אשמות כתיבי, "להשיב האשם" "האשם המושב". צריכין לחזור אחריו. ולשאול אם יש לו בנים, קודם שתתנהו לכהן. קטן. שאין איש, בידוע שאין לו בנים, יתנהו לכהנים. ומהכא נפקא לן דקטן לאו בר אולודי הוא, בסנהדרין ב"בן סורר ומורה" (דף סט.). לכהן שבאותו משמר. שהוא בא להתכפר בו. כשהוא אומר מלבד איל הכפורים. משמע: למי שזה ניתן – זה ניתן, ואיל הכפורים אין יכול להקריב אלא כהן שבאותו משמר, כדכתיב (דברים יח): "לבד ממכריו על האבות" – אני בשבתי ואתה בשבתך. הרי שהיה כהן גוזל. את הגר, וכשהגיע משמר שלו בא והודה, לאחר מיתת הגר. בשל אחרים. אם היה ישראל מביא גזל הגר במשמר זה – הריני נוטל חלקי עם אחיי הכהנים בני המשמר. בשל עצמי לא כ"ש. שאטול את הכל. מה דבר שאין לו חלק בו. כגון כהן שהתנדב קרבן, דאמרינן לקמן בשמעתין: כהן בא ומקריב קרבנותיו בכל שעה שירצה, ובשרה ועורה שלו, דכתיב: "ואיש את קדשיו לו יהיו", נמצא שאין לבני משמר חלק בו. (א) משנכנס לרשותו אין אחר יכול כו'. שאם נתנה לכהן אחר של אותו משמר – שוב אין יכול להוציאו מידו, שנאמר: "ואיש אשר יתן לכהן לו יהיה". דבר שיש לו חלק בו עד שלא נכנס ברשותו. שכיון שבא ישראל והביא גזל הגר למשמר זה, אע"פ שנתנו לאחד מאחיו – יש לו חלק בו. ל"א: מה דבר (שלא נכנס ברשותו) – כגון תרומות ומעשרות. מפי עוקר הריס. כך אין לאחרים חלק בו. לפיכך משנתנו לך מי יעכב עליך. תאמר בגזל. הגר, שהוא לכל בני משמר, וכולם תובעין. והכתיב ואיש את קדשיו [וגו']. ונפקא לן לקמן מיניה שכהן מקריב קרבנותיו בכל עת שירצה, ובשרה ועורה שלו. והכא נמי, האי איל אשם – קרבנות דכהן הוא, וזכי ביה. וכיון דמקריב ליה וזכי ביה – גזל נמי דידיה הוא, כדאמרינן: "מלבד איל הכפורים" למי שזה ניתן זה ניתן. בכהן טמא. דאין ראוי להקריב איל האשם. אי [בכהן] טמא. היכי מצי למימר דבר שיש לו חלק בו? והא קיימא לן בזבחים (דף צח:) דאין טמא חולק בקדשי המקדש, ואפילו בעורות. (ב) וגזל הגר נמי קדשי המקדש הוא!

אלא. לעולם בכהן טהור, והאי דמוציאין מידו – משום דילפינן ג"ש "כהן" "כהן" משדה אחוזה, ו"איש את קדשיו" – במילי אחריני מתוקמא. אחוזתו. "לכהן תהיה" היה לו למימר, ודיו. ומה ת"ל "אחוזתו". לשדה היוצאה לכהנים. מקדיש שדה אחוזה, ולא גאלה מן ההקדש ומכרה גזבר לאחרים, כשהיא יוצאה מיד הלוקח ביובל – מתחלקת לכהנים, משמר שנכנס בו יובל. שנאמר: "ואם לא יגאל את השדה" – בעלים, "ואם מכר את השדה" – גזבר, "לא יגאל עוד" – בעלים, אלא "והיה השדה" וגו'. והכי תניא בת"כ ובערכין. וגאלה אחד מן הכהנים. כלומר: והלוקח מן הגזבר כהן היה, ומבני המשמר של יובל היה. שבא ומקריב. אם נדר קרבן או שהיה מוטל עליו חטאת ואשם חובה – מקריב אף במשמר שאינו שלו. שעבודתה. שכר עבודתה, דהיינו בשרה. אם היה בעל מום. ראוי לאכול, ואין ראוי להקריב – אין יכול לעשות שליח להקרבה מי שירצה, אלא נותנה לבני המשמר. והואיל והוא ראוי לאכילה – קרינן ביה "ואיש את קדשיו", לפיכך עבודה ועורה שלו. לשון אחר, גרסינן: עבודה ועורה לאנשי משמר, כיון דהם הקריבוהו. ואם

אלא גזל הגר דקאמר (ג) היכי משכחת לה. ה"ה דה"מ למפרך בתחילת סוגיא, כי קאמר: ר' יוסי הגלילי לא שנא לנפשיה ולא שנא לאחריני מצי מחיל. אלא משום דהוו ליה פירכי אחריני לא חש למפרך. קטן אי אתה צריך לחזור עליו. וא"ת: גזל גר קטן היכי משכחת לה? והא אין זכיה לקטן, כדאמרינן בפ"ק דב"מ (דף יב.) דגזל קטן מדבריהם, ולא מדאורייתא! וירושה ליכא למימר, דגר אין יורש אביו דבר תורה! *וי"ל: דדוקא מציאה, דאין דעת אחרת מקנה אותו – לא הוה אלא מדבריהם, אבל כשדעת אחרת מקנה אותו – קני מדאורייתא. ובקטן שנתגייר עם אביו מיירי, דלכ"ע מטבילין אותו, אבל בלא אביו – פלוגתא היא בפרק קמא דכתובות (דף יא.) אם מטבילים אותו על דעת בית דין. [ועי' תוס' סנהדרין סח: ד"ה קטן]

לכהן שבאותו משמר. אין נראה לפרש דבשעת הודאה כשמתחייב, אלא למשמר שהיה בשעת הבאה. שהרי בכל הקרבנות חטאות ואשמות נדרים ונדבות אין אנו הולכים אחר שעת החיוב, ליתנו לאותו משמר שהיה באותה שעה שנדר או נדב או חטא שהוא מתחייב בה, אלא אחר הבאה אנו הולכים – וכמו כן בכאן.

מנין שלא יאמר. תימה דנקיט האי לישנא, כיון דלא מקרא מייתי לה, אלא מדינא.

ומה דבר שאין לו חלק בו עד שיכנס לרשותו. כגון תרומה וחלה וראשית הגז, שטובת הנאה לבעלים ליתן לאיזה כהן שירצה, משנכנס לרשותו אין אחר יכול להוציא מידו שיתחלק לבני משמר, דאין מתחלק לאנשי משמר אלא מתנות.

לא אם אמרת בדבר שאין כו'. ללשון ראשון נמי, דקאמר: ודין הוא בשל אחרים אני זוכה, יכול להקשות: דיו לבא מן הדין להיות כנדון, שלא יזכה בשל עצמו אלא כפי חלקו, כמו בשל אחרים.

אחוזתו מה ת"ל. תימה להרשב"א: למ"ל "אחוזתו" לומר שיוצאה מתחת ידו ומתחלקת לכל אחיו הכהנים? דהיכי הוה אמינא בשל אחרים אני זוכה בשל עצמי לא כ"ש? הא הכא שייך נמי למפרך כמו לעיל: דיו לבא כו'! ויש לומר: דאיצטריך "אחוזתו" משום דה"א כיון שהיא תחת ידו – תהא שלו, דהוה ילפינן "כהן" "כהן" מגזל הגר, ובגזל הגר ה"א דהוי שלו, כדקאמר "ואיש את קדשיו לו יהיו", משום הכי איצטריך "אחוזתו".

מנין ליוצאה לכהנים כו'. ברייתא היא בערכין, בפרק "אין מקדישין" (דף כה:).

דבי

קסט א מיי' פ"ח מהל' גזילה ואבידה הל' ה ועי' בהשגות ובכ"מ:
קע ב מיי' שם הל' ז:
קעא ג מיי' שם הל' ה:
קעב ד מיי' שם הל' ט:
קעג ה מיי' פ"ד מהל' ערכין הלכה כג סמג עשין קלא:
[כלאי' בקדושין יז:]
קעד ו ז מיי' פ"ד מהלכות כלי המקדש הלכה ז וע"ש בהשגות ובכ"מ:
קעה ח מיי' שם הל' ח:

ס"א משתכחת לה כ
רש"א
[סנהד' סט.]
ערכין כח:
[מנחות מה:]
ס"א שאין לו חלק
ערכין כה:
[מנחות עג.]

הגהות הב"ח

(א) רש"י ד"ה משנכנס וכו'. נ"ב עיין בסמוך במשנה דף קי ע"א: (ב) ד"ה אי [בכהן] טמא וכו' וגזל הגר. נ"ב עיין לקמן סוף דף קי: (ג) תוס' ד"ה אלא גזל הגר דקאמר רחמנא נתינה לכהנים היכי משכחת:

וְאִם הָיָה זָקֵן אוֹ חוֹלֶה – נוֹתְנָהּ לְכָל כֹּהֵן שֶׁיִּרְצֶה, וַעֲבוֹדָתָהּ וְעוֹרָהּ לְאַנְשֵׁי מִשְׁמָר. הַאי זָקֵן אוֹ חוֹלֶה הֵיכִי דָּמֵי? אִי דְּמָצֵי עָבֵיד עֲבוֹדָה – עֲבוֹדָתָהּ וְעוֹרָהּ נַמִּי תֶּיהֱוֵי דִּידֵיהּ, וְאִי דְּלָא מָצֵי עָבֵיד עֲבוֹדָה – שָׁלִיחַ הֵיכִי מְשַׁוֵּי? אָמַר רַב פַּפָּא: [א]שֶׁיָּכוֹל לַעֲשׂוֹת עַל יְדֵי הַדְּחָק; עֲבוֹדָה, דְּכִי עָבֵיד לֵיהּ ע"י הַדְּחָק – עֲבוֹדָה הִיא וּמְשַׁוֵּי שָׁלִיחַ; אֲכִילָה, *דְּכִי אָכֵיל עַל יְדֵי הַדְּחָק אֲכִילָה גַּסָּה הִיא, [ב]וַאֲכִילָה גַּסָּה לָאו כְּלוּם הוּא – מִשּׁוּם הָכִי עֲבוֹדָתָהּ וְעוֹרָהּ לְאַנְשֵׁי מִשְׁמָר. אָמַר רַב שֵׁשֶׁת: [ג]אִם הָיָה כֹּהֵן טָמֵא, בְּקָרְבַּן צִבּוּר – נוֹתְנָהּ לְכָל מִי שֶׁיִּרְצֶה, וַעֲבוֹדָתָהּ וְעוֹרָהּ לְאַנְשֵׁי מִשְׁמָר. הֵיכִי דָּמֵי? אִי דְּאִיכָּא טְהוֹרִים, טְמֵאִים מִי מָצוּ עָבְדִי? וְאִי דְּלֵיכָּא טְהוֹרִים, עֲבוֹדָתָהּ וְעוֹרָהּ לְאַנְשֵׁי מִשְׁמָר? הָא טְמֵאִים נִינְהוּ וְלָא מָצוּ אָכְלִי! אָמַר רָבָא, [ד]אֵימָא: לְבַעֲלֵי מוּמִין טְהוֹרִין שֶׁבְּאוֹתוֹ מִשְׁמָר. אָמַר רַב אַשִׁי: [ה]אִם הָיָה כֹּהֵן גָּדוֹל אוֹנֵן – נוֹתְנָהּ לְכָל כֹּהֵן שֶׁיִּרְצֶה, וַעֲבוֹדָתָהּ וְעוֹרָהּ לְאַנְשֵׁי מִשְׁמָר. מַאי קמ"ל? תְּנֵינָא:* [ו]כֹּהֵן גָּדוֹל מַקְרִיב אוֹנֵן, [ז]וְאֵינוֹ אוֹכֵל, [ח]וְאֵינוֹ חוֹלֵק לֶאֱכוֹל לָעֶרֶב! ס"ד אָמִינָא, כִּי חַס רַחֲמָנָא עֲלֵיהּ דְּכֹהֵן גָּדוֹל – לְקָרוּבֵי הוּא, אֲבָל לְשַׁוּוּיֵי שָׁלִיחַ לָא מָצֵי מְשַׁוֵּי, קמ"ל. §

מתני' [ט]הַגּוֹזֵל אֶת הַגֵּר וְנִשְׁבַּע לוֹ וּמֵת – הֲרֵי זֶה מְשַׁלֵּם קֶרֶן וְחוֹמֶשׁ לַכֹּהֲנִים וְאָשָׁם לַמִּזְבֵּחַ, שֶׁנֶּאֱמַר: °"וְאִם אֵין לָאִישׁ גּוֹאֵל לְהָשִׁיב הָאָשָׁם אֵלָיו הָאָשָׁם הַמּוּשָׁב לַה' לַכֹּהֵן מִלְּבַד אֵיל הַכִּפּוּרִים אֲשֶׁר יְכַפֶּר בּוֹ עָלָיו". [י]הָיָה מַעֲלֶה אֶת הַכֶּסֶף וְאֶת הָאָשָׁם וּמֵת – הַכֶּסֶף יִנָּתֵן לְבָנָיו, וְהָאָשָׁם יִרְעֶה עַד שֶׁיִּסְתָּאֵב, וְיִמָּכֵר וְיִפְּלוּ דָּמָיו לִנְדָבָה. (א) [כ]נָתַן הַכֶּסֶף לְאַנְשֵׁי מִשְׁמָר וּמֵת – אֵין הַיּוֹרְשִׁין יְכוֹלִין לְהוֹצִיא מִיָּדָם, שֶׁנֶּאֱמַר: °"וְאִישׁ אֲשֶׁר יִתֵּן לַכֹּהֵן לוֹ יִהְיֶה". [ל]נָתַן הַכֶּסֶף לִיהוֹיָרִיב וְאָשָׁם לִידַעְיָה – יָצָא; [מ]אָשָׁם לִיהוֹיָרִיב וְכֶסֶף לִידַעְיָה, אִם קַיָּים הָאָשָׁם – יַקְרִיבוּהוּ בְּנֵי יְדַעְיָה, וְאִם לָאו – יַחֲזִיר וְיָבִיא אָשָׁם אַחֵר, שֶׁהַמֵּבִיא גְּזֵילוֹ עַד שֶׁלֹּא הֵבִיא אֲשָׁמוֹ – יָצָא, הֵבִיא אֲשָׁמוֹ עַד שֶׁלֹּא הֵבִיא גְּזֵילוֹ – לֹא יָצָא. [נ]נָתַן אֶת הַקֶּרֶן וְלֹא נָתַן אֶת הַחוֹמֶשׁ – אֵין הַחוֹמֶשׁ מְעַכֵּב. §

גמ' ת"ר: "אָשָׁם" – זֶה קֶרֶן, "הַמּוּשָׁב" – זֶה חוֹמֶשׁ. אוֹ אֵינוֹ, אֶלָּא "אָשָׁם" זֶה אַיִל? וּלְמַאי נָפְקָא מִינַּהּ – לְאַפּוּקֵי מִדְּרָבָא, דְּאָמַר רָבָא: [ס]גֶּזֶל הַגֵּר שֶׁהֶחֱזִירוֹ בַּלַּיְלָה – לֹא יָצָא, הֶחֱזִירוֹ חֲצָאִין – לֹא יָצָא, מ"ט? אָשָׁם קַרְיֵיהּ רַחֲמָנָא. כְּשֶׁהוּא אוֹמֵר: "מִלְּבַד אֵיל הַכִּפּוּרִים", הֱוֵי אוֹמֵר: "אָשָׁם" – זֶה קֶרֶן. תַּנְיָא אִידַּךְ: "אָשָׁם" – זֶה קֶרֶן, "הַמּוּשָׁב" – זֶה חוֹמֶשׁ. אוֹ אֵינוֹ, אֶלָּא "אָשָׁם" זֶה חוֹמֶשׁ? לְמַאי נָפְקָא מִינַּהּ – לְאַפּוּקֵי מִמַּתְנִיתִין, דִּתְנַן: נָתַן לוֹ אֶת הַקֶּרֶן וְלֹא נָתַן לוֹ אֶת הַחוֹמֶשׁ – אֵין הַחוֹמֶשׁ מְעַכֵּב; אַדְּרַבָּה, חוֹמֶשׁ מְעַכֵּב. כְּשֶׁהוּא אוֹמֵר: °"וְהֵשִׁיב אֶת אֲשָׁמוֹ בְּרֹאשׁוֹ וַחֲמִישִׁיתוֹ", הֱוֵי אוֹמֵר: "אָשָׁם" – זֶה קֶרֶן. תַּנְיָא אִידַּךְ: "אָשָׁם" – זֶה קֶרֶן, "הַמּוּשָׁב" – זֶה חוֹמֶשׁ, וּבְגֶזֶל הַגֵּר הַכָּתוּב מְדַבֵּר. אוֹ אֵינוֹ, אֶלָּא "הַמּוּשָׁב" זֶה כֶּפֶל, וּבִגְנֵיבַת הַגֵּר הַכָּתוּב מְדַבֵּר? כְּשֶׁהוּא אוֹמֵר: "וְהֵשִׁיב אֶת אֲשָׁמוֹ בְּרֹאשׁוֹ וַחֲמִישִׁיתוֹ", הֲרֵי בְּמָמוֹן הַמִּשְׁתַּלֵּם בְּרֹאשׁ הַכָּתוּב מְדַבֵּר. גּוּפָא, *אָמַר רָבָא: גֶּזֶל הַגֵּר שֶׁהֶחֱזִירוֹ בַּלַּיְלָה – לֹא יָצָא, הֶחֱזִירוּהוּ חֲצָאִין – לֹא יָצָא; מַאי טַעְמָא? אָשָׁם קַרְיֵיהּ רַחֲמָנָא. וְאָמַר רָבָא: [ע]גֶּזֶל הַגֵּר שֶׁאֵין בּוֹ שָׁוֶה פְּרוּטָה לְכָל כֹּהֵן וְכֹהֵן – לֹא יָצָא יְדֵי חוֹבָתוֹ; מ"ט? דִּכְתִיב: "הָאָשָׁם הַמּוּשָׁב", עַד שֶׁיְּהֵא הֲשָׁבָה לְכָל כֹּהֵן וְכֹהֵן. בָּעֵי רָבָא: אֵין בּוֹ לְמִשְׁמֶרֶת יְהוֹיָרִיב וְיֵשׁ בּוֹ לְמִשְׁמֶרֶת

רש"י

וְאִם הָיָה זָקֵן. וְרָאוּי לַעֲבוֹדָה, כִּדְמְפָרֵשׁ לְקַמָּן, וְאֵין רָאוּי לַאֲכִילָה. נוֹתְנָהּ. לְהַקְרִיב. לְכָל כֹּהֵן שֶׁיִּרְצֶה. דְּהוֹאִיל דְּהוּא חֲזֵי לַעֲבוֹדָה – מָצֵי לְשַׁוּוּיֵיהּ שָׁלִיחַ. וַעֲבוֹדָתָהּ וְעוֹרָהּ לְאַנְשֵׁי מִשְׁמָר. דְּכֵיוָן דְּלָא חֲזֵי לַאֲכִילָה – לָא מְשַׁוֵּי שָׁלִיחַ לַאֲכִילָה. אֲכִילָה גַּסָּה. שֶׁנַּפְשׁוֹ קָצָה בָּהּ. אִם הָיָה הַכֹּהֵן. שֶׁל הַמִּשְׁמָר טָמֵא, וְיֵשׁ לוֹ קָרְבָּן לִבּוּר לְהַקְרִיב. נוֹתְנוֹ לְכָל כֹּהֵן שֶׁיִּרְצֶה. דְּהוֹאִיל דְּהוּא יָכוֹל לְהַקְרִיבוֹ, דְּהָא קָרְבַּן לִבּוּר דּוֹחֶה אֶת הַטּוּמְאָה – שָׁלִיחַ נַמִּי מָצֵי עָבֵיד. קָרְבַּן לִבּוּר בָּא בְּטוּמְאָה וְאֵין נֶאֱכָל בְּטוּמְאָה, בְּ"כֵּיצַד צוֹלִין" (פסחים ד' עו:). אִי דְּאִיכָּא טְהוֹרִין. בְּהַהוּא מִשְׁמָר. טְמֵאִים מִי מָצוּ עָבְדִי. וְכֵיוָן דְּלָא מָצוּ עָבְדִי – שָׁלִיחַ הֵיכִי מְשַׁוֵּי. לְבַעֲלֵי מוּמִין טְהוֹרִין. מִתְחַלֶּקֶת, דְּקַיְימָא לָן, זְבָחִים (ד' לח:): אִישׁ חוֹלֵק, וַאֲפִי' בַּעַל מוּם, בְּקָדָשִׁים וּבִמְנָחוֹת. אִם הָיָה כֹּהֵן גָּדוֹל אוֹנֵן. וְיֵשׁ לוֹ קָרְבַּן עַצְמוֹ לְהַקְרִיב. נוֹתְנוֹ לְכָל כֹּהֵן שֶׁיִּרְצֶה. דְּכֵיוָן דְּכֹהֵן גָּדוֹל מַקְרִיב אוֹנֵן, (ב) דִּכְתִיב: "לְאָבִיו וּלְאִמּוֹ לֹא יִטַּמָּא וּמִן הַמִּקְדָּשׁ לֹא יֵצֵא" אִם מֵת אָבִיו וְאִמּוֹ דַּהֲוֵי אוֹנֵן, אֲפִילּוּ הָכִי – מִקְּדוּשָּׁתוֹ לֹא יֵצֵא, "וְלֹא יְחַלֵּל", כְּלוֹמַר: דַּעֲבוֹדָתוֹ שֶׁיַּעֲבוֹד בַּאֲנִינוּת לֹא תִּתְחַלֵּל. הָא אַחֵר, הֶדְיוֹט שֶׁלֹּא יָצָא – חִילֵּל. וְאֵינוֹ חוֹלֵק לֶאֱכוֹל לָעֶרֶב. כְּשֶׁמִּסְתַּלֵּק אֲנִינוּתוֹ. דַּאֲנִינוּת לַיְלָה דְּרַבָּנָן. דַּאֲנִינוּת דְּאוֹרַיְיתָא אֵינוֹ אֶלָּא יוֹם מִיתָה, דִּכְתִיב (עמוס ח): "וְאַחֲרִיתָהּ כְּיוֹם מָר", אַלְמָא: אֵין מְרִירוּת אֶלָּא יוֹם אֶחָד. **מתני'** הָיָה מַעֲלֶה אֶת הַכֶּסֶף וּמֵת. בַּדֶּרֶךְ. הַכֶּסֶף יִנָּתֵן לְבָנָיו. שֶׁל גַּזְלָן. דְּהָא זָכָה בֵּיהּ מִמִּיתַת הַגֵּר, אֶלָּא דְּבָעֵי לְמֶעֱבַד הֲשָׁבָה כִּי הֵיכִי דְּתֶיהֱוֵי לֵיהּ כַּפָּרָה אַשְּׁבוּעָתֵיהּ, וְהַשְׁתָּא תּוּ לֵיכָּא כַּפָּרָה, כֵּיוָן דְּמִית לֵיהּ. הָאָשָׁם יִרְעֶה. דַּהֲוֵי אָשָׁם שֶׁמֵּתוּ בְּעָלָיו, וְקיי"ל (ג) לְקַמָּן: כָּל שֶׁבְּחַטָּאת מֵתָה – בְּאָשָׁם רוֹעֶה. לִנְדָבָה. לְשׁוֹפְרוֹת קַיִץ הַמִּזְבֵּחַ, עוֹלוֹת – בָּשָׂר לַשֵּׁם, וְעוֹרוֹת לַכֹּהֲנִים. מִשְׁמֶרֶת יְהוֹיָרִיב. רִאשׁוֹנָה לְכָל הַמִּשְׁמָרוֹת, וְשֶׁל יְדַעְיָה אַחֲרֶיהָ. נָתַן. הַגַּזְלָן אֶת הַכֶּסֶף לִיהוֹיָרִיב בְּמִשְׁמַרְתּוֹ, וְאַחַ"כ נָתַן אָשָׁם לִידַעְיָה בְּמִשְׁמַרְתּוֹ. יָצָא. כִּדְמְפָרֵשׁ וְאָזֵיל, שֶׁהַמֵּבִיא גְּזֵילוֹ עַד שֶׁלֹּא הֵבִיא קָרְבַּן אֲשָׁמוֹ – יָצָא, וְזֶה זָכָה בְּשֶׁלּוֹ וְזֶה בְּשֶׁלּוֹ. אִם קַיָּים הָאָשָׁם יַקְרִיבוּהוּ בְּנֵי יְדַעְיָה. דְּקָנְסִינְהוּ לִיהוֹיָרִיב לְהַחֲזִיר הָאָשָׁם, דְּשֶׁלֹּא כַּדִּין עָבוּד בְּנֵי יְהוֹיָרִיב דְּקַבּוּל אָשָׁם מִקַּמֵּי כֶּסֶף. וְלִידַעְיָה לֵיכָּא לְמִקְנָס מִידֵּי, דִּבְמִשְׁמָר דִּידְהוּ קַבִּילֵי. וְר' יְהוּדָה דִּפְלִיג אַבָּרַיְיתָא בַּגְּמָרָא, בְּמַתְנִיתִין מוֹדֶה. נָתַן הַקֶּרֶן. לַכֹּהֲנִים, אֵין הַחוֹמֶשׁ מְעַכֵּב מִלְּהַקְרִיב אֶת הָאָשָׁם, אִם לֹא נָתַן עֲדַיִין וּלְבַסּוֹף *נָתַן. **גמ'** אוֹ אֵינוֹ אֶלָּא אָשָׁם זֶה אַיִל. אָשָׁם, וּ"מוּשָׁב" זֶה קֶרֶן. וּלְמַאי נ"מ. דְּהָא מִמָּה נַפְשָׁךְ תַּרְוַיְיהוּ קָאָמַר קְרָא! תֵּיפּוֹק לֵיהּ מִינָּהּ לְאַפּוּקֵי מִדְּרָבָא, דְּאָמַר דְּ"אָשָׁם" קַרְיֵיהּ רַחֲמָנָא לַקֶּרֶן, וּמָה אָשָׁם אֵינוֹ בָּא בַּלַּיְלָה, דִּכְתִיב (ויקרא ז): "בְּיוֹם צַוּוֹתוֹ" וְאֵינוֹ בָּא לַחֲצָאִין – אַף קֶרֶן כו'. כְּשֶׁהוּא אוֹמֵר מִלְּבַד אֵיל הַכִּפּוּרִים הֱוֵי אוֹמֵר אָשָׁם. דְּרֵישָׁא, קֶרֶן הוּא. אוֹ אֵינוֹ אֶלָּא אָשָׁם זֶה חוֹמֶשׁ. וּ"מוּשָׁב" זֶה קֶרֶן. וְנ"מ לְאַפּוּקֵי מִמַּתְנִיתִין, דִּתְנַן: אֵין הַחוֹמֶשׁ מְעַכֵּב. אֵימָא, אַדְּרַבָּה חוֹמֶשׁ מְעַכֵּב, דְּאָשָׁם קַרְיֵיהּ רַחֲמָנָא לְשׁוֹן קָרְבָּן, כְּשֶׁהוּא אוֹמֵר כו'. מִשְׁתַּלֵּם בְּרֹאשׁ. קֶרֶן לְבַדּוֹ, שֶׁהוּא רֹאשׁ. לְכָל כֹּהֵן וְכֹהֵן. שֶׁבַּמִּשְׁמָר, וּמוֹסִיף מִשֶּׁלּוֹ עוֹד לְהַשְׁלִים. אֵין בּוֹ. שָׁוֶה פְּרוּטָה לְכָל מִשְׁמַר יְהוֹיָרִיב, וְיֵשׁ בּוֹ שָׁוֶה פְּרוּטָה לְכָל מִשְׁמַר יְדַעְיָה, שֶׁהֵן מוּעָטִין, מַהוּ? אֵין

תוספות

דכי עביד ע"י הדחק עבודה היא. דלא מלינו בכהנים פסול בשנים, אלא דנתנו חכמים שיעור עד שירתת, ב"הכל שוחטין" (חולין ד' כד:). **אכילה** גסה לאו כלום היא. מפיק (ד) מדריש לקיש, דאמר ב"החולץ" (יבמות ד' מ. ושם*): האוכל אכילה גסה ביום הכפורים – פטור מ"לא *תענו". וא"ת: דבפרק "מי שאמר הריני נזיר ושמע" (נזיר דף כג. ושם) גבי הא דאמר רבה בר בר חנה אמר ר' יוחנן: מאי דכתיב (ה) "לדיקים ילכו בם ופושעים יכשלו בם" משל לשני בני אדם שצלו פסחיהם, אחד אכלו לשם מצוה ואחד אכלו לשם אכילה גסה, זה שאכלו לשם אכילה גסה – "ופושעים יכשלו בם". א"ל ריש לקיש: רשע קרית ליה? נהי דלא עבד מצוה מן המובחר, מצוה מיהא עביד. משמע דילא ידי חובה! וי"ל: דהתם לא קאמר דילא, אלא דלא מיקרי רשע. ועוד, דהתם לא מיירי באוכלו אכילה גסה ממש, אלא כלומר שאין אוכלו לשם פסח אלא כדי להיות שבע. תדע, דלא קאמר אכילה גסה אלא "לשם אכילה גסה". ועי"ל דשתי אכילות גסות הן*. **אי** דאיכא טהורין טמאין מי מצו עבדי. לרב ששת פריך, דשמעינן ליה לרב ששת דאמר בפ"ק דיומא (דף ו:) טומאה דחויה בלבור, ואי איכא טמאים וטהורין – לא מצו עבדי טמאים. ואיכא דפליג התם, ואמר דטומאה הותרה בלבור, ואפי' איכא טמאים וטהורים – מצו עבדי טמאים.

[א]**לבעלי** מומין טהורין. תימה: ועורה אמאי הויא לבעלי מומין? **תנינא** כ"ג מקריב אונן. תימה, אמאי לא פריך נמי לרב ששת: תנינא: טמא מותר בקרבן ליבור?

למאי נ"מ לאפוקי ממתניתין. תימה: אמאי לא קאמר לאפוקי מדרבא, כדקאמר לעיל? **או** אינו אלא המושב זה כפל. תימה: היכי ס"ל זה כפל? והלא אין מתחייב כאן אלא בהודאתו, א] דכתיב "והתודה", וכפל לא מחייב בהודאה!

עין משפט נר מצוה

קעו א מיי' פ"ד מהל' כלי המקדש הל' ח:

[ד"ה אכילה]

קעז ב מיי' פ"י מהל' מעשה קרבנות הלכה יא:

קעח ג ד מיי' פ"ד מהלכות כלי המקדש הלכה ט ועיין בהשגות ובכ"מ:

קעט ה מיי' שם הלכה י סמג עשין קעב:

קפ ו מיי' פ"ב מהלכות ביאת המקדש הלכה ו ופרק ד מהלכות כלי המקדש הלכה י:

קפא ז ח מיי' פ"ב מהל' ביאת המקדש הלכה ח:

קפב ט מיי' פ"ח מהל' גזילה הלכה ד ה:

קפג י מיי' שם הל' י:

קפד כ מיי' שם הלכה יא:

[ועי' תוספות פסחים קז: ד"ה דלמא ותוספות יבמות מ. ד"ה אכילה ותוס' נזיר כג. ד"ה פסח]

קפה ל מיי' שם הלכה יב:

קפו נ מיי' שם הלכה יג:

קפז ס מיי' שם ה"ז:

קפח ע מיי' שם ה"ז:

הגהות הב"ח

(א) במשנה נתן הכסף לאנשי משמר ומת. נ"ב פירוש מת קודם שהקריבו הקרבן: (ב) רש"י ד"ה נותנו לכל כהן שירלה דכיון דכ"ג מקריב אונן משוי נמי שליח הס"ד ואח"כ מ"ה ועבודתה ועורה לאנשי משמר דהוא אינו ראוי לחלוק הלכך שליח נמי לא מלי משוי הס"ד ואח"כ מ"ה מקריב אונן דכתיב: (ג) ד"ה האשם וכו' וקיימא לן. נ"ב עי' סוף דף זה: (ד) תוס' ד"ה אכילה וכו' מפיק לה ריש לקיש בהחולץ וקאמר האוכל: (ה) בא"ד מאי דכתיב כי ישרים דרכי ה' לדיקים ילכו:

גליון הש"ס

גמ' אמר רבא. כעין זה בב"מ דף קט ע"ב גופא א"ר מניומי וכו' ובשיטה מקובלת שם כתב בשם הרא"ש אע"פ שלא חידש דבר קאמר גופא משום דבעי מימר אחריתי ודכוותה בפרק הגוזל וכו':

הגהות מהר"ב רנשבורג

א] תוס' ד"ה או אינו וכו' דכתיב והתודה וכפל לא מחייב. עיין שיטה מקובלת ודו"ק:

מסורת הש"ס

[לעיל יט: שבת עו.]

ס לט. [יומא יג: מ"ק הוריות יב: תוס' דזבחים פי"א]

במדבר ה

שם

שם

[נ"ל נתן ועי' רש"י]

הגהות הגר"א

תוס' ד"ה לבעלי וכו' בס"ד מוסגר בכ"ח למחקו (ועיין בת"ח ולא כהפ"ע):

קפט א מיי' פ"י מהלכות מעשה קרבנות הלכה טו טז:
קצ ב מיי' פ"ח מהל' גזילה הלכה ו סמג עשין עג:
קצא ג מיי' שם הל' ח:
קצב ד מיי' פ"ו מהל' בכורות הלכה יג סמג עשין ריב:
קצג ה ו מיי' שם הלכה ו:
קצד ז מיי' פ"א מהל' ביכורים הל' א:
קצה ח מיי' שם הלכה יב:
קצו ט מיי' שם הלכה יג:
קצז י מיי' שם הלכה יד:
קצח כ מיי' שם הלכה טו:
קצט ל מיי' פ"ח מהלכות גזילה הלכה ח ופ"ו מהלכות בכורות הלכה יג:
ר מ מיי' פ"ד מהלכות פסולי המוקדשין הלכה ח:
רא נ מיי' שם הלכה יד:

לְמִשְׁמֶרֶת יְדַעְיָה מַהוּ? הֵיכִי דָּמֵי? אִילֵימָא דִּיהַבֵיהּ לִידַעְיָה בְּמִשְׁמֶרֶת יְדַעְיָה, הָא *אִית בֵּיהּ! לָא צְרִיכָא, דִּיהַבֵיהּ לִידַעְיָה בְּמִשְׁמַרְתּוֹ דִּיהוֹיָרִיב, מַאי? מִי אָמְרִינַן: כֵּיוָן דְּלָאו מִשְׁמַרְתּוֹ הוּא — וְלָא כְּלוּם הוּא, אוֹ דִּלְמָא כֵּיוָן דְּלָא חָזֵי לֵיהּ, מֵעִיקָּרָא לִידַעְיָה קָאֵי? תֵּיקוּ. בָּעֵי רָבָא: כֹּהֲנִים, מַהוּ שֶׁיַּחְלְקוּ גֶּזֶל הַגֵּר כְּנֶגֶד גֶּזֶל הַגֵּר? מִי אָמְרִינַן: אָשָׁם קָרְיֵיהּ רַחֲמָנָא, מָה אָשָׁם [א]אֵין חוֹלְקִין אָשָׁם כְּנֶגֶד אָשָׁם, אַף גֶּזֶל (א) אֵין חוֹלְקִין גֶּזֶל הַגֵּר כְּנֶגֶד גֶּזֶל הַגֵּר. אוֹ דִּלְמָא גֶּזֶל הַגֵּר מָמוֹנָא הוּא? הֲדַר פְּשָׁטָהּ: אָשָׁם קָרְיֵיהּ רַחֲמָנָא. רַב אַחָא בְּרֵיהּ דְּרָבָא מַתְנֵי לָהּ בְּהֶדְיָא, אָמַר רָבָא: [ב]כֹּהֲנִים אֵין חוֹלְקִין גֶּזֶל הַגֵּר כְּנֶגֶד גֶּזֶל הַגֵּר, מ"ט? אָשָׁם קָרְיֵיהּ רַחֲמָנָא.§ בָּעֵי רָבָא: כֹּהֲנִים בְּגֶזֶל הַגֵּר, יוֹרְשִׁין הָווּ אוֹ מְקַבְּלֵי מַתָּנוֹת הָווּ? לְמַאי נָפְקָא מִינַּהּ — כְּגוֹן [א] שֶׁגָּזַל חָמֵץ (ב) שֶׁעָבַר עָלָיו הַפֶּסַח; אִי אָמְרַתְּ יוֹרְשִׁין הָווּ — הַיְינוּ הַאי דִּירָתֵי מוֹרִית, וְאִי אָמְרַתְּ מְקַבְּלֵי מַתָּנוֹת הָווּ — מַתָּנָה קָאָמַר רַחֲמָנָא דְּנֵיתִיב לְהוּ, וְהָא לָא קָא יָהֵיב לְהוּ מִידֵּי, דְּעַפְרָא בְּעָלְמָא הוּא. רַב זְעִירָא בָּעֵי הָכִי: אֲפִילּוּ אִם תִּימְצֵי לוֹמַר [ג]מְקַבְּלֵי מַתָּנָה הָווּ, הָא לָא אִיבַּעְיָא לָן דְּהַהִיא מַתָּנָה אָמַר רַחֲמָנָא דְּנֵיתִיב לְהוּ, אֶלָּא כִּי קָמִבַּעְיָא לָן — כְּגוֹן שֶׁנָּפְלוּ לוֹ עֶשֶׂר בְּהֵמוֹת בְּגֶזֶל הַגֵּר, מְחַיְּיבִי לְאַפְרוֹשֵׁי מִינַּיְיהוּ מַעֲשֵׂר אוֹ [ד]לָא? יוֹרְשִׁין הָווּ, (ג) דְּאָמַר מָר: [ה]קָנוּ בִּתְפִיסַת הַבַּיִת — חַיָּיבִין, אוֹ דִּלְמָא מְקַבְּלֵי מַתָּנוֹת הָווּ, וּתְנַן: *[ו]הַלּוֹקֵחַ וְהַנִּיתָּן לוֹ בְּמַתָּנָה — פָּטוּר מִמַּעֲשַׂר בְּהֵמָה, מַאי? ת"ש: *[ז]עֶשְׂרִים וְאַרְבַּע מַתָּנוֹת כְּהוּנָּה נִיתְּנוּ לְאַהֲרֹן וּלְבָנָיו, וְכוּלָּן נִיתְּנוּ בִּכְלָל וּפְרָט וּכְלָל וּבְרִית מֶלַח, כָּל הַמְקַיְּימָן — כְּאִילּוּ מְקַיֵּים כְּלָל וּפְרָט וּכְלָל וּבְרִית מֶלַח, כָּל הָעוֹבֵר עֲלֵיהֶם — כְּאִילּוּ עוֹבֵר עַל כְּלָל וּפְרָט וּכְלָל וּבְרִית מֶלַח; [ח]וְאֵלּוּ הֵן: עֶשֶׂר בַּמִּקְדָּשׁ, וְד' בִּירוּשָׁלַיִם, וְעֶשֶׂר בַּגְּבוּלִים; [ט]עֶשֶׂר בַּמִּקְדָּשׁ: חַטַּאת בְּהֵמָה, וְחַטַּאת הָעוֹף, וְאָשָׁם וַדַּאי, וְאָשָׁם תָּלוּי, וְזִבְחֵי שַׁלְמֵי צִבּוּר, וְלוֹג שֶׁמֶן שֶׁל מְצוֹרָע, וּמוֹתַר הָעוֹמֶר, וּשְׁתֵּי הַלֶּחֶם, וְלֶחֶם הַפָּנִים, וּשְׁיָרֵי מְנָחוֹת. [י]וְאַרְבַּע בִּירוּשָׁלַיִם: הַבְּכוֹרָה, וְהַבִּיכּוּרִים, וְהַמּוּרָם מִן הַתּוֹדָה וְאֵיל נָזִיר, וְעוֹרוֹת קָדָשִׁים. [כ]וַעֲשָׂרָה בַּגְּבוּלִין: תְּרוּמָה, וּתְרוּמַת מַעֲשֵׂר, וְחַלָּה, וְרֵאשִׁית הַגֵּז, וְהַמַּתָּנוֹת, וּפִדְיוֹן הַבֵּן, וּפִדְיוֹן פֶּטֶר חֲמוֹר, וּשְׂדֵה אֲחוּזָּה, וּשְׂדֵה חֲרָמִים, וְגֶזֶל הַגֵּר. וְקָא קָרֵי מִיהַת מַתָּנָה, ש"מ: [ל]מְקַבְּלֵי מַתָּנוֹת הָווּ, ש"מ.§ "נָתַן אֶת הַכֶּסֶף לְאַנְשֵׁי מִשְׁמָר" [וכו']§ אָמַר אַבַּיֵי, ש"מ: כֶּסֶף מְכַפֵּר מֶחֱצָה. דְּאִי לָא מְכַפֵּר, הֲוָה אָמִינָא מַהְדַר לְיוֹרְשִׁין, מ"ט? אַדַּעְתָּא דְּהָכִי לָא יָהַב לֵיהּ. אֶלָּא מֵעַתָּה, חַטָּאת שֶׁמֵּתוּ בְּעָלֶיהָ תֵּיפּוֹק לְחוּלִּין, דְּאַדַּעְתָּא דְּהָכִי לָא אַפְרְשָׁהּ! אָמְרִי: חַטָּאת שֶׁמֵּתוּ בְּעָלֶיהָ, [מ]הִלְכְתָא גְּמִירִי לָהּ דִּלְמִיתָה אָזְלָא. אֶלָּא מֵעַתָּה, אָשָׁם שֶׁמֵּתוּ בְּעָלָיו לִיפּוֹק לְחוּלִּין, דְּאַדַּעְתָּא דְּהָכִי לָא אַפְרְשֵׁיהּ! אָשָׁם נַמִי *הִלְכְתָא גְּמִירִי לָהּ: [נ]כָּל שֶׁבְּחַטָּאת מֵתָה — בְּאָשָׁם רוֹעֶה. אֶלָּא מֵעַתָּה, יְבָמָה שֶׁנָּפְלָה לִפְנֵי מוּכֵּה שְׁחִין תֵּיפּוֹק בְּלָא חֲלִיצָה, דְּאַדַּעְתָּא דְּהָכִי לָא קִדְּשָׁה עַצְמָהּ! הָתָם אֲנַן סָהֲדֵי

דְּמֵינַח

תוספות

או דלמא כיון דלא חזי ליהוריב לידעיה קאי. ויכול להביא אשם מיד, וליתבה לפני יהויריב להתכפר, אע"פ שהכסף נתון לידעיה, כדקתני בפירקין: נתן את הכסף ליהויריב והאשם לידעיה — יצא.

למאי נ"מ לגזל חמץ ועבר עליו הפסח. תימה: אמאי לא פשיט ליה מדידיה, דאמר לעיל: גזל הגר שאין בו שוה פרוטה לכל אחד ואחד — לא יצא. אלמא, מקבלי מתנות הוו, א] דאי יורשין הוו — אמאי לא יצא? מאי דשבק להון אבוהון יהב להון! ונראה דבחד מנהון גרסינן "רבה".

בכלל ופרט וכלל וברית מלח. הך שמעתא מפורש בפרק "הזרוע" (חולין דף קלג:).

וגזל הגר. תימה: אמאי חשיב גזל הגר מעשרה בגבולין? דכי היכי דאמר רבא החזירו בלילה ולחצאין לא יצא, דאשם קרייה רחמנא — ה"נ אם החזירו בגבולין לא יצא, כדין אשם!

כסף מכפר מחצה. מכאן נראה דכהן אין יכול למחול, כיון דהוי כפרה.

דאדעתא דהכי לא קדשה נפשה. נראה דבנפלה מן האירוסין איירי, דאי מן הנישואין — ודאי מקדשה נפשה כדי שתהא נשואה לבעלה, דמשום אחר מיתת בעלה לא מסקא אנפשה מלהיות נשואה. אלא מן האירוסין איירי, דמקדושין אין לה שום טובה. וא"ת: אדם שקנה מחבירו שום דבר ונתקלקל — יבטל המקח, דאדעתא דהכי לא קנה! וי"ל: דהתם לאו בלוקח לחודיה תליא מילתא, אלא כמו כן בדעת מוכר, ומוכר אקנה ליה אדעתא דהכי. אבל הכא, דקדושין בדידה קיימא, והוא אינו חושש היאך דעתה להתקדש. וכן גבי מקדיש נמי — בדידיה קאי, וכן נותן הגזל — בדידיה קאי. [ועי' בתוספות כתובות מז: ד"ה שלא]

רש"י

אין חולקים מנחות כנגד מנחות וקרבן כנגד קרבן. מ"לכל בני אהרן תהיה איש כאחיו" נפקא לן, בקידושין (דף נג.) ובמנחות פרק "אלו מנחות" (דף עג.). יורשין. הגר הן, או מקבלי מתנות גבוה הן? היינו האי דירתי. ירושה זאת נפלה להן, והרי היא לפניהן. שאילו היה הגר קיים — היה זה אומר לו: הרי שלך לפניך. רב זעירי בעי לה הכי אפילו אם תמצי לומר מקבלי מתנות הוו הא לא מבעיא לן דהא מתנה יהיב להו רחמנא. והרי הן לפניהן. כגון שנפלו לו. לכהן. קנו. יתומים שקנו בהמות. בתפיסת הבית. כלומר: נפלו להן בהמות בירושה עד שלא חלקו. הלוקח. לקח עשרה טלאים שלא נתעשרו מן השוק. פטור. ובמסכת בכורות* מפרש טעמא. בכלל ופרט וכלל. "לכל קדשי בני ישראל לך *נתונים למשחה" — כלל, "וזה יהיה לך מקדש הקדשים מן האש" — פרט, כל מתנה בפני עצמה, "וכל תרומת קדשים" חזר וכלל, והדר כתיב "ברית מלח עולם הוא" וגו', בסוף הפרשה (במדבר יח). כל המקיימן כאילו קיים. כל התורה כולה, שניתנה לדרוש בכלל ופרט וכלל, וכאילו קיים כל הקרבנות, שניתנה בהן ברית מלח. עשר במקדש. נאכל לפנים מן הקלעים. ארבע בירושלים. בכל העיר. ועשר בגבולים. בערי ארץ ישראל. אשם ודאי. חמשה הן: גזילות, מעילות, שפחה חרופה, נזיר ומצורע, וחד חשיב להו. אשם תלוי. בא על ספק כרת, שלא נודע לו שעבר ודאי שיביא חטאת. וזבחי שלמי צבור. כבשי עצרת, שנקראו שלמים, כדכתיב (ויקרא כג): "ושני כבשים בני שנה". (ד) וקדשי קדשים הן, כדכתיב (שם): "קדש יהיו לה' לכהן", ונאכלים לפנים מן הקלעים. ולוג שמן של מצורע. מה שנשאר בלוג מליקה לכף כהן של השמאלית נאכל לכהנים, דתניא במנחות (דף עג.) ובזבחים (דף מד:): "לכל קרבנם" — לרבות לוג שמן של מצורע, דהוא נמי קרוי קרבן, דכתיב: "והקריב אותו לאשם ואת לוג השמן" וסמיך ליה לקרא קמא "בקדש הקדשים תאכלנו", בפ' "ויקח קרח". מותר העומר. מנחת העומר נקמצת ושייריה נאכלים, (ה) וכל המנחות קדשי הקדשים הן, כדכתיב: "לא (*תאכל עליו חמץ)" וגו'. ושירי מנחות. כל מנחות הנקמצות: מנחת נדבה, ומנחת חוטא, ומנחת סוטה. הבכורה. בכור תם נאכל בכל העיר, וכן הבכורים צריכין חומה, כדכתיב (דברים יב): "ואכלתם שם לפני ה' אלהיכם" וגו', ואמר מר: "תרומת ידך" — אלו בכורים, במכות (דף יז.). והמורם מתודה. חזה, ושוק, וארבע חלות מארבע מינים שבה: חלות, ורקיקין, חמץ, ורבוכה. וכתיב (ויקרא ז): "והקריב ממנו אחד מכל קרבן תרומה לכהן הזורק" וגו'. והמורם מאיל נזיר. זרוע בשלה, וחלה ורקיק. וחזה ושוק של שלמים בכלל תודה הוא, דתודה שלמים אקרי, והנך תרתי, תודה ואיל נזיר, משום דדמיין להדדי — חשיב להו בחדא, כדאמר בשחיטת חולין בפרק "הזרוע"*. ועורות קדשים. עורות עולה וחטאות ואשמות. אבל קדשים קלים עורותיהן לבעלים, כדאמר בזבחים פרק "טבול יום" (דף קג.). ומש"ה קא חשיב להו בהדי הנך דבירושלים — למעוטי דאין נחשבים בהדי הנך דגבולים, דהני עורות לא מתייהבי להו אלא בירושלים. ובהדי הנך דבמקדש לא חשיב אלא הנהו דאי נפקי חוץ לקלעים מפסלי ביוצא. ושדה אחוזה. שהקדישה בעליה ולא גאלה, ומכרה גזבר, כשהלוקח מחזירה ביובל — מתחלקת לכהנים. ושדה חרמים. ישראל שהחרימו שדיהן. וגזל הגר. נמי קרי ליה מתנת גבולין, שאם נתנו לכהן המשמר חוץ לירושלים — יצא. ואיל אשמו יעלה לירושלים להקריב. אדעתא דהכי. דלא תיהוי ליה כפרה. תיפוק לחולין. ולא תיזל למיתה. באשם רועה. עד שיומם, וימכר ויפלו דמיו לקיץ המזבח, עולה (ו) לשם ועורה לכהנים. זה מדרש דרש יהוידע הכהן, בשקלים (דף ט:) ובתמורה (דף כג:). וכל זמן שהוא תם — אין יוצא לחולין לימכר, לפיכך ירעה, והוא מעצמו אין יכול להשתנות מאשם לעולה.

דמינח

נ"א זכו

[דף נה:]

[נ"ל נתתים]

בכורות נה: [ודף יא.]

חולין קלג: [תוספתא ע"ב]

ס"א תאפה חמץ וגו'. רש"א

[נזיר כה: תמורה... בכורות יז.]

[דף קלג:]

הגהות הב"ח

(א) גמ' אף גזל הגר אין חולקין: (ב) שם שגזל חמץ ועבר עליו הפסח וכו' האי דירתי דקא מורית להון אבוהון ואי אמרת מקבלי: (ג) שם יורשין הוו ואמר מר: (ד) רש"י ד"ה וזבחי וכו' בני שנה לזבח שלמים וקדשי: (ה) ד"ה מותר העומר. נ"ב אבל מותר עומר דחשיב פ"א דחלה משנה ג דנפלה ונאכל לכל אדם היינו המותר מהשני סאין שלוקח ומוציא ממנו עשירית איפה כדאיתא במנחות פרק ר' ישמעאל במשנה: (ו) ד"ה באשם רועה וכו' עולה בשר לאשם ועורה:

הגהות הגר"א

[א] גמ' שגזל חמץ ועבר. כצ"ל:

הגהות מהר"ב רנשבורג

א] תוס' ד"ה למאי נ"מ וכו' דאי יורשין הוו אמאי לא יצא. עיין מהרש"א ושיטה מקובצת ודו"ק:

תורה אור

דְּמֵינַח נִיחָא לָהּ בְּכָל דְּהוּ, (א) כְּרֵישׁ לָקִישׁ: *דְּאָמַר ר"ל: טַב לְמֵיתַב טַן דּוּ מִלְּמֵיתַב אַרְמְלוּ.§ "נָתַן אֶת הַכֶּסֶף לִיהוֹיָרִיב" וכו'.§ תָּנוּ רַבָּנַן: נָתַן אָשָׁם לִיהוֹיָרִיב וְכֶסֶף לִידַעְיָה — [א]יַחֲזִיר כֶּסֶף אֵצֶל אָשָׁם, דִּבְרֵי רַבִּי יְהוּדָה, וַחֲכָמִים אוֹמְרִים: יַחֲזִיר אָשָׁם אֵצֶל כֶּסֶף. הֵיכִי דָּמֵי? אִילֵימָא דְּיָהֵיב לֵיהּ אָשָׁם לִיהוֹיָרִיב בְּמִשְׁמַרְתּוֹ דִּיהוֹיָרִיב, וְכֶסֶף לִידַעְיָה בְּמִשְׁמַרְתּוֹ דִּידַעְיָה, זֶה זָכָה בְּשֶׁלּוֹ וְזֶה זָכָה בְּשֶׁלּוֹ! אָמַר רָבָא: [ב]הָכָא בְּמַאי עָסְקִינַן — דְּיָהֵיב אָשָׁם לִיהוֹיָרִיב בְּמִשְׁמַרְתּוֹ דִּיהוֹיָרִיב, וְכֶסֶף לִידַעְיָה בְּמִשְׁמַרְתּוֹ דִּיהוֹיָרִיב; ר' יְהוּדָה סָבַר: כֵּיוָן דְּלָאו מִשְׁמֶרֶת דִּידַעְיָה הִיא — לִידַעְיָה קָנְסִינַן לֵיהּ, הִלְכָּךְ יַחֲזִיר כֶּסֶף אֵצֶל אָשָׁם; וְרַבָּנַן סָבְרִי: שֶׁלֹּא כַּדִּין הוּא עֲבוּד בְּנֵי יְהוֹיָרִיב דְּקִיבְּלוּ אָשָׁם מִקַּמֵּי כֶּסֶף, הִלְכָּךְ לְדִידְהוּ קָנְסִינַן לְהוּ, וְיַחֲזוֹר אָשָׁם אֵצֶל כֶּסֶף. תַּנְיָא, אָמַר רַבִּי: לְדִבְרֵי רַבִּי יְהוּדָה, אִם קָדְמוּ בְּנֵי יְהוֹיָרִיב וְהִקְרִיבוּ אֶת הָאָשָׁם — יַחֲזוֹר וְיָבִיא אָשָׁם אַחֵר, וְיַקְרִיבוּהוּ בְּנֵי יְדַעְיָה, וְזָכוּ הַלָּלוּ בְּמַה שֶּׁבְּיָדָן. אָמְרִי: לְמַאי חָזֵי? אָשָׁם פָּסוּל הוּא! אָמַר רָבָא: לְעוֹרוֹ. תַּנְיָא, אָמַר רַבִּי: לְדִבְרֵי רַבִּי יְהוּדָה, אִם קַיָּים אָשָׁם — יַחֲזִיר אָשָׁם אֵצֶל כֶּסֶף. וְהָא רַבִּי יְהוּדָה, יַחֲזִיר כֶּסֶף אֵצֶל אָשָׁם אִית לֵיהּ! הָכָא בְּמַאי עָסְקִינַן — כְּגוֹן דְּנָפַק מִשְׁמַרְתּוֹ דִּיהוֹיָרִיב וְלֹא תָבְעוּ, וְהָא קמ"ל, דְּאַחוּלֵי אַחִילוּ גַּבַּיְיהוּ. תַּנְיָא אִידָךְ, אָמַר רַבִּי: לְדִבְרֵי רַבִּי יְהוּדָה, אִם קַיָּים אָשָׁם — יַחֲזוֹר כֶּסֶף אֵצֶל אָשָׁם. פְּשִׁיטָא, הָכִי אִית לֵיהּ! הָכָא בְּמַאי עָסְקִינַן — כְּגוֹן דְּנָפֵיק מִשְׁמַרְתָּם דְּהָנֵי וּדְהָנֵי וְלֹא תָבְעוּ, מַהוּ דְּתֵימָא אַחוּלֵי גַּבֵּי הֲדָדֵי, קמ"ל דְּאָמְרִינַן: כֵּיוָן דְּלָא תָּבְעֵי לַהֲדָדֵי בְּרֵישָׁא.§ "שֶׁהַמֵּבִיא גְּזֵילוֹ עַד שֶׁלֹּא הֵבִיא אֲשָׁמוֹ" [וכו']. מְנָהָנֵי מִילֵּי? אָמַר רָבָא, דְּאָמַר קְרָא: °"הָאָשָׁם הַמּוּשָׁב לַה' לַכֹּהֵן מִלְּבַד אֵיל הַכִּפּוּרִים אֲשֶׁר יְכַפֵּר בּוֹ", מִכְּלָל דְּכֶסֶף בְּרֵישָׁא. אֲמַר הַהוּא מֵרַבָּנַן לְרָבָא: אֶלָּא מֵעַתָּה, °"מִלְּבַד עוֹלַת הַבֹּקֶר" הָכִי נַמִּי מִכְּלָל דְּמוּסָפִין בְּרֵישָׁא? וְהָתַנְיָא: *[ג]מִנַּיִן שֶׁלֹּא יְהֵא דָּבָר קוֹדֵם לְתָמִיד שֶׁל שַׁחַר? תַּלְמוּד לוֹמַר: °"וְעָרַךְ עָלֶיהָ הָעוֹלָה", וְאָמַר רָבָא: "הָעוֹלָה" — עוֹלָה רִאשׁוֹנָה! אָמַר לֵיהּ: אֲנָא °מֵ"אֲשֶׁר יְכַפֶּר בּוֹ" נָפְקָא לִיהּ, וַעֲדַיִין לֹא כִּיפֵּר.§ "נָתַן לוֹ אֶת הַקֶּרֶן" וכו'.§ ת"ר: מִנַּיִן שֶׁאִם הֵבִיא מְעִילָתוֹ וְלֹא הֵבִיא אֲשָׁמוֹ, אֲשָׁמוֹ וְלֹא הֵבִיא מְעִילָתוֹ, שֶׁלֹּא יָצָא? תַּלְמוּד לוֹמַר: °"בְּאֵיל הָאָשָׁם וְנִסְלַח לוֹ". וּמִנַּיִן שֶׁאִם הֵבִיא אֲשָׁמוֹ עַד שֶׁלֹּא הֵבִיא מְעִילָתוֹ, שֶׁלֹּא יָצָא? תַּלְמוּד לוֹמַר: "בְּאֵיל הָאָשָׁם", הָאָשָׁם בִּכְבָר. יָכוֹל כְּשֵׁם שֶׁאַיִל וְאָשָׁם מְעַכְּבִים, כָּךְ חוֹמֶשׁ מְעַכֵּב? תַּלְמוּד לוֹמַר: "בְּאֵיל הָאָשָׁם וְנִסְלַח לוֹ", [ד]אַיִל וְאָשָׁם מְעַכְּבִים בְּהֶקְדֵּשׁ, [ה]וְאֵין חוֹמֶשׁ מְעַכֵּב. וְיִלָּמֵד הֶקְדֵּשׁ מֵהֶדְיוֹט וְהֶדְיוֹט מֵהֶקְדֵּשׁ; הֶקְדֵּשׁ מֵהֶדְיוֹט — מַה "אָשָׁם" דְּהָתָם קֶרֶן, אַף "אָשָׁם" דְּהָכָא קֶרֶן, וְהֶדְיוֹט מֵהֶקְדֵּשׁ — מַה הֶקְדֵּשׁ אֵין חוֹמֶשׁ מְעַכֵּב, אַף הֶדְיוֹט נַמִּי אֵין חוֹמֶשׁ מְעַכֵּב.§

הדרן עלך הגוזל עצים

רש"י

דְּמֵינַח נִיחָא לָהּ. לְהִתְקַדֵּשׁ לָרִאשׁוֹן שֶׁהוּא שָׁלֵם, עַל סָפֵק זֶה שֶׁאִם יָמוּת תִּזָּקֵק לְאָחִיו. **טַן דּוּ.** גּוּף שְׁנַיִם, כְּלוֹמַר: אִשָּׁה בְּכָל דְּהוּ נִיחָא לָהּ. **זֶה זָכָה בְּשֶׁלּוֹ וְזֶה זָכָה בְּשֶׁלּוֹ.** וּמַאי טַעְמָא לְרַבָּנַן דְּקָנְסוּ לִיהוֹיָרִיב דְּקִבְּלוּ אָשָׁם מִקַּמֵּי כֶּסֶף, אֶלָּא לְרַבִּי יְהוּדָה מ"ט דְּקָנֵיס לִידַעְיָה? לְדִבְרֵי רַבִּי יְהוּדָה. וְאע"ג דְּקָנֵיס לֵיהּ לִידַעְיָה, ה"מ הֵיכָא דְּאָשָׁם רִאשׁוֹן קַיָּים, דִּיכוֹלִין בְּנֵי יְהוֹיָרִיב לְהַקְרִיבוֹ בְּעוֹד מִשְׁמַרְתָּן קַיֶּימֶת וּבְהֶכְשֵׁר. אֲבָל אִם קָדְמוּ וְהִקְרִיבוּהוּ בְּפָסוּל, דְּאָשָׁם הַבָּא קוֹדֶם הַקֶּרֶן פָּסוּל הוּא, כִּדְמְפוֹרָשׁ לְקַמָּן — יִתֵּן אָשָׁם הַשֵּׁנִי לִידַעְיָה. **לְמַאי חָזֵי.** דְּקָתָנֵי זָכוּ. **כְּגוֹן דְּנָפַק מִשְׁמַרְתָּם.** דְּהָנֵי וּדְהָנֵי, וְלֹא תָּבְעוּ בְּנֵי יְהוֹיָרִיב אֶת הַכֶּסֶף בְּמִשְׁמַרְתָּם, וְלֹא בְּנֵי יְדַעְיָה אֶת הָאָשָׁם בְּמִשְׁמַרְתָּם. וְאִיצְטְרִיךְ לְאַשְׁמוּעִינַן, דְּלָא תֵּימָא: טַעְמָא דְּרַבִּי יְהוּדָה — בִּדְתָבְעוּ בְּנֵי יְהוֹיָרִיב, שֶׁיַּחֲזוֹר בְּעוֹד מִשְׁמַרְתָּן קַיֶּימֶת, אֲבָל הֵיכָא דְּלֹא תָּבְעוּ — מָחֲלוּ לִבְנֵי יְדַעְיָה. קמ"ל. דְּכֵיוָן דִּבְנֵי יְדַעְיָה נַמִּי לֹא תָּבְעוּ לְאָשָׁם בְּמִשְׁמַרְתָּן — יַחֲזוֹר כֶּסֶף אֵצֶל אָשָׁם, וְיַקְרִיבוּהוּ בְּנֵי יְהוֹיָרִיב כְּשֶׁיַּחֲזִיר שַׁבַּת מִשְׁמַרְתָּם. **הָאָשָׁם הַמּוּשָׁב [לַה'] לַכֹּהֵן מִלְּבַד אֵיל הַכִּפּוּרִים אֲשֶׁר יְכַפֵּר בּוֹ.** כְּלוֹמַר: לֹא קָרַב הָאַיִל עֲדַיִין. **אֲנָא מֵאֲשֶׁר יְכַפֵּר קָאָמִינָא.** דִּכְתִיב בִּלְשׁוֹן עָתִיד, מִדְּלָא כְּתִיב "אֲשֶׁר כִּיפֵּר". וּמַשְׁמַע דִּכְשֶׁהֵשִׁיב לַכֹּהֵן אֶת הָאָשָׁם, דְּהַיְינוּ קֶרֶן הַכֶּסֶף, עֲדַיִין לֹא כִּיפֵּר. **מִנַּיִן שֶׁאִם הֵבִיא מְעִילָתוֹ.** גַּבֵּי נֶהֱנָה מִן הַהֶקְדֵּשׁ קָאָמַר. **מְעִילָתוֹ.** קֶרֶן דְּהֶקְדֵּשׁ שֶׁמָּעַל בּוֹ. **בְּאֵיל הָאָשָׁם וְנִסְלַח.** מַשְׁמַע: אֵין סְלִיחָה אֶלָּא בִּשְׁנֵיהֶם "אַיִל" — כְּמַשְׁמָעוֹ, "הָאָשָׁם" — קֶרֶן. כִּדְיָלֵיף לְקַמֵּיהּ הֶקְדֵּשׁ מֵהֶדְיוֹט, מַה "הָאָשָׁם" דִּכְתִיב בִּגְזֶל הַגֵּר קֶרֶן הוּא, כִּדְאָמַר לְעֵיל (דף קי.), אַף אָשָׁם דִּכְתִיב בְּהֶקְדֵּשׁ קֶרֶן הוּא. **בְּאֵיל הָאָשָׁם.** מַשְׁמַע בָּאַיִל שֶׁהוּא בָּא חוֹבָה לְאָשָׁם שֶׁהוּא קֶרֶן, אַלְמָא: קֶרֶן בְּרֵישָׁא מַיְיתֵי. **אֵין הַחוֹמֶשׁ מְעַכֵּב.** אֶת הַכַּפָּרָה.

הדרן עלך הגוזל עצים

תוספות

אמר רבא לעורו. תימה: דהכא משמע אפילו בפסול קודם זריקה, וגם כשהעור מחובר עדיין בבשר ונעשה בו פסול קודם שחיטה, שהביא קודם הכסף — שרי בהנאה. ובזבחים, בפרק "טבול יום" (דף קד. ושם) אמר רבי: דם מרצה על העור בפני עצמו. פי': כשהוא מופשט, ואירע פסול בבשר — הדם מרצה על העור. וכשהוא עם הבשר *ונולד בו פסול קודם זריקה — הרי הוא כיוצא בו. אחר זריקה הורצה בשר שעה אחת — יפשיטנו, ועורו לכהנים. אלמא; כשהוא עם הבשר ונפסל קודם זריקה — יוצא לשריפה. והכא אירע בו פסול קודם שחיטה, שהובא קודם הכסף, ואמאי לא יצא העור לשריפה? **ת"ל** העולה עולה ראשונה. פי': ראשונה שבפרשת פנחס. וכי היכי ד"מלבד עולת הבקר" גלי לך בהדיא דמלבד דבר הקודם לו קאמר, הכי נמי "מלבד איל הכפורים" — דבר הקודם לו קאמר. ותימה: דיליף הכא מ"העולה", ובפרק "כל התדיר" (זבחים דף פט. ושם*) יליף מ"מלבד עולת הבקר" לחודיה! וי"ל: דהתם נמי א"העולה" קסמיך. ועוד יש תירוץ אחר, ואין להאריך כאן*.

וילמד הקדש מהדיוט והדיוט מהקדש. תימה: אמאי איצטריך קרא לעיל גבי הדיוט שאם הביא אשמו עד שלא הביא גזילו לא יצא? נילף מהקדש! ויש לומר: דאי לאו דאשכחן שהשוה הכתוב הדיוט להקדש להך מילתא — לא הוה ילפינן האי מהאי לענין שאר דברים. אבל השתא, דאשכחן שהשוה אותן, דבתרוייהו אם הביא אשמו תחילה לא יצא — כמו כן יש להשוותם לענין שאר דברים.

הדרן עלך הגוזל עצים

מסורת הש"ם

א) קיח: כתובות עה. קדושין ז. מא.

נח: יומא לג:
קו: ב"מ נה.
קג.] מנחות מט.
תמיד כח:

במדבר ה
שם כח
ויקרא ו
במדבר ה
ויקרא ה

עין משפט נר מצוה

רב א ב מיי' פ"ח מהל' גזילה ואבידה הלכה יב:

רג ג מיי' פ"א מהלכות תמידין הלכה ג:

ונולד בו פסול בין קודם זריקה בין לאחר זריקה הרי הוא כיוצא בו (ולהרשב"א) [ולרא"ש] כשהוא עם הבשר ונולד בו פסול קודם כנ"ל. העתק מחילופי גרסאות

רד ד מיי' פ"א מהל' מעילה הל' ה' [ועי' בהשגות ובכ"מ]:

רה ה (ו) שם הל' ד סמג עשין רי:

[ד"ה כל]

[ועיין תוספות כתובות קו: ד"ה כדאמר ותוספות זבחים פט. ד"ה כל ומנחות מט. ד"ה ת"ל ופסחים נח: ויומא לד. ד"ה העולה]

הגהות הב"ח

(א) גמ' כדריש לקיש: